Guide to Computer Forensics and Investigations: Processing Digital Evidence

Fifth Edition

Bill Nelson

Amelia Phillips

Christopher Steuart

CENGAGE
Learning·

Australia • Brazil • Mexico • Singapore • United Kingdom • United States

CENGAGE
Learning®

Guide to Computer Forensics and Investigations: Processing Digital Evidence, Fifth Edition

Bill Nelson, Amelia Phillips, Christopher Steuart

Product Director: Kathleen McMahon

Senior Director of Development:
Marah Bellegarde

Product Team Manager: Kristin McNary

Product Development Manager:
Leigh Hefferon

Senior Content Developer: Julia McGuirk

Developmental Editor: Lisa M. Lord

Product Assistant: Scott Finger

Marketing Director: Michele McTighe

Marketing Manager: Eric La Scola

Marketing Coordinator: Will Guiliani

Production Director: Patty Stephan

Senior Content Project Manager:
Brooke Greenhouse

Managing Art Director: Jack Pendleton

Cover photo or illustration: © Mega Pixel/
Shutterstock

Manufacturing Planner: Ron Montgomery

Compositor: Cenveo Publisher Services

Quality Assurance Tester: Serge Palladino

Library of Congress Control Number: 2014958600

ISBN: 978-1-285-06003-3

Cengage Learning
20 Channel Center Street
Boston, MA 02210

Cengage Learning is a leading provider of customized learning solutions with office locations around the globe, including Singapore, the United Kingdom, Australia, Mexico, Brazil, and Japan. Locate your local office at: **www.cengage.com/global**

Cengage Learning products are represented in Canada by Nelson Education, Ltd.

To learn more about Cengage Learning, visit **www.cengage.com**

Purchase any of our products at your local college store or at our preferred online store **www.cengagebrain.com**.

Printed in the United States of America

Print Number: 03   Print Year: 2016

Brief Table of Contents

Table of Contents

CHAPTER 12
Mobile Device Forensics

CHAPTER 13
Cloud Forensics

CHAPTER 14
Report Writing for High-Tech Investigations **511**

CHAPTER 15
Expert Testimony in Digital Investigations. **535**

Preface

Guide to Computer Forensics and Investigations: Processing Digital Evidence is now in its fifth edition! My sincere congratulations to the authors and publishing staff who have made this book such a great resource for thousands of students and practitioners worldwide. As digital technology and cyberspace have evolved from their early roots as basic communications platforma, so has the demand for people who have the knowledge and skills to investigate legal and technical issues involving computers and digital technology.

Today, computers, the Internet, and the world's digital ecosystem are instrumental in how we conduct our daily lives. The technological advancement of these systems over the past 10 years has changed the way we learn, socialize, and conduct business. Many of us working computer forensic cases in the security and criminal justice sectors during the late 1990s came to the conclusion that technology's rate of growth was going to have a significant impact on our operations. Currently, the organizations and agencies whose job it is to investigate both criminal and civil matters involving the use of rapidly evolving digital technology often struggle to keep up with the ever-changing digital landscape. Additionally, finding trained and qualified people to conduct these types of inquiries has been challenging as well.

In 1998, while creating an instructional program for law enforcement officers, I predicted that by the year 2005, approximately 85% of all crimes committed in the United States would have some type of digital component related to the crime. That prediction has now come true with an entire industry evolving for the purpose of investigating events occurring in cyberspace, including incidents involving international and corporate espionage, massive data breaches, and even cyberterrorism. Professionals in this exciting field of endeavor are now in wide demand and are expected to have multiple skill sets in areas such as malware analysis, software reverse-engineering, and mobile device forensics.

The study of computer forensics, which has subsequently morphed into the discipline digital forensics, has become one of the hottest and in-demand career choices for many high school and college students worldwide. *Guide to Computer Forensics and Investigations: Processing Digital Evidence* can now be found in both academic and professional environments as a reliable source of current technical information and practical exercises on investigations involving the latest digital technology. It's my belief that this book, combined with an enthusiastic and knowledgeable facilitator, will make for a fascinating course of instruction.

As I have stated to many of my students, it's not just desktop computers that harbor the binary code of 1s and 0s, but an infinite array of digital devices. If one of these devices retains evidence of a crime, it will be up to newly trained and educated digital detectives to find the evidence in a forensically sound manner. This book will assist both students and practitioners in accomplishing this goal.

Respectfully,

John A. Sgromolo

As a Senior Special Agent, John was one of the founding members of the NCIS Computer Crime Investigations Group. John left government service to run his own company, Digital Forensics, Inc., and has taught hundreds of law enforcement and corporate students nationwide the art and science of digital forensic investigations. Currently, John serves as a Senior Investigator for Verizon's RISK Team.

Introduction

Computer forensics, now most commonly called "digital forensics," has been a professional field for many years, but most well-established experts in the field have been self-taught. The growth of the Internet and the worldwide proliferation of computers have increased the need for digital investigations. Computers can be used to commit crimes, and crimes can be recorded on computers, including company policy violations, embezzlement, e-mail harassment, murder, leaks of proprietary information, and even terrorism. Law enforcement, network administrators, attorneys, and private investigators now rely on the skills of professional digital forensics experts to investigate criminal and civil cases.

This book is not intended to provide comprehensive training in digital forensics. It does, however, give you a solid foundation by introducing digital forensics to those who are new to the field. Other books on digital forensics are targeted to experts; this book is intended for novices who have a thorough grounding in computer and networking basics.

The new generation of digital forensics experts needs more initial training because operating systems, computer and mobile device hardware, and forensics software tools are changing more quickly. This book covers current and past operating systems and a range of hardware, from basic workstations and high-end network servers to a wide array of mobile devices. Although this book focuses on a few forensics software tools, it also reviews and discusses other currently available tools.

The purpose of this book is to guide you toward becoming a skilled digital forensics investigator. A secondary goal is to help you pass related certification exams. As the field of digital forensics and investigations matures, keep in mind that certifications will change. You can find more information on certifications in Chapter 2 and Appendix A.

Intended Audience

Although this book can be used by people with a wide range of backgrounds, it's intended for those with A+ and Network+ certifications or the equivalent. A networking background is necessary so that you understand how computers operate in a networked environment and can work with a network administrator when needed. In addition, you must know how to use a computer from the command line and how to use common operating systems, including Windows, Linux, and Mac OS, and their related hardware.

This book can be used at any educational level, from technical high schools and community colleges to graduate students. Current professionals in the public and private sectors can also use this book. Each group will approach investigative problems from a different perspective, but all will benefit from the coverage.

What's New in This Edition

The chapter flow of this book is organized so that you're first exposed to what happens in a forensics lab and how to set one up before you get into the nuts and bolts. Coverage of several GUI tools has been added to give you a familiarity with some widely used software. In addition, Chapter 11 now includes coverage of social media forensics, and Chapter 13 is a new chapter on forensics procedures for information stored in the cloud. Chapter 12 has also expanded to include more information on smartphones and tablets. Corrections have been made to this edition based on feedback from users, and all software packages and Web sites have been updated to reflect what's current at the time of publication. Finally, a new lab manual is now offered to go with the new fifth edition textbook (ISBN: 9781285079080).

Chapter Descriptions

Here is a summary of the topics covered in each chapter of this book:

Chapter 1, "Understanding the Digital Forensics Profession and Investigations," introduces you to the history of digital forensics and explains how the use of electronic evidence developed. It also reviews legal issues and compares public and private sector cases. This chapter also explains how to take a systematic approach to preparing a digital investigation, describes how to conduct an investigation, and summarizes requirements for workstations and software.

Chapter 2, "The Investigator's Office and Laboratory," outlines physical requirements and equipment for digital forensics labs, from small private investigators' labs to the regional FBI lab. It also covers certifications for digital investigators and building a business case for a forensics lab.

Chapter 3, "Data Acquisition," explains how to prepare to acquire data from a suspect's drive and discusses available Linux and GUI acquisition tools. This chapter also discusses acquiring data from RAID systems and gives you an overview of tools for remote acquisitions.

Chapter 4, "Processing Crime and Incident Scenes," explains search warrants and the nature of a typical digital forensics case. It discusses when to use outside professionals, how to assemble a team, and how to evaluate a case and explains the correct procedures for searching and seizing evidence. This chapter also introduces you to calculating hashes to verify data you collect.

Chapter 5, "Working with Windows and CLI Systems," discusses the most common operating systems. You learn what happens and what files are altered during computer startup and how file systems deal with deleted and slack space. In addition, this chapter covers some options for decrypting drives encrypted with whole disk encryption and explains the purpose of using virtual machines.

Chapter 6, "Current Digital Forensics Tools," explores current digital forensics software and hardware tools, including those that might not be readily available, and evaluates their strengths and weaknesses.

Chapter 7, "Linux and Macintosh File Systems," continues the operating system discussion from Chapter 5 by examining Macintosh and Linux OSs and file systems. It also gives you practice in using Linux forensics tools.

Chapter 8, "Recovering Graphics Files," explains how to recover graphics files and examines data compression, carving data, reconstructing file fragments, and steganography and copyright issues.

Chapter 9, "Digital Forensics Analysis and Validation," covers determining what data to collect and analyze and refining investigation plans. It also explains validation with hex editors and forensics software and data-hiding techniques.

Chapter 10, "Virtual Machine Forensics, Live Acquisitions, and Network Forensics," covers tools and methods for conducting forensic analysis of virtual machines, performing live acquisitions, reviewing network logs for evidence, and using network-monitoring tools to detect unauthorized access. It also examines using Linux tools and the Honeynet Project's resources.

Chapter 11, "E-mail and Social Media Investigations," examines e-mail crimes and violations and reviews some specialized e-mail and social media forensics tools. It also explains how to approach investigating social media communications and handling the challenges this content poses.

Chapter 12, "Mobile Device Forensics," covers investigation techniques and acquisition procedures for smartphones and other mobile devices. You learn where data might be stored or backed up and what tools are available for these investigations.

Chapter 13, "Cloud Forensics," summarizes the legal and technical challenges in conducting cloud forensics. It also describes how to acquire cloud data and explains how remote acquisition tools can be used in cloud investigations.

Chapter 14, "Report Writing for High-Tech Investigations," discusses the importance of report writing in digital forensics examinations; offers guidelines on report content, structure, and presentation; and explains how to generate report findings with forensics software tools.

Chapter 15, "Expert Testimony in Digital Investigations," explores the role of an expert witness or a fact witness, including developing a curriculum vitae, understanding the trial process, and preparing forensics evidence for testimony. It also offers guidelines for testifying in court and at depositions and hearings.

Chapter 16, "Ethics for the Expert Witness," provides guidance in the principles and practice of ethics for digital forensics investigators and examines other professional organizations' codes of ethics.

Appendix A, "Certification Test References," provides information on the National Institute of Standards and Technology (NIST) testing processes for validating digital forensics tools and covers digital forensics certifications and training programs.

Appendix B, "Digital Forensics References," lists recommended books, journals, e-mail lists, and Web sites for additional information and further study. It also covers the latest ISO 27000 standards that apply to digital forensics.

Appendix C, "Digital Forensics Lab Considerations," provides more information on considerations for forensics labs, including certifications, ergonomics, structural design, and communication and fire-suppression systems.

Appendix D, "DOS File System and Forensics Tools," reviews FAT file system basics and Mac legacy file systems and explains using DOS forensics tools, creating forensic boot media, and using scripts. It also reviews DriveSpy commands and X-Ways Replica and gives you an overview of the hexadecimal numbering system and how it's applied to digital information.

Features

To help you fully understand digital forensics, this book includes many features designed to enhance your learning experience:

- *Chapter objectives*—Each chapter begins with a detailed list of the concepts to be mastered in that chapter. This list gives you a quick reference to the chapter's contents and is a useful study aid.

- *Figures and tables*—Screenshots are used as guidelines for stepping through commands and forensics tools. For tools not included with the book or that aren't offered in free demo versions, figures have been added when possible to illustrate the tool's interface. Tables are used throughout the book to present information in an organized, easy-to-grasp manner.

- *Chapter summaries*—Each chapter's material is followed by a summary of the concepts introduced in that chapter. These summaries are a helpful way to review the ideas covered in each chapter.

- *Key terms*—Following the chapter summary, all new terms introduced in the chapter with boldfaced text are gathered together in the Key Terms list, with full definitions for each term. This list encourages a more thorough understanding of the chapter's key concepts and is a useful reference.

- *Review questions*—The end-of-chapter assessment begins with a set of review questions that reinforce the main concepts in each chapter. These questions help you evaluate and apply the material you have learned.

- *Hands-on projects*—Although understanding the theory behind digital technology is important, nothing can improve on real-world experience. To this end, each chapter offers several hands-on projects with software supplied with this book or free downloads. You can explore a variety of ways to acquire and even hide evidence. For the conceptual chapters, research projects are provided.

- *Case projects*—At the end of each chapter are several case projects. To complete these projects, you must draw on real-world common sense as well as your knowledge of the technical topics covered to that point in the book. Your goal for each project is to come up with answers to problems similar to those you'll face as a working digital forensics investigator.

- *Video tutorials*—The Instructor Companion Site includes video tutorials to help with learning the tools needed to perform in-chapter activities and hands-on projects. Each tutorial is a .wmv file that can be played in most OSs.

- *Software and student data files*—This book includes a DVD containing student data files and free software demo packages for use with activities and projects in the chapters. (Additional software demos or freeware can be downloaded to use in some projects.) Three software companies have graciously agreed to allow including their products with this book: Technology

Pathways (ProDiscover Basic), PassMark Software (OSForensics), and X-Ways (WinHex Demo). To check for newer versions or additional information, visit Technology Pathways, LLC at *www.arcgroupny.com/products/*, PassMark Software at *www.osforensics.com*, and X-Ways Software Technology AG at *www.x-ways.net*.

Technology Pathways recently changed its name to the ARC Group.

Text and Graphic Conventions

When appropriate, additional information and exercises have been added to this book to help you better understand the topic at hand. The following icons used in this book alert you to additional materials:

The Note icon draws your attention to additional helpful material related to the subject being covered.

Tips based on the authors' experience offer extra information about how to attack a problem or what to do in real-world situations.

The Caution icon warns you about potential mistakes or problems and explains how to avoid them.

Each hands-on project in this book is preceded by the Hands-On icon and a description of the exercise that follows.

This icon marks case projects, which are scenario-based or research assignments. In these extensive case examples, you're asked to apply independently what you have learned.

Instructor's Resources

The following additional materials are available when this book is used in a classroom setting. All the supplements available with this book are provided to instructors for download at our Instructor Companion Site. Simply search for this text at *login.cengage.com*.

- *Electronic Instructor's Manual*—The Instructor's Manual that accompanies this book includes additional instructional material to assist in class preparation, including suggestions for lecture topics, recommended lab activities, tips on setting up a lab for hands-on projects, and solutions to all end-of-chapter materials.

- *Cognero®*—Cengage Learning Testing Powered by Cognero is a flexible, online system that allows you to author, edit, and manage test bank content from multiple Cengage Learning solutions; create multiple test versions in an instant; and deliver tests from your LMS, your classroom, or wherever you want.

- *PowerPoint presentations*—This book comes with a set of Microsoft PowerPoint slides for each chapter. These slides are meant to be used as a teaching aid for classroom presentations, to be made available to students on the network for chapter review, or to be printed for classroom distribution. Instructors are also at liberty to add their own slides for other topics introduced.

- *Figure files*—All the figures in the book are reproduced on the Instructor Companion Site. Similar to the PowerPoint presentations, they're included as a teaching aid for classroom presentation, to make available to students for review, or to be printed for classroom distribution.

Student Resources

Lab Manual for Guide to Computer Forensics and Investigations (ISBN: 1285079086), a companion to *Guide to Computer Forensics and Investigations, Fifth Edition*, provides students with additional hands-on experience.

Lab Requirements

The hands-on projects in this book help you apply what you have learned about digital forensics techniques. The following sections list the minimum requirements for completing all the projects in this book. In addition to the items listed, you must be able to download and install demo versions of software.

 In Chapter 12, you use a demo version of Oxygen Forensics to search for e-mails. This software requires getting a registration code to download and install it, and you must e-mail the vendor ahead of time to get this code. Make sure you allow at least a few days to get this software ready before you start Chapter 12.

Minimum Lab Requirements

- Lab computers that boot to Windows 7, 8, or 8.1
- An external USB, FireWire, or SATA drive larger than a typical 512 MB USB drive

The projects in this book are designed with the following hardware and software requirements in mind. The lab in which most of the work takes place should be a typical network training lab with a variety of operating systems and computers available.

Operating Systems and Hardware

Windows 7, 8, or 8.1

Use a standard installation of Windows. The computer running Windows should be a fairly current model that meets the following minimum requirements:

- USB ports
- CD-ROM/DVD-ROM drive
- VGA or higher monitor

- Hard disk partition of 100 GB or more
- Mouse or other pointing device
- Keyboard
- At least 6 GB RAM (more is recommended)

Linux

For this book, it's assumed you're using an Ubuntu standard installation, although other Linux distributions will work with minor modifications. Also, some projects use specialized "live" Linux distributions, such as Kali Linux.

- Hard disk partition of 6 GB or more reserved for Linux
- Other hardware requirements are the same as those listed for Windows computers

This book contains a DVD with data files, demo software, and video tutorials. Some older computers and DVD drives might have difficulty reading data from this DVD. If you have any problems, make sure you copy the data to an external USB or FireWire drive before transferring it to your computer.

Digital Forensics Software

Three digital forensics programs, listed previously under "Features," are supplied with this book. In addition, there are projects using the following software, most of which can be downloaded from the Internet as freeware, shareware, or demo versions:

Because Web site addresses change frequently, use a search engine to find the following software online if URLs are no longer valid. Efforts have been made to provide information that's current at the time of writing, but things change constantly on the Web. Learning how to use search tools to find what you need is a valuable skill you'll use as a digital forensics investigator.

- DEFT: Download from *www.deftlinux.net*. This virtual appliance currently works only with Ubuntu 12.04.
- Device Seizure: Download from *www.paraben.com*.
- Facebook Forensics: Download from *www.facebookforensics.com*.
- HexWorkshop: Download from Breakpoint Software at *www.hexworkshop.com*.
- IrfanView: Download from *www.irfanview.com*.
- Kali Linux: Download the ISO image from *www.kali.org*.
- OpenOffice (includes OpenCalc): Download from *www.openoffice.org*.
- Oxygen Forensics: Register at *www.oxygen-forensic.com/en/* to get a code for downloading. You must use a business e-mail address or one ending in .edu. Oxygen doesn't respond to free Web-based e-mail addresses, such as Yahoo! or Gmail.
- PsTools: Download from *http://technet.microsoft.com/en-us/sysinternals/bb896649.aspx*.

- SecureClean: Download from *www.whitecanyon.com/ConsumerSecureClean*.
- SIMManager: Download from *www.dekart.com/products/card_management/sim_manager*.
- Sleuth Kit 2.08 and Autopsy Browser 2.07 for Linux and Autopsy Browser 3.1 for Windows: Download from *www.sleuthkit.org*.
- S-Tools4: Download from *http://packetstormsecurity.com/files/21688/s-tools4.zip.html* or *www.4shared.com/zip/q764vcPu/s-tools4.htm*.
- VirtualBox: Download from *www.virtualbox.org/wiki/Downloads*.
- Wireshark: Download from *www.wireshark.org*.

In addition, you use Microsoft Office Word (or other word processing software) and Excel (or other spreadsheet software) as well as a Web browser.

About the Authors

Bill Nelson has worked for more than 30 years for two global Fortune 100 companies in information technologies, with more than 18 years in corporate digital forensics and information security. In addition, he has been an instructor of digital forensics classes at the City University of Seattle and the University of Washington's Professional and Continuing Education Department for 10 years. His previous experience includes Automated Fingerprint Identification System (AFIS) software engineering and reserve police work. Bill has served as president and vice president for Computer Technology Investigators Northwest (CTIN) and is a member of Computer Related Information Management and Education (CRIME). He routinely lectures at several colleges and universities in the Pacific Northwest.

Amelia Phillips is a graduate of the Massachusetts Institute of Technology with B.S. degrees in astronautical engineering and archaeology and an MBA in technology management. She also holds an interdisciplinary Ph.D. in computer security from the University of Alaska, Fairbanks. After serving as an engineer at the Jet Propulsion Lab, she worked with e-commerce Web sites and began her training in computer forensics to prevent credit card numbers from being stolen from sensitive e-commerce databases. She designed certificate and AAS programs for community colleges in e-commerce, network security, computer forensics, and data recovery. She recently designed the Bachelor of Applied Science in cybersecurity and forensics, which was approved in 2014. She is currently tenured at Highline College in Seattle, Washington. Amelia is a Fulbright Scholar who taught at Polytechnic of Namibia in 2005 and 2006. She continues her work with developing nations and travels there frequently.

Christopher K. Steuart is a practicing attorney maintaining a general litigation practice, with experience in information systems security for a Fortune 50 company and the U.S. Army. He is also an honorary life member and the former general counsel for Computer Investigators Northwest (CTIN). He has presented computer forensics seminars in regional and national forums, including the American Society for Industrial Security (ASIS), Agora, Northwest Computer Technology Crime Analysis Seminar (NCT), and CTIN. He is currently vice president and general counsel for IT Forensics, Inc.

Acknowledgments

The team would like to express its appreciation to Product Manager Nick Lombardi, who has given us a great deal of moral support. We would like to thank the entire editorial and production staff for their dedication and fortitude during this project, including Julia McGuirk, Senior Content Developer, and Brooke Greenhouse, Senior Content Project Manager. Our special thanks go to Lisa

Lord, the Developmental Editor. We also appreciate the careful reading and thoughtful suggestions of the Technical Editor, Serge Palladino. We would like to thank the reviewers: Steve Bale, Truckee Meadows Community College; Dawn Blanche, Anne Arundel Community College; Gary Kessler, Embry-Riddle Aeronautical University; and Tenette Prevatte, Fayetteville Technical Community College. We would also like to thank our colleagues in professional groups in Washington State and Mike Lacey for his photos.

Bill Nelson

I want to express my appreciation to my wife, Tricia, for her support during the long hours spent writing. I would also like to express appreciation to my coauthors along with our editors and book reviewers for the team effort in producing this book. And special thanks for the support and encouragement from my digital forensics colleagues: Franklin Clark, retired investigator for the Pierce County Prosecutor's Office, Tacoma, Washington; Detective Mike McNown, retired, Wichita PD; Scott Larson of Larson Security, LLC; Don Allison of KoreLogic; retired detectives Brian Palmer, Barry Walden, and Melissa Rogers of the King County Sheriff's Office, Seattle, Washington; John Sgromolo of Verizon; Art Ehuan of Alvarez and Marsal; Staff Sergeant Clint Baker of the RCMP; Colin Cree of Forensic Data Recovery, Inc.; Chris Brown of Technology Pathways; Stefan Fleischmann of X-Ways; Gordon Ross, formerly of Net Nanny; and Gordon Mitchell of Future Focus, Inc. In addition, special thanks to colleagues Troy Larson of Microsoft, Brett Shavers, Numo Brito, Colin Ramsden, and other unnamed contributors for the ongoing development of WinFE.

Amelia Phillips

My deepest gratitude goes to my coauthor Bill Nelson. I want to reiterate the thanks to Lisa Lord for her patience and support and to all the people who have helped us in the past, including Teresa Mobley, Deb Buser, and Detective Melissa Rogers. Acknowledgments go to my many past and present students who have helped with research on what's happening in the field of digital forensics. Special thanks go to Jens Kircher at X-Ways, who contributed to the Macintosh and Linux chapter, for his insight into these OSs. Thanks to my friends in Namibia, without whom I would not have such a thorough understanding of the different laws on digital evidence and privacy, and special thanks to Dr. Jack Bermingham, Jeff Wagnitz, Alice Madsen, and Dr. Rolita Ezeonu, who have funded and supported me as I experienced what it means to get a Ph.D., write two textbooks, create a bachelor's program, and work full time. Thanks go to my friends for their support, and the most special thanks go to my two surviving aunties, who are both great teachers and set an excellent example for me. Without them, this would not be possible.

Christopher K. Steuart

I would like to express my appreciation to my wife, Josephine, son, Alexander, and daughter, Isobel, for their enthusiastic support of my commitment to *Guide to Computer Forensics and Investigations*, even as it consumed time and energy that they deserved. I also want to express my thanks to my parents, William and Mary, for their support of my education and development of the skills needed for this project. I thank my coauthors for inviting me to join them in this project. I would like to express my appreciation to the Boy Scouts of America for providing me with the first of many leadership opportunities in my life. I want to recognize Lieutenant General (then Captain) Edward Soriano for seeing the potential in me as a young soldier and encouraging me in learning the skills required to administer, communicate with, and command an organization within the structure of law, regulation, and personal commitment. I must also thank the faculty of Drake University Law School, particularly Professor James A. Albert, for encouraging me to think and write creatively about the law. I also note the contribution of Diane Gagon and the staff of the Church of Scientology in Seattle, Washington, in supporting my better understanding of commitment to myself and others.

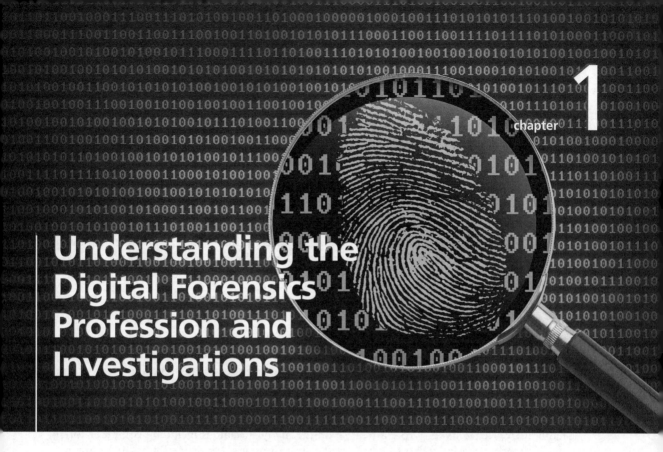

chapter 1

Understanding the Digital Forensics Profession and Investigations

After reading this chapter and completing the exercises, you will be able to:

- Describe the field of digital forensics

- Explain how to prepare for computer investigations and summarize the difference between public-sector and private-sector investigations

- Explain the importance of maintaining professional conduct

- Describe how to prepare a digital forensics investigation by taking a systematic approach

- Describe procedures for private-sector digital investigations

- Explain requirements for data recovery workstations and software

- Summarize how to conduct an investigation, including critiquing a case

In the past several years, the field of computer forensics has developed significantly, including new terminology. This chapter introduces you to computer forensics or, as it's now typically called, digital forensics and discusses issues of importance in the industry. This book blends traditional investigative methods with classic systems analysis problem-solving techniques and applies them to investigations involving computers and other digital media and systems. Understanding these disciplines combined with the use of the forensics tools will make you a skilled digital forensics examiner.

This chapter also gives you an overview of how to manage a computing investigation and use standard problem-solving techniques. You learn about the problems and challenges forensics examiners face when preparing and processing investigations, including the ideas and questions they must consider. To perform the activities and projects in this chapter, you work with forensic disk images from small USB drives and then can apply the same techniques to a large disk.

An Overview of Digital Forensics

As the world has become more of a level playing field, with more people online who have access to the same information (Thomas L. Freidman, *The World Is Flat*, Farrar, Straus, and Giroux, 2005), the need to standardize digital forensics processes has become more urgent. The definition of **digital forensics** has also evolved over the years from simply involving securing and analyzing digital information stored on a computer for use as evidence in civil, criminal, or administrative cases. The former director of the Defense Computer Forensics Laboratory, Ken Zatyko, wrote a treatise on the many specialties including computer forensics, network forensics, video forensics, and a host of others. He defined it as "[t]he application of computer science and investigative procedures for a legal purpose involving the analysis of digital evidence (information of probative value that is stored or transmitted in binary form) after proper search authority, chain of custody, validation with mathematics (hash function), use of validated tools, repeatability, reporting and possible expert presentation" ("Commentary: Defining Digital Forensics," *Forensic Magazine*, 2007).

The field of digital forensics can also encompass items such as research and incident response. With incident response, most organizations are concerned with protecting their assets and containing the situation, not necessarily prosecuting or finding the person responsible. Research in digital forensics also isn't concerned with prosecution or validity of evidence. This book is intended for digital forensics investigators and examiners at the civil, criminal, and administrative levels. Other facets of digital forensics are beyond the scope of this book. Keep in mind that depending on the jurisdiction and situation, forensic investigators and examiners might be the same or different personnel. In this book, the terms are used interchangeably.

For a more in-depth discussion of what the term "digital forensics" means, see "Digital Forensic Evidence Examination" (Fred Cohen, *www.fredcohen.net/Books/2013-DFE-Examination.pdf*, 2012).

Many groups have tried to create digital forensics certifications that could be recognized worldwide but have failed in this attempt. However, they have created certifications for specific categories of practitioners, such as government investigators. Because digital evidence is everywhere, with ubiquitous access to mobile devices, the need for a global standardized method is even more critical so that companies and governments can share and use digital evidence. In October 2012, an International Organization for Standardization (ISO) standard for digital forensics was ratified. This standard, ISO 27037 Information technology – Security techniques – Guidelines for identification, collection, acquisition and preservation of digital evidence, defines the personnel and methods for acquiring and preserving digital evidence. To address the multinational cases that continue to emerge, agencies in every country should develop policies and procedures that meet this standard.

The Federal Rules of Evidence (FRE), signed into law in 1973, was created to ensure consistency in federal proceedings, but many states' rules map to the FRE, too. In another attempt to standardize procedures, the FBI Computer Analysis and Response Team (CART) was formed in 1984 to handle the increase in cases involving digital evidence. Figure 1-1 shows the home page for the FBI CART. By the late 1990s, CART had teamed up with the Department of Defense Computer Forensics Laboratory (DCFL) for research and training. Much of the early curriculum in this field came from the DCFL.

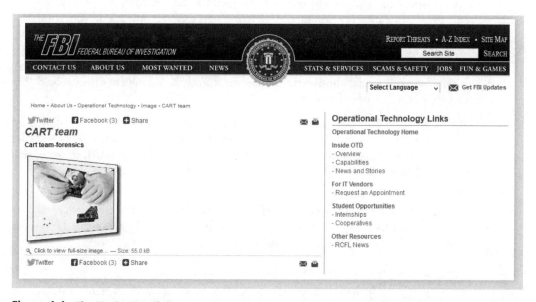

Figure 1-1   The FBI CART Web site
Source: *www.fbi.gov/about-us/otd/image/cart-team/view*

Files maintained on a computer are covered by different rules, depending on the nature of the documents. Many court cases in state and federal courts have developed and clarified how the rules apply to digital evidence. The **Fourth Amendment** to the U.S. Constitution (and each state's constitution) protects everyone's right to be secure in their person, residence, and property from search and seizure. Continuing development of the jurisprudence of this amendment has played a role in determining whether the search for digital evidence has established a different precedent, so separate **search warrants** might not be necessary. However, when preparing to search for evidence in a criminal case, many investigators still include the suspect's computer and its components in the search warrant to avoid later admissibility problems.

In an important case involving these issues, the Pennsylvania Supreme Court addressed expectations of privacy and whether evidence is admissible (see *Commonwealth v. Copenhefer*, 587 A.2d 1353, 526 Pa. 555 [1991]). Initial investigations by the FBI, state police, and local police resulted in discovering computer-generated notes and instructions—some of which had been deleted—that had been concealed in hiding places around Corry, Pennsylvania. The investigation also produced several possible suspects, including David Copenhefer, who owned a nearby bookstore and apparently had bad relationships with the victim and her husband. Examination of trash discarded from Copenhefer's store revealed drafts of the ransom note and directions. Subsequent search warrants resulted in seizure of evidence against him. Copenhefer's computer contained several drafts and amendments of the text of phone calls to the victim and the victim's husband the next day, the ransom note, the series of hidden notes, and a plan for the entire kidnapping scheme (*Copenhefer*, p. 559).

On direct appeal, the Pennsylvania Supreme Court concluded that the physical evidence, including the digital forensics evidence, was sufficient to support the bookstore owner's conviction. Copenhefer's argument was that "[E]ven though his computer was validly seized pursuant to a warrant, his attempted deletion of the documents in question created an expectation of privacy protected by the Fourth Amendment. Thus, he claims, under *Katz v. United States*, 389 U.S. 347, 357, 88 S.Ct. 507, 19 L.Ed.2d 576 (1967), and its progeny, Agent Johnson's retrieval of the documents, without first obtaining another search warrant, was unreasonable under the Fourth Amendment and the documents thus seized should have been suppressed" (*Copenhefer*, p. 561).

The Pennsylvania Supreme Court rejected this argument, stating, "A defendant's attempt to secrete evidence of a crime is not synonymous with a legally cognizable expectation of privacy. A mere hope for secrecy is not a legally protected expectation. If it were, search warrants would be required in a vast number of cases where warrants are clearly not necessary" (*Copenhefer*, p. 562).

Every U.S. jurisdiction has case law related to the admissibility of evidence recovered from computers and other digital devices. As you learn in this book, however, the laws on digital evidence vary between states as well as between provinces and countries.

The U.S. Department of Justice offers a useful guide to search and seizure procedures for computers and computer evidence at *www.justice.gov/criminal/cybercrime/docs/ccmanual.pdf*.

Digital Forensics and Other Related Disciplines

According to DIBS USA, Inc., a privately owned corporation specializing in digital forensics since the 1990s (*www.dibsforensics.com*), digital forensics involves scientifically examining and analyzing data from computer storage media so that it can be used as evidence in court. In the National Institute of Standards and Technology (NIST) document "Guide to Integrating Forensic Techniques into Incident Response" (*http://csrc.nist.gov/publications/nistpubs/800-86/SP800-86.pdf*, 2006), digital forensics is defined as "the application of science to the identification, collection, examination, and analysis of data while preserving the integrity of the information and maintaining a strict chain of custody for the data." Typically, investigating digital devices includes collecting data securely, examining suspect data to determine details such as origin and content, presenting digital information to courts, and applying laws to digital device practices.

In general, digital forensics is used to investigate data that can be retrieved from a computer's hard drive or other storage media. Like an archaeologist excavating a site, digital forensics examiners retrieve information from a computer or its components. The information retrieved might already be on the drive, but it might not be easy to find or decipher. On the other hand, network forensics yields information about how attackers gain access to a network along with files they might have copied, examined, or tampered with. Network forensics examiners use log files to determine when users logged on and determine which URLs users accessed, how they logged on to the network, and from what location. Network forensics also tries to determine what tracks or new files were left behind on a victim's computer and what changes were made. In Chapter 10, you explore when and how network forensics should be used in an investigation.

Digital forensics is also different from **data recovery**, which involves retrieving information that was deleted by mistake or lost during a power surge or server crash, for example. In data recovery, typically you know what you're looking for. Digital forensics is the task of recovering data that users have hidden or deleted, with the goal of ensuring that the recovered data is valid so that it can be used as evidence. In this regard, digital forensics differs from other types of evidence recovered from a scene. When investigators in a crime scene unit retrieve blood or hair or bullets, they can identify what it is. When a laptop, smartphone, or other digital device is retrieved, its contents are unknown and pose a challenge to the examiner. The evidence can be **inculpatory evidence** (in criminal cases, the expression is "incriminating") or **exculpatory evidence**, meaning it tends to clear the suspect. Examiners often approach a digital device not knowing whether it contains evidence. They must search storage media and piece together any data they find. Forensics software tools can be used for most cases. In extreme cases, examiners can use electron microscopes and other sophisticated equipment to retrieve information from machines that have been damaged or reformatted purposefully. This method is usually cost prohibitive, so it's not normally used.

Forensics investigators often work as part of a team to secure an organization's computers and networks. The digital investigation function can be viewed as part of a triad that makes up computing security. Rapid progress in technology has resulted in an expansion of the skills needed and varies depending on the organization using practitioners in this field. Figure 1-2 shows the investigations triad made up of these functions:

- Vulnerability/threat assessment and risk management
- Network intrusion detection and incident response
- Digital investigations

Each side of the triad in Figure 1-2 represents a group or department responsible for performing the associated tasks. Although each function operates independently, all three groups draw from one another when a large-scale computing investigation is being conducted. By combining these three groups into a team, all aspects of a digital technology investigation can be addressed without calling in outside specialists. In smaller companies, one group might perform all the tasks shown in the investigations triad, or a small company might contract with service providers to perform these tasks.

When you work in the **vulnerability/threat assessment and risk management** group, you test and verify the integrity of stand-alone workstations and network servers. This integrity check covers the physical security of systems and the security of operating systems (OSs) and applications. People working in this group (often known as penetration testers) test for vulnerabilities of OSs and applications used in the network and conduct authorized attacks on the

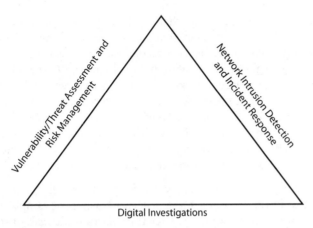

Figure 1-2   The investigations triad
© 2016 Cengage Learning®

network to assess vulnerabilities. Typically, people performing this task have several years of experience in system administration. Their job is to poke holes in the network to help an organization be better prepared for a real attack.

Professionals in the vulnerability assessment and risk management group also need skills in **network intrusion detection and incident response**. This group detects intruder attacks by using automated tools and monitoring network firewall logs. When an external attack is detected, the response team tracks, locates, and identifies the intrusion method and denies further access to the network. If an intruder launches an attack that causes damage or potential damage, this team collects the necessary evidence, which can be used for civil or criminal litigation against the intruder and to prevent future intrusions. If an internal user is engaged in illegal acts or policy violations, the network intrusion detection and incident response group might assist in locating the user. For example, someone at a community college sends e-mails containing a worm to other users on the network. The network team realizes the e-mails are coming from a node on the internal network, and the security team focuses on that node. The **digital investigations** group manages investigations and conducts forensics analysis of systems suspected of containing evidence related to an incident or a crime. For complex casework, this group draws on resources from personnel in vulnerability assessment, risk management, and network intrusion detection and incident response. However, the digital investigations group typically resolves or terminates case investigations.

A Brief History of Digital Forensics

Forty years ago, few people imagined that computers would be an integral part of everyday life. Now computer technology is commonplace, as are crimes in which a computer is the instrument of the crime, the target of the crime, and, by its nature, the location where evidence is stored.

By the 1970s, electronic crimes were increasing, especially in the financial sector. Most computers in that era were mainframes, used by trained people with specialized skills who worked in finance, engineering, and academia. White-collar fraud began when people in these industries saw a way to make money by manipulating computer data. One of the most well-known crimes of the mainframe era is the one-half cent crime. Banks commonly tracked money in accounts to the third decimal place or more. They used and still use the rounding-up accounting method when paying interest. If the interest applied to an account resulted in a fraction of a cent, that fraction was used in the calculation for the next account until the total resulted in a whole cent. It was assumed that eventually every customer would benefit from this averaging. Some computer programmers corrupted this method by opening an account for themselves and writing programs that diverted all the fractional monies into their accounts. In small banks, this practice amounted to only a few hundred dollars a month. In large banks with millions of accounts, however, the amount could reach hundreds of thousands of dollars.

During this time, most law enforcement officers didn't know enough about computers to ask the right questions or to preserve evidence for trial. Many began to attend the Federal Law Enforcement Training Center (FLETC) programs designed to train law enforcement in handling digital data.

As PCs gained popularity and began to replace mainframe computers in the 1980s, many different OSs emerged. Apple released the Apple IIe in 1983 and then the Macintosh in 1984. Computers such as the TRS-80 and Commodore 64 were the machines of the day. CP/M machines, such as the Kaypro and Zenith, were also in demand.

Disk Operating System (DOS) was available in many varieties, including PC-DOS, QDOS, DR-DOS, IBM-DOS, and MS-DOS. Forensics tools at that time were simple, and most were generated by government agencies, such as the Royal Canadian Mounted Police (RCMP, which had its own investigative tools) and the U.S. Internal Revenue Service (IRS). Most tools were written in C and assembly language and weren't available to the general public.

In the mid-1980s, a new tool, Xtree Gold, appeared on the market. It recognized file types and retrieved lost or deleted files. Norton DiskEdit soon followed and became the preferred tool for finding and recovering deleted files. You could use these tools on the most powerful PCs of that time; IBM-compatible computers had hard disks of 10 to 40 MB and two floppy drives, as shown in Figure 1-3.

Figure 1-3 An 8088 computer
© iStockPhoto.com/Maxiphoto

In 1987, Apple produced the Mac SE, a Macintosh with an external EasyDrive hard disk with 60 MB of storage (see Figure 1-4). At this time, the popular Commodore 64 still used standard audiotapes to record data, so the Mac SE represented an important advance in computer technology.

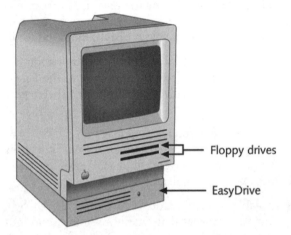

Floppy drives

EasyDrive

Figure 1-4   A Mac SE with an external EasyDrive hard disk
© Cengage Learning®

By the early 1990s, specialized tools for digital forensics were available. The **International Association of Computer Investigative Specialists (IACIS)** introduced training on software for digital forensics examinations, and the IRS created search-warrant programs. However, no commercial GUI software for digital forensics was available until ASR Data created Expert Witness for Macintosh. This software could recover deleted files and fragments of deleted files. One of the ASR Data partners later left and developed EnCase, which became a popular digital forensics tool.

As computer technology continued to evolve, more digital forensics software was developed. The introduction of large hard disks posed new problems for investigators. Most DOS-based software didn't recognize a hard disk larger than 8 GB. Because contemporary computers have hard disks of 500 GB and often much larger, changes in forensics software were needed. Later in this book, you explore the challenges of examining older software and hardware.

Other tools, such as ILook, which is currently maintained by the IRS Criminal Investigation Division and limited to law enforcement, can analyze and read special files that are copies of a disk. AccessData Forensic Toolkit (FTK) has become a popular commercial product that performs similar tasks in the law enforcement and civilian markets.

As software companies become savvier about digital forensics and investigations, they are producing more forensics tools to keep pace with technology. This book describes several tools but by no means all available tools. You should refer to trade publications, e-zines, and Web sites to stay current.

Understanding Case Law

Existing laws and statutes simply can't keep up with the rate of technological change. Therefore, when statutes or regulations don't exist, case law is used. In common law nations, such as the United States, case law allows legal counsel to apply previous similar cases to current ones in an effort to address ambiguity in laws. Examiners must be familiar with recent court rulings on search and seizure in the electronic environment to avoid mistakes such as exceeding a search warrant's authority. Recent events involving privacy incursions by government agencies have resulted in new laws and policies. Developments in technology have changed how everyday events are viewed. For example, what should be considered private conversations? Which devices are actually protected?

Although law enforcement can certainly confiscate anything an arrested person is carrying and log that a device, such as a smartphone, was on the person, they don't necessarily have the right or authority to search the device. These actions are being challenged in courts constantly. Remaining vigilant in keeping up with changing case law is critical to being an effective digital forensics investigator.

Developing Digital Forensics Resources

To be a successful digital forensics investigator, you must be familiar with more than one computing platform. In addition to older platforms, such as DOS, Windows 9x, and Windows XP, you should be familiar with Linux, Macintosh, and current Windows platforms. However, no one can be an expert in every aspect of computing. Likewise, you can't know everything about the technology you're investigating. To supplement your knowledge, you should develop and maintain contact with computing, network, and investigative professionals.

Join computer user groups in both the public and private sectors. In the Pacific Northwest, for example, **Computer Technology Investigators Network (CTIN)** meets to discuss problems that digital forensics examiners encounter. This nonprofit organization also conducts training. IACIS is an excellent group for law enforcement personnel but doesn't have local chapters. However, groups such as the High Technology Crime Investigation Association, International Information Systems Security Certification Consortium (ISC^2), and InfraGard have local chapters open to professionals in most major cities. Build your own network of digital forensics experts, and keep in touch through e-mail. Cultivate professional relationships with people who specialize in technical areas different from your own specialty. If you're a Windows expert, for example, maintain contact with experts in Linux, UNIX, and Macintosh. If you're using social media to interact with experts, exercise caution and good judgment when communicating with people you haven't met in person or whose backgrounds you don't know.

User groups can be especially helpful when you need information about obscure OSs. For example, a user group helped convict a child molester in Pierce County, Washington, in 1996. The suspect installed video cameras throughout his house, served alcohol to young women to intoxicate them, and secretly filmed them playing strip poker. When he was accused of molesting a child, police seized his computers and other physical evidence. The investigator discovered that the computers used CoCo DOS, an OS that had been out of use for years. The investigator contacted a local user group, which supplied the standard commands and other information needed to access the system. On the suspect's computer, the investigator found a diary detailing the suspect's actions over 15 years, including the molestation of more than 400 young women. As a result, the suspect received a longer sentence than if he had been convicted of molesting only one child.

Outside experts can also give you detailed information you need to retrieve digital evidence. For example, a recent murder case involved a husband and wife who owned a Macintosh store. When the wife was discovered dead, apparently murdered, investigators found that she had wanted to leave her husband but didn't because of her religious beliefs. The police got a search warrant and confiscated the home and office computers. When the detective on the case examined the home system, he found that the hard drive had been compressed and erased. He contacted a Macintosh engineer, who determined the two software programs used to compress the drive. With this knowledge, the detective could retrieve information from the hard drive, including text files indicating that the husband spent $35,000 in business funds to purchase cocaine and prostitution services. This evidence proved crucial in making it possible to convict the husband of murder.

Preparing for Digital Investigations

Digital investigations can be categorized several ways. For the purposes of this discussion, however, they fall into two categories: public-sector investigations and private-sector investigations (see Figure 1-5).

Private organizations
Company policy violations
Litigation disputes

Government agencies
Article 8 in the Charter of Rights of Canada
U.S. Fourth Amendment search
   and seizure rules

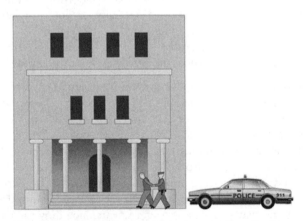

Figure 1-5   Public-sector and private-sector investigations
© Cengage Learning®

In general, public-sector investigations involve government agencies responsible for criminal investigations and prosecution. Government agencies range from municipal, county, and state or provincial police departments to federal law enforcement agencies. These organizations must observe legal guidelines of their jurisdictions, such as Article 8 in the Charter of Rights of Canada and the Fourth Amendment to the U.S. Constitution restricting government **search and seizure** (see Figure 1-6). The law of search and seizure in the United States protects the rights of people, including people suspected of crimes; as a digital forensics examiner, you must follow these laws. The Department of Justice (DOJ) updates information on computer search and seizure regularly.

The right of the people to be secure in their persons, houses, papers, and effects, against unreasonable searches and seizures, shall not be violated, and no Warrants shall issue, but upon probable cause, supported by Oath or affirmation, and particularly describing the place to be searched, and the persons or things to be seized.

Figure 1-6   The Fourth Amendment
© Cengage Learning®

Private-sector investigations focus more on policy violations, such as not adhering to Health Insurance Portability and Accountability Act of 1996 (HIPAA) regulations. However, criminal acts, such as corporate espionage, can also occur. So although private-sector investigations often start as civil cases, they can develop into criminal cases; likewise, a criminal case can have implications leading to a civil case. If you follow good forensics procedures, the evidence found in your examinations can make the transition between civil and criminal cases.

Understanding Law Enforcement Agency Investigations

When conducting public-sector investigations, you must understand laws on computer-related crimes, including standard legal processes, guidelines on search and seizure, and how to build a criminal case. In a criminal case, a suspect is charged with a criminal offense, such as burglary, murder, molestation, or fraud. To determine whether there was a computer crime, an investigator asks questions such as the following: What was the tool used to commit the crime? Was it a simple trespass? Was it a theft or vandalism? Did the perpetrator infringe on someone else's rights by cyberstalking or e-mail harassment?

Laws, including procedural rules, vary by jurisdiction. Therefore, this book points out when items accepted in U.S. courts don't stand up in other courts. Lately, a major issue has been that European Union (EU) privacy laws are more stringent than U.S. privacy laws. Issues related to international companies are still being defined. Over the past few decades, more companies have been consolidating into global entities. As a result, internal company investigations can involve laws of multiple countries. For example, a company has a subsidiary operating in Australia. An employee at that subsidiary is suspected of fraud, and as part of your investigation, you need to seize his cell phone. Under U.S. law, you can if he used it on company property and synchronized it with the company network. Under Australian law, you can't.

Computers and networks might be only tools used to commit crimes and are, therefore, analogous to the lockpick a burglar uses to break into a house. For this reason, many states have added specific language to criminal codes to define crimes involving computers. States such as Alabama have wording such as "willfully or without authorization" and specify what dollar amount qualifies as a misdemeanor or a felony. For example, they have expanded the definition of laws for crimes such as theft to include taking data from a computer without the owner's permission, so computer theft is now on a par with shoplifting or car theft. States have also enacted specific criminal statutes that address computer-related crimes but typically don't include digital issues in standard trespass, theft, vandalism, or burglary laws. The Computer Fraud and Abuse Act was passed in 1986, but specific state laws were generally developed later.

For information on how each state defines and addresses computer-related crimes, see *http://statelaws.findlaw.com/criminal-laws/computer-crimes/*.

Many serious crimes involve computers, smartphones, and other digital devices. The most notorious are those involving sexual exploitation of minors. Digital images are stored on hard disks, flash drives, removable hard drives, and the cloud and are circulated on the Internet. Other computer crimes concern missing children and adults because information about missing people is often found on computers. Drug dealers, car theft rings, and other criminals often keep information about transactions on their computers, laptops, smartphones, and other devices.

Following Legal Processes

When conducting a computer investigation for potential criminal violations of the law, the legal processes you follow depend on local custom, legislative standards, and rules of evidence. In general, however, a criminal case follows three stages: the complaint, the investigation, and the prosecution. Someone files a complaint, and then a specialist investigates the complaint and, with the help of a prosecutor, collects evidence and builds a case. If the evidence is sufficient, the case might proceed to trial.

A criminal investigation generally begins when someone finds evidence of or witnesses an illegal act. The witness or victim makes an **allegation** to the police, an accusation of fact that a crime has been committed.

A police officer interviews the complainant and writes a report about the crime. The law enforcement agency processes the report, and management decides to start an investigation or log the information into a police blotter, which provides a record of information about crimes that have been committed previously. Criminals often repeat actions in their illegal activities, and these patterns can be discovered by examining police blotters. This historical knowledge is useful when conducting investigations, especially in high-technology crimes. Blotters now are generally electronic files, often structured as databases, so they can be searched more easily than the old paper blotters.

To see an example of a police blotter, go to *http://spdblotter.seattle.gov*.

Not every police officer is a computer expert. Some are computer novices; others might be trained to recognize what they can retrieve from a computer disk. To differentiate the training and experience officers have, ISO standard 27037 (*www.iso.org/iso/catalogue_detail?csnumber=44381*) defines two categories. A **Digital Evidence First Responder (DEFR)** has the skill and training to arrive on an incident scene, assess the situation, and take precautions to acquire and preserve evidence. A **Digital Evidence Specialist (DES)** has the skill to analyze the data and determine when another specialist should be called in to assist with the analysis.

If you're an examiner assigned to a case, recognize the level of expertise of police officers and others involved in the case. You should have DES training to conduct the examination of systems and manage the digital forensics aspects of the case. You start by assessing the scope of the case, which includes the computer's OS, hardware, and peripheral devices. You then determine whether resources are available to process all the evidence. Determine whether you have the right tools to collect and analyze evidence and whether you need to call on other specialists to assist in collecting and processing evidence. After you have gathered the resources you need, your role is to delegate, collect, and process the information related to the complaint. After you build a case, the information is turned over to the prosecutor. As an investigator, you must then present the collected evidence with a report to the government's attorney. Depending on the community and the nature of the crime, the prosecutor's title varies by jurisdiction.

In a criminal or public-sector case, if the police officer or investigator has sufficient cause to support a search warrant, the prosecuting attorney might direct him or her to submit an **affidavit** (also called a "declaration"). This sworn statement of support of facts about or evidence of a crime is submitted to a judge with the request for a search warrant before seizing evidence. Figure 1-7 shows a typical affidavit. It's your responsibility to write the affidavit, which must include **exhibits** (evidence) that support the allegation to justify the warrant. You must then have the affidavit notarized under sworn oath to verify that the information in the affidavit is true. (You learn more about affidavits and declarations in Chapter 14.)

In general, after a judge approves and signs a search warrant, it's ready to be executed, meaning a DEFR can collect evidence as defined by the warrant. After you collect the evidence, you process and analyze it to determine whether a crime actually occurred. The evidence can then be presented in court in a hearing or trial. A judge or an administrative law judge then renders a judgment, or a jury hands down a **verdict** (after which a judge can enter a judgment).

Date ___ ___ ___

Based on actual inspection of spreadsheets, financial records, and invoices, Joe Smith, a computer forensics expert, is aware that computer equipment was used to generate, store, and print documents used in Jonathon Douglas's tax evasion scheme. There is reason to believe that the computer system currently located on Jonathon Douglas's premises is the same system used to produce and store the spreadsheets, financial records, and invoices, and that both the [spreadsheets, financial records, invoices] and other records relating to Jonathon Douglas's criminal enterprise will be stored on Jonathon Douglas's computer.

Source: *Searching and Seizing Computers and Obtaining Electronic Evidence in Electronic Investigations*, U.S. Department of Justice, July 2002.

Figure 1-7   Typical affidavit language
© Cengage Learning®

Understanding Private-Sector Investigations

Private-sector investigations involve private companies and lawyers who address company policy violations and litigation disputes, such as wrongful termination. When conducting an investigation for a private company, remember that business must continue with minimal interruption from your investigation. Because businesses usually focus on continuing their usual operations and making profits, many in a private-sector environment consider your investigation and apprehension of a suspect secondary to stopping the violation and minimizing damage or loss to the business. Businesses also strive to minimize or eliminate litigation, which is an expensive way to address criminal or civil issues. Private-sector computer crimes can involve e-mail harassment, falsification of data, gender and age discrimination, embezzlement, sabotage, and **industrial espionage**, which involves selling sensitive or confidential company information to a competitor. Anyone with access to a computer can commit these crimes.

Establishing Company Policies   One way that businesses can reduce the risk of litigation is to publish and maintain policies that employees find easy to read and follow. In addition, these policies can make internal investigations go more smoothly. The most important policies are those defining rules for using the company's computers and networks; this type of policy is commonly known as an "acceptable use policy." Organizations should have all employees sign this acceptable use agreement. Published company policies also provide a **line of authority** for conducting internal investigations; it states who has the legal right to initiate an investigation, who can take possession of evidence, and who can have access to evidence.

Well-defined policies give computer investigators and forensics examiners the authority to conduct an investigation. Policies also demonstrate that an organization intends to be fair-minded and objective about how it treats employees and state that the organization will follow due process for all investigations. ("Due process" refers to fairness under the law and is meant to protect all.) Without defined policies, a business risks exposing itself to litigation from current or former employees. The person or committee in charge of maintaining company policies must also stay current with applicable laws, which can vary depending on the city, state, and country. In addition, training and updates on standards and policies should be scheduled regularly to keep employees informed of what should and shouldn't be done on the organization's network.

Displaying Warning Banners Another way a private or public organization can avoid litigation is to display a warning banner on computer screens. A **warning banner** usually appears when a computer starts or connects to the company intranet, network, or virtual private network (VPN) and informs end users that the organization reserves the right to inspect computer systems and network traffic at will. (An end user is a person using a computer to perform routine tasks other than system administration.) If this right isn't stated explicitly, employees might have an assumed right of privacy when using a company's computer systems and network accesses. Figure 1-8 shows a sample warning banner.

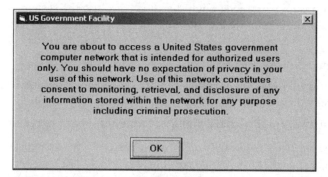

Figure 1-8 A sample warning banner
© Cengage Learning®

A warning banner asserts the right to conduct an investigation and notifies the user. By displaying a strong, well-worded warning banner, an organization owning computer equipment doesn't need a search warrant or court order as required under Fourth Amendment search-and-seizure rules to seize the equipment. In a company with a well-defined policy, this right to inspect or search at will applies to both criminal activity and company policy violations. Keep in mind, however, that your country's laws might differ. For example, in some countries, even though the company has the right to seize computers at any time, if employees are suspected of a criminal act, they must be informed at that time.

The following list recommends phrases to include in warning banners. Before using these warnings, consult with the organization's legal department for other required legal notices for your work area or department. Depending on the type of organization, the following text can be used in internal warning banners:

- Access to this system and network is restricted.
- Use of this system and network is for official business only.
- Systems and networks are subject to monitoring at any time by the owner.

- Using this system implies consent to monitoring by the owner.

- Unauthorized or illegal users of this system or network will be subject to discipline or prosecution.

- Users of this system agree that they have no expectation of privacy relating to all activity performed on this system.

The DOJ document at *www.justice.gov/criminal/cybercrime/docs/ ssmanual2009.pdf* has several examples of warning banners.

An organization such as a community college might simply state that systems and networks are subject to observation and monitoring at any time because members of the local community who aren't staff or students might use the facilities. A for-profit organization, on the other hand, could have proprietary information on its network and use all the phrases suggested in the preceding list.

Guests, such as employees of business partners, might be allowed to use the system. The text that's displayed when a guest attempts to log on can include warnings similar to the following:

- This system is the property of Company X.

- This system is for authorized use only; unauthorized access is a violation of law and violators will be prosecuted.

- All activity, software, network traffic, and communications are subject to monitoring.

As a private-sector digital investigator, make sure a company displays a clearly worded warning banner. Without a banner, your authority to inspect might conflict with the user's expectation of privacy, and a court might have to determine the issue of authority to inspect. State laws vary on the expectation of privacy, but all states accept the concept of a waiver of the expectation of privacy. Additionally, the EU and its member nations impose substantial penalties for personal information that crosses national boundaries without the person's consent. For example, if your company is conducting an investigation at its subsidiary in the EU, you might not be able to acquire a network drive without notifying certain parties or making sure consent documents are in place.

Some might argue that written policies are all that are necessary. However, in the actual prosecution of cases, warning banners have been critical in determining that a user didn't have an expectation of privacy for information stored on the system. A warning banner has the additional advantage of being easier to present in trial as an exhibit than a policy manual. Government agencies, such as the Department of Energy, NASA, Lawrence Livermore Labs, and even public libraries, now require warning banners on all computer terminals on their systems. Many corporations also require warning banners as part of the logon/startup process.

Designating an Authorized Requester As mentioned, investigations must establish a line of authority. In addition to using warning banners that state a company's rights of computer ownership, businesses are advised to specify an **authorized requester** who has the power to initiate investigations. Executive management should define a policy to avoid conflicts from competing interests in organizations. In large organizations, competition for funding or management support can become so fierce that people might create false allegations of misconduct to prevent competing departments from delivering a proposal for the same source of funds.

To avoid inappropriate investigations, executive management must also define and limit who's authorized to request a computer investigation and forensics analysis. Generally, the fewer groups with authority to request a computer investigation, the better. Examples of groups with this authority in a private-sector environment include following:

- Corporate security investigations
- Corporate ethics office
- Corporate equal employment opportunity office
- Internal auditing
- The general counsel or legal department

All other groups should coordinate their requests through the corporate security investigations group. This policy separates the investigative process from the process of employee discipline.

Conducting Security Investigations Conducting a digital investigation in the private sector is not much different from conducting one in the public sector. During public investigations, you search for evidence to support criminal allegations. During private investigations, you search for evidence to support allegations of violations of a company's rules or an attack on its assets. Three types of situations are common in private-sector environments:

- Abuse or misuse of computing assets
- E-mail abuse
- Internet abuse

Most digital investigations in the private sector involve misuse of computing assets. Typically, this misuse is referred to as "company rules violation." Computing abuse complaints often center on e-mail and Internet misuse by employees but could involve other computing resources, such as using company software to produce a product for personal profit. The scope of an e-mail investigation ranges from excessive use of a company's e-mail system for personal use to making threats or harassing others via e-mail. Some common e-mail abuses involve transmitting offensive messages. These types of messages can create a **hostile work environment** that can result in an employee civil lawsuit against a company that does nothing to prevent or respond to it (in other words, implicitly condones the e-mail abuse).

Digital investigators also examine Internet abuse. Employees' abuse of Internet privileges ranges from excessive use, such as spending all day Web surfing, to viewing pornographic pictures on the Internet while at work. An extreme instance of Internet abuse is viewing contraband (illegal) pornographic images, such as child pornography. Viewing contraband images is a criminal act in most jurisdictions, and digital investigators must handle this situation with the highest level of professionalism and notify law enforcement. By enforcing policies consistently, a company minimizes its liability exposure. The role of a digital forensics examiner is to give management personnel complete and accurate information so that they can verify and correct abuse problems in an organization. (In later chapters, you learn the procedures for conducting these types of investigations.)

Actions that seem related to internal abuse could also have criminal or civil liability. Because any civil investigation can become a criminal investigation, you must treat all evidence you collect with the highest level of security and accountability. Later in this book, you learn the Federal Rules of Evidence (processes to ensure the chain of custody) and how to apply them to computing investigations.

Similarly, your private-sector investigation might seem to involve a civil, noncriminal matter, but as you progress through your analysis, you might identify a criminal matter, too. Because of this possibility, always remember that your work can come under the scrutiny of the civil or criminal legal system. The Federal Rules of Evidence are the same for civil and criminal matters. By applying the rules to all investigations uniformly, you eliminate any concerns about the admissibility of the evidence you develop. These standards are emphasized throughout this book.

 The silver-platter doctrine used to allow a civilian or private-sector investigative agent to deliver evidence obtained in a manner that violated the Fourth Amendment to a law enforcement agency. However, this doctrine was ruled unconstitutional in 1960 (see *Elkins v. United States*, 1960).

Remember that a police officer is a law enforcement agent. A private-sector investigator's job is to minimize risk to the company. After you turn over evidence to law enforcement and begin working under their direction, you become an agent of law enforcement, subject to the same restrictions on search and seizure as a law enforcement agent. A law enforcement agent can't ask you, as a private citizen, to obtain evidence that requires a warrant. The rules controlling the use of evidence collected by private citizens vary by jurisdiction, so check the law if you're investigating a case outside the United States.

Litigation is costly, so after you have assembled evidence, offending employees are usually disciplined. However, when you discover that a criminal act involving a third-party victim has been committed, you might have a legal and moral obligation to turn the information over to law enforcement. In the next section, you learn about situations in which criminal evidence must be separated from any company proprietary information.

Distinguishing Personal and Company Property

Many company policies distinguish between personal and company computer property; however, making this distinction can be difficult with cell phones, smartphones, personal notebooks, and tablet computers. For example, an employee brings her personal tablet to work and connects it to the company's wireless network. As the employee synchronizes information on the tablet with information in the company network, she copies some data in the tablet to the company network. During the synchronization, data on the company computer or network might be placed on the tablet, too. In this case, at least one question is "Does the information on the tablet belong to the company or the employee?"

Now suppose the company gave the employee the tablet as a holiday bonus. Can the company claim rights to this device? Similar issues come up when an employee brings in a smartphone and connects it to the company network. What rules apply? Because digital devices are part of daily life, you'll encounter these issues often. These questions are still being debated, however, and companies are establishing their own policies to handle them. In today's bring your own device (BYOD) environment, more companies are forced to address the issue of personal devices accessing the company network. Some companies simply state that if you connect a personal device to the business network, it falls under the same rules as company property.

BYOD is a major challenge in company security, digital investigations, and compliance with regulations, including company policies.

Maintaining Professional Conduct

Your professional conduct as a digital investigator is critical because it determines your credibility. **Professional conduct**, discussed in more detail in Chapters 15 and 16, includes ethics, morals, and standards of behavior. As a professional, you must exhibit the highest level of professional behavior at all times. To do so, you must maintain objectivity and confidentiality during an investigation, expand your technical knowledge constantly, and conduct yourself with integrity. Maintaining objectivity means you form opinions based on your education, training, experience, and the evidence in your cases. Avoid making conclusions about your findings until you have exhausted all reasonable leads and considered the available facts. Your ultimate responsibility is to find relevant digital evidence. You must avoid prejudice or bias to maintain the integrity of your fact-finding in all investigations. For example, if you're employed by an attorney, don't allow the attorney's agenda to dictate the outcome of your investigation. Your reputation depends on maintaining your objectivity.

You must also maintain an investigation's credibility by maintaining confidentiality. Discuss the case only with people who need to know about it, such as other investigators involved in the case or someone in the line of authority. If you need advice from other professionals, discuss only the general terms and facts about the case without mentioning specifics. All investigations you conduct must be kept confidential, until you're designated as a witness or required by the attorney or court to release a report.

In the corporate environment, confidentiality is critical, especially when dealing with employees who have been terminated. The agreement between the company and the employee might have been to represent the termination as a layoff or resignation in exchange for no bad references. If you give case details and the employee's name to others, your company could be liable for breach of contract.

In some instances, your corporate case might become a criminal case, and it could be years before the case finally goes to trial or is settled. If an investigator talks about evidence with unauthorized people, the case could be damaged. When working for an attorney on an investigation, the attorney-work-product rule applies to all communications. This means you can discuss the case only with the attorney or other members of the team working with the attorney. All communication about the case to other people requires the attorney's approval.

In addition to maintaining objectivity and confidentiality, you can enhance your professional conduct by continuing your training. The field of digital investigations and forensics is changing constantly. You should stay current with the latest technical changes in computer hardware and software, networking, and forensic tools. You should also learn about the latest investigation techniques you can use in your cases.

To continue your professional training, you should attend workshops, conferences, and vendor courses. You might also need to continue or enhance your formal education, such as pursuing certifications. You improve your professional standing if you have at least an under-graduate degree in computing or a related field. If you don't have an advanced degree, consider graduate-level studies in a complementary area of study, such as business law or e-commerce. Several colleges and universities now offer associate's, bachelor's, and master's degrees and certificate programs in digital forensics. Many companies are willing to assist with employee education expenses because it's to their advantage that employees remain current in their knowledge.

In addition to education and training, membership in professional organizations adds to your credentials. These organizations often sponsor training and publications on the latest techni-cal improvements and trends in digital forensic examinations. Also, keep up to date with the most current publications on digital forensics examination tools and techniques.

As a digital investigator and forensics professional, you're expected to maintain honesty and integrity. You must conduct yourself with the highest levels of integrity in all aspects of your life. Any indiscreet actions can embarrass you and give opposing attorneys opportunities to discredit you during your testimony in court or in depositions.

Preparing a Digital Forensics Investigation

Your role as a digital forensics professional is to gather data from a suspect's computer and determine whether there's evidence that a crime was committed or company policy or indus-try regulations had been violated. If the evidence suggests that a crime or policy violation has been committed, you begin to prepare a case, which is a collection of evidence you can offer in court or at a private-sector inquiry. This process involves investigating the suspect's com-puter and then preserving the evidence on a different computer. Before you begin investigat-ing, however, you must follow an accepted procedure to prepare a case. By approaching each case methodically, you can evaluate the evidence thoroughly and document the chain of evi-dence, or **chain of custody**, which is the route the evidence takes from the time you find it until the case is closed or goes to court.

The following sections present two sample cases—one involving a computer crime and another involving a company policy violation. Each example describes the typical steps of a forensics investigation, including gathering evidence, preparing a case, and preserving the evidence.

An Overview of a Computer Crime

Law enforcement officers often find computers, smartphones, and other devices as they're investigating crimes, gathering other evidence, or making arrests. These devices can contain information that helps law enforcement officers determine the chain of events leading to a crime or information providing evidence that's more likely to lead to a conviction. As an example of a case in which computers were involved in a crime, the police raided a suspected drug dealer's home and found a desktop computer, several USB drives (also called "flash drives" or "thumb drives"), a tablet computer, and a cell phone in a bedroom (see Figure 1-9). The computer was "bagged and tagged," meaning it was placed in evidence bags along with the storage media and then labeled with tags as part of the search and seizure.

Figure 1-9   The crime scene
© Cengage Learning®

The lead detective on the case wants you to examine the computer and cell phone to find and organize data that could be evidence of a crime, such as files containing names of the drug dealer's contacts, text messages, and photos. The acquisitions officer gives you documentation of items the investigating officers collected with the computer, including a list of other storage media, such as removable disks and flash drives. The acquisitions officer also notes that the computer is a Windows 8 system, and the machine was running when it was discovered. Before shutting down the computer, the acquisitions officer photographs all open windows on the Windows desktop, including one showing File Explorer, and gives you the photos. (Before shutting down the computer, a live acquisition should be done to capture RAM, too. This procedure is discussed in Chapter 10.)

As a digital forensics investigator, you're grateful the officers followed proper procedure when acquiring the evidence. With digital evidence, it's important to realize how easily key data, such as the last access date, can be altered by an overeager investigator who's first on the scene. The U.S. DOJ has a document you can download that reviews the correct acquisition of electronic evidence, "Prosecuting Computer Crimes" (*www.justice.gov/criminal/ cybercrime/docs/ssmanual2009.pdf*, 2009). If this link has changed because of site updates, use the search feature.

In your preliminary assessment, you assume that the hard disk and storage media include intact files, such as e-mail messages, deleted files, and hidden files. A range of software is available for use in your investigation; your office uses the tool Technology Pathways ProDiscover.

This chapter introduces you to the principles applied to digital forensics. In Chapter 6, you learn the strengths and weaknesses of several software packages.

Because some cases involve computers running legacy OSs, older versions of tools often need to be used in forensics investigations. For example, Norton DiskEdit is an older tool that was last available on the Norton System Works 2000 CD.

After your preliminary assessment, you identify the potential challenges in this case. Later, you perform the steps needed to investigate the case, including how to address risks and obstacles. Then you can begin the actual investigation and data retrieval.

An Overview of a Company Policy Violation

Companies often establish policies for employee use of computers. Employees surfing the Internet, sending personal e-mail, or using company computers for personal tasks during work hours can waste company time. Because lost time can cost companies millions of dollars, digital forensics specialists are often used to investigate policy violations. The following example describes a company policy violation.

Manager Steve Billings has been receiving complaints from customers about the job performance of one of his sales representatives, George Montgomery. George has worked as a representative for several years. He's been absent from work for two days but hasn't called in sick or told anyone why he wouldn't be at work. Another employee, Martha, is also missing and hasn't informed anyone of the reason for her absence. Steve asks the IT Department to confiscate George's hard drive and all storage media in his work area. He wants to know whether any information on George's computer and storage media might offer a clue to his whereabouts and job performance concerns. To help determine George's and Martha's whereabouts, you must take a systematic approach, described in the following section, to examining and analyzing the data found on George's desk.

Taking a Systematic Approach

When preparing a case, you can apply standard systems analysis steps, explained in the following list, to problem solving. Later in this chapter, you apply these steps to cases.

- *Make an initial assessment about the type of case you're investigating*—To assess the type of case you're handling, talk to others involved in the case and ask questions about the incident. Have law enforcement or company security officers already seized the computer, disks, peripherals, and other components? Do you need to visit an office or another location? Was the computer used to commit a crime, or does it contain evidence about another crime?

- *Determine a preliminary design or approach to the case*—Outline the general steps you need to follow to investigate the case. If the suspect is an employee and you need to acquire his or her system, determine whether you can seize the computer during work hours or have to wait until evening or weekend hours. If you're preparing a criminal case, determine what information law enforcement officers have already gathered.

- *Create a detailed checklist*—Refine the general outline by creating a detailed checklist of steps and an estimated amount of time for each step. This outline helps you stay on track during the investigation.

- *Determine the resources you need*—Based on the OS of the computer you're investigating, list the software you plan to use for the investigation, noting any other software, tools, or expert assistance you might need.

- *Obtain and copy an evidence drive*—In some cases, you might be seizing multiple computers along with CDs, DVDs, USB drives, mobile devices, and other removable media. (For the examples in this chapter, you're using only USB drives.) Make a forensic copy of the disk.

- *Identify the risks*—List the problems you normally expect in the type of case you're handling. This list is known as a standard risk assessment. For example, if the suspect seems knowledgeable about computers, he or she might have set up a logon scheme that shuts down the computer or overwrites data on the hard disk when someone tries to change the logon password.

- *Mitigate or minimize the risks*—Identify how you can minimize the risks. For example, if you're working with a computer on which the suspect has likely password-protected the hard drive, you can make multiple copies of the original media before starting. Then if you destroy a copy during the process of retrieving information from the disk, you have additional copies.

- *Test the design*—Review the decisions you've made and the steps you've completed. If you have already copied the original media, a standard part of testing the design involves comparing hash values (discussed in Chapters 3 and 4) to ensure that you copied the original media correctly.

- *Analyze and recover the digital evidence*—Using the software tools and other resources you've gathered, and making sure you've addressed any risks and obstacles, examine the disk to find digital evidence.

- *Investigate the data you recover*—View the information recovered from the disk, including existing files, deleted files, e-mail, and Web history, and organize the files to help find information relevant to the case.

- *Complete the case report*—Write a complete report detailing what you did and what you found.

- *Critique the case*—Self-evaluation and peer review are essential parts of professional growth. After you complete a case, review it to identify successful decisions and actions and determine how you could have improved your performance.

The amount of time and effort you put into each step varies, depending on the nature of the investigation. For example, in most cases, you need to create a simple investigation plan so that you don't overlook any steps. However, if a case involves many computers with complex issues to identify and examine, a detailed plan with periodic review and updates is essential. A systematic approach helps you discover the information you need for your case, and you should gather as much information as possible.

For all computing investigations, you must be prepared for the unexpected, so you should always have a contingency plan for the investigation. A contingency plan can consist of anything to help you complete the investigation, from alternative software and hardware tools to other methods of approaching the investigation.

Assessing the Case As mentioned, identifying case requirements involves determining the type of case you're investigating. Doing so means you should outline the case details systematically, including the nature of the case, the type of evidence available, and the location of evidence.

In the company-policy violation case, you have been asked to investigate George Montgomery. Steve Billings had the IT Department confiscate George's storage media that might contain information about his whereabouts. After talking to George's co-workers, Steve learned that George has been conducting a personal business on the side using company computers. Therefore, the focus of the case has shifted to include possible employee abuse of company resources. You can begin assessing this case as follows:

- *Situation*—Employee abuse of resources.
- *Nature of the case*—Side business conducted on the company computer.
- *Specifics of the case*—The employee is reportedly conducting a side business on his company computer that involves registering domain names for clients and setting up their Web sites at local ISPs. Co-workers have complained that he's been spending too much time on his own business and not performing his assigned work duties. Company policy states that all company-owned computing assets are subject to inspection by company management at any time. Employees have no expectation of privacy when operating company computer systems.
- *Type of evidence*—Small-capacity USB drive connected to a company computer.
- *Known disk format*—NTFS.
- *Location of evidence*—One USB drive recovered from the employee's assigned computer.

Based on these details, you can determine the case requirements. You now know that the nature of the case involves employee abuse of company resources, and you're looking for evidence that an employee was conducting a side business using his employer's computers. On the USB drive retrieved from George's computer, you're looking for any information related to Web sites, ISPs, or domain names. You know that the USB drive uses the NTFS file system. To duplicate the USB drive and find deleted and hidden files, you need a reliable digital forensics tool. Because the USB drive has already been retrieved, you don't need to seize the drive yourself.

You call this case Montgomery_72015 (because the case opened on July 20, 2015) and determine that your task is to gather data from the storage media seized to confirm or deny the allegation that George is conducting a side business on company time and computers. Remember that he's suspected only of resource abuse, and the evidence you obtain might be exculpatory—meaning it could prove his innocence. You must always maintain an unbiased perspective and be objective in your fact-findings. If you are systematic and thorough, you're more likely to produce consistently reliable results.

Planning Your Investigation Now that you have identified the requirements of the Montgomery_72015 case, you can plan your investigation. You have already determined the kind of evidence you need; now you can identify the specific steps to gather the evidence, establish a chain of custody, and perform the forensic analysis. These steps become the basic plan for your investigation and indicate what you should do and when. To investigate the Montgomery_72015 case, you should perform the following general steps. Most of these steps are explained in more detail in the following sections.

1. Acquire the USB drive from the IT Department, which bagged and tagged the evidence.

2. Complete an evidence form and establish a chain of custody.

3. Transport the evidence to your digital forensics lab.

4. Place the evidence in an **approved secure container**.

5. Prepare your **forensic workstation**.

6. Retrieve the evidence from the secure container.

7. Make a forensic copy of the evidence drive (in this case, the USB drive).

8. Return the evidence drive to the secure container.

9. Process the copied evidence drive with your digital forensics tools.

 The approved secure container you need in Step 4 should be a locked, fireproof locker or cabinet that has limited access. Limited access means that only you and other authorized personnel can open the secure container.

The first rule for all investigations is to preserve the evidence, which means it shouldn't be tampered with or contaminated. Because the IT Department staff confiscated the storage media, you need to go to them for the evidence. The IT Department manager confirms that the storage media has been locked in a secure cabinet since it was retrieved from George's desk. Keep in mind that even though this case is a company policy matter, many cases are thrown out because the chain of custody can't be proved or has been broken. When this happens, there's the possibility that the evidence has been compromised.

To document the evidence, you record details about the media, including who recovered the evidence and when and who possessed it and when. Use an **evidence custody form**, also called a chain-of-evidence form, which helps you document what has and has not been done with the original evidence and forensic copies of the evidence. Depending on whether you're working in law enforcement or private security, you can create an evidence custody form to fit your environment. This form should be easy to read and use. It can contain information for one or several pieces of evidence. Consider creating a **single-evidence form** (which lists each piece of evidence on a separate page) and a **multi-evidence form** (see Figure 1-10), depending on the administrative needs of your investigation.

If necessary, document how to use your evidence custody form. Clear instructions help users remain consistent when completing the form and ensure that everyone uses the same definitions for collected items. Standardization helps maintain consistent quality for all investigations and prevent confusion and mistakes about the evidence you collect. An evidence custody form usually contains the following information:

- *Case number*—The number your organization assigns when an investigation is initiated.

- *Investigating organization*—The name of your organization. In large corporations with global facilities, several organizations might be conducting investigations in different geographic areas.

- *Investigator*—The name of the investigator assigned to the case. If many investigators are assigned, specify the lead investigator's name.

Figure 1-10   A sample multi-evidence form used in a private-sector environment
© Cengage Learning®

- *Nature of case*—A short description of the case. For example, in the private-sector environment, it might be "data recovery for corporate litigation" or "employee policy violation case."

- *Location evidence was obtained*—The exact location where the evidence was collected. If you're using multi-evidence forms, a new form should be created for each location.

- *Description of evidence*—A list of the evidence items, such as "hard drive, 250 GB" or "one USB drive, 8 GB." On a multi-evidence form, write a description for each item of evidence you acquire and possibly include photos.

- *Vendor name*—The name of the manufacturer of the computer component. List a 250 GB hard drive, for example, as a "Maxtor 250 GB hard drive," or describe a USB drive as a "SanDisk 8 GB USB drive." In later chapters, you see how differences among manufacturers can affect data recovery.

- *Model number or serial number*—List the model number or serial number (if available) of the computer component. Many computer components, including hard drives, memory chips, and expansion slot cards, have model numbers but not serial numbers.

- *Evidence recovered by*—The name of the investigator who recovered the evidence. The chain of custody for evidence starts with this information. If you insert your name, for example, you're declaring that you have taken control of the evidence. It's now your responsibility to ensure that nothing damages the evidence and no one tampers with it.

The person placing his or her name on this line is responsible for preserving, transporting, and securing the evidence.

- *Date and time*—The date and time the evidence was taken into custody. This information establishes exactly when the chain of custody starts.

- *Evidence placed in locker*—Specifies which approved secure container is used to store evidence and when the evidence was placed in the container.

- *Item #/Evidence processed by/Disposition of evidence/Date/Time*—When you or another authorized investigator retrieves evidence from the evidence locker for processing and analysis, list the item number and your name, and then describe what was done to the evidence.

- *Page*—The forms used to catalog all evidence for each location should have page numbers. List the page number, and indicate the total number of pages for this group of evidence. For example, if you collected 15 pieces of evidence at one location and your form has only 10 lines, you need to fill out two multi-evidence forms. The first form is noted as "Page 1 of 2," and the second page is noted as "Page 2 of 2."

Figure 1-11 shows a single-evidence form, which lists only one piece of evidence per page. This form gives you more flexibility in tracking separate pieces of evidence for your chain-of-custody log. It also has more space for descriptions, which is helpful when finalizing the investigation and creating a case report. With this form, you can accurately account for what was done to the evidence and what was found. Use evidence forms as a reference for all actions taken during your investigative analysis.

Figure 1-11 A single-evidence form
© Cengage Learning®

You can use both multi-evidence and single-evidence forms in your investigation. By using two forms, you can keep the single-evidence form with the evidence and the multi-evidence form in your report file. Two forms also provide redundancy that can be used as a quality control for evidence.

Securing Your Evidence Computing investigations demand that you adjust your procedures to suit the case. For example, if the evidence for a case includes an entire computer system and associated storage media, such as flash drives and large external hard drives, you must be flexible when you account for all these items. Some evidence is small enough to fit into an evidence bag. Other items, such as CPU cabinets, monitors, keyboards, and printers, are too large.

To secure and catalog the evidence contained in large computer components, you can use large **evidence bags**, tape, tags, labels, and other products available from police supply vendors or office supply stores. When gathering products to secure your computer evidence, make sure they are safe and effective to use on computer components. Be cautious when handling any computer component to avoid damaging the component or coming into contact with static electricity, which can destroy digital data. For this reason, make sure you use antistatic bags when collecting computer evidence. Consider using an antistatic pad with an attached wrist strap, too. Both help prevent damage to computer evidence.

This section focuses on securing computers and related hardware. Devices such as smartphones and cell phones are covered later in Chapter 12.

Be sure to place computer evidence in a well-padded container. Padding prevents damage to the evidence as you transport it to your secure evidence locker, evidence room, or computer lab. Save discarded hard drive boxes, antistatic bags, and packing material for computer hardware when you or others acquire computer devices.

Because you might not have everything needed to secure your evidence, you have to improvise. Securing evidence often requires building secure containers. If the computer component is large and contained in its own casing, you can use evidence tape to seal all openings on the cabinet. Placing evidence tape over drive bays, insertion slots for power supply cords and USB cables, and any other openings ensures the security of evidence. As a standard practice, you should write your initials on the tape before applying it to the evidence. This practice makes it possible to prove later in court that the evidence hasn't been tampered with because the casing couldn't have been opened nor could power have been supplied to the closed casing with this tape in place. If the tape had been replaced, your initials wouldn't be present, which would indicate tampering. If you transport a computer, place new disks in disk drives to reduce possible drive damage while you're moving it.

Computer components require specific temperature and humidity ranges. If it's too cold, hot, or wet, computer components and magnetic media can be damaged. Even heated car seats can damage digital media, and placing a computer on top of a two-way car radio in the trunk can damage magnetic media. When collecting computer evidence, make sure you have a safe environment for transporting and storing it until a secure evidence container is available.

Procedures for Private-Sector High-Tech Investigations

As an investigator, you need to develop formal procedures and informal checklists to cover all issues important to high-tech investigations. These procedures are necessary to ensure that correct techniques are used in an investigation. Use informal checklists to be certain that all evidence is collected and processed correctly. This section lists some sample procedures that computing investigators commonly use in private-sector high-tech investigations.

Employee Termination Cases

Most investigative work for termination cases involves employee abuse of company resources. Incidents that create a hostile work environment, such as viewing pornography in the workplace and sending inappropriate e-mails, are the predominant types of cases investigated. The following sections describe key points for conducting an investigation that might lead to an employee's termination. Consulting with your organization's general counsel and Human Resources Department for specific directions on how to handle these investigations is recommended. Your organization must have appropriate policies in place, as described previously in this chapter.

Internet Abuse Investigations

The information in this section applies to an organization's internal private network, not a public ISP. Consult with your organization's general counsel after reviewing this list, and make changes according to their directions to build your own procedures. To conduct an investigation involving Internet abuse, you need the following:

- The organization's Internet proxy server logs
- Suspect computer's IP address obtained from your organization's network administrator
- Suspect computer's disk drive
- Your preferred digital forensics analysis tool (ProDiscover, Forensic Toolkit, EnCase, X-Ways Forensics, and so forth)

The following steps outline the recommended processing of an Internet abuse case:

1. Use the standard forensic analysis techniques and procedures described in this book for the disk drive examination.
2. Using tools such as Magnet Forensics Internet Evidence Finder or Forensic Toolkit's Internet keyword search option, extract all Web page URLs and other associated information.
3. Contact the network firewall administrator and request a proxy server log, if it's available, of the suspect computer's network device name or IP address for the dates of interest. Consult with your organization's network administrator to confirm that these logs are maintained and how long the time to live (TTL) is set for the network's IP address assignments that use Dynamic Host Configuration Protocol (DHCP).
4. Compare the data recovered from forensics analysis with the network server log data to confirm that they match.
5. If the URL data matches the network server log and the forensic disk examination, continue analyzing the suspect computer's drive data, and collect any relevant photos

or Web pages that support the allegation. If there are no matches between the network server logs, and the forensic examination shows no contributing evidence, report that the allegation is unsubstantiated.

Before investigating an Internet abuse case, research your state or country's privacy laws. Many countries have unique privacy laws that restrict the use of computer log data, such as network server logs or disk drive cache files, for any type of investigation. Some state or federal laws might supersede your organization's employee policies. Always consult with your organization's attorney. For companies with international business operations, jurisdiction is a problem; what's legal in the United States, such as examining and investigating a network server log, might not be legal in Germany, for example.

For investigations in which the network server log doesn't match the forensics analysis that found inappropriate data, continue the examination of the suspect computer's disk drive. Determine when inappropriate data was downloaded to the computer and whether it was through an organization's intranet connection to the Internet. Employees might have used their employer's laptop computers to connect to their own ISPs to download inappropriate Web content. For these situations, you need to consult your organization's employee policy guidelines for what's considered appropriate use of the organization's computing resources.

E-mail Abuse Investigations

E-mail investigations typically include spam, inappropriate and offensive message content, and harassment or threats. E-mail is subject to the same restrictions as other computer evidence data, in that an organization must have a defined policy, as described previously. The following list is what you need for an investigation involving e-mail abuse:

- An electronic copy of the offending e-mail that contains message header data; consult with your e-mail server administrator
- If available, e-mail server log records; consult with your e-mail server administrator to see whether they are available
- For e-mail systems that store users' messages on a central server, access to the server; consult with your e-mail server administrator
- For e-mail systems that store users' messages on a computer as an Outlook .pst or .ost file, for example, access to the computer so that you can perform a forensic analysis on it
- Your preferred digital forensics analysis tool, such as OS Forensics or ProDiscover

The following steps outline the recommended procedure for e-mail investigations:

1. For computer-based e-mail data files, such as Outlook .pst or .ost files, use the standard forensic analysis techniques and procedures described in this book for the drive examination.
2. For server-based e-mail data files, contact the e-mail server administrator and obtain an electronic copy of the suspect's and victim's e-mail folder or data.
3. For Web-based e-mail (Gmail, for example) investigations, use tools such as Forensic Toolkit's Internet keyword search option to extract all related e-mail address information.
4. Examine header data of all messages of interest to the investigation.

Attorney-Client Privilege Investigations

When conducting a digital forensics analysis under **attorney-client privilege** (**ACP**) rules for an attorney, you must keep all findings confidential. The attorney you're working for is the ultimate authority over the investigation. For investigations of this nature, attorneys typically request that you extract all data from drives. It's your responsibility to comply with the attorney's directions. Because of the large quantities of data a drive can contain, the attorney will want to know about everything of interest on the drives.

Many attorneys like to have printouts of the data you have recovered, but printouts can pose problems when you have log files with several thousand pages of data or CAD drawing programs that can be read only by proprietary programs. You need to persuade and educate many attorneys on how digital evidence can be viewed electronically. In addition, learn how to teach attorneys and paralegals to sort through files so that you can help them efficiently analyze the huge amount of data a forensic examination produces.

You can also encounter problems if you find data in the form of binary files, such as CAD drawings. Examining these files requires using the CAD program that created them. In addition, engineering companies often have specialized drafting programs. Discovery demands for lawsuits involving a product that caused injury or death requires extracting design plans for attorneys and expert witnesses to review. You're responsible for locating the programs for these design plans so that attorneys and expert witnesses can view the evidence files.

The following list shows the basic steps for conducting an ACP case:

1. Request a memorandum from the attorney directing you to start the investigation. The memorandum must state that the investigation is privileged communication and list your name and any other associates' names assigned to the case.

2. Request a list of keywords of interest to the investigation.

3. After you have received the memorandum, initiate the investigation and analysis. Any findings you made before receiving the memorandum are subject to discovery by the opposing attorney.

4. For drive examinations, make two bit-stream images (discussed later in this chapter) of the drive using a different tool for each image, such as EnCase for the first and ProDiscover or FTK Imager for the second. This approach is advisable because every tool has its strengths and weaknesses. If you have large enough storage drives, make each bit-stream image uncompressed so that if it becomes corrupt, you can still examine uncorrupted areas with your preferred forensics analysis tool.

5. Verify the hash values on all files on the original and re-created disks.

6. Methodically examine every portion of the drive (both allocated and unallocated data areas) and extract all data.

7. Run keyword searches on allocated and unallocated disk space. Follow up the search results to determine whether the search results contain information that supports the case.

8. For Windows OSs, use specialty tools to analyze and extract data from the Registry, such as AccessData Registry Viewer or a Registry viewer program (discussed in more detail in Chapter 5). Use the Edit, Find menu option in Registry Editor, for example, to search for keywords of interest to the investigation.

9. For binary files such as CAD drawings, locate the correct program and, if possible, make printouts of the binary file content. If the files are too large, load the specialty program on a separate workstation with the recovered binary files so that the attorney can view them.

10. For unallocated data recovery, use a tool that removes or replaces nonprintable data, such as X-Ways Forensics Specialist Gather Text function.

11. Consolidate all recovered data from the evidence bit-stream image into well-organized folders and subfolders. Store the recovered data output, using a logical and easy-to-follow storage method for the attorney or paralegal.

Here are some other guidelines to remember for ACP cases:

- Minimize all written communication with the attorney; use the telephone when you need to ask questions or provide information related to the case.

- Any documentation written to the attorney must contain a header stating that it's "Privileged Legal Communication—Confidential Work Product," as defined under the attorney-work-product rule.

- Assist the attorney and paralegal in analyzing the data.

If you have difficulty complying with the directions or don't understand the directives in the memorandum, contact the attorney and explain the problem. Always keep an open line of verbal communication with the attorney during these types of investigations. If you're communicating via e-mail, use encryption or another secure e-mail service for all messages.

Industrial Espionage Investigations

Industrial espionage cases can be time consuming and are subject to scope creep problems (meaning the investigation's focus widens and becomes more time consuming). This section offers some guidelines on how to deal with industrial espionage investigations. Be aware that cases dealing with foreign nationals might be violations of International Traffic in Arms Regulations (ITAR) or Export Administration Regulations (EAR). For more information on ITAR, see the U.S. Department of State's Web site (*www.state.gov*; substitute the actual state name or a shortened version for *state*) or do an Internet search for "International Traffic in Arms Regulations." For EAR information, see the U.S. Department of Commerce Web site (*www.doc.gov*) or do an Internet search for "Export Administration Regulations."

Unlike the other private-sector investigations covered in this section, all suspected industrial espionage cases should be treated as criminal investigations. The techniques described here are for private network environments and internal investigations that haven't yet been reported to law enforcement officials. Make sure you don't become an agent of law enforcement by filing a complaint of a suspected espionage case before substantiating the allegation. The following list includes staff you might need when planning an industrial espionage investigation. This list isn't exhaustive, so use your knowledge to improve on these recommendations:

- The computing investigator who's responsible for disk forensic examinations

- The technology specialist who is knowledgeable about the suspected compromised technical data

- The network specialist who can perform log analysis and set up network monitors to trap network communication of possible suspects

- The threat assessment specialist (typically an attorney) who's familiar with federal and state laws and regulations related to ITAR or EAR and industrial espionage

The International Competition Network has established guidelines (available at *www.internationalcompetitionnetwork.org/uploads/library/doc627.pdf*) for digital evidence gathering in private-sector settings; they're used by more than 90 jurisdictions.

In addition, consider the following guidelines when initiating an international espionage investigation:

- Determine whether this investigation involves a possible industrial espionage incident, and then determine whether it falls under ITAR or EAR.

- Consult with corporate attorneys and upper management if the investigations must be conducted discreetly.

- Determine what information is needed to substantiate the allegation of industrial espionage.

- Generate a list of keywords for disk forensics and network monitoring.

- List and collect resources needed for the investigation.

- Determine the goal and scope of the investigation; consult with management and the company's attorneys on how much work you should do.

- Initiate the investigation after approval from management, and make regular reports of your activities and findings.

The following are planning considerations for industrial espionage investigations:

- Examine all e-mail of suspected employees, both company-provided e-mail and free Web-based services.

- Search Internet forums or blogs for any postings related to the incident.

- Initiate physical surveillance with cameras on people or things of interest to the investigation.

- If available, examine all facility physical access logs for sensitive areas, which might include secure areas where smart badges or video surveillance recordings are used.

- If there's a suspect, determine his or her location in relation to the vulnerable resource that was compromised.

- Study the suspect's work habits.

- Collect all incoming and outgoing phone logs to see whether any unique or unusual places were called.

When conducting an industrial espionage case, follow these basic steps:

1. Gather all personnel assigned to the investigation and brief them on the plan and any concerns.

2. Gather the resources needed to conduct the investigation.

3. Start the investigation by placing surveillance systems, such as cameras and network monitors, at key locations.

4. Discreetly gather any additional evidence, such as the suspect's computer drive, and make a bit-stream image for follow-up examination.

5. Collect all log data from networks and e-mail servers, and examine them for unique items that might relate to the investigation.

6. Report regularly to management and corporate attorneys on your investigation's status and current findings.

7. Review the investigation's scope with management and corporate attorneys to determine whether it needs to be expanded and more resources added.

Interviews and Interrogations in High-Tech Investigations

Becoming a skilled interviewer and interrogator can take many years of experience. Typically, a private-sector digital investigator is a technical person acquiring the evidence for an investigation. Many large organizations have full-time security investigators with years of training and experience in criminal and civil investigations and interviewing techniques. Few of these investigators have any computing or network technical skills, so you might be asked to assist in interviewing or interrogating a suspect when you have performed a forensic disk analysis on that suspect's machine.

An interrogation is different from an interview. An **interview** is usually conducted to collect information from a witness or suspect about specific facts related to an investigation. An **interrogation** is the process of trying to get a suspect to confess to a specific incident or crime. An investigator might change from an interview to an interrogation when talking to a witness or suspect. The more experience and training investigators have in the art of interviewing and interrogating, the more easily they can determine whether a witness is credible and possibly a suspect.

Your role as a digital investigator is to instruct the investigator conducting the interview on what questions to ask and what the answers should be. As you build rapport with the investigator, he or she might ask you to question the suspect. Watching a skilled interrogator is a learning experience in human relations skills.

If you're asked to assist in an interview or interrogation, prepare yourself by answering the following questions:

- What questions do I need to ask the suspect to get the vital information about the case?
- Do I know what I'm talking about, or will I have to research the topic or technology related to the investigation?
- Do I need additional questions to cover other indirect issues related to the investigation?

Common interview and interrogation errors include being unprepared for the interview or interrogation and not having the right questions or enough questions to increase your depth of knowledge. Make sure you don't run out of conversation topics; you need to keep the conversation friendly to gain the suspect's confidence. Avoid doubting your own skills, which might show the suspect you lack confidence in your ability. The ingredients for a successful interview or interrogation include the following:

- Being patient throughout the session
- Repeating or rephrasing questions to zero in on specific facts from a reluctant witness or suspect
- Being tenacious

Understanding Data Recovery Workstations and Software

Now you know what's involved in acquiring and documenting evidence. In Chapter 2, you examine a complete setup of a digital forensics lab, which is where you conduct your investigations and where most of your equipment and software are located, including secure evidence containers. Be aware that some companies that perform digital investigations also do data recovery, e-discovery, and other related investigations.

Remember the difference between data recovery and digital forensics. In data recovery, typically, the customer or your company just wants the data back. The other key difference is that in data recovery, you usually know what you're trying to retrieve. In digital forensics, you might have an idea of what you're searching for, but not necessarily.

To conduct your investigation and analysis, you must have a specially configured PC known as a forensic workstation, which is a computer loaded with additional bays and forensics software. Depending on your needs, a forensic workstation can use the following operating systems:

- MS-DOS 6.22
- Windows 95, 98, or Me
- Windows NT 3.5 or 4.0
- Windows 2000, XP, Vista, 7, or 8
- Linux (including Kali Linux)
- Mac OS X

Chapters 2 and 6 cover the software resources you need and the forensics lab and workstation in detail. Visit *www.digitalintelligence.com* to examine the specifications of the Forensic Recovery of Evidence Device (F.R.E.D.) unit, or go to sites such as *www.forensiccomputers.com* to look at current products.

If you start any operating system while you're examining a hard disk, the OS alters the evidence disk by writing data to the Recycle Bin and corrupts the quality and integrity of the evidence you're trying to preserve. Chapter 5 covers which files Windows updates automatically at startup. Windows XP and newer Windows OSs also record the serial numbers of hard drives and CPUs in a file, which can be difficult to recover.

Of all the Microsoft OSs, the least intrusive (in terms of changing data) to disks is MS-DOS 6.22. With the continued evolution of Microsoft OSs, it's not always practical to use older MS-DOS platforms, however. Many older digital forensics acquisition tools work in the MS-DOS environment. These tools can operate from an MS-DOS window in Windows 98 or from the command prompt in Windows 2000 and later. Some of their functions are disabled or generate error messages when run in these OSs, however.

Newer file system formats, such as NTFS, are accessible—that is, readable—only from Windows NT and later or any Linux OS. You can use one of several write-blockers that enable you to boot to Windows without writing data to the evidence drive. In Chapter 3, you learn more about write-blockers and some inexpensive alternatives for preserving data during an acquisition.

Many hardware write-blockers that connect to USB or FireWire ports are on the market. Several vendors sell write-blockers, including Technology Pathways NoWrite FPU; Digital Intelligence Ultra-Kit, UltraBlock, FireFly, FireChief 800, and USB Write Blocker; WiebeTECH Forensic DriveDock; Guidance Software FastBloc; Paralan's SCSI Write Blockers; and Intelligent Computer Solutions (*www.ics-iq.com*) Image LinkMASSter Forensics Hard Case.

Software write-blockers are available, too. Typically these write-blockers require a bootable DVD or USB flash drive that runs an independent OS in a suspect computer's RAM. For more information on software write-blockers, see *http://forensicsoft.com*.

Windows products are being developed that make performing disk forensics easier. However, because Windows has limitations in performing disk forensics, you need to develop skills in acquiring data with Linux. In later chapters, you learn more about using these other tools. Keep in mind that no single digital forensics tool can recover everything. Each tool and OS has its own strengths and weaknesses, so develop skills with as many tools as possible to become an effective computing investigator. Appendix D has additional information on how to use MS-DOS for data acquisitions.

Setting Up Your Workstation for Digital Forensics

With current digital forensics hardware and software, configuring a computer workstation or laptop as a forensic workstation is simple. All that's required are the following:

- A workstation running Windows XP or later
- A write-blocker device
- Digital forensics acquisition tool
- Digital forensics analysis tool
- A target drive to receive the source or suspect disk data
- Spare PATA or SATA ports
- USB ports

Additional useful items include the following:

- Network interface card (NIC)
- Extra USB ports
- FireWire 400/800 ports
- SCSI card
- Disk editor tool
- Text editor tool
- Graphics viewer program
- Other specialized viewing tools

In Chapter 2, you learn more about setting up and configuring a computer to be a forensic workstation.

Conducting an Investigation

Now you're ready to return to the Montgomery_72015 case. You have created a plan for the investigation, set up your forensic workstation, and installed the necessary forensic analysis software you need to examine the evidence. The type of software to install includes your preferred analysis tool, such as ProDiscover, EnCase, FTK, or X-Ways Forensics; an office suite, such as LibreOffice; and a graphics viewer, such as IrfanView. To begin conducting an investigation, you start by copying the evidence, using a variety of methods. No single method retrieves all data from a disk, so using several tools to retrieve and analyze data is a good idea.

Start by gathering the resources you identified in your investigation plan. You need the following items:

- Original storage media
- Evidence custody form
- Evidence container for the storage media, such as an evidence bag
- Bit-stream imaging tool; in this case, the ProDiscover Basic acquisition utility
- Forensic workstation to copy and examine the evidence
- Secure evidence locker, cabinet, or safe

Gathering the Evidence

Now you're ready to gather evidence for the Montgomery_72015 case. Remember that you need antistatic bags and pads with wrist straps to prevent static electricity from damaging digital evidence. To acquire George Montgomery's storage media from the IT Department and then secure the evidence, you perform the following steps:

1. Arrange to meet the IT manager to interview him and pick up the storage media.
2. After interviewing the IT manager, fill out the evidence form, have him sign it, and then sign it yourself.
3. Store the storage media in an evidence bag, and then transport it to your forensic facility.
4. Carry the evidence to a secure container, such as a locker, cabinet, or safe.
5. Complete the evidence custody form. As mentioned, if you're using a multi-evidence form, you can store the form in the file folder for the case. If you're also using single-evidence forms, store them in the secure container with the evidence. Reduce the risk of tampering by limiting access to the forms.
6. Secure the evidence by locking the container.

Understanding Bit-stream Copies

A **bit-stream copy** is a bit-by-bit copy (also known as a "forensic copy") of the original drive or storage medium and is an exact duplicate. The more exact the copy, the better chance you have of retrieving the evidence you need from the disk. This process is usually referred to as "acquiring an image" or "making an image" of a suspect drive. A bit-stream copy is different from a simple backup copy of a disk. Backup software can only copy or compress files that are stored in a folder or are of a known file type. Backup software can't copy deleted files and e-mails or recover file fragments.

A **bit-stream image** is the file containing the bit-stream copy of all data on a disk or disk partition. For simplicity, it's usually referred to as an "image," "image save," or "image file." To create an exact image of an evidence disk, copying the image to a target disk that's identical to the evidence disk is preferable (see Figure 1-12). The target disk's manufacturer and model, in general, should be the same as the original disk's manufacturer and model. If the target disk is identical to the original, the size in bytes and sectors of both disks should also be the same. Some image acquisition tools can accommodate a target disk that's a different size than the original. These imaging tools are discussed in Chapter 3. Older digital forensics tools designed for MS-DOS work only on a copied disk. Current GUI tools can work on both a disk drive and copied data sets that many manufacturers refer to as "image saves."

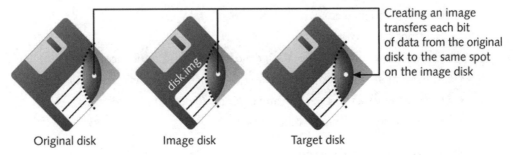

Creating an image transfers each bit of data from the original disk to the same spot on the image disk

Original disk   Image disk   Target disk

Figure 1-12   Transfer of data from original to image to target
© Cengage Learning®

Occasionally, the track and sector maps on the original and target disks don't match, even if you use disks of exactly the same size that are different makes or models. Tools such as Guidance EnCase and NTI SafeBack adjust for the target drive's geometry. Two other tools, X-Ways WinHex Specialist Edition and Technology Pathways ProDiscover, can copy sector by sector to equal-size or larger disks without needing to force changes in the target disk's geometry.

Acquiring an Image of Evidence Media

After you retrieve and secure the evidence, you're ready to copy the evidence media and analyze the data. The first rule of digital forensics is to preserve the original evidence. Then conduct your analysis only on a copy of the data—the image of the original medium. Several vendors provide MS-DOS, Linux, and Windows acquisition tools. Windows tools, however, require a write-blocking device (discussed in Chapter 3) when acquiring data from FAT or NTFS file systems.

Using ProDiscover Basic to Acquire a USB Drive

ProDiscover Basic from Technology Pathways is a forensic analysis tool. You can use it to acquire and analyze data from several different file systems, such as Microsoft FAT and NTFS; Linux Ext2, Ext3, and Ext4; and other UNIX file systems, from a Windows XP or older OS.

The DVD accompanying this book includes ProDiscover Basic. The installation program includes a user manual, `ProDiscoverManual.pdf`, in the C:\Program Files (x86)\Technology Pathways\ProDiscover folder (if the installation defaults are used; for older Windows OS, look in the C:\Program Files\Technology Pathways\ProDiscover folder). Read the user manual for instructions, and install ProDiscover Basic on your computer before you perform the following activity. In Windows Vista and later, you must be in Administrator mode.

Before starting this activity, create a work folder on your computer for data storage and other related files ProDiscover creates when acquiring and analyzing evidence. You can use any location and name for your work folder, but you'll see it referred to in activities as "C:\Work" or simply "your work folder." To keep your files organized, you should also create subfolders for each chapter. For this chapter, create a Work\Chap01\Chapter folder to store files from in-chapter activities. Note that you might see work folder pathnames in screenshots that are slightly different from your own pathname.

The following steps show how to acquire an image of a USB drive, but you can apply them to other media, such as disk drives. You can use any USB drive already containing files to see how ProDiscover acquires data. To perform an acquisition on a USB drive with ProDiscover Basic, follow these steps:

1. On the USB drive, locate the write-protect switch (if one is available) and place the drive in write-protect mode. Then connect the USB drive to your computer. (Most current USB flash drives don't have a write-block switch; for this activity, it's assumed that the USB flash drive has been write-protected.)

This activity is meant to introduce you to the ProDiscover Basic tool. Proper forensics procedures require write-protecting any evidence medium to make sure it's not altered. In Chapter 3, you learn how to use hardware and software write-blocking methods.

2. To start ProDiscover Basic in Windows 7 or earlier, click **Start**, point to **All Programs**, click **ProDiscover**, and click **ProDiscover Basic**. In Windows 8, click the **ProDiscover** icon in the Start screen. If the Launch Dialog dialog box opens (see Figure 1-13), click **Cancel**.

If you're using Windows Vista or later, right-click the ProDiscover Basic desktop icon (or menu item on the All Programs menu) and click Run as administrator. In the User Account Control (UAC) message box, click Continue or Yes (in Windows 7).

3. In the main window, click **Action, Capture Image** from the menu.

4. In the Capture Image dialog box shown in Figure 1-14, click the **Source Drive** list arrow, and select the USB drive.

5. Click the ≫ button next to the Destination text box and click **Choose Local Path**. When the Save As dialog box opens, navigate to your work folder (Work\Chap01\ Chapter) and enter a name for the image you're making, such as **InChp-prac**. Click **Save** to save the file.

Figure 1-13 The Launch Dialog dialog box in ProDiscover
Courtesy of Technology Pathways, LLC

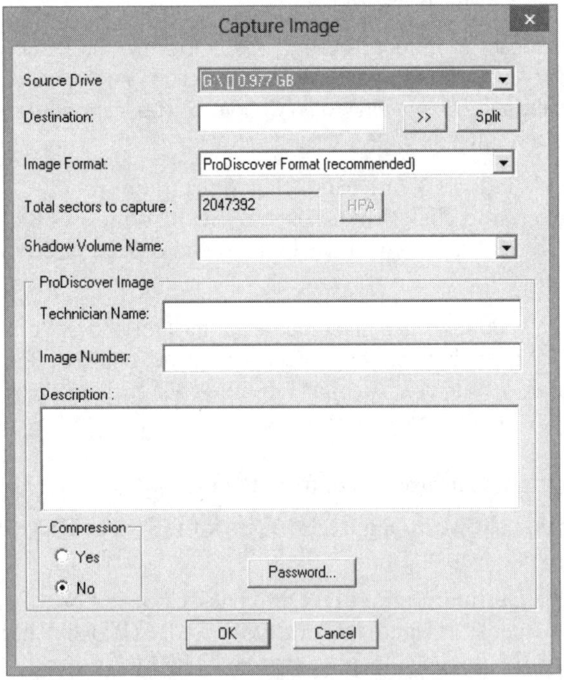

Figure 1-14 The Capture Image dialog box
Courtesy of Technology Pathways, LLC

6. Next, in the Capture Image dialog box, type your name in the Technician Name text box and **InChp-prac01** in the Image Number text box (see Figure 1-15). Click **OK**.

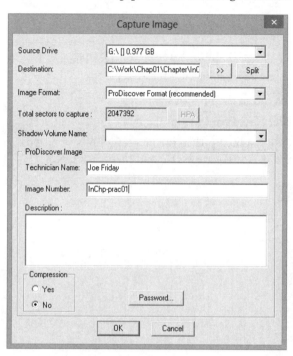

Figure 1-15   The completed Capture Image dialog box
Courtesy of Technology Pathways, LLC

ProDiscover Basic then acquires an image of the USB drive. When it's finished, it displays a notice to check the log file created during the acquisition. This log file contains additional information if errors were encountered during the data acquisition. ProDiscover also creates an MD5 hash output file. In Chapters 3 and 4, you learn how to use MD5 for forensic analysis and evidence validation.

7. When ProDiscover is finished, click **OK** in the completion message box. Click **File, Exit** from the menu to exit ProDiscover.

This activity completes your first forensics data acquisition. Next, you learn how to locate data in an acquisition.

Analyzing Your Digital Evidence

When you analyze digital evidence, your job is to recover the data. If users have deleted or overwritten files on a disk, the disk contains deleted files and file fragments in addition to existing files. Remember that as files are deleted, the space they occupied becomes free space—meaning it can be used for new files that are saved or files that expand as data is added to them. The files that were deleted are still on the disk until a new file is saved to the same physical location, overwriting the original file. In the meantime, those files can still be retrieved. Forensics tools such as ProDiscover Basic can retrieve deleted files for use as evidence.

Before beginning, extract all compressed files from the Chap01 folder on the book's DVD to your work folder.

In the following steps, you analyze George Montgomery's USB drive. The first task is loading the acquired image into ProDiscover Basic by following these steps:

1. Start ProDiscover Basic as you did in the previous activity.

2. To create a new case, click **File, New Project** from the menu.

3. In the New Project dialog box, type **InChp01** in the Project Number text box and again in the Project File Name text box (see Figure 1-16), and then click **OK**.

Figure 1-16   The New Project dialog box
Courtesy of Technology Pathways, LLC

4. In the tree view of the main window (see Figure 1-17), click to expand the **Add** item, and then click **Image File**.

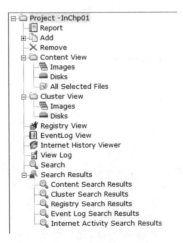

Figure 1-17   The tree view in ProDiscover
Courtesy of Technology Pathways, LLC

5. In the Open dialog box, navigate to the folder containing the image, click the
   `InChp01-prac.eve` file, and click **Open**. Click **Yes** in the Auto Image Checksum
   message box, if necessary.

The next task is to display the contents of the acquired data. Perform the following steps:

1. In the tree view, click to expand **Content View**, if necessary. Click to expand **Images**,
   and click the image filename path **C:\Work\Chap01\Chapter\InChp01-prac.eve**
   (substituting your folder path for *Work*—for example, C:*Work*\Chap01\Chapter).

2. Next, click the **+** in front of the image file pathname, and then click **All Files** under
   the image filename path. When the CAUTION dialog box opens, click **Yes**.
   The `InChp01-prac.eve` file is then loaded in the main window, as shown
   in Figure 1-18.

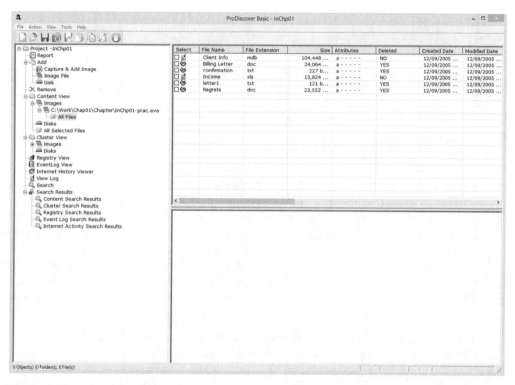

Figure 1-18   The loaded `InChp01-prac.eve` file
Courtesy of Technology Pathways, LLC

3. In the upper-right pane (the work area), click the `letter1` file to view its contents in
   the data area (see Figure 1-19).

4. In the data area, you see the contents of the `letter1` file. Continue to navigate
   through the work and data areas and inspect the contents of the recovered evidence.
   Note that many of these files are deleted files that haven't been overwritten. Leave
   ProDiscover Basic running for the next activity.

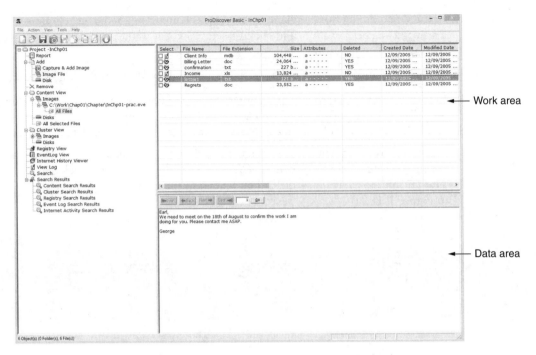

Figure 1-19   Selecting a file in the work area and viewing its contents in the data area
Courtesy of Technology Pathways, LLC

The next step is analyzing the data and searching for information related to the complaint. Data analysis can be the most time-consuming task, even when you know exactly what to look for in the evidence. The method for locating evidentiary artifacts is to search for specific known data values. Data values can be unique words or nonprintable characters, such as hexadecimal codes. There are also printable character codes that can't be generated from a keyboard, such as the copyright (©) or registered trademark (™) symbols. Many digital forensics programs can search for character strings (letters and numbers) and hexadecimal values, such as A9 for the copyright symbol or AE for the registered trademark symbol. All these searchable data values are referred to as "keywords."

With ProDiscover Basic, you can search for keywords of interest in the case. For this case, follow these steps to search for any reference to the name George:

1. In the tree view, click **Search**.
2. In the Search dialog box, click the **Content Search** tab, if necessary. Click the **Select all matches** check box, the **ASCII** option button, and the **Search for the pattern(s)** option button, if they aren't already selected.
3. Next, in the text box under the Search for the pattern(s) option button, type **George** (see Figure 1-20).

You can list keywords separately or combine words with the Boolean logic operators AND, OR, and NOT. Searching for a common keyword produces too many hits and makes it difficult to locate evidence of interest to the case. Applying Boolean logic can help reduce unrelated excessive hits, which are called "false-positive hits."

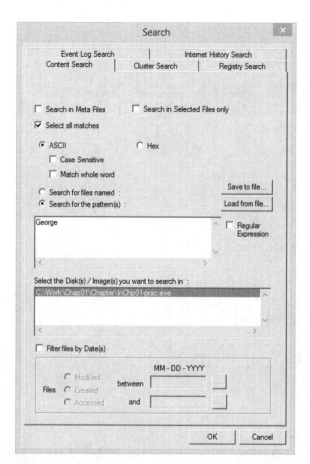

Figure 1-20   Entering a keyword in the Search dialog box
Courtesy of Technology Pathways, LLC

4. Under Select the Disk(s)/Image(s) you want to search in, click **C:\Work\Chap01\ Chapter\InChp01-prac.eve** (substituting the path to your work folder), and then click **OK** to start the search. Leave ProDiscover Basic running for the next activity.

When the search is finished, ProDiscover displays the results in the search results pane in the work area. Note the tabs labeled Search 1 and Search 2 in Figure 1-21. For each search you do in a case, ProDiscover adds a new tab to help catalog your searches.

Click each file in the search results pane and examine its content in the data area. If you locate a file of interest that displays binary (nonprintable) data in the data area, you can double-click the file to display the data in the work area. Then you can double-click the file in the work area, and an associated program, such as Microsoft Excel or LibreOffice for a spreadsheet, opens the file's content. If you want to extract the file, you can right-click it and click Copy File.

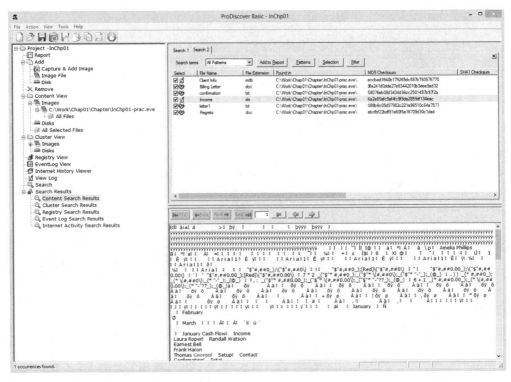

Figure 1-21 The search results pane
Courtesy of Technology Pathways, LLC

For this example, an Excel spreadsheet named Income.xls is displayed in the search results pane. The information in the data area shows mostly unreadable character data. To examine this data, you can export the data to a folder of your choice, and then open it for follow-up examination and analysis. To export the Income.xls file, perform the following steps:

1. In the search results pane, double-click the **Income.xls** file, which switches the view to the work area.

2. In the work area, right-click the **Income.xls** file and click **Copy File**.

3. In the Save As dialog box, navigate to the folder you've selected, and click **Save**.

4. Now that the Income.xls file has been copied to a Windows folder, start Excel (or another spreadsheet program, such as LibreOffice Calc) to examine the file's content. Figure 1-22 shows the extracted file open in LibreOffice Calc. Repeat this data examination and file export process for the remaining files in the search results pane. Then close all open windows except ProDiscover Basic for the next activity.

With ProDiscover's Search feature, you can also search for specific filenames. To use this feature, click the "Search for files named" option button in the Search dialog box. When you're dealing with a very large drive with several thousand files, this useful feature minimizes human error in looking at data.

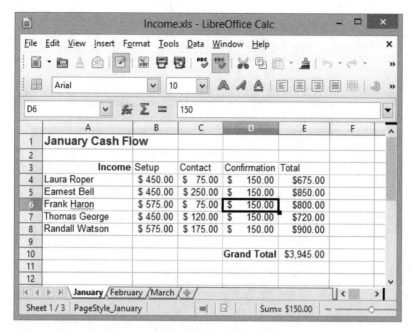

Figure 1-22   The extracted spreadsheet file
Source: The Document Foundation

After completing the detailed examination and analysis, you can then generate a report of your activities. Several digital forensics programs provide a report generator or log file of actions taken during an examination. These reports and logs are typically text or HTML files. The text files are usually in plaintext or Rich Text Format (RTF). ProDiscover Basic offers a report generator that produces an RTF or a plaintext file that most word processing programs can read.

You can also select specific items and add them to the report. For example, to select a file in the work area, click the check box in the Select column next to the file to open the Add Comment dialog box. Enter a description and click OK. The descriptive comment is then added to the ProDiscover Basic report. To create a report in ProDiscover Basic, perform the following steps:

1. In the tree view, click **Report**. The report is then displayed in the right pane, as shown in Figure 1-23.

2. To print the report, click **File**, **Print Report** from the menu.

3. In the Print dialog box, click **OK**.

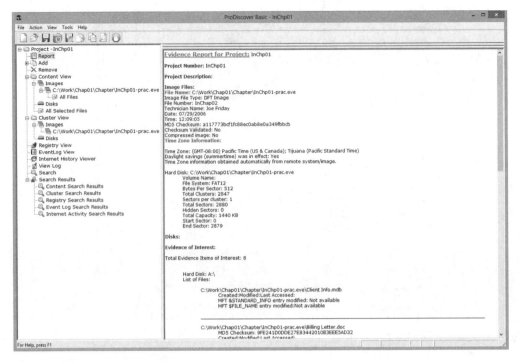

Figure 1-23   A ProDiscover report
Courtesy of Technology Pathways, LLC

If the report needs to be saved to a file, you use ProDiscover Basic's Export feature and choose RTF or plaintext for the file format. To export the report to a file, do the following:

1. In the tree view, click **Report**.

2. Click **Action, Export** from the menu.

3. In the Export dialog box, click the **RTF Format** or **Text Format** option button, type **InChp01** in the File Name text box, and then click **OK**.

> To place the report in a different folder, click the Browse button and navigate to the folder where you want to save the report. Click Save, and then click OK in the Export dialog box.

4. Review the report, and then click **File, Exit** from the menu to exit ProDiscover Basic.

This activity completes your analysis of the USB drive. In the next section, you learn how to complete the case. In later chapters, you learn how to apply more search and analysis techniques.

Completing the Case

After analyzing the disk, you can retrieve deleted files, e-mail, and items that have been purposefully hidden, which you do in Chapters 8, 9, and 11. The files on George's USB drive indicate that he was conducting a side business on his company computer. Now that you have retrieved and analyzed the evidence, you need to find the answers to the following questions to write the final report:

- How did George's manager acquire the disk?
- Did George perform the work on a laptop, which is his own property? If so, did he conduct business transactions on his break or during his lunch hour?
- At what times of the day was George using the non-work-related files? How did you retrieve this information?
- Which company policies apply?
- Are there any other items that need to be considered?

When you write your report, state what you did and what you found. The report you generated in ProDiscover gives you an account of the steps you took. As part of your final report, depending on guidance from management or legal counsel, include the ProDiscover report file to document your work. In any computing investigation, you should be able to repeat the steps you took and produce the same results. This capability is referred to as **repeatable findings**; without it, your work product has no value as evidence.

Keep a written journal of everything you do. Your notes can be used in court, so be mindful of what you write or e-mail, even to a fellow investigator. Often these journals start out as handwritten notes, but you can transcribe them to electronic format periodically.

Basic report writing involves answering the six Ws: who, what, when, where, why, and how. In addition to these basic facts, you must also explain computer and network processes. Typically, your reader is a senior personnel manager, a lawyer, or occasionally a judge who might have little computer knowledge. Identify your reader and write the report for that person. Provide explanations for processes and how systems and their components work.

Your organization might have templates to use when writing reports. Depending on your organization's needs and requirements, your report must describe the findings from your analysis. The report generated by ProDiscover lists your examination and data recovery findings. Other digital forensics tools generate a log file of all actions taken during your examination and analysis. Integrating a digital forensics log report from these other tools can enhance your final report. When describing the findings, consider writing your narrative first and then placing the log output at the end of the report, with references to it in the main narrative. Chapter 14 covers writing final reports for investigations in more detail.

In the Montgomery_72015 case, you want to show what evidence exists that George had his own business registering domain names and list the names of his clients and his income from this business. You also want to show letters he wrote to clients about their accounts. The time and date stamps on the files are during work hours, so you should include this information, too. Eventually, you hand the evidence file to your supervisor or to Steve, George's manager, who then decides on a course of action.

Critiquing the Case

After you close the case and make your final report, you need to meet with your department or a group of fellow investigators and critique the case in an effort to improve your work. Ask yourself assessment questions such as the following:

- How could you improve your performance in the case?
- Did you expect the results you found? Did the case develop in ways you did not expect?
- Was the documentation as thorough as it could have been?
- What feedback has been received from the requesting source?
- Did you discover any new problems? If so, what are they?
- Did you use new techniques during the case or during research?

Make notes to yourself in your journal about techniques or processes that might need to be changed or addressed in future investigations. Then store your journal in a secure place.

Chapter Summary

- Digital forensics applies forensics procedures to digital evidence. This process involves systematically accumulating and analyzing digital information for use as evidence in civil, criminal, and administrative cases. Digital forensics differs from network forensics and data recovery in scope, technique, and objective.

- Laws relating to digital evidence were established in the 1970s.

- To be a successful digital forensics investigator, you must be familiar with more than one computing platform. To supplement your knowledge, develop and maintain contact with computer, network, and investigative professionals.

- Investigators need specialized workstations to examine digital evidence, including additional bays for evidence drives, forensics software, and write blockers.

- Public-sector and private-sector investigations differ, in that public-sector investigations typically require a search warrant before seizing digital evidence. The Fourth Amendment to the U.S. Constitution and similar legislation in other countries apply to government search and seizure. During public-sector investigations, you search for evidence to support criminal allegations. During private-sector investigations, you search for evidence to support allegations of policy violations, abuse of assets, and, in some cases, criminal complaints.

- Warning banners should be used to remind employees and visitors of company policy on computer, e-mail, and Internet use.

- Companies should define and limit the number of authorized requesters who can start an investigation.

- Digital forensics investigators must maintain professional conduct to protect their credibility.

- Always use a systematic approach to your investigations. Follow the checklist in this chapter as a guideline for your case.

- When planning a case, take into account the nature of the case, instructions from the requester, what additional tools and expertise you might need, and how you will acquire the evidence.

- Criminal cases and company-policy violations should be handled in much the same manner to ensure that quality evidence is presented. Both criminal cases and company-policy violations can go to court.

- When you begin a case, there might be unanticipated challenges that weren't obvious when applying a systematic approach to your investigation plan. For all investigations, you need to plan for contingencies for any unexpected problems you might encounter.

- You should create a standard evidence custody form to track the chain of custody of evidence for your case. There are two types of forms: a multi-evidence form and a single-evidence form.

- Internet abuse investigations require examining server log data.

- For attorney-client privilege cases, all written communication should have a header label stating that it's privileged communication and a confidential work product.

- A bit-stream copy is a bit-by-bit duplicate of the original disk. You should use the duplicate, whenever possible, when analyzing evidence.

- Always maintain a journal to keep notes on exactly what you did when handling evidence.

- You should always critique your own work to determine what improvements you made during each case, what could have been done differently, and how to apply those lessons to future cases.

Key Terms

affidavit A notarized document, given under penalty of perjury, that investigators create to detail their findings. This document is often used to justify issuing a warrant or to deal with abuse in a corporation. Also called a "declaration" when the document is unnotarized.

allegation A charge made against someone or something before proof has been found.

approved secure container A fireproof container locked by a key or combination.

attorney-client privilege (ACP) Communication between an attorney and client about legal matters is protected as confidential communications. The purpose of having confidential communications is to promote honest and open dialogue between an attorney and client. This confidential information must not be shared with unauthorized people.

authorized requester In a private-sector environment, the person who has the right to request an investigation, such as the chief security officer or chief intelligence officer.

bit-stream copy A bit-by-bit duplicate of data on the original storage medium. This process is usually called "acquiring an image," "making an image," or "forensic copy."

bit-stream image The file where the bit-stream copy is stored; usually referred to as an "image," "image save," or "image file."

chain of custody The route evidence takes from the time the investigator obtains it until the case is closed or goes to court.

Computer Technology Investigators Network (CTIN) A nonprofit group based in Seattle-Tacoma, WA, composed of law enforcement members, private corporation security professionals, and other security professionals whose aim is to improve the quality of high-technology investigations in the Pacific Northwest.

data recovery Retrieving files that were deleted accidentally or purposefully.

Digital Evidence First Responder (DEFR) A professional who secures digital evidence at the scene and ensures its viability while transporting it to the lab.

Digital Evidence Specialist (DES) An expert who analyzes digital evidence and determines whether additional specialists are needed.

digital forensics Applying investigative procedures for a legal purpose; involves the analysis of digital evidence as well as obtaining search warrants, maintaining a chain of custody, validating with mathematical hash functions, using validated tools, ensuring repeatability, reporting, and presenting evidence as an expert witness.

digital investigations The process of conducting forensic analysis of systems suspected of containing evidence related to an incident or a crime.

evidence bags Nonstatic bags used to transport computer components and other digital devices.

evidence custody form A printed form indicating who has signed out and been in physical possession of evidence.

exculpatory evidence Evidence that indicates the suspect is innocent of the crime.

exhibits Evidence used in court to prove a case.

forensic workstation A workstation set up to allow copying forensic evidence, whether it's on a hard drive, flash drive, or the cloud. It usually has software preloaded and ready to use.

Fourth Amendment The Fourth Amendment to the U.S. Constitution in the Bill of Rights dictates that the government and its agents must have probable cause for search and seizure.

hostile work environment An environment in which employees cannot perform their assigned duties because of the actions of others. In the workplace, these actions include sending threatening or demeaning e-mail or a co-worker viewing pornographic or hate sites.

inculpatory evidence Evidence that indicates a suspect is guilty of the crime with which he or she is charged.

industrial espionage Theft of company sensitive or proprietary company information often to sell to a competitor.

International Association of Computer Investigative Specialists (IACIS) An organization created to provide training and software for law enforcement in the digital forensics field.

interrogation The process of trying to get a suspect to confess to a specific incident or crime.

interview A conversation conducted to collect information from a witness or suspect about specific facts related to an investigation.

line of authority The order in which people or positions are notified of a problem; these people or positions have the legal right to initiate an investigation, take possession of evidence, and have access to evidence.

multi-evidence form An evidence custody form used to list all items associated with a case. See also evidence custody form.

network intrusion detection and incident response Detecting attacks from intruders by using automated tools; also includes the manual process of monitoring network firewall logs.

professional conduct Behavior expected of an employee in the workplace or other professional setting.

repeatable findings Being able to obtain the same results every time from a digital forensics examination.

search and seizure The legal act of acquiring evidence for an investigation. *See also* Fourth Amendment.

search warrants Legal documents that allow law enforcement to search an office, a home, or other locale for evidence related to an alleged crime.

single-evidence form A form that dedicates a page for each item retrieved for a case. It allows investigators to add more detail about exactly what was done to the evidence each time it was taken from the storage locker. *See also* evidence custody form.

verdict The decision returned by a jury.

vulnerability/threat assessment and risk management The group that determines the weakest points in a system. It covers physical security and the security of OSs and applications.

warning banner Text displayed on computer screens when people log on to a company computer; this text states ownership of the computer and specifies appropriate use of the machine or Internet access.

Review Questions

1. Digital forensics and data recovery refer to the same activities. True or False?

2. Police in the United States must use procedures that adhere to which of the following?
   a. Third Amendment
   b. Fourth Amendment
   c. First Amendment
   d. None of the above

3. The triad of computing security includes which of the following?
   a. Detection, response, and monitoring
   b. Vulnerability assessment, detection, and monitoring
   c. Vulnerability/threat assessment and risk management, network intrusion detection and incident response, and digital investigation
   d. Vulnerability assessment, intrusion response, and monitoring

4. What's the purpose of maintaining a network of digital forensics specialists?

5. Policies can address rules for which of the following?
   a. When you can log on to a company network from home
   b. The Internet sites you can or can't access
   c. The amount of personal e-mail you can send
   d. Any of the above
6. List two items that should appear on a warning banner.
7. Under normal circumstances, a private-sector investigator is considered an agent of law enforcement. True or False?
8. List two types of digital investigations typically conducted in a business environment.
9. What is professional conduct, and why is it important?
10. What's the purpose of an affidavit?
11. What are the necessary components of a search warrant?
12. What are some ways to determine the resources needed for an investigation?
13. List three items that should be on an evidence custody form.
14. Why should you do a standard risk assessment to prepare for an investigation?
15. You should always prove the allegations made by the person who hired you. True or False?
16. For digital evidence, an evidence bag is typically made of antistatic material. True or False?
17. Why should evidence media be write-protected?
18. List three items that should be in your case report.
19. Why should you critique your case after it's finished?
20. What do you call a list of people who have had physical possession of the evidence?
21. Data collected before an attorney issues a memo for an attorney-client privilege case is protected under the confidential work product rule. True or False?

Hands-On Projects

In the following hands-on projects, continue to work at the workstation you set up in this chapter. Extract the compressed files from the Chap01\Projects folder on the book's DVD to your *Work*\Chap01\Projects folder. (If necessary, create this folder on your system to store your files.)

If needed, refer to the directions in this chapter and the ProDiscover user manual, which is in C:\Program Filesx86\Technology Pathways\ProDiscover by default.

Hands-On Project 1-1

The case in this project involves a suspicious death. Joshua Zarkan found his girlfriend's dead body in her apartment and reported it. The first responding law enforcement officer seized a USB drive. A crime scene evidence technician skilled in data acquisition made an image of the USB drive with ProDiscover and named it C1Prj01.eve. Following the acquisition, the technician transported and secured the USB drive and placed it in a secure evidence locker at the police station. You have received the image file from the detective assigned to this case. He directs you to examine it and identify any evidentiary artifacts that might relate to this case. To process this case, follow these steps to evaluate what's on the image of the USB drive:

1. Start ProDiscover Basic. (If you're using Windows Vista or later, right-click the **ProDiscover** desktop icon and click **Run as administrator**.)

2. In the Launch Dialog dialog box, click the **New Project** tab, if necessary. Enter a project number. If your company doesn't have a standard numbering scheme, you can use the date followed by the number representing the case that day in sequence, such as 20150124_01.

3. Enter **C1Prj01** as the project name, enter a brief description of the case, and then click **Open**.

4. To add an image file, click **Action** from the menu, point to **Add**, and click **Image File**.

5. Navigate to your work folder, click **C1Prj01.eve**, and then click **Open**. If the Auto Image Checksum message box opens, click **Yes**.

6. In the tree view, click to expand **Content View**. Click to expand **Images**, and then click the pathname containing the image file. In the work area, notice the files that are listed.

7. Right-click any file and click **View** to start the associated program, such as Word or Excel. View the file, and then exit the program.

8. If you decide to export a file, right-click the file and click **Copy File**. (*Note*: Creating a separate folder for exports is a good idea to keep your files organized.) In the Save As dialog box that opens, navigate to the location where you want to save the file, and then click Save.

9. To save the project to view later, click **File, Save Project** from the menu. The default project name is the one you entered in Step 3. Select the drive and folder (*Work*\Chap01\Projects, for example), and then click **Save**. After you have finished examining the files, exit ProDiscover Basic and save the project again, if prompted.

You need to export any files in this image and give them to the investigator. In addition, write a brief report (no more than two paragraphs) including any facts from the contents of the recovered data.

In ProDiscover Basic, you must exit the program before beginning a new case.

Hands-On Project 1-2

In this project, you work for a large corporation's IT security company. Your duties include conducting internal computing investigations and forensics examinations on company computing systems. A paralegal from the Law Department, Ms. Jones, asks you to examine a USB drive belonging to an employee who left the company and now works for a competitor. The Law Department is concerned that the former employee might possess sensitive company data. Ms. Jones wants to know whether the USB drive contains anything significant.

In addition, she informs you that the former employee might have had access to confidential documents because a co-worker saw him accessing his manager's computer on his last day of work. These confidential documents consist of 24 files with the text "book." She wants you to locate any occurrences of these files on the USB drive's bit-stream image.

To process this case, make sure you have extracted the C1Prj02.eve file to your work folder, and then follow these steps:

1. Start ProDiscover Basic. In the New Project tab, enter a project number, the project name **C1Prj02**, and a project description, and then click **Open**. It's a good idea to get in the habit of saving the project immediately, so click **File, Save Project** from the menu, and save the file in your work folder (*Work*\Chap01\Projects).

2. Click **Action** from the menu, point to **Add**, and click **Image File**. Navigate to and click **C1Prj02.eve** in your work folder, and then click **Open**. If the Auto Image Checksum message box opens, click **Yes**.

3. In the tree view, click to expand **Content View**, if necessary. Click to expand **Images**, and then click the pathname containing the image file. In the work area, examine the files that are listed.

4. To search for the keyword "book," click the **Search** toolbar button to open the Search dialog box.

5. If necessary, click the **Content Search** tab, and then click the **ASCII** option button and the **Search for the pattern(s)** option button. Type **book** in the list box for search keywords. Under Select the Disk(s)/Image(s) you want to search in, click the drive you're searching (see Figure 1-24), and then click **OK**.

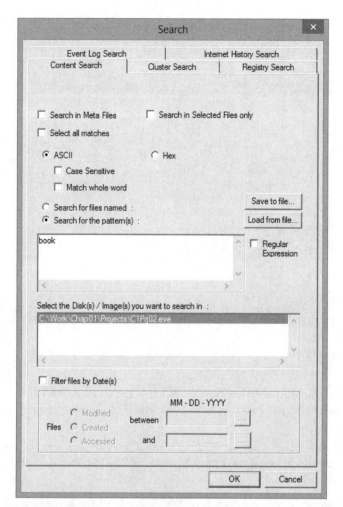

Figure 1-24   Entering search settings
Courtesy of Technology Pathways, LLC

6. In the tree view, click to expand **Search Results,** if necessary, and then click **Content Search Results** to specify the type of search. Figure 1-25 shows the search results pane.

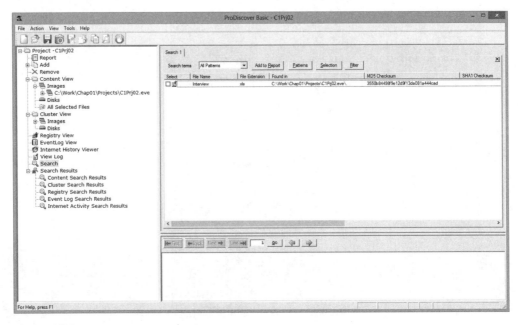

Figure 1-25   Viewing the search results
Courtesy of Technology Pathways, LLC

7. Next, open the Search dialog box again, click the **Cluster Search** tab, and run the same search. Note that it takes longer because each cluster on the drive is searched.

8. In the tree view, click **Cluster Search Results**, and view the search results pane. Remember to save your project and exit ProDiscover Basic before starting the next case.

When you're finished, write a memo to Ms. Jones with the following information: the filenames in which you found a hit for the keyword and, if the hit occurred in unallocated space, the cluster number.

Hands-On Project 1-3

Ms. Jones notifies you that the former employee has used an additional drive. She asks you to examine this new drive to determine whether it contains an account number the employee might have had access to. The account number, 461562, belongs to the senior vice president and is used to access the company's banking service over the Internet.

1. Start ProDiscover Basic. In the New Project tab, enter a project number, the project name **C1Prj03**, and a brief description, and then click **Open**. Save the project in your work folder by clicking **File, Save Project** from the menu.

2. To add the evidence, click **Action** from the menu, point to **Add**, and click **Image File**. Navigate to your work folder, click the **C1Prj03.dd** file, and then click **Open**. Click **Yes** in the Auto Image Checksum message box, if

necessary. Notice that the image file is a `.dd` file, not an `.eve` file. Like most forensics tools, ProDiscover can read standard UNIX `.dd` image files.

3. To aid in your investigation, you might want to view graphics files on the drive. To do this, click to expand **Content View** in the tree view, click to expand **Images**, and then click the pathname containing the image file.

4. Click **View, Gallery View** from the menu. Scroll through the graphics files on the drive image. You'll need to search through all folders, which can take some time. If a file is of interest, click the check box next to it in the Select column. In the Add Comment dialog box that opens, enter a description and click **OK**. These notes are added to the ProDiscover report.

5. This drive is related to the case in Hands-On Project 1-2, so you're still looking for occurrences of the word "book." Open the Search dialog box, and repeat Steps 5 through 8 of Hands-On Project 1-2 for this drive image. When you view the search results, click to select any files of interest (as described in Step 4), which opens the Add Comment dialog box where you can enter notes.

6. Next, search for the account number Ms. Jones gave you. Click the **Search** toolbar button. Click the **Content Search** tab, if necessary, and type **461562** as the search keyword. Click to select the drive you're searching, and then click **OK**. Click the **Cluster Search** tab, and repeat the search for the account number. Remember to select any files of interest and enter notes in the Add Comment dialog box.

Remember that text can be found in graphics files as well as in documents. If your search results produces no findings, you might have to search graphics and picture files separately for evidence.

7. When you're finished, click **Report** in the tree view. Scroll through the report to make sure all the items you found are listed.

8. Next, click the **Export** toolbar button. In the Export dialog box, click the **RTF Format** option button, type **Ch1Prj03Report** in the File Name text box, and then click **OK**. (If you want to store the report in a different folder, click Browse and navigate to the new location.)

9. Write a short memo to summarize what you found. Save the project and exit ProDiscover Basic.

Hands-On Project 1-4

Sometimes discovery demands from law firms require you to recover only allocated data from a disk. This project shows you how to extract just the files that haven't been deleted from an image.

1. Start ProDiscover Basic. In the New Project tab, enter a project number, a brief description, and the project name **C1Prj04**, and then click **Open**.

2. In the tree view, click to expand **Add**, and then click **Image File**. Navigate to your work folder, click the **C1Prj04.eve** file, and then click **Open**. Click **Yes** in the Auto Image Checksum message box, if necessary. Save the project in your work folder.

3. In the tree view, click to expand **Content View,** if necessary. Click to expand **Images,** and then click the pathname containing the image file. Notice the files displayed in the work area.

4. Click the column header **Deleted** to sort the files into YES and NO groups (see Figure 1-26).

Select	File Name	File Extension	Size	Attributes	Deleted	Created Date	Modified Date	Accessed Date	Parent Folder	MFT $ST
☐	All Files			- d - - - -	NO	12/31/1969 ...	12/31/1969 ...	12/31/1969 ...	C:\Work\Cha...	
☐	Botany	doc	19,96...	a - - - - -	NO	06/23/2004 ...	06/23/2004 ...	06/23/2004 ...	C:\Work\Cha...	
☐	Lin_tomb	jpg	9,95...	a - - - - -	NO	06/23/2004 ...	06/23/2004 ...	09/24/2006 ...	C:\Work\Cha...	
☐	LINC3	GIF	17,93...	a - - - - -	NO	06/23/2004 ...	06/23/2004 ...	09/24/2006 ...	C:\Work\Cha...	
☐	USDeclar	doc	29,69...	a - - - - -	NO	06/23/2004 ...	06/23/2004 ...	06/23/2004 ...	C:\Work\Cha...	
☐	USConst	doc	73,72...	a - - - - -	NO	06/23/2004 ...	06/23/2004 ...	09/24/2006 ...	C:\Work\Cha...	
☐	MagnaCt	doc	50,17...	a - - - - -	NO	06/23/2004 ...	06/23/2004 ...	06/23/2004 ...	C:\Work\Cha...	
☐	Gettysbg	jpg	58,92...	a - - - - -	NO	06/23/2004 ...	06/23/2004 ...	09/24/2006 ...	C:\Work\Cha...	
☐	Amendments to...	doc	87,04...	a - - - - -	YES	06/23/2004 ...	06/23/2004 ...	06/23/2004 ...	C:\Work\Cha...	
☐	THE UNITED ST...	doc	73,72...	a - - - - -	YES	06/23/2004 ...	06/23/2004 ...	06/23/2004 ...	C:\Work\Cha...	
☐	THE DECLARATI...	doc	29,69...	a - - - - -	YES	06/23/2004 ...	06/23/2004 ...	06/23/2004 ...	C:\Work\Cha...	
☐	Magna Carta	doc	50,17...	a - - - - -	YES	06/23/2004 ...	06/23/2004 ...	06/23/2004 ...	C:\Work\Cha...	
☐	Lincoln	jpg	18,55...	a - - - - -	YES	06/23/2004 ...	06/23/2004 ...	06/23/2004 ...	C:\Work\Cha...	
☐	USAmmend	doc	87,04...	a - - - - -	YES	06/23/2004 ...	06/23/2004 ...	06/23/2004 ...	C:\Work\Cha...	
☐	Gettysburg	jpg	58,92...	a - - - - -	YES	06/23/2004 ...	06/23/2004 ...	06/23/2004 ...	C:\Work\Cha...	

Figure 1-26   Deleted files displayed in the work area
Courtesy of Technology Pathways, LLC

5. To extract the allocated files from the image to your work folder, right-click each file containing NO in the Deleted column and click **Copy File.** (Note that in ProDiscover Basic, there's no way to select multiple files at once. You must copy each allocated file separately.) When you're finished, save the project and exit ProDiscover Basic.

Hands-On Project 1-5

This project is a continuation from the previous project; you'll create a report listing all the unallocated (deleted) files ProDiscover finds.

1. Start ProDiscover Basic. Click the **Open Project** tab, and navigate to your work folder.

2. Click the **C1Prj04.dft** file and click **Open.** Click **Yes** in the Auto Image Checksum message box, if necessary.

3. If necessary, sort the files in the work area again by clicking the **Deleted** column header. Click the check box in the Select column next to all unallocated (deleted) files, as shown in Figure 1-27. As you click each check box, the Add Comment dialog box opens, where you can enter a description of each file.

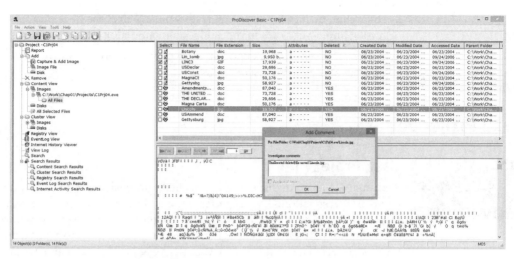

Figure 1-27   Selecting a file to include in a report
Courtesy of Technology Pathways, LLC

4. In the Investigator comments text box, add a comment noting that the file is deleted and indicating its file type, such as a Word document or an image file (.jpeg or .gif, for instance). Be sure to enter something meaningful by examining the file first.

5. When you're finished, click **Report** in the tree view. If you're satisfied, export the report by clicking the **Export** toolbar button. In the Export dialog box, select the format option you want, type **C1Prj05Report** in the File Name text box, and then click **OK**. Save the project and exit ProDiscover Basic.

Hands-On Project 1-6

In this project, another investigator asks you to examine an image and search for all occurrences of the following keywords:

- ANTONIO
- HUGH EVANS
- HORATIO

1. Start ProDiscover Basic. In the New Project tab, enter a project number, a brief description, and the project name, and then click **Open**.

2. In the tree view, click to expand **Add**, and click **Image File**. Navigate to your work folder, click the **C1Prj06.eve** file, and click **Open**. Click **Yes** in the Auto Image Checksum message box, if necessary. Save the project in your work folder.

3. Click the **Search** toolbar button. In the Search dialog box, type all keywords in the list box (placing each on a separate line), click to select the drive containing the image, and click **OK**.

4. Examine the files in the search results pane. Select the ones that look interesting and enter notes in the Add Comment dialog box.

5. Generate a report and export it, as explained in previous projects. Save the project and exit ProDiscover Basic.

Case Projects

CASE PROJECTS

Case Project 1-1

An insurance company has asked your digital forensics firm to review a case for an arson investigation. The suspected arsonist has already been arrested, but the insurance company wants to determine whether there's any contributory negligence on the part of the victims. Two files were extracted to your work folder for this project. The first, Chap01_CasePrj01a.doc, is a memo about the case from the police department. The second, Chap01_CasePrj01b.doc, is a letter from the insurance company explaining what should be investigated. Review these files, and decide the course of action your firm needs to take. Write an outline for how your firm should approach the case.

Case Project 1-2

Jonathan Simpson owns a construction company. One day a subcontractor calls him, saying that he needs a replacement check for the job he completed at 1437 West Maple Avenue. Jonathan looks up the job on his accounting program and agrees to reissue the check for $12,750. The subcontractor says that the original check was for only $10,750. Jonathan looks around the office but can't find the company checkbook or ledger. Only one other person has access to the accounting program. Jonathan calls you to investigate. How would you proceed? Write a one-page report detailing the steps Jonathan needs to take to gather the necessary evidence and protect his company.

Case Project 1-3

You are the digital forensics investigator for a law firm. The firm acquired a new client, a young woman who was fired from her job for inappropriate files discovered on her computer. She swears she never accessed the files. What questions should you ask and how should you proceed? Write a one- to two-page report describing the computer the client used, who else had access to it, and any other relevant facts that should be investigated.

Case Project 1-4

A desperate employee calls because she has accidentally deleted crucial files from her hard drive and can't retrieve them from the Recycle Bin. What are your options? Write one to two pages explaining your capabilities and listing the questions you need to ask her about her system.

chapter 2

The Investigator's Office and Laboratory

After reading this chapter and completing the exercises, you will be able to:

- Describe certification requirements for digital forensics labs
- List physical requirements for a digital forensics lab
- Explain the criteria for selecting a basic forensic workstation
- Describe components used to build a business case for developing a forensics lab

This chapter explains some options for setting up an effective digital forensics laboratory. Each digital forensics investigator in a lab should also have a private office where he or she can manage cases, conduct interviews, and communicate without eavesdropping concerns. Whether you're new to digital forensics or are an experienced examiner, your goal is to make your office and lab work smoothly and efficiently for all casework.

Digital forensics investigators must remember to consider budget and time when updating their labs to keep pace with computer technology changes. The workflow and processes you establish directly affect the quality of evidence you discover. You must balance cost, quality, and reliability when determining the kind of equipment, software, and other items you need to add to your lab. This chapter provides a foundation for organizing, controlling, and managing a safe, efficient forensics laboratory.

Understanding Forensics Lab Accreditation Requirements

A **digital forensics lab** is where you conduct investigations, store evidence, and do most of your work. You use the lab to house your instruments, current and legacy software, and forensic workstations. In general, you need a variety of digital forensics hardware and software to do your work.

You also need to make sure you have defined policies, processes, and prescribed procedures before beginning any casework to ensure the integrity of an analysis and its results. A number of organizations have created guidelines for devising your own processes and procedures. What's most important is that you follow the policies and procedures you have created to ensure consistency in your output. Checklists are a good way to ensure consistent methods of operations for staff.

 Be sure to research accrediting bodies thoroughly before pursuing any accreditation. Many accreditations are offered by software vendors; others are specific for law enforcement or started by local groups.

The **American Society of Crime Laboratory Directors (ASCLD;** *www.ascld.org*) provides guidelines to members for managing a forensics lab and acquiring crime and forensics lab accreditation. ASCLD also accredits forensics labs that analyze digital evidence as they do other criminal evidence, such as fingerprints and DNA samples. This accreditation is based on the original crime lab accreditation, ASCLD/LAB (*www.ascld-lab.org*), which regulates how crime labs are organized and managed. The ASCLD/LAB program includes specific audits on all functions to ensure that lab procedures are being performed correctly and consistently for all casework. These audits should be conducted in forensics labs to maintain the quality and integrity of analysis. The following sections discuss several key guidelines from the ASCLD/LAB program that you can apply to managing, configuring, and auditing your forensics lab. For additional information on how ASCLD conforms to an international standard, see ISO/IEC 17025:2005.

Identifying Duties of the Lab Manager and Staff

The ASCLD states that each lab should have specific objectives that a parent organization and the lab's director or manager have determined. The lab manager sets up processes for managing cases and reviews them regularly. Besides performing general management tasks, such as promoting group consensus in decision making, maintaining fiscal responsibility for lab needs,

2

and enforcing ethical standards (covered in Chapters 15 and 16) among staff members, the lab manager plans updates for the lab, such as new hardware and software purchases.

The lab manager also establishes and promotes quality assurance processes for the lab's staff to follow, such as outlining what to do when a case arrives, logging evidence, specifying who can enter the lab, and establishing guidelines for filing reports. To ensure the lab's efficiency, the lab manager also sets reasonable production schedules for processing work.

A typical investigation involves seizing a hard disk and other media, such as smartphones; making forensic copies of them; evaluating evidence; and filing a report. A forensics analysis of a 2 TB disk, for example, can take several days and often involves running imaging software overnight and on weekends. This means one of the forensic workstations in the lab is occupied for that time, which can be 20 hours or more. Based on past experience, the lab manager can estimate how many cases each investigator can handle and when to expect a preliminary and final report for each case.

The lab manager creates and monitors lab policies for staff and provides a safe and secure workplace for staff and evidence. Above all, the lab manager accounts for all activities the lab's staff conducts to complete its work. Tracking cases such as e-mail abuse, Internet misuse, and illicit activities can justify the funds spent on a lab.

Staff members in a forensics lab should have enough training to perform their tasks. Necessary skills include hardware and software knowledge, including OS and file types, and deductive reasoning. Their work is reviewed regularly by the lab manager and their peers to ensure quality. Staff members are also responsible for continuing technical training to update their investigative and computer skills and maintaining a record of the training they have completed. Many vendors and organizations hold annual or quarterly training seminars that offer certification exams.

The ASCLD Web site summarizes the requirements of managing a digital forensics lab, handling and preserving evidence, performing laboratory procedures, setting personnel requirements, and encouraging professional development. The site also provides a user license for printed and online manuals of lab management guidelines. ASCLD stresses that each lab should maintain an up-to-date library of resources in its field. For digital forensics, these resources include software, hardware information, and technical journals.

Lab Budget Planning

To conduct a professional computing investigation, you need to understand the cost of your lab operation. Lab costs can be broken down into monthly, quarterly, and annual expenses. The better you understand these expenses, the better you can delegate resources for each investigation. Using a spreadsheet program helps you keep track of past investigation expenses so that you can extrapolate expected future costs. Remember that expenses include purchasing computer hardware and software, renting facility space, and training personnel.

When creating a budget, start by estimating the number of cases your lab expects to examine and identifying the types of computers you're likely to examine, such as Windows PCs, Apple systems, or Linux workstations. For example, suppose you work for a state police agency that's planning to provide computing investigation services for the entire state. You could start by collecting state crime statistics for the current year and several previous years to determine types of computers or other devices associated with these crimes. Criminal behavior often reflects sales trends for certain computing systems. Because more than 90% of consumers use Intel and AMD PCs, and 90% of these computers run Windows, the same statistics are likely true of computers used in crimes. Verify this trend by determining how often each type of system is used in a crime. List the number of crimes committed that involve DOS/Windows, Linux/UNIX, and Apple computers.

If you can't find detailed information on the types of computers and OSs used in computer crimes, gather enough information to make an educated guess. Your goal is to build a baseline for the types and numbers of systems you can expect to investigate. In addition to the historical data you compile, identify any future trends that could affect your lab, such as a new version of an OS or an increase in the number of computers involved in crime.

Next, estimate how many investigations you might conduct involving computer systems used less often to help determine how many tools you need to examine these systems. For example, if you learn that on average, one Macintosh is involved in a criminal investigation each month, you probably need only one or two software tools to conduct a forensic analysis on Macintosh file systems.

Figure 2-1 shows a table of statistics from a **Uniform Crime Report** that identifies the number of hard disk types, such as SATA or SCSI, and the OS used to commit crimes. Annual

Crime Statistics For 2016	HDD	Window OS	Linux	OS X & 9	Other H/W	Mobile Devices	Total Systems Examined
Arson	5	3	1	1	0	0	5
Bribery	6	3	0	1	0	0	4
Burglary	6	0	0	0	0	0	0
Child Porn	29	14	2	7	0	23	46
Counterfeit & Forgery	6	6	0	0	0	1	7
Drug Narcotic	20	7	0	3	0	54	64
Embezzlement	9	9	0	1	1	0	11
Extortion & Blackmail	5	3	2	0	0	1	6
Fraud	13	4	0	7	0	41	52
Gambling	10	7	2	0	0	5	14
Homicide	13	5	0	0	0	3	8
Kidnapping & Abduction	0	0	0	0	0	1	1
Larceny Theft	2	1	0	2	0	0	3
Robbery	1	0	0	1	0	0	1
Sex Offense Forcible	6	4	0	0	0	0	4
Sex Offense Non-Forcible	8	8	0	0	0	8	16
Stalking	15	9	0	5	0	28	42
Stolen Property Offenses	1	1	0	0	0	0	1
Weapons Violations	2	2	0	0	0	0	2
Totals	157	86	7	28	1	165	287

Figure 2-1 Uniform Crime Report statistics
© 2016 Cengage Learning®

Uniform Crime Reports are generated at the federal, state, and local levels to show the types and frequency of crimes committed. For federal reports, see *www.fbi.gov/ucr/ucr.htm*, and for a summary of crimes committed at different levels, see *www.bjs.gov*.

You can also identify specialized software used with certain crimes. For example, if you find a check-writing software tool used in a large number of counterfeiting cases, you should consider adding this specialized software to your inventory.

If you're preparing to set up a forensics lab for a private company, you can determine your needs more easily because you're working in a contained environment. Start by getting an inventory of all known computing systems and applications used in the business. For example, an insurance company often has a network of Intel PCs and servers and specialized insurance software using a database for data storage. A large manufacturing company might use Intel PCs, UNIX workstations running a computer-aided design (CAD) system, super minicomputers, and mainframes. A publishing company might have a combination of Intel PCs and Macintosh systems and a variety of word processing, imaging, and composition packages. Many other organizations use cloud-based storage or supervisory control and data acquisition (SCADA) systems for data and applications.

Next, check with your Management, Human Resource, and Security departments to determine the types of complaints and problems reported in the past year. Most companies using Internet connections, for example, receive complaints about employees accessing the Web excessively or for personal use, which generate investigations of Web misuse. Be sure to distinguish investigations of excessive Web use from inappropriate Web site access and e-mail harassment.

Your budget should also take future developments in computing technology into account because drive storage capabilities improve constantly. When examining a disk, you need a target disk to which you copy evidence data. This disk should be at least one and a half times the size of the evidence (suspect) disk. For example, a lab equipped with 4 TB disks can effectively analyze disks up to 3 TB. If your company upgrades its computers to 1 TB disks, however, you need disks that are 2 TB or more or a central secure server with at least 100 TB or more of storage. (Several forensic servers on the market are in the 32 TB and higher range.) Many businesses replace their desktop computer systems every 18 months to three years. You must be informed of computer upgrades and other changes in the computing environment so that you can prepare and submit your budget for needed resources.

Like computer hardware, OSs change periodically. If your current digital forensics tool doesn't work with the next release of a Microsoft OS or file system, you must upgrade your software tools. You should also monitor or contact vendor product development teams to learn about upgrades. File systems change, too. Forensics tools had their birth in DOS, and over the years, Windows hard disks used a variety of file systems, including FAT16, FAT32, New Technology File System (NTFS), Resilient File System (ReFS), and other Windows file systems. Most DOS-based tools can't read NTFS disks. In addition, the popularity and prevalence of the Xbox requires investigators to be familiar with the FATX file system.

Time management is a major issue when choosing software and hardware to purchase. For example, you've decided to purchase eight machines for your lab. Many commercial forensics software packages require a USB dongle to operate or have a site license of five concurrent users. You or the budget manager must decide whether you're using all the machines or need only two licensed copies of each software package. As another example, you can have a command-line tool running overnight for drive imaging; while it's running; investigators can use a commercial or freeware package to evaluate a drive. Your choices depend on what tools you have verified and what's needed for your casework.

Another option for viewing file systems is to use a Linux Live CD or WinFE (modified version of WinPE, the automated installation kit), which are CD or DVD disk acquisition tools discussed in Chapter 3. It doesn't mount the hard drive automatically and, therefore, doesn't write to the drive. (A hardware write-blocker is still recommended to prevent errors caused by the forensics technician, if nothing else.) Examining tablets, USB drives, and smartphones is routine now in cases from criminal investigations to civil litigation discovery demands. Digital investigators must be prepared to deal with constant change in these devices and know what tools are available to extract data from them safely for an investigation. In Chapter 12, you learn how to acquire data from these devices.

Acquiring Certification and Training

To continue a career in computing investigations and forensic analysis, you need to upgrade your skills through training. Several organizations have developed or are currently developing certification programs for digital forensics that usually test you after you have completed one or more training sessions successfully. Certifying organizations range from nonprofit associations to vendor-sponsored groups. All these programs charge fees for certification, and some require candidates to take vendor- or organization-sponsored training to qualify for the certification. Some U.S. state legislatures now require digital forensics examiners working in a private practice or business to have a private investigator's license. These states typically require some level of training and certification in both digital forensics and investigations before applying for a license.

Before enlisting in a certification program, thoroughly research the requirements, cost, and acceptability in your area of employment. Most certification programs require continuing education credits or reexamination of candidates' skills, which can become costly.

International Association of Computer Investigative Specialists

Created by police officers who wanted to formalize credentials in computing investigations, the International Association of Computer Investigative Specialists (IACIS) is one of the oldest professional digital forensics organizations. It restricts membership to sworn law enforcement personnel or government employees working as forensic examiners. This restriction might change, so visit the IACIS Web site (*www.iacis.com*) to verify the requirements.

Candidates who complete the IACIS test successfully are designated as a **Certified Forensic Computer Examiner (CFCE)**. The CFCE process changes as technology changes. The description here is current as of this writing. IACIS requires recertification every three years to demonstrate continuing work in the field of digital forensics. Recertification is less intense than the original certification but does test examiners to make sure they're continuing their education and are still active in the field of digital forensics. For the latest information about IACIS and applying for CFCE certification or membership in IACIS, visit the IACIS Web site.

ISC² Certified Cyber Forensics Professional The Certified Cyber Forensics Professional (CCFP) program, sponsored by ISC², requires knowledge of digital forensics, malware analysis, incident response, e-discovery, and other disciplines related to cyber investigations. The CCFP Web site (*www.isc2.org/ccfp/Default.aspx*) lists requirements and processes needed for this certification.

High Tech Crime Network The High Tech Crime Network (HTCN) also offers several levels of certification. Unlike IACIS, however, HTCN requires a review of all related training, including training in one of its approved courses, and a review of the candidate's work history. HTCN certification is open to anyone meeting the criteria in the profession of computing investigations. At the time of this writing, the HTCN Web site (*www.htcn.org*) specifies requirements for the certification levels discussed in the following paragraphs. Requirements are updated without notice, so make sure you check the site periodically.

Certified Computer Crime Investigator, Basic Level
- Candidates must have three years of experience directly related to investigating computer-related incidents or crimes.
- Candidates have successfully completed 40 hours of training from an approved agency, organization, or training company.
- Candidates must provide documentation of at least 10 cases in which they participated.

Certified Computer Crime Investigator, Advanced Level

- Candidates must have five years of experience directly related to investigating computer-related incidents or crimes.
- Candidates have successfully completed 80 hours of training from an approved agency, organization, or company.
- Candidates have served as lead investigator in at least 20 cases during the past three years and were involved in at least 40 other cases as a lead investigator or supervisor or in a supportive capacity. Candidates have at least 60 hours of involvement in cases in the past three years.

Certified Computer Forensic Technician, Basic

- Candidates must have three years of experience in computing investigations for law enforcement or corporate cases.
- Candidates must have completed 40 hours of computer forensics training from an approved organization.
- Candidates must provide documentation of at least 10 computing investigations.

Certified Computer Forensic Technician, Advanced

- Candidates must have five years of hands-on experience in computer forensics investigations for law enforcement or corporate cases.
- Candidates must have completed 80 hours of computer forensics training from an approved organization.
- Candidates must have been the lead computer forensics investigator in 20 or more investigations in the past three years and in 40 or more additional computing

investigations as lead computer forensics technician, supervisor, or contributor. The candidate must have completed at least 60 investigations in the past three years.

EnCase Certified Examiner Certification Guidance Software, the creator of EnCase, sponsors the EnCase Certified Examiner (EnCE) certification program. EnCE certification is open to the public and private sectors and is specific to use and mastery of EnCase forensics analysis. Requirements for taking the EnCE certification exam don't depend on taking the Guidance Software EnCase training courses. Candidates for this certificate are required to have a licensed copy of EnCase. For more information on EnCE certification requirements, visit *www.encase.com*.

AccessData Certified Examiner AccessData sponsors the AccessData Certified Examiner (ACE) certification program. ACE certification is open to the public and private sectors and is specific to use and mastery of AccessData Ultimate Toolkit. To help prepare for the ACE exam, applicants can attend the AccessData BootCamp and Windows forensics courses. The exam has a knowledge base assessment (KBA) and a practical skills assessment (PSA). For more information on this certification, visit *www.accessdata.com/acepreparation.html*.

Other Training and Certifications The following are other organizations to consider for certification or training:

- EC-Council, *www.eccouncil.org/Certification*
- SysAdmin, Audit, Network, Security (SANS) Institute, *www.sans.org* or *http://computer-forensics.sans.org/training#408*
- Defense Cyber Investigations Training Academy (DCITA), *www.dcita.edu*
- International Society of Forensic Computer Examiners (ISFCE, *www.isfce.com*) for the **Certified Computer Examiner (CCE)** certification
- High Tech Crime Consortium, *www.hightechcrimecops.org*
- Computer Technology Investigators Network (CTIN), *www.ctin.org*
- Digital Forensics Certification Board (DFCB), *www.dfcb.org*
- Consortium of Digital Forensics Specialists (CDFS), *www.cdfs.org*

Organizations that offer training and certification for law enforcement personnel or qualified civilian government personnel include the following:

- Federal Law Enforcement Training Centers (FLETC), *www.fletc.gov*
- National White Collar Crime Center (NW3C), *www.nw3c.org*

Determining the Physical Requirements for a Digital Forensics Lab

After you have the training to become a digital forensics investigator, you conduct most of your investigations in a lab. This section discusses the physical requirements for a forensics lab. Addressing these requirements can make a lab safer, more secure, and more productive.

Your lab facility must be physically secure so that evidence isn't lost, corrupted, or destroyed. As with hardware and software costs, you must consider what's needed to maintain a safe and secure environment when determining physical lab expenses. You must also use inventory control methods to track your computing assets, which means you should maintain a complete and up-to-date inventory of all major hardware and software items in the lab. For consumable items, such as cables and storage media, maintain an inventory so that you know when to order more supplies.

Identifying Lab Security Needs

All digital forensics labs need an enclosed room where a forensic workstation can be set up. You shouldn't use an open cubicle because it allows easy access to your evidence. You need a room you can lock to control your evidence and attest to its integrity. In particular, your lab should be secure during data analysis, even if it takes several weeks to analyze a disk drive. To preserve the integrity of evidence, your lab should function as an evidence locker or safe, making it a **secure facility** or a secure storage safe.

The following are the minimum requirements for a digital forensics lab of any size:

- Small room with true floor-to-ceiling walls
- Door access with a locking mechanism, which can be a regular key lock, combination lock, or an electronic lock capable of logging who accessed it; the key or combination must be limited to authorized users, including cleaning crews
- Secure container, such as a safe or heavy-duty file cabinet with a quality padlock that prevents drawers from opening
- Visitor's log with legible entries listing all people who have accessed the lab and showing the date, time in, and time out

For daily work production, several examiners can work together in a large open area, as long as they all have the same level of authority and access need. This area should also have floor-to-ceiling walls and a locking door. In many public and private organizations, several investigators share a door to the lab that requires an ID card and entry code.

Computing investigators and forensics examiners must be briefed on the lab's security policy. Share information about a case investigation only with other examiners and personnel who need to know about the investigation.

Conducting High-Risk Investigations

High-risk investigations, such as those involving national security or murder, for example, demand more security than the minimum lab requirements provide. As technology improves and information circulates among computer attackers, keeping an investigation secure can be more difficult. For example, detecting computer eavesdropping is difficult and expensive, but sophisticated criminals and intelligence services in foreign countries can use equipment that detects network transmissions, wireless devices, phone conversations, and the use of computer equipment. Instructions for building a sniffing device that can collect computer emanations illegally can be found online and, therefore, are available to anyone. These devices can pick up anything you type on your computer.

Most electronic devices emit electromagnetic radiation (EMR). Certain kinds of equipment can intercept EMR, which can be used to determine the data the device is transmitting or displaying. The EMR from a computer monitor can be picked up as far away as a half mile.

During the Cold War, defense contractors were required to shield sensitive computing systems and prevent electronic eavesdropping of any computer emissions. The U.S. Department of Defense calls this special computer-emission shielding **TEMPEST**. (For a brief description of TEMPEST, see the National Industrial Security Program Operating Manual [NISPOM]. DoD 5220.22-M, Chapter 11, Section 1, TEMPEST, *www.dss.mil/documents/odaa/nispom2006-5220.pdf*. Another site listing reliable sources is *www.jammed.com/~jwa/tempest.html*.)

To protect your investigations, you might consider constructing a TEMPEST-qualified lab, which requires lining the walls, ceiling, floor, and doors with specially grounded conductive metal sheets. Typically, copper sheeting is used because it conducts electricity well. TEMPEST facilities must include special filters for electrical power that prevent power cables from transmitting computer emanations. All heating and ventilation ducts must have special baffles to trap emanations. Likewise, telephones inside the TEMPEST facility must have special line filters. A TEMPEST facility usually has two doors separated by dead space. The first exterior door must be shut before opening the interior door. Each door also has special copper molding to enhance electricity conduction.

Because a TEMPEST-qualified lab facility is expensive and requires routine inspection and testing, it should be considered only for large regional digital forensics labs that demand absolute security from illegal eavesdropping. To avoid these costs, some vendors have built low-emanating workstations instead of TEMPEST facilities. These workstations are more expensive than average workstations but less expensive than a TEMPEST lab.

Using Evidence Containers

Evidence storage containers, also known as evidence lockers, must be secure so that no unauthorized person can access your evidence easily. You must use high-quality locks, such as padlocks, with limited duplicate-key distribution. Also, routinely inspect the contents of evidence storage containers to make sure only current evidence is stored. The evidence custody forms should indicate what's still in the locker. Evidence for closed cases should be moved to a secure off-site facility.

Chapter 5, Section 3, of the NISPOM (*www.dss.mil/documents/odaa/nispom2006-5220.pdf*) describes the characteristics of a safe storage container. Consult with your facility management or legal counsel, such as corporate or prosecuting attorneys, to determine what your lab should do to maintain evidence integrity. The following are recommendations for securing storage containers:

- The evidence container should be located in a restricted area that's accessible only to lab personnel.
- The number of people authorized to open the evidence container should be kept to a minimum. Maintain records on who's authorized to access each container.
- All evidence containers should remain locked when they aren't under the direct supervision of an authorized person.

If a combination locking system is used for your evidence container, follow these practices:

- Provide the same level of security for the combination as for the container's contents. Store the combination in another equally secure container.
- Destroy any previous combinations after setting up a new combination.

- Allow only authorized personnel to change lock combinations.
- Change the combination every six months, when any authorized personnel leave the organization, and immediately after finding an unsecured container—that is, one that's open and unattended.

If you're using a keyed padlock, follow these practices:

- Appoint a key custodian who's responsible for distributing keys.
- Stamp sequential numbers on each duplicate key.
- Maintain a registry listing which key is assigned to which authorized person.
- Conduct a monthly audit to ensure that no authorized person has lost a key.
- Take an inventory of all keys when the custodian changes.
- Place keys in a lockable container accessible only to the lab manager and designated key custodian.
- Maintain the same level of security for keys as for evidence containers.
- Change locks and keys annually; if a key is missing, replace all associated locks and the key.
- Do not use a master key for several locks.

The storage container or cabinet should be made of steel and include an internal cabinet lock or external padlock. If possible, purchase a safe, which provides superior security and protects your evidence from fire damage. Look for specialized safes, called media safes, designed to protect electronic media. Media safes are rated by the number of hours it takes before fire damages the contents. The higher the rating, the better the safe protects evidence.

An evidence storage room is also convenient, especially if it's part of your forensics lab. Security for an evidence room must integrate the same construction and securing devices as the general lab does. Large digital forensics operations also need an evidence custodian and a service counter with a securable metal roll-up window to control evidence. With a secure evidence room, you can store large computer components, such as computers, monitors, and other peripheral devices.

Be sure to maintain a log listing every time an evidence container is opened and closed. Each time the container is accessed, the log should indicate the date it was opened and the initials of the authorized person. These records should be maintained for at least three years or longer, as prescribed by your prosecuting or corporate attorneys. Logs are discussed in more detail in Chapter 4.

Overseeing Facility Maintenance

Your lab should be maintained at all times to ensure the safety and health of lab personnel. Any damage to the floor, walls, ceilings, or furniture should be repaired immediately. Also, be sure to escort cleaning crews into the facility and monitor them as they work.

Because static electricity is a major problem when handling computer parts, consider placing antistatic pads around electronic workbenches and workstations. In addition, floors and carpets should be cleaned at least once a week to help minimize dust that can cause static electricity.

Maintain two separate trash containers, one to store items unrelated to an investigation, such as discarded CDs, and the other for sensitive material that requires special handling to make sure it's destroyed. Using separate trash containers maintains the integrity of criminal investigation processes and protects trade secrets and attorney-client privileged communication in a private corporation. Several commercially bonded firms specialize in disposing of sensitive materials, and you should hire one to help maintain the integrity of your investigations.

Considering Physical Security Needs

In addition to your lab's physical design and construction, you need to enhance security by setting security policies. How much physical security you implement depends on the nature of your lab. A regional computer crime lab has high physical security needs because of the risks of losing, corrupting, or damaging evidence. The physical security needs of a large corporation are probably not as high because the risk of evidence loss or compromise is much lower. Determining the risk for your organization dictates how much security you integrate into your digital forensics lab.

When considering digital security needs, many companies neglect physical security.

Regardless of the security risk to your lab, maintain a paper or electronic sign-in log for all visitors. The log should list the visitor's name, date and time of arrival and departure, employer's name, purpose of the visit, and name of the lab member receiving the visitor. Consider anyone who's not assigned to the lab to be a visitor, including cleaning crews, facility maintenance personnel, friends, and family. All visitors should be escorted by an assigned authorized staff member throughout their visit to the lab to ensure that they don't accidentally or intentionally tamper with an investigation or evidence. As an added precaution, use a visible or audible alarm, such as a visitor badge, to let all investigators know that a visitor is in the area. If possible, hire a security guard or have an intrusion alarm system with a guard to ensure your lab's security. Alarm systems with guards can also be used after business hours to monitor your lab.

Auditing a Digital Forensics Lab

To make sure security policies and practices are followed, conduct routine inspections to audit your lab and evidence storage containers. Audits should include, but aren't limited to, the following facility components and practices:

- Inspect the lab's ceiling, floor, roof, and exterior walls at least once a month, looking for anything unusual or new.
- Inspect doors to make sure they close and lock correctly.
- Check locks to see whether they need to be replaced or changed.
- Review visitor logs to see whether they're being used properly.
- Review log sheets for evidence containers to determine when they have been opened and closed.
- At the end of every workday, secure any evidence that's not being processed on a forensic workstation.

Determining Floor Plans for Digital Forensics Labs

How you configure the work area for your digital forensics lab depends on your budget, the amount of available floor space, and the number of computers you assign to each computing investigator. For a small operation handling two or three cases a month, one forensic work-station should be enough to handle the workload. One workstation requires only the space an average desk takes up. If you're handling many more cases per month, you can probably process two or three investigations at a time, which requires more than one workstation. The ideal configuration for multiple workstations is to have two forensic workstations plus one non-forensic workstation with Internet access.

Because you need plenty of room around each workstation, a work area containing three workstations requires approximately 150 square feet of space, meaning the work area should be about 10 feet by 15 feet. This amount of space allows for two chairs so that the computing investigator can brief another investigator, paralegal, or attorney on the case.

Small labs usually consist of one or two forensic workstations, a research computer with Internet access, a workbench (if space allows), and storage cabinets, as shown in Figure 2-2.

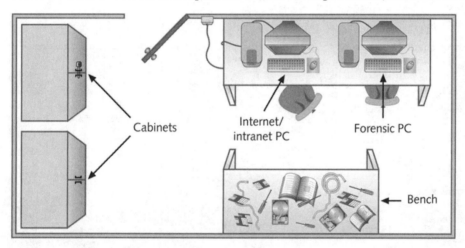

Figure 2-2 Small or home-based lab
© Cengage Learning®

Mid-size digital forensics labs, such as those in a private business, have more workstations. For safety reasons, the lab should have at least two exits, as shown in Figure 2-3. If possible, cubicles or even separate offices should be part of the layout to reinforce the need-to-know policy. These labs usually have more library space for software and hardware storage.

State law enforcement or the FBI usually runs most large or regional digital forensics labs. As shown in Figure 2-4, these labs have a separate evidence room, which is typical in police investigations, except this room is limited to digital evidence. One or more custodians might be assigned to manage and control traffic in and out of the evidence room.

As discussed, the evidence room needs to be secure. The lab should have at least two controlled exits and no windows. Separate offices for supervisors and cubicles for investiga-tors are more practical in this configuration. Remember that forensic workstations are connected to an isolated LAN, and only a few machines are connected to an outside WAN or metropolitan area network (MAN).

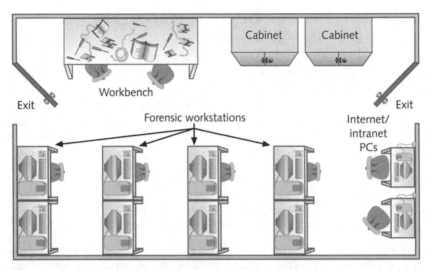

Figure 2-3   Mid-size digital forensics lab
© Cengage Learning®

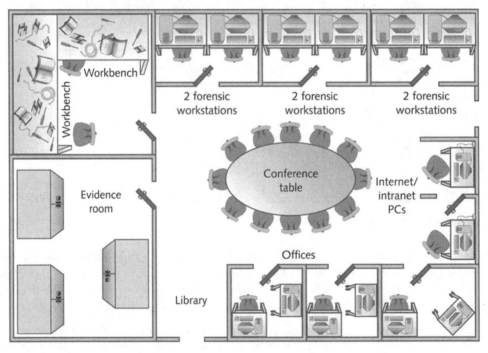

Figure 2-4   Regional digital forensics lab
© Cengage Learning®

Selecting a Basic Forensic Workstation

The workstation you use as a forensics analysis system depends on your budget and specific needs. You can find many well-designed forensic workstations that can handle most computing investigation needs. When acquiring a workstation, try to get the most powerful processor and the most RAM and disk storage available to improve the productivity of digital examinations. When you start processing a case, you use a workstation for the duration of the examination. Use less powerful workstations for mundane tasks and multipurpose workstations for resource-heavy analysis tasks.

Selecting Workstations for a Lab

If you're managing a lab for a police department in a major city, you probably have the most diverse needs for computing investigation tools because the communities it serves use a wide assortment of computing systems. Not all computer users have the latest technology, so a lab might need legacy systems and software, such as computers running CP/M or Minix, to match what's used in the community. For small, local police departments, however, most work involves Windows PCs and Macintosh systems. A small police department's digital forensics lab could be limited to one multipurpose forensic workstation with one or two basic workstations or high-end laptops.

One way to investigate older and unusual computing systems is to keep track of newsgroups or forums that you can find through an Internet search. These groups can be a valuable source of support for recovering and analyzing uncommon systems. Entering "computer forensics" or "digital forensics" as a search keyword produces several links you can follow to further your knowledge in this profession. You can also coordinate with or subcontract to larger forensics labs. Like large police departments, a regional digital forensics lab must have diverse systems to serve its community and often receives work from smaller labs involving unusual computers or OSs.

Computing systems in a lab should be able to process typical cases in a timely manner. The time it takes to process a case usually depends on the size and type of industries in the region. For example, suppose your lab is located in a region with a large manufacturing firm that employs 50,000 people. Based on crime reports you've consulted, 10% of those employees might be involved in criminal behavior, meaning 5000 employees will commit crimes such as fraud, embezzlement, and so on. These statistics can help you estimate how much time is involved in processing these types of cases.

Recent important advances in hardware technology offer more flexibility in digital forensics. You can now use a laptop PC with FireWire (IEEE 1394B standard), USB 3.0, or SATA hard disks to create a lightweight, mobile forensic workstation. Improved throughput speeds of data transfer on laptops also make it easier to create images of suspect drives, especially in the field.

Selecting Workstations for Private and Corporate Labs

For the private sector, such as a business conducting internal investigations or a commercial business providing digital forensics services to private parties, equipment resources are generally easy to determine.

Commercial businesses providing forensics analysis for other companies can tailor their services to specific markets. They can specialize in one or two platforms, such as an Intel PC running a Microsoft OS. They can also gather a variety of tools to meet a wider market. The type of equipment they need depends on their specialty, if any. For general digital forensics facilities, a multipurpose forensic workstation is sufficient.

Private companies conducting their own internal computing investigations can determine the type of forensic workstation they need based on the types of computers they use. If a company uses only Windows PCs, internal investigators don't need a wide variety of specialized equipment. If a company uses many kinds of computers, the Internal Computing Investigation Department needs systems and equipment that support the same types of computers. With some digital forensics programs, you can work from a Windows PC and examine both Windows and Macintosh disk drives.

Stocking Hardware Peripherals

In addition to workstations and software, all labs should have a wide assortment of cables and spare expansion slot cards. Consider stocking your forensics lab with the following peripheral devices:

- 40-pin 18-inch and 36-inch IDE cables, both ATA-33 and ATA-100 or faster
- Ribbon cables for floppy disks
- Extra USB 3.0 or newer cables and SATA cards and associated cables
- Extra SCSI cards, preferably ultrawide
- Graphics cards, both Peripheral Component Interconnect (PCI) and Accelerated Graphics Port (AGP)
- Assorted FireWire and USB adapters
- A variety of hard drives (as many as you can afford and in as wide a variety as possible)
- At least two 2.5-inch adapters from notebook IDE hard drives to standard IDE/ATA drives, SATA drives, and so on
- Computer hand tools, such as Phillips and flathead screwdrivers, a socket wrench, any vendor-specific tools, and a small flashlight

Maintaining Operating Systems and Software Inventories

Operating systems are an essential part of your lab's inventory. You should maintain licensed copies of as many legacy OSs as possible to handle cases involving unusual systems. Microsoft OSs should include, in addition to the most current OS, Windows 8.0 and 8.1, 7, Vista, XP, 2000, NT 4.0, NT 3.5, 9x, 3.11, and DOS 6.22. Macintosh OSs should include Mac OS X, 9.x, and 8 or older. Linux OSs can include Fedora, Ubuntu, Slackware, and Debian.

Although most high-end digital forensics tools can open or display data files created with commonly used programs, they don't support all programs. Your software inventory should include current and older versions of the following programs. If you deal with both Windows PCs and Macintosh systems, you should have programs for both.

- Microsoft Office (including current and older versions)
- Quicken (if you handle a lot of financial investigations)
- Programming languages, such as Visual Basic and Visual C++ or a programming development environment, such as Visual Studio
- Specialized viewers, such as Quick View, ACDSee, ThumbsPlus, and IrfanView
- LibreOffice, OpenOffice, or Apache OpenOffice
- Peachtree and QuickBooks accounting applications

Using a Disaster Recovery Plan

Besides planning for equipment needs, you need to plan for disasters, such as hard disk crashes, lightning strikes, power outages, floods, earthquakes, and so forth. A disaster recovery plan ensures that you can restore your workstations and file servers to their original condition or a lab-like building if a catastrophic failure occurs.

A disaster recovery plan also specifies how to rebuild a forensic workstation after it has been severely contaminated by a virus from a drive you're analyzing. Central to any disaster recovery plan is a system for backing up investigation computers. Tools such as Norton Ghost are useful for restoring files directly. As a general precaution, consider backing up your workstation once a week. You can restore programs from the original disks, USB drives, or CDs/DVDs, but recovering lost data without up-to-date backups is difficult.

Store your system backups where they are easily accessible. You should have at least one copy of backups on site and a duplicate copy or a previous copy of backups stored in a safe off-site facility. Off-site backups are usually rotated on a schedule that varies according to your needs, such as every day, week, or month.

In addition, record all updates you make to your workstation by using a process called **configuration management**. Some companies record updates in a configuration management database to maintain compliance with lab policy. Every time you add or update software on your workstation, enter the change in the database or in a simple notebook with handwritten entries to document the change. A useful tool to run regularly is Belarc Advisor (*www.belarc.com/free_download.html*), which inventories applications, hardware, and system configurations.

A disaster recovery plan can also address how to restore a workstation you reconfigured for a specific investigation. For example, if you install a suite of applications, you might not have enough disk space for normal processing needs, so you could encounter problems during reconfigurations or even simple upgrades. The disaster recovery plan should outline how to uninstall software and delete any files the uninstall program hasn't removed so that you can restore your system to its original configuration.

For labs using high-end RAID servers (such as Digital Intelligence F.R.E.D.C. or F.R.E.D.M.), you must consider methods for restoring large data sets. These large-end servers must have adequate data backup systems in case of a major failure of more than one drive. When planning a recovery procedure for RAID servers, consider whether the amount of downtime it takes to restore backup data is acceptable to the lab operation.

Planning for Equipment Upgrades

Risk management involves determining how much risk is acceptable for any process or operation, such as replacing equipment. Identify the equipment your lab depends on, and create a schedule to replace that equipment. Also, identify equipment that you can replace when it fails.

Computing components are designed to last 18 to 36 months in normal business operations, and new versions of OSs and applications that take up more disk space are released frequently. Therefore, systems periodically need more RAM, disk space, and processing speed. To keep your lab current with updates in hardware technology, schedule hardware replacements at least every 18 months and preferably every 12 months.

Building a Business Case for Developing a Forensics Lab

Before you can set up a digital forensics lab, you must enlist the support of managers and other team members. To do so, you build a **business case**, a plan you can use to sell your services to management or clients. In the business case, you justify acquiring newer and better resources to investigate digital forensics cases.

How you develop a business case depends on the organization you support. If you're the sole proprietor, creating a business case is fairly simple. If you need money to buy tools, you can save your money for the purchase or negotiate with your bank for a loan. For a public entity such as a police department, business requirements can change drastically because budgets are planned a year or more in advance. Public agency department managers present their budget proposals to upper management. If the proposal is approved, upper management makes money available to acquire resources outlined in the budget. Some public organizations might have other funds available that can be spent immediately for special needs. Managers can divert these funds for emergency or unforeseen needs.

 Like private-sector companies, police departments usually have to justify expenses to upper management. The important difference is that police departments don't always have to show cost recovery for the additional capabilities new resources and equipment offer.

Keep in mind that a private-sector business, especially a large corporation, is motivated by the need to make money. A business case should demonstrate how computing investigations could save money and avoid risks that can damage profits, such as by preventing litigation involving the company. For example, court decisions have defined viewing pornographic images in the workplace as creating a hostile environment for other employees, which is related to employee harassment and computer misuse. An employer is responsible for preventing and investigating harassment of employees and nonemployees associated with the workplace. A company is also liable if it doesn't actively prevent creating a hostile workplace by providing employee training and investigating allegations of computer misuse. A lawsuit, regardless of who wins, can cost an employer several hundred thousand dollars. In your business case, compare the cost of training and conducting computing investigations with the cost of a lawsuit.

The Internet makes it difficult for employers to provide a safe and secure environment for employees. In particular, employees can misuse free Web-based e-mail services. These free services give senders anonymity, making it possible for employees to send inappropriate e-mails, often in the form of sexual harassment. Because training rarely prevents this type of behavior, an employer needs to institute an investigation program that involves collecting network logs, such as proxy server logs, and examining computer disks to locate traces of message evidence. Chapter 11 discusses e-mail abuse and using e-mail server and network logs.

Your business case should also show how digital investigations can improve profits, such as by protecting intellectual property, trade secrets, and future business plans. For example, when employees leave one company for a competing company, they can reveal vital competitive information to their new employers. Suppose a company called Skateboard International (SI) has invested research and development funds into a new product that improves the stability of skateboards. Its main competitor is Better Skateboard; this company contacts Gwen Smith, a disgruntled SI employee, via e-mail and offers her a job. When Gwen leaves SI, she takes with her the plans for the new product. A few months later, Better Skateboard introduces a product similar to the skateboard Gwen had been researching at SI. SI recognizes that the new, improved skateboard is similar to the one Gwen had been developing and consults the noncompete agreement Gwen signed when she was hired. SI thinks the new technology Gwen might have given Better Skateboards belongs to its company. It suspects that Better Skateboard stole its trade secret and intellectual property.

SI could sue Better Skateboard and demand discovery on internal documents. Because Gwen and Better Skateboard corresponded via e-mail, a computing investigator needs to find data related to hiring and research engineering at Better Skateboard. Better Skateboard can also demand discovery on SI's research records to determine whether any discrepancies in product design could disprove the lawsuit. In this example, computing investigations can allow one company to generate revenue from a new product and prevent the other company from doing so. Information related to profit and loss makes a persuasive argument in a business case.

Preparing a Business Case for a Digital Forensics Lab

It's important to understand the need for planning in the creation and continued maintenance of a forensics lab. The reason is the constant cost-cutting efforts of upper management. Because of organizations' tendencies to look for ways to reduce costs, you must plan ahead to ensure that money is available for facilities, tools, supplies, and training for your forensics lab. The following sections describe some key elements for creating a digital forensics business case. It's a good idea to maintain a business case with annual updates.

Justification Before you can start, you need to justify to the person controlling the budget the reason a lab is needed. This justification step requires asking the following questions:

- What type of computing investigation service is needed for your organization?
- Who are the potential customers for this service, and how will it be budgeted—as an internal operation (police department or company security department, for instance) or an external operation (a for-profit business venture)?
- How will you advertise your services to customers?
- What time-management techniques will you use?
- Where will the initial and sustaining budget for business operations come from?

No matter what type of organization you work for—a public agency or a private business—operating a digital forensics lab successfully requires constant efforts to market the lab's services to previous, current, and future customers and clients. By using marketing to attract new customers or clients, you can justify future budgets for the lab's operation and staff.

Budget Development The budget needs to include all items described in the following sections. You must be as exact as possible when determining the true cost of these items. Making a mistake could cause delays and possible loss of the opportunity to start or improve your lab.

Facility Cost For a new forensics lab, startup costs might take most of the budget. Depending on how large the lab is, you must determine first how much floor space is needed. As mentioned, a good rule of thumb is 150 square feet per person. This amount of space might seem a bit larger than necessary, but consider how much storage space is needed to preserve evidence and to have enough supplies in stock. Check with your organization's facility manager on per-square-foot costs for your area or building. Here are some sample questions to answer to get started on calculating a budget:

- How many digital forensics examiners will you need?
- How much training will each examiner require per year, and what are the estimated costs?
- Will you need more than one lab?
- How many digital forensics examiners will use each lab? Will there be a need to accommodate other nonexaminers temporarily to inspect recovered evidence?
- What are the costs to construct a secure lab?
- Is there a suitable room that can be converted into a lab?
- Does the designated room have enough electrical power and heating, ventilation, and air-conditioning (HVAC) systems?
- Does the designated room have existing phone lines and network cables? If not, how much will it cost to install these items?
- Is there an adequate lock on the designated room's door?
- What will the furniture costs be?
- Will you need to install an alarm system?
- Are there any other facility costs, such as fees for janitorial services and facility maintenance services?
- If IT support is needed, how many hours of support are estimated?

Hardware Requirements Determining the types of investigations and data that will be analyzed in your forensics lab dictates what hardware equipment you need. If your organization is using Intel-based PCs with Windows 8.1 or later, for instance, your forensic workstation should be a high-end Intel-based PC, too. For a small police department, determining the types of computers the public uses is more difficult. The diversity of a community's computer systems requires a police department to be more versatile in the tools needed to conduct investigations. To determine computer hardware budget needs, here are some questions to consider in your planning:

- What types of investigations and data recovery will be performed in the lab?
- How many investigations can be expected per month of operation?
- Will there be any time-sensitive investigations that demand rapid analysis of disk data?
- What sizes and how many drives will be needed to support a typical investigation?
- Will you need a high-speed backup system, such as tape backup or DVD burners?
- What's the predominant type of computer system you will investigate?
- What will you use to store digital evidence? How long do you need to store it?

Software Requirements In the past few years, many more digital forensics tools have become available. For the private sector, the cost for these tools ranges from about $1200 and up. For the public sector, many forensics software vendors offer discounts. However, just as you select hardware for your digital forensics lab to fit specific needs, you must first determine what type of OSs and applications will be investigated and then make purchases that fit. Keep in mind that the more you spend on a forensics software package, the more function and flexibility will be available. To determine software budget needs, here are some questions to consider in your planning:

- What types of OSs will be examined?
- For less popular, uncommon, or older OSs (such as Mac OS 9.x, OS/2, and CP/M), how often will there be a need to investigate them?
- What are the minimum needs for forensics software tools? For example, how many copies of each tool will be needed? How often will each tool be used in an average week?
- What types of OSs will be needed to conduct routine examinations?
- Will there be a need for specialized software, such as QuickBooks or Peachtree?
- Is there a budget to purchase more than one forensics software tool, such as EnCase, FTK, or ProDiscover?
- Which disk-editing tool should be selected for general data analysis?

Miscellaneous Budget Needs For this section of the budget, you need to brainstorm on other items, tools, and supplies to consider purchasing for the lab, from general office supplies to specific needs for daily operations. To determine miscellaneous budget needs, here are some questions to consider in your planning:

- Will there be a need for errors and omission insurance for the lab's operation and staff?
- Will you need a budget for office supplies?

Approval and Acquisition The approval and acquisition phase for a digital forensics lab is a management function. It's your responsibility to create a business case with a budget to present to upper management for approval. As part of the approval process, you should include a risk analysis describing how the lab will minimize the risk of litigation, which is a persuasive argument for supporting the lab. You also need to make an educated guess of how many investigations are anticipated and how long they will take to complete on average. Remember that part of the approval process requires using negotiation skills to justify the business case. You might need to revise your case as needed to get approval.

As part of the business case, acquisition planning requires researching different products to determine which one is the best and most cost effective. You need to contact several vendors' sales staff and design engineers to learn more about each product and service. Another factor to investigate is annual maintenance costs. You need to budget for this expense, too, so that you can get support if you run into problems during an investigation. An additional item to research from others in the profession is the vendor's maintenance history. Do other forensics labs use the same product, and have they had any problems getting support for problems they encounter?

Another consideration is vendors' pricing structures. Vendor pricing isn't based on the cost of creating CDs and DVDs and packaging them. Product prices are based on cost for development, testing, documentation support, shipping, and research and development for future improvements. In addition, vendors are for-profit organizations; they have investors to pay, too. Keep in mind that for vendors to be around next year to provide products and services for you, they need to make money.

Implementation After approval and acquisition, you need to plan the implementation of facilities and tools. As part of your business case, describe how implementation of all approved items will be processed. A timeline showing expected delivery or installation dates and expected completion dates must be included. You should also have a coordination plan for delivery dates and times for materials and tools. Inspection of facility construction, equipment (including furniture and benches), and software tools should be included in the schedule. Make sure you schedule inspection dates, too, to ensure that what you ordered arrived and is functional.

Acceptance Testing Following the implementation scheduling and inspection, you need to develop an acceptance test plan for the digital forensics lab to make sure everything works correctly. When writing the acceptance test plan, consider the following items:

- Inspect the facility to see whether it meets the security criteria to contain and control digital evidence.

- Test all communications, such as phone and network connections, to make sure they work as expected.

- Test all hardware to verify that it operates correctly; for example, test a computer to make sure it boots to Windows.

- Install and start all software tools; make sure all software can run on the computers and OSs you have in the lab.

Correction for Acceptance The better you plan for your lab, the less likely you'll have problems. However, any lab operation has some problems during startup. Your business case must anticipate problems that can cause delays in lab production. In the business case, you need to develop contingencies to deal with system or facility failures. For example, devise workarounds for problems such as the wrong locks being installed on lab doors or electrical power needing additional filtering.

Production After all essential corrections have been made, your digital forensics lab can then go into production. At this time, you implement the lab operations procedures that have been described in this chapter.

For additional information on how to write a business case, see *www.sba.gov/smallbusinessplanner/plan/writeabusinessplan/ index.html*.

Chapter Summary

- A digital forensics lab is where you conduct investigations, store evidence, and do most of your work. You use the lab to house your instruments, current and legacy software, and forensic workstations. In general, you need a variety of digital forensics hardware and software.

- To continue a career in digital investigations and forensics analysis, you need to upgrade your skills through training. Several organizations offer training and certification programs for digital forensics that test you after you have successfully completed training. Some state and federal government agencies are also considering establishing certification programs that address minimum skills needed to conduct digital investigations at different levels.

- Your lab facility must be physically secure so that evidence is not lost, corrupted, or destroyed.

- Police departments in major cities need a wide assortment of computing systems, including older, outdated technology. Most digital investigations in small, local police departments involve Windows PCs and Macintosh systems. As a general rule, there should be at least one law enforcement digital investigator for every 250,000 people in a geographic region. Commercial services providing forensics analysis for other businesses can tailor their services to specific markets.

- A forensic workstation needs to have adequate memory, storage, and ports to deal with the common types of cases that come through your lab.

- Before you can set up a digital forensics lab, you must enlist the support of your managers and other team members by building a business case, a plan you can use to sell your services to management or clients. In the business case, you justify acquiring newer and better resources to investigate digital forensics cases.

Key Terms

American Society of Crime Laboratory Directors (ASCLD) A national society that sets the standards, management, and audit procedures for labs used in crime analysis, including digital forensics labs used by the police, FBI, and similar organizations.

business case A document that provides justification to upper management or a lender for purchasing new equipment, software, or other tools when upgrading your facility. In many instances, a business case shows how upgrades will benefit the company.

Certified Computer Examiner (CCE) A certification from the International Society of Forensic Computer Examiners.

Certified Cyber Forensics Professional (CCFP) A certification from ISC^2 for completing the education and work experience and passing the exam.

Certified Forensic Computer Examiner (CFCE) A certificate awarded by IACIS at completion of all portions of the exam.

configuration management The process of keeping track of all upgrades and patches you apply to your computer's OS and applications.

digital forensics lab A lab dedicated to digital investigations; typically, it has a variety of computers, OSs, and forensics software.

High Tech Crime Network (HTCN) A national organization that provides certification for computer crime investigators and digital forensics technicians.

risk management The process of determining how much risk is acceptable for any process or operation, such as replacing equipment.

secure facility A facility that can be locked and allows limited access to the room's contents.

TEMPEST A term referring to facilities that have been hardened so that electrical signals from digital devices, computer networks, and telephone systems can't be monitored or accessed easily by someone outside the facility.

Uniform Crime Report Information collected at the federal, state, and local levels to determine the types and frequencies of crimes committed.

Review Questions

1. An employer can be held liable for e-mail harassment. True or False?

2. Building a business case can involve which of the following?
   a. Procedures for gathering evidence
   b. Testing software
   c. Protecting trade secrets
   d. All of the above

3. The ASCLD mandates the procedures established for a digital forensics lab. True or False?

4. The manager of a digital forensics lab is responsible for which of the following? (Choose all that apply.)
   a. Making necessary changes in lab procedures and software
   b. Ensuring that staff members have enough training to do the job
   c. Knowing the lab objectives
   d. None of the above

5. To determine the types of operating systems needed in your lab, list two sources of information you could use.

6. What items should your business plan include?

7. List two popular certification systems for digital forensics.

8. Why is physical security so critical for digital forensics labs?

9. If a visitor to your digital forensics lab is a personal friend, it's not necessary to have him or her sign the visitor's log. True or False?

10. What three items should you research before enlisting in a certification program?

11. Large digital forensics labs should have at least _____ exits.

12. Typically, a(n) _____ lab has a separate storage area or room for evidence.

13. Digital forensics facilities always have windows. True or False?

14. Evidence storage containers should have several master keys. True or False?

15. A forensic workstation should always have a direct broadband connection to the Internet. True or False?

16. Which organization provides good information on safe storage containers?

17. Which organization has guidelines on how to operate a digital forensics lab?

18. What term refers to labs constructed to shield EMR emissions?

Hands-On Projects

Hands-On Project 2-1

You have just been hired to perform digital investigations and forensics analysis for a company. You find that no policies, processes, or procedures are currently in place. Do an Internet search to find information, and then create a policy and processes document to provide the structure necessary for your lab environment. Be sure to cite your online sources.

Hands-On Project 2-2

As mentioned, new forensics certifications are offered constantly. Research certifications online and find one not discussed in this chapter. Write a short paper stating what organization offers the certification, who endorses the certification, how long the organization has been in business, and so forth.

Hands-On Project 2-3

Physical security of a lab must always be maintained. In your classroom lab, get permission to make observations at different times of the day when classes are and aren't in session. Record how many people go in and out during a period. Do you know all the people or can you identify them? Are they all students or faculty? Who monitors the lab when classes aren't in session? Are the rooms locked? How often are things stolen from the labs? Write one to two pages about your observations. If it were a digital forensics lab, what changes would you have to make?

Hands-On Project 2-4

Write a disaster recovery plan of not more than three pages for a fictitious company's digital forensics lab. Include backup schedules, note the programs and OS installed on each machine, and list other information you would have to recover after a disaster. You should also note where the original disks and backups are located.

Hands-On Project 2-5

A law firm has hired you to assist with digital evidence cases involving divorces. The main evidence consists of e-mail, spreadsheets, and documents. Before hiring you, the firm used an outside group to conduct investigations. You have to decide what equipment and software to purchase. What would you do to build a business plan that would be approved?

Case Projects

CASE PROJECTS

Case Project 2-1

Your manager informs you that she needs to prepare for next year's budget and wants you to prepare a list of hardware and software for two new workstations and one laptop, all Windows computers. Conduct Internet research, and create a spreadsheet listing hardware and software for each computer with estimated costs. For the computers, include specifications such as processor speeds, RAM, internal disk storage, and type of monitor. For software, include an OS, an office suite, and two digital forensics tools.

Case Project 2-2

A new version of Windows has been released. What do you need to do to be ready in 6 to 10 months when you encounter cases involving the new OS? Include research, user groups, and others you need to contact. Write a one-page paper on the procedures you should use.

Case Project 2-3

Research your state, province, or neighboring states and provinces to determine whether digital forensics examiners require licenses. Write a one-page summary of the licensing requirements in the region you selected. If your region doesn't have any licensing requirements, research one of the following states: Michigan, Texas, or Georgia.

chapter 3

Data Acquisition

After reading this chapter and completing the exercises, you will be able to:

- List digital evidence storage formats
- Explain ways to determine the best acquisition method
- Describe contingency planning for data acquisitions
- Explain how to use acquisition tools
- Describe how to validate data acquisitions
- Describe RAID acquisition methods
- Explain how to use remote network acquisition tools
- List other forensics tools available for data acquisitions

Data acquisition is the process of copying data. For digital forensics, it's the task of collecting digital evidence from electronic media. There are two types of data acquisition: static acquisitions and live acquisitions. In this chapter, you learn how to perform static acquisitions from magnetic disk media and flash drives. In Chapter 12, you learn how to forensically acquire digital evidence from solid-state devices, typically found in smartphones and tablets.

Because of the use of whole disk encryption, data acquisitions are shifting toward live acquisitions with newer operating systems (OSs). In addition to encryption concerns, collecting any data that's active in a suspect's computer RAM is becoming more important to digital investigations. Techniques for acquiring live disk and RAM data are covered in Chapter 10. The processes and data integrity requirements for static and live acquisitions are similar, in that static acquisitions capture data that's not accessed by other processes that can change. With live acquisitions, file metadata, such as date and time values, changes when read by an acquisition tool. With static acquisitions, if you have preserved the original media, making a second static acquisition should produce the same results. The data on the original disk isn't altered, no matter how many times an acquisition is done. Making a second live acquisition while a computer is running collects new data because of dynamic changes in the OS.

Your goal when acquiring data for a static acquisition is to preserve the digital evidence. Many times, you have only one chance to create a reliable copy of disk evidence with a data acquisition tool. Although these tools are generally dependable, you should still take steps to make sure you acquire an image that can be verified. In addition, failures can and do occur, so you should learn how to use several acquisition tools and methods; you work with a few different tools in this chapter. Other data acquisition tools that work in Windows, MS-DOS 6.22, and Linux are described briefly in the last section, but the list of vendors and methods is by no means conclusive. You should always search for newer and better tools to ensure the integrity of your forensics acquisitions.

For additional information on older acquisition methods and tools, see Appendix D. You can perform most digital evidence acquisitions for your investigations with a combination of the tools discussed in this chapter.

Understanding Storage Formats for Digital Evidence

Chapter 1 introduced the process of acquiring data from a USB drive and storing it in a data file. The acquisition tool you used, ProDiscover Basic, performed a bit-by-bit (or sector-by-sector) copy of the USB drive and wrote it to an image file, which was an exact duplicate of the source device (the USB drive).

For additional information on digital evidence handling and documenting, see ISO/IEC 27037: 2012, *www.iso.org/iso/catalogue_detail?csnumber=44381*. Downloading ISO documents requires paying a fee, so you might check with a college or public library about getting a copy.

The data a forensics acquisition tool collects is stored as an image file, typically in an open-source or proprietary format. Each vendor has unique features, so several different proprietary formats are available. Depending on the proprietary format, many forensics analysis tools can read other vendors' formatted acquisitions. Many forensics acquisition tools create a disk-to-image file in an older open-source format, known as raw, as well as their own proprietary formats. The new open-source format, Advanced Forensic Format (AFF), is gaining recognition from some forensics examiners.

Each data acquisition format has unique features along with advantages and disadvantages. The following sections summarize each format to help you choose which one to use.

Raw Format

In the past, there was only one practical way of copying data for the purpose of evidence preservation and examination. Examiners performed a bit-by-bit copy from one disk to another disk the same size or larger. As a practical way to preserve digital evidence, vendors (and some OS utilities, such as the Linux/UNIX dd command) made it possible to write bit-stream data to files. This copy technique creates simple sequential flat files of a suspect drive or data set. The output of these flat files is referred to as a **raw format**. This format has unique advantages and disadvantages to consider when selecting an acquisition format.

The advantages of the raw format are fast data transfers and the capability to ignore minor data read errors on the source drive. In addition, most forensics tools can read the raw format, making it a universal acquisition format for most tools. One disadvantage of the raw format is that it requires as much storage space as the original disk or data set. Another disadvantage is that some raw format tools, typically freeware versions, might not collect marginal (bad) sectors on the source drive, meaning they have a low threshold of retry reads on weak media spots on a drive. Many commercial tools have a much higher threshold of retry reads to ensure that all data is collected.

Several commercial acquisition tools can produce raw format acquisitions and typically perform a validation check by using Cyclic Redundancy Check (CRC32), Message Digest 5 (MD5), and Secure Hash Algorithm (SHA-1 or later) hashing functions. These validation checks, however, usually create a separate file containing the hash value.

Proprietary Formats

Most commercial forensics tools have their own formats for collecting digital evidence. Proprietary formats typically offer several features that complement the vendor's analysis tool, such as the following:

- The option to compress or not compress image files of a suspect drive, thus saving space on the target drive
- The capability to split an image into smaller segmented files for archiving purposes, such as to CDs or DVDs, with data integrity checks integrated into each segment
- The capability to integrate metadata into the image file, such as date and time of the acquisition, hash value (for self-authentication) of the original disk or medium, investigator or examiner name, and comments or case details

Forensics examiners have several ways of referring to copying evidence data to files: bit-stream copy, bit-stream image, image, mirror, and sector copy, to name a few. For the purposes of this book, "image" is generally used to refer to all forensics acquisitions saved to a data file.

One major disadvantage of proprietary format acquisitions is the inability to share an image between different vendors' computer forensics analysis tools. For example, the ILookIX imaging tool IXimager produces three proprietary formats—IDIF, IRBF, and IEIF—that can be read only by ILookIX (see *www.perlustro.com* for additional information on ILookIX). If necessary, IXimager can copy IDIF, IRBF, and IEIF formats to a raw format image file that can be read by other tools.

Another problem with proprietary and raw formats is a file size limitation for each segmented volume. Typically, proprietary format tools produce a segmented file of 650 MB. The file size can be adjusted up or down, with a maximum file size per segment of no more than 2 GB. Most proprietary format tools go up to only 2 GB because many examiners use a target drive formatted as FAT, which has a file size limit of 2 GB.

Of all the proprietary formats for image acquisitions, the Expert Witness format is currently the unofficial standard. This format, the default for Guidance Software EnCase, produces both compressed and uncompressed image files. These files (or volumes) write an extension starting with `.e01` and incrementing it for each additional segmented image volume.

Several forensics analysis tools can generate generic versions of the Expert Witness format and analyze it, including X-Ways Forensics, AccessData Forensic Toolkit (FTK), and SMART. For more information on the Expert Witness format, see *http://asrdata.com/E01-format.html*.

Advanced Forensic Format

Dr. Simson L. Garfinkel developed an open-source acquisition format called **Advanced Forensic Format (AFF)**. This format has the following design goals:

- Capable of producing compressed or uncompressed image files
- No size restriction for disk-to-image files
- Space in the image file or segmented files for metadata
- Simple design with extensibility
- Open source for multiple computing platforms and OSs
- Internal consistency checks for self-authentication

File extensions include `.afd` for segmented image files and `.afm` for AFF metadata. Because AFF is open source, digital forensics vendors have no implementation restrictions on this format. For more information on AFF, see *www.afflib.sourceforge.net* and *www.basistech.com/wp-content/uploads/datasheets/Digital-Forensics-Toolsets-EN.pdf*.

For more information on forensics acquisition file formats, see *www.sleuthkit.org/informer*, issues #19 and #23.

Determining the Best Acquisition Method

As mentioned, there are two types of acquisitions: **static acquisitions** and **live acquisitions**. Typically, a static acquisition is done on a computer seized during a police raid, for example. If the computer has an encrypted drive, a live acquisition is done if the password or passphrase is available—meaning the computer is powered on and has been logged on to by the suspect. Static acquisitions are always the preferred way to collect digital evidence. However, they do have limitations in some situations, such as an encrypted drive that's readable only when the computer is powered on or a computer that's accessible only over a network. Some solutions can help decrypt a drive that has been encrypted with whole disk encryption, such as Elcomsoft Forensic Disk Decryptor (*www.elcomsoft.com/efdd.html*).

In Chapter 10, you learn how to perform live acquisitions, including data collection of digital media and dynamic/volatile memory (RAM) on a computing system.

For both types of acquisitions, data can be collected with four methods: creating a disk-to-image file, creating a disk-to-disk copy, creating a logical disk-to-disk or disk-to-data file, or creating a sparse copy of a folder or file. Determining the best acquisition method depends on the circumstances of the investigation.

See ISO/IEC 27037: 2012 (section 5.4.4 Acquisition and section 6.5 Use reasonable care) for additional discussions on when to perform sparse acquisitions.

Creating a disk-to-image file is the most common method and offers the most flexibility for your investigation. With this method, you can make one or many copies of a suspect drive. These copies are bit-for-bit replications of the original drive. In addition, you can use other forensics tools, such as ProDiscover, EnCase, FTK, SMART, Sleuth Kit, X-Ways Forensics, and ILookIX, to read the most common types of disk-to-image files you create. These programs read the disk-to-image file as though it were the original disk. MS-DOS tools can only read data from a drive. To use MS-DOS tools, you have to duplicate the original drive to perform the analysis. GUI programs save time and disk resources because they can read and interpret directly from the disk-to-image file of a copied drive.

Sometimes you can't make a disk-to-image file because of hardware or software errors or incompatibilities. This problem is more common when you have to acquire older drives. For these drives, you might have to create a disk-to-disk copy of the suspect drive. Several imaging tools can copy data exactly from an older disk to a newer disk. These programs can adjust the target disk's geometry (its cylinder, head, and track configuration) so that the copied data matches the original suspect drive. These imaging tools include EnCase and X-Ways Forensics. See the vendors' manuals for instructions on using these tools for disk-to-disk copying.

For more information on current and older drives, see *www.t13.org*.

Collecting evidence from a large drive can take several hours. If your time is limited, consider using a **logical acquisition** or **sparse acquisition** data copy method. A logical acquisition captures only specific files of interest to the case or specific types of files. A sparse acquisition is similar but also collects fragments of unallocated (deleted) data; use this method only when you don't need to examine the entire drive. An example of a logical acquisition is an e-mail investigation that requires collecting only Outlook .pst or .ost files. Another example is collecting only specific records from a large RAID server. If you have to recover data from a RAID or storage area network (SAN) server with several exabytes (EB) or more of data storage, the logical method might be the only way you can acquire the evidence. In e-discovery for the purpose of litigation, a logical acquisition is becoming the preferred method, especially with large data storage systems.

To determine which acquisition method to use for an investigation, consider the size of the source (suspect) disk, whether you can retain the source disk as evidence or must return it to the owner, how much time you have to perform the acquisition, and where the evidence is located.

If the source disk is very large, such as 4 terabytes (TB) or more, make sure you have a target disk that can store a disk-to-image file of the large disk. If you don't have a target disk of comparable size, review alternatives for reducing the size of data to create a verifiable copy of the suspect drive. Older Microsoft disk compression tools, such as DoubleSpace or DriveSpace, eliminate only slack disk space between files. Other compression methods use an algorithm to reduce file size. Popular archiving tools, such as PKZip, WinZip, and WinRAR, use an algorithm referred to as "lossless compression." Compression algorithms for graphics files use what's called "lossy compression," which can change data. For example, lossy compression is used with .jpeg files to reduce file size and doesn't affect image quality when the file is restored and viewed. Because lossy compression alters original data, however, it isn't used for forensics acquisitions. Both compression methods are discussed in more detail in Chapter 8.

Most imaging tools have an option to use lossless compression to save disk space, which means the target drive doesn't have to be as large as the suspect drive. For example, if you have a SATA 3 TB suspect drive, you might be able to use lossless compression to create the disk-to-image file on a 2 TB target drive. Image files can be reduced by as much as 50% of the original. If the suspect drive already contains compressed data, such as several large zip files, the imaging tool can't compress the data any further, however.

An easy way to test lossless compression is to perform an MD5 or SHA-1 hash on a file before and after it's compressed. If the compression is done correctly, both versions have the same hash value. If the hashes don't match, that means something corrupted the compressed file, such as a hardware or software error. As an added precaution, perform two separate hashes with different algorithms, such as MD5 and SHA-1. This step isn't mandatory; however, it's a good way to establish that nothing has changed during data processing.

If you can't retain the original evidence drive and must return it to the owner, as in a discovery demand for a civil litigation case, check with the requester (your lawyer or supervisor, for example), and ask whether a logical acquisition is acceptable. If not, you have to refer the matter back to the requester. When performing an acquisition under these conditions, make sure you have a good copy because most discovery demands give you only one chance to capture data. In addition, make sure you have a reliable forensics tool that you know how to use.

Contingency Planning for Image Acquisitions

Because you're working with digital evidence, you must take precautions to protect it from loss. You should also make contingency plans in case software or hardware doesn't work or you encounter a failure during an acquisition. The most common and time-consuming technique for preserving evidence is creating a duplicate of your disk-to-image file. Many digital investigators don't make duplicates of their evidence because they don't have enough time or resources to make a second image. However, if the first copy doesn't work correctly, having a duplicate is worth the effort and resources. Be sure you take steps to minimize the risk of failure in your investigation.

As a standard practice, make at least two images of the digital evidence you collect. If you have more than one imaging tool, such as ProDiscover, FTK, and X-Ways Forensics, make the first copy with one tool and the second copy with the other tool. If you have only one tool, consider making two images of the drive with the same tool, especially for critical investigations. With tools such as EnCase, X-Ways Forensics, FTK Imager, and ProDiscover, you can make one copy with no compression and compress the other copy. Remember that Murphy's Law applies to digital forensics, too: If anything can go wrong, it will.

Some acquisition tools don't copy data in the **host protected area** (**HPA**) of a disk drive. Check the vendor's documentation to verify that its tool can copy a drive's HPA. For these situations, consider using a hardware acquisition tool that can access the drive at the BIOS level, such as ProDiscover with a write-blocker, ImageMASSter Solo, or X-Ways Replica. These tools can read a disk's HPA.

Microsoft has added **whole disk encryption** with BitLocker to its newer operating systems, such as Windows 7 and 8, which makes performing static acquisitions more difficult. (Several other third-party whole disk encryption tools are available, and you should be familiar with as many as possible.) As part of contingency planning, you must be prepared to deal with encrypted drives. A static acquisition on most whole disk–encrypted drives currently involves decrypting the drives, which requires the user's cooperation in providing the decryption key. Most whole disk encryption tools at least have a manual process for decrypting data, which is converting the encrypted disk to an unencrypted disk. This process can take several hours, depending on the disk size. One good thing about encryption is that data isn't altered, in that free and slack space aren't changed. The biggest concern with whole disk encryption is getting the decryption key—that is, the password or code used to access encrypted data. If you can recover the whole disk key with tools such as Elcomsoft Forensic Disk Decryptor, mentioned previously, you need to learn how to use it to decrypt the drive. In criminal investigations, this might be impossible because if a disk contains evidence supporting the crime, a suspect has a strong motivation *not* to supply the decryption key.

NOTE

Researchers at Princeton University have produced a technique to recover passwords and passphrases from RAM; for more information, visit *http://citp.princeton.edu/pub/coldboot.pdf*

Using Acquisition Tools

Many forensics software vendors have developed acquisition tools that run in Windows. These tools make acquiring evidence from a suspect drive more convenient, especially when you use them with hot-swappable devices, such as USB-3, FireWire 1394A and 1394B, or SATA, to connect disks to your workstation.

Windows acquisition tools have some drawbacks, however. Because Windows can easily contaminate an evidence drive when it mounts it, you must protect it with a well-tested write-blocking hardware device. The automatic mounting process updates boot files by changing metadata, such as the most recent access time. (Chapter 6 discusses write-blocking devices in more detail.) Another drawback is that most Windows tools can't acquire data from a disk's host protected area. In addition, some countries haven't yet accepted the use of write-blocking devices for data acquisitions. Check with your legal counsel for evidence standards in your community or country.

Mini-WinFE Boot CDs and USB Drives

Accessing a computer's disk drive directly might not be practical for a forensics acquisition. For example, a laptop's design could make removing the disk drive to mount it on a write-blocker difficult, or you might not have the right connector for a drive. In these situations, a forensic boot CD/DVD or USB drive gives you a way to acquire data from a suspect computer and write-protect the disk drive. These forensic boot discs or drives can be Windows or Linux.

One forensically sound Windows boot utility is Mini-WinFE. It enables you to build a Windows forensic boot CD/DVD or USB drive with a modification in its Windows Registry file so that connected drives are mounted as read-only. Before booting a suspect's computer with Mini-WinFE, you need to connect your target drive, such as a USB drive. After Mini-WinFE is booted, you can list all connected drives and alter your target USB drive to read-write mode so that you can run an acquisition program, such as FTK Imager Lite or X-Ways Forensics.

To create your own Mini-WinFE boot CD or USB drive, review the documentation and download the software from the following Web sites:

- For an overview of WinFE, see *http://winfe.wordpress.com*. For the latest information and instructions, review the Downloads and Using WinFE menus.
- For download instructions on Mini-WinFE, see *http://winfe.wordpress.com/downloads-2/mini-winfe*.
- Another download site for Mini-WinFE is *http://reboot.pro/files/file/375-mini-winfe*.
- For complete instructions on Mini-WinFE, see *http://mistype.reboot.pro/mini-winfe.docs/readme.html*.

In addition, you need a Windows installation DVD (version 8 or later) and FTK Imager Lite or X-Ways Forensics installed on your workstation. Follow the instructions in the preceding Web sites to create the Mini-WinFE ISO file and then burn it to CD or transfer it to a USB drive. If you want to use a USB drive, you need a tool to transfer an ISO image to a USB drive. A freeware tool called ISO to USB is available at *www.isotousb.com*.

For a history of the evolution of WinFE and the people involved in its development, see Appendix B.

Acquiring Data with a Linux Boot CD

The Linux OS has many features that are applicable to digital forensics, especially data acquisitions. One unique feature is that Linux can access a drive that isn't mounted. Physical access for the purpose of reading data can be done on a connected media device, such as a disk drive, a USB drive, or other storage devices. In Windows OSs and newer Linux kernels, when you connect a drive via USB, FireWire, external SATA, or even internal PATA or SATA controllers, both OSs automatically mount and access the drive. On Windows drives, an acquisition workstation can access and alter data in the Recycle Bin; on Linux drives, the workstation most likely alters metadata, such as mount point configurations for an Ext3 or Ext4 drive. If you need to acquire a USB drive that doesn't have a write-lock switch, use one of the forensic Linux Live CDs (discussed in the next section) to access the device.

Use caution when working with newer Linux distributions with KDE or Gnome GUIs. Many newer distributions mount most media devices automatically. If you're using a nonforensic Linux distribution, you should test it before using it on actual evidence to see how it handles attached storage devices. If in doubt, always use a physical write-blocker for an acquisition from Linux.

Using Linux Live CD Distributions Several Linux distributions, such as Ubuntu, openSUSE, Arch Linux, Fedora, and Slackware, provide ISO images that can be burned to a CD or DVD. They're called "Linux Live CDs." Most of these Linux distributions are for Linux OS recovery, not for digital forensics acquisition and analysis. For a list of the most current Linux Live CDs, see *www.frozentech.com* or *http://livecdlist.com.*

A few Linux ISO images are designed specifically for digital forensics, however. These images contain additional utilities that aren't typically installed in normal Linux distributions. They're also configured not to mount, or to mount as read-only, any connected storage media, such as USB drives. This feature protects the media's integrity for the purpose of acquiring and analyzing data. To access media, you have to give specific instructions to the Live CD boot session through a GUI utility or a shell command prompt. Mounting drives from a shell gives you more control over them. See the man page for the mount command (by typing man mount at the shell prompt) to learn what options are available for your Linux distribution.

The man command displays pages from the online help manual for information on Linux commands and their options.

Linux can read data from a physical device without having to mount it. As a usual practice, don't mount a suspect media device as a precaution against any writes to it. Later in this section, you learn how to make a forensics acquisition in Linux without mounting the device.

The following are some well-designed Linux Live CDs for digital forensics:

- Penguin Sleuth (*www.linux-forensics.com*)
- F.I.R.E (*http://fire.dmzs.com*)
- CAINE (*www.caine-live.net*)
- Deft (*www.deftlinux.net*)

- Kali Linux (*www.kali.org*), previously known as BackTrack (*www.backtrack-linux. org/wiki/index.php/Forensics_Boot*)

- Knoppix (*www.knopper.net/knoppix/index-en.html*)

- SANS Investigate Forensic Toolkit (SIFT; *http://computer-forensics.sans.org/ community/downloads*)

You can download these ISO images to any computer, including a Windows system, and then burn them to CD/DVD with burner software, such as Roxio or Nero. Creating a bootable image from an ISO file is different from copying data or music files to a CD or DVD. If you aren't familiar with how to do it, see the Help menu in your burner software for instructions on creating a bootable CD or DVD. For example, Roxio Creator Classic and Nero Express have a Bootable CD or DVD option. An alternative is using a USB drive instead of a CD or DVD. For this option, you need a tool such as ISO to USB, mentioned previously (or another tool for transferring an ISO image to a USB drive).

After creating a Linux Live CD, test it on your workstation. Remember to check your workstation's BIOS to see whether it boots first from the CD or DVD on the system. To test the Live CD, simply place it in the CD or DVD drive and reboot your system. If successful, Linux loads into your computer's memory, and a common GUI for Linux is displayed. If you have problems with the video display on your workstation, try another computer with a different video card. No one Live CD distribution has all video drivers. Linux Live CDs load the OS into a computer's RAM, so performance can be affected when you're using GUI tools. The following sections explain how to use Linux to make forensically sound data acquisitions.

Preparing a Target Drive for Acquisition in Linux
The Linux OS has many tools you can use to modify non-Linux file systems. Current Linux distributions can create Microsoft FAT and NTFS partition tables. Linux kernel version 2.6.17.7 and earlier can format and read only the FAT file system, although an NTFS driver, NTFS-3G, is available that allows Linux to mount and write data only to NTFS partitions. You can download this driver from *http://sourceforge.net/projects/ntfs-3g*, where you can also find information about NTFS and instructions for installing the driver. For information on Mac OS X file systems and acquisitions, see Chapter 7.

In this section, you learn how to partition and format a Microsoft FAT drive from Linux so that you don't have to switch OSs or computers to prepare a FAT target disk. If you have a previously used target drive, you can use the following procedure to format it as a FAT32 drive. After you make the acquisition, you can then transfer the FAT disk to a Windows system to use a Windows analysis tool.

When preparing a drive to be used on a Linux system for forensics acquisition or analysis, do it in a separate boot session with no suspect drive attached.

Linux/UNIX commands are case sensitive, so make sure you type commands exactly as shown in this section's steps.

Assuming you have a functioning Linux computer or one running with a Linux Live CD, perform the following steps from a shell prompt:

Depending on which version and distribution of Linux you use, your screen prompts might be slightly different from those mentioned in this section.

1. First, boot Linux on your computer.
2. Connect the USB, FireWire, or SATA external drive to the Linux computer and power it on.
3. If a shell window isn't already open, start one.
4. At the shell prompt, type **su** and press **Enter** to log in as the superuser (root). Then type the root password and press **Enter**.

If you're using one of the Live CDs listed previously, these distributions are typically already in superuser (root) mode, so there's no need to use the su command. Other Linux Live CDs might have no password set and simply require pressing Enter.

5. To list the current disk devices connected to the computer, type **fdisk -l** (lowercase L) and press **Enter**. You should see output similar to the following:

Linux lists all IDE (also known as PATA) drives as hda, hdb, and so on. All SCSI, SATA, FireWire, and USB-connected drives are listed as sda, sdb, and so forth.

```
Disk /dev/hda: 40.0 GB, 40007761920 bytes
255 heads, 63 sectors/track, 4864 cylinders
Units = cylinders of 16065 * 512 = 8225280 bytes

Device Boot      Start    End      Blocks      Id   System
/dev/hda1   *    1        13       104391      83   Linux
/dev/hda2        14       4864     38965657+   8e   Linux LVM

Disk /dev/sda: 6448 MB, 6448619520 bytes
199 heads, 62 sectors/track, 1020 cylinders
Units = cylinders of 12338 * 512 = 6317056 bytes

Disk /dev/sda doesn't contain a valid partition table
```

In the preceding output, the /dev/sda device has no partition listed. These steps show how to create a Microsoft FAT partition on this disk. If there's a partition on this drive, it can be deleted with the Linux fdisk utility. For additional information on fdisk, refer to the man page.

6. Type **fdisk /dev/sda** and press **Enter** to partition the disk drive as a FAT file system. You should see output similar to the following:

```
Welcome to fdisk (util-linux 2.21.2).
Changes will remain in memory only, until you decide to write them.
Be careful before using the write command.

Command (m for help): m
```

7. Display `fdisk` menu options by typing **m** and pressing **Enter**. You should see output similar to the following:

```
Command action
a   toggle a bootable flag
b   edit bsd disklabel
c   toggle the dos compatibility flag
d   delete a partition
l   list known partition types
m   print this menu
n   add a new partition
o   create a new empty DOS partition table
p   print the partition table
q   quit without saving changes
s   create a new empty Sun disk label
t   change a partition's system id
u   change display/entry units
v   verify the partition table
w   write table to disk and exit
x   extra functionality (experts only)
```

8. Determine whether there are any partitions on /dev/sda by typing **p** and pressing **Enter**. You should see output similar to the following:

```
Disk /dev/sda: 6448 MB, 6448619520 bytes
199 heads, 62 sectors/track, 1020 cylinders
Units = cylinders of 12338 * 512 = 6317056 bytes

Device Boot     Start   End     Blocks      Id    System
/dev/sda1       1       1020    6292349 b   W95   FAT32
```

In this example, the disk has no previously configured partitions. If it did, there would be data under each column heading describing each partition's configuration.

9. Next, you create a new primary partition on /dev/sda. To use the defaults and select the entire drive, type **n** and press **Enter**. To create a primary partition table, type **p** and press **Enter**, and then type **1** (the numeral) to select the first partition and press **Enter**. At the remaining prompts, press **Enter**. Your output should be similar to the following:

```
Command action
e   extended
p   primary partition (1-4)
p
Partition number (1-4): 1
```

```
First cylinder (1-1020, default 1):
Using default value 1
Last cylinder or +size or +sizeM or +sizeK (1-1020, default 1020):
Using default value 1020
```

In Linux, the first logical partition created after the primary and extended partitions is numbered 5; any additional logical partitions are numbered 6, 7, and so on. For example, the C partition is typically `/dev/hda1`, and the D partition is `/dev/hda2`.

10. List the newly defined partitions by typing **p** and pressing **Enter**, which produces the following output:

```
Disk /dev/sda: 6448 MB, 6448619520 bytes
199 heads, 62 sectors/track, 1020 cylinders
Units = cylinders of 12338 * 512 = 6317056 bytes

Device Boot      Start      End      Blocks      Id      System
/dev/sda1        1          1020     6292349     83      Linux
```

11. To list the menu again so that you can select the change partition ID, type **m** and press **Enter**. You should see output similar to the following:

```
Command action
a   toggle a bootable flag
b   edit bsd disk label
c   toggle the dos compatibility flag
d   delete a partition
l   list known partition types
m   print this menu
n   add a new partition
o   create a new empty DOS partition table
p   print the partition table
q   quit without saving changes
s   create a new empty Sun disk label
t   change a partition's system id
u   change display/entry units
v   verify the partition table
w   write table to disk and exit
x   extra functionality (experts only)
```

12. To change the newly created partition to the Windows 95 FAT32 file system, first type **t** and press **Enter**, which produces the following output:

```
Selected partition 1
Hex code (type L to list codes):
```

13. List available file systems and their code values by typing **l** (lowercase L) and pressing **Enter**. You should see output similar to what's shown in Figure 3-1.

```
Command (m for help): l
```

0 Empty	24 NEC DOS	81 Minix / old Lin	bf Solaris
1 FAT12	27 Hidden NTFS Win	82 Linux swap / So	c1 DRDOS/sec (FAT-
2 XENIX root	39 Plan 9	83 Linux	c4 DRDOS/sec (FAT-
3 XENIX usr	3c PartitionMagic	84 OS/2 hidden C:	c6 DRDOS/sec (FAT-
4 FAT16 <32M	40 Venix 80286	85 Linux extended	c7 Syrinx
5 Extended	41 PPC PReP Boot	86 NTFS volume set	da Non-FS data
6 FAT16	42 SFS	87 NTFS volume set	db CP/M / CTOS / .
7 HPFS/NTFS/exFAT	4d QNX4.x	88 Linux plaintext	de Dell Utility
8 AIX	4e QNX4.x 2nd part	8e Linux LVM	df BootIt
9 AIX bootable	4f QNX4.x 3rd part	93 Amoeba	e1 DOS access
a OS/2 Boot Manag	50 OnTrack DM	94 Amoeba BBT	e3 DOS R/O
b W95 FAT32	51 OnTrack DM6 Aux	9f BSD/OS	e4 SpeedStor
c W95 FAT32 (LBA)	52 CP/M	a0 IBM Thinkpad hi	eb BeOS fs
e W95 FAT16 (LBA)	53 OnTrack DM6 Aux	a5 FreeBSD	ee GPT
f W95 Ext'd (LBA)	54 OnTrackDM6	a6 OpenBSD	ef EFI (FAT-12/16/
10 OPUS	55 EZ-Drive	a7 NeXTSTEP	f0 Linux/PA-RISC b
11 Hidden FAT12	56 Golden Bow	a8 Darwin UFS	f1 SpeedStor
12 Compaq diagnost	5c Priam Edisk	a9 NetBSD	f4 SpeedStor
14 Hidden FAT16 <3	61 SpeedStor	ab Darwin boot	f2 DOS secondary
16 Hidden FAT16	63 GNU HURD or Sys	af HFS / HFS+	fb VMware VMFS
17 Hidden HPFS/NTF	64 Novell Netware	b7 BSDI fs	fc VMware VMKCORE
18 AST SmartSleep	65 Novell Netware	b8 BSDI swap	fd Linux raid auto
1b Hidden W95 FAT3	70 DiskSecure Mult	bb Boot Wizard hid	fe LANstep
1c Hidden W95 FAT3	75 PC/IX	be Solaris boot	ff BBT
1e Hidden W95 FAT1	80 Old Minix		

```
Command (m for help):
```

Figure 3-1 Listing code values for available file systems
Source: Adapted from Linux commands

14. Change the newly created partition to the Windows 95 FAT32 file system by typing **c** and pressing **Enter**. Your output should look similar to the following:

```
Changed system type of partition 1 to c (W95 FAT32 (LBA))
```

15. To display partitions of the newly changed drive, type **p** and press Enter, which produces the following output:

```
Disk /dev/sda: 6448 MB, 6448619520 bytes
199 heads, 62 sectors/track, 1020 cylinders
Units = cylinders of 12338 * 512 = 6317056 bytes

Device Boot     Start     End     Blocks     Id     System
/dev/sda1       1         1020    6292349    c      W95 FAT32 (LBA)
```

16. Save (write) the newly created partition to the /dev/sda drive by typing **w** and pressing **Enter**. Your output should look similar to the following:

```
The partition table has been altered!
```

```
Calling ioctl() to re-read partition table.
```

```
WARNING: If you have created or modified any DOS 6.x partitions,
please see the fdisk manual page for additional information.
Syncing disks.
```

Fdisk exits back to the shell prompt after updating the partition table on the /dev/sda drive.

17. Show the known drives connected to your computer by typing **fdisk -l** and pressing **Enter**, which produces the following output:

```
Disk /dev/hda: 40.0 GB, 40007761920 bytes
255 heads, 63 sectors/track, 4864 cylinders
Units = cylinders of 16065 * 512 = 8225280 bytes

Device Boot     Start     End     Blocks      Id     System
/dev/hda1   *   1         13      104391      83     Linux
/dev/hda2       14        4864    38965657+   8e     Linux LVM

Disk /dev/sda: 6448 MB, 6448619520 bytes
199 heads, 62 sectors/track, 1020 cylinders
Units = cylinders of 12338 * 512 = 6317056 bytes

Device Boot     Start     End     Blocks      Id     System
/dev/sda1       1         1020    6292349     b      W95 FAT32
```

18. To format a FAT file system from Linux, type **mkfs.msdos -vF32 /dev/sda1** and press **Enter**, which produces the following output:

If your Linux distribution is missing the mkfs.msdos command, you need to download and install your distribution's dosfstools package. To find these files, search for mkfs.msdos Fedora or dostools Debian, for example.

```
mkfs.msdos 2.8 (28 Feb 2001)
Selecting 8 sectors per cluster
/dev/sde1 has 33 heads and 61 sectors per track,
logical sector size is 512,
using 0xf8 media descriptor, with 2047966 sectors;
file system has 2 32-bit FATs and 8 sectors per cluster.
FAT size is 1997 sectors, and provides 255492 clusters.
Volume ID is 420781ea, no volume label.
```

Newer Linux distributions automatically sync the newly created partition and format the drive. The sync feature eliminates the need to reboot the computer.

19. Close the shell window for this session by typing **exit** and pressing **Enter**.

This drive can now be mounted and used to receive an image of a suspect drive. Later in this section, you learn how to mount and write to this Microsoft FAT target drive.

Acquiring Data with `dd` in Linux A unique feature of a forensics Linux Live CD is that it can mount and read most drives. To perform a data acquisition on a suspect computer, all you need are the following:

- A forensics Linux Live CD
- A USB, FireWire, or SATA external drive with cables
- Knowledge of how to alter the suspect computer's BIOS to boot from the Linux Live CD
- Knowledge of which shell commands to use for the data acquisition

If you want to learn more about Linux and shell commands, review a Linux tutorial, such as Nix Tutor at *www.nixtutor.com/linux/all-the-best-linux-cheat-sheets*.

The `dd` command, available on all UNIX and Linux distributions, means "data dump." This command, which has many functions and switches, can be used to read and write data from a media device and a data file. The `dd` command isn't bound by a logical file system's data structures, meaning the drive doesn't have to be mounted for `dd` to access it. For example, if you list a physical device name, the `dd` command copies the entire device—all data files, slack space, and free space (unallocated data) on the device. The `dd` command creates a raw format file that most forensics analysis tools can read, which makes it useful for data acquisitions.

Use extreme caution with the `dd` command. Make sure you know which drives are the suspect drive and target drive. Although you might not have mounted the suspect drive, if you reverse the input field (`if=`) of the suspect and target drives with the output field (`of=`), data is written to the wrong drive, thus destroying the original evidence drive.

As powerful as this command is, it does have some shortcomings. One major problem is that it requires more advanced skills than the average computer user might have. Also, because it doesn't compress data, the target drive needs to be equal to or larger than the suspect drive. It's possible to divide the output to other drives if a large enough target drive isn't available, but this process can be cumbersome and prone to mistakes when you're trying to keep track of which data blocks to copy to which target drive.

The `dd` command combined with the `split` command segments output into separate volumes. Use the `split` command with the `-b` switch to adjust the size of segmented volumes the `dd` command creates. As a standard practice for archiving purposes, create segmented volumes that fit on a CD or DVD. For additional information on `dd` and `split`, see their man pages.

Follow these steps to make an image of an NTFS disk on a FAT32 disk by using the `dd` command:

1. Assuming that your workstation is the suspect computer and is booted from a Linux Live CD, connect the USB, FireWire, or SATA external drive containing the FAT32 target drive, and turn the external drive on.

2. If you're not at a shell prompt, start a shell window, switch to superuser (su) mode, type the root password, and press **Enter**.

3. At the shell prompt, list all drives connected to the computer by typing **fdisk -l** and pressing **Enter**, which produces the following output:

```
Disk /dev/hda: 40.0 GB, 40007761920 bytes
255 heads, 63 sectors/track, 4864 cylinders
Units = cylinders of 16065 * 512 = 8225280 bytes

Device Boot      Start       End       Blocks       Id     System
/dev/hda1  *     1           13        104391       83     Linux
/dev/hda2        14          4864      38965657+    8e     Linux LVM

Disk /dev/sda: 163.9 GB, 163928605184 bytes
255 heads, 63 sectors/track, 19929 cylinders
Units = cylinders of 16065 * 512 = 8225280 bytes

Device Boot      Start       End       Blocks       Id     System
/dev/sda1        1           12000     96389968+    b      W95 FAT32
/dev/sda2        12001       19929     63689692+    5      Extended
/dev/sda5        12001       19929     63689661     c      W95 FAT32 (LBA)

Disk /dev/sdb: 6448 MB, 6448619520 bytes
199 heads, 62 sectors/track, 1020 cylinders
Units = cylinders of 12338 * 512 = 6317056 bytes

Device Boot      Start     End     Blocks     Id    System
/dev/sdb1        1         1020    6292349    7     HPFS/NTFS
```

4. To create a mount point for the USB, FireWire, or SATA external drive and partition, make a directory in /mnt by typing **mkdir /mnt/sda5** and pressing **Enter**.

5. To mount the target drive partition, type **mount -t vfat /dev/sda5 /mnt/sda5** and press **Enter**.

6. To change your default directory to the target drive, type **cd /mnt/sda5** and press **Enter**.

7. List the contents of the target drive's root level by typing **ls -al** and pressing **Enter**. Your output should be similar to the following:

```
total 40
drwxr-xr-x 2 root root 32768 Dec 31 1969 .
drwxr-xr-x 5 root root 4096 Feb 6 17:22 ..
```

8. To make a target directory to receive image saves of the suspect drive, type **mkdir case01** and press **Enter**.

9. To change to the newly created target directory, type **cd case01** and press **Enter**. Don't close the shell window.

Next, you perform a raw format image of the entire suspect drive to the target directory. To do this, you use the split command with the dd command. The split command creates a two-letter extension for each segmented volume. The -d switch creates numeric rather than letter extensions. As a general rule, if you plan to use a Windows forensics tool to examine a dd image file created with this switch, the segmented volumes shouldn't exceed 2 GB each because of FAT32 file size limits. This 2 GB limit allows you to copy only up to 198 GB of a suspect's disk. If you need to use the dd command, it's better to use the split command's default of incremented letter extensions and make smaller segments. To adjust the segmented volume size, change the value for the -b switch from the 650 MB used in the following example to 2000 MB.

1. First, type **dd if=/dev/sdb | split -b 650m - image_sdb .** and press **Enter**. You should see output similar to the following:

```
12594960+0 records in
12594960+0 records out
```

When using the split command, type a period at the end of the line as shown, with no space between it and the filename. Otherwise, the extension is appended to the filename with no "." delimiter.

2. Now list the raw images that have been created from the dd and split commands by typing **ls -l** and pressing **Enter**. You should see output similar to the following:

```
total 6297504
-rwxr-xr-x    1    root root 681574400 Feb    6 17:26 image_sdb.aa
-rwxr-xr-x    1    root root 681574400 Feb    6 17:28 image_sdb.ab
-rwxr-xr-x    1    root root 681574400 Feb    6 17:29 image_sdb.ac
-rwxr-xr-x    1    root root 681574400 Feb    6 17:30 image_sdb.ad
-rwxr-xr-x    1    root root 681574400 Feb    6 17:32 image_sdb.ae
-rwxr-xr-x    1    root root 681574400 Feb    6 17:33 image_sdb.af
-rwxr-xr-x    1    root root 681574400 Feb    6 17:34 image_sdb.ag
-rwxr-xr-x    1    root root 681574400 Feb    6 17:36 image_sdb.ah
-rwxr-xr-x    1    root root 681574400 Feb    6 17:37 image_sdb.ai
-rwxr-xr-x    1    root root 314449920 Feb    6 17:37 image_sdb.aj
```

3. To complete this acquisition, dismount the target drive by typing **umount /dev/sda5** and pressing **Enter**.

Depending on the Windows forensics analysis tool you're using, renaming each segmented volume's extension with incremented numbers instead of letters might be necessary. For example, rename image_sdb.aa as image_sdb.01, and so on. Several Windows forensics tools can read only disk-to-image segmented files that have numeric extensions. Most Linux forensics tools can read segments with numeric or lettered extensions.

Acquiring a specific partition on a drive works the same way as acquiring the entire drive. Instead of typing /dev/sdb as you would for the entire drive, add the partition number to the device name, such as /dev/sdb1. For drives with additional partitions, use the number that would be listed in the fdisk -l output. For example, to copy only the partition of the previous NTFS drive, you use the following dd command:

```
dd if=/dev/sdb1 | split -b 650m - image_sdb1
```

Remember to use caution with the dd command in your forensics data acquisitions.

Acquiring Data with dcfldd in Linux The dd command is intended as a data management tool; it's not designed for forensics acquisitions. Because of these shortcomings, Nicholas Harbour of the Defense Computer Forensics Laboratory (DCFL) developed a tool that can be added to most UNIX/Linux OSs. This tool, the dcfldd command, works similarly to the dd command but has many features designed for forensics acquisitions. The following are important functions dcfldd offers that aren't possible with dd:

- Specify hexadecimal patterns or text for clearing disk space.
- Log errors to an output file for analysis and review.
- Use the hashing options MD5, SHA-1, SHA-256, SHA-384, and SHA-512 with logging and the option of specifying the number of bytes to hash, such as specific blocks or sectors.
- Refer to a status display indicating the acquisition's progress in bytes.
- Split data acquisitions into segmented volumes with numeric extensions (unlike dd's limit of 99).
- Verify the acquired data with the original disk or media data.

When using dcfldd, you should follow the same precautions as with dd. The dcfldd command can also write to the wrong device, if you aren't careful.

The following examples show how to use the dcfldd command to acquire data from a 64 MB USB drive, although you can use the command on a larger media device. All commands need to be run from a privileged root shell session. To acquire an entire media device in one image file, you type the following command at the shell prompt:

```
dcfldd if=/dev/sda of=usbimg.dat
```

If the suspect media or disk needs to be segmented, use the dcfldd command with the split command, placing split before the output file field (of=), as shown here:

```
dcfldd if=/dev/sda split=2M of=usbimg hash=md5
```

This command creates segmented volumes of 2 MB each. To create segmented volumes that fit on a CD of 650 MB, change the split=2M to split=650M. This command also displays the MD5 value of the acquired data.

For additional information on the dcfldd command, see *http://dcfldd. sourceforge.net*. Information on how to download and install dcfldd is available for many UNIX, Linux, and Macintosh OSs. You can also use the man page to find more information on dcfldd features and switches.

Capturing an Image with ProDiscover Basic

In Chapter 2, you learned how to acquire an image of a USB drive. ProDiscover automates many acquisition functions, unlike current Linux tools. Because USB drives are typically small, a single image file can be acquired with no need to segment it. In this section, you learn how to make an image of a larger drive and apply the Split function in ProDiscover Basic to create segmented files of 650 MB each that can be archived to CDs.

Before acquiring data directly from a suspect drive with ProDiscover Basic, always use a hardware write-blocker device.

The following activity assumes you have removed the suspect drive and connected it to a USB or FireWire write-blocker device connected to your forensic workstation. The acquisition is written to a work folder on your C drive, assuming it has enough free space for the acquired data. Follow these steps to perform the first task of connecting the suspect's drive to your workstation:

1. Document the chain of evidence for the drive you plan to acquire.

2. Remove the drive from the suspect's computer.

3. For IDE drives, configure the suspect drive's jumpers as needed. (*Note*: This step doesn't apply to SATA or USB drives.)

4. Connect the suspect drive to the USB or FireWire write-blocker device.

5. Create a storage folder on the target drive. For this activity, you use your work folder (C:*Work*\\Chap03\\Chapter), but in real life, you'd use a folder name such as C:\\Evidence.

The work folder shown in screenshots might differ from the work folder you've created for this chapter's activities.

Using ProDiscover's Proprietary Acquisition Format
Follow these steps to perform the second task, starting ProDiscover Basic and configuring settings for the acquisition:

1. Start ProDiscover Basic. (Remember to click the **Run as administrator** option if you're using Windows Vista or later.) If the Startup dialog box opens, click **Cancel**.

2. In the ProDiscover Basic window, click **Action, Capture Image** from the menu.

3. In the Capture Image dialog box, click the **Source Drive** list arrow, and then click **PhysicalDrive1 *xxxx* GB**.

With Windows 7 and later, the source (or suspect) drive might differ from your computer when it's displayed in the Capture Image dialog box. In this example, it's listed as PhysicalDrive 1 7.500 GB. If you have additional drives connected to your workstation, the PhysicalDrive number varies, such as PhysicalDrive2. Always verify your current drives and their numbers before connecting your source drive so that you know which new drive is your target drive after it's connected. To verify all drives on a Windows computer, start the Computer Management utility in the Computer window, and click Disk Management.

4. Click the >> button next to the Destination text box, and click **Choose Local Path**. In the Save As dialog box, navigate to the work folder you set up. In the File name text box, type **InChp031**, and then click **Save**.

5. Click the **Split** button. In the Split Image dialog box shown in Figure 3-2, type **650** for a small drive or **2000** for a larger drive in the "Split into equal sized image of" text box, click **Split**, and then click **OK**.

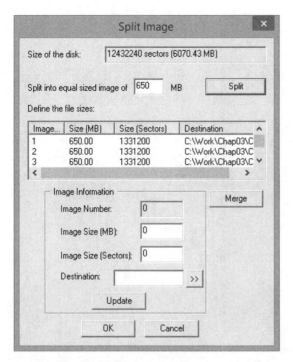

Figure 3-2 The Split Image dialog box
Courtesy of Technology Pathways, LLC

NOTE

If your target drive is FAT32, you're limited to 2 GB (2000 MB) split file sizes. For larger files, you need an NTFS-formatted drive.

6. In the Capture Image dialog box, click the **Image Format** list arrow, and click **ProDiscover Format (recommended)**, if it's not already selected.

7. In the Technician Name text box, type your name, and in the Image Number text box, type **InChp03** (see Figure 3-3). If you like, in the Description text box, type any comments related to the case.

8. If you needed to save space on your target drive, you would click the Yes option button in the Compression section. For this and other activities in this book, click **No**.

9. If additional security is needed for the acquired image, click **Password**. In the Password dialog box, enter a new password once, type it again to confirm it, and then click **OK**.

10. When you're finished entering information in the Capture Image dialog box, click **OK** to begin the acquisition. ProDiscover then creates a segmented image file in your work folder. During this acquisition, ProDiscover displays a status bar in the lower-right corner to show the progress for each volume segment it's creating.

11. When the acquisition is done, ProDiscover displays a message box instructing you to examine a log file for errors. Click **OK** to finish the acquisition, and then exit ProDiscover Basic.

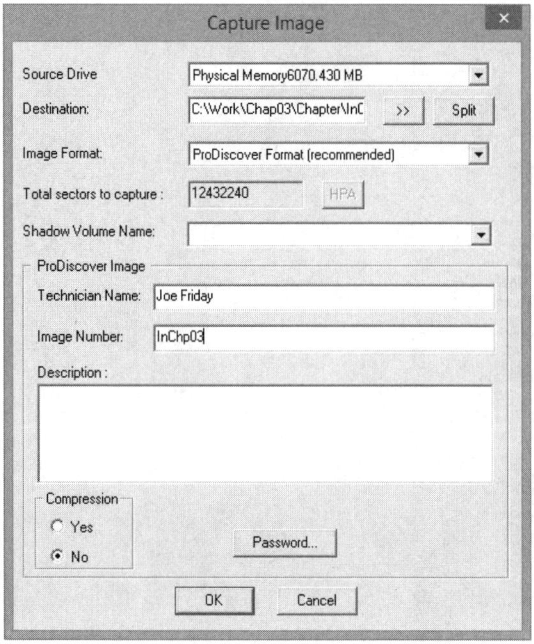

Figure 3-3 The Capture Image dialog box
Courtesy of Technology Pathways, LLC

ProDiscover then creates image files (segmented volumes) with an .eve extension, a log file (.log extension) listing any errors that occurred during the acquisition, and a special inventory file (.pds extension) that tells ProDiscover how many segmented volumes were created. All these files have the prefix you specified in the Capture Image dialog box. ProDiscover uses the .pds file to load all segmented volumes in the correct order for analysis.

For this activity, ProDiscover produced four files. Two are segments of the suspect drive's split image, one is the log file, and one is the .pds file. A larger drive would have more than two segmented volumes. The first segmented volume (volume one) has the extension .eve, and all other segmented volumes have the suffix -Split1, -Split2, -Split3, and so on before the .eve extension. If the compression option was selected, ProDiscover uses a .cmp rather than an .eve extension on all segmented volumes.

Using ProDiscover's Raw Acquisition Format For versatility, ProDiscover can produce raw format acquisitions that many other forensics tools can read. To perform a raw format acquisition, follow the same steps as for the proprietary format in the Capture Image dialog box, but select the "UNIX style dd" format in the Image Format list box. When you select this option, the input fields at the bottom of the Capture Image dialog box are grayed out. To segment the image acquisition, click the Split button as you would for the proprietary format.

To initiate the raw acquisition, click OK, and then click Proceed in the warning box, which simply advises you that the raw acquisition saves only the image data and hash value. When the raw acquisition is finished, click OK in the message box.

The raw format creates a log file (.pds extension) and segmented volume files, just like the proprietary format acquisition. Another file with the .md5 extension is created, which contains the MD5 hash for the acquired drive. In the proprietary format, the hash value, the time zone where the acquisition occurred, the password if it was specified, the investigator's name, and any comments entered in the Description text box are stored in the .eve file.

Capturing an Image with AccessData FTK Imager Lite

FTK Imager is a data acquisition tool that's included with a licensed copy of AccessData Forensic Toolkit. Like most Windows data acquisition tools, it requires using a USB dongle for licensing. FTK Imager Lite is free and requires no dongle license and can be downloaded at *www.accessdata.com/support/product-downloads*. FTK Imager is available for both Windows and Macintosh. Find FTK Imager in the Current Releases section, click to expand the available tools, and select FTK Imager Lite. After downloading this tool, install it on your workstation.

FTK Imager is designed for viewing evidence disks and disk-to-image files created from other proprietary formats. It can read AccessData .ad1, Expert Witness (EnCase) .e01, SMART .s01, Advanced Forensic Format, and raw format files. In addition to disk media, FTK Imager can read CD and DVD file systems. This program shows a view of a disk partition or an image file as though it's a mounted partition, with additional panes showing the contents of the selected file (see Figure 3-4).

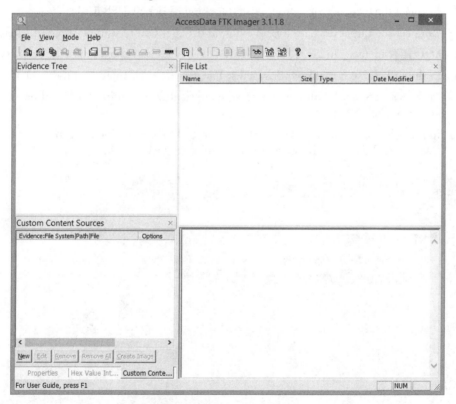

Figure 3-4   The FTK Imager main window
© 2014 AccessData Group, Inc. All Rights Reserved

FTK Imager can make disk-to-image copies of evidence drives and enables you to acquire an evidence drive from a logical partition level or a physical drive level. You can also define the size of each disk-to-image file volume, allowing you to segment the image into one or many split volumes. For example, you can specify 650 MB volume segments if you plan to store volumes on 650 MB CD-Rs or 2.0 GB volume segments so that you can record volumes on DVD-/+Rs. An additional feature of FTK Imager is that it can image RAM on a live computer. The evidence drive you're acquiring data from must have a hardware write-blocking device or run from a Live CD, such Mini-WinFE.

FTK Imager can't acquire a drive's host protected area, however. In other words, if the drive's specifications indicate it has 11,000,000 sectors and the BIOS display indicates 9,000,000, a host protected area of 2,000,000 sectors might be assigned to the drive. If you suspect an evidence drive has a host protected area, you must use an advanced acquisition tool, such as ProDiscover, OS Forensics, or X-Ways Replica, to include this area when copying data. With older MS-DOS tools, you might have to define the exact sector count to make sure you include more than what the BIOS shows as the number of known sectors on a drive. Review vendors' manuals to determine how to account for a drive's host protected area.

In the following activity, you use FTK Imager Lite to make an image file. Use a write-blocking device to protect the suspect drive, and then follow these steps:

1. Boot your forensic workstation to Windows, using an installed write-blocker.

2. Connect the evidence drive to a write-blocking device or USB device.

3. Connect the target drive to a USB external drive, if you're using a write-blocker.

4. Start FTK Imager Lite. If prompted by the User Account Control message box, click **Yes**.

5. In the FTK Imager main window, click **File**, **Create Disk Image** from the menu.

6. In the Select Source dialog box, click the **Physical Drive** option button, if necessary, and then click **Next**.

7. In the Select Drive dialog box, click the **Source Drive Selection** list arrow (see Figure 3-5), click the suspect drive, and then click **Finish**.

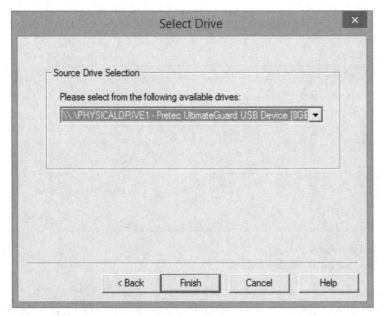

Figure 3-5   The Select Drive dialog box
© 2014 AccessData Group, Inc. All Rights Reserved

8. In the Create Image dialog box, click to select the **Verify images after they are created** check box, if necessary, and then click **Add**. In the Select Image Type dialog box that opens (see Figure 3-6), click the **Raw (dd)** option button, if necessary, and then click **Next**.

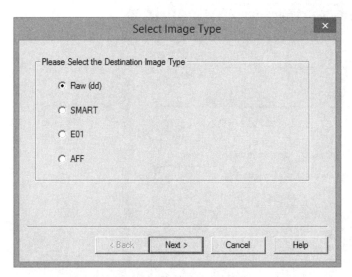

Figure 3-6   The Select Image Type dialog box
© 2014 AccessData Group, Inc. All Rights Reserved

9. In the Evidence Item Information dialog box, complete the case information, as shown in Figure 3-7, and then click **Next**.

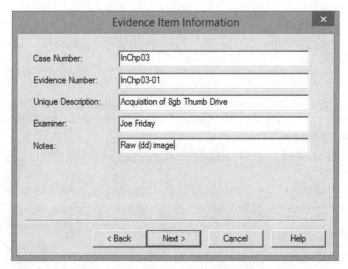

Figure 3-7   The Evidence Item Information dialog box
© 2014 AccessData Group, Inc. All Rights Reserved

10. In the Select Image Destination dialog box (see Figure 3-8), click **Browse**, navigate to the location for the image file (your work folder), and click to clear the **Use AD Encryption** check box, if necessary.

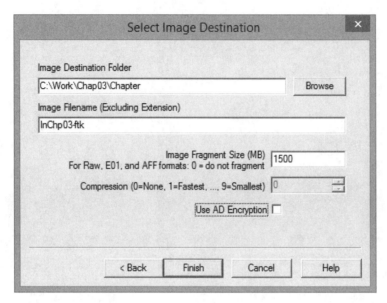

Figure 3-8 Selecting where to save the image file
© 2014 AccessData Group, Inc. All Rights Reserved

 You can adjust the segmented volume size in this dialog box, but for this activity, leave the default value of 1500 MB.

11. In the Image Filename (Excluding Extension) text box, type **InChp03-ftk**, and then click **Finish**.

12. Next, in the Create Image dialog box, click **Start** to initiate the acquisition.

13. When FTK Imager finishes the acquisition, review the information in the Drive/Image Verify Results dialog box, and then click **Close**. Click **Close** again in the Creating Image dialog box (see Figure 3-9).

14. Exit FTK Imager Lite by clicking **File, Exit** from the menu.

 For additional information, see the Help menu in FTK Imager to learn more about its many features.

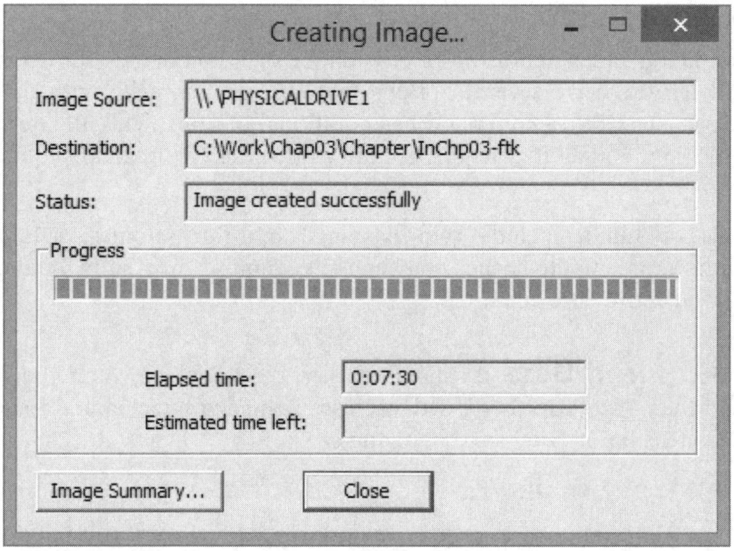

Figure 3-9   A completed image save
© 2014 AccessData Group, Inc. All Rights Reserved

Validating Data Acquisitions

Probably the most critical aspect of computer forensics is validating digital evidence. The weakest point of any digital investigation is the integrity of the data you collect, so validation is essential. In this section, you learn how to use several tools to validate data acquisitions.

Validating digital evidence requires using a hashing algorithm utility, which is designed to create a binary or hexadecimal number that represents the uniqueness of a data set, such as a file or disk drive. This unique number is referred to as a "digital fingerprint." With a few exceptions, making any alteration in one of the files—even changing one letter from upper-case to lowercase—produces a completely different hash value.

These exceptions, known as "collisions," have been found to occur in a small number of files with MD5, and SHA-1 might also be subject to collisions. For forensic examinations of data files on a disk drive, however, collisions are of little concern. If two files with different content have the same MD5 hash value, a comparison of each byte of a file can be done to see the differences. Currently, several tools can do a byte-by-byte comparison of files. Programs such as X-Ways Forensics, X-Ways WinHex, and IDM Computing Solution's UltraCompare can analyze and compare data files. For more information on MD5 collisions, see *www.x-ways.net/md5collision.html* or *www.mscs.dal.ca/~selinger/md5collision/*. Chapter 4 discusses methods of using MD5 and SHA-1.

For imaging an evidence drive, many tools offer validation techniques ranging from CRC-32, MD5, and SHA-1 to SHA-512. These hashing algorithm utilities are available as stand-alone programs or are integrated into many acquisition tools. The following sections discuss how to perform validation with some currently available acquisition programs.

Linux Validation Methods

Linux is rich in commands and functions. The two Linux shell commands shown earlier in this chapter, dd and dcfldd, have several options that can be combined with other commands to validate data. The dcfldd command has additional options that validate data collected from an acquisition. Validating acquired data with the dd command requires using other shell commands.

Current distributions of Linux include two hashing algorithm utilities: md5sum and sha1sum. Both utilities can compute hashes of a single file, multiple files, individual or multiple disk partitions, or an entire disk drive.

Validating dd Acquired Data   As shown earlier, the following command produces segmented volumes of the /dev/sdb drive, with each segmented volume named image_sdb and an incrementing extension of .aa, .ab, .ac, and so on:

```
dd if=/dev/sdb | split -b 650m - image_sdb
```

To validate all segmented volumes of a suspect drive with the md5sum utility, you use the Linux shell commands in the following steps. For the saved images, remember to change to the directory where the data was saved, or list the exact path for the saved images. To use sha1sum instead of md5sum, just replace all md5sum references in commands with sha1sum. The drive should still be connected to your acquisition workstation.

1. If necessary, start Linux, open a shell window, and navigate to the directory where image files are saved. To calculate the hash value of the original drive, type **md5sum /dev/sdb > md5_sdb.txt** and press **Enter**.

The redirect (>) option saves the computed MD5 hash value in the md5_sdb.txt file. This file should be saved with image files as validation of the evidence.

2. To compute the MD5 hash value for the segmented volumes and append the output to the md5_sdb.txt file, type **cat image_sdb.* | md5sum >> md5_sdb.txt** and press **Enter**.

By using the cat (concatenate) command with an asterisk (*) as the extension value, all segmented volumes are read sequentially as one big contiguous file, as though they were the original drive or partition. The pipe (|) function outputs the cat command read data to the input of the md5sum command. The >> option adds the md5sum hash results to the end of the md5_sdb.txt file's content.

3. Examine the md5_sdb.txt file to see whether both hashes match by typing **cat md5_sdb.txt** and pressing **Enter**. If the data acquisition is successful, the two hash numbers should be identical. If not, the acquisition didn't work correctly. You should see output similar to the following:

```
34963884a4bc5810b130018b00da9de1  /dev/sdb
34963884a4bc5810b130018b00da9de1
```

4. Close the Linux shell window by typing **exit** and pressing **Enter**.

With the `dd` command, the `md5sum` or `sha1sum` utilities should be run on all suspect disks and volumes or segmented volumes.

Validating `dcfldd` Acquired Data Because dcfldd is designed for forensics data acquisition, it has validation options integrated: `hash` and `hashlog`. You use the `hash` option to designate a hashing algorithm of md5, sha1, sha256, sha384, or sha512. The `hashlog` option outputs hash results to a text file that can be stored with image files.

To create an MD5 hash output file during a dcfldd acquisition, you enter the following command (in one line) at the shell prompt:

```
dcfldd if=/dev/sda split=2M of=usbimg hash=md5
 hashlog=usbhash.log
```

To see the results of files generated with the `split` command, you enter the list directory (`ls`) command at the shell prompt. You should see the following output:

```
usbhash.logusbimg.004 usbimg.010 usbimg.016 usbimg.022 usbimg.028
usbseghash.logusbimg.005 usbimg.011 usbimg.017 usbimg.023 usbimg.029
usbimg.000 usbimg.006 usbimg.012 usbimg.018 usbimg.024 usbimg.030
usbimg.001 usbimg.007 usbimg.013 usbimg.019 usbimg.025
usbimg.002 usbimg.008 usbimg.014 usbimg.020 usbimg.026
usbimg.003 usbimg.009 usbimg.015 usbimg.021 usbimg.027
```

Note that the first segmented volume has the extension `.000` rather than `.001`. Some Windows forensics tools might not be able to read segmented file extensions starting with `.000`. They are typically looking for `.001`. If your forensics tool requires starting with an `.001` extension, the files need to be renamed incrementally. So segmented file `.000` should be renamed `.001`, `.001` should be renamed `.002`, and so on.

Another useful dcfldd option is `vf` (verify file), which compares the image file to the original medium, such as a partition or drive. The `vf` option applies only to a nonsegmented image file. To validate segmented files from dcfldd, use the `md5sum` or `sha1sum` command described previously. To use the `vf` option, you enter the following command at the shell prompt:

```
dcfldd if=/dev/sda vf=sda_hash.img
```

For additional information on dcfldd, see the man page.

Windows Validation Methods

Unlike Linux, Windows has no built-in hashing algorithm tools for digital forensics. However, many Windows third-party programs do have a variety of built-in tools. These third-party programs range from hexadecimal editors, such as X-Ways WinHex or Breakpoint Software Hex Workshop, to forensics programs, such as ProDiscover, EnCase, and FTK. In Chapter 9, you learn how to hash specific data by using a hexadecimal editor to locate and verify groups of data that have no file association or are sections within a file.

Commercial forensics programs also have built-in validation features. Each program has its own validation technique used with acquisition data in its proprietary format. For example, ProDiscover's `.eve` files contain metadata in the acquisition file or segmented files, including the hash value for the suspect drive or partition. Image data loaded into ProDiscover is hashed and then compared with the hash value in the stored metadata. If the hashes don't match, ProDiscover notifies you that the acquisition is corrupt and can't be considered reliable evidence. This function is called Auto Verify Image Checksum.

In ProDiscover and many other forensics tools, however, raw format image files don't contain metadata. As mentioned, a separate manual validation is recommended for all raw acquisitions at the time of analysis. The previously generated validation file for raw format acquisitions is essential to the integrity of digital evidence. The saved validation file can be used later to check whether the acquisition file is still good.

In FTK Imager, when you select the Expert Witness (.e01) or the SMART (.s01) format, additional options for validation are displayed. This validation report also lists the MD5 and SHA-1 hash values. The MD5 hash value is added to the proprietary format image or segmented files. When this image is loaded into FTK, SMART, or X-Ways Forensics (which can read only .e01 and raw files), the MD5 hash is read and compared with the image to verify whether the acquisition is correct.

You can find other open-source hashing tools online; just search for "windows open source hash" to find the latest available Windows hashing tools. For example, a recent search turned up SourceForge md5deep at *http://md5deep.sourceforge.net* and Software Informer at *http://softwaresolution.informer.com/Hash-Tool.*

Performing RAID Data Acquisitions

Acquisitions of RAID drives can be challenging and frustrating for digital forensics examiners because of how RAID systems are designed, configured, and sized. Size is the biggest concern because many RAID systems are now pushing into terabytes of data. The following sections review common RAID configurations and discuss ways to acquire data on these large storage devices.

Understanding RAID

Redundant array of independent (formerly "inexpensive") **disks (RAID)** is a computer configuration involving two or more physical disks. Originally, RAID was developed as a dataredundancy measure to minimize data loss caused by a disk failure. As technology improved, RAID also provided increased storage capabilities.

Several levels of RAID can be implemented through software or special hardware controllers. For Windows XP, 2000, and NT servers and workstations, RAID 0 or 1 is available. For a high-end data-processing environment, RAID 5 is common and is often based in special RAID towers. These high-end RAID systems usually have integrated controllers that connect to high-end servers or mainframes. These systems provide redundancy and high-speed data access and can make many small disks appear as one very large drive.

Other variations of RAID besides 0, 1, and 5 are specific to their vendor or application.

RAID 0 provides rapid access and increased data storage (see Figure 3-10). In RAID 0, two or more disk drives become one large volume, so the computer views the disks as a single disk. The tracks of data on this mode of storage cross over to each disk. The logical

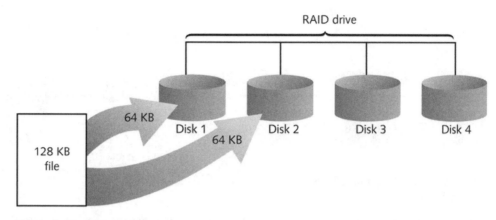

Figure 3-10   RAID 0: Striping
© Cengage Learning®

addressing scheme makes it seem as though each track of data is continuous throughout all disks. If you have two disks configured as RAID 0, track one starts on the first physical disk and continues to the second physical disk. When viewed from a booted OS, such as Windows XP or later, the two disks appear as one large disk. The advantage of RAID 0 is increased speed and data storage capability spread over two or more disks that can be one large disk partition. Its biggest disadvantage is lack of redundancy; if a disk fails, data isn't continuously available.

RAID 1, shown in Figure 3-11, is made up of two disks for each volume and is designed for data recovery in the event of a disk failure. The contents of the two disks in RAID 1 are identical. When data is written to a volume, the OS writes the data twice—once to each disk at the same time. If one drive fails, the OS switches to the other disk.

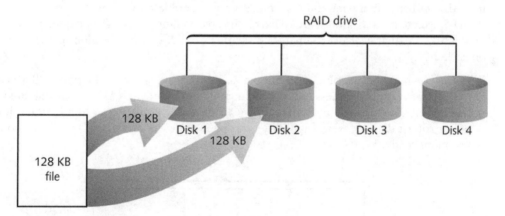

Figure 3-11   RAID 1: Mirroring
© Cengage Learning®

RAID 1 ensures that data isn't lost and helps prevent computer downtime. The main disadvantage of RAID 1 is that it takes two disks for each volume, which doubles the cost of disk storage.

Like RAID 1, RAID 2 (see Figure 3-12) provides rapid access and increased storage by configuring two or more disks as one large volume. The difference with RAID 2 is that data is written to disks on a bit level. An error-correcting code (ECC) is used to verify whether the

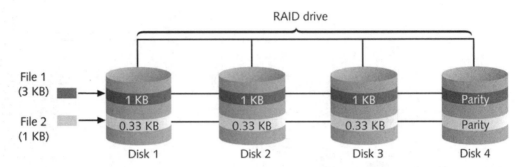

Figure 3-12 RAID 2: Striping (bit level)
© Cengage Learning®

write is successful. RAID 2, therefore, has better data integrity checking than RAID 0. Because of the bit-level writes and the ECC, however, RAID 2 is slower than RAID 0.

RAID 3 uses data striping and dedicated parity and requires at least three disks. Similar to RAID 0, RAID 3 stripes tracks across all disks that make up one volume. RAID 3 also implements dedicated parity of data to ensure recovery if data is corrupted. Dedicated parity is stored on one disk in the RAID 3 array. Like RAID 3, RAID 4 uses data striping and dedicated parity (block writing), except data is written in blocks rather than bytes.

RAID 5 (see Figure 3-13) is similar to RAID 0 and RAID 3 in that it uses distributed data and distributed parity and stripes data tracks across all disks in the RAID array. Unlike RAID 3, however, RAID 5 places parity data on each disk. If a disk in a RAID array has a data failure, the parity on other disks rebuilds the corrupt data automatically when the failed drive is replaced.

In RAID 6, distributed data and distributed parity (double parity) function the same way as RAID 5, except each disk in the RAID array has redundant parity. The advantage of RAID 6 over RAID 5 is that it recovers any two disks that fail because of the additional parity stored on each disk.

RAID 10, or mirrored striping, also known as RAID 1+0, is a combination of RAID 1 and RAID 0. It provides fast access and redundancy of data storage. RAID 15, or mirrored striping with parity, also known as RAID 1+5, is a combination of RAID 1 and RAID 5. It offers the most robust data recovery capability and speed of access of all RAID configurations and is also more costly.

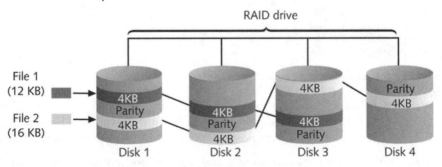

Figure 3-13 RAID 5: Block-level striping with distributed parity
© Cengage Learning®

Acquiring RAID Disks

There's no simple method for getting an image of a RAID server's disks. You need to address the following concerns:

- How much data storage is needed to acquire all data for a forensics image?
- What type of RAID is used? Is it Windows RAID 0 or 1 or an integrated hardware-firmware vendor's RAID 5, 10, or 15? Is it another unknown configuration or OS (Linux, UNIX, mainframe)?
- Do you have an acquisition tool capable of copying the data correctly?
- Can the tool read a forensic copy of a RAID image?
- Can the tool read split data saves of each RAID disk, and then combine all images of each disk into one RAID virtual drive for analysis?

With the larger disks now available, copying small RAID systems to one large disk is possible, similar to the way non-RAID suspect drives are copied. For example, a small server running eight 36 GB SCSI drives in a RAID 0 tower requires about a 300 GB SATA or IDE (PATA) drive. Less data storage is needed if a proprietary format acquisition is used with compression applied. All forensics analysis tools can analyze an image because they see the acquired data as one large drive, not eight separate drives.

Several forensics vendors have added RAID recovery features. These vendors typically specialize in one or two types of RAID formats. The following are some vendors offering RAID acquisition functions:

- Technology Pathways ProDiscover
- Guidance Software EnCase
- X-Ways Forensics
- AccessData FTK
- Runtime Software
- R-Tools Technologies

You should know which vendor supports which RAID format and keep up to date on the latest improvements in these products.

ProDiscover can acquire RAID disks at the physical level. After all disks have been acquired, a ProDiscover Group file (.pdg extension) is created, which includes instructions for how ProDiscover should load each physical disk's image data. It also lists the paths to each physical disk's image data if the RAID acquisition takes several storage drives.

Being able to separate each physical disk into smaller save sets eliminates the need to have one large drive for storing acquired data. Acquiring RAID data requires only similar-size drives that match each disk in the RAID array. For example, with a RAID 0 array of three 250 GB disks, all you need are three target drives of the same size. If each acquisition is compressed, you might be able to get by with slightly smaller target drives.

With ProDiscover, all you need are three 250 GB target drives to collect the image's segmented files for each disk. This feature eliminates the need for a 750 GB drive to collect the combined data from all three 250 GB drives. EnCase and X-Ways Forensics also have similar features for RAID 0 and 5 acquisitions.

Other tools, such as Runtime Software (*www.runtime.org*) and R-Tools Technologies (*www.r-tt.com*), are designed as data recovery tools. Although not intended as forensics acquisition tools, they have unique features that can aid in recovering corrupted RAID data and can perform raw format acquisitions and repair broken RAID 0 and 5 systems. The Runtime RAID Reconstructor tool copies the original RAID to a raw format file, which must then be restored on another RAID-configured system where repairs can be performed. It also scans and corrects errors on the newly copied RAID. R-Tools R-Studio creates a virtual volume of the RAID image file. All repairs are made on the virtual volume, which can then be restored to the original RAID.

Occasionally, a RAID system is too large for a static acquisition. Under ideal circumstances, your goal is to collect a complete image of evidence drives. Because RAID systems can have dozens or more terabytes of data storage, copying all data isn't always practical. For these occasions, retrieving only the data relevant to the investigation with the sparse or logical acquisition method is the only practical solution. When dealing with very large RAID servers, consult with the forensics vendor to determine how to best capture RAID data. Another possible solution is renting portable RAIDBanks for your acquisition.

Using Remote Network Acquisition Tools

Recent improvements in forensics tools include the capability to acquire disk data or data fragments (sparse or logical) remotely. With this feature, you can connect to a suspect computer remotely via a network connection and copy data from it. Remote acquisition tools vary in configurations and capabilities. Some require manual intervention on remote suspect computers to initiate the data copy. Others can acquire data surreptitiously through an encrypted link by pushing a remote access program to the suspect's computer. From an investigation perspective, being able to connect to a suspect's computer remotely to perform an acquisition has tremendous appeal. It saves time because you don't have to go to a suspect's computer, and it minimizes the chances of a suspect discovering that an investigation is taking place. Most remote acquisitions have to be done as live acquisitions, not static acquisitions. When performing remote acquisitions, advanced privileges are required to push agent applications to the remote system.

There are some drawbacks to consider, such as antivirus, antispyware, and firewall tools. Most of these security programs can be configured to ignore remote access programs. However, if suspects have administrator rights on their computers, they could easily install their own security tools that trigger an alarm to notify them of remote access intrusions.

The following section describes how to perform remote acquisitions in ProDiscover. Chapter 10 covers other resources for data copying and explains how to perform a live forensics acquisition.

Remote Acquisition with ProDiscover

ProDiscover Incident Response is designed to be integrated as a network intrusion analysis tool and is useful for performing remote acquisitions. When connected to a remote computer, it uses the same ProDiscover acquisition method described previously. After the connection is established, the remote computer is displayed in the Capture Image dialog box. This tool offers all the functions and features of other tools in the ProDiscover suite plus the following:

- Capture volatile system state information.
- Analyze current running processes on a remote system.
- Locate unseen files and processes on a remote system that might be running malware or spyware.
- Remotely view and listen to IP ports on a compromised system.
- Run hash comparisons on a remote system to search for known Trojans and rootkits.
- Create a hash inventory of all files on a system remotely (a negative hash search capability) to establish a baseline if it gets attacked.

The ProDiscover utility for remote access is the PDServer remote agent, which must be loaded on the suspect computer before ProDiscover Incident Response can access it. This remote agent can be installed in three different ways:

- *Trusted CD*—For this manual installation method, ProDiscover can create a special CD/DVD or USB drive containing the PDServer remote agent. It's used to load PDServer manually on the suspect computer.
- *Preinstallation*—For networks with a configured OS, the PDServer remote agent can be added to the standard installation of high-risk computers, which enables network security administrators to respond to network attacks and malware contaminations quickly. Any network management tool, such as DameWare (*www.dameware.com*) or Hyena (*www.systemtools.com/hyena/*), can be used to initiate a connection with ProDiscover. This is a remote method of installing the remote acquisition tool.
- *Pushing out and running remotely*—Downloading PDServer to a remote computer helps investigators respond quickly to incidents. Data is collected in real time when using this function. This is a remote method of installing the remote acquisition tool.

With PDServer, you have the option of running it in a stealth mode to hide it from the suspect. Note that Windows Task Manager lists the process as PDServer. To disguise it, you can change the process name so that it appears to be an OS function in the suspect computer's Task Manager. In addition, the following security features are available for remote connections:

- *Password protection*—PDServer on the target computer is password-protected, and the password is encrypted at all times.
- *Encryption*—All communication between PDServer on the suspect's and investigator's computers can be encrypted. ProDiscover provides 256-bit Advanced Encryption Standard (AES) or Twofish encryption for the connection.
- *Secure communication protocol*—All connections between the suspect's and examiner's computers have globally unique identifiers (GUIDs) to prevent inserting packets in the data stream.
- *Write-protected trusted binaries*—PDServer can run from a write-protected device, such as a CD.
- *Digital signatures*—PDServer and its removal device driver, PARemoval.sys, are digitally signed to verify that they haven't been tampered with before and during the remote connection.

For more information on ProDiscover and PDServer, see *www.techpathways.com.*

Remote Acquisition with EnCase Enterprise

Guidance Software was the first forensics vendor to develop a remote acquisition and analysis tool based on its desktop tool EnCase. This remote tool, EnCase Enterprise, comes with several capabilities. The following are some of its remote acquisition features:

- Remote data acquisition of a computer's media and RAM data
- Integration with intrusion detection system (IDS) tools that copy evidence of intrusions to an investigation workstation automatically for further analysis over the network
- Options to create an image of data from one or more systems
- Preview of systems to determine whether future actions, such as an acquisition, are needed
- A wide range of file system formats, such as NTFS, FAT, Ext2/3, Reiser, Solaris UFS, AIX Journaling File System (JFS), LVM8, FFS, Palm, Macintosh HFS/HFS+, CDFS, ISO 9660, UDF, DVD, and more
- RAID support for both hardware and software

EnCase Enterprise is set up with an Examiner workstation and a Secure Authentication for EnCase (SAFE) workstation. Acquisition and analysis are conducted on the Examiner workstation. The SAFE workstation provides secure encrypted authentication for the Examiner workstation and the suspect's system.

The remote access program in EnCase Enterprise is Servlet, a passive utility installed on the suspect computer. Servlet connects the suspect computer to the Examiner and SAFE workstations and can run in stealth mode on the suspect computer.

Remote Acquisition with R-Tools R-Studio

The R-Tools suite of software is designed for data recovery. As part of this recovery capability, the R-Studio network edition can remotely access networked computer systems. Its remote connection uses Triple Data Encryption Standard (3DES) encryption. Data acquired with R-Studio network edition creates raw format acquisitions, and it's capable of recovering many different file systems, including ReFS. For more information on R-Studio, see *www.r-tt.com.*

Remote Acquisition with WetStone US-LATT PRO

US-LATT PRO, part of a suite of tools developed by WetStone, can connect to a networked computer remotely and perform a live acquisition of all drives connected to it. For more information on this tool, see *www.wetstonetech.com/product/14.*

Remote Acquisition with F-Response

F-Response is a vendor-neutral specialty remote access utility designed to work with any digital forensics program. When installed on a remote computer, it sets up a security read-only connection that allows forensics examiners to access it. With F-Response, examiners can access remote drives at the physical level and view raw data. After the F-Response connection has been set up, any forensics acquisition tool can be used to collect digital evidence.

F-Response is sold in four different versions: Enterprise Edition, Consultant + Convert Edition, Consultant Edition, and TACTICAL Edition. For the latest information on F-Response, see *www.f-response.com*.

Using Other Forensics Acquisition Tools

In addition to ProDiscover, FTK Imager, and X-Ways Forensics, you can use other commercial acquisition tools, described in the following sections. Prices for some tools are discounted for law enforcement officers working in digital forensics.

PassMark Software ImageUSB

PassMark Software has an acquisition tool called ImageUSB for its OSForensics analysis product. To create a bootable flash drive, you need Windows XP or later and ImageUSB downloaded from the OSForensics Web site. For more information on ImageUSB, see *www.osforensics.com/tools/write-usb-images.html*.

ASRData SMART

ASRData SMART is a Linux forensics analysis tool that can make image files of a suspect drive. SMART can produce proprietary or raw format images and includes the following capabilities:

- Robust data reading of bad sectors on drives
- Mounting suspect drives in write-protected mode
- Mounting target drives, including NTFS drives, in read/write mode
- Optional compression schemes to speed up acquisition or reduce the amount of storage needed for acquired digital evidence

For more information on SMART, see *www.asrdata.com*.

Runtime Software

In addition to RAID Reconstructor, Runtime Software offers several compact shareware programs for data acquisition and recovery, including DiskExplorer for FAT and DiskExplorer for NTFS. Runtime has designed its tools to be file system specific, so DiskExplorer versions for both FAT and NTFS are available. These tools offer the following features for acquisition needs:

- Create a raw format image file.
- Segment the raw format or compressed image for archiving purposes.
- Access network computers' drives.

For more information on Runtime Software, see *www.runtime.org*.

ILookIX Investigator IXimager

IXimager runs from a bootable thumb drive or CD/DVD. It's a stand-alone proprietary format acquisition tool designed to work only with ILookIX Investigator. It can acquire single drives and RAID drives. It supports IDE (PATA), SCSI, USB, and FireWire devices. The IXimager proprietary format can be converted to a raw format if other analysis tools are used. For more information on IXimager, see *www.perlustro.com/solutions/e-forensics/iximager*.

SourceForge

SourceForge provides several applications for security, analysis, and investigations. For a listing of its current tools, see *http://sourceforge.net/directory/security-utilities/storage/archiving/os:windows/freshness:recently-updated*. SourceForge also offers a Windows version of dcfldd; for updates, go to *http://dcfldd.sourceforge.net*.

Chapter Summary

- Forensics data acquisitions are stored in three different formats: raw, proprietary, and AFF. Most proprietary formats and AFF store metadata about the acquired data in the image file.

- The four methods of acquiring data for forensics analysis are disk-to-image file, disk-to-disk copy, logical disk-to-disk or disk-to-data file, or sparse data copy of a folder or file.

- Lossless compression for forensics acquisitions doesn't alter the data when it's restored, unlike lossy compression. Lossless compression can compress up to 50% for most data. If data is already compressed on a drive, lossless compression might not save much more space.

- If there are time restrictions or too much data to acquire from large drives or RAID drives, a logical or sparse acquisition might be necessary. Consult with your lead attorney or supervisor first to let them know that collecting all the data might not be possible.

- You should have a contingency plan to ensure that you have a forensically sound acquisition and make two acquisitions if you have enough data storage. The first acquisition should be compressed, and the second should be uncompressed. If one acquisition becomes corrupt, the other one is available for analysis.

- Write-blocking devices or utilities must be used with GUI acquisition tools in both Windows and Linux. Practice with a test drive rather than suspect drive, and use a hashing tool on the test drive to verify that no data was altered.

- Always validate your acquisition with built-in tools from a forensics acquisition program, a hexadecimal editor with MD5 or SHA-1 hashing functions, or the Linux md5sum or sha1sum commands.

- A Linux Live CD, such as SIFT, Kali Linux, or Deft, provides many useful tools for digital forensics acquisitions.

- The preferred Linux acquisition tool is dcfldd instead of dd because it was designed for forensics acquisition. The dcfldd tool is also available for Windows. Always validate the acquisition with the hashing features of dcfldd and md5sum or sha1sum.

- When using the Linux dd or dcfldd commands, remember that reversing the output field (of=) and input field (if=) of suspect and target drives could write data to the wrong drive, thus destroying your evidence. If available, you should always use a physical write-blocker device for acquisitions.

■ To acquire RAID disks, you need to determine the type of RAID and which acquisition tool to use. With a firmware-hardware RAID, acquiring data directly from the RAID server might be necessary.

■ Remote network acquisition tools require installing a remote agent on the suspect computer. The remote agent can be detected if suspects install their own security programs, such as a firewall.

Key Terms

Advanced Forensic Format (AFF) An open-source data acquisition format that stores image data and metadata. File extensions include .afd for segmented image files and .afm for AFF metadata.

host protected area (HPA) An area of a disk drive reserved for booting utilities and diagnostic programs. It's not visible to the computer's OS.

live acquisitions A data acquisition method used when a suspect computer can't be shut down to perform a static acquisition. Captured data might be altered during the acquisition because it's not write-protected. Live acquisitions aren't repeatable because data is continually being altered by the suspect computer's OS.

logical acquisition This data acquisition method captures only specific files of interest to the case or specific types of files, such as Outlook .pst files. *See also* sparse acquisition.

raw format A data acquisition format that creates simple sequential flat files of a suspect drive or data set.

redundant array of independent disks (RAID) Two or more disks combined into one large drive in several configurations for special needs. Some RAID systems are designed for redundancy to ensure continuous operation if one disk fails. Another configuration spreads data across several disks to improve access speeds for reads and writes.

sparse acquisition Like logical acquisitions, this data acquisition method captures only specific files of interest to the case, but it also collects fragments of unallocated (deleted) data. *See also* logical acquisition.

static acquisitions A data acquisition method used when a suspect drive is write-protected and can't be altered. If disk evidence is preserved correctly, static acquisitions are repeatable.

whole disk encryption An encryption technique that performs a sector-by-sector encryption of an entire drive. Each sector is encrypted in its entirety, making it unreadable when copied with a static acquisition method.

Review Questions

1. What's the main goal of a static acquisition?

2. Name the three formats for digital forensics data acquisitions.

3. What are two advantages and disadvantages of the raw format?

4. List two features common with proprietary format acquisition files.

5. Of all the proprietary formats, which one is the unofficial standard?

6. Name two commercial tools that can make a forensic sector-by-sector copy of a drive to a larger drive.

7. What does a logical acquisition collect for an investigation?

8. What does a sparse acquisition collect for an investigation?

9. What should you consider when determining which data acquisition method to use?

10. Why is it a good practice to make two images of a suspect drive in a critical investigation?

11. When you perform an acquisition at a remote location, what should you consider to prepare for this task?

12. With newer Linux kernel distributions, what happens if you connect a hot-swappable device, such a USB drive, containing evidence?

13. In a Linux shell, the fdisk -l command lists the suspect drive as /dev/hda1. Is the following dcfldd command correct?

```
dcfldd if=image_file.img of=/dev/hda1
```

14. What's the most critical aspect of digital evidence?

15. What is a hashing algorithm?

16. In the Linux dcfldd command, which three options are used for validating data?

17. What's the maximum file size when writing data to a FAT32 drive?

18. What are two concerns when acquiring data from a RAID server?

19. With remote acquisitions, what problems should you be aware of? (Choose all that apply.)
    a. Data transfer speeds
    b. Access permissions over the network
    c. Antivirus, antispyware, and firewall programs
    d. The password of the remote computer's user

20. How does ProDiscover Incident Response encrypt the connection between the examiner's and suspect's computers?

21. What's the ProDiscover remote access utility?

22. Which forensics tools can connect to a suspect's remote computer and run surreptitiously?

23. EnCase, FTK, SMART, and ILookIX treat an image file as though it were the original disk. True or False?

24. FTK Imager can acquire data in a drive's host protected area. True or False?

Hands-On Projects

If necessary, extract all data files in the Chap03\Projects folder on the book's DVD to the *Work*\Chap03\Projects folder on your system. (Create this folder on your system before starting the projects.)

Hands-On Project 3-1

In this project, you learn how to restore an image file to a drive. Subsequent projects in this book require using these steps. To prepare for this project, you need the following items:

- A USB or FireWire drive that can hold up to 100 MB or a secondary internally connected drive

- ProDiscover Basic installed on your workstation

- The **GCFI-datacarve-FAT.eve** data file (extracted from GCFI-data-carve-FAT.exe in the Chap03\Projects folder on the book's DVD)

Data-Loading Procedure in ProDiscover Basic The first task is to transfer data from the GCFI-datacarve-FAT.eve file to the target drive. Follow these steps:

1. Boot your acquisition workstation.

2. Connect a hot-swappable media storage device to receive the data, such as a 100+ MB USB drive, a FireWire drive, or an internally connected drive. This device is referred to as the target drive.

3. Start ProDiscover Basic (running it as administrator), and in the main window, click **Tools, Copy Disk** from the menu.

4. In the Copy source disk or image to destination disk dialog box, click the **Image to Disk** tab.

5. Click **Browse** next to the Image File text box, and navigate to the location where you copied this chapter's data files. Click the **GCFI-datacarve-FAT.eve** file, and then click **Open**.

6. In the Copy source disk or image to destination disk dialog box, click in the space under the Disk Name column at the bottom, as shown in Figure 3-14.

7. Click the **Disk Name** list arrow, click the target drive, and then click **OK**.

8. In the Copy dialog box that opens, click the **Write All 0's** option button, and then click **OK** to start the data loading.

9. Click **OK** in the "Copy successful" message box to terminate the loading.

10. Exit ProDiscover Basic, shut down your acquisition workstation, and remove the target drive.

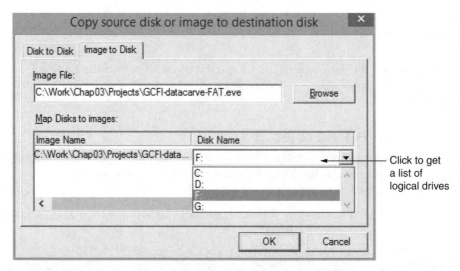

Figure 3-14 The Copy source disk or image to destination disk dialog box
Courtesy of Technology Pathways, LLC

Hands-On Project 3-2

In this project, you make a ProDiscover image file of the data load in Hands-On Project 3-1. To prepare, you need to do the following:

- Make sure you have the suspect drive containing the data load from Hands-On Project 3-1.

- Review the steps in "Using ProDiscover's Raw Acquisition Format" for creating an image file.

- Verify that you have enough free space on your computer's internal drive to receive the image file (about 120 MB).

 For the purposes of this project, you don't need a write-blocker. For actual casework, however, always use a write-blocker.

To make this acquisition on an internally connected drive, follow these steps:

1. Use a write-blocking hardware device to protect the suspect drive.

2. Turn on your acquisition workstation.

3. Start ProDiscover. Follow the steps in this chapter for making a raw format acquisition, making sure you click **UNIX style dd format** in the Image Format drop-down list box. Then click **OK** in the Capture Image dialog box.

4. When the acquisition is finished, exit ProDiscover. Shut down the acquisition workstation, remove the suspect drive, and secure it as evidence.

Hands-On Project 3-3

In this project, you prepare a drive and create a FAT32 disk partition using Linux. You need the following:

- A Linux distribution or Linux Live CD
- A disk drive
- A method of connecting a disk drive to your workstation, such as USB, FireWire, external SATA, or internal connections, such as PATA or SATA
- A review of the steps in the "Preparing a Target Drive for Acquisition in Linux" section

    To format a drive as FAT32 in Linux, follow these steps:

1. Connect the target drive to be partitioned and formatted as FAT32 to your workstation.
2. Start your workstation, and log on or boot the Linux Live CD.
3. Follow the steps in the "Preparing a Target Disk for Acquisition in Linux" section.
4. When you've finished formatting the target drive, leave it connected for the next project.

Hands-On Project 3-4

In this project, you use the Linux dd command to make an acquisition split into 30 MB segmented volumes. Then you validate the data by using the Linux md5sum command on the original drive and the image files. The output for md5sum is then redirected to a data file kept with the image files. For this project, you need the following:

- A Linux distribution or Linux Live CD
- The FAT32 drive partitioned and formatted in Hands-On Project 3-3
- A method of connecting the FAT32 drive and the drive created in Hands-On Project 3-1 to your workstation, such as USB, FireWire, external SATA, or internal connections, such as PATA or SATA
- A review of the "Acquiring Data with dd in Linux" and "Validating dd Acquired Data" sections

    Follow these steps:

1. Make sure you've connected the drive you prepared in Hands-On Project 3-3 to your Linux workstation.
2. Start your workstation, if necessary, and log on to Linux or boot the Linux Live CD.
3. Reboot the Linux system, and make the dd acquisition, following the steps in "Acquiring Data with dd in Linux." For the split -b command, make the segmented size **30m**, and use the **-d** switch to create numeric extensions for each segmented file.

4. When the acquisition is done, perform a validation of the suspect drive and the acquired image files. Follow the steps in the "Validating dd Acquired Data" section. When you're finished, close the shell window, and log off Linux.

Case Projects

CASE PROJECTS

Case Project 3-1

Your supervisor has asked you to research current acquisition tools. Using your preferred Internet search engine and the vendors listed in this chapter, prepare a report containing the following information for each tool and stating which tool you would prefer to use:

- Forensics vendor name
- Acquisition tool name and latest version number
- Features of the vendor's product

With this data collected, prepare a spreadsheet listing vendors in the rows. For the column headings, list the following features:

- Raw format
- Proprietary format
- AFF format
- Other proprietary formats the tool can read
- Compression of image files
- Remote network acquisition capabilities
- Method used to validate (MD5, SHA-1, and so on)

Case Project 3-2

At a murder scene, you have started making an image of a computer's drive. You're in the back bedroom of the house, and a small fire has started in the kitchen. If the fire can't be extinguished, you have only a few minutes to acquire data from a 10 GB hard disk. Write one to two pages outlining your options for preserving the data.

Case Project 3-3

You need to acquire an image of a disk on a computer that can't be removed from the scene, and you discover that it's a Linux computer. What are your options for acquiring the image? Write a brief paper specifying the hardware and software you would use.

Case Project 3-4

A bank has hired your firm to investigate employee fraud. The bank uses four 20 TB machines on a LAN. You're permitted to talk to the network administrator, who is familiar with where the data is stored. What diplomatic strategies should you use? Which acquisition method should you use? Write a two-page report outlining the problems you expect to encounter, explaining how to rectify them, and describing your solution. Be sure to address any customer privacy issues.

Case Project 3-5

You're investigating a case involving a 2 GB drive that you need to copy at the scene. Write one to two pages describing three options you have to copy the drive accurately. Be sure to include your software and media choices.

Processing Crime and Incident Scenes

chapter 4

After reading this chapter and completing the exercises, you will be able to:

- Explain the rules for controlling digital evidence
- Describe how to collect evidence at private-sector incident scenes
- Explain guidelines for processing law enforcement crime scenes
- List the steps in preparing for an evidence search
- Describe how to secure a computer incident or crime scene
- Explain guidelines for seizing digital evidence at the scene
- List procedures for storing digital evidence
- Explain how to obtain a digital hash
- Review a case to identify requirements and plan your investigation

In this chapter, you learn how to process a digital investigation scene. Because this chapter focuses on investigation needs for computing systems and digital devices, you should supplement your training by studying police science or U.S. Department of Justice (DOJ) procedures to understand field-of-evidence recovery tasks. If you're in another country, be aware of laws relating to privacy, searches, and the rules of evidence for your region. In addition, consult local authorities, and refer to the excellent guidelines in ISO standard 27037 (introduced in Chapter 1).

Evidence rules are critical, whether you're on a corporate or a criminal case. As you'll see, a civil case can quickly become a criminal case, and a criminal case can have civil implications larger than the criminal case. This chapter examines rules of evidence in the United States, but similar procedures apply in most courts worldwide. This chapter also describes differences between a business (private entity) and a law enforcement organization (public entity) in needs and concerns and discusses incident-scene processing for both types of investigations. Private-sector security officers often begin investigating corporate digital crimes and then coordinate with law enforcement as they complete the investigation. Law enforcement investigators should, therefore, know how to process and manage incident scenes. Because public agencies usually don't have the funding to train officers continuously in technology advances, they must learn to work with private-sector investigators, whose employers can often afford to maintain their investigators' computing skills.

This chapter also discusses how the Fourth Amendment relates to corporate and law enforcement digital investigations in the United States. Many countries have similar statutes or charters. As the world becomes more global or "flat" in nature, you need to be aware of how laws are interpreted in other countries. In addition, the laws must be applied consistently as more countries establish e-laws and more cases go to court. Cases of fraud and money laundering are becoming more of a global issue, and crimes against consumers can originate from anywhere in the world. Computers and digital evidence seized in one jurisdiction might affect a case that's worldwide in scope.

To address these issues, this chapter explains how to apply standard crime scene practices and rules for handling evidence to corporate and law enforcement digital investigations. You must handle digital evidence systematically so that you don't inadvertently alter or lose data. In addition, you should apply the same security controls to evidence for a civil lawsuit as evidence for a major crime. Federal and state rules of evidence govern both civil and criminal cases. However, the restrictions on how the government can proceed, as opposed to a private company, are much stricter. For example, as long as a policy exists, a company doesn't need a search warrant to examine a company-owned machine; however, the government would. These rules are similar in English-speaking countries because they have a common ancestor in English common law (judge-made law), dating back to the late Middle Ages.

Identifying Digital Evidence

Digital evidence can be any information stored or transmitted in digital form. Because you can't see or touch digital data directly, it's difficult to explain and describe. Is digital evidence real or virtual? Does data on a disk or other storage medium physically exist, or does it merely represent real information? U.S. courts accept digital evidence as physical evidence, which means digital data is treated as a tangible object, such as a weapon, paper document, or visible injury, that's related to a criminal or civil incident. In addition, the ISO standard 27037 gives guidance on what procedures countries should have in place for digital evidence. However, each country has its own interpretation of what can or can't be presented in court or accepted as evidence. Some countries used to require that all digital evidence be printed to be presented in court. Groups such as the **Scientific Working Group on Digital Evidence (SWGDE;** *www.swgde.org*) set standards for recovering, preserving, and examining digital evidence.

NOTE For more information on digital evidence, go to *https://www.ncjrs.gov/ pdffiles1/nij/219941.pdf* and read "Electronic Crime Scene Investigation: A Guide for First Responders, 2nd edition," which has guidelines for U.S. law enforcement and other responders who protect an electronic crime scene and search for, collect, and preserve electronic evidence.

Following are the general tasks investigators perform when working with digital evidence:

- Identify digital information or artifacts that can be used as evidence.
- Collect, preserve, and document evidence.
- Analyze, identify, and organize evidence.
- Rebuild evidence or repeat a situation to verify that the results can be reproduced reliably.

Collecting digital devices while processing a criminal or incident scene must be done systematically. To minimize confusion, reduce the risk of losing evidence, and avoid damaging evidence, only one team should collect and catalog digital evidence at a crime scene or lab, if practical. If there's too much evidence or too many systems to make it practical for one team to perform these tasks, all examiners must follow the same established operating procedures, and a lead or managing examiner should control collecting and cataloging evidence. You should also use standardized forms (discussed later in "Documenting Evidence") for tracking evidence to ensure that you consistently handle evidence in a safe, secure manner.

An important challenge investigators face today is establishing recognized standards for digital evidence. For example, there are cases involving police raids being conducted simultaneously in many countries as well as anti-cartel investigations taking place in several locations around the world. As a result, you have multiple sites where evidence was seized and hundreds of pieces of digital evidence, including hard drives, cell phones, and other storage devices. If law enforcement and civil organizations in these countries have agreed on proper procedures (generally, the highest control standard should be applied to evidence collection in all jurisdictions), the evidence can be presented in any jurisdiction confidently.

Understanding Rules of Evidence

Consistent practices help verify your work and enhance your credibility, so you must handle all evidence consistently. Apply the same security and accountability controls for evidence in a civil lawsuit as in a major crime to comply with your state's rules of evidence or with the Federal Rules of Evidence (FRE). Also, keep in mind that evidence admitted in a criminal case might also be used in a civil suit, and vice versa. For example, suppose someone is charged with murder and acquitted at the criminal trial because the jury isn't convinced beyond a reasonable doubt of the person's guilt. If enough evidence shows that the accused's negligence contributed to a wrongful death, however, the victim's relatives can use the evidence in a civil lawsuit to recover damages.

You can review the Federal Rules of Evidence at *www.uscourts.gov/ uscourts/rules/rules-evidence.pdf*.

As part of your professional growth, keep current on the latest rulings and directives on collecting, processing, storing, and admitting digital evidence. The following sections discuss some key concepts of digital evidence. You can find additional information at the U.S. Department of Justice Web site (*www.usdoj.gov*) and by searching the Internet for "digital evidence," "best evidence rule," "hearsay," and other relevant keywords. Consult with your prosecuting attorney, Crown attorney, corporate general counsel, or the attorney who retained you to learn more about managing evidence for your investigation.

In Chapter 2, you learned how to make an image of a disk as part of gathering digital evidence. The data you discover from a forensic examination falls under your state's rules of evidence or the FRE. However, digital evidence is unlike other physical evidence because it can be changed more easily. The only way to detect these changes is to compare the original data with a duplicate. Furthermore, distinguishing a duplicate from the original electronically is challenging, so digital evidence requires special legal consideration.

If you're working in a country outside the United States, you need to verify its rules of evidence for electronic evidence.

Another concern when dealing with digital records is the concept of hearsay, which is a statement made while testifying at a hearing by someone other than an actual witness to the event. For example, a rumor has been circulating around an office about an incident, or a friend mentioned it to the person being questioned; both situations would be considered hearsay. The concept of what is or isn't hearsay can become particularly challenging when examining the contents of documents, text messages, e-mails, and other electronic files. The fact that the documents or text messages exist can't be disputed; however, the contents require eyewitness testimony or corroborating evidence. The definition of hearsay isn't difficult to understand, but it can become confusing when considering all the exceptions to the general rule against hearsay.

Like most common law nations, the United States excludes hearsay as spelled out in the FRE Article VIII, Rule 802. Rules 803 and 804 cite more than 20 exceptions for when hearsay can be used. The following are some that apply to digital forensics investigations:

- Business records, including those of a public agency
- Certain public records and reports
- Evidence of the absence of a business record or entry
- Learned treatises used to question an expert witness
- Statements of the absence of a public record or entry

To see more exceptions to the hearsay rule, consult sources such as *www.FindLaw.com*.

The business-record exception, for example, allows "records of regularly conducted activity," such as business memos, reports, records, or data compilations. Business records are authenticated by verifying that they were created "at or near the time by, or from information transmitted by, a person with knowledge ..." and are admissible "if the record was kept in the course of a regularly conducted business activity, and it was the regular practice of that business activity to make the record" (FRE, 803(6); see Section V, "Evidence," in *Searching and Seizing Computers and Obtaining Electronic Evidence in Criminal Investigations, www.justice.gov/criminal/cybercrime/docs/ssmanual2009.pdf*).

In other common law countries, a distinction is made between "real computer evidence" and "hearsay computer evidence." A simplified explanation of the condition states that you can, for example, prove an e-mail was sent and perhaps opened by a logged-in user. However, you can't necessarily verify the e-mail's contents. Generally, digital records are considered admissible if they qualify as a business record.

Another way of categorizing computer records is by dividing them into **computer-generated records** and **computer-stored records**. Computer-generated records are data the system maintains, such as system log files and proxy server logs. They are output generated from a computer process or algorithm, not usually data a person creates. Computer-stored records, however, are electronic data that a person creates and saves on a computer or digital device, such as a spreadsheet or word processing document. Some records combine computer-generated and computer-stored evidence, such as a spreadsheet containing mathematical operations (computer-generated records) generated from a person's input (computer-stored records).

Computer and digitally stored records must also be shown to be authentic and trustworthy to be admitted into evidence. Computer-generated records are considered authentic if the program that created the output is functioning correctly. These records are usually considered exceptions to the hearsay rule. For computer-stored records to be admitted into court, they must also satisfy an exception to the hearsay rule, usually the business-record exception, so they must be authentic records of regularly conducted business activity. To show that computer-stored records are authentic, the person offering the records must demonstrate that a person created the data and the data is reliable and trustworthy—in other words, that it wasn't altered when it was acquired or afterward.

Collecting evidence according to approved steps of evidence control helps ensure that the computer evidence is authentic, as does using established forensics software tools. Courts have consistently ruled that forensics investigators don't have to be subject matter experts on the tools they use. In *United States v. Salgado* (250 F.3d 438, 453, 6th Cir., 2001), the court stated, "It is not necessary that the computer programmer testify in order to authenticate computer-generated records." In other words, the witness must have firsthand knowledge only of facts relevant to the case. If you have to testify about your role in acquiring, preserving, and analyzing evidence, you don't have to know the inner workings of the tools you use, but you should understand their purpose and operation. For example, Message Digest 5 (MD5) and Secure Hash Algorithm (SHA-1) tools use complex algorithms. During a cross-examination, an opposing attorney might ask you to describe how these forensics tools work. You can safely testify that you don't know how the MD5 hashing algorithm works, but you can describe the steps for using the MD5 function in OSForensics, for instance.

Even though research has forced collisions (meaning duplicate values) of the MD5 hash, it's still useful for forensic validation. Keep in mind that you can't generate the source string from the hash value. In addition, the probability of collisions affecting a case is remote.

When attorneys challenge digital evidence, often they raise the issue of whether computer-generated records were altered or damaged after they were created. In the case of *American Express v. Vinhnee* (9th Cir. Bk. App. Panel, 2005), the judge determined that American Express hadn't established that the records presented in court were authentic and the same as the original bill sent to Mr. Vinhnee. The company lost on appeal, too. Attorneys might also question the authenticity of computer-generated records by challenging the program that created them. To date, courts have been skeptical of unsupported claims about digital evidence. Asserting that the data changed without specific evidence isn't sufficient grounds to discredit the digital evidence's authenticity. Most federal courts that evaluate digital evidence from computer-generated records assume that the records contain hearsay. Federal courts then apply the business-records exception to hearsay as it relates to digital evidence.

As mentioned, one test to prove that computer-stored records are authentic is to demonstrate that a specific person created the records. Establishing who created digital evidence can be difficult, however, because records recovered from slack space or unallocated disk space usually don't identify the author. The same is true for other records, such as anonymous e-mail messages or text messages from instant-messaging programs. To establish authorship of digital evidence in these cases, attorneys can use circumstantial evidence, which requires finding other clues associated with the suspect's computer or location. The circumstantial evidence might be that the computer has a password consistent with the password the suspect used on other systems, a witness saw the suspect at the computer at the time the offense occurred, or additional trace evidence associates the suspect with the computer at the time of the incident. In a recent case, the attorney chose not to use the digital evidence because although it could be proved that a particular camera was used to create the suspect's movies, CDs, and DVDs, there was no way to prove that the suspect was the person using the camera. Therefore, there was no circumstantial or corroborating evidence to prove that the suspect was guilty.

Although some files might not contain the author's name, in the arrest of the BTK strangler, the author of a Microsoft Word document was identified by using file metadata. In February 2005, the man claiming to be the BTK strangler sent a floppy disk to FOX News in Wichita. The police he had been taunting told him that they wouldn't be able to trace him via the floppy disk. Forensics examination of the disk came back with the name of the church and a user named Dennis, who turned out to be Dennis Rader, president of the congregation. The police had enough physical evidence to link him to the crimes. They arrested him, and he confessed to the murders of 10 people over the course of 30 years. He was sentenced to 10 life terms. (For the full story, visit the TruTV Web site at *www.crimelibrary.com/serial_killers/unsolved/btk/index_1.html.*)

The following activity shows an easy way to identify this file metadata. Follow these steps in the demo version of OSForensics:

These steps are designed for OSForensics, which is included on this book's DVD. If you haven't installed it, do so now. In addition, create a *Work*\Chap04\Chapter work folder on your system.

1. Start Microsoft Word, and in a new document, type **By creating a file, you can identify the author with file metadata.** Save it in your work folder as `InChap04-01.docx` (or `InChap04-01.doc` in earlier Word versions), and then exit Microsoft Word.

2. To start OSForensics in Windows 7 or earlier, click **Start,** point to **All Programs,** click the **OSForensics** folder, and click **OSForensics.** In Windows 8 or 8.1, go to the Start screen and click **OSForensics.** If Windows prompts you to confirm that you trust this program, click **OK** or **Yes.**

3. If you see a message asking whether you want to upgrade to the professional version, click the **Continue Using Free Version** button.

4. In the OSForensics main window, notice the Viewers section in the right pane. Click **File and Hex Viewer.** In the "Select a file to open" dialog box that opens, navigate to your work folder and double-click the file you created in Step 1.

5. The dialog box that opens (see Figure 4-1) has five tabs. Click the **File Info** tab, where you can see where the file is located along with the date and time it was created. Notice that the file size and its size on the disk are different.

Figure 4-1 Examining a file in OSForensics
Source: PassMark Software, *www.osforensics.com*

6. Click the **Metadata** tab. The information in this tab includes file permissions, file type, file size, and other items. Scroll to the bottom of this tab, where you can see who created the file and who last modified the file (see Figure 4-2).

Figure 4-2 Viewing file metadata
Source: PassMark Software, *www.osforensics.com*

7. Close the dialog box, and exit OSForensics by scrolling to the bottom of the left pane and clicking the **Exit** button.

In addition to revealing the author, computer-stored records must be proved authentic, which is the most difficult requirement to prove when you're trying to qualify evidence as an exception to the hearsay rule. The process of establishing digital evidence's trustworthiness originated with written documents and the "best evidence rule," which states that to prove the content of a written document, recording, or photograph, ordinarily the original writing, recording, or photograph is required (as stated in Article X, Rule 1001, of the FRE). In addition, the original of a document is preferred to a duplicate. The best evidence, therefore, is the document created and saved on a computer's hard disk. However, Rule 1001, section (e), defines a duplicate done in a manner, including electronic, that "accurately reproduces the original." Rule 1003 states that the duplicate can be used unless the original's authenticity is challenged.

Agents and prosecutors occasionally express concern that a printout of a computer-stored electronic file might not qualify as an original document, according to the best evidence rule. In its most fundamental form, the original file is a collection of 0s and 1s; in contrast, the printout is the result of manipulating the file through a complicated series of electronic and mechanical processes (FRE, 803(6); see *Searching and Seizing from Computers and Obtaining Electronic Evidence in Criminal Investigations*, 2009). To address this concern about original evidence, the FRE states: "[I]f data are stored in a computer or similar device, any printout or other output readable by sight, shown to reflect the data accurately, is an 'original.'" Instead of producing hard disks in court, attorneys can submit printed copies of files as evidence. In contrast, some countries used to allow only the printed version to be presented in court, not hard disks.

In addition, the FRE allows duplicates instead of originals when the duplicate is "produced by the same impression as the original ... by mechanical or electronic re-recording ... or by other equivalent techniques which accurately reproduce the original." Therefore, as long as bit-stream copies of data are created and maintained correctly, the copies can be admitted in court, although they aren't considered best evidence. The copied evidence can be a reliable working copy, but it's not considered the original. Courts understand that the original evidence might not be available, however. For example, you could make one image of the evidence drive successfully but lose access to the original drive because it has a head crash when you attempt to make a backup image. Your first successful copy then becomes secondary evidence. The attorney must be able to explain to the judge that circumstances beyond the examiner's control resulted in loss of the original evidence; in this case, the hard drive is no longer available to be examined or imaged. Mishaps with evidence happen routinely in all aspects of evidence recovery; the majority are caused by user error. Adhering to approved procedures can help prevent these mishaps.

Another example of not being able to use original evidence is investigations involving network servers. Removing a server from the network to acquire evidence data could cause harm to a business or its owner, who might be an innocent bystander to a crime or civil wrong. For example, Steve Jackson Games was the innocent party in a case in which evidence of criminal activity had been stored in e-mail on company computers. The network administrator had reported evidence of a crime committed by users of the company's bulletin board system (BBS) to the Secret Service. Secret Service agents seized all the computers at Steve Jackson Games and effectively put the company out of business. Steve Jackson Games sued the Secret Service, which was found liable for damages under the Privacy Protection Act and Title II of the Electronic Communications Privacy Act. For more information, see *Steve Jackson Games v. United States Secret Service and United States of America* (36 F.3d 457, USCA 5, 1994). In this situation, you might not have the authority to create an image or remove the original drive. Instead, make your best effort to acquire the digital evidence with a less intrusive or disruptive method. In this context, the recovered materials become the best evidence because of the circumstances.

In summary, computer-generated records, such as system logs or the results of a mathematical formula in a spreadsheet, aren't hearsay. Computer-stored records that a person generates are subject to rules governing hearsay, however. For the evidence to qualify as a business-record exception to the hearsay rule, a person must have created the computer-stored records, and the records must be original. The FRE treats images and printouts of digital files as original evidence.

Collecting Evidence in Private-Sector Incident Scenes

Private-sector organizations include small to medium businesses, large corporations, and non-government organizations (NGOs), which might get funding from the government or other agencies. In the United States, NGOs and similar agencies must comply with state public disclosure and federal Freedom of Information Act (FOIA) laws and make certain documents available as public records. State public disclosure laws define state public records as open and available for inspection. For example, divorces recorded in a public office, such as a courthouse, become matters of public record unless a judge orders the documents sealed. Anyone can request a copy of a public divorce decree. Figure 4-3 shows an excerpt of a public disclosure law for the state of Idaho.

9-338. PUBLIC RECORDS -- RIGHT TO EXAMINE.

(1) Every person has a right to examine and take a copy of any public record of this state and there is a presumption that all public records in Idaho are open at all reasonable times for inspection except as otherwise expressly provided by statute.

(2) The right to copy public records shall include the right to make photographs or photographic or other copies while the records are in the possession of the custodian of the records using equipment provided by the public agency or independent public body corporate and politic or using equipment designated by the custodian.

(4) The custodian shall make no inquiry of any person who applies for a public record, except to verify the identity of a person requesting a record in accordance with section 9-342, Idaho Code, to ensure that the requested record or information will not be used for purposes of a mailing or telephone list prohibited by section 9-348, Idaho Code, or as otherwise provided by law. The person may be required to make a written request and provide their name, a mailing address and telephone number. [The custodian shall make no inquiry of any person who applies for a public record, except that the person may be required to make a written request and provide a mailing address and telephone number, and except as required for purposes of protecting personal information from disclosure under chapter 2, title 49, Idaho Code, and federal law.]

(5) The custodian shall not review, examine or scrutinize any copy, photograph or memoranda in the possession of any such person and shall extend to the person all reasonable comfort and facility for the full exercise of the right granted under this act.

Figure 4-3 Idaho public disclosure law
© Cengage Learning®

State public disclosure laws apply to state records, but the FOIA allows citizens to request copies of public documents created by federal agencies. The FOIA was originally enacted in the 1960s, and several subsequent amendments have broadened its laws. Some Web sites now provide copies of publicly accessible records for a fee.

A special category of private-sector businesses is ISPs and other communication companies. ISPs can investigate computer abuse committed by their employees but not by customers. ISPs must preserve customer privacy, especially when dealing with e-mail. However, federal regulations related to the Homeland Security Act and the PATRIOT Act of 2001 have redefined how ISPs and large corporations operate and maintain their records. ISPs and other communication companies can be called on to investigate customers' activities that are deemed to create an emergency situation. An emergency situation under the PATRIOT Act is defined as the immediate risk of death or personal injury, such as finding a bomb threat in an e-mail.

As recent events have shown, the government monitors e-mails for the occurrence of keywords. Incidents such as the Edward Snowden case have made public the amount of electronic surveillance done by the U.S. government and the governments of other countries. Some provisions of these federal regulations have been revised over the past few years, so you should stay abreast of their implications.

Investigating and controlling computer incident scenes in corporate environments is much easier than in crime scenes. In the private sector, the incident scene is often a workplace, such as a contained office or manufacturing area, where a policy violation is being investigated. Everything from the computers used to violate a company policy to the surrounding facility is under a controlled authority—that is, company management. Typically, businesses have inventory databases of computer hardware and software. Having access to these databases and knowing what applications are on suspected computers help identify the forensics tools needed to analyze a policy violation and the best way to conduct the analysis. For example, companies might have a preferred Web browser, such as Microsoft Internet Explorer, Mozilla Firefox, or Google Chrome. Knowing which browser a suspect used helps you develop standard examination procedures to identify data downloaded to the suspect's workstation.

To investigate employees suspected of improper use of company digital assets, a company policy statement about misuse of digital assets allows corporate investigators to conduct covert surveillance with little or no cause and access company computer systems and digital devices without a warrant, which is an advantage for corporate investigators. Law enforcement investigators can't do the same, however, without sufficient reason for a warrant.

However, if a company doesn't display a warning banner or publish a policy stating that it reserves the right to inspect digital assets at will, employees have an expectation of privacy (as explained in Chapter 1). When an employee is being investigated, this expected privacy prevents the employer from legally conducting an intrusive investigation. A well-defined corporate policy, therefore, should state that an employer has the right to examine, inspect, or access any company-owned digital assets. If a company issues a policy statement to all employees, the employer can investigate digital assets at will without any privacy right restrictions; this practice might violate the privacy laws of countries in the EU, for example. As a standard practice, companies should use both warning banners and policy statements. For example, if an incident is escalated to a criminal complaint, prosecutors prefer showing juries warning banners instead of policy manuals. A warning banner leaves a much stronger impression on a jury.

In addition to making sure a company has a policy statement or a warning banner, corporate investigators should know under what circumstances they can examine an employee's computer. With a policy statement, an employer can freely initiate any inquiry necessary to protect the company or organization. However, organizations must also have a well-defined process describing when an investigation can be initiated. At a minimum, most company policies require that employers have a "reasonable suspicion" that a law or policy is being violated. For example, if a policy states that employees can't use company computers for outside business and a supervisor notices a change in work behavior that could indicate an employee is violating this rule, generally it's enough to warrant an investigation. However, some countries require notifying employees that they're being investigated if they're suspected of criminal behavior at work.

If a corporate investigator finds that an employee is committing or has committed a crime, the employer can file a criminal complaint with the police. Some businesses, such as banks, have a regulatory requirement to report crimes. In the United States, the employer must turn over all evidence to the police for prosecution. If this evidence had been collected by a law enforcement officer, it would require a warrant, which would be difficult to obtain without sufficient probable cause. In "Processing Law Enforcement Crime Scenes" later in this chapter, you learn more about probable cause and how it applies to a criminal investigation.

Employers are usually interested in enforcing company policy, not seeking out and prosecuting employees, so typically they approve digital investigations only to identify employees who are misusing company assets. Corporate investigators are, therefore, concerned mainly with protecting company assets, such as intellectual property. Finding evidence of a criminal act during an investigation escalates the investigation from an internal civil matter to an external criminal complaint. In some situations, such as the discovery of child pornography or identity theft, the company or its agents must notify law enforcement immediately.

If you discover evidence of a crime during a company policy investigation, first determine whether the incident meets the elements of criminal law. You might have to consult with your corporate attorney to determine whether the situation is a potential crime. Next, inform management of the incident; they might have other concerns, such as protecting confidential business data that might be included with the criminal evidence (called "commingled data"). In this case, coordinate with management and the corporate attorney to determine the best way to protect commingled data. After you submit evidence containing sensitive information to the police, it becomes public record. Public record laws do include exceptions for protecting sensitive corporate information; ultimately, however, a judge decides what to protect.

After you discover illegal activity and document and report the crime, stop your investigation to make sure you don't violate Fourth Amendment restrictions on obtaining evidence. If the information you supply is specific enough to meet the criteria for a search warrant, the police are responsible for obtaining a warrant that requests any new evidence. If you follow police instructions to gather additional evidence without a search warrant after you have reported the crime, you run the risk of becoming an agent of law enforcement. Instead, consult with your corporate attorney on how to respond to a police request for information. The police and prosecutor should issue a subpoena for any additional new evidence, which minimizes your exposure to potential civil liability. In addition, you should keep all documentation of evidence collected to investigate an internal company policy violation. Later in this section, you learn more about using affidavits in an internal investigation.

One example of a company policy violation involves employees observing another employee accessing pornographic Web sites. If your organization's policy requires you to determine whether any evidence supports this accusation, you could start by extracting log file data from the proxy server (used to connect a company LAN to the Internet) and conducting a forensic examination of the subject's computer. Suppose that during your examination, you find adult and child pornography. Further examination of the subject's hard disk reveals that the employee has been collecting child pornography in separate folders on his workstation's hard drive. In the United States, possessing child pornography is a crime under federal and state criminal statutes. These situations aren't uncommon and make life difficult for investigators who don't want to be guilty of possession of contraband, such as child pornography, on their forensic workstations.

You survey the remaining content of the subject's drive and find that he's a lead engineer for the team developing your company's latest high-tech bicycle. He placed the child pornography images in a subfolder where the bicycle plans are stored. By doing so, he has commingled contraband with the company's confidential design plans for the bicycle. Your discovery poses two problems in dealing with this contraband evidence. First, you must report the crime to the police; all U.S. states and most countries have legal and moral codes when evidence of sexual exploitation of children is found. Second, you must also protect sensitive company information. Letting the high-tech bicycle plans become part of the criminal evidence might make it public record, and the design work will then be available to competitors. Your first step is to ask your corporate attorney how to deal with the commingled contraband data and sensitive design plans.

Your next step is to work with the corporate attorney to write an affidavit confirming your findings. The attorney should indicate in the affidavit that the evidence is commingled with company secrets and releasing the information will be detrimental to the company's financial health. When the affidavit is completed, you sign it before a notary, and then deliver the affidavit and the recovered evidence with log files to the police, where you make a criminal complaint. At the same time, the corporate attorney goes to court and requests that all evidence recovered from the hard disk that's not related to the complaint and is a company trade secret be protected from public viewing. You and the corporate attorney have reported the crime and taken steps to protect the sensitive data.

Now suppose the detective assigned to the case calls you. In the evidence you've turned over to the police, the detective notices that the suspect is collecting most of his contraband from e-mail attachments. The prosecutor needs you to collect more evidence to determine whether the suspect is transmitting contraband pictures to other potential suspects. The detective realizes that collecting more evidence might make you an agent of law enforcement and violate the employee's Fourth Amendment rights, so she writes an affidavit for a search warrant, ensuring that any subsequent instructions to you are legal. Before collecting any additional information, you wait until you or your corporate attorney get a subpoena, search warrant, or other court order.

Processing Law Enforcement Crime Scenes

To process a crime scene correctly, you must be familiar with criminal rules of search and seizure. You should also understand how a search warrant works and what to do when you process one. For all criminal investigations in the United States, the Fourth Amendment limits how governments search and seize evidence. A law enforcement officer can search for and seize criminal evidence only with probable cause. **Probable cause** refers to the standard specifying whether a police officer has the right to make an arrest, conduct a personal or property search, or obtain a warrant for arrest. With probable cause, a police officer can obtain a search warrant from a judge that authorizes a search and the seizure of specific evidence related to the criminal complaint.

The Fourth Amendment states that only warrants "particularly describing the place to be searched and the persons or things to be seized" can be issued. Note that this excerpt uses the word "particularly." The courts have determined that this phrase means a warrant can authorize a search only of a specific place for a specific thing. Without *specific* evidence and the description of a particular location, a warrant might be weak and create problems later during prosecution. For example, stating that the evidence is in a house on Elm Avenue between Broadway and Main Street is too general, unless only one house fits that description, because several houses might be located in this area. Instead, provide specific information, such as "123 Elm Avenue." Most courts have allowed more general wording for digital evidence, however. For example, you can state that you want to seize a "computer and all associated parts" instead of specifying a "Dell Optiplex GXA." The DOJ document "Searching and Seizing Computers and Obtaining Electronic Evidence in Criminal Investigations" (*www.justice.gov/criminal/cybercrime/docs/ssmanual2009.pdf*, 2009) has an example of a search warrant affidavit for computer searches on premises.

Although several court cases have allowed latitude when searching and seizing digital evidence, making your warrant as specific as possible to avoid challenges from defense attorneys is a good practice. Often a warrant is written and issued in haste because of the nature of the investigation. Law enforcement officers might not have the time to research the correct language for stating the nature of the complaint to meet probable cause requirements. However, because a judge can exclude evidence obtained from a poorly worded warrant, you should review these issues with your local prosecutor before investigating a case.

Understanding Concepts and Terms Used in Warrants

You should be familiar with warrant terminology that governs the type of evidence that can be seized. Many digital investigations involve large amounts of data you must sort through to find evidence; the Enron case, for example, involved terabytes of information. Unrelated information (referred to as **innocent information**) is often included with the evidence you're trying to recover. It might be personal records of innocent people or confidential business information, for example. When you find commingled evidence, judges often issue a **limiting phrase** to the warrant, which allows the police to separate innocent information from evidence. The warrant must list which items can be seized.

When approaching or investigating a crime scene, you might find evidence related to the crime but not in the location the warrant specifies. You might also find evidence of another unrelated crime. In these situations, this evidence is subject to the plain view doctrine. The **plain view doctrine** states that objects falling in the direct sight of an officer who has the right to be in a location are subject to seizure without a warrant and can be introduced into evidence. For the plain view doctrine to apply, three criteria must be met:

- The officer is where he or she has a legal right to be.
- Ordinary senses must not be enhanced by advanced technology in any way, such as with binoculars.
- Any discovery must be by chance.

For the officer to seize the item, he or she must have probable cause to believe the item is evidence of a crime or is contraband. In addition, the police aren't permitted to move objects to get a better view. In *Arizona v. Hicks* (480 U.S. 321, 1987), the officer was found to have acted unlawfully because he moved stereo equipment, without probable cause, to record the serial numbers. The plain view doctrine has also been expanded to include the subdoctrines of plain feel, plain smell, and plain hearing.

In *Horton v. California* (496 U.S. 128, 1990), the court eliminated the requirement that the discovery of evidence in plain view be inadvertent. Previously, "inadvertent discovery" was required, which led to difficulties in defining this term. The three-prong Horton test requires the following:

- The officer must be lawfully present at the place where the evidence can be plainly viewed.

- The officer must have a lawful right of access to the object.

- The incriminating character of the object must be "immediately apparent."

The plain view doctrine doesn't extend to supporting a general exploratory search from one object to another unless something incriminating is found (*Coolidge v. New Hampshire*, 403 U.S. 443, 466, 1971).

However, the plain view doctrine's applicability in the digital forensics world is being rejected. The U.S. Court of Appeals for the Ninth Circuit has directly addressed this doctrine and used it to give wide latitude to law enforcement (*United States v. Wong*, 334 F.3d 831, 9th Cir., 2003). Other circuit courts have been less willing to address applying the doctrine to computer searches. For example, police investigating a case have a search warrant authorizing the search of a computer for evidence related to illegal drug trafficking; during the search, the examiner observes an .avi file, opens it, and sees that it's child pornography. At that point, he must get an additional warrant or an expansion of the existing warrant to continue the search for child pornography. This approach is consistent with rulings in *United States v. Carey* (172 F.3d 1268, 10th Cir., 1999) and *United States v. Walser* (275 F.3d 981, 10th Cir. 2001). In a more recent case that went to the Ninth Circuit Court of Appeals, the original search warrant was for 10 major league baseball players suspected of steroid use (*United States v. Comprehensive Drug Testing*, 2010). During the examination of files and e-mails, 200 more players were implicated. Forensics investigators see many files when they're searching for evidence, so in this case, their opinion was that the data was in plain view. However, the court disagreed. As with the example of discovering child pornography, a separate warrant for all other players should have been issued.

Preparing for a Search

Preparing for search and seizure of computers or digital devices is probably the most important step in digital investigations. The better you prepare, the smoother your investigation will be. The following sections discuss the tasks you should perform before you search for evidence. For these tasks, you might need to get answers from the victim (the complainant) and an informant, who could be a police detective assigned to the case, a law enforcement witness, or a manager or co-worker of the **person of interest** to the investigation.

Identifying the Nature of the Case

Recall from Chapter 1 that when you're assigned a digital investigation case, you start by identifying the nature of the case, including whether it involves the private or public sector. For example, a corporate investigation might involve an employee abusing Internet privileges by surfing the Web excessively or an employee who has filed an equal employment opportunity (EEO) or ethics complaint. Serious cases might involve an employee abusing company digital assets to acquire or deliver contraband. Law enforcement cases could range from a check fraud ring to a homicide. The nature of the case dictates how you proceed and what types of assets or resources you need to use in the investigation (discussed in more detail in "Determining the Tools You Need" later in this chapter).

Identifying the Type of OS or Digital Device

Next, determine the type of OSs involved in the investigation. For law enforcement, this step might be difficult because the crime scene isn't controlled. You might not know what kinds of digital devices were used to commit a crime or how or where they were used. In this case, you must draw on your skills, creativity, and sources of knowledge, such as the Uniform Crime Report discussed in Chapter 2, to deal with the unknown.

If you can identify the OS or device, estimate the size of the storage device on suspect computers and determine how many digital devices you have to process at the scene. Also, determine what hardware might be involved and whether the evidence is on a Microsoft, Linux, Apple, or mainframe computer. For corporate investigators, configuration management databases (discussed in Chapter 2) make this step easier. Consultants to the private sector or law enforcement officers might have to investigate more thoroughly to determine these details.

Determining Whether You Can Seize Computers and Digital Devices

Generally, the ideal situation for incident or crime scenes is seizing computers and digital devices and taking them to your lab for further processing. However, the type of case and location of the evidence determine whether you can remove digital equipment from the scene. Law enforcement investigators need a warrant to remove computers from a crime scene and transport them to a lab. If removing the computers will irreparably harm a business, the computers shouldn't be taken offsite, unless you have disclosed the effect of the seizure to the judge. An additional complication is files stored offsite that are accessed remotely. You must decide whether the drives containing these files need to be examined. Another consideration is the availability of cloud storage, which essentially can't be located physically. The data is stored on drives where data from many other subscribers might be stored.

If you aren't allowed to take the computers and digital devices to your lab, determine the resources you need to acquire digital evidence and which tools can speed data acquisition. With large drives, such as a terabyte or more, acquisition times can increase to several hours. In Chapter 3, you examined data acquisition software and learned which tools meet needs for acquiring disk images. Some software, such as EnCase, compresses data while making forensic images. For large drives, this compression might be necessary.

Getting a Detailed Description of the Location

The more information you have about the location of a digital crime, the more efficiently you can gather evidence from the crime scene. Environmental and safety issues are the main concerns during this process. Before arriving at an incident or crime scene, identify potential hazards to your safety as well as that of other examiners.

Some cases involve dangerous settings, such as a drug bust of a methamphetamine lab or a terrorist attack using biological, chemical, or nuclear contaminants. For these types of investigations, you must rely on the skills of **hazardous materials (HAZMAT)** teams to recover evidence from the scene. The recovery process might include decontaminating digital components needed for the investigation, if possible. If the decontamination procedure might destroy electronic evidence, a HAZMAT specialist or an investigator in HAZMAT gear should make an image of a suspect's drive. If you have to rely on a HAZMAT specialist to acquire data, coach the specialist on how to connect cables and how to run the software. You must be exact and articulate in your instructions.

Ambiguous or incorrect instructions could destroy evidence. Ideally, a digital forensics investigator trained in dealing with HAZMAT environments should acquire drive images. However, not all organizations have funds available for this training.

Whether you or a HAZMAT technician is the one acquiring an image, you should keep some guidelines in mind. Before acquiring the data, a HAZMAT technician might suggest that you put the target drive in a special HAZMAT bag, leaving the data and power cables out of the bag but creating an airtight seal around the cables to prevent any contaminants from entering the bag and affecting the target drive. When the data acquisition is finished, power down the computer and then disconnect the data and power cables from the target drive. The HAZMAT technician can then decontaminate the bag. When dealing with extreme conditions, such as biological or chemical hazardous contaminants, you might have to sacrifice equipment, such as data and power cables, to perform a task. In certain instances, such as a methamphetamine lab bust, the contaminants might be so toxic that hazards to the safety of others prohibit acquiring any digital evidence.

In addition, if the temperature in the contaminated room is higher than 80 degrees, you should take measures to avoid damage to the drive from overheating. In a dry desert region, consider cooling the target drive by using sealed ice packs or double-wrapped bags of ice so that moisture doesn't leak out and damage the drive. In extreme conditions, consider the risks to evidence and your equipment. You'll need to brainstorm for solutions to overcome these problems. Moving the equipment to a controlled environment is ideal; however, doing so isn't always possible.

Determining Who Is in Charge

As discussed in Chapter 1, a company needs an established line of authority to specify who can instigate or authorize an investigation. Corporate investigations usually require only one person to respond to an incident or crime scene. Processing evidence usually involves acquiring an image of a suspect's drive. In law enforcement, however, many investigations need additional staff to collect all evidence quickly. For large-scale investigations, a crime or incident scene leader should be designated. Anyone assigned to a large-scale investigation scene should cooperate with the designated leader to ensure that the team addresses all details when collecting evidence.

Using Additional Technical Expertise

After you collect evidence data, determine whether you need specialized help to process the incident or crime scene. For example, suppose you're assigned to process a crime scene at a data center running Windows servers with several RAID drives and high-end Linux servers. If you're the lead on this investigation, you must identify the additional skills needed to process the crime scene, such as enlisting help with a high-end server OS. Other concerns are how to acquire data from RAID drives and how much data you can acquire. RAID servers typically process several terabytes of data, and standard imaging tools might not be able to handle such large data sets.

When working at high-end computing facilities, identify the applications the suspect uses, such as Oracle databases. You might need to recruit an Oracle specialist or site support staff to help extract data for the investigation. Finding the right person can be an even bigger challenge than conducting the investigation.

If you do need to recruit a specialist who's not an investigator, develop a training program to educate the specialist in investigative techniques. This advice also applies to specialists you plan to supervise during search-and-seizure tasks. When dealing with digital evidence, an untrained specialist can easily destroy evidence unintentionally, no matter how careful you are in giving instructions and monitoring his or her activities.

Determining the Tools You Need

After you have gathered as much information as possible about the incident or crime scene, you can start listing what you need at the scene. Being overprepared is better than being underprepared, especially when you determine that you can't transfer the computer to your lab for processing.

To manage your tools, consider creating an initial-response field kit and an extensive-response field kit. Using the right kit makes processing an incident or crime scene much easier and minimizes how much you have to carry from your vehicle to the scene.

Your **initial-response field kit** should be lightweight and easy to transport. With this kit, you can arrive at a scene, acquire the data you need, and return to the lab as quickly as possible. Figure 4-4 shows some items you might need, and Table 4-1 lists the tools you might need in an initial-response field kit.

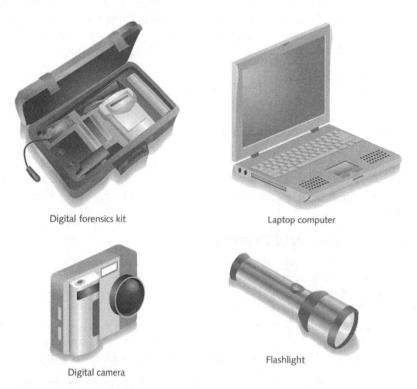

Digital forensics kit

Laptop computer

Digital camera

Flashlight

Figure 4-4 Items in an initial-response field kit
© Cengage Learning®

Table 4-1   Tools in an initial-response field kit

Number needed	Tools
1	Small computer toolkit
1	Large-capacity drive
1	IDE ribbon cable (ATA-33 or ATA-100)
1	SATA cables
1	Forensic boot media containing an acquisition utility
1	Laptop IDE 40- to 44-pin adapter, other adapter cables
1	Laptop or tablet computer
1	FireWire or USB dual write-protect external bay
1	Flashlight
1	Digital camera with extra batteries or 35mm camera with film and flash
10	Evidence log forms
1	Notebook or digital dictation recorder
10	Computer evidence bags (antistatic bags)
20	Evidence labels, tape, and tags
1	Permanent ink marker
10	External USB devices or a portable hard drive

© 2016 Cengage Learning®

An **extensive-response field kit** should include all the tools you can afford to take to the field. When you arrive at the scene, you should extract only those items you need to acquire evidence. Doing so protects your equipment and minimizes how many items you have to keep track of at the scene. Table 4-2 lists the tools you might need in an extensive-response field kit, including external USB drives.

Table 4-2   Tools in an extensive-response field kit

Number needed	Tools
Varies	Assorted technical manuals, ranging from OS references to forensic analysis guides
1	Initial-response field kit
1	Laptop or tablet with cables and connectors
2	Electrical power strips
1	Additional hand tools, including bolt cutters, pry bar, and hacksaw
1	Leather gloves and disposable latex gloves (assorted sizes)
1	Hand truck and luggage cart
10	Large garbage bags and large cardboard boxes with packaging tape
1	Rubber bands of assorted sizes
1	Magnifying glass
1	Ream of printer paper
1	Small brush for cleaning dust from digital devices

(*continues*)

Table 4-2   Tools in an extensive-response field kit (*Continued*)

Number needed	Tools
10	USB drives of varying sizes
2	External hard drives (1 TB or larger) with power cables
Assorted	Converter cables
5	Additional assorted hard drives or flash drives for data acquisition

© 2016 Cengage Learning®

When deciding what items to include in initial-response and extensive-response field kits, you should also analyze needs specific to your region or organization. Refer to Tables 4-1 and 4-2 for guidelines.

Preparing the Investigation Team

Before you initiate the search and seizure of digital evidence at an incident or a crime scene, you must review all the available facts, plans, and objectives with the investigation team you have assembled. The goal of scene processing is to collect and secure digital evidence successfully. The better prepared you are, the fewer problems you encounter when you carry out the plan to collect data.

Keep in mind that digital evidence is volatile. Develop the skills to assess the facts quickly, make your plan, gather the needed resources, and collect data from the incident or crime scene. In some digital investigations, responding slowly might result in the loss of important evidence for the case.

Securing a Computer Incident or Crime Scene

Investigators secure an incident or crime scene to preserve the evidence and to keep information about the incident or crime confidential. Information made public could jeopardize the investigation. If you're in charge of securing a digital incident or crime scene, use barrier tape to prevent bystanders from entering the scene accidentally, and ask police officers or security guards to prevent others from entering the scene or taking photos and videos with smartphones and other digital devices. Legal authority for a corporate incident scene includes trespassing violations; for a crime scene, it includes obstructing justice or failing to comply with a police officer. Access to the scene should be restricted to only those people who have a specific reason to be there. The reason for the standard practice of securing an incident or crime scene is to expand the area of control beyond the scene's immediate location. In this way, you avoid overlooking an area that might be part of the scene. Shrinking the scene's perimeter is easier than expanding it.

For major crime scenes, digital investigators aren't usually responsible for defining a scene's security perimeter. These cases involve other specialists and detectives who are collecting physical evidence and recording the scene. For incidents involving mostly computers, the computers can be a crime scene within a crime scene or a secondary crime scene, containing evidence to be processed. The evidence is in the computer, but the courts consider it physical evidence. Computers and other digital devices can also contain actual physical evidence, such as DNA evidence or fingerprints on keyboards. Crime labs can use special vacuums to extract

DNA residue from a keyboard to compare with other DNA samples. In a major crime scene, law enforcement usually retains the keyboard and other peripherals.

Evidence is commonly lost or corrupted because of **professional curiosity**, which involves the presence of police officers and other professionals who aren't part of the crime scene–processing team. They just have a compelling interest in seeing what happened, but their presence could contaminate the scene directly or indirectly. Keep in mind that even those authorized and trained to search crime scenes can alter the scene or evidence inadvertently.

For example, during one homicide investigation, the lead detective collected a good latent fingerprint from the crime scene. He compared it with the victim's fingerprints and those of others who knew the victim, but he couldn't find a matching fingerprint. The detective suspected he had the murderer's fingerprint and kept it on file for several years until his police department purchased an **Automated Fingerprint Identification System (AFIS)** computer. During acceptance testing, the software vendor processed sample fingerprints to see how quickly and accurately the system could match fingerprints in the database. The detective asked the testing team to run the fingerprint he found at the homicide scene. He believed the suspect's fingerprints were in the AFIS database. The testing team complied and within minutes, AFIS found a near-perfect match of the latent fingerprint: It belonged to the detective.

Always remember that professional curiosity can destroy or corrupt evidence, including digital evidence. When working at an incident or crime scene, be aware of what you're doing and what you have touched, physically or virtually. A police detective can take elimination prints of everyone who had access to the crime scene to identify the fingerprints of known people; digital evidence doesn't have an equivalent elimination process. You must protect all digital evidence, so make sure no one examines a suspect's computer before you can capture and preserve an image of the hard disk. For example, starting a computer without forensic boot media alters important data, such as the date and timestamps of last access to certain files.

Seizing Digital Evidence at the Scene

With proper search warrants, law enforcement can seize all digital systems and peripherals. In corporate investigations, you might have similar authority; however, you might have the authority only to make an image of the suspect's drive. Depending on company policies, corporate investigators rarely have the authority to seize all computers and peripherals.

When seizing digital evidence in criminal investigations, follow the U.S. DOJ standards for seizing digital data (described later in this chapter, or see *www.justice.gov/criminal/cybercrime/docs/ssmanual2009.pdf*). Another good source for both criminal and civil procedures is ISO standard 27037. For civil investigations, follow the same rules of evidence as for criminal investigation. You might be looking for specific evidence, such as a particular e-mail or spreadsheet. In a criminal matter, investigators seize entire drives to preserve as much information as possible and make sure no evidence is overlooked. If you have any questions, doubts, or concerns, consult with your attorney for additional guidance.

Preparing to Acquire Digital Evidence

The evidence you acquire at the scene depends on the nature of the case and the alleged crime or violation. For a criminal case involving a drug dealer's computer, for example, you need to take the entire computer along with any peripherals and media in the area, including smartphones, USB devices, CDs/DVDs, printers, cameras, and scanners. Seizing peripherals and other media ensures that you leave no necessary system components behind; often, predicting what components might be critical to the system's operation is difficult. On the other hand, if you're investigating employee misconduct, you might need only a few specific items.

Before you collect digital evidence, ask your supervisor or senior forensics examiner in the organization the following questions:

- Do you need to take the entire computer and all peripherals and media in the immediate area? How are you going to protect the computer and media while transporting them to your lab?
- Is the computer powered on when you arrive? (This question is discussed in more detail later in "Processing an Incident or a Crime Scene.")
- Is the suspect you're investigating in the immediate area of the computer? Is it possible the suspect damaged or destroyed the computer, peripherals, or media? Will you have to separate the suspect from the computer?

For example, suppose a company employee, Edward Braun, is suspected of using a company computer at his desk to write a book. You suspect that Edward is saving personal files on the computer's hard drive. Using imaging software, you can copy the hard drive onto another drive, install the duplicate hard drive in the computer, and take the original drive to your forensics lab for examination. This procedure doesn't create a bit-for-bit copy; you're creating a working copy for continued business operations and taking the original for examination.

Because Edward's supervisors don't want him to know he's being investigated, you must create the working copy when he's not at his desk and isn't expected to return. Because most people notice when something is out of order on their desks, you should photograph the scene, measure the height of his chair, and record the position of items on his desk you need to move before removing the hard drive. (The following section has more tips on photographing and documenting the scene.) After you create an image of his hard drive and substitute the copy, return Edward's belongings to their original locations.

Processing an Incident or a Crime Scene

The following guidelines offer suggestions on how to process an incident or crime scene. As you gain experience in performing searches and seizures, you can add to or modify these guidelines to meet the needs of specific cases. Use your judgment to determine what steps to take when processing a civil or criminal investigation. For any difficult issues, seek out legal counsel or other technical experts.

Keep a journal to document your activities. Include the date and time you arrive on the scene, the people you encounter, and notes on every important task you perform. Update the journal as you process the scene.

To secure the scene, use whatever is practical to make sure only authorized people can access the area. Remove anyone who isn't investigating the scene unless you need his or her help to process the scene. For example, the company's network administrator might need to help you collect and recover data. As mentioned, you should secure a wider scene perimeter than necessary. Make sure nothing in this area, including digital evidence, moves until you have had time to record it. Be professional and courteous to any curious onlookers, but don't offer information about the investigation or incident or answer questions. Refer journalists to a public information officer or the organization's public relations manager.

Take video and still recordings of the area around the computer or digital device. Start by recording the overall scene, and then record details with close-up shots, including the back of all computers. Before recording the back of each computer, place numbered or lettered labels on each cable to help identify which cable is connected to which plug, in case you need to reassemble components at the lab. Make sure you take close-ups of all cable connections, including keyloggers (devices used to record keystrokes) and dongle devices used with software as part of the licensing agreement. Record the area around the computer, including the floor and ceiling, and all access points to the computer, such as doors and windows. Be sure to look under any tables or desks for anything taped to the underside of a table or desk drawer or on the floor out of view. If the area has ceiling panels—false ceiling tiles—remove them and record that area, too. Slowly pan or zoom the camera to prevent blurring in the video image, and maintain a camera log for all shots you take.

When you finish videotaping or photographing the scene, sketch the incident or crime scene. This sketch is usually a rough draft with notes on objects' dimensions and distances between fixed objects. For example, a note might read "The suspect's computer is on the south wall, three meters from the southeast corner of the room." When you prepare your report, you can make a clean, detailed drawing from your sketch, preferably using drawing software so that the sketch is in electronic form.

Because digital data is volatile, check the state of each computer or device at the scene as soon as possible. Determine whether the computer is powered on or off or in hibernation or sleep mode. If it's off, leave it off. If it's on, use your professional judgment on what to do next. Standard digital forensics practice has been to kill the computer's power to make sure data doesn't become corrupt through covert means. Typically, this procedure is still acceptable on legacy Windows and MS-DOS systems because turning off the power usually preserves data. On Windows, UNIX, and Linux computers, generally you should do an orderly shutdown first. Every shutdown process has inherent risks, however; to avoid data loss, you or your supervisor might have to determine the best shutdown procedure.

In addition, there are many urban legends about criminals placing self-destruct mechanisms—both hardware and software devices—in computers. Many years ago, a common trick was altering the DOS program command.com by changing the dir (directory) command to the deltree (delete the directory tree) command. When an investigator entered the dir command on a suspect's computer, he would inadvertently start the deltree command, which deletes all files and folders and their contents. More advanced criminals have been known to create similar command-altering methods that overwrite a drive's contents. In addition, computer owners who suspect someone will investigate their computers might set the computer to delete the hard drive's contents if the correct screensaver password isn't entered.

As a general rule, don't cut electrical power to a running system unless it's an older Windows or MS-DOS system. However, it's a judgment call because of recent trends in digital crimes. More digital investigations now revolve around network- and Internet-related cases, which rely heavily on log file data. Certain files, such as the Event log and Security log in Windows, might lose essential network activity records if power is terminated without a proper shutdown. Some government agencies, however, still teach investigators to "pull the plug"; it's the Digital Evidence First Responder's (DEFR's) judgment call.

If you're working on a network or Internet investigation and the computer is on, save data in any current applications as safely as possible and record all active windows or shell sessions. Don't examine folders or network connections or press any keys unless it's necessary. For systems that are powered on and running, photograph the screens. If windows are open but minimized, expanding them so that you can photograph them is safe. As a precaution, write down the contents of each window.

As you're copying data on a live suspect computer, make notes in your journal about everything you do so that you can explain your actions in your formal report to prosecutors and other attorneys. When you've finished recording screen contents, save them to external media. For example, if one screen shows a Word file, save it to an external drive. Keep in mind that the suspect might have changed the file since last using the Save command. If another screen is a Web browser, take a screenshot or save the Web page to a USB drive or an external hard drive. If the suspect computer has an active connection to a network server with enough storage, you can save large files to a folder on the server. To do so, you need the cooperation of the network administrator to help direct you to the correct server and folder for storing the file.

If you can't save an open application to external media, save the open application to the suspect drive with a new filename. Changing the filename avoids overwriting an existing file that might not have been updated already. This method isn't ideal and should be done only in extreme emergency conditions. Remember that your goal is to preserve as much evidence in as good a condition as is practical.

After you have saved all active files on the suspect computer, you can close all applications. If an application prompts you to save before closing, don't save the files. When all applications are closed, perform an orderly shutdown. If you're not familiar with the correct shutdown method for the system you're examining, consult someone who has expertise in this procedure.

After you record the scene and shut down the system, bag and tag the evidence, following these steps:

1. Assign one person, if possible, to collect and log all evidence. Minimize the number of people handling evidence to ensure its integrity.

2. Tag all the evidence you collect with the current date and time, serial numbers or unique features, make and model, and name of the person who collected it.

3. Maintain two separate logs of collected evidence to be reconciled for audit control purposes and to verify everything you have collected.

4. Maintain constant control of the collected evidence and the crime or incident scene.

If the nature of the case doesn't permit you to seize the computer or digital device, create an image of the hard drive, as you learned in Chapter 3. Be sure to use critical investigative methods and look for other physical drives, and verify that the image you created corresponds to the device's physical size.

In Chapter 10, you learn how to use forensics tools to acquire RAM. Many studies are being conducted on how to analyze RAM systematically, in an effort to find relevant information in what seems to look like random garbage data.

During the data acquisition or immediately after collecting the evidence, look for information related to the investigation, such as passwords, passphrases, personal identification numbers (PINs), and bank account numbers (particularly offshore bank accounts, often used to hide evidence of financial transactions). This information might be in plain view or out of sight in a drawer or trashcan. At the scene, collect as much personal information as possible about the suspect or victim. Collect all information related to facts about the crime or incident, particularly anything that connects the suspect to the victim.

To finish your analysis and processing of a scene, collect all documentation and media related to the investigation, including the following material:

- Hardware, including peripheral devices
- Software, including OSs and applications
- All media, such as USB drives, backup tapes, and disks
- All documentation, manuals, printouts, and handwritten notes

Processing Data Centers with RAID Systems

Digital investigators sometimes perform forensics analysis on RAID systems or server farms, which are rooms filled with extremely large disk systems and are typical of large business data centers, such as banks, insurance companies, and ISPs. As you learned in Chapter 3, one technique for extracting evidence from large systems is called sparse acquisition. This technique extracts only data related to evidence for your case from allocated files and minimizes how much data you need to analyze. A drawback of this technique is that it doesn't recover data in free or slack space. If you have a computer forensics tool that accesses unallocated space on a RAID system, work with the tool on a test system first to make sure it doesn't corrupt the RAID system.

Using a Technical Advisor

When working with advanced technologies, recruit a technical advisor who can help you list the tools you need to process the incident or crime scene. At large data centers, the technical advisor is the person guiding you about where to locate data and helping you extract log records or other evidence from large RAID servers. In law enforcement cases, the technical advisor can help create the search warrant by itemizing what you need for the warrant. If you use a technical advisor for this purpose, you should list his or her name in the warrant. At the scene, a technical advisor can help direct other investigators to collect evidence correctly. Technical advisors have the following responsibilities:

- Know all aspects of the system being seized and searched.
- Direct investigators on how to handle sensitive media and systems to prevent damage.
- Help ensure security of the scene.
- Help document the planning strategy for the search and seizure.
- Conduct ad hoc training for investigators on the technologies and components being seized and searched.
- Document activities during the search and seizure.
- Help conduct the search and seizure.

Documenting Evidence in the Lab

After you collect digital evidence at the scene, you transport it to a forensics lab, which should be a controlled environment that ensures the security and integrity of digital evidence. In any investigative work, be sure to record your activities and findings as you work. To do so, you can maintain a journal to record the steps you take as you process evidence. Your goal is to be able to reproduce the same results when you or another investigator repeat the steps you took to collect evidence.

If you get different results when you repeat the steps, the credibility of your evidence becomes questionable. At best, the evidence's value is compromised; at worst, the evidence will be disqualified. Because of the nature of electronic components, failures do occur. For example, you might not be able to repeat a data recovery because of a hardware failure, such as a disk drive head crash. Be sure to report all facts and events as they occur.

Besides verifying your work, a journal serves as a reference that documents the methods you used to process digital evidence. You and others can use it for training and guidance on other investigations.

Processing and Handling Digital Evidence

You must maintain the integrity of digital evidence in the lab as you do when collecting it in the field. Your first task is to preserve the disk data. If you have a suspect computer that hasn't been copied with an imaging tool, you must create a copy. When you do, be sure to make the suspect drive read-only (typically by using a write-blocking device), and document this step. If the disk has been copied with an imaging tool, you must preserve the image files. With most imaging tools, you can create smaller, compressed volume sets to make archiving your data easier.

In Chapter 3, you learned how to use imaging tools, and in Chapter 1, you examined the steps for preserving digital evidence with chain-of-custody controls. You use the following steps to create image files:

1. Copy all image files to a large drive. Most forensics labs have several machines set up with disk-imaging software and multiple hard drives that can be exchanged as needed for your cases. You can use these resources to copy image files to large drives. Some might be equipped with large network storage devices for ongoing cases.

2. Start your forensics tool to access and open the image files.

3. Run an MD5 or SHA-1 hashing algorithm on the image files to get a digital hash. Later in "Obtaining a Digital Hash," you learn how to compare MD5 or SHA-1 hashes to make sure the evidence hasn't changed.

4. When you finish copying image files to a larger drive, secure the original media in an evidence locker. Don't work with the original media; it should be stored in a locker that has an evidence custody form. Be sure to fill out the form and date it.

Storing Digital Evidence

With digital evidence, you need to consider how and on what type of media to save it and what type of storage device is recommended to secure it. The media you use to store digital evidence usually depends on how long you need to keep it. If you investigate criminal matters, store the evidence as long as you can. The ideal media on which to store digital data are CDs, DVDs, DVD-Rs, DVD+Rs, or DVD-RWs. (CDs from the 1980s could last up to 5 years. The expected lifespan of CDs and DVDs is now 2 to 5 years.)

You can also use magnetic tape to preserve evidence data. The 4-mm DAT magnetic tapes store between 40 to 72 GB or more of data, but like CD-Rs, they are slow at reading and writing data. If you're using these tapes, test stored data by copying the contents from the tape back to a disk drive. Then verify that the data is good by examining it with forensics tools or doing an MD5 hash comparison of the original data and the newly restored data.

If a 30-year lifespan for data storage is acceptable for your digital evidence, older DLT magnetic tape cartridge systems are a good choice. Keep in mind that you never know how long it will take for a case to go to trial. DLT systems have been used with mainframe computers for several decades and are reliable data-archiving systems. Depending on the size of the DLT cartridge, one cartridge can store up to 80 GB of data in compressed mode. Speed of data transfer from a hard drive to a DLT tape is also faster than transferring data to a CD-R or DVD. The only major drawback of a DLT drive and tapes is cost. A drive can cost from $400 to $800, and each tape is about $40. However, with the current large disk drives, the DLT system does offer substantial labor savings over other systems.

Recently, manufacturers such as Quantum Corp. have introduced a high-speed, high-capacity tape cartridge drive system called Super Digital Linear Tape (Super-DLT or SDLT). These systems are specifically designed for large RAID data backups and can store more than 1 TB of data. Smaller external SDLT drives can connect to a workstation through a SCSI card. In addition, many external USB drives can hold 1 or more TB of information. Reliable offsite storage and encrypted cloud storage are other options.

However, don't rely on one media storage method to preserve your evidence—be sure to make two copies of every image to prevent data loss. Also, if practical, use different tools to create the two images because every tool has strengths and weaknesses. For example, you can use the Linux dd command to create the first image and ProDiscover to create the second image.

Evidence Retention and Media Storage Needs

To help maintain the chain of custody for digital evidence so that it's accepted in court or by arbitration, restrict access to your lab and evidence storage area. When your lab is open for operations, authorized personnel must keep these areas under constant supervision. When your lab is closed, at least two security workers should guard evidence storage cabinets and lab facilities.

As a good security practice, your lab should have a sign-in roster for all visitors. Most labs use a manual log system that an authorized technician maintains when an evidence storage container is opened and closed. These logs should be maintained for a period based on legal requirements, including the statute of limitations, the maximum sentence, and expiration of appeal periods. Make the logs available for management to inspect. The evidence custody form should contain an entry for every person who handles the evidence (see Figure 4-5).

Item description:				
Item tag number:				
Person	Date logged out	Time logged out	Date logged in	Time logged in

Figure 4-5 A sample log file
© Cengage Learning®

If you're supporting a law enforcement agency, you might need to retain evidence indefinitely, depending on the type of crime. Check with your local prosecuting attorney's office or state laws to make sure you're in compliance. For the private sector or corporate environments, check with your company's legal department (the general counsel), which is responsible for setting your organization's standards for evidence retention. Cases involving child pornography are the exception: The evidence must be turned over to law enforcement. This material is contraband and must not be stored by any person or organization other than a law enforcement agency.

Documenting Evidence

To document evidence, create or use an evidence custody form (shown in Chapter 1). Because of constant changes in technologies and methods for acquiring data, create an electronic evidence custody form that you can modify as needed. An evidence custody form serves the following functions:

- Identifies the evidence
- Identifies who has handled the evidence
- Lists dates and times the evidence was handled

After you have established these pieces of information, you can add others to your form, such as a section listing MD5 and SHA-1 hash values. Include any detailed information you might need to reference.

Evidence bags also include labels or evidence forms you can use to document your evidence. Commercial companies offer a variety of sizes and styles of paper and plastic evidence bags. Be sure to write on the bag when it's empty, not when it contains digital evidence, to make sure your writing is legible and to avoid damaging the evidence. You should use antistatic bags for electronic components.

Obtaining a Digital Hash

To verify data integrity, different methods of obtaining a unique identity for file data have been developed. One of the first methods, the **Cyclic Redundancy Check (CRC)** is a mathematical algorithm that determines whether a file's contents have changed. The most recent version is CRC-32. CRC, however, is not considered a forensic hashing algorithm. The first algorithm used for digital forensics was **Message Digest 5 (MD5)**. Like CRC, MD5 is a mathematical formula that generates a hexadecimal code value, or **hash value**, based on the contents of a file, a folder, or an entire drive. If a bit or byte in the file changes, it alters the hash value, a unique hexadecimal value that can be used to verify that a file or drive hasn't changed or been tampered with. Before you process or analyze a file, you can use a software tool to calculate its hash value. After you process the file, you produce another digital hash. If it's the same as the original one, you can verify the integrity of your digital evidence with mathematical proof that the file didn't change.

According to work done by Wang Xiaoyun and her associates from Beijing's Tsinghua University and Shandong University of Technology, there are three rules for forensic hashes:

- You can't predict the hash value of a file or device.
- No two hash values can be the same. (Note that collisions have occurred in research using supercomputers.)
- If anything changes in the file or device, the hash value must change.

Another hashing algorithm is **Secure Hash Algorithm version 1 (SHA-1)**, developed by the **National Institute of Standards and Technology (NIST)**. SHA-1 has slowly replaced MD5 and CRC-32, although MD5 is still widely used. (For more information on SHA-1, see *http://csrc.nist.gov/publications/fips/fips180-4/fips-180-4.pdf*.) In both MD5 and SHA-1, collisions have occurred, meaning two different files have the same hash value. Collisions are rare, however, and despite flaws in MD5 and SHA-1, both are still used for validating digital evidence collected from files and storage media. If a collision is suspected, you can do a byte-by-byte comparison to verify that all bytes are identical. Byte-by-byte comparisons can be done with the MS-DOS `comp` command or the Linux/UNIX `diff` command. New developments in this field happen constantly, however, so staying current by investigating the NIST Web site and reading related journals is a good idea. New versions, such as SHA 256, are already being used.

Most digital forensics hashing needs can be satisfied with a **nonkeyed hash set**, which is a unique hash number generated by a software tool, such as the Linux `md5sum` command. The advantage of this type of hash is that it can identify known files, such as executable programs or viruses, that hide themselves by changing their names. For example, many people who view or transmit pornographic material change filenames and extensions to obscure the nature of the contents. However, even if a file's name and extension change, the hash value doesn't.

The alternative to a nonkeyed hash is a **keyed hash set**, which is created by an encryption utility's secret key. You can use the secret key to create a unique hash value for a file. Although a keyed hash set can't identify files as nonkeyed hash methods can, it can produce a unique hash set for digital evidence.

You can use the MD5 function in FTK Imager to obtain the digital signature of a file or an entire drive. In the following activity, you use a thumb drive, although you often work with hard drives in actual investigations. First, you create a test file and then generate an MD5 hash value for it. Then you change the file and produce another MD5 hash value, this time noting the change in the hash value. You need a blank, formatted USB drive and a Windows computer for the following steps:

1. Power on your forensic workstation, booting it to Windows.

2. Insert a blank, formatted USB drive into your computer.

3. Start Notepad. In a new text file, type **This is a test to see how an MD5 digital hash works.**

4. Click **File, Save As** from the menu. In the File name text box, type **InChap04.txt**. Navigate to your thumb drive, and then click **Save**.

5. Exit Notepad.

Next, you use FTK Imager Lite to determine the MD5 and SHA-1 hash values:

If you didn't install FTK Imager Lite in Chapter 3, do so before performing these steps.

1. Start FTK Imager Lite. In Windows 7 and 8, click **Yes** in the UAC message box, if necessary.

2. Click **File, Add Evidence Item** from the menu. In the Select Source dialog box, click the **Logical Drive** option button, and then click **Next**.

3. In the Select Drive dialog box, click the **Source Drive Selection** list arrow, click your USB drive in the drop-down list, and then click **Finish**.

4. Right-click the USB drive at the upper left and click **Verify Drive/Image**. The verification process takes a few minutes. When it finishes, you should see a window similar to Figure 4-6. Copy the MD5 and SHA-1 hash values for this file to a text file in Notepad, and then click **Close**. Click **Save**, and save the text file in your work folder with a filename of your choosing. Close the Drive/Image Verify Results dialog box.

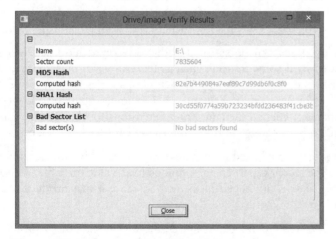

Figure 4-6   Using FTK Imager to verify hash values

5. In FTK Imager, click **File, Remove Evidence Item** from the menu. (You're about to make changes to the file and don't want it open in FTK Imager while you do so.) Leave FTK Imager running for the next set of steps.

Now you change the text file:

1. Start Notepad, and open the **InChap04.txt** file.

2. Delete one word from the sentence. Click **File, Save**, and save the file with the same filename.

3. Repeat the previous activity's steps in FTK Imager to generate MD5 and SHA-1 hash values. Open the file containing the original hash values from Step 4 in the preceding activity to compare the hash values. They should be different from the original hash values you found for this file. When you're finished, exit FTK Imager.

Reviewing a Case

Chapter 1 introduced tasks for planning your investigation, some of which are repeated in the following list. Later in this section, you apply each task to a hypothetical investigation to create a preparation plan for searching an incident or crime scene. The following are the general tasks you perform in any digital forensics case:

- Identify the case requirements.
- Plan your investigation.
- Conduct the investigation.
- Complete the case report.
- Critique the case.

The following sections give you an example of civil and criminal investigations, and then you review how to perform some of these general tasks in a case involving a hypothetical company.

Sample Civil Investigation

Most cases in the corporate environment are considered **low-level investigations,** or noncriminal cases. This doesn't mean corporate digital investigations are less important; it means they require less effort than a major criminal case. The example of a low-level civil investigation in this section is an e-mail investigation that resulted in a lawsuit between two businesses. An investigation of this nature requires examining only e-mail messages, not a complete disk forensics analysis.

Mr. Jones at Company A claims to have received an order for $200,000 in widgets from the purchasing manager, Mr. Smith, at Company B. Company A manufactures the widgets and notifies Company B that they're ready for shipment. Mr. Smith at Company B replies that they didn't order any widgets and won't pay for them. Company A locates an e-mail requesting the widgets that appears to be from Mr. Smith and informs Company B about the e-mail. Company B tells Company A that the e-mail didn't originate from its e-mail server, and it won't pay for the widgets.

Company A files a lawsuit against Company B based on the widget order in Mr. Smith's e-mail. The lawyers for Company A contact the lawyers for Company B and discuss the lawsuit. Company A's lawyers make discovery demands to conduct a digital forensics analysis on Mr. Smith's computer in hopes of finding the original message that caused the problem. At the same time, Company B's lawyers demand discovery on Mr. Jones's computer because they believe the e-mail is a fake.

As a digital investigator, you receive a call from your boss asking you to fulfill the discovery demands from Company B's lawyers to locate and determine whether the e-mail message on Mr. Jones's computer is real or fake. Because it's an e-mail investigation, not a major crime involving computers, you're dispatched to Company A. When you get there, you find Mr. Jones's computer powered on and running Microsoft Outlook. The discovery order authorizes you to recover only Mr. Jones's Outlook e-mail folder, the .pst file. You aren't authorized to do anything else. You would take the following steps in this situation:

1. Close the Outlook program on Mr. Jones's computer.

2. Use Windows Explorer to locate the Outlook .pst file containing his business e-mail. You might need to use the Windows Search feature to find files with the .pst extension.

3. Determine how large the .pst file is and connect the appropriate media device, such as an external USB drive, to Mr. Jones's computer.

4. Copy the .pst file to your external USB drive, and then remove the USB drive.

5. Fill out your evidence form, stating where on Mr. Jones's disk you located the .pst file, along with the date and time you performed this task.

6. Leave Company A and return to your computer forensics lab. Place the USB drive in your evidence safe.

For most civil investigations, you collect only specific items that have been determined germane by lawyers or the Human Resources Department.

Another activity common in the corporate environment is **covert surveillance** of employees who are abusing their computing and network privileges. The use of covert surveillance of employees must be well defined in company policy before it can be carried out. If a company doesn't have a policy that informs employees they have no privacy rights when using company computers and digital devices, no surveillance can be conducted without exposing the company to civil or even criminal liability. If no policy exists, the company must create a policy and notify all employees about the new rules. Your legal department should create policy language appropriate for your state or country and define the rights and authority the company has in conducting surveillance of employees according to provincial, state, or country privacy laws.

For covert surveillance, you set up monitoring tools that record a suspect's activity in real time. Real-time surveillance requires **sniffing** data transmissions between a suspect's computer and a network server. Sniffing software, such as Wireshark, allows network administrators and others to determine what data is being transmitted over the network. Other data-collecting tools (called keylogger programs—Spector and TrueActive Sofware, for example) are screen capture programs that collect most or all screens and keystrokes on a suspect's computer. Most of these tools run on Windows and usually collect data through remote network connections. The tools are hidden or disguised as other programs in Windows Task Manager and process logs.

Another covert surveillance product is Guidance Software EnCase Enterprise Edition (EEE), which is a centrally located server with specialized software that can activate servlets over a network to remote workstations. Digital investigators can perform forensics examinations in real time through this remote connection to a suspect's computer.

Sample Criminal Investigation

Crime scenes involving computers range from fraud cases to homicides. Because high-quality printers are now available, one of the most common computer-related crimes is check fraud. Many check fraud cases also involve making and selling false ID cards, such as driver's licenses.

In one case, the police received a tip that a check-forging operation was active in an apartment building. After the detective contacted a reliable informant, he had enough information for a search warrant and asked the patrol division to assist him in serving the warrant. When the detective entered the suspect's apartment and conducted a preliminary search, he found a network of six high-end workstations with cables connected to devices in the adjacent apartment through a hole in the wall (see Figure 4-7). Unfortunately, the warrant specified a search of only one apartment.

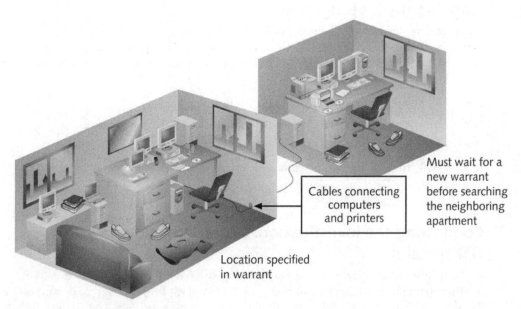

Cables connecting computers and printers

Must wait for a new warrant before searching the neighboring apartment

Location specified in warrant

Figure 4-7   Search warrant limits
© 2016 Cengage Learning®

The detective contacted the deputy prosecutor, who instructed him to stand guard at both apartments until she could have a judge issue an additional warrant for the neighboring apartment. When he received the second search warrant, the detective entered the adjoining apartment and continued his search, finding more computers, high-quality color laser printers, checks, and stolen blank driver's licenses. The outcome of the investigation revealed that the perpetrators were three enterprising high school students who were selling fake IDs to fellow students. The check fraud scheme was a new sideline they were developing to improve their cash flow.

Reviewing Background Information for a Case

Throughout this book, you're using data files from the hypothetical M57 Patents case. These files have been made available through a National Science Foundation (NSF) grant for digital forensics students that makes full images of drives (with Microsoft proprietary information redacted) available on bit-torrent sites for download. In this case, a new startup company, M57 Patents, was in business for about a month, doing art patent searches. Later, a computer sold on Craigslist was discovered to contain "kitty" porn. It was traced back to M57 Patents, and an employee is suspected of downloading the porn.

For more details of the case, go to *http://digitalcorpora.org/corpora/scenarios/m57-patents-scenario*, scroll down to the Exercise slides section, and read the PowerPoint slides.

Planning the Investigation

To determine what has happened, you need some background information on the case. The main players are the CEO, Pat McGoo; the IT person, Terry; and the patent researchers, Jo and Charlie. The police seized the digital evidence at the scene and made forensic copies of the following evidence:

- The image of the computer sold on Craigslist
- The images of five other machines found at the M57 Patents office
- The images of four USB drives found at M57 Patents
- RAM from the imaged machines
- Network data from the M57 Patents servers

Conducting the Investigation: Acquiring Evidence with OSForensics

In the following activity, you use OSForensics to analyze an image file. In Chapters 1 and 3, you learned how to acquire an image of a drive with ProDiscover Basic and other tools. To prepare OSForensics for analyzing the image of a suspect USB drive, follow these steps:

1. If you haven't downloaded the M57 files yet, start a Web browser and go to **http://digitalcorpora.org/corpora/scenarios/m57-patents-scenario**. Scroll down, click the **USB Drive Images** link, and download all four images to your work folder. Next, create a subfolder of your work folder called **InChap** (so the path is *Work*\Chap04\InChap).

2. Start OSForensics. If prompted to allow the program to make changes to your computer, click **OK** or **Yes**. In the OSForensics message box, click **Continue Using Free Version**.

3. Click **Start** in the left pane, if necessary. In the right pane, click **Create Case**.

4. In the New Case dialog box, enter your name. For the case name, type **M57 - USB drives**. Fill in the contact details and the organization, and then click **Investigate Disk(s) from Another Machine**.

5. Click **Custom Location** for the case folder. Click the **Browse** button on the lower right, navigate to and click your **Work\Chap04\InChap** folder, and then click **OK** twice. You should see the Manage Case window (see Figure 4-8).

Figure 4-8   The Manage Case window
Source: PassMark Software, *www.osforensics.com*

6. Click the **Add Device** button to open the Select device to add dialog box, and then click the **Image File** option button. Click the browse button, navigate to your work folder where you copied the USB drive images, click **charlie-work-usb-2009-12-11.E01**, and click **Open**.

7. In the message box asking which partition to use, leave the default setting **use entire image file**, and then click **OK**. The completed "Select device to add" dialog box should be similar to Figure 4-9. Click **OK**.

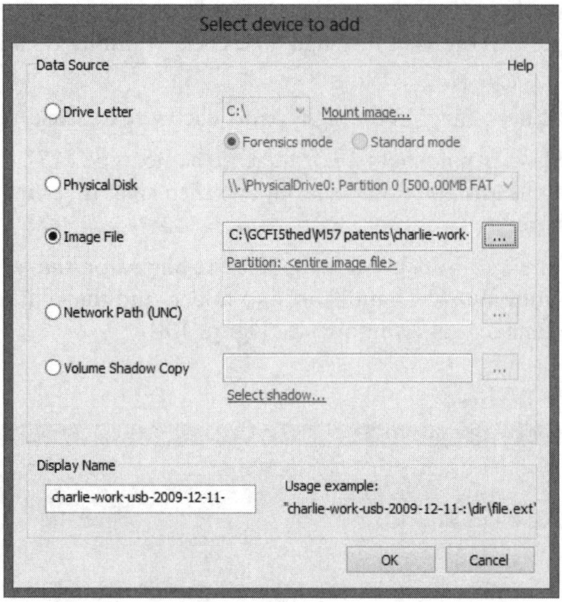

Figure 4-9 The "Select device to add" dialog box
Source: PassMark Software, *www.osforensics.com*

8. Click the `charlie-work-usb-2009-12-11.E01` filename in the bottom pane on the right, and then click the **Open** button to the left to open the File System Browser window shown in Figure 4-10. Although viewing the files on a USB drive in this window is fairly easy, tools to search for specific files are available. Close the window.

9. Click the **File Name Search** button in the left pane of the main window. Type **charlie*** in the Search String text box. Verify that the Start Folder specifies Charlie's USB image file. On the far right, click the **Search** button. The results should be similar to Figure 4-11. You can use the tabs at the top of the search results to see thumbnails of files and the timeline for files on the device.

10. Next, click the **Create Index** button in the left pane to start the Create Index Wizard. In the Step 1 of 5 window, click the **Pre-determined File Types** option button, if necessary. Click all the file types listed (see Figure 4-12), and then click **Next**.

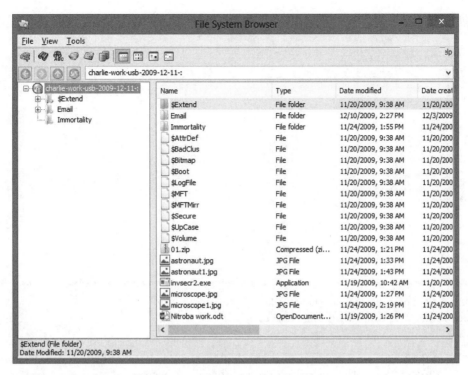

Figure 4-10 The File System Browser window
Source: PassMark Software, *www.osforensics.com*

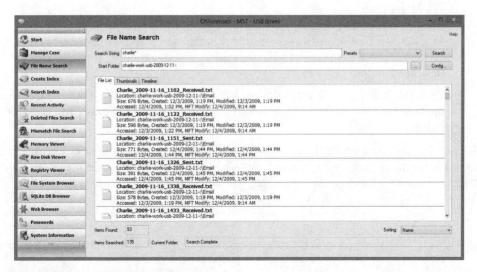

Figure 4-11 The File Name Search window
Source: PassMark Software, *www.osforensics.com*

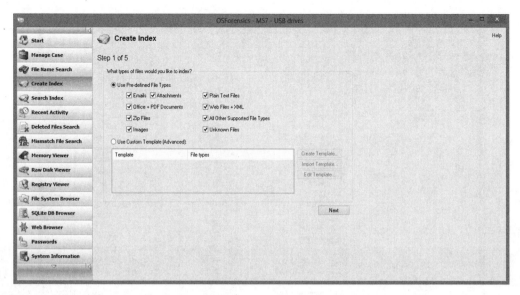

Figure 4-12 Specifying the file types to index
Source: PassMark Software, *www.osforensics.com*

11. In the Step 2 of 5 window, click the **Add** button, click the `charlie-work-usb-2009-12-11.E01` file, click **OK**, and then click **Next**.

12. In the Step 3 of 5 window, type **Index all file types** in the Index Title text box, and then click **Start Indexing**. The Step 4 of 5 window flashes by quickly, and then the Step 5 of 5 window shows the files processing. When the indexing is finished, click **OK** in the message box informing you that some errors might have occurred in the indexing process.

13. Click the **Open Log** button at the lower right of the Step 5 of 5 window. The window that opens shows you the files that were indexed, any errors that occurred, and a summary of what was done. After examining the summary, close the window.

14. Click the **Manage Case** button in the left pane. Notice that the index is now listed in the bottom pane on the right. Scroll to the bottom of the left pane, and click the **Exit** button.

This activity has given you a chance to see how indexing is done in the OSForensics tool you use throughout the book. You should now be able to create a case, add it to your inventory, scan the files, and perform indexing, which will be useful later for searching.

Chapter Summary

- Digital evidence is anything stored or transmitted on electronic or optical media. It's extremely fragile and easily altered.

- In the private sector, an incident scene is often a place of work, such as a contained office or manufacturing area. Because everything from the computers used to violate a company policy to the surrounding facility is under a controlled authority, investigating and controlling the scene are easier than at a crime scene.

- Companies should publish policies stating that they reserve the right to inspect digital assets at will; otherwise, employees' expectation of privacy prevents an employer from legally conducting an intrusive investigation or covert surveillance. A well-defined company policy states that an employer has the right to examine, inspect, or access any company-owned digital asset.

- Approved procedures must be followed, even in private-sector investigations, because civil cases can easily become criminal cases. If an internal corporate case is turned over to law enforcement because of criminal activity, the corporate investigator must avoid becoming an agent of law enforcement.

- Criminal cases require a correctly executed and well-defined search warrant. A specific crime and location must be spelled out in the warrant. For all criminal investigations in the United States, the Fourth Amendment specifies that a law enforcement officer can search for and seize criminal evidence only with probable cause, which is facts or circumstances that lead a reasonable person to believe a crime has been committed or is about to be committed.

- The plain view doctrine applies when investigators find evidentiary items that aren't specified in a warrant or under probable cause.

- When preparing for a case, describe the nature of the case, identify the type of OS, determine whether you can seize the computer or digital device, and obtain a description of the location.

- If you deal with situations involving hazardous materials often, you might need to get HAZMAT certification or have someone else with this certification collect the evidence.

- Always take pictures or use a video camera to document the scene. Prevent professional curiosity from contaminating evidence by limiting who enters the scene.

- As you collect digital evidence, guard against physically destroying or contaminating it. Take precautions to prevent static electricity discharge to electronic devices. If possible, bag or box digital evidence and any hardware you collect from the scene. As you collect hardware, sketch the equipment, including exact markings of where components are located. Tag and number each cable, port, and other connection and record its number and description in a log.

- Selecting a medium for storing digital evidence usually depends on how long you need to keep the evidence. The ideal storage media are CDs, DVD-Rs, DVD-RWs, or offsite storage. You can also use magnetic tape, such as 4-mm DAT and DLT magnetic tapes.

- Forensic hash values are used to verify that data or storage media haven't been altered. The two most common hashing algorithms for forensics purposes are currently MD5 and SHA-1. A forensic hash can't be predicted, each file produces a unique hash value, and if the file changes, the hash value must change.

- To analyze digital forensics data, learn to use more than one vendor tool. Vendors offer different methods for recovering data from digital media.

- You must handle all evidence the same way every time you handle it. Apply the same security and accountability controls for evidence in a civil lawsuit as for evidence from a crime scene to comply with state or federal rules of evidence.

- After you determine that an incident scene has digital data or devices, identify the information or artifacts that can be used as evidence. Next, catalog or document the evidence you find. Your goal is to preserve evidence integrity, which means you must not modify the evidence as you collect and catalog it. An incident scene should be photographed and sketched, and then each item labeled and put in an evidence bag. Collect, preserve, document, analyze, identify, and organize the evidence. Then rebuild evidence or repeat a situation to verify that you get the same results every time.

Key Terms

Automated Fingerprint Identification System (AFIS) A computerized system for identifying fingerprints that's connected to a central database; used to identify criminal suspects and review thousands of fingerprint samples at high speed.

computer-generated records Data generated by a computer, such as system log files or proxy server logs.

computer-stored records Digital files generated by a person, such as electronic spreadsheets.

covert surveillance Observing people or places without being detected, often using electronic equipment, such as video cameras or key stroke/screen capture programs.

Cyclic Redundancy Check (CRC) A mathematical algorithm that translates a file into a unique hexadecimal value.

digital evidence Evidence consisting of information stored or transmitted in electronic form.

extensive-response field kit A portable kit designed to process several computers and a variety of operating systems at a crime or incident scene involving computers. This kit should contain two or more types of software or hardware computer forensics tools, such as extra storage drives.

hash value A unique hexadecimal value that identifies a file or drive.

hazardous materials (HAZMAT) Chemical, biological, or radiological substances that can cause harm to people.

initial-response field kit A portable kit containing only the minimum tools needed to perform disk acquisitions and preliminary forensics analysis in the field.

innocent information Data that doesn't contribute to evidence of a crime or violation.

keyed hash set A value created by an encryption utility's secret key.

limiting phrase Wording in a search warrant that limits the scope of a search for evidence.

low-level investigations Corporate cases that require less investigative effort than a major criminal case.

Message Digest 5 (MD5) An algorithm that produces a hexadecimal value of a file or storage media. Used to determine whether data has been changed.

National Institute of Standards and Technology (NIST) One of the governing bodies responsible for setting standards for some U.S. industries.

nonkeyed hash set A unique hash number generated by a software tool and used to identify files.

person of interest Someone who might be a suspect or someone with additional knowledge that can provide enough evidence of probable cause for a search warrant or arrest.

plain view doctrine When conducting a search and seizure, objects in plain view of a law enforcement officer, who has the right to be in position to have that view, are subject to seizure without a warrant and can be introduced as evidence. As applied to executing searches of computers, the plain view doctrine's limitations are less clear.

probable cause The standard specifying whether a police officer has the right to make an arrest, conduct a personal or property search, or obtain a warrant for arrest.

professional curiosity The motivation for law enforcement and other professional personnel to examine an incident or crime scene to see what happened.

Scientific Working Group on Digital Evidence (SWGDE) A group that sets standards for recovering, preserving, and examining digital evidence.

Secure Hash Algorithm version 1 (SHA-1) A forensic hashing algorithm created by NIST to determine whether data in a file or on storage media has been altered.

sniffing Detecting data transmissions to and from a suspect's computer and a network server to determine the type of data being transmitted over a network.

Review Questions

1. Corporate investigations are typically easier than law enforcement investigations for which of the following reasons?

    a. Most companies keep inventory databases of all hardware and software used.

    b. The investigator doesn't have to get a warrant.

    c. The investigator has to get a warrant.

    d. Users can load whatever they want on their machines.

2. In the United States, if a company publishes a policy stating that it reserves the right to inspect computing assets at will, a corporate investigator can conduct covert surveillance on an employee with little cause. True or False?

3. If you discover a criminal act, such as murder or child pornography, while investigating a corporate policy abuse, the case becomes a criminal investigation and should be referred to law enforcement. True or False?

4. As a corporate investigator, you can become an agent of law enforcement when which of the following happens? (Choose all that apply.)

    a. You begin to take orders from a police detective without a warrant or subpoena.

    b. Your internal investigation has concluded, and you have filed a criminal complaint and turned over the evidence to law enforcement.

    c. Your internal investigation begins.

    d. None of the above.

5. The plain view doctrine in computer searches is well-established law. True or False?

6. If a suspect computer is found in an area that might have toxic chemicals, you must do which of the following? (Choose all that apply.)

    a. Coordinate with the HAZMAT team.

    b. Determine a way to obtain the suspect computer.

    c. Assume the suspect computer is contaminated.

    d. Do not enter alone.

7. What are the three rules for a forensic hash?

8. In forensic hashes, a collision occurs when _____.

9. List three items that should be in an initial-response field kit.

10. When you arrive at the scene, why should you extract only those items you need to acquire evidence?

11. Computer peripherals or attachments can contain DNA evidence. True or False?

12. If a suspect computer is running Windows 7, which of the following can you perform safely?

    a. Browsing open applications

    b. Disconnecting power

    c. Either of the above

    d. None of the above

13. Describe what should be videotaped or sketched at a digital crime scene.

14. Which of the following techniques might be used in covert surveillance? (Choose all that apply.)

    a. Keylogging

    b. Data sniffing

    c. Network logs

15. Commingling evidence means what in a corporate setting?

16. List two hashing algorithms commonly used for forensic purposes.

17. Small companies rarely need investigators. True or False?

18. If a company doesn't distribute a computing use policy stating an employer's right to inspect employees' computers freely, including e-mail and Web use, employees have an expectation of privacy. True or False?

19. You have been called to the scene of a fatal car crash where a laptop computer is still running. What type of field kit should you take with you?

20. You should always answer questions from onlookers at a crime scene. True or False?

Hands-On Projects

Create a *Work\Chap04\Projects* folder on your system before starting these projects. If you haven't downloaded the drive images for the M57 Patents case, go to *http://digitalcorpora. org/corpora/scenarios/m57-patents-scenario* and do so now. In addition, download all files under the heading "Detective reports, warrant and affidavit."

Hands-On Project 4-1

Read the four detective reports and the combined affidavit and warrant. Write a one- to two-page paper describing the evidence the police found and explaining whether they had enough information for the search warrant. Did the information justify taking all the computers and USB drives? Why or why not?

Hands-On Project 4-2

You're investigating an internal policy violation when you find an e-mail about a serious assault for which a police report needs to be filed. What should you do? Write a two-page paper specifying who in your company you need to talk to first and what evidence must be turned over to the police.

Hands-On Project 4-3

This chapter introduced the M57 Patents case, which is a hypothetical case created for new investigators to practice on real data. In this project, you examine the USB drive of Terry, the IT person. Your job is to ascertain whether Terry is involved in anything illicit or against company policy.

1. Start OSForensics. If prompted to allow the program to make changes to your computer, click **OK** or **Yes**. In the OSForensics message box, click **Continue Using Free Version**.

2. Click **Start** in the left pane, if necessary. In the right pane, click **Create Case**.

3. In the New Case dialog box, enter your name in the Investigator text box. In the Case Name text box, type **M57 - Terrys USB drive**. Fill in the contact details and the organization, and then click **Investigate Disk(s) from Another Machine**.

4. Click **Custom Location** for the case folder. Click the **Browse** button on the lower right, navigate to and click your *Work\Chap04\Projects* folder, and then click **OK** twice. You should see the Manage Case window.

5. Click the **Add Device** button to open the "Select device to add" dialog box, and then click the **Image File** option button. Click the browse button, navigate to the folder you copied images to, and click `terry-work-usb-2009-12-11.E01`. Click **Open**.

6. In the message box asking which partition to use, leave the default setting **use entire image file**, and then click **OK**. Click **OK** to close the "Select device to add" dialog box.

7. Click the `terry-work-usb-2009-12-11.E01` filename at the lower right, and then click the **Open** button to the left to open the File System Browser window.

8. Click the **File Name Search** icon in the File System Browser window or the left pane of the main window. In the Search String text box, type **kitty***. On the far right, click the **Search** button. Notice that the "kitty porn" isn't on his USB drive.

9. Click the **Create Index** button in the left pane. (*Note*: You might have to click New Index if the window is showing the results from the index of Charlie's USB drive.) In the Step 1 of 5 window, click the **Pre-determined File Types** option button, click all the file types listed, and then click **Next**.

10. In the Step 2 of 5 window, click Charlie's USB image and click **Remove** to delete it from the list box, if necessary. Click **Add**, click `terry-work-usb-2009-12-11.E01`, click **OK**, and then click **Next**.

11. In the Step 3 of 5 window, type **Index all file types** in the Index Title text box, and then click **Start Indexing**. When the indexing is finished, which might take up to an hour, click **OK** in the message box.

12. Click the **Open Log** button at the lower right, and examine the log. Notice whether any errors were reported and the number of files processed, and then close the log.

13. Click the **Manage Case** button in the left pane. In the lower right pane, double-click **Terrys USB** under the Devices heading, open any text or picture files, and examine them.

14. Scroll to the bottom of the left pane, and click the **Exit** button. Write a one- to two-page paper explaining the importance of the files you examined. How might they affect a patent case?

Hands-On Project 4-4

In this project, you create a file on a USB drive and calculate its hash value in FTK Imager. Then you change the file and calculate the hash value again to compare the files. You need a Windows computer and a USB drive.

1. Create a folder called **C4Prj04** on your USB drive, and then start Notepad.

2. In a new text file, type **This is a test of hash values. One definition of a forensic hash is that if the file changes, the hash value changes.**

3. Save the file as `hash1.txt` in the C4Prj04 folder on your USB drive, and then exit Notepad.

4. Start FTK Imager (clicking **OK** or **Yes** in the UAC message box, if necessary), and click **File, Add Evidence Item** from the menu. In the Select Source dialog box, click the **Logical Drive** option button, and then click **Next**.

5. In the Select Drive dialog box, click the **Source Drive Selection** list arrow, click to select your USB drive, and then click **Finish**.

6. In the upper-left pane, click to expand your USB drive and continue expanding until you can click the C4Prj04 folder. In the upper-right pane, you should see the hash1.txt file you created.

7. Right-click the file and click **Export File Hash List**. Save the file as **original hash** in the C4Prj04 folder on your USB drive. FTK Imager saves it as a .csv file. Exit FTK Imager, and start Notepad.

8. Open **hash1.txt** in Notepad. Add one letter to the end of the file, save it, and exit Notepad.

9. Start FTK Imager again. Repeat Steps 4 to 7 (but without starting Notepad), but this time when you export the file hash list, save the file as **changed hash**.

10. Open the **original hash** and **changed hash** files on your USB drive in Excel (or another spreadsheet program). Compare the hash values in both files to see whether they are different, and then exit Excel.

Hands-On Project 4-5

In this project, you create a file on your USB drive and calculate its hash values in FTK Imager. Then you change the filename and extension and calculate the hash values again to compare them. You need a Windows computer and a USB drive.

1. Create a folder called **C4Prj05** on your USB drive, and then start Notepad.

2. In a new text file, type **This project shows that the file, not the filename, has to change for the hash value to change.**

3. Click **File, Save As** from the menu, and save the file as **testhash.txt** in the C4Prj05 folder on your USB drive. Exit Notepad, and start FTK Imager (clicking **OK** or **Yes** in the UAC message box, if necessary).

4. Click **File, Add Evidence Item** from the menu. In the Select Source dialog box, click the **Logical Drive** option button, and then click **Next**.

5. In the Select Drive dialog box, click the **Source Drive Selection** list arrow, click to select your USB drive, and then click **Finish**.

6. In the upper-left pane, click to expand your USB drive and continue expanding until you can click the C4Prj05 folder. In the upper-right pane, you should see the testhash.txt file you created.

7. Right-click the file and click **Export File Hash List**. Save the file as **original hash value** in the C4Prj05 folder on your USB drive. FTK Imager saves it as a .csv file.

8. Click to select your USB drive in the upper-left pane, if necessary, and then click **File, Remove Evidence Item** from the menu. Exit FTK Imager.

9. Open Windows Explorer. Right-click the `testhash.txt` file on your USB drive, and rename it as `testhash.doc`. In the warning message about the change in extension, click **Yes**.

10. Start FTK Imager. Follow Steps 4 to 7, but this time when you export the file hash list, save the file as `changed hash value`. Exit FTK Imager.

11. Open `original hash value` and `changed hash value` in Excel (or another spreadsheet program). Compare the hash values in both files to see whether they are different, and then exit Excel.

Case Projects

CASE PROJECTS

Case Project 4-1

You're a detective for the local police. Thomas Brown, the primary suspect in a murder investigation, works at a large local firm and is reported to have two computers at work in addition to one at home. What do you need to do to gather evidence from these computers, and what obstacles can you expect to encounter during this process? Write a two- to three-page report stating what you would do if the company had its own Computer Forensics and Investigations Department and what you would do if the company did not.

Case Project 4-2

A murder in a downtown office building has been widely publicized. You're a police detective and receive a phone call from a digital forensics investigator employed by the police department. His name is Gary Owens, and he says he has information that might relate to the murder case. Gary says he ran across a few files while investigating another case at a company in the same office building. Considering the plain view doctrine, what procedures might you and he, as public officials, have to follow? Write a one-page paper detailing what you might do.

Case Project 4-3

Your spouse works at a middle school and reports rumors of a teacher, Zane Wilkens, molesting some students and taking illicit pictures of them. Zane allegedly viewed these pictures in his office. Your spouse wants you to take a disk image of Zane's computer and find out whether the rumors are true. Write a one- to two-page paper outlining how you would tell your spouse and school administrators to proceed. Also, explain why walking into Zane's office to acquire a disk image wouldn't preserve the integrity of the evidence.

Case Project 4-4

As a digital investigator for your local sheriff's department, you have been asked to go with a detective to a local school that received a bomb threat in an anonymous e-mail. The detective already has information from a subpoena sent to the last known ISP where the anonymous e-mail originated, and the message was sent from a residence in the school's neighborhood. The detective tells you the school principal also stated that the school's Web server had been defaced by an unknown computer attacker. The detective has just obtained a warrant for the search and seizure of a computer at the residence the ISP identified. Prepare a list of what items should be included in an initial-response field kit to ensure the preservation of digital evidence when the warrant is carried out.

4

Working with Windows and CLI Systems

After reading this chapter and completing the exercises, you will be able to:

- Explain the purpose and structure of file systems
- Describe Microsoft file structures
- Explain the structure of NTFS disks
- List some options for decrypting drives encrypted with whole disk encryption
- Explain how the Windows Registry works
- Describe Microsoft startup tasks
- Explain the purpose of a virtual machine

This chapter and Chapter 7 give you an overview of digital data and drives. In this chapter, you review how data is stored and managed in Microsoft OSs, including Windows and command-line interface (CLI) OSs. To become proficient in recovering data for digital investigations, you should understand file systems and their OSs, including legacy (MS-DOS, Windows 9x, and Windows Me, for example) and current OSs. In this chapter, you examine the tasks an OS performs when it starts so that you can avoid altering evidence when you examine data on a drive. You also learn how to use a Virtual PC environment to further analyze Windows digital evidence. Chapter 7 discusses Linux and Macintosh file systems and covers hardware devices, such as CDs/DVDs, CD/DVD-RWs, and SCSI, IDE, and SATA drives.

Understanding File Systems

To investigate digital evidence effectively, you must understand how the most commonly used OSs work and how they store files. In addition to this section on file systems, you should review books on Computer Technology Industry Association (CompTIA) A+ certifications in hardware and firmware startup tasks and operations.

A **file system** gives an OS a road map to data on a disk. The type of file system an OS uses determines how data is stored on the disk. When you need to access a suspect's computer to acquire or inspect data related to your investigation, you should be familiar with both the computer's OS and file system so that you can access and modify system settings when necessary. This chapter examines Windows and CLI OSs in detail; Chapter 7 covers information on Linux and Macintosh. For other OSs, consult system administrators and vendor manuals.

Understanding the Boot Sequence

This section explains the boot sequence for desktop and laptop computers. For tablets and smartphones, it's best to review vendors' documentation. To ensure that you don't contaminate or alter data on a suspect's system, you must know how to access and modify Complementary Metal Oxide Semiconductor (CMOS), BIOS, Extensible Firmware Interface (EFI), and Unified Extensible Firmware Interface (UEFI) settings. A computer stores system configuration and date and time information in the CMOS when power to the system is off. The system BIOS or EFI contains programs that perform input and output at the hardware level. BIOS is designed for x86 computers and typically used on disk drives with Master Boot Records (MBR). EFI is designed for x64 computers and uses GUID Partition Table (GPT)-formatted disks. BIOS and EFI are designed for specific firmware. In an effort to reduce the relationship with firmware, Intel developed UEFI, which defines the interface between a computer's firmware and the OS. (For more information on Windows boot processes, see *Windows 8 Administration*, by William R. Stanek, Microsoft Press 2012.)

 The following paragraph describes how a BIOS boot works. For more information on the differences in these boot utilities, see *www.cs.rutgers.edu/~pxk/416/notes/02-boot.html*.

When a subject's computer starts, you must make sure it boots to a forensically configured CD, DVD, or flash drive, as described in Chapters 1 and 3, because booting to the hard disk overwrites and changes evidentiary data. To do this, you access the CMOS setup by monitoring the computer during the **bootstrap process** to identify the correct key or keys to use. The bootstrap process, which is contained in ROM, tells the computer how to proceed. As the computer starts, the screen usually displays the key or keys, such as the Delete key, you press to open the CMOS setup screen. You can also try unhooking the keyboard to force the system to tell you what keys to use. The key you press to access CMOS depends on the computer's BIOS. Many BIOS manufacturers use the Delete key to access CMOS; other manufacturers use Ctrl+Alt+Insert, Ctrl+A, Ctrl+S, or Ctrl+Fl, F2, or F10. A safe method for verifying the BIOS is removing all hard drives from the computer, which enables you to start the computer to verify its BIOS date and time without accessing the disk drive.

Figure 5-1 shows a typical CMOS setup screen, where you check a computer's boot sequence. If necessary, you can change the boot sequence so that the OS accesses the CD/DVD drive, for example, before any other boot device. Each BIOS vendor's screen is different, but you can refer to the vendor's documentation or Web site for instructions on changing the boot sequence.

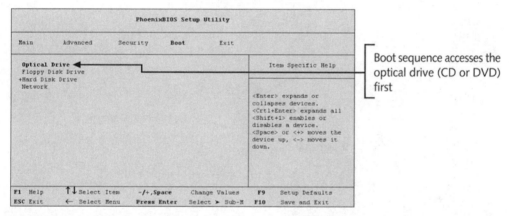

Figure 5-1   A typical CMOS setup screen
Courtesy of Phoenix Technologies, Ltd.

Understanding Disk Drives

You should be familiar with disk drives and how data is organized on a disk so that you can find data effectively. Disk drives are made up of one or more platters coated with magnetic material, and data is stored on platters in a particular way. Following is a list of disk drive components, illustrated in Figure 5-2:

- *Geometry*—**Geometry** refers to a disk's logical structure of platters, tracks, and sectors.
- *Head*—The **head** is the device that reads and writes data to a drive. There are two heads per platter that read and write the top and bottom sides.
- *Tracks*—**Tracks** are concentric circles on a disk platter where data is located.
- *Cylinders*—A **cylinder** is a column of tracks on two or more disk platters. Typically, each platter has two surfaces: top and bottom.
- *Sectors*—A **sector** is a section on a track, usually made up of 512 bytes.

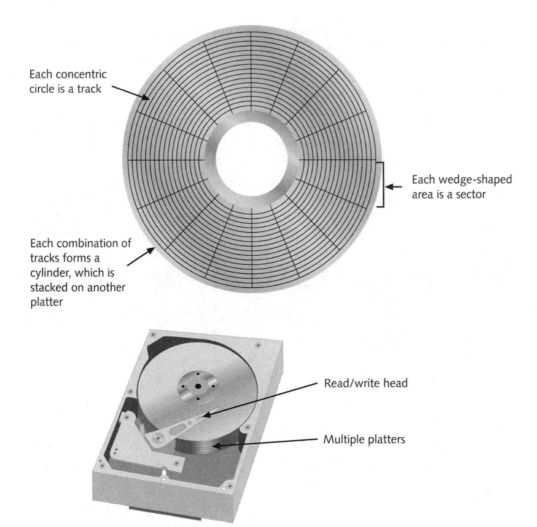

Each concentric circle is a track

Each wedge-shaped area is a sector

Each combination of tracks forms a cylinder, which is stacked on another platter

Read/write head

Multiple platters

Figure 5-2   Components of a disk drive
© Cengage Learning®

For more information on disk drive configurations, see
www.storagereview.com/guide2000/ref/hdd/index.html.

The manufacturer engineers a disk to have a certain number of sectors per track, and a typical disk drive stores 512 bytes per sector. (For Advanced Format disks, 4096 bytes per sector are stored; see *http://msdn.microsoft.com/en-us/library/windows/desktop/hh848035%28v=vs. 85%29.aspx.*) To determine the total number of addressable bytes on a disk, multiply the number of cylinders by the number of heads (actually tracks) and by the number of sectors (groups of 512 or more bytes), as shown in Figure 5-3. Disk drive vendors refer to this formula as a cylinder, head, and sector (CHS) calculation. Tracks also follow a numbering scheme starting from 0, which is the first value in computing. If a disk lists 79 tracks, you actually have 80 tracks from 0 to 79.

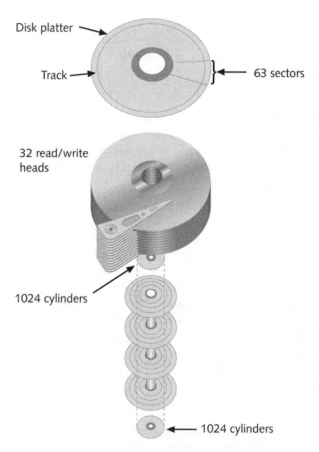

Disk platter

Track

63 sectors

32 read/write
heads

1024 cylinders

1024 cylinders

1024 cylinders × 32 heads × 63 sectors = 2,064,384 sectors

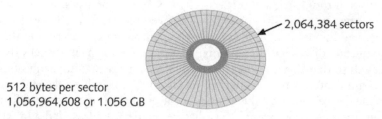

2,064,384 sectors

512 bytes per sector
1,056,964,608 or 1.056 GB

Figure 5-3 CHS calculation
© Cengage Learning®

Other disk properties, such as **zone bit recording (ZBR)**, **track density**, **areal density**, and **head and cylinder skew**, are handled at the drive's hardware or firmware level. ZBR is how most manufacturers deal with a platter's inner tracks having a smaller circumference (and, therefore, less space to store data) than its outer tracks. Grouping tracks by zones ensures that all tracks hold the same amount of data.

Track density is the space between each track. As with old vinyl records, the smaller the space between each track, the more tracks you can place on the platter.

Areal density refers to the number of bits in one square inch of a disk platter. This number includes the unused space between tracks. Head and cylinder skew are used to improve disk performance. As the read-write head moves from one track to another, starting sectors are offset to minimize lag time.

Solid-State Storage Devices

Flash memory storage devices used in USB drives, laptops, tablets, and cell phones can be a challenge for digital forensics examiners because if deleted data isn't recovered immediately, it might be lost forever. The reason is a feature all flash memory devices have: **wear-leveling**.

When data is deleted on a hard drive, only the references to it are removed, which leaves the original data in unallocated disk space. With forensics recovery tools, recovering data from magnetic media is fairly easy by copying the unallocated space. USB drives are different, in that memory cells shift data at the physical level to other cells that have had fewer reads and writes continuously. The purpose of shifting (or rotating) data from one memory cell to another is to make sure all memory cells on the flash drive wear evenly. Memory cells are designed to perform only 10,000 to 100,000 reads/writes, depending on the manufacturer's design. When they reach their defined limits, they can no longer retain data. When you attempt to connect to the device, you get an access failure message. This process is controlled on the flash device's firmware.

In addition, when data is rotated to another memory cell, the old memory cell addresses are listed in a firmware file called a "garbage collector." At some point, the flash drive's firmware erases data in unallocated cells by overwriting the value of 1 in all cells listed in the garbage collector file.

When dealing with solid-state devices, making a full forensic copy as soon as possible is crucial in case you need to recover data from unallocated disk space. You can test this feature with a USB drive easily by copying data to it, deleting it, and then making a forensic acquisition with any acquisition tool, such as ProDiscover or X-Ways Forensics, immediately after the data is deleted. The first acquisition produces recoverable artifacts. If you let the USB drive sit and write no additional data to it, wear-leveling automatically overwrites the unallocated space. All solid-state drives have an internal power source for memory cells (both allocated and unallocated) so that they can preserve data. If you make another acquisition of the USB drive a day or more later, it reveals that the previously recoverable deleted data no longer exists. For mobile device forensics, this feature is extremely important, especially if a suspect deleted relevant messages, for example, just before the device was seized and taken into evidence.

Depending on your jurisdiction and country's laws on search and seizure, there might be some limitations on when an acquisition can take place in criminal cases. For criminal investigations, you should get guidance from your local prosecutor's office on how to handle this type of evidence.

Exploring Microsoft File Structures

Because most PCs use Microsoft software products, you should understand Microsoft file systems so that you know how Windows and DOS computers store files. In particular, you need to understand clusters, File Allocation Table (FAT), and NT File System (NTFS). The method an OS uses to store files determines where data can be hidden. When you examine a computer for forensic evidence, you need to explore these hiding places to determine whether they contain files or parts of files that might be evidence of a crime or policy violation.

In Microsoft file structures, sectors are grouped to form **clusters**, which are storage allocation units of one or more sectors. Clusters range from 512 bytes up to 32,000 bytes each. Combining sectors minimizes the overhead of writing or reading files to a disk. The OS groups one or more sectors into a cluster. The number of sectors in a cluster varies according to the disk size. For example, a double-sided floppy disk has one sector per cluster; a hard disk has four or more sectors per cluster.

Clusters are numbered sequentially, starting at 0 in NTFS and 2 in FAT. The first sector of all disks contains a system area, the boot record, and a file structure database. The OS assigns these cluster numbers, which are referred to as **logical addresses**. These addresses point to relative cluster positions; for example, cluster address 100 is 98 clusters from cluster address 2. Sector numbers, however, are referred to as **physical addresses** because they reside at the hardware or firmware level and go from address 0 (the first sector on the disk) to the last sector on the disk. Clusters and their addresses are specific to a logical disk drive, which is a disk partition.

Disk Partitions

Many hard disks are partitioned, or divided, into two or more sections. A **partition** is a logical drive. Windows OSs can have three primary partitions followed by an extended partition that can contain one or more logical drives. Someone who wants to hide data on a hard disk can create hidden partitions or voids—large unused gaps between partitions on a disk drive. For example, partitions containing unused space can be created between the primary partitions or logical partitions. This unused space between partitions is called the **partition gap**. It's possible to create a partition, add data to it, and then remove references to the partition so that it can be hidden in Windows. If data is hidden in this partition gap, a disk editor utility could be used to access it. Another technique is to hide incriminating digital evidence at the end of a disk by declaring a smaller number of bytes than the actual drive size. With disk-editing tools, however, you can access these hidden or empty areas of the disk.

One way to examine a partition's physical level is to use a disk editor, such as WinHex or Hex Workshop. These tools enable you to view file headers and other critical parts of a file. Both tasks involve analyzing the key hexadecimal codes the OS uses to identify and maintain the file system. Table 5-1 lists the hexadecimal codes in a partition table and identifies some common file system structures.

To understand hexadecimal numbering better, see *www.i-programmer. info/babbages-bag/478-hexadecimal.html*.

TIP

Table 5-1 Hexadecimal codes in the partition table

Hexadecimal code	File system
01	DOS 12-bit FAT (floppy disks)
04	DOS 16-bit FAT for partitions smaller than 32 MB
05	Extended partition
06	DOS 16-bit FAT for partitions larger than 32 MB
07	NTFS and exFAT
08	AIX bootable partition
09	AIX data partition
0B	DOS 32-bit FAT
0C	DOS 32-bit FAT for interrupt 13 support
0F	Extended Partition with Logical Block Address (LBA)
17	Hidden NTFS partition (XP and earlier)
1B	Hidden FAT32 partition
1E	Hidden VFAT partition
3C	Partition Magic recovery partition
66–69	Novell partitions
81	Linux
82	Linux swap partition (can also be associated with Solaris partitions)
83	Linux native file systems (Ext2, Ext3, Ext4, Reiser, Xiafs)
86	FAT16 volume/stripe set (Windows NT)
87	High Performance File System (HPFS) fault-tolerant mirrored partition or NTFS volume/stripe set
A5	FreeBSD and BSD/386
A6	OpenBSD
A9	NetBSD
C7	Typical of a corrupted NTFS volume/stripe set
EB	BeOS

© Cengage Learning®

The partition table is in the **Master Boot Record** (**MBR**), located at sector 0 of the disk drive. In a hexadecimal editor, such as WinHex, you can find the first partition starting at offset 0x1BE. The second partition starts at 0x1CE, the third partition starts at 0x1DE, and the fourth partition starts at 0x1EE (see Figure 5-4).

The file system's hexadecimal code is offset 3 bytes from 0x1BE for the first partition. The sector address of where this partition starts on the drive is offset 8 bytes from 0x1BE. The number of sectors assigned to the partition are offset 12 bytes for position 0x1BE. These offsets are duplicated for any additional partitions created on the disk, as shown in Figure 5-4. For the extended part of the drive, all partitions are logical partitions. In the first logical partition's boot sector, there's a partition table similar to the MBR.

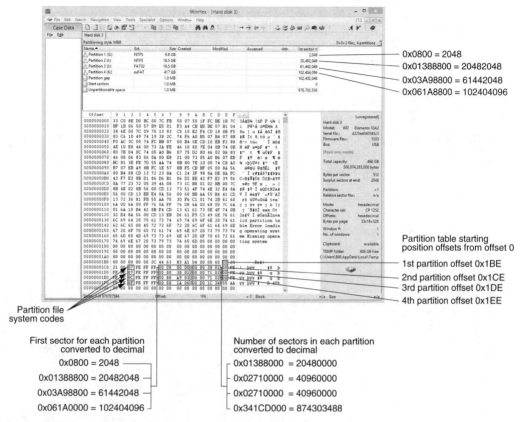

Figure 5-4 The partition table in a hexidecimal editor
Courtesy of X-Ways AG, *www.x-ways.net*

NOTE

Before beginning the following activity, create a *Work*Chap05\
Chapter work folder on your system.

In some instances, you might need to identify the OS on an unknown disk. You can use WinHex or another hexadecimal editor, such as Hex Workshop, for this task. The following steps show you how to determine a disk's OS by using WinHex:

1. Copy WinHex from this book's DVD (or download WinHex at *http://x-ways.net/winhex/index-m.html*) and install it. Check with your instructor about where you should install it on your computer.

2. Insert a USB drive into a USB port.

3. In Windows 8 or later, go to the Start screen, type **WinHex**, and press **Enter**. Right-click the **WinHex** icon and click **Run as administrator**. In older Windows OSs, right-click the **WinHex** desktop icon and click **Run as administrator**, and then click **Continue** or **Yes** in the UAC message box. (In Windows XP or earlier, simply double-click the **WinHex** desktop icon.)

In Windows 8 or later, it's recommended that you create a shortcut in File Explorer for the `WinHex.exe` file, which is usually in the C:\Program Files (x86)\WinHex folder. To start the program, you right-click the WinHex desktop icon and click "Run as administrator."

When starting WinHex in Windows 8, you might get a "Windows Protected your PC" warning message. In this case, click More Info, and then click "Run anyway." When attempting to access a disk drive in WinHex, if you get an error message stating that administrator privileges are missing, click Yes in the Restart WinHex now message box. When restarting WinHex, click Yes in the UAC message box.

4. Click **Tools, Open Disk** from the menu to see a list of logical drives. Click the **C** drive (or your working drive), and click **OK**. Figure 5-5 shows a typical hard disk in the WinHex window. If an error message is displayed, you can ignore it because it won't affect your analysis for this activity.

Indicates the file system

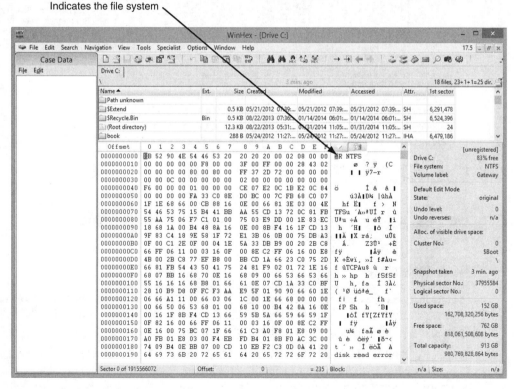

Figure 5-5 WinHex identifying the file system
Courtesy of X-Ways AG, *www.x-ways.net*

The C drive displays ".R.NTFS" if the partition is formatted as an NTFS drive. If it's a FAT drive, it displays MSDOS5.0 or MSWIN4.1 in the first logical sector, which is sector 0 of the partition. Note that the physical drive's sector 0 is the drive's boot sector and is not associated with the partition's sector 0 location.

5. Click **Tools, Open Disk** again, but this time, click your USB drive in the Edit Disk list, and then click **OK**. Compare the file system label for this drive with the one you saw in Step 4. Leave WinHex open for the next activity.

With tools such as WinHex, you can also identify file headers to determine the file types, with or without an extension. Before performing the following steps in WinHex, use File Explorer or My Computer to find a folder on your system containing a bitmap (.bmp) file and a folder containing a Word document (.doc). (In the Hands-On Projects, you apply these techniques to other file types.) Then follow these steps:

1. To open a bitmap file on your computer, click **File, Open** from the WinHex menu (the main menu, not the File item in the Case Data menu). In the Open Files dialog box, navigate to a folder containing a bitmap file, and then double-click the .bmp file. If you get a WinHex evaluation warning message, click **OK** to continue.

2. As shown in Figure 5-6, the WinHex window identifies the file type for the graphic. For .bmp files, it shows "BM6," "BM," or "BMF." As shown in the figure, "42 4D" is also displayed to indicate a BM file signature.

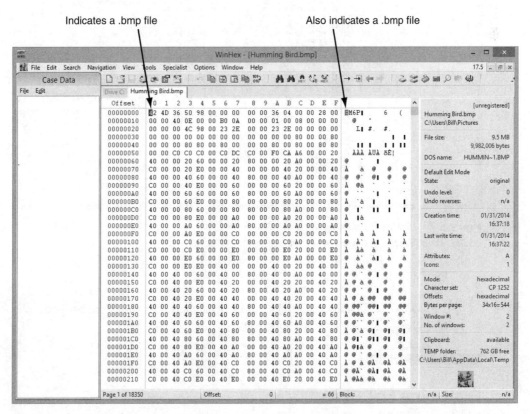

Figure 5-6 WinHex indicating a .bmp file
Courtesy of X-Ways AG, *www.x-ways.net*

3. To open an Office 2003 or later Word document, click **File, Open** from the menu. Navigate to a folder containing a Word document file, and then double-click the .doc file. As shown in Figure 5-7, the first line contains a row of 0s followed by "D0 CF 11

E0 A1 B1 1A E1," which identifies the file as a Microsoft Office (before Office 2007) document. The same file header is displayed for an Excel or a PowerPoint file but doesn't apply to Access databases. For Microsoft Office 2007 and later, the first two characters are "PK" or "OOXML," which represent a compressed file.

Indicates a Microsoft Office 2003 file

Figure 5-7   WinHex indicating a Microsoft Office file
Courtesy of X-Ways AG, *www.x-ways.net*

4. Exit WinHex.

Depending on the hexadecimal editor, hex values can be grouped in sets of two or four digits.

TIP

Examining FAT Disks

File Allocation Table (FAT) is the file structure database that Microsoft designed for floppy disks. It's used to organize files on a disk so that the OS can find the files it needs. Since its development, other OSs, such as Linux and Macintosh, can format, read, and write to FAT storage devices such as USB drives and SD cards. The FAT database is typically written to a disk's outermost track and contains filenames, directory names, date and time stamps, the starting cluster number, and file attributes (archive, hidden, system, and read-only).

There are three current versions of FAT—FAT16, FAT32, and exFAT (used by Xbox game systems)—and three older FAT formats, which are FATX, Virtual FAT (VFAT), and FAT12. The FAT version in Microsoft DOS 6.22 had a limitation of eight characters for filenames and three characters for extensions. The following list summarizes the evolution of FAT versions:

- *FAT12*—This version is used specifically for floppy disks, so it has a limited amount of storage space. It was originally designed for MS-DOS 1.0, the first Microsoft OS, used for floppy disk drives and drives up to 16 MB.

- *FAT16*—To handle larger disks, Microsoft developed FAT16, which is still used on older Microsoft OSs, such as MS-DOS 3.0 through 6.22, Windows 95 (first release), and Windows NT 3.5 and 4.0. FAT16 supports disk partitions with a maximum storage capacity of 4 GB.

- *FAT32*—When disk technology improved and disks larger than 2 GB were developed, Microsoft released FAT32, which can access larger drives.

- *exFAT*—Developed for mobile personal storage devices, such as flash memory devices, secure digital eXtended capacity (SDCX), and memory sticks. The exFAT file system can store very large files, such as digital images, video, and audio files.

- *VFAT*—Developed to handle files with more than eight-character filenames and three-character extensions; introduced with Windows 95. VFAT is an extension of other FAT file systems.

Cluster sizes vary according to the hard disk size and file system. Table 5-2 lists the number of sectors and bytes assigned to a cluster on FAT16 disk according to hard disk size. For FAT32 file systems, cluster sizes are determined by the OS. Clusters can range from 1 sector consisting of 512 bytes to 128 sectors of 64 KB.

Table 5-2 Sectors and bytes per cluster

Drive size	Sectors per cluster	FAT16
8–32 MB	1	512 bytes
32–64 MB	2	1 KB
64–128 MB	4	2 KB
128–256 MB	8	4 KB
256–512 MB	16	8 KB
512–1024 MB	32	16 KB
1024–2048 MB	64	32 KB
2048–4096 MB	128	64 KB

© 2016 Cengage Learning®

Microsoft OSs allocate disk space for files by clusters. This practice results in **drive slack**, composed of the unused space in a cluster between the end of an active file's content and the end of the cluster. Drive slack includes **RAM slack** (found mainly in older Microsoft OSs) and **file slack**. In newer Windows OSs, when data is written to disk, the remaining RAM slack is zeroed out and contains no RAM data.

For example, suppose you create a text document containing 5000 characters—that is, 5000 bytes of data. If you save this file on a FAT16 1.6 GB disk, a Microsoft OS reserves one cluster for it automatically. For a 1.6 GB disk, the OS allocates about 32,000 bytes, or 64 sectors (512 bytes per sector), for your file. The unused space, 27,000 bytes, is the file slack (see Figure 5-8). That is, RAM slack is the portion of the last sector used in the last assigned cluster, and the remaining sectors are referred to as "file slack." The 5000-byte text document uses up 10 sectors, or 5120 bytes, so 120 bytes of a sector aren't used; however, DOS must write in full 512-byte chunks of data (sectors). The data to fill the 120-byte void is pulled from RAM and placed in the area between the end of the file (EOF) and the end of the last sector used by the active file in the cluster. Any information in RAM at that point, such as logon IDs or passwords, is placed in RAM slack on older Microsoft OSs when you save a file. File fragments, deleted e-mails, and passwords are often found in RAM and file slack.

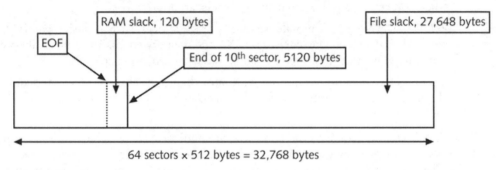

Figure 5-8   File slack space
© Cengage Learning®

An unintentional side effect of FAT16 allowing large clusters was that it reduced fragmentation as cluster size increased. The OS added extra data to the end of the file and allowed the file to expand to this assigned cluster until it consumed the remaining reserved 27,000 bytes. This increased cluster size resulted in inefficient use of disk space. Because of this inefficient allocation of sectors to clusters, when nearly full FAT16 drives were converted to FAT32, users discovered they had a lot of extra free disk space because the files wasted less space.

When you run out of room for an allocated cluster, the OS allocates another cluster for your file. As files grow and require more disk space, assigned clusters are chained together. Typically, chained clusters are contiguous on the disk. However, as some files are created and deleted and other files are expanded, the chain can be broken or fragmented. With a tool such as ProDiscover, you can view the cluster-chaining sequence and see how FAT addresses linking clusters to one another (see Figure 5-9).

When the OS stores data in a FAT file system, it assigns a starting cluster position to a file. Data for the file is written to the first sector of the first assigned cluster. When this first assigned cluster is filled and runs out of room, FAT assigns the next available cluster to the file. If the next available cluster isn't contiguous to the current cluster, the file becomes fragmented. In the FAT for each cluster on the volume (the partitioned disk), the OS writes the

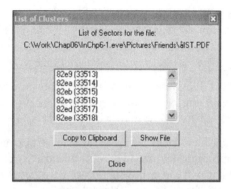

Figure 5-9 Chained sectors associated with clusters as a result of increasing file size
Courtesy of Technology Pathways, LLC

address of the next assigned cluster. Think of clusters as buckets that can hold a specific number of bytes. When a cluster (or bucket) fills up, the OS allocates another cluster to collect the extra data.

On rare occasions, such as a system failure or sabotage, these cluster chains can break. If they do, data can be lost because it's no longer associated with the previous chained cluster. FAT looks forward for the next cluster assignment but doesn't provide pointers to the previous cluster. Rebuilding these broken chains can be difficult.

 Many recent disk forensics tools have automated much of the file-rebuilding process. These improved features make recovering data easier.

Deleting FAT Files When a file is deleted in Windows Explorer or with the MS-DOS `delete` command, the OS inserts a HEX E5 (0xE5) in the filename's first letter position in the associated directory entry. This value tells the OS that the file is no longer available and a new file can be written to the same cluster location.

In the FAT file system, when a file is deleted, the only modifications made are that the directory entry is marked as a deleted file, with the HEX E5 character replacing the first letter of the filename, and the FAT chain for that file is set to 0. The data in the file remains on the disk drive. The area of the disk where the deleted file resides becomes **unallocated disk space** (also called "free disk space"). The unallocated disk space is now available to receive new data from newly created files or other files needing more space as they grow. Most forensics tools can recover data still residing in this area.

Examining NTFS Disks

NT File System (NTFS) was introduced when Microsoft created Windows NT and is still the main file system in Windows 8. Each generation of Windows since NT has included minor changes in NTFS configuration and features. The NTFS design was partially based on, and incorporated many features from, Microsoft's project for IBM with the OS/2 operating system;

in this OS, the file system was **High Performance File System (HPFS)**. When Microsoft created Windows NT, it provided backward-compatibility so that NT could read OS/2 HPFS disk drives. Since the release of Windows 2000, this backward-compatibility is no longer available. For a detailed explanation of NTFS structures, see *www.ntfs.com/ntfs_basics.htm*.

NTFS offers substantial improvements over FAT file systems. It provides more information about a file, including security features, file ownership, and other file attributes. With NTFS, you also have more control over files and folders (directories) than with FAT file systems.

NTFS was Microsoft's move toward a journaling file system. The system keeps track of transactions such as file deleting or saving. This journaling feature is helpful because it records a transaction before the system carries it out. That way, in a power failure or other interruption, the system can complete the transaction or go back to the last good setting.

In NTFS, everything written to the disk is considered a file. On an NTFS disk, the first data set is the **Partition Boot Sector**, which starts at sector [0] of the disk and can expand to 16 sectors. Immediately after the Partition Boot Sector is the **Master File Table (MFT)**. The MFT, similar to FAT in earlier Microsoft OSs, is the first file on the disk. An MFT file is created at the same time a disk partition is formatted as an NTFS volume and usually consumes about 12.5% of the disk when it's created. As data is added, the MFT can expand to take up 50% of the disk. (The MFT is covered in more detail in "NTFS System Files.")

An important advantage of NTFS over FAT is that it results in much less file slack space. Compare the cluster sizes in Table 5-3 with Table 5-2, which showed FAT cluster sizes. Clusters are smaller for smaller disk drives. This feature saves more space on all disks using NTFS.

Table 5-3 Cluster sizes in an NTFS disk

Drive size	Sectors per cluster	Cluster size
7–512 MB	8	4 KB
512 MB–1 GB	8	4 KB
1–2 GB	8	4 KB
2 GB–2 TB	8	4 KB
2–16 TB	8	4 KB
16–32 TB	16	8 KB
32–64 TB	32	16 KB
64–128 TB	64	32 KB
128–256 TB	128	64 KB

© 2016 Cengage Learning®

For more information on Microsoft file system sizes, see *http://support.microsoft.com/kb/140365*.

NTFS (and VFAT for long filenames) also uses **Unicode**, an international data format. Unlike the **American Standard Code for Information Interchange (ASCII)** 8-bit configuration,

Unicode uses an 8-bit, a 16-bit, or a 32-bit configuration. These configurations are known as **UTF-8 (Unicode Transformation Format)**, UTF-16, and UTF-32. For Western-language alphabetic characters, UTF-8 is identical to ASCII (see *www.unicode.org/versions* for more details). Knowing this feature of Unicode comes in handy when you perform keyword searches for evidence on a disk drive. (This feature is discussed in more detail in Chapter 9.) Because NTFS offers many more features than FAT, more utilities are used to manage it.

NTFS System Files

Because everything on an NTFS disk is a file, the first file, the MFT, contains information about all files on the disk, including the system files the OS uses. In the MFT, the first 15 records are reserved for system files. Records in the MFT are referred to as **metadata**. Table 5-4 lists the first 16 metadata records you find in the MFT.

Table 5-4 Metadata records in the MFT

Filename	System file	Record position	Description
$Mft	MFT	0	Base file record for each folder on the NTFS volume; other record positions in the MFT are allocated if more space is needed.
$MftMirr	MFT 2	1	The first four records of the MFT are saved in this position. If a single sector fails in the first MFT, the records can be restored, allowing recovery of the MFT.
$LogFile	Log file	2	Previous transactions are stored here to allow recovery after a system failure in the NTFS volume.
$Volume	Volume	3	Information specific to the volume, such as label and version, is stored here.
$AttrDef	Attribute definitions	4	A table listing attribute names, numbers, and definitions.
$	Root filename index	5	This is the root folder on the NTFS volume.
$Bitmap	Cluster bitmap	6	A map of the NTFS partition shows which clusters are in use and which are available.
$Boot	Boot sector	7	Used to mount the NTFS volume during the bootstrap process; additional code is listed here if it's the boot drive for the system.
$BadClus	Bad cluster file	8	For clusters that have unrecoverable errors, an entry of the cluster location is made in this file.
$Secure	Security file	9	Unique security descriptors for the volume are listed in this file. It's where the access control list (ACL) is maintained for all files and folders on the NTFS volume.
$Upcase	Upcase table	10	Converts all lowercase characters to uppercase Unicode characters for the NTFS volume.
$Extend	NTFS extension file	11	Optional extensions are listed here, such as quotas, object identifiers, and reparse point data.
		12–15	Reserved for future use.

© 2016 Cengage Learning®

MFT and File Attributes

When Microsoft introduced NTFS, the way the OS stores data on disks changed substantially. In the NTFS MFT, all files and folders are stored in separate records of 1024 bytes each. Each record contains file or folder information. This information is divided into record fields containing metadata about the file or folder and the file's data or links to the file's data. A record field is referred to as an **attribute ID**.

File or folder information is typically stored in one of two ways in an MFT record: resident and nonresident. For very small files, about 512 bytes or less, all file metadata and data are stored in the MFT record. These types of records are called resident files because all their information is stored in the MFT record.

Files larger than 512 bytes are stored outside the MFT. The file or folder's MFT record provides cluster addresses where the file is stored on the drive's partition. These cluster addresses are called **data runs**. This type of MFT record is referred to as "nonresident" because the file's data is stored in its own separate file outside the MFT.

Each MFT record starts with a header identifying it as a resident or nonresident attribute. The first 4 bytes (characters) for all MFT records are FILE. The header information contains additional data specifying where the first attribute ID starts, which is typically at offset 0x14 from the beginning of the record. Each attribute ID has a length value in hexadecimal defining where it ends and where the next attribute starts. The length value is located 4 bytes from the attribute ID.

Table 5-5 lists the types of attributes in an MFT record. For more details on how the MFT is configured, search on MFT and NTFS at *http://technet.microsoft.com/en-us/library/cc781134.aspx*.

Table 5-5   Attributes in the MFT

Attribute ID	Purpose
0x10	$Standard Information This field contains data on file creation, alterations, MFT changes, read dates and times, and DOS file permissions.
0x20	$Attribute_List Attributes that don't fit in the MFT (nonresident attributes) are listed here along with their locations.
0x30	$File_Name The long and short names for a file are contained here. Up to 255 Unicode bytes are available for long filenames. For POSIX requirements, additional names or hard links can also be listed. Files with short filenames have only one attribute ID 0x30. Long filenames have two attribute ID 0x30s in the MFT record: one for the short name and one for the long name.
0x40	$Object_ID ($Volume_Version in Windows NT) Ownership and who has access rights to the file or folder are listed here. Every MFT record is assigned a unique GUID. Depending on your NTFS setup, some file records might not contain this attribute ID.
0x50	$Security_Descriptor Contains the access control list (ACL) for the file.

Table 5-5 Attributes in the MFT (*Continued*)

Attribute ID	Purpose
0x60	$Volume_Name The volume-unique file identifier is listed here. Not all files need this unique identifier.
0x70	$Volume_Information This field indicates the version and state of the volume.
0x80	$Data File data for resident files or data runs for nonresident files.
0x90	$Index_Root Implemented for use of folders and indexes.
0xA0	$Index_Allocation Implemented for use of folders and indexes.
0xB0	$Bitmap A bitmap indicating cluster status, such as which clusters are in use and which are available.
0xC0	$Reparse_Point This field is used for volume mount points and Installable File System (IFS) filter drivers. For the IFS, it marks specific files used by drivers.
0xD0	$EA_Information For use with OS/2 HPFS.
0xE0	For use with OS/2 HPFS.
0x100	$Logged_Utility_Stream This field is used by Encrypting File System (EFS) in Windows 2000 and later

© 2016 Cengage Learning®

Figure 5-10 is an MFT record showing the resident attributes of a small file viewed in a hexadecimal editor. Note that on line 035B3530 near the bottom, there's text data in the right pane. In Figure 5-11, the bottom half of the hexadecimal editor window shows the remaining portion of this resident file's MFT record.

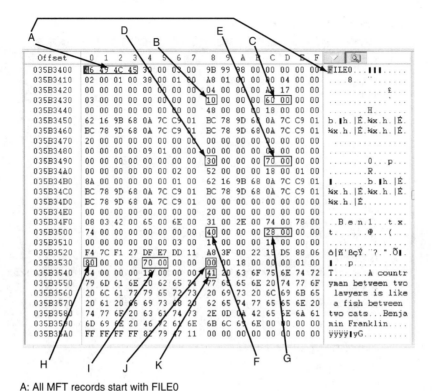

A: All MFT records start with FILE0
B: Start of attribute 0x10
C: Length of attribute 0x10 (value 60)
D: Start of attribute 0x30
E: Length of attribute 0x30 (value 70)
F: Start of attribute 0x40
G: Length of attribute 0x40 (value 28)
H: Start of attribute 0x80
I: Length of attribute 0x80 (value 70)
J: Attribute 0x80 resident flag
K: Starting position of resident data

Figure 5-10   Resident file in an MFT record
Courtesy of X-Ways AG, *www.x-ways.net*

A: Starting position of attribute 0x80 $Data

B: Length of attribute 0x80 in little endian format

C: Interpreted little endian value

```
035B3530  80 00 00 00 70 00 00 00   00 00 18 00 00 00 01 00   I...p...........
035B3540  54 00 00 00 18 00 00 00   41 20 63 6F 75 6E 74 72   T.......A countr
035B3550  79 6D 61 6E 20 62 65 74   77 65 65 6E 20 74 77 6F   yman between two
035B3560  20 6C 61 77 79 65 72 73   [Data Interpreter  X]  6B 65   lawyers is like
035B3570  20 61 20 66 69 73 68 20   [16 Bit (±): 112]      6E 20   a fish between
035B3580  74 77 6F 20 63 61 74 73   E 6A 61   two cats...Benja
035B3590  6D 69 6E 20 46 72 61 6E   6B 6C 69 6E 00 00 00 00   min Franklin....
035B35A0  FF FF FF FF 82 79 47 11   00 00 00 00 00 00 00 00   ÿÿÿÿ‚yG.........
```

Figure 5-11   File data for a resident file
Courtesy of X-Ways AG, *www.x-ways.net*

Figure 5-12 is an example of a nonresident file's hexadecimal view. Notice that on line 35B3D50 near the bottom, there's no text data. This file is a longer version of the file shown in Figure 5-10. Current forensics tools, such as ProDiscover, EnCase, FTK, and X-Ways Forensics, can interpret the MFT from an image file.

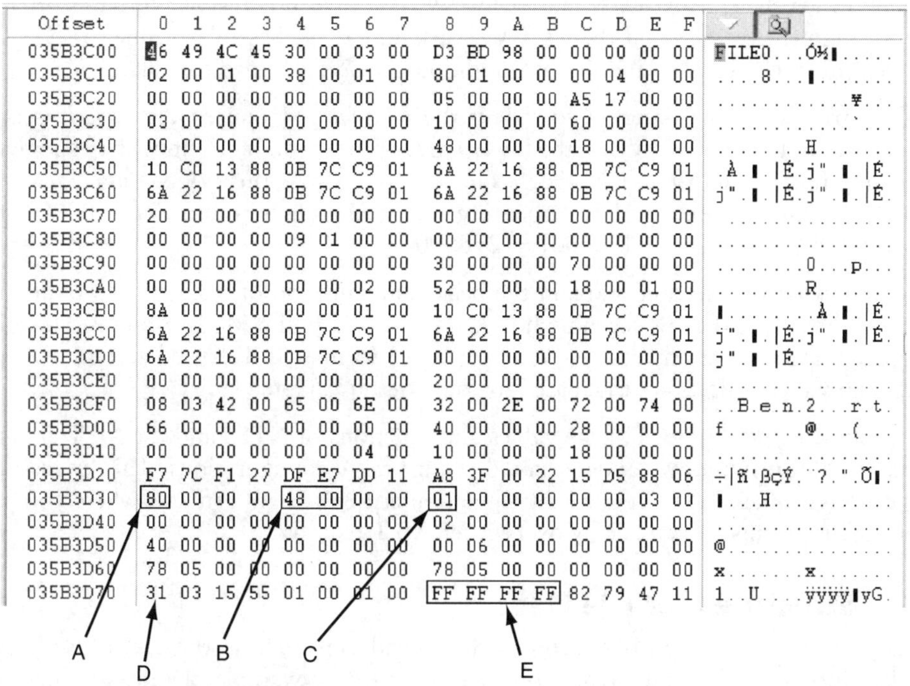

A: Start of nonresident attribute 0x80
B: Length of nonresident attribute 0x80
C: Attribute 0x80 nonresident flag
D: Starting point of data run
E: End-of-record marker (FF FF FF FF) for the MFT record

Figure 5-12   Nonresident file in an MFT record
Courtesy of X-Ways AG, *www.x-ways.net*

To understand how data runs are assigned for nonresident MFT records, you should know that when a disk is created as an NTFS file structure, the OS assigns logical clusters to the entire disk partition. These assigned clusters, called **logical cluster numbers** (LCNs), are sequentially numbered from the beginning of the disk partition, starting with the value 0. LCNs become the addresses that allow the MFT to link to nonresident files (files outside the MFT) on the disk's partition.

When data is first written to nonresident files, an LCN address is assigned to the file in the attribute 0x80 field of the MFT. This LCN becomes the file's **virtual cluster number** (VCN), which is listed as zero: VCN(0). If there's not enough space at VCN(0)'s location because of excessive disk fragmentation another data run is added. More VCNs are added as needed, and each additional VCN is sequentially numbered as VCN(1), VCN(2), and so on until all data is written to the drive.

The value in VCN(0) is the first cluster for the file; this value is the cluster's actual LCN. VCN(1) and other VCNs are the offset of the cluster's number from the previous VCN cluster position in the data run. For example, to determine the next data run location for VCN(0) for a fragmented file, simply add VCN(0)'s LCN value to the next VCN's offset value. So if VCN(0)'s LCN is 10000 and VCN(1) is 120, add VCN(1)'s 120 to VCN(0)'s LCN value of 10000 to get the starting LCN cluster for VCN(1), which is the LCN address 10120. If the file is fragmented more and there's a VCN(2), add VCN(1)'s LCN value to VCN(2)'s LCN value. This process is repeated for any additional VCNs assigned to a file.

VCNs are also signed integers so that if the next largest unused disk space is at a lower address than the previous VCN, the lower value address can be computed by simply adding a negative number to the VCN. For example, if the previous VCN data run is at offset 3000000 and the next available open area to receive data is at LCN 2900000, the VCN is -100000 (3000000 + [-100000] = 2900000).

The following two sections explain the basic configuration of resident and nonresident files managed by the MFT. By learning how data is stored in the MFT, a forensics examiner can manually reconstruct any residual data on NTFS-formatted disk media. You need to understand how these offsets are calculated for activities in Chapter 16.

The following descriptions of the values and functions of NTFS and the MFT aren't exhaustive, and future Windows updates could change these configurations. This discussion should be used as a quick reference for locating and interpreting data artifacts where you might find residual fragments from partially overwritten MFT records.

MFT Structures for File Data

When you're viewing an MFT record with a hexadecimal editor, the data is displayed in little endian format, meaning it's read from right to left. For example, the hexadecimal value 400 is displayed as 00 04 00 00, and the number 0x40000 is displayed as 00 00 04 00.

The first section of an MFT record is the header that defines the size and starting position of the first attribute. Following the header are attributes that are specific for the file type, such as an application file or a data file. MFT records for directories and system files have additional attributes that don't appear in a file MFT record. The following sections explain how data files are configured in the MFT. In Chapter 16, you see how these fields apply to data recovery.

MFT Header Fields For the header of all MFT records, the record fields of interest are as follows:

- *At offset 0x00*—The MFT record identifier FILE; the letter F is at offset 0.
- *At offset 0x1C to 0x1F*—Size of the MFT record; the default is 0x400 (1024) bytes, or two sectors.
- *At offset 0x14*—Length of the header, which indicates where the next attribute starts; it's typically 0x38 bytes.
- *At offset 0x32 and 0x33*—The update sequence array, which stores the last 2 bytes of the first sector of the MFT record. It's used only when MFT data exceeds 512 bytes. The update sequence array is used as a checksum for record integrity validation.

Figure 5-13 shows these fields and their relationships in the MFT record.

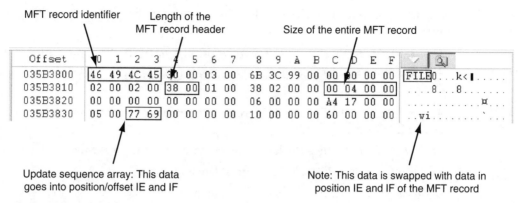

Figure 5-13 An MFT header
Courtesy of X-Ways AG, *www.x-ways.net*

Attribute 0x10: Standard Information Following the MFT header for a data file is the Standard Information attribute, 0x10, which has the following fields (see Figure 5-14):

- *At offset 0x38 from the beginning of the MFT record*—The start of attribute 0x10.

- *At offset 0x04 and 0x05 from the beginning of attribute 0x10*—Size of the 0x10 attribute.

- *At offset 0x18 to 0x1F*—The file's create date and time; all dates and times are stored in the Win32 Filetime format.

- *At offset 0x20 to 0x27*—The last modified date and time for the file.

- *At offset 0x28 to 0x2F*—The last access date and time.

- *At offset 0x30 to 0x2F*—The record access date and time.

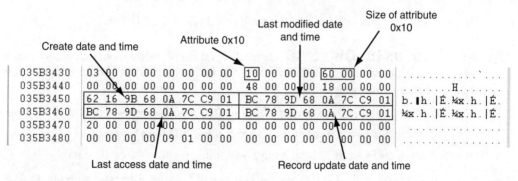

Figure 5-14 Attribute 0x10: Standard Information
Courtesy of X-Ways AG, *www.x-ways.net*

Attribute 0x30: File_Name For files with filenames of eight or fewer characters, the MFT record has only one attribute 0x30. If a filename is longer than eight characters, there are two attribute 0x30s. The following description shows an MFT record with a short and long filename in attribute 0x30. The fields of interest for the short filename attribute 0x30 are as follows:

- *At offset 0x04 and 0x05 from the beginning of attribute 0x30*—The size of attribute 0x30.
- *At offset 0x5A from the 0x30 attribute's starting position*—The short filename; note that it's in Unicode.
- *At offset 0x20 to 0x27*—The file's create date and time; all dates and times are stored in Win32 Filetime format.
- *At offset 0x28 to 0x2F*—The last modified date and time for the file.
- *At offset 0x30 to 0x37*—The last access date and time.
- *At offset 0x38 to 0x3F*—The record update date and time.

The date and time values in attribute 0x30 are usually the same as in attribute 0x10. On occasion, depending how data is copied to a disk and the Windows OS version, these values might differ substantially.

The following are fields of interest for the long filename attribute 0x30:

- *At offset 0x04 and 0x05 from the beginning of attribute 0x30*—The size of attribute 0x30.
- *At offset 0x5A from the 0x30 attribute's starting position*—The long filename; note that it's in Unicode.
- *At offset 0x20 to 0x27*—The file's create date and time; all dates and times are stored in Win32 Filetime format.
- *At offset 0x28 to 0x2F*—The last modified date and time for the file.
- *At offset 0x30 to 0x37*—The last access date and time.
- *At offset 0x38 to 0x3F*—The record update date and time.

Figure 5-15 shows these fields and their relationships in the MFT record.

Attribute 0x40: Object_ID Depending on the Windows version, sometimes attribute 0x40 is listed in the MFT. This attribute contains file ownership and access control information and has the following fields:

- *At offset 0x04 and 0x05 from the beginning of attribute 0x40*—The size of attribute 0x40
- *At offset 0x14*—Starting offset position for GUID data
- *At offset 0x18 to 0x27*—Starting position for GUID Object_ID data

In this example, only the GUID Object_ID is listed. In large enterprise systems, typically additional information is listed, such as the following:

- GUID Birth Volume ID
- GUID Birth Object ID
- GUID Birth Domain ID

Figure 5-16 shows these fields and their relationships in the MFT record.

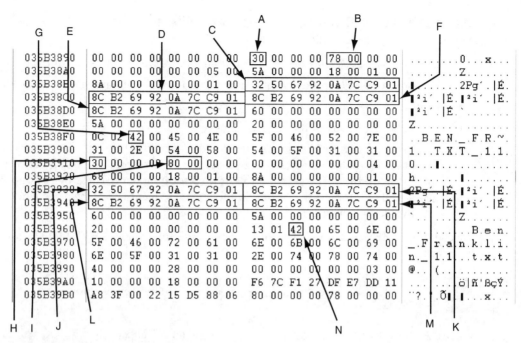

Figure 5-15 Attributes 0x30: short and long filenames
Courtesy of X-Ways AG, *www.x-ways.net*

A: Attribute 0x30 short filename
B: Size of attribute 0x30 short filename
C: Short create date and time
D: Short last modified date and time
E: Short last access date and time
F: Short record update date and time
G: Starting position of short filename
H: Attribute 0x30 long filename
I: Size of attribute 0x30 long filename
J: Long create date and time
K: Long last modified date and time
L: Long last access date and time
M: Long record update date and time
N: Starting position of long filename

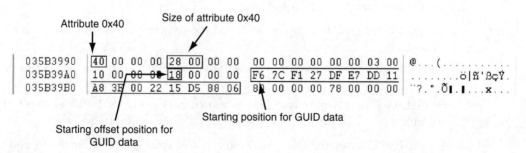

Figure 5-16 Attribute 0x40: Object_ID
Courtesy of X-Ways AG, *www.x-ways.net*

Attribute 0x80: Data for a Resident File

For a resident file's attribute 0x80, the fields of interest are as follows (see Figure 5-17):

- *At offset 0x04 and 0x05 from the beginning of attribute 0x80*—Size of the attribute.
- *At offset 0x08*—The resident/nonresident flag; for resident data, it's set to 0x00.
- *At offset 0x10*—Number of bytes in the data run.
- *At offset 0x18*—Start of the resident data run.
- *At offset 0x1E and 0x1F from the beginning of the MFT header*—The sector checksum value, used to validate the first 512 bytes of the MFT record. The break between the first and second sectors is referred to as the sector boundary. The 2 bytes at positions 0x32 and 0x33 of the MFT header in the update sequence array field are where the actual values for these bytes are stored.

The end of the MFT record is indicated by the hexadecimal values FF FF FF FF at the end of the record.

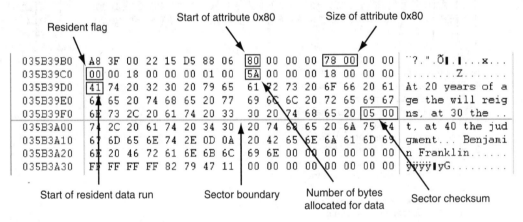

Figure 5-17 Attribute 0x80: Data for a resident file
Courtesy of X-Ways AG, *www.x-ways.net*

Attribute 0x80: Data for a Nonresident File

For a nonresident file, the fields of interest for attribute 0x80 are as follows:

- *At offset 0x04 and 0x05 from the beginning of attribute 0x80*—Size of the attribute.
- *At offset 0x08*—The resident/nonresident flag; for nonresident data, it's set to 0x01.
- *At offset 0x40*—The start of the data run. The first run is the LCN; if the file is fragmented, additional data runs follow, as shown in Figure 5-18. In this example, there are a total of six data runs, which means this file has several fragments.

Following the last data run, the value 0x00 indicates the end of the Data attribute. Figure 5-18 shows these fields and their relationships in the MFT record.

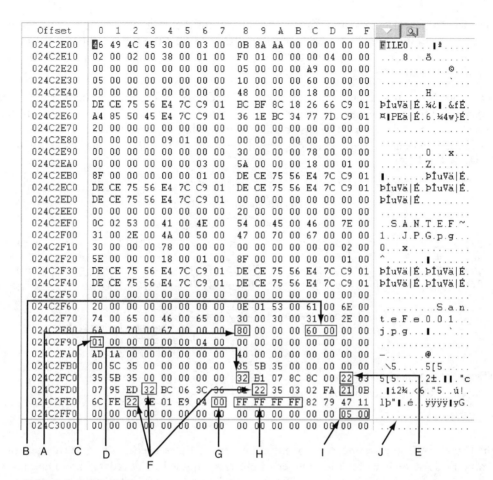

Offset	0	1	2	3	4	5	6	7	8	9	A	B	C	D	E	F		
024C2E00	46	49	4C	45	30	00	03	00	0B	8A	AA	00	00	00	00	00	FILE0....¦ª.....
024C2E10	02	00	02	00	38	00	01	00	F0	01	00	00	00	04	00	00	....8...ð......
024C2E20	00	00	00	00	00	00	00	00	05	00	00	00	A9	00	00	00	..............©...
024C2E30	05	00	00	00	00	00	00	00	10	00	00	00	60	00	00	00	............`...
024C2E40	00	00	00	00	00	00	00	00	48	00	00	00	18	00	00	00	........H......
024C2E50	DE	CE	75	56	E4	7C	C9	01	BC	BF	8C	18	26	66	C9	01	ÞÎuVä	É.¼¿Œ.&fÉ.
024C2E60	A4	85	50	45	E4	7C	C9	01	36	1E	BC	34	77	7D	C9	01	¤…PEä	É.6.¼4w}É.
024C2E70	20	00	00	00	00	00	00	00	00	00	00	00	00	00	00	00	....
024C2E80	00	00	00	00	09	01	00	00	00	00	00	00	00	00	00	00	....
024C2E90	00	00	00	00	00	00	00	00	30	00	00	00	78	00	00	00	........0...x...
024C2EA0	00	00	00	00	00	00	03	00	5A	00	00	00	18	00	01	00	........Z......
024C2EB0	8F	00	00	00	00	00	01	00	DE	CE	75	56	E4	7C	C9	01	........ÞÎuVä	É.
024C2EC0	DE	CE	75	56	E4	7C	C9	01	DE	CE	75	56	E4	7C	C9	01	ÞÎuVä|É.ÞÎuVä|É.
024C2ED0	DE	CE	75	56	E4	7C	C9	01	00	00	00	00	00	00	00	00	ÞÎuVä	É......
024C2EE0	00	00	00	00	00	00	00	00	20	00	00	00	00	00	00	00	....
024C2EF0	0C	02	53	00	41	00	4E	00	54	00	45	00	46	00	7E	00	..S.A.N.T.E.F.~.
024C2F00	31	00	2E	00	4A	00	50	00	47	00	70	00	67	00	00	00	1...J.P.G.p.g...
024C2F10	30	00	00	00	78	00	00	00	00	00	00	00	00	00	02	00	0...x..........
024C2F20	5E	00	00	00	18	00	01	00	8F	00	00	00	00	00	01	00	^.........I...
024C2F30	DE	CE	75	56	E4	7C	C9	01	DE	CE	75	56	E4	7C	C9	01	ÞÎuVä|É.ÞÎuVä|É.
024C2F40	DE	CE	75	56	E4	7C	C9	01	DE	CE	75	56	E4	7C	C9	01	ÞÎuVä|É.ÞÎuVä|É.
024C2F50	00	00	00	00	00	00	00	00	00	00	00	00	00	00	00	00	....
024C2F60	20	00	00	00	00	00	00	00	0E	01	53	00	61	00	6E	00	.........S.a.n.
024C2F70	74	00	65	00	46	00	65	00	30	00	30	00	31	00	2E	00	t.e.F.e.0.0.1...
024C2F80	6A	00	70	00	67	00	00	00	80	00	00	00	60	00	00	00	j.p.g...I...`...
024C2F90	01	00	00	00	00	00	04	00	00	00	00	00	00	00	00	00	....
024C2FA0	AD	1A	00	00	00	00	00	00	40	00	00	00	00	00	00	00	-.......@....
024C2FB0	00	5C	35	00	00	00	00	00	35	5B	35	00	00	00	00	00	.\5.....5[5.....
024C2FC0	35	5B	35	00	00	00	00	00	32	B1	07	8C	8C	00	22	03	5[5.....2±.ŒŒ."c
024C2FD0	07	95	ED	32	BC	06	3C	36	0E	22	35	03	02	FA	21	0B	.•í2¼.<6.."5..ú!.
024C2FE0	6C	FE	22	9E	01	E9	04	00	FF	FF	FF	FF	82	79	47	11	lþ"ž.é...ÿÿÿÿ‚yG.
024C2FF0	00	00	00	00	00	00	00	00	00	00	00	00	00	00	05	00	....
024C3000	00	00	00	00	00	00	00	00	00	00	00	00	00	00	00	00	....

B   A   C   D   F   G   H   I   J   E

A: Start of attribute 0x80
B: Size of attribute 0x80
C: Nonresident flag
D: First data run
E: Second data run
F: Additional data runs
G: End of data run
H: End of MFT record
I: Sector checksum
J: Sector boundary

Figure 5-18   Attribute 0x80: Data for a nonresident file
Courtesy of X-Ways AG, *www.x-ways.net*

Interpreting a Data Run

As discussed, the first data run for a nonresident attribute 0x80 field starts at offset 0x40 from the beginning of the attribute. In this discussion, a file called SanteFe001.jpg is used as an example of how data runs are interpreted. Data runs have three components: The first component declares how many bytes in the attribute field are needed to store the values for the second and third components. The second component stores the number of clusters assigned to the data run, and the third component contains the starting cluster address value (the LCN or the VCN). This discussion uses a file with six fragments (data runs).

For the first component—the 32 shown in Figure 5-19 as the data run's starting position—the second digit, 2, means that the next 2 bytes contain the number of clusters assigned to this data run. The first digit, 3, means that the next 3 bytes (after the number of clusters assigned) contain the cluster address value VCN(0); for the first data run, this value is the LCN.

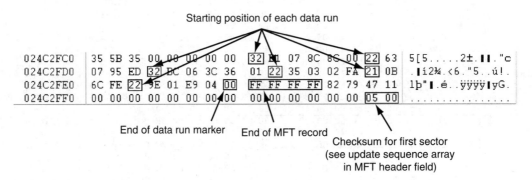

Figure 5-19 Multiple data runs
Courtesy of X-Ways AG, *www.x-ways.net*

In Figure 5-20, the second component shows the 2 bytes needed to store the hexadecimal value (in little endian) for the number of clusters assigned to this data run. The number of clusters assigned to this data run is 7B1 (hexadecimal) or 1969 in decimal.

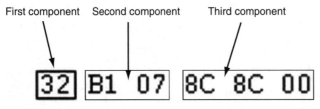

Figure 5-20 Data run components
Courtesy of X-Ways AG, *www.x-ways.net*

As shown in Figure 5-21, for the third component, the starting assigned cluster address is 0x8C8C (hexadecimal), or 35980 in decimal. Because it's the first data run of the file, this address is the LCN.

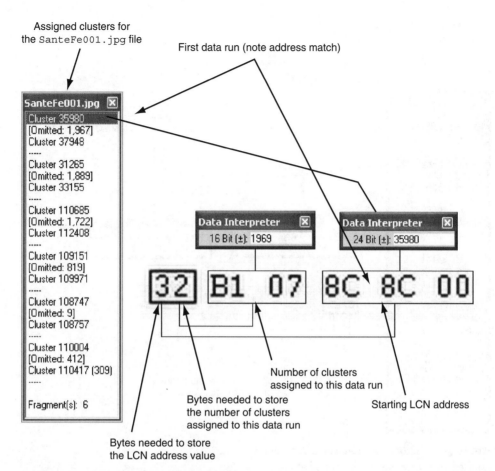

Figure 5-21 First data run with an LCN address
Courtesy of X-Ways AG, *www.x-ways.net*

Figures 5-22 and 5-23 show the second and third data runs for the SanteFe001.jpg file. For the second and all other data runs, the third component is a signed integer; for example, in Figure 5-22, this value is converted from a hexadecimal number to a negative decimal number. In NTFS, if the next available open area of a highly fragmented disk is at a lower address, a negative number is assigned as the VCN value. The way NTFS navigates to this second open area is by adding the VCN to the previous LCN. For example, the first data run has the LCN address 35980, and the second data run has the value -4715. The OS adds the two numbers, but because the second data run has a negative number, they're actually subtracted: 35980 + (-4715) = 31265.

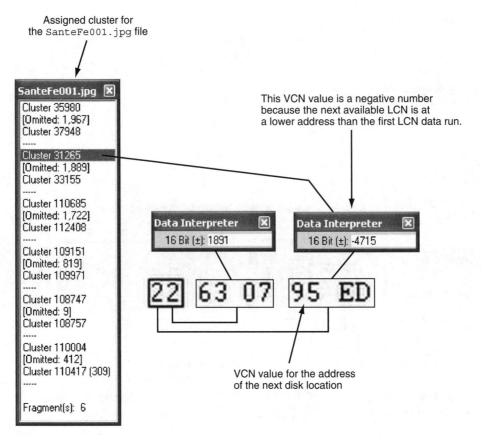

Assigned cluster for the `SanteFe001.jpg` file

This VCN value is a negative number because the next available LCN is at a lower address than the first LCN data run.

Data Interpreter
16 Bit (±): 1891

Data Interpreter
16 Bit (±): -4715

VCN value for the address of the next disk location

Figure 5-22 Second data run with a VCN address
Courtesy of X-Ways AG, *www.x-ways.net*

As you can see in the assigned cluster lists in Figure 5-23, the second fragment has a starting cluster number (an LCN) of 31265. In the third data run, the VCN value is a positive number.

For additional information on NTFS and its design, see *http://dubeyko. com/development/FileSystems/NTFS/ntfsdoc.pdf* or *http://download. paragon-software.com/doc/manual_NTFS-HFS_for_Linux_8.1_User_ Manual.pdf*.

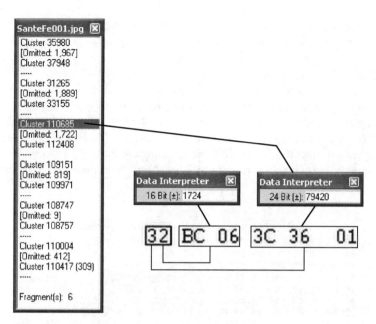

Figure 5-23 Third data run with a VCN address
Courtesy of X-Ways AG, *www.x-ways.net*

NTFS Alternate Data Streams

Of particular interest when you're examining NTFS disks are **alternate data streams,** which are ways data can be appended to existing files. When you're examining a disk, be aware that alternate data streams can obscure valuable evidentiary data, intentionally or by coincidence.

In NTFS, an alternate data stream becomes an additional file attribute and allows the file to be associated with different applications. As a result, it remains one data unit. You can also store information about a file in an alternate data stream. In its resource documentation Web page, Microsoft states: "For example, a graphics program can store a thumbnail image of a bitmap in a named data stream within the NTFS file containing the image." At a command prompt in Windows NT and later, you can create an alternate data stream with this DOS command:

```
C:\echo text_string > myfile.txt:stream_name
```

You can also use the following type command to redirect the contents of a small file to an alternate data stream:

```
C:\type textfile.txt > myfile.txt:stream1
```

In these commands, the alternate data stream is defined in the MFT by the colon between the file extension and the stream label. To display an alternate data stream's content as a simple text string, use this command:

```
C:\more < myfile.txt:stream1
```

If you save a file with alternate data streams attached to a FAT volume, the alternate data streams aren't transferred.

If you perform a keyword search and retrieve a file associated with a keyword, you might not be able to open the alternate data stream. An alternate data stream isn't displayed when you open a file in a text editor. The only way you can tell whether a file has an alternate data stream attached is by examining the file's MFT record entry. Figure 5-24 shows the MFT record of a file containing a text alternate data stream. Note that there are two attribute 0x80 fields.

Offset	0	1	2	3	4	5	6	7	8	9	A	B	C	D	E	F		
024C0E00	46	49	4C	45	30	00	03	00	41	FD	AA	00	00	00	00	00	FILE0...Aýª....
024C0E10	03	00	01	00	38	00	01	00	B8	01	00	00	00	04	00	00	....8....,....
024C0E20	00	00	00	00	00	00	00	00	07	00	00	00	A1	00	00	00	.........i...
024C0E30	07	00	00	00	00	00	00	00	10	00	00	00	60	00	00	00	............`...
024C0E40	00	00	00	00	00	00	00	00	48	00	00	00	18	00	00	00	........H....
024C0E50	B2	4C	07	BB	D3	7C	C9	01	14	4A	A3	3D	C8	7D	C9	01	²L.»Ó	É..J£=È}É.
024C0E60	14	4A	A3	3D	C8	7D	C9	01	96	75	F5	6A	54	7E	C9	01	.J£=È}É..uõjT~É.
024C0E70	20	4A	00	00	00	00	00	00	00	00	00	00	00	00	00	00	.J..............
024C0E80	00	00	00	00	09	01	00	00	00	00	00	00	00	00	00	00	....
024C0E90	00	00	00	00	00	00	00	00	30	00	00	00	70	00	00	00	........0...p...
024C0EA0	00	00	00	00	00	00	02	00	54	00	00	00	18	00	01	00	........T.......
024C0EB0	8A	00	00	00	00	00	01	00	B2	4C	07	BB	D3	7C	C9	01	I.......²L.»Ó	É.
024C0EC0	B2	4C	07	BB	D3	7C	C9	01	B2	4C	07	BB	D3	7C	C9	01	²L.»Ó|É.²L.»Ó|É.
024C0ED0	B2	4C	07	BB	D3	7C	C9	01	00	00	00	00	00	00	00	00	²L.»Ó	É.........
024C0EE0	00	00	00	00	00	00	00	00	20	00	00	00	00	00	00	00	....
024C0EF0	09	03	42	00	46	00	31	00	5F	00	34	00	2E	00	74	00	..B.F.1._.4...t.
024C0F00	78	00	74	00	00	00	00	00	80	00	00	00	50	00	00	00	x.t.....I...P...
024C0F10	00	00	18	00	00	00	05	00	38	00	00	00	18	00	00	00	........8.......
024C0F20	57	65	6C	6C	20	64	6F	6E	65	20	69	73	20	62	65	74	Well done is bet
024C0F30	74	65	72	20	74	68	61	6E	20	77	65	6C	6C	20	73	61	ter than well sa
024C0F40	69	64	2E	0D	0A	20	20	42	65	6E	6A	61	6D	69	6E	20	id... Benjamin
024C0F50	46	72	61	6E	6B	6C	69	6E	80	00	00	00	58	00	00	00	Franklin I...X...
024C0F60	01	06	40	00	00	00	06	00	00	00	00	00	00	00	00	00	..@.............
024C0F70	00	00	00	00	00	00	00	00	50	00	00	00	00	00	00	00	........P.......
024C0F80	00	02	00	00	00	00	00	00	3B	00	00	00	00	00	00	00	........;.......
024C0F90	3B	00	00	00	00	00	00	00	68	00	69	00	64	00	64	00	;.......h.i.d.d.
024C0FA0	65	00	6E	00	00	00	00	00	31	01	31	A2	00	00	21	E4	e.n.....1.1¢..!ä
024C0FB0	FF	FF	FF	FF	82	79	47	11	00	00	00	00	00	00	00	00	ÿÿÿÿ IyG........

Second attribute 0x80

Start of data run for second attribute
0x80 (location of hidden alternate data stream)

Size of second attribute 0x80

Figure 5-24 A text alternate data stream
Courtesy of X-Ways AG, *www.x-ways.net*

Figure 5-25 shows what larger nonresident files look like in an MFT record. Note that the sector boundary's checksum value (item R) must be swapped with the update sequence array's value (item C).

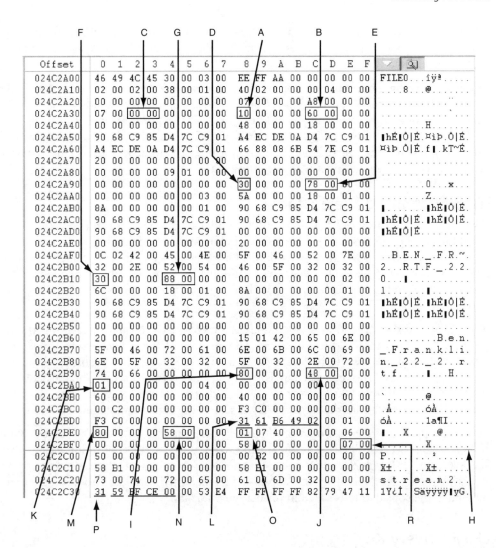

Figure 5-25   A nonresident alternate data stream
Courtesy of X-Ways AG, *www.x-ways.net*

A: Attribute 0x10
B: Attribute 0x10 size
C: Update sequence array
D: Attribute 0x30 short filename
E: Attribute 0x30 size short filename
F: Attribute 0x30 long filename
G: Attribute 0x30 size long filename
H: Sector boundary
I: First attribute 0x80

J: Size of attribute
K: Nonresident flag
L: Start of first data run
M: Second attribute 0x80
N: Size of attribute
O: Nonresident flag
P: Start of second data run
R: Sector boundary's checksum

NTFS Compressed Files

To improve data storage on disk drives, NTFS provides compression similar to FAT Drive-Space 3, a Windows 98 compression utility. With NTFS, you can compress files, folders, or entire volumes. With FAT16, you can compress only a volume. On a Windows NT or later system, compressed data is displayed normally when you view it in Windows Explorer or applications such as Microsoft Word.

During an investigation, typically you work from an image of a compressed disk, folder, or file. Most forensics tools can uncompress and analyze compressed Windows data, including data compressed with the Lempel-Ziv-Huffman (LZH) algorithm and in formats such as PKZip, WinZip, and GNU gzip. However, forensics tools might have difficulty with third-party compression utilities, such as the .rar format. If you identify third-party compressed data, you need to uncompress it with the utility that created it.

NTFS Encrypting File System

When Microsoft introduced Windows 2000, it added optional built-in encryption to NTFS called **Encrypting File System (EFS)**. EFS uses **public key** and **private key** methods of encrypting files, folders, or disk volumes (partitions). Only the owner or user who encrypted the data can access encrypted files. The owner holds the private key, and the public key is held by a certification authority, such as a global registry, network server, or company such as VeriSign.

When EFS is used in Windows 2000 and later, a **recovery certificate** is generated and sent to the local Windows administrator account. The purpose of the recovery certificate is to provide a mechanism for recovering files encrypted with EFS if there's a problem with the user's original private key. The recovery key is stored in one of two places. When a network user initiates EFS, the recovery key is sent to the local domain server's administrator account. On a stand-alone workstation, the recovery key is sent to the local administrator account.

Users can apply EFS to files stored on their local workstations or a remote server. Windows 2000 and later decrypt the data automatically when a user or an application accesses an EFS file, folder, or disk volume. In Windows Server 2003 and later, users can grant other users access to their EFS data. If a user copies a file encrypted with EFS to a folder that isn't encrypted, the copied data is saved in unencrypted format.

EFS Recovery Key Agent

The Recovery Key Agent implements the recovery certificate, which is in the Windows administrator account. Windows administrators can recover a key in two ways: through Windows or from an MS-DOS command prompt. These three commands are available from the MS-DOS command prompt:

- cipher
- copy
- efsrecvr (used to decrypt EFS files)

For information on how to use these commands, enter the question mark switch after each command. For example, type cipher /? and press Enter. Encrypted files aren't part of the FAT12, FAT16, or FAT32 file systems, so cipher and efsrecvr work only on NTFS systems running Windows 2000 Professional, XP Professional, Vista Business Edition, and 7 and 8 Professional and Enterprise editions. The copy command, however, works in both FAT and NTFS.

In Vista Business Edition and later, Microsoft has added features to the `cipher` command that aren't available when encrypting data in Windows Explorer or File Explorer. One is the `/w` switch that overwrites all deleted files, making them impossible to recover with data recovery or forensics carving tools.

If you copy an encrypted file from an EFS-enabled NTFS disk or folder to a non-EFS storage media or folder, it's unencrypted automatically.

5

To recover an encrypted EFS file, a user can e-mail it or copy the file to the administrator. The administrator can then run the Recovery Key Agent function to restore the file. For additional information, review the Microsoft Security Guidance documentation (*http://technet.microsoft.com/en-us/library/cc700811.aspx#XSLTsection125121120120*) for the latest procedures on how to recover EFS files.

Deleting NTFS Files

Typically, you use Windows or File Explorer to delete files from a disk. When a file is deleted in Windows NT and later, the OS renames it and moves it to the Recycle Bin. Another method is using the `del` (delete) MS-DOS command. This method doesn't rename and move the file to the Recycle Bin, but it eliminates the file from the MFT listing in the same way FAT does.

When you delete a file in Windows or File Explorer, you can restore it from the Recycle Bin. The OS takes the following steps when you delete a file or a folder in Windows or File Explorer:

1. Windows changes the filename and moves the file to a subdirectory with a unique identity in the Recycle Bin.

2. Windows stores information about the original path and filename in the **Info2 file**, which is the control file for the Recycle Bin. It contains ASCII data, Unicode data, and the date and time of deletion for each file or folder.

NTFS files deleted at an MS-DOS command prompt function much like FAT files. (The following steps also apply when a user empties the Recycle Bin.) The OS performs the following tasks:

1. The associated clusters are designated as free—that is, marked as available for new data.

2. The $Bitmap file attribute in the MFT is updated to reflect the file's deletion, showing that this space is available.

3. The file's record in the MFT is marked as being available.

4. VCN/LCN cluster locations linked to deleted nonresident files are then removed from the original MFT record.

5. A run list is maintained in the MFT of all cluster locations on the disk for nonresident files. When the list of links is deleted, any reference to the links is lost.

NTFS is more efficient than FAT at reclaiming deleted space. Deleted files are overwritten more quickly.

Resilient File System

With the release of Windows Server 2012, Microsoft created a new file system: **Resilient File System (ReFS)**. ReFS is designed to address very large data storage needs, such as the cloud. The following features are incorporated into ReFS's design:

- Maximized data availability
- Improved data integrity
- Designed for scalability

ReFS is an outgrowth of NTFS designed to provide a large-scale data storage access capability. It's intended only for data storage, so as of this writing, it can't be used as a boot drive. Windows 8/8.1 and Windows Server 2012 are the only Windows OSs that can access ReFS disk drives.

ReFS uses disk structures similar to the MFT in NTFS. Its storage engine uses a B+-tree sort method for fast access to large data sets. It also uses a method called "allocate-on-write" that copies updates of data files to new locations; similar to shadow paging, it prevents overwriting the original data files. The purpose of writing updates to new locations is to ensure that the original data can be recovered easily if a failure occurs in the update write to disk.

For more information on ReFS and other storage methods, see *http://msdn. microsoft.com/en-us/library/windows/desktop/hh848060(v=vs.85).aspx* or *http://technet.microsoft.com/en-us/library/hh831724.aspx*.

Understanding Whole Disk Encryption

Loss of **personal identity information (PII)** and trade secrets caused by computer theft has become more of a concern. Company PII might consist of employees' full names, home addresses, and Social Security numbers. With this information, criminals could easily apply for credit card accounts in these employees' names. Trade secrets are any information a business keeps confidential because it provides a competitive edge over other companies. The inadvertent public release of this information could devastate a business's competitive edge.

Of particular concern is the theft of laptop computers and other handheld devices, such as smartphones. If data on these devices isn't secured correctly, the owners could be liable for any damages incurred, such as stolen identities, credit card fraud, or loss of business caused by the release of trade secrets to the competition. Because of the PII problem, many states have enacted laws requiring any person or business to notify potential victims of the loss as soon as possible. To help prevent loss of information, software vendors, including Microsoft, now provide whole disk encryption (WDE, introduced in Chapter 3). This feature creates new challenges in examining and recovering data from drives.

Whole disk encryption tools offer the following features that forensics examiners should be aware of:

- Preboot authentication, such as a single sign-on password, fingerprint scan, or token (USB device)
- Full or partial disk encryption with secure hibernation, such as activating a password-protected screen saver
- Advanced encryption algorithms, such as Advanced Encryption Standard (AES) and International Data Encryption Algorithm (IDEA)
- Key management function that uses a challenge-and-response method to reset passwords or passphrases

WDE tools encrypt each sector of a drive separately. Many of these tools encrypt the drive's boot sector to prevent any efforts to bypass the secured drive's partition. To examine an encrypted drive, you must decrypt it first. An encryption tool's key management function typically uses a challenge-and-response method for decryption, which means you must run a vendor-specific program to decrypt the drive. Many vendors use a bootable CD or USB drive that prompts for a **one-time passphrase** generated by the key management function. If you need to decrypt the same computer a second time, you need a new one-time passphrase.

The biggest drawback to decrypting a drive is the several hours required to read, decrypt, and write each sector. The larger the drive, the longer decryption takes. After you've decrypted the drive, however, you can use standard acquisition methods to retrieve data.

Examining Microsoft BitLocker

BitLocker, introduced briefly in Chapter 3, is Microsoft's utility for protecting drive data. It's available in Windows Vista Enterprise and Ultimate editions, Windows 7 and 8 Professional and Enterprise editions, and Windows Server 2008 and 2012. Guidance Software Encase can decrypt BitLocker drives, although the process can take a lot of time. BitLocker's current hardware and software requirements are as follows:

- A computer capable of running Windows Vista or later (non-home editions)
- The Trusted Platform Module (TPM) microchip, version 1.2 or newer
- A computer BIOS compliant with Trusted Computing Group (TCG)
- Two NTFS partitions for the OS and an active system volume with available space
- The BIOS configured so that the hard drive boots first before checking the CD/DVD drive or other bootable peripherals

For more information on BitLocker, see *http://technet.microsoft.com/ en-us/library/cc732774.aspx* or go to *http://technet.microsoft.com* and search on "BitLocker."

Examining Third-Party Disk Encryption Tools

Several vendors offer third-party WDE utilities that often have more features than BitLocker. For example, BitLocker can encrypt only NTFS drives. If you want to encrypt a FAT drive, you need a third-party solution. Decrypting with third-party utilities typically follows the same process as in BitLocker, with some exceptions. Before using one of these utilities, make sure you investigate its features thoroughly. The following list describes some available third-party WDE utilities:

- PGP Full Disk Encryption (*www.symantec.com/drive-encryption*) can be used on PCs, laptops, and removable media to secure an entire disk volume. This tool works in Windows 2000, XP Professional (SP1 and SP2), and Mac OS X 10.4 and can also encrypt FAT volumes.

- Voltage SecureFile (*www.voltage.com/products/voltage-securefile/*) is designed for an enterprise computing environment.

- Jetico BestCrypt Volume Encryption (*www.jetico.com/products/personal-privacy/ bestcrypt-volume-encryption*) provides WDE for older MS-DOS and Windows NTFS systems.

- TrueCrypt (*www.truecrypt.org*) creates a virtual encrypted volume—a file mounted as though it were a disk drive. Data is encrypted automatically and in real time.

With improved encryption methods, extracting digital evidence will become more difficult. Because of these challenges, you need to know how to make remote live acquisitions, discussed in Chapter 10.

Understanding the Windows Registry

When Microsoft created Windows 95, it consolidated initialization (.ini) files into the **Registry**, a database that stores hardware and software configuration information, network connections, user preferences (including usernames and passwords), and setup information. The Registry has been updated and is still used in Windows Vista and later.

For investigative purposes, the Registry can contain valuable evidence. To view the Registry, you can use the Regedit (Registry Editor) program for Windows 9x and Regedt32 for Windows 2000, XP, and Vista. For Windows 7 and 8, both Regedit and Regedt32 are available.

For more information on using Regedit and Regedt32, see the Windows Resource Kit documentation for the OS version. You can find it at *http://support.microsoft.com/kb/141377*.

In general, you can use the Edit, Find menu command in Registry Editor to locate entries that might contain trace evidence, such as information identifying the last person who logged on to the computer, which is usually stored in user account information. You can also use the Registry to determine the most recently accessed files and peripheral devices. In addition, all installed programs store information in the Registry, such as Web sites accessed, recent files, and even chat rooms accessed.

As a digital forensics investigator, you should explore the Registry of all Windows systems. On a live system, be careful not to alter any Registry setting to avoid corrupting the system and possibly making it unbootable.

Several third-party tools, such as FTK Registry Viewer, are also available for accessing the Registry.

Exploring the Organization of the Windows Registry

The Windows Registry is organized in a specific way that has changed slightly with each new version of Windows. However, the major Registry sections have been consistent, with some minor changes, since Windows 2000; they're slightly different in Windows 9x/Me. Before proceeding, review the following list of Registry terminology:

- *Registry*—A hierarchical database containing system and user information.

- *Registry Editor*—A Windows utility for viewing and modifying data in the Registry. There are two Registry Editors: Regedit and Regedt32 (introduced in Windows 2000).

- *HKEY*—Windows splits the Registry into categories with the prefix HKEY_. Windows 9x systems have six HKEY categories and Windows 2000 and later have five. Windows programmers refer to the "H" as the handle for the key.

- *Key*—Each HKEY contains folders referred to as keys. Keys can contain other key folders or values.

- *Subkey*—A key displayed under another key is a subkey, similar to a subfolder in Windows or File Explorer.

- *Branch*—A key and its contents, including subkeys, make up a branch in the Registry.

- *Value*—A name and value in a key; it's similar to a file and its data content.

- *Default value*—All keys have a default value that may or may not contain data.

- *Hives*—Hives are specific branches in HKEY_USER and HKEY_LOCAL_MACHINE. Hive branches in HKEY_LOCAL_MACHINE\Software are SAM, Security, Components, and System. For HKEY_USER, each user account has its own hive link to Ntuser.dat.

The next piece of the puzzle is learning where data files that the Registry reads are located. The number of files the Registry uses depends on the Windows version. In Windows 9x/Me, it uses only two files, User.dat and System.dat. In Windows NT and later, there are six files: `Ntuser.dat`, `System.dat`, `SAM.dat`, `Software.dat`, `Security.dat`, and `Default.dat`. When examining Registry data from a suspect drive after you have made an acquisition and are reviewing it in a forensics tool, you need to know the location of these files. Table 5-6 shows how Registry data files are organized and explains these files' purposes in Windows Vista and later. For information on older Windows Registry files, see *http://support.microsoft.com/kb/250410*.

Table 5-6   Registry file locations and purposes

Filename and location	Purpose of file
Users*user-account*\\`Ntuser.dat`	User-protected storage area; contains the list of most recently used files and desktop configuration settings
Windows\\system32\\config\\`Default.dat`	Contains the computer's system settings
Windows\\system32\\config\\`SAM.dat`	Contains user account management and security settings
Windows\\system32\\config\\`Security.dat`	Contains the computer's security settings
Windows\\system32\\config\\`Software.dat`	Contains installed programs' settings and associated usernames and passwords
Windows\\system32\\config\\`System.dat`	Contains additional computer system settings
Windows\\system32\\config\\systemprofile	Contains additional NTUSER information

© 2016 Cengage Learning®

When viewing the Registry with Registry Editor, you can see the HKEYs used in Windows (see Figure 5-26).

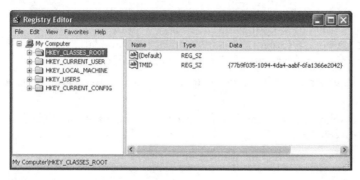

Figure 5-26   Viewing HKEYs in Registry Editor
Courtesy of Microsoft Corporation

Table 5-7 describes the functions of Registry HKEYs.

TIP

For additional information on the Registry, see *http://support.microsoft.com/default.aspx?scid=kb;EN-US;256986*, *http://regripper.wordpress.com*, and *www.computerhope.com/registry.htm*. For a detailed listing of HKEYs, see *www.accessdata.com/technical*.

Table 5-7 Registry HKEYs and their functions

HKEY	Function
HKEY_CLASS_ROOT	A symbolic link to HKEY_LOCAL_MACHINE\SOFTWARE\Classes; provides file type and file extension information, URL protocol prefixes, and so forth
HKEY_CURRENT_USER	A symbolic link to HKEY_USERS; stores settings for the currently logged-on user
HKEY_LOCAL_MACHINE	Contains information about installed hardware and software
HKEY_USERS	Stores information for the currently logged-on user; only one key in this HKEY is linked to HKEY_CURRENT_USER
HKEY_CURRENT_CONFIG	A symbolic link to HKEY_LOCAL_MACHINE\SYSTEM\CurrentControlSet\Hardware Profile\xxxx (with xxxx representing the current hardware profile); contains hardware configuration settings
HKEY_DYN_DATA	Used only in Windows 9x/Me systems; stores hardware configuration settings

© 2016 Cengage Learning®

Examining the Windows Registry

Some forensics tools, such as ProDiscover, X-Ways Forensics, OSForensics, and FTK, have built-in or add-on Registry viewers. For this next activity, your company's Legal Department has asked you to search for any references to an e-mail addresses containing the name Denise or Robinson with the domain name outlook.com. A paralegal gives you a raw (dd) image file containing InCh05.img, a forensic image of a Windows 8 computer's hard drive used by Superior Bicycle employee Denise Robinson.

For this activity, you use OSForensics to examine Denise Robinson's NTUser.dat file. If you find any items of interest, add them to an OSForensics case report that you can give to the paralegal. The following steps explain how to generate a case report in OSForensics.

 Before beginning this activity, extract compressed files from the Chap05 folder on the book's DVD to your *Work*\Chap05\Chapter folder. If necessary, create the Chap05 and Chapter folders first. The work folder pathname you see in screenshots might differ.

To examine Registry files with OSForensics, follow these steps:

1. Start OSForensics with the **Run as administrator** option, and click the **Continue Using Free Version.**

2. In the left pane, click **Manage Case**, if necessary. In the Manage Case pane on the right, click the **New Case** button. In the New Case dialog box, type **InChap05** in the Case Name text box and your name in the Investigator text box. For the Acquisition Type setting, click the **Investigate Disk(s) from Another Machine** option button (see Figure 5-27). Click **Custom Location** for the Case Folder option. Click the **Browse** button on the lower right, navigate to and click your *Work***Chap05** folder, and then click **OK** twice.

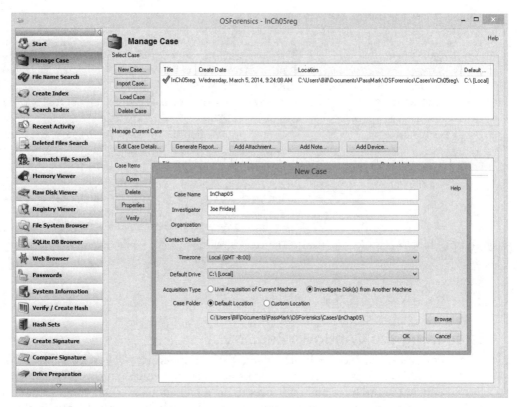

Figure 5-27   The New Case dialog box
Source: PassMark Software, *www.osforensics.com*

Notice the drive letter in the OSFMount - Mount drive dialog box, which you use in Step 4. This image is mounted as read-only as an attached drive on your computer and becomes accessible to OSForensics.

3. To mount the disk image, scroll down the navigation bar on the left, and click **Mount Drive Image**. In the Mounted virtual disks window, click the **Mount new** button. In the OSFMount - Mount drive dialog box that opens (see Figure 5-28), click the **...** button next to the Image file text box, navigate to your work folder, click **InCh05.img**, click **Open**, and then click **OK**.

4. In the navigation bar on the left, click **Registry Viewer**. In the "Select registry hive file to open" dialog box, click the **Select Drive** list arrow, and then click the drive letter that was shown in Step 3 (see Figure 5-29). The drive letter on your system is likely to be different. In the list of files on the right, click *DriveLetter***users****Denise****NTUSER. DAT**, and then click **Open**.

Figure 5-28 Mounting a drive in OSForensics
Source: PassMark Software, *www.osforensics.com*

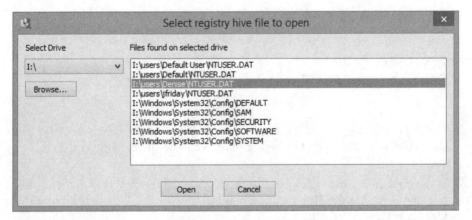

Figure 5-29 The "Select registry hive file to open" dialog box
Source: PassMark Software, *www.osforensics.com*

5. In the OSForensics Registry Viewer, click **Search, Find** from the menu to open the Find dialog box. In the Search For text box, type **Outlook.com** (see Figure 5-30), and then click the **Find** button.

6. In the Registry Viewer pane on the right, right-click the first search hit and click **Add to Case** to open the Please Enter New Case Item Details dialog box. In the Title text box, type **Outlook e-mail address for Denise Robinson**, and then click **OK**.

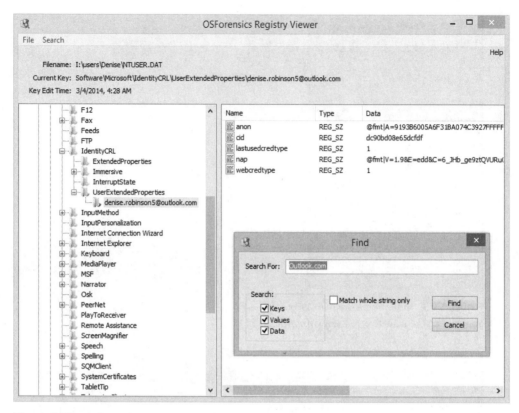

Figure 5-30   Entering a search term
Source: PassMark Software, *www.osforensics.com*

7. In the Find dialog box, click **Find** again. Right-click the next search hit and click **Add to Case**. Type **Outlook e-mail Web site** in the Title text box, and then click **OK**.

8. In the Find dialog box, click **Find** again. Right-click the next search hit and click **Add to Case**. Type **Denise Robinson's e-mail address** in the Title text box, and then click **OK**. Exit Registry Viewer.

9. In the main OSForensics window, click **Manage Case** in the navigation bar on the left. In the Manage Current Case pane on the right, click the **Generate Report** button. In the Export Report window, click **Browse** next to the Output Location text box, navigate to your work folder, click **OK**, and then click **OK** again to open the report in your Web browser. In the Mounted virtual disks window, click the **Dismount** button. Click **Yes**, and then click **Exit**.

An extensive amount of information is stored in the Registry. With Registry data, you can ascertain when users went online, when they accessed a printer, and many other events. A lot of the information in the Registry is beyond the scope of this book, so you're encouraged to expand your knowledge by attending training sessions or classes.

Understanding Microsoft Startup Tasks

You should have a good understanding of what happens to disk data at startup. In some investigations, you must preserve data on the disk exactly as the suspect last used it. Any access to a computer system after it was used for illicit purposes alters your disk evidence. As you learned in Chapter 3, altering disk data lessens its evidentiary quality considerably. In some instances, accessing a suspect computer incorrectly could make the digital evidence corrupt and less credible for litigation.

In the following sections, you learn what files are accessed when Windows starts. This information helps you determine when a suspect's computer was last accessed, which is particularly important with computers that might have been used after an incident was reported.

Startup in Windows 7 and Windows 8

Since Windows Vista, Microsoft has changed its approach to OS boot processes. In addition, Windows 8 is a multiplatform OS that can run on desktops, laptops, tablets, and smartphones. This discussion covers desktop and laptop computers running Windows 8, although Windows Vista and 7 are very similar.

All Windows 8 boot processes are designed to run on multiple devices, ranging from desktop or laptop systems to tablets and smartphones. In Windows Vista and later, the boot process uses a boot configuration data (BCD) store. For desktops and laptops (BIOS-designed systems), a BCD Registry file in the \Boot\Bcd folder is maintained to control the boot process. To access this file, you use the BCD Editor; Regedit and Regedt32 aren't associated with this file.

In Windows 8, the BCD contains the boot loader that initiates the system's bootstrap process when Windows starts. To access the Advanced Boot Options menu during the bootstrap process, press F8 or F12 when the system is starting. This menu enables you to choose between Safe Mode (or Enable Safe Mode, in Windows 8), Enable boot logging, or Disable Driver Signature Enforcement.

To access the computer's firmware to modify the boot priority order, press F2 or Delete. Follow the onscreen instructions to save the updates and reboot the computer. For additional information on Windows 8 boot processes, refer to *Windows 8 Administration Pocket Consultant* (William R. Stanek, Microsoft Press, 2012, ISBN 978-0-7356-6613-9).

Startup in Windows NT and Later

Although Windows NT is much different from Windows 95 and 98, the startup method for the NT OSs—NT, 2000, and XP—is about the same. There are some minor differences in how certain system start files function, but they accomplish the same orderly startup.

Any computer using NTFS performs the following steps when the computer is turned on:

- Power-on self test (POST)
- Initial startup
- Boot loader
- Hardware detection and configuration

- Kernel loading
- User logon

Windows OSs use the files discussed in the following sections to start. These files can be located on the system partition or boot partition.

Startup Files for Windows Vista   When Microsoft developed Vista, it updated the boot process to use the new Extensible Firmware Interface (EFI) as well as the older BIOS system. The EFI boot firmware is designed to provide better protection against malware than BIOS does. EFI Vista's boot processes have also changed since Windows XP. The Ntldr program in Windows XP used to load the OS has been replaced with these three boot utilities:

- Bootmgr.exe—The Windows Boot Manager program controls boot flow and allows booting multiple OSs, such as booting Vista along with XP.
- Winload.exe—The Windows Vista OS loader installs the kernel and the Hardware Abstraction Layer (HAL) and loads memory with the necessary boot drivers.
- Winresume.exe—This tool restarts Vista after the OS goes into hibernation mode.

Windows Vista also includes the BCD editor for modifying boot options and updating the BCD registry file. The BCD store replaces the Windows XP Boot.ini file. For additional information on the BCD, see *www.microsoft.com/whdc/system/platform/firmware/bcd.mspx*.

Startup Files for Windows XP   Unless otherwise specified, most startup files for Windows XP are in the root folder of the system partition. **NT Loader (Ntldr)** loads the OS. When the system is powered on, Ntldr reads the **Boot.ini** file, which displays a boot menu. After you select the mode to boot to, Boot.ini runs Ntoskrnl.exe and reads Bootvid.dll, Hal.dll, and startup device drivers. Boot.ini specifies the Windows XP path installation and contains options for selecting the Windows version.

If a system has multiple boot OSs, including older ones such as Windows 9x or DOS, Ntldr reads **BootSect.dos** (a hidden file), which contains the address (boot sector location) of each OS.

When the boot selection is made, Ntldr runs **NTDetect.com**, a 16-bit real-mode program that queries the system for device and configuration data, and then passes its findings to Ntldr. This program identifies components and values on the computer system, such as the following:

- CMOS time and date value
- Buses attached to the motherboard, such as Industry Standard Architecture (ISA) or Peripheral Component Interconnect (PCI)
- Disk drives connected to the system
- Mouse input devices connected to the system
- Parallel ports connected to the system

NTBootdd.sys is the device driver that allows the OS to communicate with SCSI or ATA drives that aren't related to the BIOS. (On some workstations, a SCSI disk is used as the primary boot disk.) Controllers that don't use Interrupt 13 (INT-13) use NTBootdd.sys. It runs in privileged processor mode with direct access to hardware and system data.

Ntoskrnl.exe is the Windows XP OS kernel, located in the %*systemroot*% \Windows\System32 folder.

Hal.dll is the Hardware Abstraction Layer (HAL) dynamic link library, located in the %*systemroot*%\Windows\System32 folder. The HAL allows the OS kernel to communicate with the computer's hardware.

At startup, data and instruction code are moved in and out of the **Pagefile.sys** file to optimize the amount of physical RAM available.

The HKEY_LOCAL_MACHINE\SYSTEM Registry key contains information the OS requires to start system services and devices. This system Registry file is located in the %*systemroot*%\Windows\System32\Config\System folder.

Device drivers contain instructions for the OS for hardware devices, such as the keyboard, mouse, and video card, and are stored in the %*systemroot*%\Windows\System32\Drivers folder.

To identify the specific path for %*systemroot*% at a DOS prompt, type set with no switches or parameters and press Enter. This command displays all current %*systemroot*% paths.

Windows XP System Files Next, you need to examine the core OS files that Windows XP, 2000, and NT use, usually located in %*systemroot*%\Windows\System32 or %*systemroot*%\Winnt\System32. Table 5-8 lists the system files Windows XP uses. Although a few of these files are repeats of previous table entries, you should be aware of their key roles.

Table 5-8 Windows XP system files

Filename	Description
Ntoskrnl.exe	The XP executable and kernel
Ntkrnlpa.exe	The physical address support program for accessing more than 4 GB of physical RAM
Hal.dll	The Hardware Abstraction Layer (described earlier)
Win32k.sys	The kernel-mode portion of the Win32 subsystem
Ntdll.dll	System service dispatch stubs to executable functions and internal support functions
Kernel32.dll	Core Win32 subsystem DLL file
Advapi32.dll	Core Win32 subsystem DLL file
User32.dll	Core Win32 subsystem DLL file
Gdi32.dll	Core Win32 subsystem DLL file

© 2016 Cengage Learning®

Contamination Concerns with Windows XP When you start a Windows XP NTFS workstation, several files are accessed immediately. When any of these or other related OS files are accessed at startup, the last access date and time stamp for the files changes to the current date and time. This change destroys any potential evidence that shows when a Windows XP workstation was last used. For this reason, you should have a strong working knowledge of the startup process.

Understanding Virtual Machines

New versions of OSs and applications are released frequently, but older versions are still widely used. As an investigator, you'll face the challenge of having enough resources to support the variety of software you're likely to encounter. More companies are turning to virtualization to reduce the cost of hardware purchases, so the number of investigations involving virtual machines will increase as this practice continues.

As an investigator, you might need a virtual server to view legacy systems, and you might need to forensically examine suspects' virtual machines. **Virtual machines** enable you to run another OS on an existing physical computer (known as the host computer) by emulating a computer's hardware environment. Figure 5-31 shows an Oracle VM VirtualBox virtual machine running Windows 8.1 on the desktop of a host computer. Typically, a virtual machine consists of several files. The two main files are the configuration file containing hardware settings, such as RAM, network configurations, port settings, and so on, and the virtual hard disk file, which contains the boot loader program, OS files, and users' data files. (Depending on the virtualization software, these files might be organized differently.)

Figure 5-31   A virtual machine running on the host computer's desktop
Source: Courtesy of Oracle VirtualBox

Another reason for using a virtual machine in an investigation is to emulate actions taken by a suspect or even by malware. Several forensics analysis tools can convert a forensic image to an **ISO image** or a **virtual hard disk (VHD)** file, which enables you to run a suspect's computer in a virtual environment. This feature is useful for analyzing malware to see how it behaves without corrupting or contaminating your workstation.

A virtual machine acts like any other computer but with a twist: It performs all the tasks the OS running on the physical computer can, up to a certain point. The virtual machine recognizes hardware components of the host computer it's loaded on, such as the mouse, keyboard, and CD/DVD drive. However, the guest OS (the one running on a virtual machine) is limited by the host computer's OS, which might block certain operations. For example, most virtual machines recognize a CD/DVD drive because the host computer defaults to autodetect. Some virtual machines don't recognize a USB drive; this capability varies with the virtualization software. Although networking capabilities are beyond the scope of this book, be aware that virtual machines can use bridged, Network Address Translation (NAT), or other network configurations to determine how they access the Internet and communicate with systems on the local network.

Say your company has upgraded to Windows 8, but you still have a few applications that require Windows XP. Not a problem! Choose your virtualization software, install the Windows XP OS and the applications you want to run, and you're ready to go. Depending on the host computer's hard drive size and amount of RAM, you can have an entire virtual network running on one physical computer. One advantage is that if you're running several virtual machines, you can pause some of the guest OSs to keep them from consuming CPU cycles and then resume them when needed.

In digital forensics, virtual machines make it possible to restore a suspect drive on a virtual machine and run nonstandard software the suspect might have loaded, for example. You can browse through the drive's contents, and then go back to the forensic image and test the items you found. Remember that in forensics, everything should be reproducible. Therefore, anything you found in the virtual machine re-creation of the suspect drive should exist in the forensic image, too.

From a network forensics standpoint, you need to be aware of some potential issues, such as a virtual machine used to attack another system or network. The technology is still developing, so it's unclear how much of the physical drive is represented in the virtual disk file. File slack, unallocated space, and so forth don't exist on a virtual machine, so many standard items don't work on virtual drives.

Creating a Virtual Machine

Some common applications for creating virtual machines are VMware Server, VMware Player and VMware Workstation, Oracle VM VirtualBox, Microsoft Virtual PC, and Hyper-V, available in current versions of Windows Server. VirtualBox is an open-source program that can be downloaded at *www.virtualbox.org/wiki/Downloads*.

The Microsoft Academic Alliance issues ISO images to schools and students for an inexpensive annual fee.

Consult with your instructor before doing the following activity, which shows you how to create a virtual machine in VirtualBox. Follow these steps:

1. If you haven't already done so, download and install VirtualBox.

2. In Windows 8 or later, go to the Start screen, type **VirtualBox**, and press **Enter**.

3. In the Oracle VM VirtualBox Manager, click the **New** icon at the upper left (see Figure 5-32) to start the Create Virtual Machine Wizard.

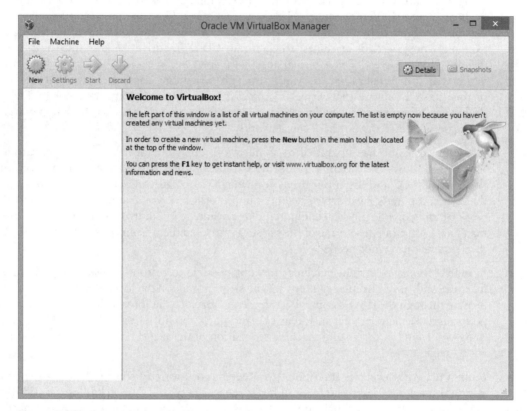

Figure 5-32   The Oracle VM VirtualBox Manager
Source: Courtesy of Oracle VirtualBox

4. In the Name and operating system window, type **Windows 7 GCFI** for the virtual machine name (see Figure 5-33). If necessary, click the **Type** list arrow, and click **Microsoft Windows;** then click the **Version** list arrow, and click **Windows 7** (32-bit if you have Windows 7 x86 or 64-bit if you have x64). Click **Next**.

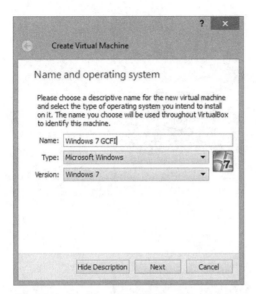

Figure 5-33 Entering a virtual machine name
Source: Courtesy of Oracle VirtualBox

5. In the Memory size window, adjust the allocated memory to about 50% of your work-station's total amount of RAM, and then click **Next**.

6. In the Hard drive window, click **Create a virtual drive now**, and then click **Create**.

7. In the Hard drive file type window, click **VHD (Virtual Hard Disk)**, and then click **Next**.

VirtualBox offers versatility in its virtual hard disk file options. By select-ing the VHD option, you can load the virtual hard disk file into other virtualization programs, such as VMware.

8. In the Storage on physical hard drive window, click **Dynamically allocated,** and then click **Next**.

9. In the File location and size window, expand the default of 25 GB if you think you need more storage space allocated, and then click **Create**. When VirtualBox finishes creating the virtual machine, the window shown in Figure 5-34 is displayed. Leave VirtualBox running for the next activity.

Figure 5-34   Displaying a created virtual machine
Source: Courtesy of Oracle VirtualBox

In the following activity, you use an ISO image that your instructor will provide on the network or a CD for installing Windows 7 as a guest OS. (You can also install other Windows OSs and most Linux distributions as guest OSs.) For any guest OS, you must have a valid product key to install it. You can get the product key from your instructor.

1. In the Oracle VM VirtualBox Manager, click the **Settings** icon. In the Windows 7 - Settings dialog box, click **System** in the left pane, and click to clear the **Floppy** check box for the boot order (leaving the **CD/DVD** and **Hard Disk** check boxes selected).

2. Next, click **Display** in the left pane, and click the **Video** tab, if necessary. Adjust the **Video Memory** slider to at least 27 MB (see Figure 5-35).

Depending on the amount of video memory on your workstation, you might need to adjust it so that your monitor can display the virtual session correctly. For more information on this setting and other Virtual-Box features, see *www.virtualbox.org/wiki/Documentation*.

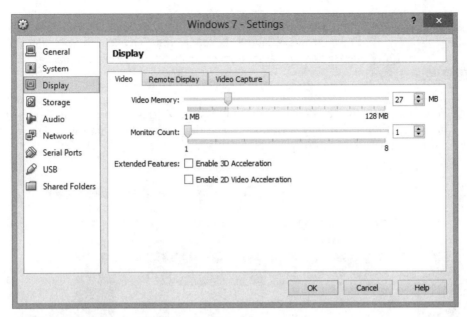

Figure 5-35 Adjusting the video memory
Source: Courtesy of Oracle VirtualBox

3. Click **Storage** in the left pane, click **Empty** in the Storage Tree section, and then click the down arrow with the disk icon, as shown in Figure 5-36. If you have a Windows ISO file, click **Choose a virtual CD/DVD disk file**, click an ISO image to install, and then click **OK**. If you have a Windows installation DVD, click **Host Drive 'E:'**, and then click **OK**. In the Oracle VM VirtualBox Manager, click **Start**.

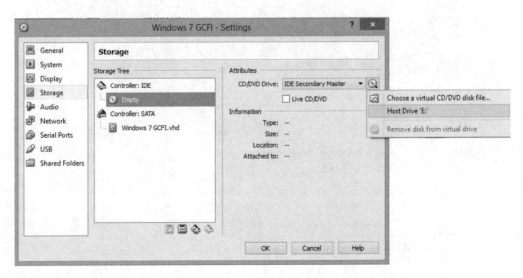

Figure 5-36 Selecting a source drive
Source: Courtesy of Oracle VirtualBox

In this example, the installation disc for the source OS, Windows 7, is in the DVD drive, lettered E. Your workstation might show a different drive letter, such as D:, if your hard drive has only one partition.

4. Follow the prompts to continue installing Windows 7 as a guest OS on your virtual machine. If the "Which type of installation do you want?" window is displayed, click **Custom (advanced)**, as shown in Figure 5-37.

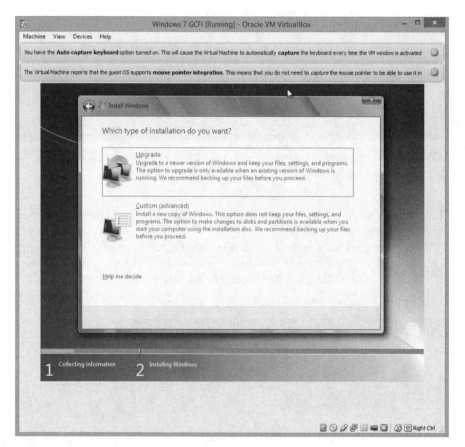

Figure 5-37 Selecting a Windows installation option
Source: Courtesy of Oracle VirtualBox

To start a virtual session in VirtualBox, select a virtual machine you created, and then click the Start icon (see Figure 5-38). You see standard boot prompts for the logon name and password you defined during the OS installation. The guest OS works as though it were running on a stand-alone workstation. You can add other applications to this virtual environment to perform tasks as needed. To terminate the session, simply perform the usual Windows shutdown procedure.

Select the virtual machine by clicking here

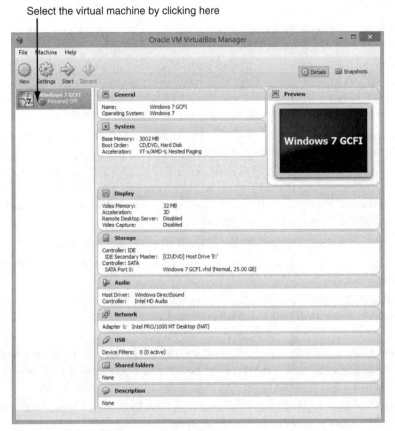

Figure 5-38 Starting a virtual machine session
Source: Courtesy of Oracle VirtualBox

Be aware that as you install software and perform other tasks, you might encounter problems with recognition of the CD/DVD drive, for example. Virtual machines present some challenges because they are limited by the host computer they're loaded on. For this reason, many legal issues need to be addressed before these systems are accepted for use in court.

Chapter Summary

- When booting a suspect's computer, using boot media, such as forensic boot CDs or USB drives, is important to ensure that disk evidence isn't altered. You should access a suspect computer's BIOS to configure the computer to boot to these CDs or USB drives.

- The Master Boot Record (MBR) stores information about partitions on a disk.

- Microsoft used FAT12 and FAT16 on older operating systems, such as MS-DOS, Windows 3.x, and Windows 9x. The maximum partition size is 2 GB. Newer systems use FAT32. FAT12 is now used mainly on floppy disks and small USB drives. VFAT, created for Windows 95, allows filenames longer than eight characters.

- To find a hard disk's capacity, use the cylinders, heads, and sectors (CHS) calculation. To find a disk's byte capacity, multiply the number of heads, cylinders, and sectors.

- Sectors are grouped into clusters and clusters are chained because the OS can track only a given number of allocation units (65,536 in FAT16 and 4,294,967,296 in FAT32).

- Solid-state disk drives use wear-leveling to ensure even use of memory cells. It transfers data to unused memory cells so that all cells have an equal amount of reads and writes. The previously assigned memory cells are listed as unallocated space. After a predetermined time, the unallocated memory cells are overwritten with binary 1s.

- When files are deleted in a FAT file system, the hexadecimal value 0x05 is inserted in the first character of the filename in the directory.

- NTFS is more versatile because it uses the Master File Table (MFT) to track file information. Approximately the first 512 bytes of data for small files (called resident files) are stored in the MFT. Data for larger files (called nonresident files) is stored outside the MFT and linked by using cluster addresses.

- Records in the MFT contain attribute IDs that store metadata about files.

- In NTFS, alternate data streams can obscure information that might be of evidentiary value to an investigation.

- File slack, RAM slack (in older Windows OSs), and drive slack are areas in which valuable information, such as downloaded files, swap files, passwords, and logon IDs, can reside on a drive.

- NTFS can encrypt data with Encrypting File System (EFS) and BitLocker. Decrypting data with these methods requires using recovery certificates. BitLocker is Microsoft's whole disk encryption (WDE) utility that can be decrypted by using a one-time passphrase.

- The Resilient File System (ReFS), available only in Windows 8 and Windows Server 2012, provides access to large disk storage systems.

- With a hexadecimal editor, you can determine information such as file type and OS configurations.

- NTFS can compress files, folders, or an entire volume. FAT16 can compress only entire volumes.

- The Registry in Windows keeps a record of attached hardware, user preferences, network connections, and installed software. It also contains information such as passwords in two binary files: System.dat and User.dat.

- Every user with an account on a Windows computer has his or her own Ntuser.dat file. Windows 9x user information is stored in User.dat.

- Virtualization software enables you to run other OSs on a host computer. Virtual machines are beneficial if, for example, you need to run a previous OS to test old software that won't run on newer OSs.

Key Terms

alternate data streams Ways in which data can be appended to a file (intentionally or not) and potentially obscure evidentiary data. In NTFS, alternate data streams become an additional file attribute.

American Standard Code for Information Interchange (ASCII) An 8-bit coding scheme that assigns numeric values to up to 256 characters, including letters, numerals, punctuation marks, control characters, and other symbols.

areal density The number of bits per square inch of a disk platter.

attribute ID In NTFS, an MFT record field containing metadata about the file or folder and the file's data or links to the file's data.

Boot.ini A file that specifies the Windows path installation and a variety of other startup options.

BootSect.dos If a machine has multiple booting OSs, NTLDR reads BootSect.dos, which is a hidden file, to determine the address (boot sector location) of each OS. *See also* NT Loader (Ntldr).

bootstrap process Information contained in ROM that a computer accesses during startup; this information tells the computer how to access the OS and hard drive.

clusters Storage allocation units composed of groups of sectors. Clusters are 512, 1024, 2048, or 4096 bytes each.

cylinder A column of tracks on two or more disk platters.

data runs Cluster addresses where files are stored on a drive's partition outside the MFT record. Data runs are used for nonresident MFT file records. A data run record field consists of three components; the first component defines the size in bytes needed to store the second and third components' content.

device drivers Files containing instructions for the OS for hardware devices, such as the keyboard, mouse, and video card.

drive slack Unused space in a cluster between the end of an active file and the end of the cluster. It can contain deleted files, deleted e-mail, or file fragments. Drive slack is made up of both file slack and RAM slack. *See also* file slack *and* RAM slack.

Encrypting File System (EFS) A public/private key encryption first used in Windows 2000 on NTFS-formatted disks. The file is encrypted with a symmetric key, and then a public/private key is used to encrypt the symmetric key.

File Allocation Table (FAT) The original Microsoft file structure database. It's written to the outermost track of a disk and contains information about each file stored on the drive. PCs use the FAT to organize files on a disk so that the OS can find the files it needs. The variations are FAT12, FAT16, FAT32, VFAT, and FATX.

file slack The unused space created when a file is saved. If the allocated space is larger than the file, the remaining space is slack space and can contain passwords, logon IDs, file fragments, and deleted e-mails.

file system The way files are stored on a disk; gives an OS a road map to data on a disk.

geometry A disk drive's internal organization of platters, tracks, and sectors.

Hal.dll The Hardware Abstraction Layer dynamic link library allows the OS kernel to communicate with hardware.

head The device that reads and writes data to a disk drive.

head and cylinder skew A method manufacturers use to minimize lag time. The starting sectors of tracks are slightly offset from each other to move the read-write head.

High Performance File System (HPFS) The file system IBM uses for its OS/2 operating system.

Info2 file In Windows NT through Vista, the control file for the Recycle Bin. It contains ASCII data, Unicode data, and date and time of deletion.

ISO image A bootable file that can be copied to CD or DVD; typically used for installing operating systems. It can also be read by virtualization software when creating a virtual boot disk.

logical addresses When files are saved, they are assigned to clusters, which the OS numbers sequentially starting at 2. Logical addresses point to relative cluster positions, using these assigned cluster numbers.

logical cluster numbers (LCNs) The numbers sequentially assigned to each cluster when an NTFS disk partition is created and formatted. The first cluster on an NTFS partition starts at count 0. LCNs become the addresses that allow the MFT to read and write data to the disk's nonresident attribute area. *See also* data runs *and* virtual cluster number (VCN).

Master Boot Record (MBR) On Windows and DOS computers, this boot disk file contains information about partitions on a disk and their locations, size, and other important items.

Master File Table (MFT) NTFS uses this database to store and link to files. It contains information about access rights, date and time stamps, system attributes, and other information about files.

metadata In NTFS, this term refers to information stored in the MFT. *See also* Master File Table (MFT).

NTBootdd.sys A device driver that allows the OS to communicate with SCSI or ATA drives that aren't related to the BIOS.

NTDetect.com A 16-bit program that identifies hardware components during startup and sends the information to Ntldr.

NT File System (NTFS) The file system Microsoft created to replace FAT. NTFS uses security features, allows smaller cluster sizes, and uses Unicode, which makes it a more versatile system. NTFS is used mainly on newer OSs, starting with Windows NT.

NT Loader (Ntldr) A program located in the root folder of the system partition that loads the OS. *See also* BootSect.dos.

Ntoskrnl.exe The kernel for the Windows NT family of OSs.

one-time passphrase A password used to access special accounts or programs requiring a high level of security, such as a decryption utility for an encrypted drive. This passphrase can be used only once, and then it expires.

Pagefile.sys At startup, data and instruction code are moved in and out of this file to optimize the amount of physical RAM available during startup.

partition A logical drive on a disk. It can be the entire disk or part of the disk.

Partition Boot Sector The first data set of an NTFS disk. It starts at sector [0] of the disk drive and can expand up to 16 sectors.

partition gap Unused space or void between the primary partition and the first logical partition.

personal identity information (PII) Any information that can be used to create bank or credit card accounts, such as name, home address, Social Security number, and driver's license number.

physical addresses The actual sectors in which files are located. Sectors reside at the hardware and firmware level.

private key In encryption, the key used to decrypt the file. The file owner keeps the private key.

public key In encryption, the key used to encrypt a file; it's held by a certificate authority, such as a global registry, network server, or company such as VeriSign.

RAM slack The unused space between the end of the file (EOF) and the end of the last sector used by the active file in the cluster. Any data residing in RAM at the time the file is saved, such as logon IDs and passwords, can appear in this area, whether the information was saved or not. RAM slack is found mainly in older Microsoft OSs.

recovery certificate A method NTFS uses so that a network administrator can recover encrypted files if the file's user/creator loses the private key encryption code.

Registry A Windows database containing information about hardware and software configurations, network connections, user preferences, setup information, and other critical information.

Resilient File System (ReFS) A new file system developed for Windows Server 2012. It allows increased scalability for disk storage and improved features for data recovery and error checking.

sector A section on a track, typically made up of 512 bytes.

track density The space between tracks on a disk. The smaller the space between tracks, the more tracks on a disk. Older drives with wider track densities allowed the heads to wander.

tracks Concentric circles on a disk platter where data is stored.

unallocated disk space Partition disk space that isn't allocated to a file. This space might contain data from files that have been deleted previously.

Unicode A character code representation that's replacing ASCII. It's capable of representing more than 64,000 characters and non-European-based languages.

UTF-8 (Unicode Transformation Format) One of three formats Unicode uses to translate languages for digital representation.

virtual cluster number (VCN) When a large file is saved in NTFS, it's assigned a logical cluster number specifying a location on the partition. Large files are referred to as nonresident files. If the disk is highly fragmented, VCNs are assigned and list the additional space needed to store the file. The LCN is a physical location on the NTFS partition; VCNs are the offset from the previous LCN data run. *See also* data runs *and* logical cluster numbers (LCNs).

virtual hard disk (VHD) A file representing a system's hard drive that can be booted in a virtualization application and allows running a suspect's computer in a virtual environment.

virtual machines Emulated computer environments that simulate hardware and can be used for running OSs separate from the physical (host) computer. For example, a computer running Windows Vista could have a virtual Windows 98 OS, allowing the user to switch between OSs.

wear-leveling An internal firmware feature used in solid-state drives that ensures even wear of read/writes for all memory cells.

zone bit recording (ZBR) The method most manufacturers use to deal with a platter's inner tracks being shorter than the outer tracks. Grouping tracks by zones ensures that all tracks hold the same amount of data.

Review Questions

1. On a Windows system, sectors typically contain how many bytes?
   a. 256
   b. 512
   c. 1024
   d. 2048

2. What does CHS stand for?

3. Zone bit recording is how disk manufacturers ensure that a platter's outer tracks store as much data as possible. True or False?

4. Areal density refers to which of the following?
   a. Number of bits per disk
   b. Number of bits per partition
   c. Number of bits per square inch of a disk platter
   d. Number of bits per platter

5. Clusters in Windows always begin numbering at what number?

6. How many sectors are typically in a cluster on a disk drive?
   a. 1
   b. 2 or more
   c. 4 or more
   d. 8 or more

7. List three items stored in the FAT database.

8. What does the Ntuser.dat file contain?

9. In FAT32, a 123 KB file uses how many sectors?

10. What is the space on a drive called when a file is deleted? (Choose all that apply.)
    a. Disk space
    b. Unallocated space
    c. Drive space
    d. Free space

11. List two features NTFS has that FAT does not.

12. What does MFT stand for?

13. In NTFS, files smaller than 512 bytes are stored in the MFT. True or False?

14. In Windows 7 and later, how much data from RAM is loaded into RAM slack on a disk drive?

15. What's a virtual cluster number?

16. Why was EFI boot firmware developed?

17. Device drivers contain what kind of information?

18. Which of the following Windows 8 files contains user-specific information?
    a. `User.dat`
    b. `Ntuser.dat`
    c. `System.dat`
    d. `SAM.dat`

19. Virtual machines have which of the following limitations when running on a host computer?
    a. Internet connectivity is restricted to virtual Web sites.
    b. Applications can be run on the virtual machine only if they're resident on the physical machine.
    c. Virtual machines are limited to the host computer's peripheral configurations, such as mouse, keyboard, CD/DVD drives, and other devices.
    d. Virtual machines can run only OSs that are older than the physical machine's OS.

20. An image of a suspect drive can be loaded on a virtual machine. True or False?

21. EFS can encrypt which of the following?
    a. Files, folders, and volumes
    b. Certificates and private keys
    c. The global Registry
    d. Network servers

22. What happens when you copy an encrypted file from an EFS-enabled NTFS disk to a non-EFS disk or folder?
    a. The file can no longer be encrypted.
    b. EFS protection is maintained on the file.
    c. The file is unencrypted automatically.
    d. Only the owner of the file can continue to access it.

23. What are the functions of a data run's field components in an MFT record?

5

Hands-On Projects

There are no data files to extract for this chapter's projects, but create a *Work*\Chap05\Projects folder on your system before starting the projects.

Hands-On Project 5-1

In this project, you compare two files created in Microsoft Office to determine whether the files are different at the hexadecimal level. Keep a log of what you find. Follow these steps:

1. Start Word, and in a new document, type **This is a test**.

2. Save the file as **Mywordnew.doc** in your work folder, using **Word 97-2003 Document (*.doc)** as the file type. Exit Word.

3. Start Excel, and in a new workbook, enter a few random numbers. Save the file in your work folder as **Myworkbook.xls**, using **Excel 97 - 2003 Workbook (*.xls)** as the file type.

4. Exit Excel, and start WinHex (running it as an Administrator).

5. Click **File, Open** from the menu. In the Open dialog box, navigate to your work folder and double-click **Mywordnew.doc**.

6. Notice the file hexadecimal header D0 CF 11 E0 Al Bl 1A El starting at offset 0. Click **Edit, Copy All** from the menu, and then click **Editor Display**.

7. Start Notepad, and in a new document, press **Ctrl+V** to paste the copied data. Leave this window open.

8. Click **File, Open** from the WinHex menu. In the Open dialog box, navigate to your work folder and double-click **Myworkbook.xls**.

9. Repeat Step 6.

10. Paste the data you just copied under the Word document header information you pasted previously.

11. In the Notepad window, add your observations about the two files' header data. Save this file as **C5Prj01.txt** and turn it in to your instructor.

12. Exit WinHex.

Hands-On Project 5-2

In this project, you explore the MFT and learn how to locate date and time values in the metadata of a file you create. These steps help you identify previously deleted fragments of MFT records that you might find in unallocated disk space or in residual data in Pagefile.sys. You need the following for this project:

- A system running Windows Vista or later, with the C drive formatted as NTFS

- Notepad to create a small text file

- WinHex to analyze the metadata in the MFT (available on the book's DVD)

1. Start Notepad, and create a text file with one or more of the following lines:
   - A countryman between two lawyers is like a fish between two cats.
   - A slip of the foot you may soon recover, but a slip of the tongue you may never get over.
   - An investment in knowledge always pays the best interest.
   - Drive thy business or it will drive thee.

2. Save the file in your work folder as **C5Prj02.txt**, and exit Notepad. (If your work folder isn't on the C drive, make sure you save the file on your C drive to have it entered in the $MFT files you copy later.)

3. Next, review the material in "MFT and File Attributes," paying particular attention to attributes 0x10 and 0x30 for file dates and times. The following charts show the offset byte count starting at position FILE of the file's MFT record for the date and time stamps:

The offsets listed in the following charts are from the first byte of the MFT record, not the starting position of the specific attributes 0x10 and 0x30.

0x10 $Standard Information (data starts at offset 0x18)

Description of field	Offset position	Byte size
C Time (file creation)	0x50	8
A Time (file altered)	0x58	8
L Time (Last accessed)	0x60	8

© 2016 Cengage Learning®

0x30 $File_Name (data starts at offset 0x18)

Description of field	Offset position	Byte size
C Time (file creation)	0xB8	8
A Time (file altered)	0xC0	8
R Time (file read)	0xC8	8
M Time (MFT change)	0xD0	8

© 2016 Cengage Learning®

Next, you examine the metadata of the C5Prj02.txt file stored in the $MFT file. Follow these steps:

1. Start WinHex with the **Run as administrator** option. If you see an evaluation warning message, click **OK**.

2. As a safety precaution, click **Options, Edit Mode** from the menu. In the Select Mode (globally) dialog box, click **Read-only Mode (=write protected)**, as shown in Figure 5-39, and then click **OK**.

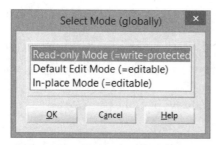

Figure 5-39   Changing WinHex to read-only mode
Courtesy of X-Ways AG, *www.x-ways.net*

 WinHex defaults to an editable mode, which means you can alter data in important system files and possibly corrupt them. When using a disk editor such as WinHex, always set it to read-only mode, unless you need to make specific modifications to data.

3. Click **Tools, Open Disk** from the menu. In the View Disk dialog box, click the **C:** drive (or the drive where you saved `C5Prj02.txt`), as shown in Figure 5-40, and then click **OK**. If you're prompted to take a new snapshot, click **Take new one**. Depending on the size and quantity of data on your disk, it might take several minutes for WinHex to traverse all the files and paths on your disk drive.

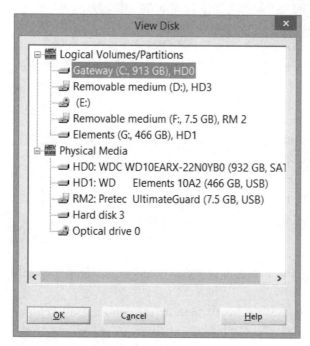

Figure 5-40   Selecting the drive in WinHex
Courtesy of X-Ways AG, *www.x-ways.net*

By default, WinHex displays a floating Data Interpreter window that converts hex values to decimal values and can also convert date and time codes. If you don't see this window, activate it by clicking View, pointing to Show, and clicking Data Interpreter.

4. Click **Options, Data Interpreter** from the menu. In the Data Interpreter Options dialog box, click the **Win32 FILETIME (64 bit)** check box, shown in Figure 5-41, and then click **OK**. The Data Interpreter should then have FILETIME as an additional display item.

Data Interpreter Options   ✕

- ☑ 8 bit, signed   ☐ DOS Date+Time (32 bit)
- ☐ 8 bit, unsigned   ☑ Win32 FILETIME (64 bit)
- ☑ 16 bit, signed   ☐ OLE 2.0 Date+Time (64 bit)
- ☐ 16 bit, unsigned   ☐ ANSI SQL Date+Time (64 bit)
- ☐ 24 bit, signed   ☐ UNIX/C Date+Time (32 bit)
- ☐ 24 bit, unsigned   ☐ Min's instead of sec's
- ☑ 32 bit, signed   ☐ HFS+ Date+Time (32 bit)
- ☐ 32 bit, unsigned   ☐ Java Date+Time (64 bit)
- ☐ 48 bit, unsigned
- ☐ 64 bit, signed   ☐ Binary (8 bit)
                                           ☐ Assembler opcodes
- ☐ Float (=Single, 32 bit)   ☐ GUID
- ☐ Real (48 bit)   ☐ SID
- ☐ Double (64 bit)   ☐ IP address
- ☐ Long Double (=Ext., 80 bit)   ☐ Packed 7-bit ASCII

☐ Big Endian   ☐ Hexadecimal [3]   ☐ Digit grouping

[OK]   [Cancel]   [Help]

Figure 5-41 The Data Interpreter Options dialog box
Courtesy of X-Ways AG, *www.x-ways.net*

5. Now you need to navigate to your work folder (C:\ *Work* \Chap05\Projects) in WinHex. In the upper-right pane of WinHex, scroll down until you see your work folder. Double-click each folder in the path (see Figure 5-42), and then click the **C5Prj02.txt** file.

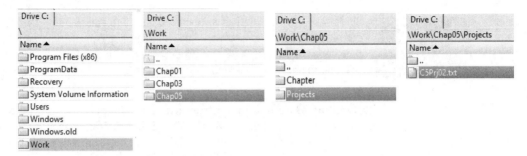

Figure 5-42 Navigating through folders in WinHex
Courtesy of X-Ways AG, *www.x-ways.net*

6. Click at the beginning of the record, on the letter **F** in FILE, and then drag down and to the right while you monitor the hexadecimal counter in the lower-right corner. (*Note:* 50 hexadecimal bytes is the "offset position" for the first date and time stamp for this record, as described in the previous charts for 0x10 $Standard Information.) When the counter reaches 50 (see Figure 5-43), release the mouse button.

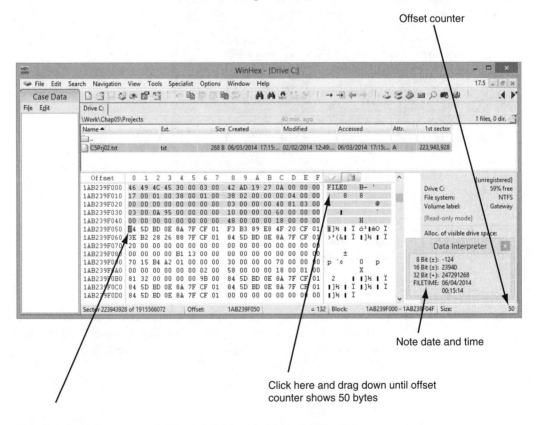

Offset counter

Note date and time

Click here and drag down until offset counter shows 50 bytes

After dragging, release mouse button and click here to interpret date and time

Figure 5-43 Locating the date and time value in the MFT record
Courtesy of X-Ways AG, *www.x-ways.net*

7. Move the cursor one position to the next byte (down one line and to the left), and record the date and time of the Data Interpreter's FILETIME values.

8. Reposition the mouse cursor on the remaining offsets listed in the previous charts, and record their values.

9. When you're finished, exit WinHex and hand in the date and time values you recorded.

Hands-On Project 5-3

In this project, you use WinHex to become familiar with different file types. Follow these steps:

1. Locate or create Microsoft Excel (.xls), Microsoft Word (.doc), .gif, .jpg, and .mp3 files. If you're creating a Word document or an Excel spreadsheet, save it as an Office 97-2003 file.

2. Start WinHex.

3. Open each file type in WinHex. Record the hexadecimal codes for each file in a text editor, such as Notepad or WordPad. For example, for the Word document, record **Word Header: D0 CF 11 E0**.

4. Save the file, and then print it to give to your instructor.

Hands-On Project 5-4

This project is a continuation of the in-chapter activity done with OSForensics. The paralegal has asked you to see whether any passwords are listed in the image of Denise Robinson's computer. Follow these steps:

1. Start OSForensics. If prompted to allow the program to make changes to your computer, click **OK** or **Yes**. In the OSForensics message box, click **Continue Using Free Version**.

2. Mount the **InCh05.img** file as described in the in-chapter activity.

3. In the main window, click **Manage Case** in the navigation bar on the left, if necessary. In the Select Case pane on the right, double-click **InChap05** if a green checkmark isn't displayed next to it.

4. In the navigation bar on the left, click **Passwords**. In the pane on the right, click the **Find Browser Passwords** tab, if necessary. Click the **Scan Drive** button, and then click the drive letter for the InCh05.img mounted virtual drive.

5. In the navigation bar on the left, click **Retrieve Passwords**. In the pane on the right, right-click the first item and click **Export List to Case**. In the Title text box, type **Denise Robinson's additional e-mail and password**, and then click **OK**. Repeat this step for all browser passwords that were recovered.

6. In the Passwords window, click the **Windows Login Passwords** tab. Click the **Scan Drive** button, and then click the drive letter for the InCh05.img mounted virtual drive.

7. Click **Retrieve Hashes**, and then click **Save to File**. In the Save to dialog box, navigate to your work folder, type **Denise-Robinson-Win-Passwords-Hashes** in the File name text box, and then click **Save**.

8. In the navigation bar on the left, click **Manage Case**. In the Manage Current Case pane on the right, click the **Add Attachment** button. Navigate to where you saved the Denise-Robinson-Win-Password file, click the file, and click **Open**. In the Export Title text box, type **Denise-Robinson-Win-Passwords**, and then click **Add**.

9. In the navigation bar at the top, click **Generate Report**. In the Export Report dialog box, click **OK**. If you get a warning message that the report already exists, click **Yes** to overwrite the previous report.

10. Exit OSForensics, and print the report displayed in your Web browser. Turn the report in to your instructor.

Case Projects

Case Project 5-1

Using the information you gathered in Hands-On Project 5-4, write a one-page memo to the paralegal, Ms. D. K. Jones, explaining the process you used to find the e-mail and password data.

Case Project 5-2

An employee suspects that his password has been compromised. He changed it two days ago, yet it seems someone has used it again. What might be going on?

Case Project 5-3

To continue your learning in digital forensics, you should research new tools and methods often. For this project, download the user manuals for VirtualBox and ProDiscover. Write a guide on how to load a VHD file converted from a ProDiscover .eve image file into VirtualBox. You can download the user guide for VirtualBox at *www.virtualbox.org/wiki/Downloads*. The ProDiscover manual should be in the following path, under the folder where you installed ProDiscover: Program Files (x86)\Technology Pathways\ProDiscover\ProDiscoverManual.pdf.

chapter # 6

Current Digital Forensics Tools

After reading this chapter and completing the exercises, you will be able to:

- Explain how to evaluate needs for digital forensics tools
- Describe available digital forensics software tools
- List some considerations for digital forensics hardware tools
- Describe methods for validating and testing forensics tools

Chapter 2 outlined how to set up a forensics laboratory. This chapter explores many software and hardware tools used during digital forensics investigations. No specific tools are recommended; instead, the goal is to explain how to select tools for digital investigations based on specific criteria.

Forensics tools are constantly being developed, updated, patched, revised, and discontinued. Therefore, checking vendors' Web sites routinely to look for new features and improvements is important. These improvements might address a difficult problem you're having in an investigation.

Before purchasing any forensics tools, consider whether the tool can save you time during investigations and whether that time savings affects the reliability of data you recover. Many GUI forensics tools require a lot of resources and demand computers with more memory and faster processor speeds or more processors. Sometimes they require more resources than a typical workstation has because of other applications, such as antivirus programs, running in the background. These background programs compete for resources with a digital forensics program, and a forensics program or the OS can stop running or hang, causing delays in your investigation.

Finally, when planning purchases for your forensics lab, determine what a new forensics tool can do better than one you're currently using. In particular, assess how well the software performs in validation tests, and then verify the integrity of the tool's results.

As software continues to develop and investigators have new needs, vendors will address these needs. The tools listed in this chapter are in no way a complete list of tools available for Windows, Linux, or Mac OS.

Evaluating Digital Forensics Tool Needs

As described in Chapter 2, you need to develop a business plan to justify the acquisition of digital forensics hardware and software. When researching options, consider open-source tools, which sometimes include technical support. The goal is to find the best value for as many features as possible. Some questions to ask when evaluating tools include the following:

- On which OS does the forensics tool run? Does the tool run on multiple OSs?
- Is the tool versatile? For example, does it work in both Windows and Linux?
- Can the tool analyze more than one file system, such as FAT, NTFS, and Ext4?
- Can a scripting language be used with the tool to automate repetitive functions and tasks?
- Does the tool have any automated features that can help reduce the time needed to analyze data?
- What is the vendor's reputation for providing product support? For open-source tools, how good are the support forums?

As you learn more about digital investigations, you'll have more questions about tools for conducting these investigations. When you search for tools, keep in mind what OSs and file types you'll be analyzing. For example, if you need to analyze Microsoft Access or SQL Server databases, look for a product designed to read these files. If you're analyzing e-mail messages, look for a forensics tool that specializes in reading e-mail content.

When you're selecting tools for your lab, keep an open mind, and compare platforms and applications for different tasks. Although many investigators are most comfortable using Windows tools, check into other options, such as Linux and Macintosh platforms.

Types of Digital Forensics Tools

Digital forensics tools are divided into two major categories: hardware and software. Each category has subcategories discussed in more depth later in this chapter. The following sections outline basic features required and expected of most digital forensics tools.

Hardware Forensics Tools Hardware forensics tools range from simple, single-purpose components to complete computer systems and servers. For example, the Tableau T35es-R2 SATA/IDE eSATA bridge is a single-purpose component that makes it possible to access a SATA or an IDE drive with one device. Some examples of complete systems are Digital Intelligence F.R.E.D. systems (*www.digitalintelligence.com/cart/ComputerForensicsProducts/Hardware-p1.html*), DIBS Advanced Forensic Workstations (*www.dibsforensics.com/index.html*), Forensic Computers' Forensic Examination Stations and portable units (*www.forensic-computers.com*), and H-11 Digital Forensics systems (*www.h11dfs.com/products/products/forensic-hardware/*).

Software Forensics Tools Software forensics tools are grouped into command-line applications and GUI applications. Some tools are specialized to perform one task. For example, SafeBack was designed as a command-line disk acquisition tool from New Technologies, Inc. (NTI). It's no longer supported, but you can still find it distributed online. However, it's used more as a reliable fallback when all else fails than a primary tool. Other tools are designed to perform many different tasks. For example, PassMark Software OSForensics, Technology Pathways ProDiscover, X-Ways Forensics, Guidance Software EnCase, and AccessData FTK are GUI tools designed to perform most forensics acquisition and analysis functions.

Software forensics tools are commonly used to copy data from a suspect's drive to an image file. Many GUI acquisition tools can read all structures in an image file as though the image were the original drive and have the capability to analyze image files. In Chapter 5, you learned how some of these tools are used to acquire data from suspects' drives.

Tasks Performed by Digital Forensics Tools

All digital forensics tools, both hardware and software, perform specific functions. When you're testing new tools, you might find it helpful to follow guidelines set up by NIST's **Computer Forensics Tool Testing (CFTT)** program, ASTM International's (formerly the American Society of Testing and Materials) E2678 standard, and the International Organization on Computer Evidence (IOCE). In addition, ISO standard 27037 states that Digital Evidence First Responders (DEFRs) should use validated tools. The following categories of functions are meant as guidelines for evaluating digital forensics tools, with subfunctions for refining data analysis and recovery and ensuring data quality:

- Acquisition
- Validation and verification
- Extraction
- Reconstruction
- Reporting

NIST's CFTT and other groups include additonal functions, such as data acquistion, data extraction from mobile devices, file reconstruction, and string searching, that aren't included in these guidelines ("Verification of Digital Forensics Tools", Jim Lyle, May 2010, Montana Supreme Court Spring Training Conference). In the following sections, you learn how these functions and subfunctions apply to digital investigations.

Acquisition Acquisition, the first task in digital forensics investigations, is making a copy of the original drive. As described in Chapter 3, this procedure preserves the original drive to make sure it doesn't become corrupt and damage the digital evidence. In Chapter 4, you learned how to handle digital evidence correctly, and in Chapter 8, you learn more about using acquisition tools. Subfunctions in the acquisition category include the following:

- Physical data copy
- Logical data copy
- Data acquisition format
- Command-line acquisition
- GUI acquisition
- Remote, live, and memory acquisitions

ISO standard 27037 states that the most important factors in data acquisition are the DEFR's competency and the use of validated tools, and it includes guidelines on how to approach acquisition in different situations. What's most important is documenting what was done and why. For example, if you're acquiring data at a scene with hazardous materials, clearly speed is critical, so you might decide to forgo acquiring RAM and focus on collecting devices. You can also find decision-marking flowcharts on whether to copy an entire physical disk or concentrate on only a partition or folder, for instance. Section 7 of the standard addresses acquiring volatile memory, an important part of live acquisitions. Other situations that affect acquisitions include encrypted devices or mission-critical systems that can't be turned off.

Some digital forensics software suites, such as AccessData FTK, have separate tools for acquiring an image. However, some investigators opt to use hardware devices, such as Tableau TD2, Logicube Talon, VOOM HardCopy 3P, or Image MASSter Solo-4 Forensic unit from Intelligent Computer Solutions, Inc., for acquiring an image. These hardware devices have built-in software for data acquisition. No other device or program is needed to make a duplicate drive; however, you still need forensics software to analyze the data.

To see specifications for the Logicube Talon, go to *www.logicube.com/ shop/talon-enhanced/*. To see the Image MASSter Solo-4 unit, search at *www.ics-iq.com*. To see VOOM HardCopy 3, search at *www.voomtech.com*.

Other acquisition tools require combining hardware devices and software programs to make disk acquisitions. For example, many software tools mount drives as read-only, and others might require a physical write-blocker. Any tool that has a built-in software write-blocker should be verified to make sure evidence hasn't been altered.

Two types of data-copying methods are used in software acquisitions: physical copying of the entire drive and logical copying of a disk partition. Most software acquisition tools include the option of imaging an entire physical drive or just a logical partition. Usually, the situation dictates whether you make a physical or logical acquisition. One reason to choose a logical acquisition is drive encryption. With the increasing emphasis on data security, drive encryption is used more commonly now. As mentioned in Chapter 5, making a physical acquisition of a drive with whole disk encryption can result in unreadable data. With a logical acquisition, however, you can still read and analyze the files. Of course, this method requires a live acquisition (covered in Chapter 10) because you need to log on to the system.

Disk acquisition formats vary from raw data to vendor-specific proprietary, as you learned in Chapter 5. The raw data format, typically created with the UNIX/Linux dd command, is a simple bit-for-bit copy of a data file, a disk partition, or an entire drive. A raw imaging tool can copy data from one drive to another disk or to segmented files. Because it's a true unaltered copy, you can view a raw image file's contents with any hexadecimal editor, such as Hex Workshop or WinHex. These tools give you a hexadecimal view (see Figure 6-1) or a plaintext view of the data.

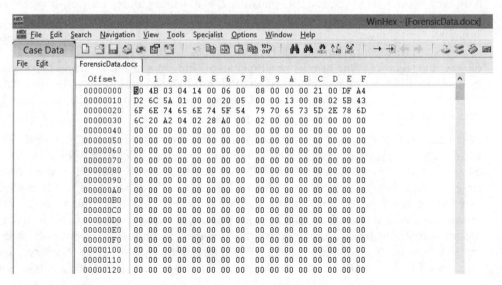

Figure 6-1 Viewing data in WinHex
Courtesy of X-Ways AG, *www.x-ways.net*

Creating smaller segmented files is a typical feature in vendor acquisition tools. Their purpose is to make it easier to store acquired data on smaller media, such as CDs or USB drives.

Remote acquisition of files is common in larger organizations. Enterprise-level companies are geographically diverse, so investigators might not be able to get physical access to systems without traveling long distances. Popular tools, such as AccessData and EnCase, can do remote acquisitions of forensics drive images on a network, and these acquisitions can also be done with a dd command.

Validation and Verification Validation and verification functions work hand in hand. **Validation** is a way to confirm that a tool is functioning as intended, and **verification** proves that two sets of data are identical by calculating hash values or using another similar method. Another related process is filtering, which involves sorting and searching through investigation findings to separate good data and suspicious data. Validating tools and verifying data are what allow filtering.

To validate a tool, you can use forensic images that have been created for desktop and mobile devices; these files are posted on Web sites such as NIST's CFTT or the Scientific Working Group on Digital Evidence (SWGDE) and tell you what the tool should find as evidence on the drives. They can also give you ranges of results so that you can determine, for example, that a tool is good for Linux images but has problems with older Windows systems. These groups also publish the results of testing hardware acquisition tools. After validating a tool, you must also make sure all forensic copies of a particular device have the same hash value.

All forensics acquisition tools have a method for verification of the data-copying process that compares the original drive with the image. For example, EnCase prompts you to obtain the MD5 hash value of acquired data, and FTK validates MD5 and SHA-1 hash sets during data acquisition. Hardware acquisition tools, such as Image MASSter Solo-4, can perform simultaneous MD5 and CRC-32 hashing during data acquisition. Whether you choose a software or hardware solution for acquisition, make sure the tool has a hashing function for verification purposes. How data hashing is used depends on the investigation, but using a hashing algorithm on the entire suspect drive and all its files is a standard practice. This method produces a unique hexadecimal value for ensuring that the original data hasn't changed and copies are of the same unchanged data or image.

When performing filtering, you separate good data from suspicious data. Good data consists of known files, such as OS files, common programs (Microsoft Word, for example), and standard files used in a company's day-to-day business. You can also use hash values to create a known good hash value list of a fresh installation of an OS, all applications, and known good images and documents (spreadsheets, text files, and so on). With this information, an investigator could ignore all files on this known good list and focus on other files that aren't on this list. Filtering can also be used to find data for evidence in criminal investigations or to build a case for terminating an employee. The **National Software Reference Library (NSRL)** has compiled a list of known file hashes for a variety of OSs, applications, and images that you can download from *www.nsrl.nist.gov/Downloads.htm* (see Figure 6-2). It's also adding hash values for mobile apps, specifically iOS and Android. You learn more about the NSRL in "Validating and Testing Forensics Software" later in this chapter.

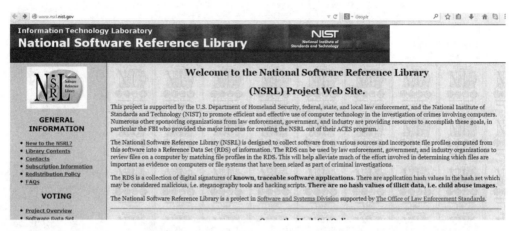

Figure 6-2   The home page of the National Software Reference Library
Source: *www.nsrl.nist.gov*

Organizations such as the National Center for Missing and Exploited Children maintain hash sets of photos of known victims. These files are sorted into the "suspicious" or known bad category.

Several digital forensics tools can integrate known good file hash sets and compare them with file hashes from a suspect drive to see whether they match. With this process, you can eliminate large amounts of data quickly so that you can focus your evidence analysis. You can also begin building your own hash sets. Another feature to consider is hashing and comparing sectors of data. It's useful for identifying fragments of data in slack and free disk space that might be partially overwritten.

Another way to filter data is analyzing and verifying header values for known file types. Each file type has a header value associated with a file extension, and many forensics tools include a list of common file headers. To view these file headers, you use a hexadecimal editor, which can tell you whether a file extension is incorrect for the file type. Renaming file extensions is often done to disguise or hide data, and you could miss pertinent data if you don't check file headers. A standard indicator for graphics files is the hex value "FF D8," shown in the first line of output in the `File_Filter.docx` file shown in Figure 6-3. (You examine graphics files in more detail in Chapter 8.) After some practice in viewing file headers, you'll learn to recognize common header values.

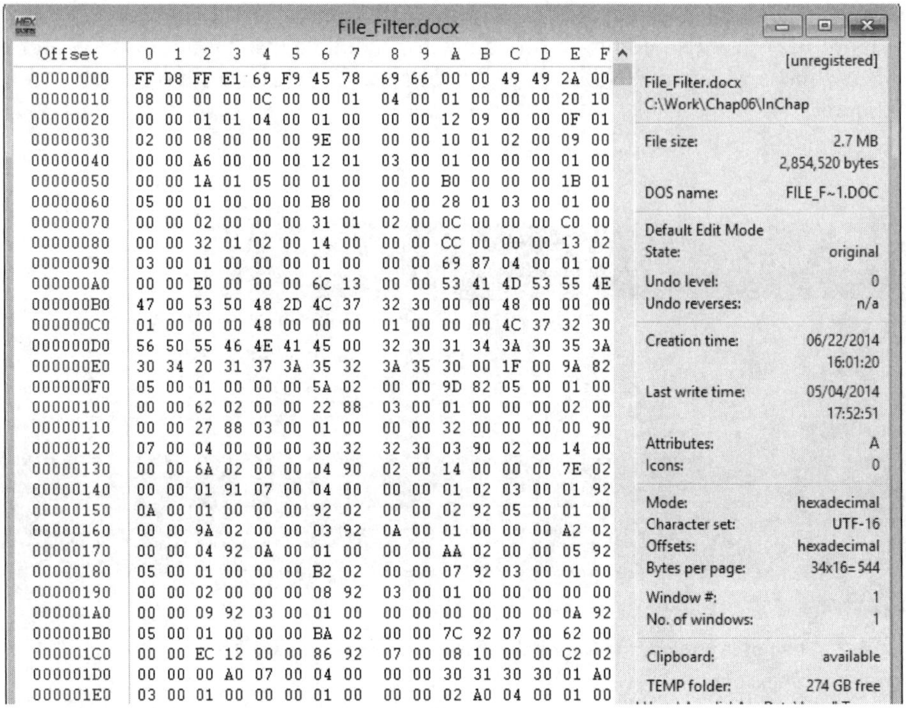

Figure 6-3 The file header indicates a `.jpeg` file
Courtesy of X-Ways AG, *www.x-ways.net*

Because the `File_Filter.docx` file has "FF D8" in the header, it's a `.jpeg` image, not a `.docx` file. If you try to open this file in Microsoft Word, you see the error message shown in Figure 6-4.

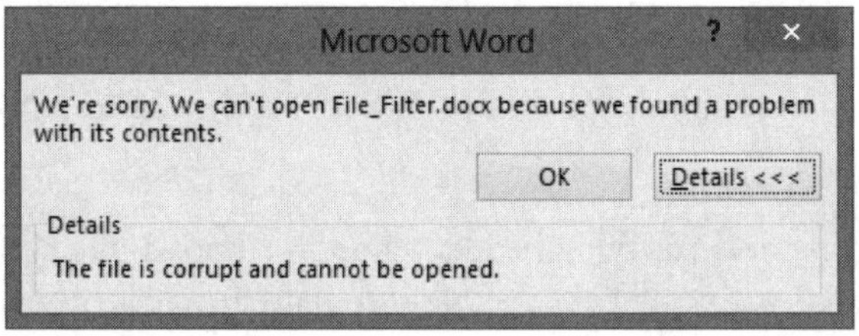

Figure 6-4 Error message displayed when trying to open a `.jpeg` file in Word
Courtesy of Microsoft Corporation

If you open the file with an image viewer, such as Microsoft Paint, you see the image shown in Figure 6-5.

Figure 6-5 `File_Filter.docx` opened in Paint
Courtesy of Microsoft Corporation and © 2016 Cengage Learning®

Searching and comparing file headers rather than file extensions improves filtering. With this feature, you can locate files that might have been altered intentionally. In Chapters 8 and 9, you see how to use this feature to locate hidden data.

Extraction The **extraction** function is the recovery task in a digital investigation and is the most challenging of all tasks to master. In Chapter 1, you learned how system analysis applies to an investigation. Recovering data is the first step in analyzing an investigation's data. The following subfunctions of extraction are used in investigations:

- Data viewing
- Keyword searching
- Decompressing or uncompressing
- Carving
- Decrypting
- Bookmarking or tagging

 Mobile devices have added some complexity to forensic extraction because so much data can be retrieved from them: call records, URLs, GPS data, SMS and text messages, and more. You explore mobile device forensics in Chapter 12.

Many digital forensics tools include a data-viewing mechanism for digital evidence and offer several ways to view data, including logical drive structures, such as folders and files. These tools also display allocated file data and unallocated disk areas with special file and disk viewers. Being able to view this data in its normal form makes analyzing and collecting clues for the investigation easier.

A common task in digital investigations is searching for and recovering relevant data. Forensics tools have functions for searching for keywords of interest to the investigation. Using a **keyword search** speeds up the analysis process, if used correctly; however, a poor selection of keywords generates too much information. Another way to narrow down a search is by using word lists created for a specific case. Figure 6-6 shows an OSForensics built-in file called "banned sports drugs" used to do an indexed search for the keyword "nucleic acids" in Charlie's hard drive from the M57 Patents case.

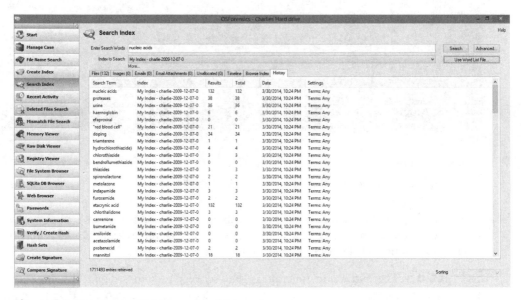

Figure 6-6   Using a word list to search in OSForensics
Source: PassMark Software, *www.osforensics.com*

With some tools, you can set filters to select file types to search, such as searching only PDF files. Another function in some forensics tools, such as X-Ways Forensics and OSForensics, is indexing all words on a drive. These features speed up keyword searches, which speeds up analysis.

Another feature to consider for extraction is the format the forensics tool can read. For example, as you saw in Chapter 4, OSForensics has a feature for reading and indexing data from Microsoft .pst and .ost files, and EnCase has a third-party add-on that indexes and analyzes Microsoft .pst files. In addition, EnCase, X-Ways Forensics, and ProDiscover enable you to create scripts for extracting data, but FTK doesn't have this feature. Often you have to use a combination of tools to retrieve and report on evidence from digital devices accurately.

The investigation process also involves reconstructing fragments of files that have been deleted from a suspect drive. In North America, this reconstruction is called "carving"; in Europe, it's called "salvaging." (Carving is covered in more depth in Chapters 8 and 16.) Investigators often need to be able to extract data from unallocated disk space. Locating file header information, as mentioned in "Validation and Verification," is a reliable method for carving data. Most forensics tools analyze unallocated areas of a drive or a forensic image and locate fragments or entire file structures that can be carved and copied into a newly reconstructed file. Some investigators prefer carving fragmented data manually with a command-line tool, but advanced GUI tools with built-in carving functions are more common now. Figure 6-7 shows the data-carving feature in OSForensics.

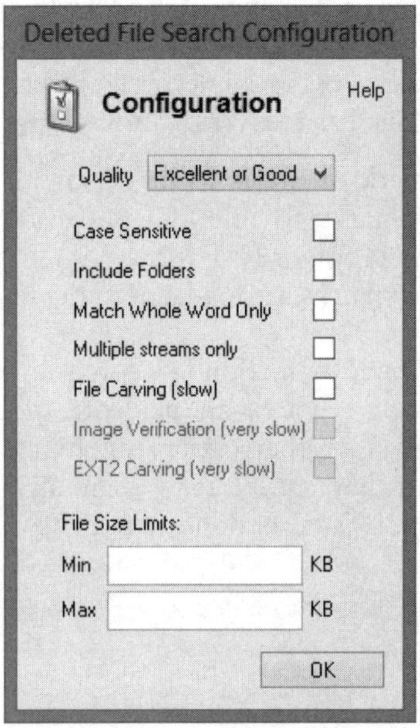

Figure 6-7 Data-carving options in OSForensics
Source: PassMark Software, *www.osforensics.com*

Some tools, such as Simple Carver Suite (*www.simplecarver.com*) and DataLifter (*http://datalifter. software.informer.com*), are specifically designed to carve known data types from exported unallocated disk space. DataLifter includes a feature that enables you to add other header values.

There are many compression or zip utilities, such as WinZip, 7Zip, and pzip. When a forensics tool encounters a compressed file or a zip archive as part of a forensic image, it applies the correct algorithm for uncompressing the files. For example, uncompressing Windows files is done with the Lempel-Ziv algorithm, Lz32.dll. Other OSs and compression utilities use other algorithms.

A major challenge in digital investigations is analyzing, recovering, and decrypting data from encrypted files or systems. Encryption can be used on a drive, disk partition, or file. Many e-mail services, such as Microsoft Outlook, provide encryption protection for .pst folders and messages. Encryption can be platform specific, such as Windows Encrypting File System (EFS) and BitLocker, or done with third-party tools, such as Pretty Good Privacy (PGP) and GnuPG.

From an investigation perspective, encrypted files and systems are a problem. Many password recovery tools have a feature for generating potential password lists for a **password dictionary attack**. Passwords are typically stored as hash values, not in plaintext, and are meant to be one-way hashes, meaning you can't apply an algorithm to break them. Password lists give you a starting point for guessing passwords; in addition, you can try words that are applicable to a suspect's profession and hobbies. Passwords are sometimes written to a temporary file or system file, such as `Pagefile.sys`, so examining these files is a useful technique, too. OSForensics, like many forensics tools, has a built-in password cracker. First, it attempts to retrieve browser and OS passwords, especially if you're examining a live system. Next, it generates rainbow tables (files containing password hash values; explained in Chapter 9) and compares hash values to see whether it can find a match with the password. If it fails, the next step is to run a **brute-force attack** on the encrypted file. OSForensics, for example, attempts to recover Windows logon passwords and has additional features, such as recovering browser passwords.

After locating the evidence, the next task is to bookmark or tag it so that you can refer to it later when needed. Many forensics tools use bookmarks to insert digital evidence into a report generator, which produces a technical report in HTML or RTF format of the examination's findings. When the report generator is started, bookmarks are loaded into the report.

Reconstruction The purpose of having a **reconstruction** function in a forensics tool is to re-create a suspect drive to show what happened during a crime or an incident. Another reason for duplicating a suspect drive is to create a copy for other digital investigators, who might need a fully functional copy of the drive so that they can perform their own acquisition, test, and analysis of the evidence. Reconstruction is also done if a drive has been compromised by malware or a suspect's actions.

The following are methods of reconstruction:

- Disk-to-disk copy
- Partition-to-partition copy
- Image-to-disk copy
- Image-to-partition copy
- Disk-to-image copy
- Rebuilding files from data runs and carving

There are several ways to re-create an image of a suspect drive. A decade ago, the ideal method was using the same make and model disk as the suspect disk, as discussed in Chapter 5, but disk-to-disk copies are rarely used now. (A partition-to-partition copy is very similar, but you use partitions instead of disks.) Typically, you copy an image to another location, such as a partition, a physical disk, or a virtual machine (covered in Chapter 10). The simplest method of duplicating a drive is using a tool that makes a direct disk-to-image copy from the suspect disk to the target location. Many tools can perform this task. One free tool is the Linux `dd` command, but it has a major disadvantage: It produces a flat, uncompressed file that's the same size as the source drive.

Some tools have proprietary formats that can be restored only by the same application that created them. For example, a ProDiscover image (`.eve` format) can be restored only by using ProDiscover. Most tools, however, can convert files to the `.E01` or `.001` format so that you can use files in a variety of tools to take advantage of their different strengths.

Forensic analysis is often complicated by time-critical cases, such as those involving kidnapping or homicides, but shadowing drives is a useful technique in these situations. It requires a hardware device, such as Voom Technologies Shadow Drive, that connects a suspect's drive to a read-only IDE port and another drive to a read-write port that's called a "shadow drive." When the Voom device is connected to a computer, you can access and run applications on the suspect's drive. All data that would normally be written to the suspect's drive is redirected to the shadow drive ("Voom Technologies' Shadow 3 said to provide a quick way to investigate computers without compromising evidence," *Government Security News*, February 2014). This tool has been used in court so that expert witnesses could easily show evidence on a drive and how a suspect could have used the information.

Reporting To perform a forensics disk analysis and examination, you need to create a report. Before Windows forensics tools were available, this process required copying data from a suspect drive and extracting the digital evidence manually. The investigator then copied the evidence to a separate program, such as a word processor, to create a report. File data that couldn't be read in a word processor—databases, spreadsheets, and graphics, for example—made it difficult to insert nonprintable characters, such as binary data, into a report. Typically, these reports weren't stored electronically because investigators had to collect printouts from several different applications to consolidate everything into one large paper report.

Newer forensics tools can produce electronic reports in a variety of formats, such as word-processing documents, HTML Web pages, and Acrobat PDF files. The following are subfunctions of the reporting function:

- Bookmarking or tagging
- Log reports
- Report generator

As part of the validation process, often you need to document the steps you took to acquire data from a suspect drive. Many forensics tools can produce a log report that records an investigator's activities and incorporates evidence that was bookmarked or tagged during extraction. Then a built-in report generator is used to create a report in a variety of formats. Some tools with report generators that display bookmarked evidence are EnCase, FTK, OSForensics, ILookIX, X-Ways Forensics, and ProDiscover.

You can add a log report to your final report as documentation of the steps you took during the examination, which can be useful if repeating the examination is necessary. For a case that requires peer review, log reports confirm what activities were performed and what results were found in the original analysis and examination. Keep in mind that reports generated by forensics tools are no substitute for an investigator's report. Investigators need to be able to explain their decisions and the output in more detail than a tool-generated report can produce.

Tool Comparisons

To help determine which forensics tool to purchase, a comparison table of functions, subfunctions, and vendor products is useful. Cross-referencing functions and subfunctions with vendor products makes it easier to identify the forensics tool that best meets your needs. Table 6-1 is an example of how to compare forensics vendors' tools. Your needs might differ from the functions and subfunctions listed in this table. When developing your own table, add other functions and subfunctions you think are necessary to determine which tools you should acquire for an investigation.

Table 6-1 Comparison of forensics tool functions

Function	ProDiscover Basic	OSForensics, demo version	AccessData FTK	Guidance Software EnCase
Acquisition				
Physical data copy	✓	✓	✓	✓
Logical data copy	✓	✓	✓	
Data acquisition formats	✓	✓	✓	✓
Command-line processes				✓
GUI processes	✓	✓	✓	✓
Remote acquisition		✓	✓	✓
Validation and verification				
Hashing	✓	✓	✓	✓
Verification	✓	✓	✓	✓
Filtering		✓	✓	✓
Analyzing file headers		✓	✓	✓
Extraction				
Data viewing	✓	✓	✓	✓
Keyword searching	✓	✓	✓	✓
Decompressing			✓	✓
Carving		✓	✓	✓
Decrypting		✓	✓	
Bookmarking	✓	✓	✓	✓
Reconstruction				
Disk-to-disk copy	✓	✓	✓	✓
Partition-to-partition copy	✓	✓	✓	✓
Image-to-disk copy	✓	✓	✓	✓
Image-to-partition copy	✓	✓	✓	✓
Disk-to-image copy	✓	✓	✓	✓
Rebuilding files	✓	✓	✓	✓
Reporting				
Bookmarking/tagging	✓	✓	✓	✓
Log reports		✓	✓	✓
Report generator	✓	✓	✓	
Automation and other features				
Scripting language				✓
Mount virtual machines		✓	✓	✓
E-discovery		✓	✓	✓

© 2016 Cengage Learning®

Other Considerations for Tools

As part of the business planning for your lab, you should determine which tools offer the most flexibility, reliability, and future expandability. The software tools you select should be compatible with the next generation of OSs; for example, Windows 7 and later added features for compatibility with mobile devices. As an investigator, it's your responsibility to find information on changes in new hardware or software releases and changes planned for the next release. Because OS vendors don't always supply adequate information about future file system upgrades, you must research and prepare for these changes and develop resources for finding new specifications if the vendor fails to provide them. For example, when NTFS was introduced with Windows NT, forensics software vendors revised their products for this new file system, but addressing the file system changes took some time. Therefore, investigators had to look for alternatives to getting the data they needed, such as consulting Microsoft resource kits for Windows NT.

Another consideration when maintaining a forensics lab is creating a software library containing older versions of forensics utilities, OSs, and other programs. When purchasing newer and more versatile tools, you should also ensure that your lab maintains older versions of software and OSs, such as Windows and Linux. If a new software version fixes one bug but introduces another, you can use the previous version to overcome problems caused by the new bug.

6

Digital Forensics Software Tools

Whether you use a suite of tools or a task-specific tool, you have the option of selecting one that enables you to analyze digital evidence through the command line or in a GUI. The following sections explore some options for command-line and GUI tools in both Windows and UNIX/Linux.

Macintosh has made a comeback, and more people are using it. Installing Windows on Mac machines is fairly easy, so you can use most forensics tools on a Mac machine.

Command-Line Forensics Tools

As mentioned in Chapter 1, computers used several OSs before Windows and MS-DOS dominated the market. During this time, digital forensics wasn't a major concern. After people started using PCs, however, they figured out how to use them for illegal and destructive purposes and to commit crimes and civil infractions with them. Software developers began releasing forensics tools to help private- and public-sector investigators examine PCs. The first tools that analyzed and extracted data from floppy disks and hard disks were MS-DOS tools for IBM PC file systems.

One of the first MS-DOS tools used for digital investigations was Norton DiskEdit. This tool used manual processes that required investigators to spend considerable time on a typical 500 MB drive. Eventually, programs designed for digital forensics were developed for DOS, Windows, Apple, NetWare, and UNIX systems. Some of these early programs could extract data from slack and free disk space; others were capable only of retrieving deleted files. Current programs are more powerful and can search for specific words or characters, import a keyword list to search, calculate hash values, recover deleted items, conduct physical and logical analyses, and more.

One advantage of using command-line tools for an investigation is that they require few system resources because they're designed to run in minimal configurations. In fact, most tools fit on bootable media (USB drives, CDs, and DVDs). Conducting an initial inquiry or a complete investigation with bootable media can save time and effort. Most tools also produce a text report that fits on a USB drive or other removable media.

Some command-line forensics tools are created specifically for Windows command-line interface (CLI) platforms; others are created for Macintosh and UNIX/Linux. Because there are many different versions of UNIX and Linux, these OSs are often referred to as "Linux platforms." In Chapter 5, you were introduced to using some command-line tools in Linux, such as the dd and dcfldd commands. For Windows platforms, a number of companies, such as NTI, Digital Intelligence, Maresware, DataLifter, and ByteBack, are recognized for their work in command-line forensics tools.

Some tools that are readily available in the command line are often overlooked. For example, in Windows 2000 and later, the `dir` command shows you the file owner if you have multiple users on the system or network. Try it by following these steps:

1. Open a command prompt window.

2. At the command prompt, type **cd ** and press **Enter** to take you to the root directory. Create a work folder for this chapter by typing **md *Work*\Chap06\Chapter** (replacing *Work* with the name of your work folder) and pressing **Enter**.

3. Make sure you're at the root directory, and type
   dir /q > C:*Work*\Chap06\Chapter\Fileowner.txt and press **Enter**.

4. In any text editor, open **Fileowner.txt** to see the results. You should see your file structure and whether the files were generated by the system or by a user. When you're finished, exit the text editor and close the command prompt window.

Linux Forensics Tools

Although UNIX has been around for many decades, it's been mostly replaced by Linux; however, you might still encounter systems running UNIX. Many people haven't used Linux platforms much. However, with GUIs now readily available with Linux platforms, these OSs are becoming more popular with home and business end users. Because most are free, they're increasingly popular in developing and emerging nations. This newfound popularity and the staggering number of versions give investigators a challenge: learning the Linux command line and investigating the Linux environment. In Chapter 7, you learn more about several Linux tools for forensics analysis, such as SMART, Kali Linux, and Autopsy with Sleuth Kit.

This book isn't geared toward the Linux platform for forensics analysis, but using a Linux tool for the processes described in this book works as well as on a Microsoft platform. Also, keep in mind that Linux tools work well on Windows systems, as you see in Chapter 7.

SMART SMART is designed to be installed on numerous Linux versions, including Gentoo, Fedora, SUSE, Debian, Knoppix, Ubuntu, Slackware, and more. You can analyze a variety of file systems with SMART; for a list of file systems or to download an evaluation ISO image for SMART and SMART Linux, go to *www.asrdata.com/forensic-software/software-download/*.

SMART includes several plug-in utilities. This modular approach makes it possible to upgrade SMART components easily and quickly. SMART can also take advantage of multi-threading capabilities in OSs and hardware, a feature lacking in other forensics utilities. This tool is one of the few that can mount different file systems, such as journaling file systems, in a read-only format.

Another useful option in SMART is the hex viewer, which color-codes hex values to make it easier to see where a file begins and ends. SMART also offers a reporting feature. Everything you do during your investigation with SMART is logged, so you can select what you want to include in a report, such as bookmarks.

Helix 3 One of the easiest suites to use is Helix because of its user interface. Although Helix is no longer a free package, you can go to *www.e-fense.com/products.php* to learn more about it. What's unique about Helix is that you can load it on a live Windows system, and it loads as a bootable Linux OS from a cold boot. Its Windows component is used for live acquisitions. Be aware, however, that some international courts haven't accepted live acquisitions as a valid forensics practice.

During corporate investigations, often you need to retrieve RAM and other data, such as the suspect's user profile, from a workstation or server that can't be seized or turned off. This data is extracted while the system is running and captured in its state at the time of extraction. Make sure to keep a journal to record what you're doing, however. To do a live acquisition, insert the Helix CD/DVD into the suspect's machine.

Kali Linux Kali Linux, formerly known as BackTrack, is another Linux Live CD used by many security professionals and forensics investigators. It includes a variety of tools and has an easy-to-use KDE interface. You can download the ISO image from *www.kali.org*. Kali includes several tools, such as Autopsy and Sleuth Kit (discussed next), ophcrack, dcfldd, MemFetch, and MBoxGrep.

Autopsy and Sleuth Kit Sleuth Kit is a Linux forensics tool, and Autopsy is the GUI browser interface for accessing Sleuth Kit's tools. Chapter 7 explains how to use these tools, but if you're accessing them from Kali, for example, shut down your Windows computer with the Kali disc in the CD/DVD drive, making sure your system is set to boot from the CD/DVD drive before the hard drive. Then do a hard boot to the computer. In the options that are displayed, select Expert Mode. (Note that this mode is forensically sound.) If you're booting from a laptop, you might have display issues. You can click "scan" to have Kali find the correct settings. (If Kali fails to find these settings, experiment until you find a setting that works.) After the correct display setting is applied, a GUI is displayed. If prompted, specify whether to load SCSI modules or additional modules from a floppy disk.

On your desktop, you should see what drives have been detected. For example, say that /dev/hda1 and /dev/hda2 are displayed at the upper left. If you click the Kali button, which is similar to the Start button in Windows, you see the GUI selection. When you select Forensic Tools, the Autopsy option is displayed. From here, you can open an existing case or start a new case. For more information on these tools, visit *www.sleuthkit.org*.

6

Other GUI Forensics Tools

Several software vendors have introduced forensics tools that work in Windows. Because GUI forensics tools don't require the same understanding of the Windows CLI and file systems that command-line tools do, they can simplify digital forensics investigations. These GUI tools have also simplified training for beginning examiners; however, you should continue to learn about and use command-line tools because some GUI tools might miss critical evidence.

Most GUI tools are put together as suites of tools. For example, the largest GUI tool vendors—AccessData and Guidance Software—offer tools that perform most of the tasks discussed in this chapter. As with all software, each suite has its strengths and weaknesses.

GUI tools have several advantages, such as ease of use, the capability to perform multiple tasks, and no requirement to learn older OSs. Their disadvantages range from excessive resource requirements (needing large amounts of RAM, for example) and producing inconsistent results because of the type of OS used. Another concern with using GUI tools is that they create investigators' dependence on using only one tool. In some situations, GUI tools don't work and a command-line tool is required, so it's essential for investigators to be familiar with more than one type of tool.

Digital Forensics Hardware Tools

This section discusses computer hardware used for forensics investigations. Technology changes rapidly, and hardware manufacturers have designed most computer components to last about 18 months between failures. Hardware is hardware; whether it's a rack-mounted server or a forensic workstation, eventually it fails. For this reason, you should schedule equipment replacements periodically—ideally, every 18 months if you use the hardware full-time. Most digital forensics operations use a workstation 24 hours a day for a week or longer between complete shutdowns.

You should plan your hardware needs carefully, especially if you have budget limitations. Include the amount of time you expect the forensic workstation to be running, how often you expect hardware failures, consultant and vendor fees to support the hardware, and how often to anticipate replacing forensic workstations. The longer you expect the forensic workstation to be running, the more you need to anticipate physical equipment failure and the expense of replacement equipment.

Forensic Workstations

Many hardware vendors offer a wide range of forensic workstations that you can tailor to meet your investigation needs. The more diverse your investigation environment, the more options you need. In general, forensic workstations can be divided into the following categories:

- *Stationary workstation*—A tower with several bays and many peripheral devices
- *Portable workstation*—A laptop computer with almost as many bays and peripherals as a stationary workstation
- *Lightweight workstation*—Usually a laptop computer built into a carrying case with a small selection of peripheral options

When considering options to add to a basic workstation, keep in mind that PCs have limitations on how many peripherals they can handle. The more peripherals you add, the more potential problems you might have, especially if you're using an older version of Windows. You must learn to balance what you actually need with what your system can handle. In addition, remember that RAM and storage need updating as technology advances.

If you're operating a digital forensics lab for a police agency, you need as many options as possible to handle any investigation. If possible, use two or three hardware configurations to handle diverse investigations. You should also keep a hardware inventory in addition to your software library. In the corporate environment, however, consider streamlining your workstation to meet the needs of only the types of systems used in your business.

Building Your Own Workstation To decide whether you want to build your own workstation, first ask "How much do I have to spend?" Building a forensic workstation isn't as difficult as it sounds but can quickly become expensive if you aren't careful. If you have the time and skill to build your own forensic workstation, you can customize it to your needs and save money, although you might have trouble finding support for problems that develop. For example, peripheral devices might conflict with one another, or components might fail. If you build your own forensic workstation, you should be able to support the hardware. You also need to identify what you intend to analyze. If you're analyzing SPARC disks from workstations in a company network, for example, you need to include a SPARC drive with a write-protector on your forensic workstation. (Note that SPARC disks are commonly used with Sun Solaris systems.)

If you decide that building a forensic workstation is beyond your skills, some vendors still offer workstations designed for digital forensics, such as the F.R.E.D. unit from Digital Intelligence or hardware mounts from ForensicPC that convert a standard server or PC into a forensic workstation. Having a vendor-supplied workstation has its advantages. If you aren't skilled in hardware maintenance and repair, having vendor support can save you time and frustration when you have problems. Of course, you can always mix and match components to get the capabilities you need for your forensic workstation.

 If you don't have the skills to build and support a PC, you might want to consider taking an A+ certification course.

Using a Write-Blocker

The first item you should consider for a forensic workstation is a **write-blocker**. Write-blockers protect evidence disks by preventing data from being written to them. Software and hardware write-blockers perform the same function but in a different fashion.

Software write-blockers, such as PDBlock from Digital Intelligence, typically run in a shell mode (such as a Windows CLI). PDBlock changes interrupt 13 of a workstation's BIOS to prevent writing to the specified drive. If you attempt to write data to the blocked drive, an alarm sounds, advising that no writes have occurred. PDBlock can run only in a true DOS mode, however, not in a Windows CLI.

With hardware write-blockers, you can connect the evidence drive to your workstation and start the OS as usual. Hardware write-blockers, which act as a bridge between the suspect drive and the forensic workstation, are ideal for GUI forensics tools. They prevent Windows or Linux from writing data to the blocked drive.

In the Windows environment, when a write-blocker is installed on an attached drive, the drive appears as any other attached disk. You can navigate to the blocked drive with any Windows application, such as File Explorer, to view files or use Word to read files. When you copy data to the blocked drive or write updates to a file with Word, Windows shows that the data copy is successful. However, the write-blocker actually discards the written data—in other words, data is written to null. When you restart the workstation and examine the blocked drive, you won't see the data or files you copied to it previously.

Many vendors have developed write-blocking devices that connect to a computer through FireWire, USB 2.0 and 3.0, SATA, PATA, and SCSI controllers. Most of these write-blockers enable you to remove and reconnect drives without having to shut down your workstation, which saves time in processing the evidence drive. For more information on write-blocker specifications, visit *www.cftt.nist.gov*. The following vendors offer write-blocking devices:

- *www.digitalintelligence.com*
- *www.forensicpc.com*
- *www.guidancesoftware.com*
- *www.voomtech.com*
- *www.mykeytech.com*
- *www.lc-tech.com*
- *www.logicube.com*
- *www.forensic-computers.com*
- *www.cru-inc.com*
- *www.paraben.com*
- *www.usbgear.com/USB-FORENSIC.html*

Recommendations for a Forensic Workstation

Before you purchase or build a forensic workstation, determine where your data acquisitions will take place. If you acquire data in the field, consider streamlining the tools you use. With the newer FireWire and USB write-blocking devices, you can acquire data easily with Digital Intelligence FireChief and a laptop computer, for example. If you want to reduce the hardware you carry, consider a product such as the WiebeTech Forensic DriveDock with its regular DriveDock FireWire bridge or the Logicube Talon.

When choosing a computer as a stationary or lightweight forensic workstation, you want a full tower to allow for expansion devices, such as a 2.5-inch drive converter to analyze a laptop hard drive on a 3.5-inch IDE write-protected drive controller. You want as much memory and processor power as your budget allows and different sizes of hard drives. In addition, consider a 400-watt or better power supply with battery backup, extra power and data cables, a SCSI controller card, external FireWire and USB ports, an assortment of drive adapter bridges to connect SATA to IDE (PATA) drives, an ergonomic keyboard and mouse, and a good video card with at least a 17-inch monitor. If you plan to conduct many investigations, a high-end video card and dual monitors are recommended. If you have a limited budget, one option for outfitting your lab is to use high-end game PCs from a local computer store. With some minor modifications and additions of hardware components, these systems perform extremely well.

As with any technology, what your forensic workstation includes is often a matter of preference. Whatever vendor you choose, make sure the devices you select perform the functions you expect to need as an investigator.

Validating and Testing Forensics Software

Now that you have selected some tools to use, you need to make sure the evidence you recover and analyze can be admitted in court. To do this, you must test and validate your software. The following sections discuss validation tools available at the time of this writing and how to develop your own validation protocols.

Using National Institute of Standards and Technology Tools

The National Institute of Standards and Technology (NIST) publishes articles, provides tools, and creates procedures for testing and validating computer forensics software. Software should be verified to improve evidence admissibility in judicial proceedings. NIST sponsors the CFTT project to manage research on forensics tools. For additional information on this testing project, visit *www.cftt.nist.gov*. The Computer Forensic Reference Data Sets (CFReDS; *www.cfreds.nist.gov*) has been created recently to provide data sets for tools, training, and hardware testing.

NIST also created criteria for testing forensics tools, which are included in the article "General Test Methodology for Computer Forensic Tools" (version 1.9, November 7, 2001), available at *www.cftt.nist.gov/testdocs.html*. This article addresses the lack of specifications for what forensics tools should do and the importance of tools meeting judicial scrutiny. The criteria are based on standard testing methods and ISO 17025 criteria for testing when no current standards are available. Your lab must meet the following criteria and keep accurate records so that when new software and hardware become available, testing standards are in place for your lab:

- *Establish categories for digital forensics tools*—Group digital forensics software according to categories, such as forensics tools designed to retrieve and trace e-mail.

- *Identify forensics category requirements*—For each category, describe the technical features or functions a forensics tool must have.

- *Develop test assertions*—Based on the requirements, create tests that prove or disprove the tool's capability to meet the requirements.

- *Identify test cases*—Find or create types of cases to investigate with the forensics tool, and identify information to retrieve from a sample drive or other media. For example, use the image of a closed case file created with a trusted forensics tool to test a new tool in the same category and see whether it produces the same results.

- *Establish a test method*—Considering the tool's purpose and design, specify how to test it.

- *Report test results*—Describe the test results in a report that complies with ISO 17025, which requires accurate, clear, unambiguous, and objective test reports.

Another standards document, ISO 5725, demands accuracy for all aspects of the testing process, so results must be repeatable and reproducible. "Repeatable results" means that if you work in the same lab on the same machine, you generate the same results. "Reproducible results" means that if you're in a different lab working on a different machine, the tool still retrieves the same information.

NIST has also developed several tools for evaluating drive-imaging tools. These tools are posted on the CFTT Web site at *www.cftt.nist.gov/ disk_imaging.htm*.

In addition, NIST created the NSRL project (*www.nsrl.nist.gov*) with the goal of collecting all known hash values for commercial software and OS files. The primary hash NSRL uses is SHA-1, which generates known digital signatures called the Reference Data Set (RDS). SHA-1 has better accuracy than other hashing methods, such as MD5. The purpose of collecting known hash values is to reduce the number of known files, such as OS or program files, included in a forensics examination of a drive so that only unknown files are left. You can also use the RDS to locate and identify known bad files, such as illegal images and computer viruses, on a suspect drive.

Using Validation Protocols

After retrieving and examining evidence data with one tool, you should verify your results by performing the same tasks with other similar forensics tools. For example, after you use one forensics tool to retrieve disk data, you use another to see whether you retrieve the same information. Although this step might seem unnecessary, you might be asked on the witness stand "How did you verify your results?" To satisfy the need for verification, you need at least two tools to validate software or hardware upgrades. The tool you use to validate the results should be well tested and documented. A hands-on project at the end of this chapter gives you a chance to validate tools.

Investigators must be confident in a tool's capability to produce consistent and accurate findings during analysis. Understanding how the tool works is equally important, as you might not have vendor support in a courtroom. One way to compare results and verify a new tool is by using a disk editor, such as Hex Workshop or WinHex, to view data on a disk in its raw format. Disk editors typically show files, file headers, file slack, and other data on the physical disk. Although disk editors aren't known for their flashy interfaces, they're reliable and capable of accessing sectors of the digital evidence to verify your findings.

Although a disk editor gives you the most flexibility in testing, it might not be capable of examining a compressed file's contents, such as a `.zip` file or an Outlook `.pst` file. This is another reason that testing and validating your tools' capabilities are essential.

If you decide to use a GUI forensics tool, use the recommended steps in the following sections to validate your findings.

Digital Forensics Examination Protocol

1. First, conduct your investigation of the digital evidence with one GUI tool.

2. Then perform the same investigation with a disk editor to verify that the GUI tool is seeing the same digital evidence in the same places on the test or suspect drive's image.

3. If a file is recovered, obtain the hash value with the GUI tool and the disk editor, and then compare the results to verify whether the file has the same value in both tools.

Many investigators in both the public and private sectors use FTK and EnCase as their choice of "flagship" forensics software suites, but they don't rely on them solely; investigators' software libraries often include other forensics utilities to supplement these tools' capabilities.

Digital Forensics Tool Upgrade Protocol
In addition to verifying your results by using two disk-analysis tools, you should test all new releases and OS patches and upgrades to make sure they're reliable and don't corrupt evidence data. New releases and OS upgrades and patches can affect the way your forensics tools perform. If you determine that a patch or upgrade isn't reliable, don't use it on your forensic workstation until the problem has been fixed. If you have a problem, such as not being able to read old image files with the new release or the disk editor generating errors after you apply the latest service pack, you can file an error report with the vendor. In most cases, the vendor addresses the problem and provides a new patch, which you should check with another round of validation testing.

One of the best ways to test patches and upgrades is to build a test hard disk to store data in unused space allocated for a file, also known as file slack. You can then use a forensics tool to retrieve it. If you can retrieve the data with that tool and verify your findings with a second tool, you know the tool is reliable.

As digital forensics tools continue to evolve, you should check the Web for new editions, updates, patches, and validation tests for your tools. Always validate what the hardware or software tool is doing as opposed to what it's supposed to be doing, and remember to test and document why a tool does or doesn't work the way it's supposed to.

Chapter Summary

- Consult your business plan to get the best hardware and software solution for your digital investigation needs.

- The functions required for digital forensics tools are acquisition, validation and verification, extraction, reconstruction, and reporting.

- For your forensics lab, you should create a software library for older versions of forensics utilities, OSs, and applications and maintain older versions of software you have used and retired, such as previous versions of Windows and Linux.

- Some forensics tools run in a command-line interface, including those that can find file slack and free space, recover data, and search by keyword. They are designed to run in minimal configurations and can fit on a bootable disk.

- Hardware required for digital forensics includes workstations and devices, such as write-blockers, to prevent contamination of evidence. Before you purchase or build a forensic workstation, consider where you acquire data, which determines the hardware configuration you need.

- Tools that run in Windows and other GUI environments don't require the same level of computing expertise as command-line tools and can simplify training and investigations.

- Before upgrading to a new version of a forensics tool, run a validation test on the new version. The National Institute of Standards and Technology has standard guidelines for verifying forensics tools.

Key Terms

acquisition The process of creating a duplicate image of data; one of the required functions of digital forensics tools.

brute-force attack The process of trying every combination of characters—letters, numbers, and special characters typically found on a keyboard—to find a matching password or passphrase value for an encrypted file.

Computer Forensics Tool Testing (CFTT) A project sponsored by the National Institute of Standards and Technology to manage research on digital forensics tools.

extraction The process of pulling relevant data from an image and recovering or reconstructing data fragments; one of the required functions of digital forensics tools.

keyword search A method of finding files or other information by entering relevant characters, words, or phrases in a search tool.

National Software Reference Library (NSRL) A NIST project with the goal of collecting all known hash values for commercial software and OS files.

password dictionary attack An attack that uses a collection of words or phrases that might be passwords for an encrypted file. Password recovery programs can use a password dictionary to compare potential passwords to an encrypted file's password or passphrase hash values.

reconstruction The process of rebuilding data files; one of the required functions of digital forensics tools.

validation A way to confirm that a tool is functioning as intended; one of the functions of digital forensics tools.

verification The process of proving that two sets of data are identical by calculating hash values or using another similar method.

write-blocker A hardware device or software program that prevents a computer from writing data to an evidence drive. Software write-blockers typically alter interrupt-13 write functions to a drive in a PC's BIOS. Hardware write-blockers are usually bridging devices between a drive and the forensic workstation.

Review Questions

1. Forensic software tools are grouped into _____ and _____ applications.

2. According to ISO standard 27037, which of the following is an important factor in data acquisition? (Choose all that apply.)
   a. The DEFR's competency
   b. The DEFR's skills in using the command line
   c. Use of validated tools
   d. Conditions at the acquisition setting

3. One reason to choose a logical acquisition is an encrypted drive. True or False?

4. Hashing, filtering, and file header analysis make up which function of digital forensics tools?
   a. Validation and verification
   b. Acquisition
   c. Extraction
   d. Reconstruction

5. Hardware acquisition tools typically have built-in software for data analysis. True or False?

6. The reconstruction function is needed for which of the following purposes? (Choose all that apply.)
   a. Re-create a suspect drive to show what happened.
   b. Create a copy of a drive for other investigators.
   c. Recover file headers.
   d. Re-create a drive compromised by malware.

7. List three subfunctions of the extraction function.

8. Data can't be written to disk with a command-line tool. True or False?

9. Hash values are used for which of the following purposes? (Choose all that apply.)
   a. Determining file size
   b. Filtering known good files from potentially suspicious data
   c. Reconstructing file fragments
   d. Validating that the original data hasn't changed

10. In testing tools, the term "reproducible results" means that if you work in the same lab on the same machine, you generate the same results. True or False?

11. The verification function does which of the following?
   a. Proves that a tool performs as intended
   b. Creates segmented files
   c. Proves that two sets of data are identical via hash values
   d. Verifies hex editors

12. What's the advantage of a write-blocking device that connects to a computer through a FireWire or USB controller?

13. Building a forensic workstation is more expensive than purchasing one. True or False?

14. A live acquisition is considered an accepted practice in digital forensics. True or False?

15. Which of the following is true of most drive-imaging tools? (Choose all that apply.)
    a. They perform the same function as a backup.
    b. They ensure that the original drive doesn't become corrupt and damage the digital evidence.
    c. They create a copy of the original drive.
    d. They must be run from the command line.

16. The standards for testing forensics tools are based on which criteria?
    a. U.S. Title 18
    b. ASTD 1975
    c. ISO 17025
    d. All of the above

17. A log report in forensics tools does which of the following?
    a. Tracks file types
    b. Monitors network intrusion attempts
    c. Records an investigator's actions in examining a case
    d. Lists known good files

18. When validating the results of a forensic analysis, you should do which of the following? (Choose all that apply.)
    a. Calculate the hash value with two different tools.
    b. Use a different tool to compare the results of evidence you find.
    c. Repeat the steps used to obtain the digital evidence, using the same tool, and recalculate the hash value to verify the results.
    d. Use a command-line tool and then a GUI tool.

19. The primary hash the NSRL project uses is SHA-1. True or False?

Hands-On Projects

If necessary, go to the M57 Patents site (*http://digitalcorpora.org/corpora/ scenarios/m57-patents-scenario*) and download the PowerPoint files, Charlie's hard drive (dated 7 Dec 2009), and the warrants. In addition, create a *Work/ Chap06/Projects* folder on your system before starting the projects; it's referred to as your "work folder" in steps.

Hands-On Project 6-1

In this project, you create and delete Word and Excel files on a USB drive (or small disk partition, if you don't have a USB drive), and then use OSForensics to examine the drive. Follow these steps:

1. Create a **C6Prj01** folder on your USB drive or disk partition.

2. Open a new document in Word, and type **This is to test deleting files and then wiping them.** Save the file in the C6Prj01 folder as **Test 6-1.docx**, and exit Word.

3. Open a new workbook in Excel. Type a few numbers, and then save the workbook in the C6Prj01 folder as **Test 6-2.xlsx**. Exit Excel.

4. Use Windows Explorer or My Computer to delete both files from the USB or disk drive.

5. Start OSForensics, and start a new case. Type **C6Prj01** for the case name, and enter your name for the investigator. Leave the Acquisition Type option as **Live Acquisition of Current Machine,** and specify the work folder you created for this chapter. Create a subfolder called **C6Prj01**, and click **OK**.

6. If necessary, click **Manage Case** in the left pane, and then click the **Add Device** button in the right pane. Click the drive letter of your USB device, make sure the **Forensics mode** option button is selected, and click **OK**.

7. Make sure the case you just created has a green check mark next to it; if not, double-click the case name, and then click **Start** in the left pane. Using the scroll bar on the far right, scroll down and click the **Deleted Files & Data Carving** icon. In the Deleted Files Search window, click the **Disk** list arrow, and then click the USB drive in the list of options. Click the **Search** button. Because you're searching for deleted files, you don't need to enter a file string or filter.

8. Double-click the **Test 6-1.docx** file in the lower pane to view its contents. You can also click the **File Info** tab to verify the file's MAC time. Repeat this process with the **Test 6-2.xlsx** file.

9. Close all open windows, and exit OSForensics.

Hands-On Project 6-2

In this project, you research and download a disk-cleaning and wiping tool and verify that it works. Make sure you aren't on a production machine. Do an Internet search for disk-cleaning and wiping software, and download and install at least one tool. Then follow these steps:

1. Create a **C6Prj02** folder on your USB or disk drive. Start the tool you just installed.

2. Select your USB drive. Following instructions in the software documentation, wipe the drive.

6

3. Start OSForensics, and start a new case. Type your name for the investigator's name, type **C6Prj02** for the case name, and enter your work folder as the case path. Create a subfolder called **C6Prj02**, and click **OK**.

4. Click the **Add Device** button. Click the **Drive Letter** option button, if necessary, and in the drop-down list box, click the drive letter for your USB drive. Click **OK**.

5. Click **Start** in the left pane, if necessary, and click the **Deleted Files Search** button on the left. (*Note*: This is another way to open the Deleted Files Search window.)

6. Click the **Disk** list arrow, and then click the USB drive in the list of options. Click the **Search** button. Because you're searching for deleted files, you don't need to enter a file string.

7. Double-click any file in the lower pane to open it.

8. If necessary, click the **Hex/String Viewer** tab (see Figure 6-8). It should show hexadecimal 0 values, which verifies that the disk wipe worked. Take a screenshot, and then exit OSForensics. Write a short report on the tool's effectiveness, and turn it in to your instructor with the screenshot.

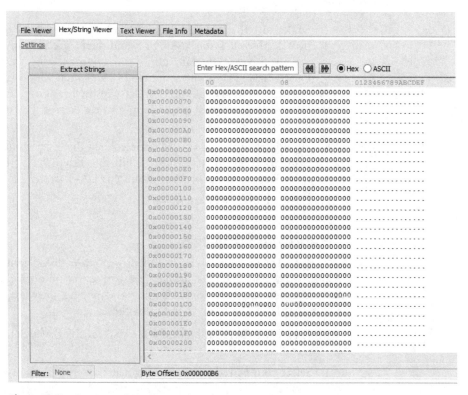

Figure 6-8   The Hex/String Viewer tab
Source: PassMark Software, *www.osforensics.com*

Hands-On Project 6-3

In this project, you create a test drive by planting evidence in the file slack space on a USB drive or small disk partition. Then you use Hex Workshop (which you downloaded in a previous chapter from *www.hexworkshop.com*) to verify that the drive contains evidence. Follow these steps:

1. First, you format the drive in File Explorer. Right-click the drive icon and click **Format**, click to clear the **Quick Format** check box, if necessary, and then click **Start**. If you see a warning message, click **OK** to continue, and then click **OK** in the Format Complete message box.

2. Create a **C6Prj03** folder on the USB or disk drive. *Warning*: This drive should contain data you no longer need.

3. Open a new document in Word, and type **Testing for string Millennium**. Save the file in the C6Prj03 folder as **C6Prj03a.docx**.

4. Close the file, start a new Word document, and type **Testing for string XYZX**. Save the file in the C6Prj03 folder as **C6Prj03b.docx**. Exit Word.

Next, you use Hex Workshop to hide information in file slack space:

1. Start Hex Workshop. On a sheet of paper, create a chart with two columns. Label the columns **Item** and **Sector**.

2. In Hex Workshop, click **Disk, Open Drive** from the menu. (*Note*: Whenever you see the UAC message box, click **Yes**.) Make sure the USB or disk drive is selected, and then click **OK**.

3. Click **File, Open** from the menu. Navigate to and double-click **C6Prj03a.docx**. Scroll down until you see "Testing for string Millennium."

4. Click the tab corresponding to your USB or disk drive, and then click at the beginning of the right column. Click **Edit, Find** from the menu. In the Find dialog box, make sure **Text String** is selected in the Type list box. Type **Millennium** in the Value text box, and then click **OK**. (If Hex Workshop doesn't find "Millennium" the first time, repeat this step.)

5. In the Item column on your chart, write **C6Prj03a.docx**. In the Sector column, write the sector number containing the search text, as shown on the Hex Workshop title bar.

6. Scroll to the bottom of the sector, if necessary. Type **Murder She Wrote** *near* the end of the sector in the right pane, and then click the **Save** toolbar button. (*Note*: If you're asked to enable Insert mode, click **OK**, press **Insert**, click to select the **Disable notification message** check box, and click **OK**, if necessary.)

7. Click the **C6Prj03a.docx** tab. Click **Edit, Find** from the menu, make sure **Text String** is selected in the Type list box, type **Murder** in the Value text box, and then click **OK**. Hex Workshop can't find this text in **C6Prj03a.docx**. Click **Edit, Find** from the menu, and then click **OK** to verify that Hex Workshop doesn't find "Murder" in the document. Close the file by clicking the lower **Close** button in the upper-right corner.

6

8. Click **File, Open** from the menu. Navigate to and double-click `C6Prj03b.docx`. Scroll down, if needed, until you see the "Testing for string XYZX" text you entered earlier. (*Hint*: You might need to use the Find command more than once to find this text.)

9. Click the tab for your USB or disk drive, if necessary, and then click at the beginning of the right column. Click **Edit, Find** from the menu, type **XYZX** as the value you want to find, and then click **OK**. On your chart, write **C6Prj03b.docx** as the filename in the Item column, and in the Sector column, note the sector number containing the search text, as shown on the Hex Workshop title bar.

10. In the tab for your USB or disk drive, type **I Spy** *near* the end of the sector in the right pane, in the slack space, and then click the **Save** toolbar button.

11. Verify that "I Spy" doesn't appear as part of the file by clicking the **C6Prj03b.docx** tab and searching for this string twice.

12. Close the `C6Prj03b.docx` file, and exit Hex Workshop.

In a forensics lab, you would generate the drive's MD5, SHA-1, or other hash value with a tool such as `md5sum`, and then generate a copy with one of the GUI tools covered in this chapter.

Hands-On Project 6-4

You should test new or updated digital forensics tools to make sure they're performing correctly. When complex software applications are updated, they might create new problems and function failures the vendor wasn't aware of. In this project, you test two competing digital forensics analysis tools to see how they compare in locating and recovering data. Keep in mind that even though tools have different strengths, they should yield similar results. To compare OSForensics and ProDiscover Basic, you need the following:

• ProDiscover Basic installed on your workstation

• OSForensics installed on your workstation

• Charlie's hard drive file from the M57 Patents case (available at *http://digitalcorpora.org/corp/nps/scenarios/2009-m57-patents/drives-redacted/*) extracted to your work folder

First, you use ProDiscover Basic to examine the file:

1. Start ProDiscover Basic. To start your analysis, click the **New Project** toolbar button. In the New Project dialog box, type **C6Prj04PD** for the project number and project filename, and then click **OK**. (*Note*: If you get an error when starting a new project, exit ProDiscover and start it again.)

2. In the tree view, click to expand **Add**, and then click **Image File**. In the Open dialog box, navigate to your work folder, click `charlie-2009-12-07.E01`, and then click **Open**.

3. In the tree view, click to expand **Content View** and then **Images**. Click to expand the image file, expand the **C** drive, and then click **All Files**. If necessary, click **Yes** in the ProDiscover message box that opens.

4. Next, click the **Search** toolbar button. Search terms have been created for the M57 case. In the Search dialog box, click the **Content Search** tab, if necessary. In the Search for the pattern(s) text box, type **project2400** on one line and **craigslist** on a second line. Under Select the Disk(s)/Image(s) you want to search in, click the `.e01` image file, and then click **OK**.

This search might take quite a while.

5. In the Search 1 tab of the search results, click the **Filter** button, and then click **project2400**. Read the files, and then click the **Selection** button and click **Select All**. (Close the Add Comment dialog box, if it opens.) When you're finished, click **Add to Report**.

6. Click the **Search** toolbar button. In the Search dialog box, click the **Content Search** tab, if necessary. In the Search for the pattern(s) text box, type **kitty** and **kitten** on separate lines. Under Select the Disk(s)/Image(s) you want to search in, click the `.e01` image file, and then click **OK**.

7. In the Search 2 tab of the search results, click the **Filter** button, and then click **kitty**. Click the check box next to the one file that doesn't have an extension, and then click **Add to Report**.

8. In the tree view, click **Report**, and then click the **Export** toolbar button. In the Export dialog box, click the **RTF Format** option button, click **Browse**, and navigate to and double-click your work folder. Type **Chap6-4-PD.rtf** in the File name text box, and then click **Save**. Click **OK** in the Export dialog box, and then click **File, Print Report** from the menu to print your report.

9. When you're finished, click **File, Exit** from the menu. When prompted, click **Yes**, and then click **Save**.

Next, you perform the same searches in OSForensics:

Before starting this part of the project, create a subfolder of your work folder called C6Prj04.

1. Start OSForensics. Click **Start** in the left pane, if necessary, and in the right pane, click **Create Case**.

2. In the New Case dialog box, enter your name for the investigator, type **C6Prj04** for the case name, and click the **Investigate Disk(s) from Another Machine** option button for the acquisition type. Click **Custom Location** for the case folder, click the **Browse** button, navigate to and click your *Work*/C6Prj04 folder, and then click **OK** twice.

3. Click the **Add Device** button. Click the **Image File** option button, and then browse to your work folder, click the `charlie-2009-12-07.E01` image file, and click **Open**. Click **OK** twice.

4. Click the **Create Index** button in the left pane. In the Step 1 of 5 window, click the **Use Pre-defined File Types** option button, click all the file types listed, and then click **Next**. In the Step 2 of 5 window, click the **Add** button, click `charlie-2009-12-07.E01`, click **OK**, and then click **Next**. In the Step 3 of 5 window, type **Index all file types** in the Index Title text box, and then click **Start Indexing**.

5. When OSForensics finishes indexing the image file, click **OK** in the message box.

Indexing might take an hour or more, so make sure you allow enough time.

6. Click the **Search Index** button in the left pane. In the Enter Search Words text box, type **project2400**, and then click **Search** in the right pane. Right-click each file in the results, point to **Bookmark**, and click **Red**.

7. In the Enter Search Words text box, type **craigslist**, and then click **Search** in the right pane. Right-click each file in the results, point to **Bookmark**, and click **Yellow**. Repeat this procedure with the search terms **kitty** and **kitten**, assigning the bookmark color red to kitty and the bookmark color yellow to kitten. (*Note*: In ProDiscover, you simply selected the file without an extension for the search term "kitty.")

8. When you're done, click the **Start** button, and then click the **Generate Report** button. Accept the default settings, and click **OK**. In the report, notice your bookmarked files toward the bottom.

9. Compare the files you found with those found in ProDiscover, and note any discrepancies. Write a two- to three-page report, including screenshots, to submit to your instructor. Explain which tool you prefer to use and why.

10. Exit your Web browser, and exit OSForensics.

Case Projects

Case Project 6-1

Do Internet research on two widely used GUI tools, Guidance Software EnCase and AccessData FTK, and compare their features with other products, such as ProDiscover (*www.techpathways.com*) and Ontrack EasyRecover Professional (*www.ontrack.com/easyrecoveryprofessional*). Create a chart outlining each tool's current capabilities, and write a one- to two-page report on the features you found most beneficial for your lab.

Case Project 6-2

Research hex editors available for Mac OS and Linux. Based on the documentation, how easy would validating these tools be? Select at least two hex editors for each OS, and write a one- to two-page paper describing what you would do to validate them, based on what you have learned in this chapter.

Case Project 6-3

You need to establish a procedure for your organization on how to validate a new forensics software package. Write two to three pages outlining the procedure you plan to use in your lab. Be sure to cite references, such as the ISO standard or NIST, to support your procedure.

6

chapter 7

Linux and Macintosh
File Systems

After reading this chapter and completing the exercises, you will be able to:

- Describe Linux file structures
- Describe Macintosh file structures
- Use Linux forensics tools

In Chapter 5, you explored Microsoft OSs and file systems. Because digital forensics investigators must understand how OSs store and manage data, this chapter continues this exploration by examining Linux and Mac file structures. In addition, this chapter introduces some hands-on approaches to identifying Linux file structures with tools such as X-Ways Forensics, OSForensics, and WinHex.

Examining Linux File Structures

UNIX was created in the early 1970s to be a multiuser, multithreaded, secure OS, and many UNIX-based OSs followed. They came in many "flavors" (the term often used for different distributions), but the Open Group was created as a neutral standards consortium that determines and certifies when an OS meets UNIX requirements. For more information, see *www.unix.org/online.html*.

Some notable UNIX distributions included Silicon Graphics, Inc. (SGI) IRIX, Santa Cruz Operation (SCO) UnixWare, Sun Solaris, IBM AIX, and HP-UX. Most are no longer available, however. Referring to Linux as a "UNIX system" or "UNIX variety" isn't technically correct, as it isn't UNIX certified. However, it's available in even more flavors than UNIX had in its heyday. In addition, the Linux kernel is usually packaged with other software components, such as a GUI and applications, so that users don't have to combine several open-source elements to create a working environment.

The most widely used distributions include Ubuntu (a Debian-based OS), Debian, Red Hat, OpenSUSE, and Slackware. The term "kernel" is often used when discussing Linux because technically, Linux is only the core of the OS. Linus Torvalds, the inventor of Linux, maintains the official kernel. All other tools, graphical interfaces, and so forth are maintained and developed by others. Despite the association of the word "kernel" with Linux terminology, all UNIX-like OSs have a kernel, and so do all Windows OSs.

 Ubuntu 14.04 is a long-term support (LTS) version of Ubuntu, meaning it will be supported for the next five years. In some activities in this book, Ubuntu 12.04 is used; it's also an LTS version.

Table 7-1 lists several Linux system files containing information about users and their activities, and Table 7-2 lists important top-level directories in Linux.

Table 7-1   Linux system files

System file	Contents
/etc/exports	File systems exported to remote hosts; might include remote drive mappings
/etc/fstab	File system table of devices and mount points
/var/log/lastlog	User's last logon
/var/log/wtmp	Logon and logoff history information
/var/run/utmp	Current user's logon information
/var/log/dmesg	System messages log

Table 7-1   Linux system files (*Continued*)

System file	Contents
/var/log/syslog	System log, occasionally called `system.log` or `kernel.log`
/etc/shadow	Master password file, containing hashed passwords for the local system
/etc/group	Group memberships for the local system
/etc/passwd	Account information for the local system

© 2016 Cengage Learning®

Table 7-2   Core top-level directories of a Linux system

Directory	Contents
/usr	Most applications and commands are in this directory or its subdirectories `bin` (stands for "binary" and contains binary files required at boot time) and `sbin` (which requires superuser permission to run the binaries in it).
/etc	Most system configuration files are stored in this directory.
/home	The home directories for all users, usually named after their usernames.
/root	The home directory for the root user (superuser), which is kept separate from other user home directories.
/dev	Device files that act as stand-ins for the devices they represent, as described in Chapter 3; for example, `/dev/sda` is the first non-IDE disk drive on the system, usually the main hard drive.
/var	Subdirectories such as `log` (often useful for investigations), `mail` (storing e-mail accounts), and `spool` (where print jobs are spooled).

© 2016 Cengage Learning®

NOTE Before beginning this activity, create a C:*Work*\\Chap07\\Chapter folder (referred to as your "work folder" in steps). Extract all files in the Chap07 folder on the DVD to your C:*Work*\\Chap07\\Chapter folder.

Chapter 3 covered Linux commands for acquiring images. In this section, you use standard commands to find information about your Linux system. Most of the commands used in this activity work the same in all UNIX-like OSs, including Mac OSs. Remember that UNIX and Linux commands are case sensitive, as you learned in Chapter 3. The wrong capitalization can mean your commands are rejected as incorrect or interpreted as something different. If you don't have Ubuntu 14.04 installed, follow these steps to create a virtual machine for running it.

1. Start VirtualBox, and click the **New** icon at the upper left to start the Create Virtual Machine Wizard.

2. In the Name and operating system window, type **Ubuntu 14.04** for the virtual machine name. Accept the default settings, and click **Next**.

3. In the Memory size window, increase the setting to **1024**, and then click **Next**.

4. In the Hard drive window, click **Create a virtual hard drive now,** and then click **Create**. In the Hard drive file type window, click **Virtual Machine Disk (VMDK),** and then click **Next**. In the "Storage on physical hard drive" window, click the **Dynamically allocated** option button, and then click **Next**.

5. In the File location and size window, increase the setting to **20 GB**, and then click **Create**. Leave VirtualBox open.

6. Start a Web browser, go to **www.ubuntu.com/download**, and download the ISO image for Ubuntu 14.04.

7. In the Oracle VM VirtualBox Manager, click the **Settings** icon.

8. Click **Storage** in the left pane. In the Storage Tree section, click **Empty** under Controller: IDE. In the Attributes section on the right, click the down arrow next to the CD icon (see Figure 7-1). Click **Choose a virtual CD/DVD disk file**. Navigate to the folder where the ISO file is stored, double-click the ISO file, and then click **OK**.

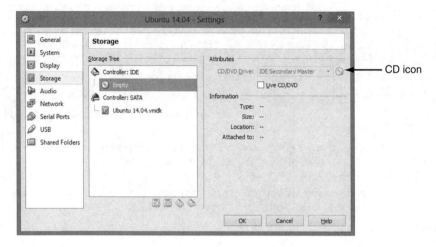

Figure 7-1 Selecting the source for an ISO file
Source: Oracle VirtualBox

9. In the Oracle VM VirtualBox Manager, click the **Ubuntu 14.04** virtual machine, and then click the **Start** icon. The VM should follow a standard OS installation. Accept the default settings. Leave the virtual machine running for the next activity.

Before moving on to working with Linux forensics tools, the following activity gives you a chance to review some commands. For example, being able to find a machine's name is always useful; the uname command is used for this task. Displaying file listings and permissions are also useful for investigators. To help with these tasks, you can use the > character to redirect the output of the command preceding it to a file you specify. If the file exists, it's overwritten with a new one; if the file doesn't exist, it's created. The double >> adds output at the *end* of a specified file, if it already exists.

For all the commands in the following activity, you can see their output in the terminal window or add the output to your log file by entering >> ~/my.log at the end of each command. (The ~ character specifies the current user's home directory.) Use the echo command to add notes or headings in the log, and add blank lines to make the contents easier to read. Just don't forget that a single > character replaces the entire file instead of appending to it. You aren't prompted that you're overwriting the file.

As you've learned, Linux commands use options to create variations of a command. There's no difference between grouping letter arguments (such as l and a) after a single - or entering them separately. Therefore, `ls -la` functions the same as `ls -l -a`. Arguments consisting of multiple letters must be preceded by two -- characters instead of one and can't be grouped together, as in `ls --all`.

As you've learned in previous chapters, the pipe (|) character also redirects the output of the command preceding it. Unlike the > character, however, it redirects output as input for the following command. As you see in this activity, the output of the `cat` command (which would have displayed the entire file in the terminal window) is sent to the `grep` command to search for occurrences of your username. The `grep` command then displays only lines matching search criteria.

1. Start Ubuntu 14.04, if necessary. On the left side of the desktop are icons for different categories of applications. You can use these desktop icons to select an application, or click the Ubuntu icon and start typing the name of the application you want to have the system make a suggestion (see Figure 7-2). Type **term** (in this case, to suggest opening the terminal window), and click the **Terminal** icon.

Figure 7-2   Opening the terminal window
Source: *www.ubuntu.com*

2. To find the name of your computer and the Linux kernel revision number, type **uname -a** and press **Enter**. To record the results in a file, type **uname -a > ~/my.log** and press **Enter**. Nothing is displayed in the terminal window, but a file called my.log is created in your user profile folder, and the output of the uname -a command is redirected to it.

3. To identify your current path, type **pwd** (which stands for "print working directory") and press **Enter**. In a new terminal window, it's likely the user's home directory.

4. To see a list of the directory's contents, type **ls** and press **Enter**. For comparison, try typing **ls -l** and pressing **Enter**, and then typing **ls -la** and pressing **Enter**. (*Note*: In listings, all files beginning with the . character are usually omitted, unless you add the a option, which stands for "all.")

5. To record the full listing in the same log file you created earlier, type **echo "" >> ~/my.log** and press **Enter**, and then type **echo "Full listing:" >> ~/my.log** and press **Enter**. Finally, type **ls -la >> ~/my.log** and press **Enter**. These commands add a blank line, followed by the heading Full listing:, and finally the listing of the directory's contents in your log file.

6. To see the updated contents of your log file, type **cat ~/my.log** and press **Enter**.

In current versions of Gnome, which is the Ubuntu desktop, the terminal window's scrollbar doesn't show, but you can display it by moving your mouse pointer to where a scrollbar is usually placed.

7. Type **ifconfig** and press **Enter** to see your network interfaces: wired, wireless, FireWire, lo (the loopback device), and so forth. They're displayed with their MAC addresses (in the "HWaddr" column) and currently assigned IP addresses (in the "inet addr" column). Try the same command with **-a**, and observe the difference in the output. Append the output of this command to your log file.

8. Navigate to the root directory by typing **cd /** and pressing **Enter**. Confirm that you're at the top of the directory tree by typing **pwd** and pressing **Enter**.

9. To identify the username you're currently using, type **whoami** and press **Enter**.

10. To see a listing of all user accounts configured on the system, type **sudo cat /etc/passwd** and press **Enter**, and then type the password and press **Enter**. The output displays the contents of the user account configuration file, passwd. It contains the superuser account "root," the regular user account you're currently using, and a long list of system accounts for system services, such as lp, sys, daemon, and sync. For each account, you see the username, numeric user and group IDs, possibly a formatted display name, the home directory (which is /root for the superuser), and the standard command shell, which is usually /bin/bash for regular and root users.

11. To see just the information for your user account, type **cat /etc/passwd | grep *user*** (replacing *user* with your own username) and press **Enter**.

12. Append the /etc/passwd file to your log file by typing **cat /etc/passwd >> ~/my.log** and pressing **Enter**. The /etc/passwd file doesn't contain user passwords, although it used to store hashed passwords. Because everyone can read this file, storing even hashed passwords was considered a security risk, so they were moved to the /etc/shadow file, which can be accessed only by the root user.

13. To get a detailed listing of the /etc/shadow file, type **ls -l /etc/shadow** and press **Enter**. If permission is denied, repeat this command preceded by **sudo**.

14. Type **sudo cat /etc/shadow** and press **Enter**, and then type the password and press **Enter**. The file's contents are shown, but only regular user accounts contain a password hash. You should see this information for your user account.

15. To append just the entry for your user account to your log file, type **sudo cat /etc/shadow | grep** *user* **>> ~/my.log** (replacing *user* with your username) and press **Enter**. This command redirects the output of cat as input to grep, which leaves only the line containing your username, and then appends it to your log file. You can have multiple | pipes in a single command but only one redirection to a file (using > or >>) because the file is a like a dead end—there can be no output after it's redirected to a file.

16. Close the terminal window by typing **exit** and pressing **Enter**, and leave Ubuntu running for the next activity.

Next, you examine deconstructing password hash values in the etc/shadow file. The entries in /etc/shadow are separated by colons. The first field is the username, and the second is the password hash, if available. (For more details, see *www.cyberciti.biz/faq/ understanding-etcshadow-file/*.) The remaining fields are numeric settings, including the maximum time before a password must be changed. Take a look at a typical password hash field:

```
$digit$ShortHashString$LongHashString
```

It begins with a $ symbol, followed by a digit representing the hashing algorithm (which is 6 for SHA-512). Next is another $ symbol followed by a short hash string, which is the password salt, used to make password hashes different even if two users have the same password. Finally, there's another $ symbol followed by a long hash string, which is the salted password hash. Even though passwords aren't stored in plaintext, two users having the same password normally results in identical hashes, which could make cracking passwords easier. In addition, without password salting, it's possible for others to create rainbow tables (discussed in more detail in Chapter 9) to look up passwords.

The salt and hash are stored in an encoded format with letters, numbers, dots, and slashes that's similar to base-64 encoding. Assuming the password hash field starts with 6, meaning SHA-512 is being used, you can use the following command to find a salted password hash, replacing *ShortHashString* and *password* with the information from your own entry in the /etc/shadow file:

```
mkpasswd --method=sha-512 --salt=ShortHashString password
```

This command returns the salted password hash and is used internally by the OS to check whether the correct password was entered. However, knowing how password hash values are created is helpful in case you need to attempt cracking passwords.

File Structures in Ext4

Linux supports a wide range of file systems. The early standard was **Second Extended File System (Ext2)**, and then **Third Extended File System (Ext3)** replaced Ext2 in most Linux distributions. Its major difference from Ext2 was being a journaling file system, which has a built-in file recovery mechanism used after a crash.

A few years later, **Fourth Extended File System (Ext4)** was introduced. Among other features, it added support for partitions larger than 16 TB, improved management of large files, and offered a more flexible approach to adding file system features. Because these changes affected the way the Linux kernel interacts with the file system, adoption of Ext4 was slower in some Linux distributions, but it's now considered the standard file system for most distributions. The Ubuntu version you used previously, for example, has an Ext4 partition at its core, unless you select another file system during installation.

In UNIX and Linux, everything is considered a file, including disk drives, monitors, tape drives, network interface cards, system memory, and directories. UNIX files are defined as objects, which means a file, like an object in an object-oriented programming language, has properties and methods (actions such as writing, deleting, and reading) that can be performed on it.

UNIX/Linux has four components defining the file system: boot block, superblock, inode block, and data block. A block is the smallest disk allocation unit in the UNIX/Linux file system and can be 512 bytes and up; block size depends on how the disk volume is initiated. The **boot block** contains the bootstrap code—instructions for startup. A UNIX/Linux computer has only one boot block, on the main hard disk.

The **superblock** contains vital information about the system and is considered part of the metadata. It specifies the disk geometry and available space and keeps track of all inodes (discussed in more detail in the following section). The superblock also manages the file system, including configuration information, such as block size for the drive, file system names, blocks reserved for inodes, and volume name. Multiple copies of the superblock are kept in different locations on the disk to prevent losing such important information.

Inode blocks contain the first data after the superblock. An inode is assigned to every file allocation unit. As files or directories are created or deleted, inodes are also created or deleted. The link between inodes associated with files and directories controls access to those files or directories.

The **data block** is where directories and files are stored on a disk drive. This location is linked directly to inodes. As in Microsoft file systems, the Linux file system on a PC has 512-byte sectors. A data block is equivalent to a cluster of disk sectors on a FAT or NTFS volume. Blocks range from 1024 to 4096 bytes each on a Linux volume.

Inodes Inodes contain file and directory metadata and provide a mechanism for linking data stored in data blocks. When a file or directory is created on a Linux file system, an inode is assigned that contains the following information:

- The mode and type of the file or directory
- The number of links to a file or directory
- The UID and GID of the file's or directory's owner
- The number of bytes in the file or directory
- The file's or directory's last access time and last modified time
- The inode's last file status change time
- The block address for the file data
- The indirect, double-indirect, and triple-indirect block addresses for the file data
- Current usage status of the inode

- The number of actual blocks assigned to a file
- File generation number and version number
- The continuation inode's link

The only pieces of metadata not in an inode are the filename and path. Inodes contain modification, access, and creation (MAC) times, not filenames. An assigned inode has 13 pointers that link to data blocks and other pointers where files are stored. Pointers 1 through 10 link directly to data storage blocks in the disk's data block and contain block addresses indicating where data is stored on the disk. These pointers are direct pointers because each one is associated with one block of data storage.

As a file grows, the OS provides up to three layers of additional inode pointers. In a file's inode, the first 10 pointers are called **indirect pointers**. The pointers in the second layer are called **double-indirect pointers**, and the pointers in the last or third layer are called **triple-indirect pointers**.

To expand storage allocation, the OS initiates the original inode's 11th pointer, which links to 128 pointer inodes. Each pointer links directly to 128 blocks located in the drive's data block. If all 10 pointers in the original inode are consumed with file data, the 11th pointer links to another 128 pointers. The first pointer in this indirect group of inodes points to the 11th block. The last block of these 128 inodes is block 138.

The term "indirect inode" refers to the 11th pointer in the original inode, which points to another group of inode pointers. In other words, it's linked indirectly to the original inode.

If more storage is needed, the 12th pointer of the original inode is used to link to another 128 inode pointers. From each of these pointers, another 128 pointers are created. This second layer of inode pointers is then linked directly to blocks in the drive's data block. The first block these double-indirect pointers point to is block 139. If more storage is needed, the 13th pointer links to 128 pointer inodes, each pointing to another 128 pointers, and each pointer in this second layer points to a third layer of 128 pointers. File data is stored in these data blocks, as shown in Figure 7-3.

All disks have more storage capacity than the manufacturer states. For example, a 240 GB disk might actually have 240.5 GB free space because disks always have bad sectors. Windows doesn't keep track of bad sectors, but Linux does in an inode called the **bad block inode**. The root inode is inode 2, and the bad block inode is inode 1. Some forensics tools ignore inode 1 and fail to recover valuable data for cases. Someone trying to mislead an investigator can access the bad block inode, list good sectors in it, and then hide information in these supposedly "bad" sectors.

To find bad blocks on your Linux computer, you can use the `badblocks` command, although you must log in as root to do so. Linux includes two other commands that supply bad block information: `mke2fs` and `e2fsck`. The `badblocks` command can destroy valuable data, but the `mke2fs` and `e2fsck` commands include safeguards that prevent them from overwriting important information.

Inode pointers

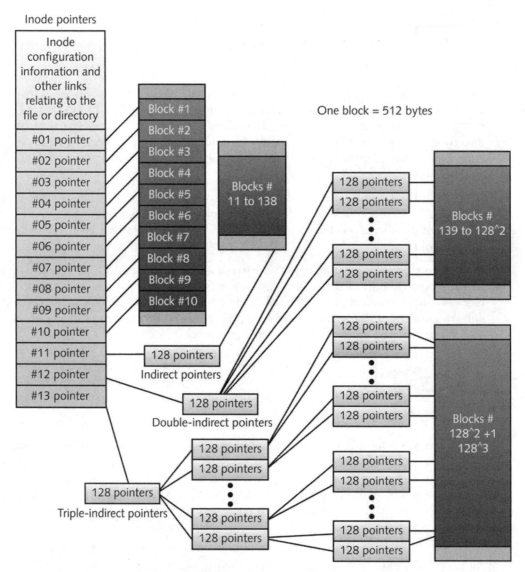

Figure 7-3 Inode pointers in the Linux file system
© Cengage Learning®

Hard Links and Symbolic Links A **hard link** is a pointer that allows accessing the same file by different filenames (Rute-Users-Guide/Linux Dictionary V 0.16, *www.tldp.org/ LDP/Linux-Dictionary/html/index.html*). The filenames refer to the same inode and physical location on a drive. Originally, hard links were used so that people with different logins could access the same physical file. If one person changed the file, the changes would be apparent when another user opened the file.

Figure 7-4 shows three hard-linked files pointing to the same inode: 23509. You use the `ln` command to create a hard link. The main requirement is that all files pointing to the same inode have to be on the same physical drive, not on another volume.

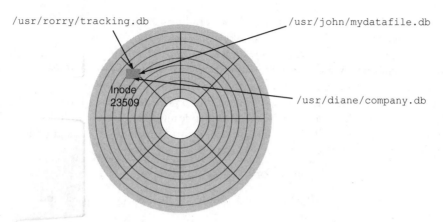

Figure 7-4 Hard-linked files with different filenames
© 2016 Cengage Learning®

To see files and their inode numbers, you use the `ls -ia` command. Inside each inode is a field called **link count** that specifies the number of hard links. The link count for directories is higher than for other file types. If two files have the same inode number, the link count is two. If one file is deleted, the link count drops by one. When the hard link count drops to zero, the file is effectively deleted. Most forensics tools, however, can retrieve these files.

To see the contents of a directory, you use the `ls -a` command. The first two items are . (called "dot"), which refers to the directory, and .. (called "dot-dot"), which refers to the parent directory (see Figure 7-5). Both dot and dot-dot count as links, so most directories have at least two hard links. Every subdirectory has a dot-dot reference to the corresponding parent directory; therefore, each one adds to the parent directory's link count.

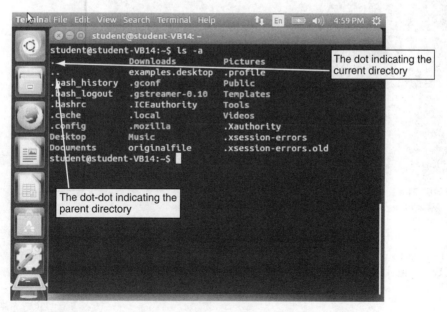

Figure 7-5 The `ls -a` command showing the dot and dot-dot notation
Source: *www.ubuntu.com*

Symbolic links (also known as "soft links" or "symlinks") are simply pointers to other files and aren't included in the link count. Unlike hard links, they can point to items on other drives or other parts of the network; they simply need an absolute path. Symbolic links have an inode of their own, which isn't the same as the inode of the item they're pointing to. Unlike hard links, they depend on the continued existence of the destination they're pointing to, and they're easier to identify on a running Linux system than hard links are. Unlike hard links, which point to their destination with an inode number, symbolic links identify their destination by name and path. If a name and path no longer exist, the symbolic link stops working. You create symbolic links with the `ln -s` command.

To see how hard and symbolic links work, follow these steps:

1. Start Ubuntu, if necessary, and open a terminal window. Type **ls -l** and press **Enter**.

2. The number in the second column shows the hard link count (see Figure 7-6). Notice the number of hard links for the `Music` directory. Type **cd Music** and press **Enter**. Create a subdirectory called `PopTunes` by typing **mkdir PopTunes** and pressing **Enter**.

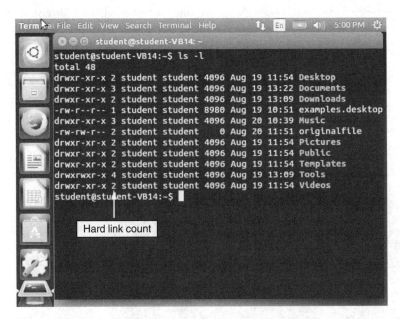

Figure 7-6 The `ls -l` command showing the hard link count
Source: *www.ubuntu.com*

3. Return to your home directory by typing **cd** and pressing **Enter**. Next, type **ls -l** and press **Enter**, and notice that the link count for the `Music` directory has increased.

4. To create a hard link, first create a new file by typing **touch originalfile** and pressing **Enter**. Then create a new subdirectory in the /tmp directory by typing **mkdir /tmp/chap07** and pressing **Enter**. Switch to your home directory again, if necessary, and type **ln originalfile /tmp/chap07/newfile** and press **Enter**.

5. Type **ls -i** and press **Enter** to see originalfile's inode number. Change to the /tmp/chap07 directory and repeat this command. Newfile should have the same inode number as originalfile (see Figure 7-7).

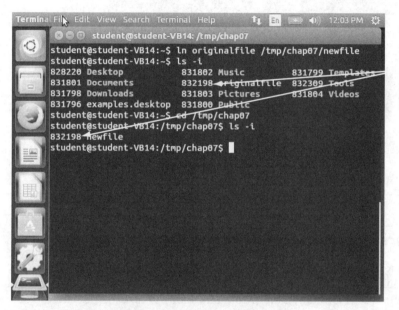

Same inode number

Figure 7-7 Comparing inode numbers for a hard link
Source: www.ubuntu.com

6. To create a symbolic link, switch to the **/tmp** directory, and type **mkdir testsym** and press **Enter** to create a new subdirectory. Switch to this subdirectory, and create two files by typing **touch test1 test2** and pressing **Enter**. Finally, create the symbolic link by typing **ln -s /tmp/testsym mysym** and pressing **Enter**.

7. Type **ls -1 mysym** (using the numeral one, not a lowercase L, for the option after the hyphen) and press **Enter**. The files you created in the testsym directory are also in mysym. Finally, type **ls -1 mysym** and press **Enter**. An arrow points from mysym to the testsym directory, as shown in Figure 7-8, to indicate the symbolic link.

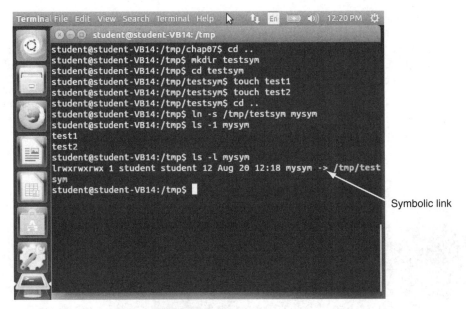

Figure 7-8   Creating a symbolic link
Source: *www.ubuntu.com*

8. Leave Ubuntu running and the terminal window open for the next activity.

Understanding Macintosh File Structures

The current Mac OS is Mac OS X, version 10.9, code-named Mavericks. Yosemite, version 10.10, is scheduled to be released October 2014. Other versions still in use include 10.6 (Snow Leopard), 10.7 (Lion), and 10.8 (Mountain Lion). Mac OS X is built on a core called Darwin, which consists of a Berkeley Software Distribution (BSD) UNIX application layer built on a Mach microkernel. Apple's OSs have been developing since 1984 with the introduction of Apple System 1. In 1997, Apple introduced Mac OS 8, followed by Mac OS 9 and then OS X. With OS X, Macintosh moved to the Intel processor and became UNIX based.

The newest version of Mac OS X, version 10.10 (code-named Yosemite), was released for beta testing in June 2014. You can find updated information on it at *https://www.apple.com/osx/preview/*.

Before OS X, the **Hierarchical File System (HFS)** was used, in which files are stored in directories (folders) that can be nested in other directories. With Mac OS 8.1, Apple introduced **Extended Format File System (HFS+)**, which continues to be an optional format in Mac OS X. The main difference between HFS and HFS+ is that HFS was limited to 65,536 blocks (512 bytes per block) per volume, and HFS+ raised the number of blocks to more than 4 billion. Consequently, HFS+ supports smaller file sizes on larger volumes, resulting in more efficient disk use. Mac OS X also supports the Unix File System (UFS), which isn't covered in this book.

An Overview of Mac File Structures

In Mac, a file consists of two parts: a **data fork**, where data is stored, and a **resource fork**, where file metadata and application information are stored (see Figure 7-9). Both forks contain the following essential information for each file:

- Resource map
- Resource header information for each file
- Window locations
- Icons

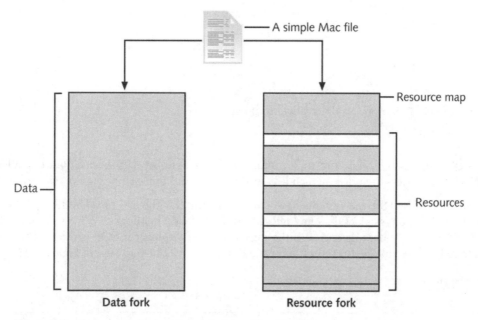

Figure 7-9   The resource fork and data fork in a Mac OS X file
© Cengage Learning®

The data fork typically contains data the user creates, such as text or spreadsheets. Applications, such as Microsoft Word or Excel, also read and write to the data fork. When you're working with an application file, the resource fork contains additional information, such as menus, dialog boxes, icons, executable code, and controls. In the Mac OS, the resource or data fork can be empty.

A volume is any storage medium used to store files. It can be all or part of the storage media for hard disks; however, in Mac OS 9 and earlier, a volume on a floppy disk was always the entire floppy. With larger disks, the user or administrator now defines a volume.

Volumes have allocation blocks and logical blocks. A **logical block** is a collection of data that can't exceed 512 bytes. When you save a file, it's assigned to an **allocation block**, which is a group of consecutive logical blocks. As volumes increase in size, one allocation block might be composed of three or more logical blocks. Figure 7-10 shows the relationship between these two types of blocks. If a file contains information, it always occupies one allocation

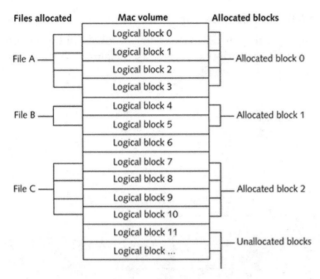

Figure 7-10 Logical and allocation block structures
© Cengage Learning®

block. For example, if a data fork contains only 11 bytes of data, it occupies one allocation block (512 bytes) on a disk, which leaves more than 500 bytes empty in the data fork.

The HFS and HFS+ file systems have two descriptors for the end of a file (EOF)—the logical EOF and the physical EOF. The **logical EOF** is the actual ending of a file's data, so if file B has 510 bytes of data, byte 510 is the logical EOF. The **physical EOF** is the number of bytes allotted on the volume for a file, so for file B, it's byte 1023, as shown in Figure 7-11.

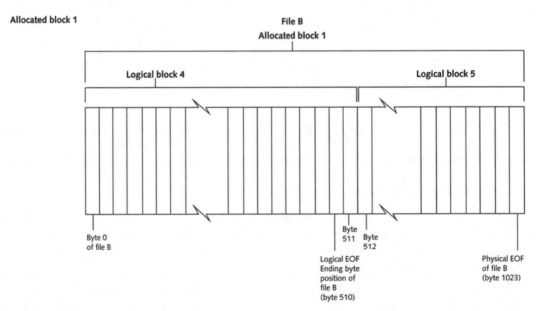

Figure 7-11 Logical EOF and physical EOF
© Cengage Learning®

Mac reduces file fragmentation by using **clumps,** which are groups of contiguous allocation blocks. As a file increases in size, it occupies more of the clump. Volume fragmentation is kept to a minimum by adding more clumps to larger files.

For older HFS-formatted drives, the first two logical blocks, 0 and 1, on the volume (or disk) are the boot blocks containing system startup instructions. Optional executable code for system files can also be placed in boot blocks.

Older Mac OSs use the **Master Directory Block (MDB)** for HFS, which is the Volume Information Block (VIB) in HFS+. All information about a volume is stored in the MDB and written to it when the volume is initialized. A copy of the MDB is also written to the next-to-last block on the volume to support disk utility functions. When the OS mounts a volume, some information from the MDB is written to a **Volume Control Block (VCB),** stored in system memory. When a user no longer needs the volume and unmounts it, the VCB is removed.

The copy of the MDB is updated when the extents overflow file or catalog increases in size. The **extents overflow file** is used to store any file information not in the MDB or a VCB. The **catalog** is the listing of all files and directories on the volume and is used to maintain relationships between files and directories on a volume.

Volume Bitmap, a system application, tracks each block on a volume to determine which blocks are in use and which ones are available to receive data. Volume Bitmap has information about the blocks' use but not about their content. Volume Bitmap's size depends on the number of allocated blocks for the volume.

File-mapping information is stored in two locations: the extents overflow file and the file's catalog entry. In earlier Mac versions, the **B*-tree** file system is also used to organize the directory hierarchy and file block mapping. In this file system, files are nodes (records or objects) containing file data. Each node is 512 bytes. The nodes containing actual file data are called leaf nodes; they're the bottom level of the B*-tree. The B*-tree also has the following nodes that handle file information:

- The **header node** stores information about the B*-tree file.
- The **index node** stores link information to previous and next nodes.
- The **map node** stores a node descriptor and map record.

For more information on HFS and HFS+, see *http://wiki.sleuthkit.org/index.php?title=HFS* and *https://developer.apple.com/library/mac/documentation/Darwin/Reference/Manpages/man1/RezWack.1.html.*

Forensics Procedures in Mac

Although understanding Linux file structures can help you learn about Mac file structures, there *are* some differences between the Linux and Mac OS X file systems. For example, Linux has the /home/*username* and /root directories. In Mac, the corresponding folders are /users/*username* and /private/var/root. The /home directory exists in the Mac OS, but it's empty. In addition, Mac users have limited access to other user accounts' files, and the guest account is disabled by default. If it's enabled, it has no password, and guest files are deleted at logout.

For forensics procedures in Mac OS X, you must know where file system components are located and how both files and file components are stored. Application settings are in three formats: plaintext, plist files (which include plain XML plists and binary plists, which are condensed XML), and the SQLite database. Plaintext files, of course, can be viewed in any text editor. **Plist files** are preference files for installed applications on a system, usually stored in /Library/Preferences. To view them, you use special editors, such as the one available at the Apple Developer Web site (*https://developer.apple.com*) or PlistEdit Pro (*www.macupdate.com/app/mac/14363/plistedit-pro*). To view the SQLite database, use the SQLite Database Browser (*http://sqlitebrowser.org*).

Other files that might contain information useful for an investigation include the following:

- /System/Library/CoreServices/SystemVersion.plist—Contains the OS version.
- /Library/Preferences/SystemConfiguration/NetworkInterfaces. plist—Shows all existing network interfaces. If an interface has been used recently, it's listed in the /private/var/db/dhcpclient/leases directory.
- /private/var/db/DirectoryService/flatfile.db—A list of users on a system; used before Mac OS X v10.7 and is similar to the Linux/UNIX /etc/passwd file.
- /private/var/db/dslocal/nodes/Default/users—Contains users' plist files in Mac OS X version after 10.7.
- /private/var/db/shadow/hash—Contains account passwords.

FileVault, introduced with version 10.3, is used to encrypt and decrypt a user's /users directory. It has master keys and recovery keys, which research later proved could be retrieved from RAM and used to crack encryption. In response to these security vulnerabilities, Mac improved FileVault by introducing FileVault2, which encrypts the whole disk with 128-bit AES encryption.

Other encrypted information you're likely to find during an investigation is passwords. Since Mac OS 8.6, **keychains** have been used to manage passwords for applications, Web sites, and other system files (*www.macworld.com/article/2013756/how-to-manage-passwords-with-keychain-access.html*). You can find keychain files in a variety of places, including /System/Library/Keychains and /Library/Keychains, and they can be useful to show what applications and files require passwords. The Mac application Keychain Access enables you to restore passwords.

You need to find deleted files in most investigations, too. In Mac OS X, deleted files are in the Trashes folder. If a file is deleted at the command line, however, it doesn't show up in the trash, which is similar to the Recycle Bin in Windows.

Unlike Windows, Mac files retain their filenames in the trash. In addition, when you copy a file in Windows, the timestamp is reset. In Mac OS X, the creation time is copied, so Mac timestamps are more accurate.

Several vendors have software for examining the Mac OS X file system. In the following section, you look at BlackBag Technologies (*https://www.blackbagtech.com/software-products.html*).

Another product for Mac forensics is SubRosaSoft MacForensicsLab (*www.macforensicslab.com*). Other vendors have added the capability to analyze Mac file systems, such as ProDiscover Forensic Edition and the freeware tools Sleuth Kit and Autopsy (*www.sleuthkit.org*). Sleuth Kit is discussed in "Using Linux Forensics Tools" later in this chapter.

Mac Acquisition Methods To examine a Mac computer, you need to make an image of the drive, using the same techniques described in Chapter 5. You should be aware of some exceptions, however, caused by Mac design and engineering. (In addition, removing the drive from a Mac Mini case is difficult, and attempting to do so without Apple factory training could damage the computer. A MacBook Air poses similar problems, as you need special Apple screwdrivers to open the case.) You need a Mac-compatible forensic boot CD/DVD to make an image, which then must be written to an external drive, such as a FireWire or USB drive. Larger Macs are constructed much like desktop PCs, making removal of the hard drive easier.

BlackBag Technologies sells acquisition tools for OS 9 and OS X and offers a forensic boot CD called MacQuisition for making an image of a Mac drive (see *https://www.blackbagtech.com/software-products/macquisition-2/macquisition.html*). BlackBag Technologies has also written a guide for forensic examination of Macs (*www.macforensicslab.com/ProductsAndServices/index.php?main_page=document_general_info &products_id=134*). Although this guide is older, it's still useful.

After making an acquisition, the next step is examining the image of the file system with a forensics tool. The tool you use depends on the image file's format. For example, if you used EnCase, FTK, or X-Ways Forensics to create an Expert Witness (.e01) image, you must use one of these tools to analyze the image. If you made a raw format image, you can use any of the following tools:

- BlackBag Technologies Macintosh Forensic Software (OS X only)
- SubRosaSoft MacForensicsLab (OS X only)
- Guidance Software EnCase
- X-Ways Forensics
- AccessData FTK

BlackBag Technologies Macintosh Forensic Software and SubRosaSoft MacForensicsLab have a feature for disabling and enabling Disk Arbitration, which is a Mac OS X feature for disabling and enabling automatic mounting when a drive is connected via a USB or FireWire device (see *www.appleexaminer.com*). Being able to turn off the mount function in OS X allows you to connect a suspect drive to a Mac without a write-blocking device.

Using Linux Forensics Tools

Learning how to use Linux forensics tools can come in handy when Windows tools don't work or you're having trouble getting a Windows machine to boot. Several commercial and freeware tools are available for analyzing UNIX and Linux file systems. Most commercial forensics tools, such as OSForensics, X-Ways Forensics, Guidance Software EnCase, AccessData FTK, and ProDiscover Forensic Edition, can analyze Linux Ext2, Ext3, Ext4, ReiserFS, and Reiser4 file systems. (ProDiscover Basic can analyze only FAT and NTFS file systems.)

Freeware tools include Sleuth Kit and its Web browser interface, Autopsy Forensic Browser, maintained by Brian Carrier (see *www.sleuthkit.org*). Sleuth Kit, previously called TASK, is partially based on The Coroner's Toolset (TCT) by Dan Farmer and Wietse Venema and designed as a network analysis tool for investigating attackers.

The U.S. Air Force Office of Special Investigations and the Center for Information Systems Security Studies and Research developed another specialized freeware tool called Foremost (see *http://foremost.sourceforge.net*). Foremost is a carving tool that can read many image file formats, such as raw and Expert Witness. It has a configuration file, `foremost.conf`, listing the most common file headers, footers, and data structures. If a file format isn't included in this file, it can be added by using a hex editor to determine the new format's header and footer values and a text editor to update the file. This file is typically in the `/usr/local/etc` directory and contains instructions on updating it. If your installation is different, read the `makefile` script in the Foremost tarball to see how the current version is installed. A **tarball** is a highly compressed data file containing one or more files or directories and their contents. It's similar to Windows zip utilities and typically has a `.tar` or `.gz` extension.

Installing Sleuth Kit and Autopsy

Sleuth Kit and Autopsy can be installed on 32-bit or 64-bit Windows versions, and version 2 can be installed in Linux or Mac OS X. You can find current and past versions of Sleuth Kit and Autopsy Forensic Browser at *www.sleuthkit.org*.

Older versions of Sleuth Kit and Autopsy are available at Web sites listed on Sleuth Kit's main page. The RPM Package Manager utility makes installing these tools in Red Hat and Fedora Linux much easier. Several other Linux distributions have tools for installing RPM packages. Check their documentation to see how they handle RPM packages.

In Linux, Sleuth Kit must be installed before Autopsy Forensic Browser, or Autopsy isn't installed correctly. In Windows, however, the order of installation isn't critical. In addition, when you're running Autopsy Forensic Browser in Mac or Linux, you must preface all commands with `sudo`.

To install Sleuth Kit and Autopsy Forensic Browser in Ubuntu 14.04, you need root user privileges. Follow these steps:

1. If necessary, start Ubuntu and open a terminal window.
2. To install Sleuth Kit, type **sudo apt-get install sleuthkit** and hit **Enter**, and then install Autopsy by typing **sudo apt-get install autopsy** and pressing **Enter**.

3. To confirm that you're in your home directory, type **pwd** and press **Enter**. Next, create the evidence locker for storing files by typing `mkdir Documents/Evidence_Locker` and pressing **Enter**.

4. To start Autopsy and let it know where to store files, type `autopsy -d /home/`*`username`*`/Documents/Evidence_Locker` (see Figure 7-12) and press **Enter**.

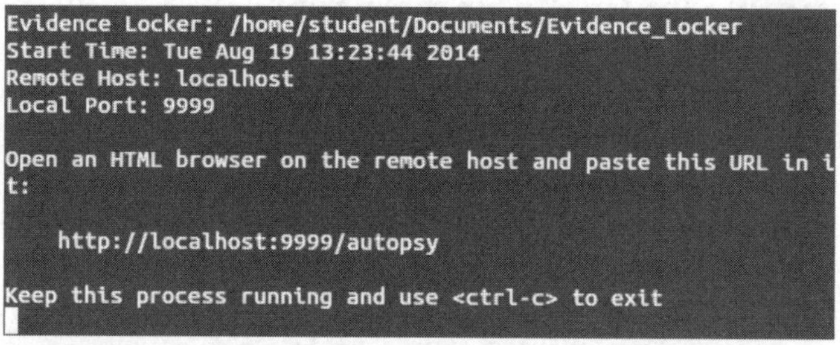

```
Evidence Locker: /home/student/Documents/Evidence_Locker
Start Time: Tue Aug 19 13:23:44 2014
Remote Host: localhost
Local Port: 9999

Open an HTML browser on the remote host and paste this URL in i
t:

    http://localhost:9999/autopsy

Keep this process running and use <ctrl-c> to exit
```

Figure 7-12 Starting Autopsy in Linux
Source: *www.sleuthkit.org*

5. Right-click the URL **http://localhost:9999/autopsy** shown in the terminal window and click **Open Link**. Figure 7-13 shows the Autopsy main window.

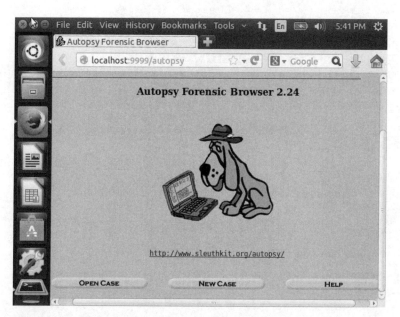

Figure 7-13 The Autopsy main window
Source: *www.sleuthkit.org*

If you see a warning message at the top stating that JavaScript is enabled, you have to reconfigure your browser to disable it. After reconfiguring the browser, you might have to exit and restart. If the Autopsy terminal session is still running, simply paste the Autopsy URL into the Address text box again.

6. Leave Autopsy running and your Web browser open for the next activity.

Examining a Case with Sleuth Kit and Autopsy In this section, you use Sleuth Kit and Autopsy Forensic Browser to examine an older Linux file system. In digital forensics, sometimes you have to reevaluate cases that are several years old, and this activity gives you a chance to do that. Before starting the examination, copy the GCFI-LX.00*n* (with *n* representing a number from 1 to 5) image files from the DVD (or your work folder) to the evidence locker you set up in the previous activity. Autopsy uses the evidence locker to save results from examinations. To start the examination, follow these steps:

1. In Autopsy's main window, click the **New Case** button shown previously in Figure 7-13. When the Create a New Case dialog box opens, enter **InChap7** for the case name (see Figure 7-14), a description (optional), and your name, and then click the **New Case** button to continue.

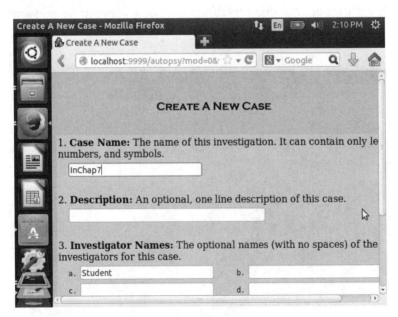

Figure 7-14   The Create a New Case dialog box
Source: *www.sleuthkit.org*

2. In the Creating Case dialog box, click **Add Host** to continue. In the Add a New Host dialog box, enter **TestUbuntu12-04** for the hostname (see Figure 7-15), and then click **Add Host**.

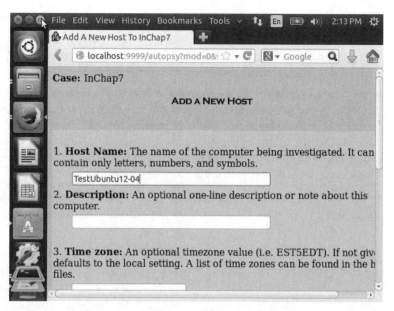

Figure 7-15 The Add a New Host dialog box
Source: *www.sleuthkit.org*

3. In the Adding host dialog box, click **Add Image** to continue. In the Open Image dialog box, click **Add Image File**.

4. In the Add a New Image dialog box, type the complete path to the evidence locker in the Location text box, click the **Partition** and **Move** option buttons, and then click **Next**. (Remember that Linux commands are case sensitive. If you enter a lowercase filename and the filename is uppercase, Autopsy can't find and load the file.)

 If you don't click Partition in Step 4, the image is read as raw data, and file and directory structures aren't visible to Autopsy.

 If you have multiple segment volumes that are sequentially numbered or lettered (the dd command with the split option without the -d switch), use an asterisk as the extension (for example, GCFI-LX.*) so that all segments are read sequentially.

5. In the Split Image Confirmation dialog box, verify that all images are correctly loaded; if they are, click **Next**. If not, click **Cancel**. (If this data is incorrect, it's probably caused by an error in the pathname to the evidence locker or image files.)

6. In the Image File Details section, click the **Calculate the hash value for this image** option button, and then click **Add**. In the Calculating MD5 message box, click **OK**.

7. In the "Select a volume to analyze or add a new image file" dialog box, click **Analyze** and then **Keyword Search** to start a search for keywords of interest to the investigation.

8. In the Keyword Search of Allocated and Unallocated Space dialog box, type the name **martha** in the text box, and then click **Search**.

9. When the search is finished, Autopsy displays a summary of the search results. To see detailed search results, click the **link to results** link at the upper left.

10. Examine the search results by scrolling through the left pane, and then click the **Fragment 236019 "Ascii"** link to view details of the search. Repeat this examination by clicking other ASCII and Hex links for the remaining hits. When you're finished examining the search hits, close the Searching for ASCII and Searching for Unicode dialog box to return to the "Select a volume to analyze or add a new image file" dialog box. Exit Autopsy, and log off Ubuntu.

Many investigators use a Windows machine as their main forensic workstation, so Autopsy now offers a Windows version for both 32-bit and 64-bit systems. Follow these steps to try this version:

1. Create a subfolder of your work folder called **Autopsy**. Start a Web browser, if necessary, and go to **www.sleuthkit.org**. Download the 32-bit or 64-bit .msi file for the Windows version of Autopsy.

2. On your Windows workstation, start Autopsy. Figure 7-16 shows the opening window. Click **Create New Case**.

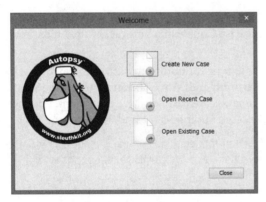

Figure 7-16   The Autopsy for Windows opening window
Source: *www.sleuthkit.org*

3. In the New Case Information dialog box, type **InChap7Windows** in the Case Name text box. Click the **Browse** button next to the Base Directory text box, navigate to and click the **Autopsy** subfolder you created, and click **Select**. Click **Next** and then **Finish**.

4. In the Add Data Source dialog box, click the **Browse** button next to the "Browse for an image" text box. Navigate to where you downloaded the M57 case files previously, click **charlie-work-usb-2009-12-11.E01**, and click **Open**. Click **Next**.

5. Keep the default settings in the Configure Ingest Modules dialog box. Click **Next** and then **Finish**. The workspace should be displayed. Click to expand the image file in the left pane, and review its contents in the right pane (see Figure 7-17).

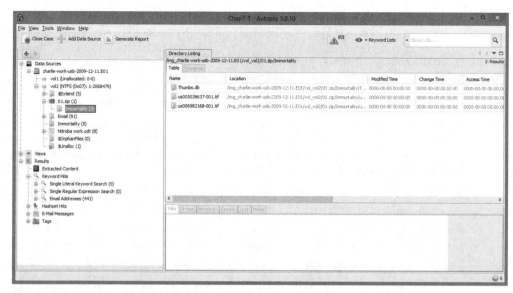

Figure 7-17   Charlie's USB drive open in Autopsy
Source: *www.sleuthkit.org*

6. Click **File, Exit** from the menu to exit Autopsy.

With Sleuth Kit and Autopsy, you can conduct additional analysis and produce other output files in subdirectories of the evidence locker. You can then use these files in a narrative report, as explained in Chapter 16.

Chapter Summary

- UNIX was created to be a multiuser, multithreaded, secure OS. The Open Group was formed as a neutral standards consortium that determines and certifies when an OS meets UNIX requirements.

- The Linux kernel is usually packaged with other software components, such as a GUI and applications. The most widely used distributions include Ubuntu (a Debian-based OS), Debian, Red Hat, OpenSUSE, and Slackware.

- Linux supports a wide range of file systems. The most recent, Ext4, added support for partitions larger than 16 TB, improved management of large files, and offered a more flexible approach to adding file system features.

- UNIX and Linux have four components defining the file system: boot block, super-block, inode block, and data block. In addition, an inode is assigned to each file allocation unit that contains file and directory metadata (except the filename and path) and provides a mechanism for linking data stored in data blocks.

- In the Linux file system, a hard link is a pointer that allows accessing the same file by different filenames, which refer to the same inode and physical location on the drive. Symbolic links are pointers to other files; they can point to items on other drives or other parts of the network and don't affect the link count.

- Before Mac OS X, the file systems HFS and HFS+ were used. The main difference between them is that HFS was limited to 65,536 blocks (512 bytes per block) per volume, and HFS+ raised the number of blocks to more than 4 billion. Consequently, HFS+ supports smaller file sizes on larger volumes, resulting in more efficient disk use.

- In Mac, a file consists of two parts: a data fork, where data is stored, and a resource fork, where file metadata and application information are stored.

- A volume is any storage medium used to store files. Volumes have allocation blocks and logical blocks. When you save a file, it's assigned to an allocation block, which is a group of consecutive logical blocks. Mac reduces file fragmentation by using clumps, which are groups of contiguous allocation blocks.

- Plist files, which are preference files for installed applications on a Mac system, can be useful sources of information for a forensics investigation.

- The biggest challenge in acquiring images from Mac systems is often physical access to the drive. With many Mac devices, special tools and training from Apple are needed.

- Linux forensics tools are often freeware, so forensics investigators can use them to help keep costs down. Tools such as Sleuth Kit and Autopsy are commonly used.

Key Terms

allocation block In the Mac file system, a group of consecutive logical blocks assembled in a volume when a file is saved. *See also* logical block.

B*-tree A Mac file that organizes the directory hierarchy and file block mapping for File Manager. Files are represented as nodes (objects); leaf nodes contain the actual file data.

bad block inode In the Linux file system, the inode that tracks bad sectors on a drive.

boot block A block in the Linux file system containing the bootstrap code used to start the system.

catalog An area of the Mac file system used to maintain the relationships between files and directories on a volume.

clumps In the Mac file system, groups of contiguous allocation blocks used to keep file fragmentation to a minimum.

data block A block in the Linux file system where directories and files are stored on a drive.

data fork The part of a Mac file containing the file's actual data, both user-created data and data written by applications, as well as resource map and header information, window locations, and icons. *See also* resource fork.

double-indirect pointers The inode pointers in the second layer or group of an OS. *See also* inodes.

Extended Format File System (HFS+) File system used by Mac OS 8.1 and later. HFS+ supports smaller file sizes on larger volumes, resulting in more efficient disk use.

extents overflow file A file in HFS and HFS+ that's used by the catalog to coordinate file allocations to a volume when the list of a file's contiguous blocks becomes too long. Any file extents not in the MDB or a VCB are also contained in this file. *See also* catalog, Master Directory Block (MDB), *and* Volume Control Block (VCB).

Fourth Extended File System (Ext4) A Linux file system that added support for partitions larger than 16 TB, improved management of large files, and offered a more flexible approach to adding file system features.

hard link In the Linux file system, a pointer that allows accessing the same file by different filenames, which refer to the same inode and physical location on the drive.

header node A node that stores information about the B*-tree file. *See also* B*-tree.

Hierarchical File System (HFS) An older Mac OS file system, consisting of directories and subdirectories that can be nested.

index node A B*-tree node that stores link information to the previous and next nodes. *See also* B*-tree.

indirect pointers The inode pointers in the first layer or group of an OS. *See also* inodes.

inode blocks Blocks in the Linux file system that contain the first data after the superblock and consist of a grouping of inodes. *See also* inodes.

inodes A key part of the Linux file system, these information nodes contain descriptive file or directory data, such as UIDs, GIDs, modification times, access times, creation times, and file locations.

keychains A Mac feature used to track a user's passwords for applications, Web sites, and other system files.

link count A field in each inode that specifies the number of hard links. *See also* hard link.

logical block In the Mac file system, a collection of data that can't exceed 512 bytes. Logical blocks are assembled in allocation blocks to store files in a volume. *See also* allocation block.

logical EOF In the Mac file system, the actual ending of a file's data.

map node A B*-tree node that stores a node descriptor and map record. *See also* B*-tree.

Master Directory Block (MDB) On older Mac systems, the location where all volume information is stored. A copy of the MDB is kept in the next-to-last block on the volume. Called the Volume Information Block (VIB) in HFS+.

physical EOF In the Mac file system, the number of bytes allotted on a volume for a file.

plist files In Mac, preference files for installed applications on a system.

resource fork The part of a Mac file containing file metadata and application information, such as menus, dialog boxes, icons, executable code, and controls. Also contains resource map and header information, window locations, and icons. *See also* data fork.

Second Extended File System (Ext2) An early Linux file system.

superblock A block in the Linux file system that specifies and keeps track of the disk geometry and available space and manages the file system.

symbolic links Pointers to other files; they can point to items on other drives or other parts of the network and don't affect the link count. *See also* hard link.

tarball A highly compressed data file containing one or more files or directories and their contents.

Third Extended File System (Ext3) A Linux file system that made improvements to Ext2, such as adding journaling as a built-in file recovery mechanism.

triple-indirect pointers The inode pointers in the third layer or group of an OS. *See also* inodes.

Volume Control Block (VCB) An area of the Mac file system containing information from the MDB. *See also* Master Directory Block (MDB).

Review Questions

1. Explain the differences in resource and data forks used in the Mac OS.

2. Which of the following is the main challenge in acquiring an image of a Mac system? (Choose all that apply.)
   a. Most commercial software doesn't support Mac.
   b. Vendor training is needed.
   c. Macs are incompatible with most write-blockers.
   d. You need special tools to remove drives from a Mac system or open its case.

3. To recover a password on a Mac system, which tool do you use?
   a. Finder
   b. PRTK
   c. Keychain Access
   d. Password Access

4. What are the major improvements in the Linux Ext4 file system?

5. How does the Mac OS reduce file fragmentation?

6. Linux is the only OS that has a kernel. True or False?

7. Hard links work in only one partition or volume. True or False?

8. Which of the following Linux system files contains hashed passwords for the local system?
   a. `/var/log/dmesg`
   b. `/etc/passwd`
   c. `/var/log/syslog`
   d. `/etc/shadow`

9. Which of the following describes the superblock's function in the Linux file system? (Choose all that apply.)
   a. Stores bootstrap code
   b. Specifies the disk geometry and available space
   c. Manages the file system, including configuration information
   d. Contains links between inodes

10. What's the Disk Arbitration feature used for in Mac OS X?

11. In Linux, which of the following is the home directory for the superuser?

    a. home

    b. root

    c. super

    d. /home/superuser

12. Which of the following certifies when an OS meets UNIX requirements?

    a. IEEE

    b. UNIX Users Group

    c. The Open Group

    d. SUSE Group

13. On most Linux systems, current user login information is in which of the following locations?

    a. /var/log/dmesg

    b. /var/log/wmtp

    c. /var/log/usr/

    d. /var/log/utmp

14. Hard links are associated with which of the following?

    a. Dot notation

    b. A specific inode

    c. An absolute path to a file

    d. Hidden files

15. Which of the following describes plist files? (Choose all that apply.)

    a. You must have a special editor to view them.

    b. They're found only in Linux file systems.

    c. They're preference files for applications.

    d. They require special installers.

16. Data blocks contain actual files and directories and are linked directly to inodes. True or False?

Hands-On Projects

Create a *Work*\Chap07\Projects folder on your system before starting the projects; it's referred to as your "work folder" in steps. All the data files you use in these projects are from previous chapters.

Hands-On Project 7-1

In this project, you explore another free Linux forensics tool. The Digital Evidence and Forensics Toolkit (DEFT) was created at the University of Bologna, Italy.

1. Start a Web browser, if necessary, and go to **www.deftlinux.net**. Download the DEFT ISO file and the user's manual. Use the ISO file to create a bootable DVD. (You aren't installing it on your hard drive. You might need to change the BIOS to boot from the CD/DVD drive.)

2. Start DEFT. The opening window should look similar to Figure 7-18. Click **Start, DEFT**.

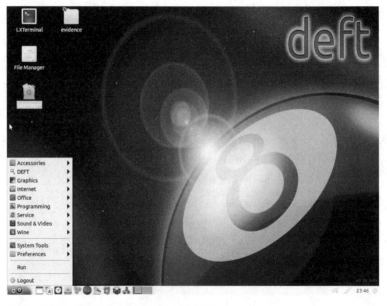

Figure 7-18   The opening window in DEFT
Source: DEFT Linux, *www.deftlinux.net*

3. Open the **MountManager** tool, and take a screenshot of this window for your report. In the DEFT 8 - Warning! message box, click **I know what I'm doing** to continue. Next, click **Start, DEFT**. Point to **Hashing**, and click **Dhash2**. Make a note of the types of hashes that are available, and then close this tool.

4. Click the **Autopsy** icon to open the Autopsy Forensic Browser window and the text interface. Take a screenshot of these windows, and then exit both.

5. Click the **Digital Forensics Framework (DFF)** icon. Examine its interface to get an idea of what functions it has. If you have time, go to its Web site to learn more about it.

6. Finally, click the **GHex** icon. This tool is a simple hex and binary editor. Examine its interface, and take a screenshot.

7. Write a one- to three-page paper explaining how this tool could be used in the field, and include your screenshots.

Hands-On Project 7-2

The purpose of this project is to become more familiar with the Linux version of Sleuth Kit and Autopsy. The best way to learn a tool, especially one that isn't well documented, is to explore its functions. You're encouraged to work in teams for this project and share your findings with other students. For this project, you convert the image file GCFI-datacarve-FAT.eve from Chapter 3 to a raw dd image by using ProDiscover Basic, and then analyze it with Sleuth Kit and Autopsy. You need the following:

- A PC running Windows with ProDiscover Basic installed

- A Linux or UNIX system with Sleuth Kit and Autopsy installed

- Disk storage of at least 200 MB to convert the .eve file to a dd file

Follow these steps:

1. Start ProDiscover Basic with the **Run as administrator** option. To convert the GCFI-datacarve-FAT.eve file to GCFI-datacarve-FAT.dd on a PC, click **Tools, Image Conversion Tools** from the menu and then click **Convert ProDiscover Image to "DD"**. In the Convert ProDiscover Image to "DD" Image dialog box, click the **Browse** button next to Source ProDiscover Image, navigate to and click the location in your work folder where you saved GCFI-datacarve-FAT.eve, and then click **Open**. Click **OK**, and then exit ProDiscover Basic.

2. Copy the converted file to your Linux virtual machine with Sleuth Kit and Autopsy installed. Start Sleuth Kit and Autopsy. In the main window, click **New Case**. In the Create a New Case dialog box, fill in your information (using **GCFI-datacarve-FAT** for the case name), and then click **New Case**.

3. In the Creating Case dialog box, click **Add Host,** and in the Add a New Host dialog box, enter your information, and click **Add Host**.

4. In the Adding host dialog box, click **Add Image** to continue. In the Open Image dialog box, click **Add Image File**. In the Add a New Image dialog box, type the full pathname and the **GCFI-datacarve-FAT.dd** image filename in the Location text box, click the **Partition** option button, click the **Copy** option button for the import method, and then click **Next**.

5. In the Image File Details section, click **Add**, and in the Testing partitions dialog box, click **OK**. In the "Select a volume to analyze or add a new image file" dialog box, click the **Analyze** button.

6. In the Analysis dialog box, click **File Analysis**, and then click **Generate MD5 List of Files**. In the MD5 results window, save the list as `GCFI-datacarve-FAT-MD5.txt` in your work folder, and close the MD5 results window.

7. Next, in the Analysis dialog box, click **File Type**, click **Sort Files by Type**, and then click **OK**. When the analysis is finished, print the Results Summary frame of the Web page.

8. Click **Image Details**, and in the General File System Details dialog box, print the frame containing the results.

9. Write a report describing the information each function asks for and what information it produces so that you can begin building your own user manual for this tool. Leave Sleuth Kit and Autopsy running for the next project.

Hands-On Project 7-3

This project is a continuation of Hands-On Project 7-2, using Sleuth Kit and Autopsy. First, convert the image files `C1Prj01.eve` and `C1Prj04.eve` from Chapter 1 to raw dd images in ProDiscover Basic. Second, use Sleuth Kit and Autopsy to perform the same tasks described in Hands-On Project 7-2 for these two image files. When examining these image files, compare the results with your findings in Hands-On Project 7-2, and write a brief report on any similarities or differences to continue adding to your user manual.

Case Projects

Case Project 7-1

Research and compare forensics tools that can examine Mac, iPod, and iPhone devices. Create a table listing the features they have in common, differences in functions, and price. Write a short paper stating which one you would choose if you were an investigator for a small firm, and explain why.

Case Project 7-2

This chapter introduced Autopsy for Windows, which is freeware. Compare it with ProDiscover Basic and another free tool of your choice. Describe how each tool performs in Linux based on research you do using blogs, user groups, and user manuals.

8

Recovering Graphics Files

After reading this chapter and completing the exercises, you will be able to:

- Describe types of graphics file formats
- Explain types of data compression
- Explain how to locate and recover graphics files
- Describe how to identify unknown file formats
- Explain copyright issues with graphics

Many digital forensics investigations involve graphics, especially those downloaded from the Web and circulated via e-mail. To examine and recover graphics files, you need to understand the basics of computer graphics, including file characteristics, common file formats, and compression methods for reducing file size. This chapter begins with an overview of computer graphics and data compression, and then explains how to locate and recover graphics files based on information stored in file headers. You learn how to identify and reconstruct graphics file fragments, analyze graphics file headers, and repair damaged file headers.

This chapter also explores tools for viewing graphics files you recover and discusses two issues related to computer graphics: steganography and copyrights. Steganography involves hiding data, including images, in files. Copyrights determine the ownership of media, such as images downloaded from a Web site, and the right to use media.

Recognizing a Graphics File

Graphics files contain digital photographs, line art, three-dimensional images, text data converted to images, and scanned replicas of printed pictures. You might have used a graphics program, such as Microsoft Paint, Adobe Photoshop, or Gnome GIMP, to create or edit an image. A graphics program creates one of three types of graphics files: bitmap, vector, and metafile. **Bitmap images** are collections of dots, or pixels, in a grid format that form a graphic. **Vector graphics** are based on mathematical instructions that define lines, curves, text, ovals, and other geometric shapes. **Metafile graphics** are combinations of bitmap and vector images.

You can use two types of programs to work with graphics files: graphics editors and image viewers. You use graphics editors to create, modify, and save bitmap, vector, and metafile graphics. You use image viewers to open and view graphics files, but you can't change their contents. When you use a graphics editor or an image viewer, you can open a file in one of many graphics file formats, such as BMP, GIF, and JPEG. Each format has different qualities, including the amount of color and compression it uses. If you open a graphics file in a graphics editor that supports multiple file formats, you can save the file in another file format. However, converting graphics files in this way can change the image quality, as you see in a hands-on project at the end of this chapter.

Understanding Bitmap and Raster Images

Bitmap images store graphics information as grids of **pixels**, short for "picture elements." **Raster images** are also collections of pixels, but they store pixels in rows to make images easy to print. In most cases, printing an image converts (rasterizes) it to print pixels line by line instead of processing the complete collection of pixels.

A bitmap's image quality on a monitor is governed by **resolution**, which determines the amount of detail that's displayed. Resolution is related to the density of pixels onscreen and depends on a combination of hardware and software. Monitors can display a range of resolutions; the higher the resolution, the sharper the image. Computers also use a video card containing a certain amount of memory for displaying images. The more advanced the video card's electronics and the more memory it has, the more detailed instructions it can accept, resulting in higher-quality images.

For example, the monitor and video card on a Windows computer might support a 4096 $\times$ 2160 resolution, which means displaying 4096 pixels horizontally and 2160 pixels vertically. Because a bitmap image is defined by pixel size, high-resolution images use smaller pixels than low-resolution images do.

Software also contributes to image quality. Software includes drivers, which are coded instructions that set a video card's display parameters, and programs used to create, modify, and view images. With some programs, such as IrfanView (*www.irfanview.com*), you can view many types of images; with other programs, you can view or work with only the graphics files they create. Digital graphics professionals use programs that support high resolutions to have more control over the display of bitmap images. However, bitmaps, especially those with low resolution, usually lose quality when you enlarge them.

Another setting that affects image quality is the number of colors the monitor displays. Graphics files can have different amounts of color per pixel, but each file must support colors with bits of space. The following list shows the number of bits per colored pixel:

- 1 bit = 2 colors
- 4 bits = 16 colors
- 8 bits = 256 colors
- 16 bits = 65,536 colors
- 24 bits = 16,777,216 colors
- 32 bits = 4,294,967,296 colors

Bitmap and raster files use as much of the color palette as possible. However, when you save a bitmap or raster file, the resolution and color might change, depending on the colors in the original file and whether the file format supports these colors.

Understanding Vector Graphics

Vector graphics, unlike bitmap and raster images, use lines instead of dots to make up an image. A vector file stores only the calculations for drawing lines and shapes; a graphics program converts these calculations into an image. Because vector files store calculations, not images, they are generally smaller than bitmap files, thereby saving disk space. You can also enlarge a vector graphic without affecting image quality—to make an image twice as large, a vector graphics program, such as CorelDRAW and Adobe Illustrator, computes the image mathematically.

Understanding Metafile Graphics

Metafile graphics combine raster and vector graphics and can have the characteristics of both file types. For example, if you scan a photograph (a bitmap image) and then add text or arrows (vector drawings), you create a metafile graphic. Although metafile graphics have the features of both bitmap and vector files, they share the limitations of both. For example, if you enlarge a metafile graphic, the area created with a bitmap loses some resolution, but the vector-formatted area remains sharp and clear.

Understanding Graphics File Formats

Graphics files are created and saved in a graphics editor, such as Microsoft Paint, Adobe Freehand MX, Adobe Photoshop, or Gnome GIMP. Some graphics editors, such as Freehand

MX, work only with vector graphics, and some programs, such as Photoshop, work with both.

Most graphics editors enable you to create and save files in one or more of the **standard graphics file formats**. Standard bitmap file formats include Portable Network Graphic (.png), Graphics Interchange Format (.gif), Joint Photographic Experts Group (.jpg or .jpeg), Tagged Image File Format (.tif or .tiff), and Windows Bitmap (.bmp). Standard vector file formats include Hewlett-Packard Graphics Language (.hpgl) and AutoCad (.dxf).

Nonstandard graphics file formats include less common formats, such as Targa (.tga) and Raster Transfer Language (.rtl); proprietary formats, such as Photoshop (.psd), Illustrator (.ai), and Freehand (.fh11); newer formats, such as Scalable Vector Graphics (.svg); and formats for old or obsolete formats, such as Paintbrush (.pcx). Because you can open standard graphics files in most or all graphics programs, they are easier to work with in a digital forensics investigation. If you encounter files in nonstandard formats, you might need to rely on your investigative skills to identify the file as a graphics file, and then find the right tools for viewing it.

To determine whether a file is a graphics file and to find a program for viewing a nonstandard graphics file, you can search the Web or consult a dictionary Web site. For example, suppose you find a file with a .tga extension during an investigation. None of the programs on your forensic workstation can open the file, and you suspect it could provide crucial evidence. To learn more about this file format, see *www.garykessler.net/library/file_sigs.html*, or follow these steps:

1. Start your Web browser, and go to **www.webopedia.com**.
2. Type **tga** in the "Enter a term" text box, and click **Search**. Webopedia lists links to additional Web pages describing the .tga file format.
3. In the Webopedia search results Web page, click the Data Format and File Extensions: T Web link, **www.webopedia.com/quick_ref/fileextensionst.asp**.
4. Scroll down until you find a definition of this format, and write it down. When you're finished, exit your Web browser.

Understanding Digital Camera File Formats

Digital cameras' popularity has had quite an impact on digital forensics because witnesses or suspects can create their own digital photos. As a digital forensics investigator, you might need to examine a digital photo created by a witness to an accident, for example. Crimes such as child pornography might involve hundreds of digital photos of alleged victims, and knowing how to analyze the data structures of graphics files can give you additional evidence for a case. In addition, knowing how digital photos are created and how they store unique information can contribute to your credibility when presenting evidence. Most, if not all, digital cameras produce digital photos in raw or Exif format, described in the following sections.

Examining the Raw File Format Referred to as a digital negative, the **raw file format** is typically used on many higher-end digital cameras. A camera performs no enhancement processing—hence the term "raw" for this format. Sensors in a digital camera simply record pixels on the memory card. One advantage of this format is that it maintains the best picture quality.

From a digital forensics perspective, the biggest disadvantage of the raw file format is that it's proprietary, and not all image viewers can display these formats. To view a raw graphics file, you might need to get the viewing and conversion software from the camera manufacturer. Each manufacturer has its own program with an algorithm to convert raw data to other standard formats, such as JPEG or TIF. The process of converting raw picture data to another format is called **demosaicing**.

For more information on raw format images, see *http://helpx.adobe.com/photoshop/digital-negative.html*.

Examining the Exchangeable Image File Format Most digital cameras use the **Exchangeable Image File (Exif)** format to store photos. The Japan Electronics and Information Technology Industries Association (JEITA) developed it as a standard for storing metadata in JPEG and TIF files (see *http://home.jeita.or.jp/tsc/std-pdf/CP3451C.pdf*). When a digital photo is taken, information about the camera (such as model, make, and serial number) and settings (such as shutter speed, focal length, resolution, date, and time) are stored in the graphics file. Most digital cameras store graphics files as Exif JPEG files. In addition, if the camera has GPS capability, the latitude and longitude location data might be recorded in the Exif section of the picture file. Location data stored in digital images is discussed in more detail in Chapter 12.

Because the Exif format collects metadata, investigators can learn more about the type of digital camera and the environment in which photos were taken. Viewing an Exif JPEG file's metadata requires special programs, such as Exif Reader (*www.takenet.or.jp/~ryuuji/minisoft/exifread/english/*), IrfanView (*www.irfanview.com*), or ProDiscover, which has a built-in Exif viewer.

Originally, JPEG and TIF formats were designed to store only digital photo data. Exif is an enhancement of these formats that modifies the beginning of a JPEG or TIF file so that metadata can be inserted. In the similar photos in Figure 8-1, the one on the left is an Exif JPEG file, and the one on the right is a standard JPEG file.

Exif picture file   JPEG picture file

Figure 8-1 Similar Exif and JPEG photos
© 2016 Cengage Learning®

Figure 8-2 shows the differences between file headers in Exif and standard JPEG files. `Sawtoothmt.jpg` is an Exif file, and `Sawtoothmtn.jpg` is a standard JPEG file. The first 160 (hexadecimal 0x9F) bytes are displayed for both files.

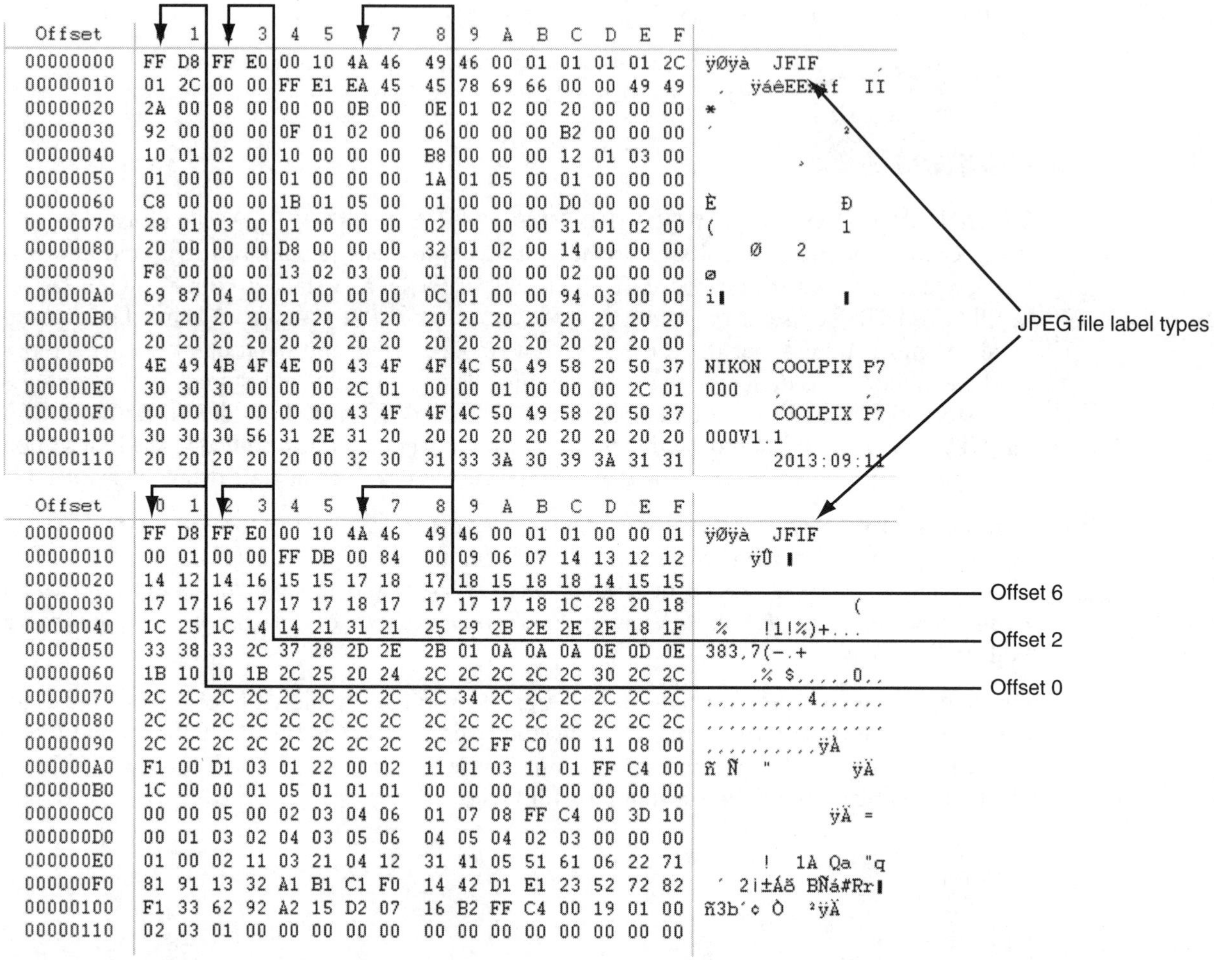

Offset	0	1	2	3	4	5	6	7	8	9	A	B	C	D	E	F		
00000000	FF	D8	FF	E0	00	10	4A	46	49	46	00	01	01	01	01	2C	ÿØÿà JFIF	,
00000010	01	2C	00	00	FF	E1	EA	45	45	78	69	66	00	00	49	49	, ÿáêExif II	
00000020	2A	00	08	00	00	00	0B	00	0E	01	02	00	20	00	00	00	*	
00000030	92	00	00	00	0F	01	02	00	06	00	00	00	B2	00	00	00	'	²
00000040	10	01	02	00	10	00	00	00	B8	00	00	00	12	01	03	00	,	
00000050	01	00	00	00	01	00	00	00	1A	01	05	00	01	00	00	00		
00000060	C8	00	00	00	1B	01	05	00	01	00	00	00	D0	00	00	00	È	Ð
00000070	28	01	03	00	01	00	00	00	02	00	00	00	31	01	02	00	(	1
00000080	20	00	00	00	D8	00	00	00	32	01	02	00	14	00	00	00	Ø 2	
00000090	F8	00	00	00	13	02	03	00	01	00	00	00	02	00	00	00	ø	
000000A0	69	87	04	00	01	00	00	00	0C	01	00	00	94	03	00	00	i‡ ”	
000000B0	20	20	20	20	20	20	20	20	20	20	20	20	20	20	20	20		
000000C0	20	20	20	20	20	20	20	20	20	20	20	20	20	20	20	00		
000000D0	4E	49	4B	4F	4E	00	43	4F	4F	4C	50	49	58	20	50	37	NIKON COOLPIX P7	
000000E0	30	30	30	00	00	00	2C	01	00	00	01	00	00	00	2C	01	000 ,	,
000000F0	00	00	01	00	00	00	43	4F	4F	4C	50	49	58	20	50	37	COOLPIX P7	
00000100	30	30	30	56	31	2E	31	20	20	20	20	20	20	20	20	20	000V1.1	
00000110	20	20	20	20	20	00	32	30	31	33	3A	30	39	3A	31	31	2013:09:11	

JPEG file label types

Offset	0	1	2	3	4	5	6	7	8	9	A	B	C	D	E	F		
00000000	FF	D8	FF	E0	00	10	4A	46	49	46	00	01	01	01	00	00	01	ÿØÿà JFIF
00000010	00	01	00	00	FF	DB	00	84	00	09	06	07	14	13	12	12	ÿÛ „	
00000020	14	12	14	16	15	15	17	18	17	18	15	18	18	14	15	15		
00000030	17	17	16	17	17	18	17	17	17	17	18	1C	28	20	18		(	
00000040	1C	25	1C	14	14	21	31	21	25	29	2B	2E	2E	2E	18	1F	% !1!%)+...	
00000050	33	38	33	2C	37	28	2D	2E	2B	01	0A	0A	0A	0E	0D	0E	383,7(-.+	
00000060	1B	10	10	1B	2C	25	20	24	2C	2C	2C	2C	2C	30	2C	2C	,% $,,,,,0,,	
00000070	2C	2C	2C	2C	2C	2C	2C	2C	2C	34	2C	2C	2C	2C	2C	2C	,,,,,,,,,4,,,,,,	
00000080	2C	2C	2C	2C	2C	2C	2C	2C	2C	2C	2C	2C	2C	2C	2C	2C	,,,,,,,,,,,,,,,,	
00000090	2C	2C	2C	2C	2C	2C	2C	2C	2C	2C	FF	C0	00	11	08	00	,,,,,,,,,,ÿÀ	
000000A0	F1	00	D1	03	01	22	00	02	11	01	03	11	01	FF	C4	00	ñ Ñ "	ÿÄ
000000B0	1C	00	00	01	05	01	01	01	00	00	00	00	00	00	00	00		
000000C0	00	00	05	00	02	03	04	06	01	07	08	FF	C4	00	3D	10	ÿÄ =	
000000D0	00	01	03	02	04	03	05	06	04	05	04	02	03	00	00	00		
000000E0	01	00	02	11	03	21	04	12	31	41	05	51	61	06	22	71	! 1A Qa "q	
000000F0	81	91	13	32	A1	B1	C1	F0	14	42	D1	E1	23	52	72	82	' 2¡±Áð BÑá#Rr‚	
00000100	F1	33	62	92	A2	15	D2	07	16	B2	FF	C4	00	19	01	00	ñ3b'¢ Ò ²ÿÄ	
00000110	02	03	01	00	00	00	00	00	00	00	00	00	00	00	00	00		

Offset 6

Offset 2

Offset 0

Figure 8-2 Differences in Exif and JPEG file header information
Courtesy of X-Ways AG, *www.x-ways.net*

All JPEG files, including Exif, start from offset 0 (the first byte of a file) with hexadecimal FFD8. The current standard header for regular JPEG files is JPEG File Interchange Format (JFIF), which has the hexadecimal value FFE0 starting at offset 2. For Exif JPEG files, the hexadecimal value starting at offset 2 is FFE1. In addition, the hexadecimal values at offset 6 specify the label name (refer to Figure 8-2). For all JPEG files, the ending hexadecimal marker, also known as the end of image (EOI), is FFD9 (see Figure 8-3).

```
Offset   | 0  1  2  3  4  5  6  7   8  9  A  B  C  D  E  F |
00019110 | 00 F8 B5 E0 F9 5B A7 F4  AC AC A0 0F 7F E9 05 BE | øµàù[§ô¬¬  é ¾
00019120 | 7F FC 62 F8 7F F9 0B FD  2A 1B AE D0 A2 C0 C6 1D | übø ù ý* ®Ð¢ÀÆ
00019130 | 5A FE 49 71 E1 5D 8A A0  9F 9E 2B 2B 28 02 AD 77 | ZþIqá] ▌ ▌▌++( -w
00019140 | 78 D7 32 BC B7 0C EE EF  F7 99 8F 26 A1 EF 95 73 | x×2¼· îï÷ &¡ï▌s
00019150 | B4 64 7B 81 59 59 4C 46  C2 75 C7 DD 15 82 E3 3D | ´d{ YYLFÂuÇÝ ▌ã=
00019160 | 16 B2 B2 80 08 D3 F5 19  6C AF 62 B8 87 EF C6 D9 | ²²¢ Óõ l¯b,▌ïÆÙr
00019170 | C7 A8 F3 1F 51 5D 4A 3B  D1 3C 09 22 16 D8 EA 18 | Ç¨ó Q]J;Ñ< " Øê
00019180 | 67 D0 8A CA CA 00 A1 76  AA C8 D8 DD 89 60 20 41 | gÐ▌ÊÊ ¡vªÈØÝ▌` A
00019190 | 36 48 5F F0 9F 31 F2 A4  5B DF FC 46 B2 B2 80 21 | 6H_ð▌1ò¤[ßüF²²▌!
000191A0 | 37 60 1C 17 23 E9 5B AC  84 91 86 AC AC A0 0D BC | 7` #é[¬▌¬¬ ¼
000191B0 | 47 D7 F1 AD 79 27 CC 7D  6B 2B 28 03 C2 39 C6 6B | G×ñy'Ì}k+( Â9Æk
000191C0 | 30 3D 7F 2A CA CA 00 F3  03 1E 75 E6 D1 E8 2B 2B | 0= *ÊÊ ó uæÑè++
000191D0 | 28 03 49 19 63 5C 95 15  E2 C9 BB EE 2E 01 F5 35 | ( I c\▌ âÉ»î. õ5
000191E0 | 95 94 08 90 92 46 09 3F  4A D7 38 E8 2B 2B 28 02 | ▌▌ ▌F ?J×8è++(
000191F0 | 32 E7 38 C5 6A 4F AF E9  59 59 40 11 93 CD 65 65 | 2ç8Åj O¯éYY@ ▌Íee
00019200 | 65 00 7F FF D9                                    | e ÿÙ
```
                                                                    JPEG file EOI marker

```
Offset   | 0  1  2  3  4  5  6  7   8  9  A  B  C  D  E  F |
00001ED0 | 92 49 00 24 92 49 00 24  92 49 00 3A 9E A3 C5 5A | ´I $´I $´I :▌£ÅZ
00001EE0 | A8 E1 1A AA 6E 51 07 C5  C2 00 6F 1A A3 9E 93 87 | ¨á ªnQ ÅÂ o £▌▌▌
00001EF0 | 43 F2 5E 6F 86 EC F4 D4  21 D3 E6 BD 1E AD 72 87 | Cò^o▌ìôÔ!Óæ½ r▌
00001F00 | 56 A7 72 63 CD 2E CE 86  57 D8 3F 01 C3 5B 45 B6 | VSrcÍ.Î▌WØ? Ã[E¶
00001F10 | 12 ED 91 36 B6 18 D1 37  26 66 53 18 35 E8 A3 AB | í▌6¶ Ñ7&fS 5è£«
00001F20 | 75 89 C8 D6 C7 82 49 89  BE CA 60 22 35 54 19 5C | u▌ÈÖÇ▌I▌¾Ê`"5T \
00001F30 | 03 28 9D 33 9B 45 19 2B  8F 25 8A 34 5A 6E 2C 77 | ( 3▌E + %▌4Zn,w
00001F40 | 5A FE CF 53 86 2C 7B 24  5D 6D 7B 37 7A 40 A7 FA | ZþÏS▌,{$]m{7z@Sú
00001F50 | 7E C5 5A B0 83 4C 09 E1  45 29 ED 5A CC C4 81 25 | ~ÅZ°▌L áE)íZÌÄ %
00001F60 | C6 94 94 A0 63 80 5D 01  36 57 42 00 EA E8 0B 90 | Æ▌▌ c▌] 6WB êè
00001F70 | 9C 14 80 A1 25 D4 94 01  8C 49 24 94 12 03 5C 49 | ▌ ▌¡%Ô▌ ▌I$▌ \I
00001F80 | 24 00 92 49 24 00 92 49  24 00 9C A0 7A E2 48 02 | $ ´I$ ´I$ ▌ zâH
00001F90 | 2A 8A 0A FA 24 92 5D 9D  0C AF B3 3A 7A 15 13 F4 | *▌ ú$´] ¯²:z ô
00001FA0 | 29 24 B0 4B B3 5B 2B 3B  64 47 87 EA 12 49 4C BA | )$°K³[+;dG▌ê ILº
00001FB0 | 2B E0 26 DD 96 C3 B3 7F  E9 04 92 5A 3D 3F 91 57 | +à&Ý▌Ã³ é ´Z=?▌W
00001FC0 | 74 15 4F 6A EA 4B 62 32  B1 C1 75 71 25 08 96 75 | t Oj êKb2±Áuq% ▌u
00001FD0 | 3D 89 24 80 1C 92 49 20  0E A4 92 4A 40 FF D9     | =▌$▌ ´I ¤´J@ÿÙ
```

Figure 8-3 EOI marker FFD9 for all JPEG files
Courtesy of X-Ways AG, *www.x-ways.net*

With tools such as ProDiscover and Exif Reader, you can extract metadata as evidence for your case. As you can see in Figure 8-4, ProDiscover shows that the picture was taken on September 11, 2013, at 1:09 a.m. You might have noticed in Figure 8-1 that there's a lot of sunlight in the photos, but the metadata shows the time of day as 1:09 a.m., when sunlight is unlikely.

As in any digital forensics investigation, determining date and time for a file is important. Getting this information might not be possible, however, for a variety of reasons, such as suspects losing cameras after transferring photo files to their computers. You should list this type of evidence as subjective in your report because intentional and unintentional acts make date and time difficult to confirm. For example, suspects could alter a camera's clock intentionally to record an incorrect date and time when a picture is taken. An unintentional act could be the battery or camera's electronics failing, for example, which causes an incorrect date and time to be recorded. When you're dealing with date and time values in Exif metadata, always look for corroborating information, such as where the picture was taken or whether the

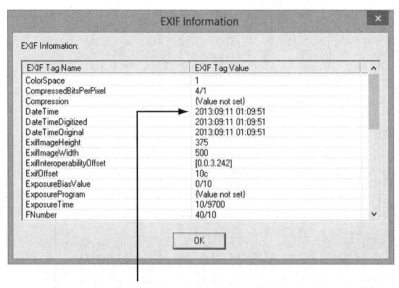

Camera-recorded date and time of photo

Figure 8-4 ProDiscover displaying metadata from an Exif JPEG file
Courtesy of Technology Pathways, LLC

device is set to Coordinated Universal Time (abbreviated as UTC), to help support what you find in metadata.

For example, the photograph in Figure 8-1 was taken in Sante Fe, New Mexico, on September 10, 2013. If the camera's date and time had been set to UTC, you need to adjust for local time. In September, Sante Fe's local time is mountain daylight saving (MDT), which is -6 hours from UTC time. So the actual local time might be 7:09 p.m. MDT. Because 7:09 p.m. is early evening, you should determine when sunset occurred on that date by using online tools, such as Time and Date (*www.timeanddate.com/worldclock/sunrise.html*) or SunriseSunset (*www.sunrisesunset.com/sun.html*). The Time and Date Web site shows that sunset for this location and time happened at 7:18 p.m. If the camera is set to 7:09 p.m. local time, you might assume sunlight would cast long shadows. Because the shadows look short, the date and time might not be accurate. In addition, if latitude and longitude values are available in the Exif file, you could approximate the time of day based on the length and angle of shadows to the sun. Of course, this calculation applies only to photos taken outside on sunny days.

Understanding Data Compression

Most graphics file formats, including GIF and JPEG, compress data to save disk space and reduce the file's transmission time. Other formats, such as BMP, rarely compress data or do so inefficiently. In this case, you can use compression tools to compact data and reduce file size. **Data compression** is the process of coding data from a larger form to a smaller form. Graphics files and most compression tools use one of two data compression schemes: lossless or lossy. You need to understand how compression schemes work to know what happens when an image is altered.

Lossless and Lossy Compression

This section describes how lossless and lossy compression work, explains their advantages and disadvantages, and discusses what they mean in terms of digital forensics.

Lossless compression techniques reduce file size without removing data. When you uncompress a file that uses lossless compression, you restore all its information. GIF and Portable Network Graphics (PNG) file formats reduce file size with lossless compression, which saves file space by using mathematical formulas to represent data in a file. These formulas generally use one of two algorithms: Huffman or Lempel-Ziv-Welch (LZW) coding. Each algorithm uses a code to represent redundant bits of data. For example, if a graphics file contains a large red area, the algorithm can set 1 byte to red and set another byte to specify 200 red bytes instead of having to store 200 red bytes. Therefore, only 2 bytes are used.

Lossy compression is much different because it compresses data by permanently discarding bits of information in the file. Some discarded bits are redundant, but others are not. When you uncompress a graphics file that uses lossy compression, you lose information, although most people don't notice the difference unless they print the image on a high-resolution printer or increase the image size. In either case, the removed bits of information reduce image quality. The JPEG format is one that uses lossy compression. If you open a JPEG file in a graphics program, for example, and save it as a JPEG file with a different name, lossy compression is reapplied automatically, which removes more bits of data and, therefore, reduces image quality. If you simply rename a file by using File Explorer or the command line, however, the file doesn't lose any more data.

Another form of lossy compression, **vector quantization** (VQ), uses complex algorithms to determine what data to discard based on vectors in the graphics file. In simple terms, VQ discards bits in much the same way rounding off decimal values discards numbers.

Some widely used lossless compression utilities include WinZip, PKZip, Stufflt, and FreeZip. Lzip is a lossy compression utility. You use compression tools to compact folders and files for data storage and transmission. Remember that the difference between lossless and lossy compression is the way data is represented after it has been uncompressed. Lossless compression produces an exact replica of the original data after it has been uncompressed; lossy compression typically produces an altered replica of the data.

Locating and Recovering Graphics Files

In a digital forensics investigation involving graphics files, you need to locate and recover all graphics files on the suspect drive and determine which ones are pertinent to your case. Because images aren't always stored in standard graphics file formats, you should examine all files your forensics tools find, even if they aren't identified as graphics files.

Some OSs have built-in tools for recovering graphics files, but they're time consuming, and the results are difficult to verify. Instead, you can use digital forensics tools dedicated to analyzing graphics files. As you work with these tools and built-in OS tools, develop standard procedures for your organization and continue to refine them so that other investigators can benefit from your experience. You should also follow standard procedures for each case to make sure your analysis is thorough.

As discussed earlier in "Examining the Exchangeable Image File Format," you can use digital forensics tools to analyze images based on information in graphics files. Each graphics file contains a header with instructions for displaying the image; this header information helps you identify the file format. The header is complex and difficult to remember, however; instead of memorizing header information, you can compare a known good file header with that of a suspected file. For example, if you find an image that you suspect is a JPEG file but can't display it with a bitmap graphics program, compare its file header with a known JPEG file header to determine whether the header has been altered. You could then use the information in the known JPEG file header to supply instructions for displaying the image. In other words, you use the known JPEG header information to create a baseline analysis.

Before you can examine a graphics file header, often you need to reconstruct a fragmented graphics file. To do so, you need to identify the data patterns the graphics file uses. If part of the file header has been overwritten with other data, you might also need to repair the damaged header. By rebuilding the file header, you can then perform a forensics analysis on the graphics file. These techniques are described in the following sections.

Identifying Graphics File Fragments

If a graphics file is fragmented across areas on a disk, you must recover all the fragments before re-creating the file. Recovering any type of file fragments is called **carving**, also known as **salvaging** outside North America. To carve a graphics file's data from file slack space and free space, you should be familiar with the data patterns of known graphics file types. Many digital forensics programs, such as ProDiscover, X-Ways Forensics, OS Forensics, EnCase, and FTK, can recognize these data patterns and carve the graphics files from slack and free space automatically, however. After you recover fragments of a graphics file, you restore them to continue your examination. You use ProDiscover Basic and WinHex later in this chapter to copy known data patterns from files you recover, and then restore this information to view the graphics file.

Repairing Damaged Headers

When you're examining recovered fragments from files in slack or free space, you might find data that appears to be a header for a common graphics file type. If you locate header data that's partially overwritten, you must reconstruct the header to make it readable by comparing the hexadecimal values of known graphics file formats with the pattern of the file header you found.

Each graphics file type has a unique header value. As you become familiar with these header values, you can spot data from partially overwritten headers in file slack or free space. For example, a JPEG file has the hexadecimal header value FFD8, followed by the label JFIF for a standard JPEG or Exif file at offset 6.

Suppose you're investigating a possible intellectual property theft by a contract employee of Exotic Mountain Tour Service (EMTS). EMTS has just finished an expensive marketing and customer service analysis with Superior Bicycles, LLC. Based on this analysis, EMTS plans to release advertising for its latest tour service with a joint product marketing campaign with Superior Bicycles. Unfortunately, EMTS suspects that a contract travel consultant, Bob Aspen, might have given sensitive marketing data to another bicycle competitor. EMTS is under a nondisclosure agreement with Superior Bicycles and must protect this advertising campaign material.

An EMTS manager found a USB drive on the desk Bob Aspen was assigned to. Your task is to determine whether the drive contains proprietary EMTS or Superior Bicycles data. The EMTS manager also gives you some interesting information he gathered from the Web server administrator. EMTS filters all Web-based e-mail traffic traveling through its network and detects suspicious attachments. When a Web-based e-mail with attachments is received, the Web filter is triggered. The EMTS manager gives you two screen captures, shown in Figures 8-5 and 8-6, of partial e-mails intercepted by the Web filter that lead him to believe Bob Aspen might have engaged in questionable activities.

From: terrysadler@goowy.com
To: baspen99@aol.com
Sent: Sun, 4 Feb 2015 9:21 PM

Bob, check these photos out and let me know what EMTS is up to too. Terry

_____

your personal webtop. @ http://www.goowy.com

From: Jim Shu[mailto:jim_shu1@yahoo.com]
Sent: Monday, February 5, 2015 5:17 AM -08:00
To: terrysadler [terrysadler@goowy.com]
Subject: New announcement

Terry, tell Bob to change these file extensions from
.txt to .jpg to see photos of the new kayak construction. Jim

--- terrysadler <terrysadler@goowy.com> wrote:

> Jim, I can't mail this to Bob, his email service

Figure 8-5 First intercepted capture of an e-mail from Terry Sadler
© 2016 Cengage Learning®

From:denisesuperbic@hotmail.com
To: baspen99@aol.com
Sent: Sun, 4 Feb 2015 9:29 PM
Subject: RE:New Announcement

Can you read the attachment yet? Denise

>From: Jim Shu <jim_shu1@yahoo.com>
>To: terrysadler <terrysadler@goowy.com>
>CC: nautieriko@lycos.com
>Subject: New announcement
>Date: Sun, 4 Feb 2015 20:57:37 -0800 (PST)
>
>Terry,
>
>I had a tour of the new kayak factory. I think we can
>run with this to the other party interested in
>competing. I smuggled these files out, they are JPEG
>files I edited with my hex editor so that the email
>monitor won't pick up on them. So to view them you
>have to re-edit each file to the proper JPEG header of
>offset 0x FF D8 FF E0 and offset 6 of 4A. Then you
>have to rename them to a .jpg extension to view
>them.

>See attached, Bob Aspen I think is working for EMTS he

Figure 8-6 Second intercepted capture of an e-mail from denisesuperbic@hotmail.com
© 2016 Cengage Learning®

For this examination, you need to search for all possible places data might be hiding. To do this, in the next section you use ProDiscover's cluster search function with hexadecimal search strings to look for known data.

Searching for and Carving Data from Unallocated Space

At this time, you have little information on what to look for on the USB drive Bob Aspen used. You need to ask some basic questions and make some assumptions based on available information to proceed in your search for information.

The first message from terrysadler@goowy.com is addressed to baspen99@aol.com, which matches the contract employee's name, Bob Aspen. Next, look at the time and date stamps in this message. The first is 4 Feb 2015 9:21 PM, and the second, farther down, is a header from Jim Shu with a time and date stamp of February 5, 2015, 5:17 AM -08:00.

Therefore, it seems Jim Shu sent the original message, which was forwarded to the terrysadler@goowy.com account. Because the timestamp for Jim Shu is later than the timestamp for terrysadler@goowy.com, Terry Sadler's location might be in a different time zone, somewhere west of Jim Shu, or one of the two e-mail server's time values is off because e-mail servers, not users, provide timestamps. In Chapter 11, you learn more about e-mail header information.

Continuing with the first message, note that Jim is telling Terry to have Bob alter the file extensions from .txt to .jpg, and the files are about new kayaks. The last line appears to be a previous response from terrysadler@goowy.com commenting that Bob (assuming it's Bob Aspen) can't receive this message.

So far, you have the following facts:

- Jim Shu's e-mail refers to JPEG files.
- Jim Shu's attached JPEG files need to have the extension renamed from .txt to .jpg.
- Jim Shu's attachments might be photographs of new kayaks.
- The e-mail account names in this message are terrysadler@goowy.com, baspen99@aol.com, and jim_shu1@yahoo.com.

Now examine the second e-mail, which contains the following pieces of information:

- Jim Shu had a tour of the new kayak factory.
- Another party might be interested in competing in manufacturing kayaks.
- Jim Shu smuggled out JPEG photos he modified with a hexadecimal editor so that they wouldn't be detected by any Web or e-mail filters.
- Jim Shu provides instructions on how to reedit the digital photos and add the .jpeg extension so that they can be viewed.
- Jim Shu thinks Bob Aspen is working at EMTS.
- Jim Shu sent a copy (CC) to nautieriko@lycos.com.

With these collected facts and your knowledge of JPEG file structures, you can use the steps in the following sections to determine whether these allegations are true.

Planning Your Examination In the second e-mail from Jim Shu to Terry Sadler, Jim states, "So to view them you have to re-edit each file to the proper JPEG header of offset 0x FF D8 FF E0 and offset 6 of 4A." From this statement, you can assume that any kayak photographs on the USB drive contain unknown characters in the first four bytes and the sixth byte. Because this is all Jim Shu said about the JPEG files, you need to assume that the seventh, eighth, and ninth bytes have the original correct information for the JPEG file.

In "Examining the Exchangeable Image File Format," you learned the difference between a standard JFIF JPEG and an Exif JPEG file: The JFIF format has 0x FFD8 FFE0 in the first four bytes, and the Exif format has 0x FFD8 FFE1. In the sixth byte, the JPEG label is listed as JFIF or Exif. In the second e-mail, Jim Shu mentions 0x FF D8 FF E0, which is a JFIF JPEG format. He also says to change the sixth byte to 0x 4A, which is the uppercase letter "J" in ASCII.

Because the files might have been downloaded to the USB drive, Bob Aspen could have altered or deleted them, so you should be thorough in your examination and analysis. You need to search all sectors of the drive for deleted files, both allocated space (in case Bob didn't modify the files) and unallocated space. In the next section, you use ProDiscover to search for and recover these JPEG files.

Searching for and Recovering Digital Photograph Evidence In this section, you learn how to use ProDiscover to search for and extract (recover) possible evidence of JPEG files from the USB drive the EMTS manager gave you. The search string to use for this examination is "FIF." Because it's part of the label name of the JFIF JPEG format, you might have several false hits if the USB drive contains several other JPEG files. These false hits, referred to as **false positives**, require examining each search hit to verify whether it's what you are looking for.

The image file of the USB drive is included on the book's DVD. You should extract all files in the Chap08 folder on the DVD to your C:*Work*\Chap08\Chapter folder (referred to as your "work folder" in steps). Create this folder on your system first, if necessary.

 Remember that the work folder you create most likely has a different name from what's shown in screenshots.

To begin the examination, follow these steps to load the image file:

1. Start ProDiscover Basic (with the **Run as administrator** option, if necessary), and click the **New Project** toolbar button. In the New Project dialog box, type **C08InChp** for the project number and filename, and then click **OK**.

2. Click **Action** from the menu, point to **Add**, and click **Image File**.

3. In the Open dialog box, navigate to your work folder, click **C08InChp.dd**, and then click **Open**.

4. To begin a search, click the **Search** toolbar button or click **Action, Search** from the menu to open the Search dialog box.

5. Click the **Cluster Search** tab, and then click the **Case Sensitive** check box. Under Search for the pattern(s), type **FIF** (see Figure 8-7). Under Select the Disk(s)/Image(s) you want to search in, click the **C08InChp.dd** file, and then click **OK**.

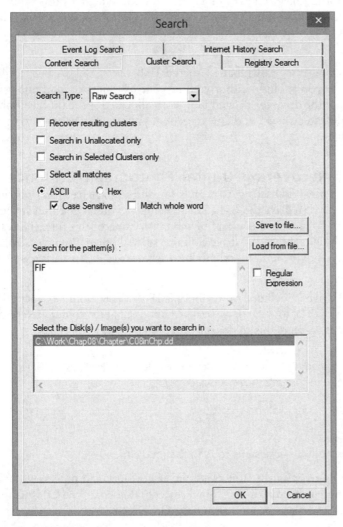

Figure 8-7   Searching clusters in ProDiscover
Courtesy of Technology Pathways, LLC

6. When the search is done, click the search hit, **AC4(2756)**, to display the cluster's content (see Figure 8-8).

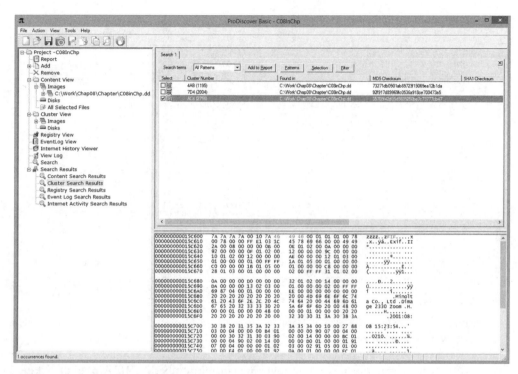

Figure 8-8 Completed cluster search for FIF
Courtesy of Technology Pathways, LLC

In Figure 8-9, the header for this JPEG file has been overwritten with zzzz. This unique header information might give you additional search values that could minimize false-positive hits in subsequent searches.

File header overwritten with zzzz

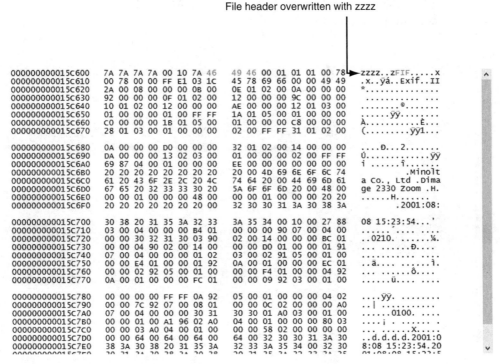

Figure 8-9   Content of cluster AC4(2756)
Courtesy of Technology Pathways, LLC

7. Next, locate the file by right-clicking cluster number **AC4(2756)** and clicking **Find File**, and then click **Yes** in the warning message.

8. In the List of Clusters dialog box, click **Show File** (see Figure 8-10), and then click **Close**.

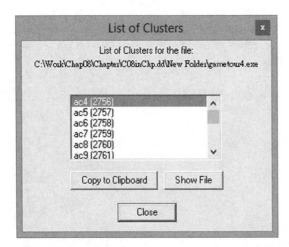

Figure 8-10   Viewing all clusters used by the `gametour4.exe` file
Courtesy of Technology Pathways, LLC

9. In the work area, right-click the **gametour4.exe** file (see Figure 8-11) and click **Copy File**. In the Save As dialog box, navigate to your work folder, type **Recover1.jpg** for the filename, and then click **Save**.

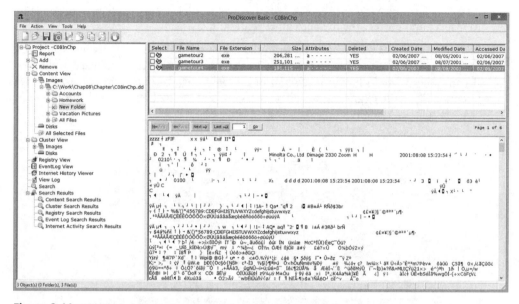

Figure 8-11 Mislabeled file that appears to be altered intentionally
Courtesy of Technology Pathways, LLC

10. Click **File, Exit** from the menu, and then click **Yes** and **Save** to save this project in your work folder.

In WinHex Demo, you can save only up to 200 KB of data in a file. That's why for activities in this book involving data extractions larger than 200 KB, ProDiscover Basic or OS Forensics is used.

NOTE

The next section shows you how to rebuild header data from this recovered file by using WinHex, although any hexadecimal editor has the capability to examine and repair damaged file headers. From a digital forensics view, this procedure can be considered corrupting the evidence, but knowing how to reconstruct data, as in the preceding example, is part of an investigator's job. When you change data as part of the recovery and analysis process, make sure you document each step as part of your reporting procedures. Your documentation should be detailed enough that other investigators could repeat the steps, which increases the credibility of your findings. When you're rebuilding a corrupted evidence image file, create a new file and leave the original file in its initial corrupt condition.

Rebuilding File Headers

Before attempting to edit a graphics file you have recovered, try to open it with an image viewer, such as the default Microsoft tool. To test whether you can view the image, double-click the recovered file in its current location in File Explorer. If you can open and view the image, you have recovered the graphics file successfully. If the image isn't displayed, you have to inspect and correct the header values manually.

If some of the data you recovered from the graphics file header is corrupt, you might need to recover more pieces of the file before you can view the image, as you'll see in the next section. Because the deleted file you recovered in the previous activity, Recover1.jpg, was altered intentionally, you might see an error message similar to the one in Figure 8-12 when you attempt to open the file.

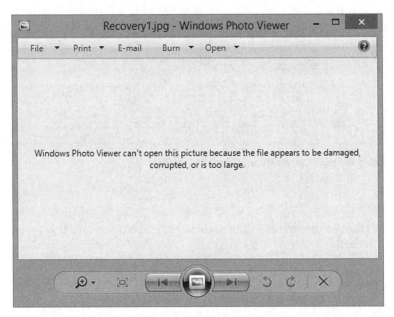

Figure 8-12   Error message indicating a damaged or an altered graphics file
Courtesy of Microsoft Corporation

If you can't open a graphics file in an image viewer, the next step is to examine the file's header data to see whether it matches the header in a good JPEG file. If the header doesn't match, you must insert the correct hexadecimal values manually with a hexadecimal editor. To inspect a file with WinHex, follow these steps:

1. Start WinHex, and click **File, Open** from the menu. Navigate to your work folder, and then double-click **Recover1.jpg**. Figure 8-13 shows this file open in WinHex.

Offset position 0   Offset position 6

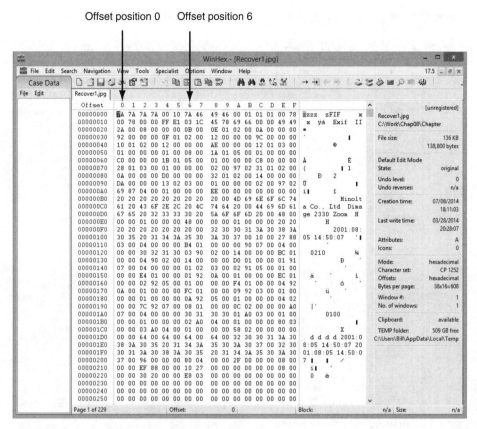

Figure 8-13 `Recover1.jpg` open in WinHex
Courtesy of X-Ways AG, *www.x-ways.net*

2. At the top of the WinHex window, notice that the hexadecimal values starting at the first byte position (offset 0) are 7A 7A 7A 7A, and the sixth position (offset 6) is also 7A. Leave WinHex open for the next activity.

As mentioned, a standard JFIF JPEG file has a header value of FF D8 FF E0 from offset 0 and the label name JFIF starting at offset 6. Using WinHex, you can correct this file header manually by following these steps:

1. In the center pane, click to the left of the first 7A hexadecimal value. Then type **FF D8 FF E0**, which are the correct hexadecimal values for the first 4 bytes of a JPEG file.

2. In the right pane at offset 6, click the **z**, and then type **J**, as shown in Figure 8-14.

Insert FF D8 FF E0 starting at offset 0   Insert an uppercase J here

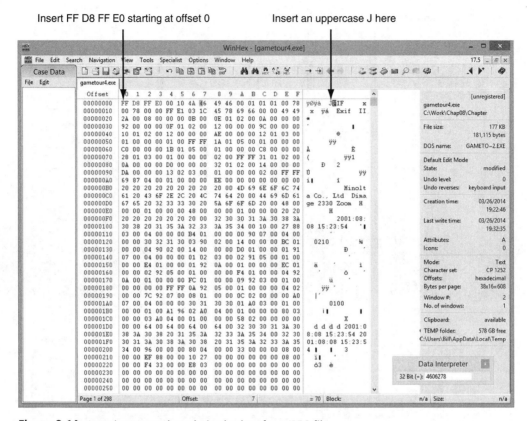

Figure 8-14   Inserting correct hexadecimal values for a JPEG file
Courtesy of X-Ways AG, *www.x-ways.net*

In WinHex, when you type a keyboard character in the right pane, the corresponding hexadecimal value appears in the center pane. So, for example, when you type J in the right pane, the hexadecimal value 4A appears in the center pane.

3. Click **File, Save As** from the menu. In the Save File As dialog box, navigate to your work folder, type **Fixed1.jpg** as the filename, and then click **Save**. Exit WinHex.

Every two hexadecimal values you entered in the previous steps are equivalent to one ASCII character. For example, an uppercase "A" has the hexadecimal value 41, and a lowercase "a" has the hexadecimal value 61. Most disk editors have a reference chart for converting hexadecimal values to ASCII characters, such as in Figure 8-15.

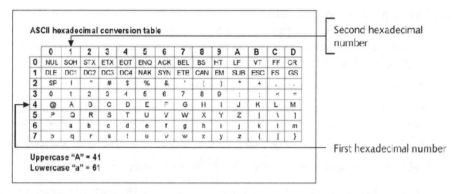

Figure 8-15 ASCII equivalents of hexadecimal values
© Cengage Learning®

After you repair a graphics file header, you can test the updated file by opening it in an image viewer, such as Windows Photo Viewer, IrfanView, ThumbsPlus, Quick View, or ACDSee. If the file displays the image, as shown in Figure 8-16, you have performed the recovery correctly.

Figure 8-16 `Fixed1.jpg` open in an image viewer
© 2016 Cengage Learning®

The process of repairing file headers isn't limited to JPEG files. You can apply the same technique to any file you can determine the header value for, including Microsoft Word, Excel, and PowerPoint documents and other image formats. You need to know only the correct header format for the type of file you're attempting to repair.

Reconstructing File Fragments

You might occasionally encounter corrupt data that prevents you from recovering data fragments for files. Whether the data corruption is accidental or intentional, you need to know how to examine a suspect drive and extract possible data fragments to reconstruct files for evidentiary purposes. In this section, you learn how to locate noncontiguous clusters that make up a deleted file. Current digital forensics tools can typically follow the links between clusters for FAT and NTFS file systems. However, sometimes the pointer information in a FAT or an NTFS Master File Table (MFT) file doesn't list this information.

The JPEG file you recovered in the previous activity was fragmented into several clusters. The following activity shows you how to recover a fragmented graphics file on a suspect drive. To perform this data-carving task, you need to locate the starting and ending clusters for each fragmented group of clusters. Here's an overview of the procedure:

1. Locate and export all clusters of the fragmented file.

2. Determine the starting and ending cluster numbers for each fragmented group of clusters.

3. Copy each fragmented group of clusters in their correct sequence to a recovery file.

4. Rebuild the file's header to make it readable in a graphics viewer.

Use the project you created previously, C08InChp, to analyze the fragmentation:

1. Start ProDiscover Basic (with the **Run as administrator** option, if necessary). Click **File, Open Project** from the menu, navigate to your work folder, click the **C08InChp.dft** file you saved previously when you exited ProDiscover, and then click **Open**.

2. In the tree view, click **Cluster Search Results**, and then in the work area, click **AC4(2756)**. Right-click the cluster row **AC4(2756)** and click **Find File**. When prompted, click **Yes** in the Continue search message box.

3. In the List of Clusters dialog box, click **Copy to Clipboard**. Start Notepad, paste the cluster into a new document, and save the file as **AC4-carve.txt** in your work folder. Leave Notepad open for the following steps.

4. In ProDiscover's List of Clusters dialog box, click **Close**.

5. In the tree view, click to expand **Cluster View**, if necessary, click to expand **Images**, and then click the **C08InChp.dd** image file to view the cluster (Figure 8-17).

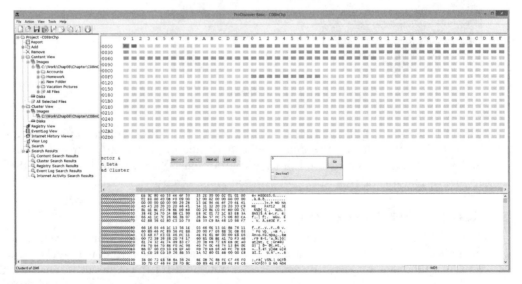

Figure 8-17   Cluster view of C08InChp.dd
Courtesy of Technology Pathways, LLC

6. Examine the `AC4-carve.txt` file in Notepad to determine the clusters that are grouped together and see the range for each cluster group. For example, locate the first cluster number, AC4, and count downward until you find a cluster number that's not sequential. Make note of the last contiguous cluster number before the change to determine the first cluster group for this fragmented file. Continue through the list of cluster numbers to determine all fragments. The following list shows the cluster groups you should find:

- *Fragment range 1*—AC4 to B20
- *Fragment range 2*—1D6 to 229
- *Fragment range 3*—3CC to 406
- *Fragment range 4*—14B to 182
- *Fragment range 5*—938 to 96D
- *Fragment range 6*—6 to D

NOTE The first fragment starts at hexadecimal AC4 (decimal 2756) and continues to hexadecimal B29. The next fragment starts at 1D6 and continues to 229, and so on until the last segment of fragmented clusters. This file is very fragmented.

7. In ProDiscover's tree view, click **Cluster View, Images,** and the `C08InChp.dd` file, if necessary. In the work area's Cluster text box at the lower right, type **AC4** (see Figure 8-18) and click **Go**.

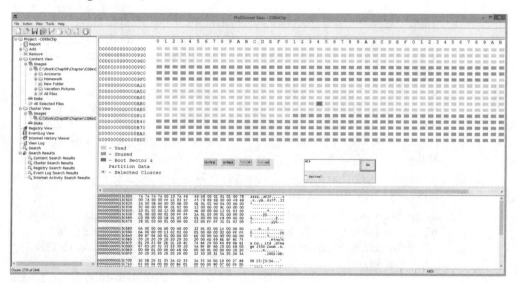

Figure 8-18   Cluster view of sector AC4
Courtesy of Technology Pathways, LLC

TIP To view all cluster columns in the work area, as shown in Figures 8-18 and 8-19, you need to maximize ProDiscover Basic's view and increase the work area's size. Drag its left border to the left, into the tree view, until you can see all 30 hexadecimal columns, and then release the mouse button.

8. In the work area, click cluster **AC4** and drag to the right until you've highlighted all clusters to **B20** (see Figure 8-19).

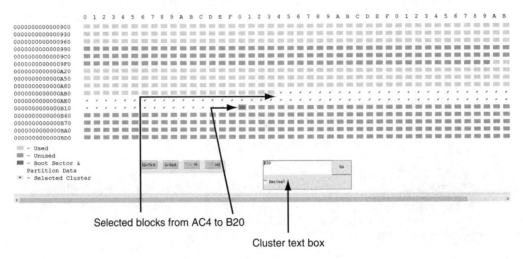

Selected blocks from AC4 to B20

Cluster text box

Figure 8-19   Selecting blocks from cluster AC4 to B20
Courtesy of Technology Pathways, LLC

9. Right-click the highlighted blocks (clusters) in the work area and click **Select**. In the Add Comment dialog box, click the **Apply to all items** check box. In the Investigator comments text box, type **Fragment 1 to recover**, and then click **OK**.

10. Repeat Steps 7 through 9 to select the remaining fragmented blocks for these sectors: 1D6 to 229, 3CC to 406, 14B to 182, 938 to 96D, and 6 to D. In the Add Comment dialog box, increase the comment's fragment number by 1 for each block: Fragment 2 to recover, Fragment 3 to recover, and so on.

11. After all clusters have been selected, click **Tools**, point to **Copy Evidence of Interest**, and click **Copy All Selected Clusters** from the menu.

12. In the Recover Clusters dialog box, click the **Recover all clusters to a single file** option button and the **Recover Binary** check box (see Figure 8-20). Click **Browse**, navigate to and click your work folder, and then click **OK**. Click **OK** again.

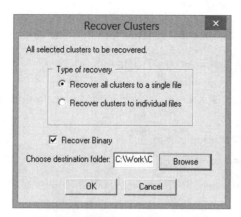

Figure 8-20 Copying all selected clusters to a file

Courtesy of Technology Pathways, LLC

13. Exit ProDiscover Basic, saving this project in your work folder if prompted. Exit Notepad, saving the file if prompted. The next step would be rebuilding the header of this recovered file, as you did in a previous activity.

When you copy the selected data with ProDiscover's Recover Clusters function, a file named `C08InChp-00000000-00000353.txt` is created. ProDiscover adds a `.txt` extension automatically on all copied clusters the Recover Clusters function exports. To view and rebuild this file, you would use the techniques described previously in "Rebuilding File Headers." (Remember to save the updated recovered data with a `.jpg` extension.) You would notice that it's the same data that enabled you to re-create `Fixed1.jpg`. Other JPEG files, such as `gametour4.exe`, can be recovered by using the same techniques. Because `gametour4.exe` is larger than 200 KB, you would have to extract its data into two separate files if you were using WinHex. Next, you would repair the first file containing the overwritten data of `zzzz`, such as `fragment1.txt`, and then combine the two files into one file. To combine them, you can use the DOS command `type fragment2.txt >> fragment1.txt`, and then use the DOS command `ren` to rename `fragment1.txt` as `Fixed2.jpg`. Another disk editor you can use is Hex Workshop (*www.hexworkshop.com*), which has a 30-day use policy for a demo version and no file size limits.

Identifying Unknown File Formats

With the continuing changes in technology and digital graphics, eventually you'll encounter graphics file formats you're not familiar with. In addition, suspects might use older systems with programs that create files in uncommon or obsolete file formats. Therefore, you must research both old and new file types. Knowing the purpose of each format and how it stores data is part of the investigation process.

The Internet is the best source for learning more about file formats and their extensions. You have already used the Webopedia site to research the TGA file format. You can also use a search engine to search for "file type" or "file format" and find the latest list of Web sites with information on file extensions. If you still can't find a specific file extension, try refining your search by entering the file extension along with the words "file format" in a search engine. One nonstandard graphics file format is XIF. To search for information on this file format, follow these steps:

1. Start your Web browser, and go to **www.google.com**.

2. Type **XIF file format** in the text box and press **Enter**.

3. Click a few links in the search results to learn more about this file format. When you're finished, exit your Web browser.

Nuance PaperPort is a scanning program that produces images in the XIF (also referred to as XIFF) format, which is derived from the TIF file format. (It's not related to the Exif format.) Older versions of PaperPort had a free viewer utility for XIF files, but you can also use Solvusoft FileViewPro (*www.solvusoft.com/en/file-extensions/file-extension-xif/*) to view these files.

The following sites have information to help you analyze file formats. Keep in mind that information on the Web changes frequently; use a search engine to find graphics file information if you can't access these Web sites:

- *www.fileformat.info/format/all.htm*
- *http://extension.informer.com/*
- *www.martinreddy.net/gfx/*

Analyzing Graphics File Headers

You should analyze graphics file headers when you find new or unique file types that forensics tools don't recognize. The simplest way to access a file header is to use a hexadecimal editor, such as WinHex. You can then record the hexadecimal values in the header and use them to define a file type.

For example, suppose you encounter an XIF file. Because this format is so old, not much information on it is available. If you need to look for hidden or deleted XIF files, you must build your own header search string. To do this, you need a hexadecimal editor, such as WinHex. To see the differences between XIF and TIF, viewing and comparing header values for these file formats is good practice.

TIF is a well-established file format for transmitting faxes and for use in printed publications. All TIF files start at offset 0 with hexadecimal 49 49 2A. These hexadecimal values translate to the letters "II" in ASCII. Figure 8-21 shows a sample TIF file open in WinHex.

TIF file headers start with hexadecimal 49 49 2A, equivalent to ASCII II

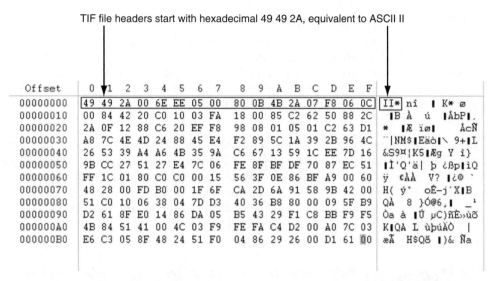

Figure 8-21 A TIF file open in WinHex
Courtesy of X-Ways AG, *www.x-ways.net*

The first 3 bytes of an XIF file are the same as a TIF file, followed by other hexadecimal values that distinguish it from a TIF file (see Figure 8-22). As you can see, the XIF header starts with hexadecimal 49 49 2A and has an offset of 4 bytes of 5C 01 00 00 20 65 58 74 65 6E 64 65 64 20 03. (Some values have been cut off in this figure to conserve space.) With this information, you can configure your forensics tool to detect an XIF file header. For more information on XIF, go to *www.fileformat.info/info/mimetype/image/vnd.xiff/index.htm* or *www.vincent-net.com/luc/papers/99isdm_document_talk.pdf*.

XIF file header   ASCII equivalent shows the same beginning values as a TIF extension

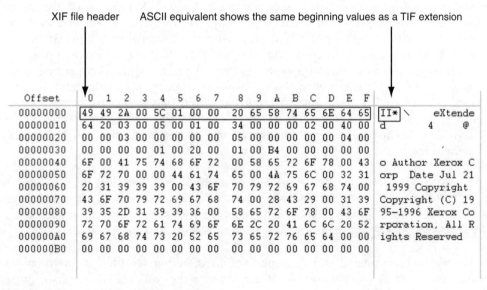

Figure 8-22 An XIF file open in WinHex
Courtesy of X-Ways AG, *www.x-ways.net*

Tools for Viewing Images

Throughout this chapter, you have been learning about recognizing file formats, using compression techniques, salvaging header information, recovering graphics files, and saving your modifications. After you recover a graphics file, you can use an image viewer to open and view it. Several hundred image viewers are available that can read many graphics file formats, although no one viewer program can read every file format. Therefore, having many different viewer programs for investigations is best.

Many viewer utilities are freeware or shareware programs that can be used to view a wide range of graphics file formats. Most GUI forensics tools include image viewers that display only common image formats, especially GIF and JPEG, which are often found in Internet-related investigations. For less common file formats, such as PCX, integrated viewers often simply identify the data as a graphics file or might not recognize the data at all. Being unable to view all formats can prevent you from finding critical evidence for a case. Be sure that you analyze, identify, and inspect every unknown file on a drive.

With many forensics tools, you can open files with external viewers.

Understanding Steganography in Graphics Files

When you open some graphics files in an image viewer, they might not seem to contain information related to your investigation. However, someone might have hidden information inside the image by using a data-hiding technique called steganography (discussed in more detail in Chapter 9), which uses a host file to cover the contents of a secret message.

Steganography has been used since ancient times. Greek rulers used this technique to send covert messages to diplomats and troops via messengers. To hide messages, rulers shaved their messengers' heads and tattooed messages on their scalps. After the messengers' hair grew enough to cover the message, they left for their destinations, where they shaved their heads so that recipients could read the message. This method was a clever way to send and retrieve encrypted information, but it was inefficient because the messengers' hair took a long time to grow back, and only a limited amount of space was available to write messages. However, it enabled the Greeks to send secret messages until their enemies discovered this early form of steganography and began intercepting messengers.

Contemporary steganography has limits because a graphics file can hide only a certain amount of information before its size and structure change. However, it does allow someone to send covert information to a recipient, unless someone else detects the hidden data.

The two major forms of steganography are insertion and substitution. Insertion places data from the secret file into the host file. When you view the host file in its associated program, the inserted data is hidden unless you analyze the data structure carefully. For example, if you create a Web page with HTML, you can display images and text in a Web browser without revealing the HTML code. Figure 8-23 shows a typical Web page intended to be viewed in a Web browser. It contains hidden text, which is shown in Figure 8-24 along with the source HTML code. To detect hidden text, you need to compare what the file displays and what the file contains. Depending on your skill level, this process can be difficult and time consuming.

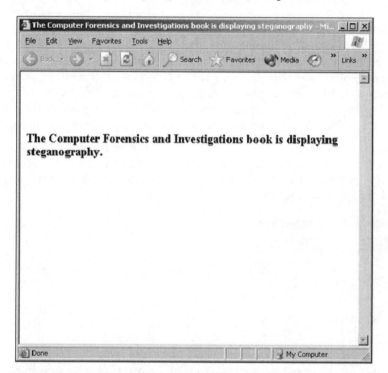

Figure 8-23   A simple Web page displayed in a Web browser
Courtesy of Microsoft Corporation

Figure 8-24   The HTML code reveals hidden text
Courtesy of Microsoft Corporation

The second type of steganography, substitution, replaces bits of the host file with other bits of data. With a bitmap file, for example, you could replace bits used for pixels and colors with hidden data. To avoid detection, you substitute only those bits that result in the least amount of change.

For example, if you use an 8-bit graphics file, each pixel is represented by 8 bits of data containing information about the color each pixel displays onscreen. The bits are prioritized from left to right, such as 11101100. The first bit on the left is the **most significant bit (MSB)**, and the last bit on the right is the **least significant bit (LSB)**. As the names suggest, changing the MSB affects the pixel display more than changing the LSB does. Furthermore, you can usually change only the last two LSBs in an image without producing a noticeable change in the shade of color the pixel displays. To detect a change to the last two LSBs in a graphics file, you need to use a steganalysis tool, which is software designed to identify steganography techniques.

For example, if your secret message is converted to binary form to equal 01101100 and you want to embed this secret message into a picture, you alter the last 2 bits of four pixels. You break the binary form into sections of two, as in 01 10 11 00, and insert the bits into the last 2 bits of each pixel, as shown in Table 8-1.

Table 8-1   **Bit breakdown of a secret message**

Original pixel	Altered pixel
1010 1010	1010 1001
1001 1101	1001 1110
1111 0000	1111 0011
0011 1111	0011 1100

© 2016 Cengage Learning®

The sequence of 2 bits is substituted for the last 2 bits of the pixel. This bit substitution can't be detected by the human eye, which can see only about 6 bits of color. Figure 8-25 shows the original image on the left and the altered image on the right. The altered image contains the hidden message shown in Figure 8-26.

Original image file   Altered image file

Figure 8-25   Original and altered images
© 2016 Cengage Learning®

```
My secret bank accounts:

Country        Bank                       Account No.   Passcode    Currency Amt.
Swiss          Swiss National SA          26845622      Y1115AQ     1.2 million CHF
Caymen Is.     Caribbean Intn. Bank Ltd.  5589999       SAMMM242    5.82 million KYD
Malta          Valletta Nat. Bank Limited 57896165      558TF558    2.3 million EUR
Hong Kong      Chan Wag Bank              A5AA59        665308888   8.9 million HKD|
South Africa   Rand Bank of Cape Town     6982543       AAF8        0.53 million ZAL
```

Figure 8-26 A hidden message in the altered image
© 2016 Cengage Learning®

Whether insertion or substitution is used, you should inspect files for evidence of steganography, especially if your suspect is technically savvy or you see signs that steganography has been used. Clues to look for are duplicate files, such as images, with different hash values, or steganography programs installed on the suspect's drive.

Steganography can be used with file formats other than graphics files, such as MPEG and AVI files.

Using Steganalysis Tools

You can use several different steganalysis tools (also called "steg tools") to detect, decode, and record hidden data, even in files that have been renamed to protect their contents. A steganalysis tool can also detect variations of an image. If a graphics file has been renamed, a steganalysis tool can identify the file format from the file header and indicate whether the file contains an image. Although steganalysis tools can help identify hidden data, steganography is generally difficult to detect. In fact, if steganography is done correctly, in most cases you can't detect the hidden data unless you can compare the altered file with the original file. Check to see whether the file size, image quality, or file extensions have changed. If so, you might be dealing with a steganography image. As an example of the difficulty of detecting the use of steganography, Niels Provos and Peter Honeyman at the University of Michigan conducted a study of more than two million images used in eBay auctions to see whether hidden data might have been placed in photos (see *www2.sans.org/reading-room/whitepapers/stenganography/steganography-whats-real-risk-555*). They were unable to determine whether any graphics files contained hidden messages.

Steganography and steganalysis tools change as rapidly as some OSs. Current steg tools include Steg Suite from WetStone and Outguess StegDetect and StegBreak. For a list of other steg tools, do an Internet search on "steganography," "steganalysis," or "blind steganalysis."

For more information on steganography, read "Steganography: Hiding Data Within Data" at *www.garykessler.net/library/steganography.html*.

Understanding Copyright Issues with Graphics

Steganography has also been used to protect copyrighted material by inserting digital watermarks into a file. When working with graphics files, digital investigators need to be aware of copyright laws, especially in the corporate environment, where they often work closely with the legal department to guard against copyright violations. Investigators might also need to determine whether a photo is from a known copyrighted source, such as a news photo being posted on a Web page without permission.

The U.S. Copyright Office Web site defines precisely how copyright laws pertain to graphics (see *www.copyright.gov* for information on the 1976 Copyright Act). Copyright laws as they pertain to the Internet, however, aren't as clear. For example, a server in another country might host a Web site, which could mean it's regulated by copyright laws in that country. Because each country has its own copyright laws, enforcement can be difficult. Contrary to what some might believe, there's no international copyright law that applies to all countries, but there are international copyright treaties between several countries. Typically, enforcing international copyright treaties requires legal action in the country where the infringement occurred. For more information, see *www.mondaq.com/unitedstates/x/171306/Copyright/ International+Copyright+Protection+How+Does+It+Work* or *www.rightsdirect.com/ content/rd/en/toolbar/copyright_education/International_Copyright_Basics.html*.

The U.S. Copyright Office (*www.copyright.gov/circs/circ01.pdf*) identifies what can and can't be covered under copyright law in the United States:

Copyright protects "original works of authorship" that are fixed in a tangible form of expression. The fixation need not be directly perceptible so long as it may be communicated with the aid of a machine or device. Copyrightable works include the following categories:

1. *literary works;*
2. *musical works, including any accompanying words;*
3. *dramatic works, including any accompanying music;*
4. *pantomimes and choreographic works;*
5. *pictorial, graphic, and sculptural works;*
6. *motion pictures and other audiovisual works;*
7. *sound recordings;*
8. *architectural works.*

These categories should be viewed broadly. For example, computer programs and most "compilations" may be registered as "literary works"; maps and architectural plans may be registered as "pictorial, graphic, and sculptural works."

Anything that would ordinarily be copyrighted through noncomputer means and is now being created on digital media is considered to be copyrighted, as long as the process for obtaining a copyright has been followed.

Digital watermarks can be visible or imperceptible in media such as digital photos and audio files. Visible watermarks are usually an image, such as the copyright symbol or a company logo, layered on top of a photo. Imperceptible watermarks don't change the appearance or sound quality of a copyrighted file. Methods used for imperceptible watermarks sometimes involve modifying a file's LSBs into a unique pattern.

Chapter Summary

- A graphics file contains an image, such as a digital photo, line art, a three-dimensional image, or a scanned replica of a printed picture. A graphics program creates and saves one of three types of graphics files: bitmap, vector, and metafile. Bitmap images are collections of dots, or pixels, that form an image. Vector graphics are mathematical instructions that define lines, curves, text, and geometric shapes. Metafile graphics are combinations of bitmap and vector images.

- When you use a graphics editor or an image viewer, you can open a file in one of many graphics file formats. Each format has different qualities, including the amount of color and compression it uses. If you open a graphics file in a program that supports multiple file formats, you can save the file in a different file format. However, converting graphics files this way can change image quality.

- Bitmap images store graphics information as grids of pixels (short for "picture elements"). The quality of a bitmap image displayed onscreen is governed by resolution, which determines the amount of detail displayed. Vector graphics, unlike bitmap and raster files, use lines instead of dots. A vector graphic stores only the calculations for drawing lines and shapes; a graphics program converts these calculations into images. You can enlarge a vector graphic without affecting image quality. Metafile graphics combine bitmap and vector graphics and can have the characteristics of both image types.

- Most graphics editors enable you to create files in one or more of the standard graphics file formats, such as Graphic Interchange Format (.gif), Joint Photographic Experts Group (.jpeg), Windows Bitmap (.bmp), and Tagged Image File Format (.tif or .tiff). Nonstandard graphics file formats include less common formats, such as Targa (.tga) and Raster Transfer Language (.rtl); proprietary formats, such as Photoshop (.psd); newer formats, such as Scalable Vector Graphics (.svg); and old or obsolete formats, such as Paintbrush (.pcx).

- Most graphics file formats, including GIF and JPEG, compress data to save disk space and reduce transmission time. Other formats, such as BMP, rarely compress data or do so inefficiently. You can use compression tools to compact data and reduce file size. Lossless compression saves file space by using mathematical formulas to represent data in a file. Lossy compression compresses data by permanently discarding bits of information in the file.

- Digital camera photos are typically in raw and Exif JPEG formats. The raw format is the proprietary format of the camera's manufacturer. The Exif format is different from the standard JFIF JPEG format because it contains metadata about the camera and picture, such as shutter speed and date and time a picture was taken.

- In a digital forensics investigation involving graphics files, you need to locate and recover all graphics files on a drive and determine which ones are pertinent to your case. Because these files aren't always stored in standard graphics file formats, you should examine all files your forensics tools find, even if they aren't identified as graphics files. A graphics file contains a header with instructions for displaying the image. Each type of graphics file has its own header that helps you identify the file format. Because the header is complex and difficult to remember, you can compare a known good file header with that of a suspect file.

8

- When you're examining recovered data remnants from files in slack or free space, you might find data that appears to be a header for a common graphics file type. If you locate header data that's partially overwritten, you must reconstruct the header to make it readable again by comparing the hexadecimal values of known graphics file formats to the pattern of the file header you found. After you identify fragmented data, you can use a forensics tool to recover the fragmented file.

- If you can't open a graphics file in an image viewer, the next step is to examine the file header to see whether it matches the header in a known good file. If the header doesn't match, you must insert the correct hexadecimal values manually with a hex editor.

- The Internet is the best source for learning more about file formats and their extensions. You can search for "file type" or "file format" and find a list of Web sites with information on file extensions.

- You should analyze graphics file headers when you find new or unique file types that digital forensics tools don't recognize. The simplest way to do this is with a hex editor. You can record the hexadecimal values in the header for future reference.

- Many viewer utilities are freeware or shareware and enable you to view a wide range of graphics file formats. Most GUI forensics tools include image viewers that display common image formats, especially GIF and JPEG.

- Steganography is a method of hiding data by using a host file to cover the contents of a secret message. The two major techniques are insertion and substitution. Insertion places data from the secret file into the host file. When you view the host file in its associated program, the inserted data is hidden unless you analyze the data structure. Substitution replaces bits of the host file with other bits of data.

- Steganalysis tools can detect hidden data in graphics files, even in files that have been renamed to protect their contents. If the file has been renamed, steganalysis tools can use the file header to identify the file format and indicate whether the file contains an image. Steganalysis tools can also detect variations in a graphics file.

Key Terms

bitmap images Collections of dots, or pixels, in a grid format that form a graphic.

carving The process of recovering file fragments that are scattered across a disk.

data compression The process of coding data from a larger form to a smaller form.

demosaicing The process of converting raw picture data to another format, such as JPEG or TIF.

Exchangeable Image File (Exif) A file format the Japan Electronics and Information Technology Industries Association (JEITA) developed as a standard for storing metadata in JPEG and TIF files.

false positives The results of keyword searches that contain the correct match but aren't relevant to the investigation.

least significant bit (LSB) The lowest bit value in a byte. In Microsoft OSs, bits are displayed from right to left, so the rightmost bit is the LSB. OSs that read bits from right to left are called "little endian." OSs that display the LSB from left to right are called "big endian."

lossless compression A compression method in which no data is lost. With this type of compression, a large file can be compressed to take up less space and then uncompressed without any loss of information.

lossy compression A compression method that permanently discards bits of information in a file. The removed bits of information reduce image quality.

metafile graphics Graphics files that are combinations of bitmap and vector images.

most significant bit (MSB) The highest bit value in a byte.

nonstandard graphics file formats Less common graphics file formats, including proprietary formats, newer formats, formats that most image viewers don't recognize, and old or obsolete formats.

pixels Small dots used to create images; the term comes from "picture element."

raster images Collections of pixels stored in rows rather than a grid, as with bitmap images, to make graphics easier to print; usually created when a vector graphic is converted to a bitmap image.

raw file format A file format typically found on higher-end digital cameras; the camera performs no enhancement processing—hence the term "raw." This format maintains the best picture quality, but because it's a proprietary format, not all image viewers can display it.

resolution The density of pixels displayed onscreen, which governs image quality.

salvaging Another term for carving, used outside North America. *See* carving.

standard graphics file formats Common graphics file formats that most graphics programs and image viewers can open.

vector graphics Graphics based on mathematical instructions to form lines, curves, text, and other geometric shapes.

vector quantization (VQ) A form of compression that uses an algorithm similar to rounding off decimal values to eliminate unnecessary bits of data.

Review Questions

1. Graphics files stored on a computer can't be recovered after they are deleted. True or False?

2. When you carve a graphics file, recovering the image depends on which of the following skills?
   a. Recovering the image from a tape backup
   b. Recognizing the pattern of the data content
   c. Recognizing the pattern of the file header content
   d. Recognizing the pattern of a corrupt file

3. Explain how to identify an unknown graphics file format that your digital forensics tool doesn't recognize.

4. What type of compression uses an algorithm that allows viewing the graphics file without losing any portion of the data?

5. When investigating graphics files, you should convert them into one standard format. True or False?

6. Digital pictures use data compression to accomplish which of the following goals? (Choose all that apply.)
   a. Save space on a hard drive.
   b. Provide a crisp and clear image.
   c. Eliminate redundant data.
   d. Produce a file that can be e-mailed or posted on the Internet.

7. The process of converting raw images to another format is called which of the following?
   a. Data conversion
   b. Transmogrification
   c. Transfiguring
   d. Demosaicing

8. In JPEG files, what's the starting offset position for the JFIF label?
   a. Offset 0
   b. Offset 2
   c. Offset 6
   d. Offset 4

9. Each type of graphics file has a unique header containing information that distinguishes it from other types of graphics files. True or False?

10. Copyright laws don't apply to Web sites. True or False?

11. When viewing a file header, you need to include hexadecimal information to view the image. True or False?

12. When recovering a file with ProDiscover, your first objective is to recover cluster values. True or False?

13. Bitmap (.bmp) files use which of the following types of compression?
    a. WinZip
    b. Lossy
    c. Lzip
    d. Lossless

14. A JPEG file uses which type of compression?
    a. WinZip
    b. Lossy
    c. Lzip
    d. Lossless

15. Only one file format can compress graphics files. True or False?

16. A JPEG file is an example of a vector graphic. True or False?

17. Which of the following is true about JPEG and TIF files?

    a. They have identical values for the first 2 bytes of their file headers.

    b. They have different values for the first 2 bytes of their file headers.

    c. They differ from other graphics files because their file headers contain more bits.

    d. They differ from other graphics files because their file headers contain fewer bits.

18. What methods do steganography programs use to hide data in graphics files? (Choose all that apply.)

    a. Insertion

    b. Substitution

    c. Masking

    d. Carving

19. Some clues left on a drive that might indicate steganography include which of the following? (Choose all that apply.)

    a. Multiple copies of a graphics file

    b. Graphics files with the same name but different file sizes

    c. Steganography programs in the suspect's All Programs list

    d. Graphics files with different timestamps

20. What methods are used for digital watermarking? (Choose all that apply.)

    a. Implanted subroutines that link to a central Web server automatically when the watermarked file is accessed

    b. Invisible modification of the LSBs in the file

    c. Layering visible symbols on top of the image

    d. Using a hex editor to alter the image data

Hands-On Projects

If necessary, extract all data files in the Chap08\Projects folder on the book's DVD to the C:\Work\Chap08\Projects folder on your system. (You might need to create this folder on your system before starting the projects; it's referred to as your "work folder" in steps.)

Hands-On Project 8-1

In this project, you use ProDiscover Basic to locate and extract JPEG files with altered extensions. Some of these files are embedded in files with non-JPEG extensions. Find the C08frag.dd file in your work folder, and then follow these steps:

1. Start ProDiscover Basic (with the **Run as administrator** option, if necessary) and begin a new project. In the New Project dialog box, type **C08frag** in the Project Number and Project File Name text boxes, and then click **OK**.

2. In the tree view, click to expand **Add**, and then click **Image File**. In the Open dialog box, navigate to your work folder and click `C08frag.dd`. Click **Open**, and then click **Yes**, if necessary, in the Auto Image Checksum message box.

3. Click the **Search** toolbar button. In the Search dialog box, click the **Content Search** tab, if necessary. Under Search for the pattern(s), type **JFIF**, and under Select the Disk(s)/Image(s) you want to search in, click C:\ *Work*\C08frag.dd. Click **OK**.

4. Click each file in the work area's search results that doesn't have a `.jpg` extension, and in the data area, scroll through and examine the entire content of each file to find any occurrences of a JFIF label. Click the check box next to each file with a JFIF label. When the Add Comment dialog box opens, type **Recovered hidden .jpg file**, click the **Apply to all items** check box, and then click **OK**.

5. In the tree view, click **Report**, and then click **File, Print Report** from the menu. Click **OK**. You can also save your report by clicking the **Export** toolbar button, and in the Export dialog box's File Name text box, type **C08Prj01**. Click **Browse**, navigate to your work folder, click **Save**, and then click **OK**.

6. Exit ProDiscover Basic, saving your project when prompted.

Hands-On Project 8-2

In this project, you continue the search for files Bob Aspen downloaded. In the in-chapter activity, you recovered three files containing zzzz for the first 4 bytes of altered JPEG files. These altered files had different extensions to hide the fact that they're graphics files.

Find the C08carve.dd file in your work folder. This image file is a new acquisition of another USB drive the EMTS manager retrieved. He wants to know whether any similar files on this drive match the files you recovered from the first USB drive. Because you know that the files you recovered earlier have zzzz for the first 4 bytes, you can use it as your search string to see whether similar files exist on this USB drive.

1. Start ProDiscover Basic (with the **Run as administrator** option, if necessary) and begin a new project. In the New Project dialog box, type **C08carve** for the project number and project filename, and then click **OK**.

2. In the tree view, click to expand **Add**, and then click **Image File**. In the Open dialog box, navigate to your work folder and click `C08carve.dd`. Click **Open**, and then click **Yes**, if necessary, in the Auto Image Checksum message box.

3. Next, click the **Search** toolbar button. In the Search dialog box, click the **Content Search** tab, if necessary, and then click the **ASCII** option button and the **Case Sensitive** check box. Under Search for the pattern(s), type **zzzz**, and under Select the Disk(s)/Image(s) you want to search in, click `C08carve.dd`. Click **OK**.

4. Click each file in the work area's search results to display it in the data area. If the file contains zzzz at the beginning of the sector, click the **Select** check box next to it. In the Add Comment dialog box, type **Similar file located on first USB drive**, click the **Apply to all items** check box, and then click **OK**.

5. In the work area, click the **Add to Report** button.

6. Double-click the **gametour5.txt** file. In the work area, click the **File Name** column heading to sort all files in this pane. Scroll through the list of files and click the **Select** check box for gametour1.txt, gametour2.txt, gametour3.txt, gametour4.txt, and gametour6.txt files. When the Add Comment dialog box opens, type **Additional similar files on USB drive**, and then click **OK**. Repeat this step for each gametour file you find in this list.

7. Right-click the **gametour1.txt** file and click **Copy All Selected Files**. In the Choose Destination dialog box, click **Browse**, navigate to and double-click your work folder, and then click **OK** to copy the files. When prompted, click **OK** in the message box about files being copied successfully.

8. To complete your examination, click **Report** in the tree view, and then click **File, Print Report** from the menu. You can also save your report by clicking the **Export** toolbar button, and in the Export dialog box's File Name text box, type **C08Prj02**. Click **Browse**, navigate to and click your work folder, click **Save**, and then click **OK**.

9. Save the project and exit ProDiscover Basic.

Hands-On Project 8-3

In this project, you use IrfanView to open graphics files and save them in a compressed graphics format different from the original format. You should note any changes in image quality after converting files to a different format. Download IrfanView from *www.irfanview.com* and install it, and then follow these steps:

1. Start IrfanView.

2. Click **File, Open** from the menu. In the Open dialog box, navigate to your work folder, and then double-click **SPIDER.bmp** to open the file.

3. Click **File, Save as** from the menu. Change the file type to **JPG** and save the file as **Spider.jpg** in the same location.

4. Save Spider.jpg as **Spider2.bmp** in the same location.

5. Open these three graphics files in new sessions of IrfanView and compare the files. Document any changes you notice.

6. Open **FLOWER.gif** from your work folder, and save it as **Flower.jpg** in the same location.

If your screen is cluttered with too many open IrfanView windows, close a few that you're no longer working with.

7. Save `Flower.jpg` as **`Flower2.gif`** in the same location.

8. Open these three graphics files in new sessions of IrfanView, and document any changes you see when comparing the files.

9. Open **`Cartoon.bmp`** from your work folder, and save it as **`Cartoon.gif`** in the same location.

10. Save `Cartoon.gif` as **`Cartoon2.bmp`** in the same location.

11. Open these three graphics files in new sessions of IrfanView, and document any changes you see when comparing the files.

12. Exit all instances of IrfanView. Summarize your conclusions in a brief report and submit it to your instructor.

Hands-On Project 8-4

In this project, you use S-Tools4 to create a steganography file for hiding an image. Download S-Tools4 from *http://packetstormsecurity.com/files/21688/s-tools4.zip.html* or *www.4shared.com/zip/q764vcPu/s-tools4.htm*, install the program, and then follow these steps:

1. In File Explorer, navigate to where you installed S-Tools4, and start the program by double-clicking **`S-Tools.exe`**. If necessary, click **Run**, and then click **Continue**, if necessary.

2. Drag **`RUSHMORE.bmp`** from your work folder to the S-Tools window.

3. To hide text in the `RUSHMORE.bmp` file, drag **`Findme.txt`** from your work folder to the **`RUSHMORE.bmp`** image.

4. In the Hiding dialog box, type **FREEDOM** in the Passphrase and Verify passphrase text boxes, and then click **OK**. A hidden data window opens in the S-Tools window.

5. Right-click the hidden data window and click **Save as**. Save the image as **`Steg.bmp`** in your work folder.

6. Close the `Steg.bmp` and `RUSHMORE.bmp` windows, but leave S-Tools open for the next project.

Hands-On Project 8-5

In this project, you use S-Tools4 to create a secret message in a bitmap file and compare this steganography file with the original file by using the DOS `comp` command. You need S-Tools4 and the `Mission.bmp` and `USDECINP.rtf` files in your work folder. Follow these steps to create a steganography file:

1. If you have exited S-Tools4, start it by double-clicking **`S-Tools.exe`** in File Explorer.

2. Drag **`Mission.bmp`** from your work folder to the S-Tools window.

3. Next, drag **`USDECINP.rtf`** from your work folder to the **`Mission.bmp`** image.

4. Type **hop08-5** in the Passphrase and Verify passphrase text boxes, and then click **OK**. A hidden data window opens in the S-Tools window.

5. Right-click the hidden data window and click **Save As**. Save the image as **Mission-steg.bmp** in your work folder. Exit S-Tools.

Next, you use the DOS comp command to compare these two files and redirect the output to a text file for further analysis:

1. To open a command prompt window in Windows 8 or later, click the **Search** icon, type **cmd**, and then press **Enter**. In Windows 7 or earlier, click **Start**, type **cmd** in the "Search for programs and files" text box, and then press **Enter**.

2. Change to your work folder by typing **cd *Work*\\Chap08\\Projects** (substituting the path to your work folder) and pressing **Enter**.

3. Type **comp Mission.bmp Mission-steg.bmp > Mission-compare.txt** and press **Enter**, and then at the Compare more files (Y/N) ? prompt, type **n** and press **Enter**.

4. In File Explorer, navigate to your work folder, and open the **Mission-compare.txt** file to see what discrepancies were found. When you're finished, close the file, and exit the command prompt window by typing **exit** and pressing **Enter**.

5. To complete this project, write a one-page report on the number of mismatches and the deviation in each mismatch between the two files. In addition, state your observations of the differences in the two files, such as hexadecimal values and their patterns.

Case Projects

CASE PROJECTS

Case Project 8-1

Do an Internet search to find current steganography tools. Create a spreadsheet listing at least five steganography tools and their features. The spreadsheet should have the following columns: name of tool, vendor (with URL for purchasing or downloading the tool), cost (or note that it's freeware, if applicable), file formats of data that can be hidden, and Web site.

Case Project 8-2

You're investigating a case involving an employee who's allegedly sending inappropriate photos via e-mail in attachments that have been compressed with a zip utility. As you examine the employee's hard disk, you find a file named Orkty.zip, which you suspect is a graphics file. When you try to open the file in an image viewer, a message is displayed indicating that the file is corrupt. Write a two- to three-page report explaining how to recover Orkty.zip for further investigation.

Case Project 8-3

You work for a mid-size corporation known for its inventions that does a lot of copyright and patent work. You're investigating an employee suspected of selling and distributing animations created for your corporation. During your investigation of the suspect's drive, you find some files with the unfamiliar extension .xde. The network administrator mentions that other .xde files have been sent through an FTP server to another site. Describe your findings after conducting an Internet search for this file extension.

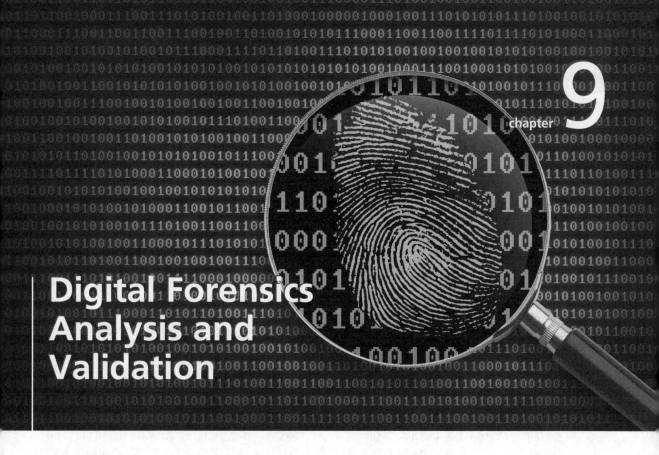

Digital Forensics Analysis and Validation

chapter 9

After reading this chapter and completing the exercises, you will be able to:

- Determine what data to analyze in a digital forensics investigation
- Explain tools used to validate data
- Explain common data-hiding techniques

This chapter explains how to apply your forensics skills and techniques to a digital investigation. One of the most critical functions is validating evidence during the analysis process. In Chapter 3, you learned how data acquisitions are validated for Windows and Linux file systems; in Chapter 4, you were introduced to hashing algorithms; and in Chapter 6, you learned about validating forensics software tools. In this chapter, you learn more about using hashing algorithms in forensics analysis to validate data. You also learn how to refine and modify an investigation plan, use data analysis tools and practices to process digital evidence, determine whether data-hiding techniques have been used, and learn methods for performing a remote acquisition.

Determining What Data to Collect and Analyze

Examining and analyzing digital evidence depend on the nature of the investigation and the amount of data to process. Criminal investigations are limited to finding data defined in the search warrant, and civil investigations are often limited by court orders for discovery. Corporate investigators might be searching for company policy violations that require examining only specific items, such as e-mail. Therefore, investigations often involve locating and recovering a few specific items, which simplifies and speeds processing.

In the corporate environment, however, especially if litigation is involved or anticipated, the company attorney often directs the investigator to recover as much information as possible. Satisfying this demand becomes a major undertaking with many hours of tedious work. These types of investigations can also result in **scope creep**, in which an investigation expands beyond the original description because of unexpected evidence you find, prompting the attorney to ask you to examine other areas to recover more evidence. Scope creep increases the time and resources needed to extract, analyze, and present evidence. Be sure to document any requests for additional investigation, in case you must explain why the investigation took longer than planned, why the scope widened during the course of the investigation, and so forth.

One reason scope creep has become more common is that criminal investigations increasingly require more detailed examination of evidence just before trial to help prosecutors fend off attacks from defense attorneys. Because defense attorneys typically have the right of full discovery of digital evidence used against their clients, it's possible for new evidence to come to light while complying with the defense request for full discovery. However, this new evidence often isn't revealed to the prosecution; instead, the defense uses it to defend the accused. For this reason, it's become more important for prosecution teams to ensure that they have analyzed the evidence exhaustively before trial. (It should be noted that the defense request for full discovery applies only to criminal cases in the United States; civil cases are handled differently.)

Approaching Digital Forensics Cases

Recall from Chapter 1 that you begin a digital forensics case by creating an investigation plan that defines the investigation's goal and scope, the materials needed, and the tasks to perform. Although there are some basic principles that apply to almost all digital forensics cases, the approach you take depends largely on the type of case you're investigating.

For example, gathering evidence for an e-mail harassment case might involve little more than accessing network logs and e-mail server backups to locate specific messages. Your approach, however, depends on whether the case is an internal corporate investigation or a civil or criminal investigation carried out by law enforcement. In an internal investigation, evidence collection tends to be fairly easy and straightforward because corporate investigators usually have ready access to the necessary records and files. In contrast, when investigating a criminal cyberstalking case, you need to contact the ISP and e-mail service. Some companies have systems set up to handle these situations, but others do not. Most companies don't keep e-mail for longer than 90 days, and many keep it for far less time.

An investigation of an employee suspected of industrial espionage can require the most work. Before initiating this type of investigation, make sure the company, whether it's a private organization or a public agency, has set up rules of use and limitations of privacy rights, as described in Chapter 1. For these investigations, you might need to set up a surveillance camera to monitor the employee's activities in the office. You might also need to plant a software or hardware keylogger (for capturing keystrokes remotely), and you need to engage the network administrator's services to monitor Internet and network activities. In this situation, you might want to do a remote acquisition of the employee's drive, and then use another tool to determine what peripheral devices have been accessed.

As a standard practice, you should follow these basic steps for all digital forensics investigations:

For more information on basic processes and recommendations, refer to Chapter 2 for guidelines on setting up a forensic workstation.

1. For target drives, IACIS recommends using recently wiped media that have been reformatted and inspected for viruses. At the very least, media should be inspected and cleared of any possible malware before using them on a case. With advanced digital forensics tools that can access network storage media, apply standard network security practices, such as access restrictions (through an access control list), securely configured routers, and a firewall. With disk-to-disk forensic copying, the original drive reformats the target drive to the same configuration. If you need to wipe media, you can use several different tools, such as ProDiscover's Secure Wipe Disk option, X-Ways Security, Digital Intelligence PDWipe, or WhiteCanyon SecureClean to clean all data from the target media.

2. Inventory the hardware on the suspect's computer, and note the condition of the computer when seized. Document all physical hardware components as part of your evidence acquisition process.

3. For static acquisitions, remove the original drive from the computer, if practical, and then check the date and time values in the system's CMOS.

4. Record how you acquired data from the suspect drive—note, for example, that you created a bit-stream image and which tool you used. The tool you use should also create an MD5 or SHA-1 hash for validating the image.

5. When examining the image of the drive's contents, process the data methodically and logically.

6. List all folders and files on the image or drive. For example, FTK can generate a Microsoft Access or Oracle database listing all files and folders on a suspect drive. Note where specific evidence is found, and indicate how it's related to the investigation.

7. If possible, examine the contents of all data files in all folders, starting at the root directory of the volume partition. The exception is for cases with the defined scope of work stated in a search warrant or discovery demand. For these cases, you look for only the specific items listed in the warrant or discovery demand.

8. For all password-protected files that might be related to the investigation, make your best effort to recover file contents. You can use password-recovery tools for this purpose, such as OS Forensics Password Recovery and Decryption, AccessData Password Recovery Toolkit (PRTK), or Passware Kit Enterprise.

9. Identify the function of every executable (binary or .exe) file that doesn't match known hash values. Make note of any system files or folders, such as the System32 folder or its content, that are out of place. If you can't find information on an executable file by using a disk editor, examine the file to see what it does and how it works.

10. Maintain control of all evidence and findings, and document everything as you progress through your examination.

Refining and Modifying the Investigation Plan In civil and criminal cases, the scope is often defined by search warrants or subpoenas, which specify what data you can recover. However, private sector cases, such as employee abuse investigations, might not specify limitations in recovering data. For these cases, it's important to refine the investigation plan as much as possible by trying to determine what the case requires. Generally, you want the investigation to be broad enough to encompass all relevant evidence yet not so wide-ranging that you waste time and resources analyzing data that's not going to help your case.

Of course, even if your initial plan is sound, at times you'll find that you need to deviate from it and follow where the evidence leads you. Even in these cases, having a plan that you revise deliberately along the way is much better than searching for evidence haphazardly.

Suppose, for example, an employee is accused of operating an online business using company resources during work hours. You use this timeframe to narrow the set of data you're searching, and because you're looking for unauthorized Internet use, you focus the search on temporary Internet files, Internet history, and e-mail communication. Knowing the types of data you're looking for at the outset helps you make the best use of your time and prevents you from casting too wide a net. However, in the course of reviewing e-mails related to the case, you might find references to spreadsheets or Word documents containing financial information related to the online business. In this case, it makes sense to broaden the range of data you're looking for to include these types of files. Again, the key is to start with a plan but remain flexible in the face of new evidence.

Using OSForensics to Analyze Data

OSForensics can perform forensics analysis on the following file systems:

- Microsoft FAT12, FAT16, and FAT32
- Microsoft NTFS
- Mac HFS+ and HFSX
- Linux Ext2fs, Ext3fs, and Ext4fs

In addition, it can analyze data from several sources, including image files from other vendors. Its OSFMount utility can access many formats, including raw, Expert Witness, and Advanced Forensics Format (AFF). It can also mount and examine VMware images (`.vmdk`), SMART images (`.s01`), and VHD images (`.vhd`). You can run OSFMount separately or access it via the Mount Drive Image menu option. It mounts a forensic image file as an attached drive that's read only to ensure that data isn't altered. If you're doing a nonforensic examination of data, you can access the drive in File Explorer.

Other OSForensics utilities are OSFClone, which creates CD/DVD or USB boot media for performing a forensic acquisition, and ImageUSB, which is used to make multiple copies of USB devices. For more information on these utilities, see *www.osforensics.com/products.html*.

To enhance searching for and eliminating known OS and application files, OSForensics can use the NIST National Software Reference Library (NSRL). Unlike some other digital forensics tools, OSForensics enables you to mount the NSRL ISO image by using the OSFMount utility. From the mounted ISO image, you can extract the reference zip files and create a database for OSForensics. You can then import the extracted NSRL reference hashes for both MD5 and SHA-1 into a hash database. For more information on how to use NSRL data with OSForensics, see *www.osforensics.com/faqs-and-tutorials/import-nsrl-hashsets-from-nist.html*.

Using the Index Feature in OSForensics Like other digital forensics tools, OSForensics indexes text data so that you can perform searches immediately when conducting an analysis. To index a case, you must have created a case first, as described in Chapter 4. Follow these steps:

Before beginning this activity, extract all files in the Chap09 folder on the DVD to your C:*Work*\\Chap09\\Chapter folder (referred to as your "work folder" in steps). Create this folder on your system first.

1. Start OSForensics. Click **Start** in the left pane, if necessary. In the right pane, click **Create Case**. In the New Case dialog box, enter your name in the Investigator text box. For the case name, type **InChap09**. Fill in the contact details and the organization, and then click **OK**.

2. To mount the disk image, scroll down the navigation bar on the left, and click **Mount Drive Image**. In the Mounted virtual disks window, click the **Mount new** button. In the OSFMount - Mount drive dialog box that opens, click the **...** button next to the Image file text box, navigate to your work folder, click `gcfi-ntfs.dd`, click **Open**, and then click **OK**.

3. Click the **Create Index** button in the left pane to start the Create Index Wizard. In the Step 1 of 5 window, click the **Use Pre-defined File Types** option button, if necessary. Click the **Emails**, **Attachments**, **Office + PDF Documents**, and **Web Files + XML** check boxes, as shown in Figure 9-1, and then click **Next**.

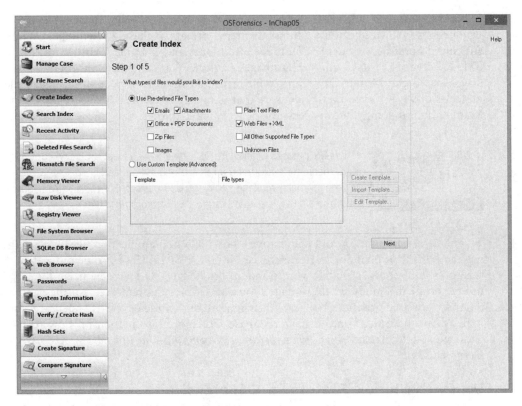

Figure 9-1 Specifying file types to index
Source: PassMark Software, *www.osforensics.com*

4. In the Step 2 of 5 window, click the **Add** button. In the Add Start Location dialog box, click the **Whole Drive** option button if necessary, click the list arrow, click the mounted image drive letter (see Figure 9-2), and then click **OK**. Click **Next**.

Your mounted drive letter might be different from what's shown in Figure 9-2. If you need help finding the assigned drive letter, click the Mount Drive Image button again to display all mounted drives.

Figure 9-2 The Add Start Location dialog box
Source: PassMark Software, *www.osforensics.com*

5. In the Step 3 of 5 window, click **Start Indexing**. The Step 4 of 5 window displays a progress bar, and then the Step 5 of 5 window shows the files being indexed.

6. When the indexing has finished, click **OK** in the message box informing you that errors reading some files might have occurred in the indexing process, if necessary. Click **Search Index** in the left pane. Type **project** in the Enter Search Words text box (see Figure 9-3), and then click **Search**.

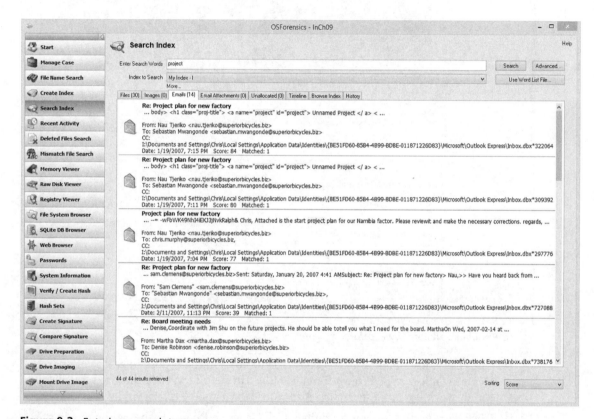

Figure 9-3   Entering a search term
Source: PassMark Software, *www.osforensics.com*

7. Click the **Emails** tab, if necessary, and then double-click the first e-mail message in the results. In the E-mail Viewer window (see Figure 9-4), select all e-mail messages in the upper pane.

The Add E-mail to Case icon

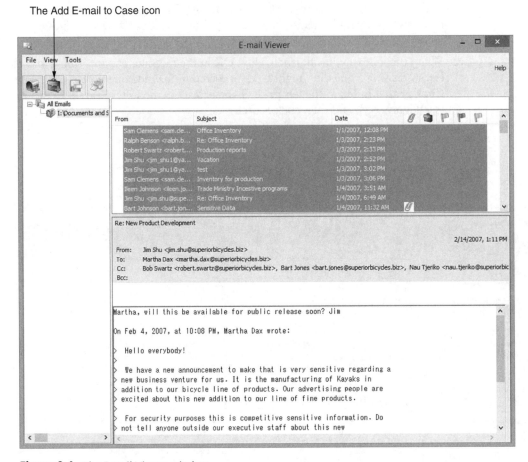

Figure 9-4 The E-mail Viewer window
Source: PassMark Software, *www.osforensics.com*

8. Click the **Add E-mail to Case** icon on the toolbar. In the Please Enter Case Export Details window, type **Project E-mails** in the Title text box, click the **Use same details for all** check box, and then click **Add**. Close the E-mail Viewer window.

9. Click **Start** in the left pane, and then click **Generate Report** in the right pane. In the Export Report dialog box, click the **Copy files to report location** button, click **Browse,** navigate to and click your work folder, and then click **OK**. OSForensics opens the report in your default Web browser.

10. After reviewing the report, close the Web browser. Click **Exit** in the left pane of OSForensics.

Validating Forensic Data

One of the most critical aspects of digital forensics is validating digital evidence because ensuring the integrity of data you collect is essential for presenting evidence in court. Chapter 4 introduced forensic hashing algorithms, and in this section, you learn more about validating an acquired image before you analyze it.

Most forensics tools offer hashing of image files. For example, when ProDiscover loads an image file, it runs a hash and compares that value with the original hash calculated when the image was first acquired. Digital forensics tools have some limitations in performing hashing, however, so using advanced hexadecimal editors is necessary to ensure data integrity.

Validating with Hexadecimal Editors

Advanced hexadecimal editors offer many features not available in digital forensics tools, such as hashing specific files or sectors. Learning how to use these tools is important, especially when you need to find a particular file—for example, a known contraband image. With the hash value in hand, you can use a forensics tool to search for a suspicious file that might have had its name changed to look like an innocuous file. (Recall that two files with exactly the same content have the same hash value, even if they have different names.) Getting hash values with a full-featured hexadecimal editor can be faster and easier than with a digital forensics tool.

WinHex provides several hashing algorithms, such as MD5 and SHA-1. Sometimes you need the hash value of specific files or sectors to validate whether data or fragments (sectors) match the contents of a known file, or you need to verify data immediately after a sparse acquisition, for example. To use the hashing functions of WinHex, follow these steps:

1. Start Word, and in a new document, type a sentence or two, and save the file as **test_hex.docx** in your work folder. When you're finished, exit Word.

2. Start WinHex, using the **Run as administrator** option. (If necessary, when the UAC message box opens, click **Yes**.) Click **File**, **Open** from the main menu. In the Open dialog box, navigate to your work folder, click **test_hex.docx**, and click **Open**. Figure 9-5 shows the file open in WinHex.

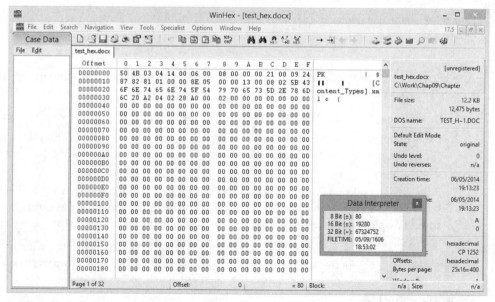

Figure 9-5 Viewing a file opened in WinHex
Courtesy of X-Ways AG, *www.x-ways.net*

3. To compute an MD5 hash of this file, click **Tools, Compute Hash** from the menu to open the Compute hash dialog box (see Figure 9-6). Click the list arrow, click **MD5 (128 bit)**, if necessary, and then click **OK**.

Figure 9-6 The Compute hash dialog box
Courtesy of X-Ways AG, *www.x-ways.net*

4. In the MD5 (128 bit) dialog box, right-click the hash value (see Figure 9-7) and click **Copy**. Start Notepad, and paste the hash value into a new text document. Save the file as **test_hex_hashvalue.txt** in your work folder, exit Notepad, and then click **Close** in the MD5 (128 bit) dialog box. Leave WinHex running for the next activity.

Figure 9-7 MD5 hash results
Courtesy of X-Ways AG, *www.x-ways.net*

Another feature of WinHex generates the hash value of selected data in a file or any sector on a disk. To see how this feature works, follow these steps:

1. In WinHex, open the **Jeffersonian quotes.doc** file from your work folder.

2. Place the mouse pointer at the beginning of the byte address 00000000; the pointer should be positioned on the hexadecimal D0 because you're examining the first sector of the file.

3. Now drag to select a complete sector (512 bytes or x200 bytes). To know when you've selected the sector, watch the Offset counter at the lower center in the status bar. It should display "Offset: 1FF" when you've highlighted the entire sector.

 As you drag the mouse, note that the offset counter increments or decrements according to the direction of the mouse's movement across the window. This counter defaults to hexadecimal but can be altered to decimal counting.

4. Click **Tools**, **Compute Hash** from the menu to open the Compute hash dialog box. Click the list arrow, click **MD5 (128 bit)**, if necessary, and then click **OK**.

5. Right-click the hash value in the MD5 (128 bit) dialog box and click **Copy**. Start Notepad, and paste the hash value into a new text document. Save the file as `Quotes_hashvalue.txt` in your work folder, exit Notepad, and then click **Close** in the MD5 (128 bit) dialog box.

6. Exit Notepad and WinHex.

The advantage of recording hash values is that you can determine whether data has changed. As shown in the preceding steps, you can use this method for specific sectors or entire files. One advantage of using hashes of sectors is that you can look for known file fragments, a process called **block-wise hashing**. This process builds a data set of hashes of sectors from the original file, and then examines sectors on the suspect's drive to see whether any other sectors match. If an identical hash value is found, you have confirmed that the file was stored on the suspect's drive. For example, say you have a known Word document from a victim, and it was stored and then deleted on a suspect's computer. The attempted recovery of deleted files reveals no trace of the original file, but you can search for fragments of deleted files by using block-wise hashing. X-Ways Forensics and many other forensics tools offer this feature. For more information on how it detects data remnants, see *www.x-ways.net/winhex/manual.pdf*.

Using Hash Values to Discriminate Data In Chapter 6, you learned about using the discrimination function to sort known good files from suspicious files. This function is useful in limiting the amount of data you have to examine, and many current digital forensics tools offer it. AccessData has its own hashing database, **Known File Filter (KFF)**, which is available only with FTK. KFF filters known program files, such as `winword.exe`, from view and contains the hash values of known illegal files, such as child pornography. It then compares known file hash values with files on your evidence drive or image files to see whether they contain suspicious data. Periodically, AccessData updates these known hash values and posts an updated KFF. As mentioned in Chapter 6, the NIST National Software Reference Library (NSRL; *www.nsrl.nist.gov/index.html*) maintains a national database of updated file hash values for a variety of OSs, applications, and images; however, it doesn't list hash values of known illegal files. Other digital forensics tools, such as X-Ways Forensics and OSForensics, can import the NSRL database and run hash comparisons. In addition, ProDiscover includes a method for creating your own hashes in HashKeeper format; for more information, see *www.techpathways.com/webhelp/Comparing_Hashkeeper_hash_sets.htm*.

Validating with Digital Forensics Tools

As mentioned, commercial digital forensics tools have built-in validation features. For example, ProDiscover's `.eve` files contain metadata that includes the hash value. ProDiscover also has a preference you can enable for using the Auto Verify Image Checksum feature when image files are loaded. If the Auto Verify Image Checksum and the hashes in the `.eve` file's metadata don't match, ProDiscover notifies you that the acquisition is corrupt and can't be considered reliable evidence. When this feature is used, the hashing verification might take several minutes to a few hours, depending on the image file's size.

In ProDiscover and other digital forensics tools, however, raw format image files (.dd extension) don't contain metadata, so you must validate them manually to ensure the integrity of data. You can also use these hash values to check whether the image file has been corrupted. Sometimes you work on a case for several months, and during that time, files can become corrupted, so you should check for this possibility periodically.

In AccessData FTK Imager, when you select the Expert Witness (.e01) or SMART (.s01) format, additional options for validating the acquisition are available. This validation report also lists MD5 and SHA-1 hash values. The MD5 hash value is added to the proprietary format image file. When this image file is loaded in a forensics tool, the MD5 hash value is read and compared with the hash value for the original acquisition to verify whether the image file is correct.

Follow these steps to see how ProDiscover's built-in validation feature works:

1. Start ProDiscover Basic with the **Run as administrator** option. Click **File, Preferences** from the menu. In the Preferences dialog box, click the **On** check boxes under Warnings and Auto Verify Image Checksum (see Figure 9-8). Click **OK**.

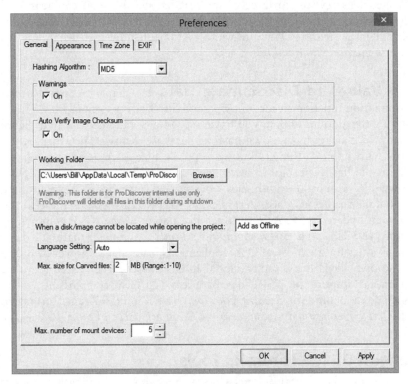

Figure 9-8 Enabling the Auto Verify Image Checksum feature
Courtesy of Technology Pathways, LLC

2. Start a new project. Enter today's date for the project number, **GCFI-Win98** for the project name, and **Denise Robinson, Superior Bicycles - suspected of industrial espionage** for the description, and then click **OK**.

3. In the tree view, click to expand **Add**, and click **Image File**.

4. Navigate to your work folder, click the `GCFI-Win98.eve` file, and click **Open**. In the Auto Verify Image Checksum message box, click **Yes**.

5. After the checksum verification has finished validating the image file, click the **Save Project** button on the toolbar. Save the file as `Denise Robinson, Superior Bicycles - suspected of industrial espionage.dft` in your work folder.

6. In the tree view, click to expand **Content View**, if necessary, and then click to expand **Images**.

7. Next, click to expand the `GCFI-Win98` image file. You should see the folders on this drive listed.

8. Click to expand the **My Documents** folder and the **New Folder** folder, and then click the first **temp** folder. Notice that a few files in this folder are graphics files. Click **View**, **Gallery View** from the menu (see Figure 9-9).

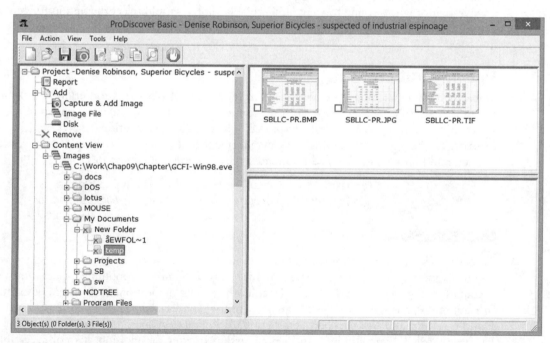

Figure 9-9   The Gallery view
Courtesy of Technology Pathways, LLC

9. In this view, you can right-click any file and export it, view the cluster numbers, compare it with a database containing hashes of known files, mark it as evidence, and so on. When you're finished exploring this view, exit ProDiscover.

Addressing Data-Hiding Techniques

Data hiding involves changing or manipulating a file to conceal information. Data-hiding techniques include hiding entire partitions, changing file extensions, setting file attributes to hidden, bit-shifting, using encryption, and setting up password protection. Some of these techniques are discussed in the following sections.

Hiding Files by Using the OS

One of the first techniques used to hide data was changing file extensions, as you learned in Chapter 8. For example, a suspect wanting to hide an Excel spreadsheet containing incriminating evidence could change its extension from .xlsx to .jpg. An investigator who tries to open the file in Excel will get an error message stating that the file can't be opened. Advanced digital forensics tools, however, check file headers and compare the file extension to verify that it's correct. If there's a discrepancy, the tool flags the file as a possible altered file that requires more analysis.

Another hiding technique is selecting the Hidden attribute in a file's Properties dialog box, so an investigator who's trying to view files in File Explorer should select the option to view hidden files, folders, and drives. Digital forensics tools can identify hidden files for investigators, however.

Hiding Partitions

One way to hide partitions you create is with the Windows disk partition utility, diskpart. By using the diskpart remove letter command, you can unassign the partition's letter, which hides it from view in File Explorer. To unhide the partition, use the diskpart assign letter command. Other disk management tools, such as Partition Magic, Partition Master, and Linux Grand Unified Bootloader (GRUB), are available, too.

To learn more about hiding and unhiding partitions, see *http://pcomtricks.blogspot.com/2013/07/how-to-hide-hard-disk-partition-in.html* or *http://infocurse.com/how-to-hide-hard-drive-partition-windows-7-8-xp-vista/*.

To detect whether this technique has been used, be sure to account for all disk space when you're examining an evidence drive. Analyze any disk areas containing space you can't account for so that you can determine whether they contain additional evidence. For example, in Figure 9-10, the Windows Disk Management tool shows two partitions for Disk 2, labeled F and G, and a 200 MB gap between these partitions. For demonstration purposes, this gap has been labeled "Part Hidden" and has no assigned letter. In addition, it's not accessible in File Explorer, but most digital forensics tools or hexadecimal editors could access it. Partition gaps are 128 bytes in Windows Vista and later. The disk space between partitions F and G is 200 MB, however, which indicates you should examine this larger-than-normal gap to see whether it contains any relevant evidence.

In ProDiscover, a hidden partition appears as the highest available drive letter set in the BIOS. Figure 9-11 shows three partitions, similar to Figure 9-10, except the hidden partition is shown as the drive letter Z. This is a feature of ProDiscover; other forensics tools have their own methods of assigning drive letters to hidden partitions. These assigned drive letters allow a digital forensics tool to access and examine the hidden partition.

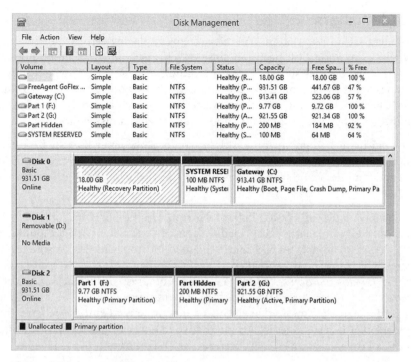

Figure 9-10   The Disk Management window
Courtesy of Microsoft Corporation

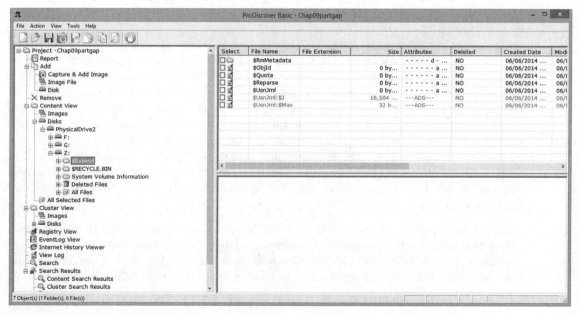

Figure 9-11   Viewing a hidden partition in ProDiscover
Courtesy of Technology Pathways, LLC

Marking Bad Clusters

Another data-hiding technique used in FAT file systems is placing sensitive or incriminating data in free or slack space on disk partition clusters. This technique, although not common now, involves using old utilities such as Norton DiskEdit, developed by Symantec as part of its Norton Utilities suite. In Norton DiskEdit, you can mark good clusters as bad clusters in the FAT table. The OS then considers these clusters unusable. The only way they can be accessed from the OS is by changing them to good clusters with a disk editor.

To mark a good cluster as bad in Norton DiskEdit, you type the letter B in the FAT entry corresponding to that cluster when examining the FAT table. You can then use any DOS disk editor to write and read data to this cluster, which is effectively hidden because it appears as bad to the OS.

DiskEdit was last available in version 8.0 of Norton Utilities. It runs only in MS-DOS and can access only FAT-formatted disk media. You can't run it by using Windows command prompts. You can find MS-DOS and Symantec Norton Utilities at sources such as MyOldSoftware (which can be downloaded from *http://myoldsoftware.blogspot.com/2009/04/norton-utilities-for-dos-windows-31.html* in RAR compressed format) and Vetusware (*http://vetusware.com/manufacturer/Symantec%20Corporation/?author=741*, which can be downloaded as dd image files). Note that dd image files are intended to be bit-stream copied to floppy disks or other external media. An alternative to extracting these files is using a forensics tool, such as ProDiscover, X-Ways Forensics, or OSForensics.

If a FAT partition containing clusters marked as bad is converted to an NTFS partition, the bad clusters remain marked as bad, so the conversion to NTFS doesn't affect the content of these clusters. Most GUI tools skip clusters marked as bad in FAT and NTFS, and these clusters might contain valuable evidence for your investigation.

Bit-Shifting

Some home computer users developed programming skills in computer manufacturers' assembly languages and learned how to create a low-level encryption program that changes the order of binary data, making the altered data unreadable when accessed with a text editor or word processor. These programs rearrange bits for each byte in a file. To secure a file containing sensitive or incriminating information, these users run an assembler program (also called a "macro") on the file to scramble the bits. To access the file, they run another program that restores the scrambled bits to their original order. Some of these programs are still used today and can make it difficult for investigators to analyze data on a suspect drive. You should start by identifying any files you're not familiar with that might lead to new evidence. Training in assembly language—as well as higher-level programming languages, such as Visual Basic, Visual C++, or Perl—is also helpful.

A related, and well-known, technique for hiding data is shifting bit patterns to alter the byte values of data. **Bit-shifting** changes data from readable code to data that looks like binary executable code. WinHex and Hex Workshop include a feature for shifting bits and altering byte patterns of entire files or specified data. To shift bits in a text file, follow these steps:

1. Start Notepad, and in a text document, type **TEST FILE. Test file is to see how shifting bits will alter the data in a file.**

2. Save the file as **Bit_shift.txt** in your work folder, and exit Notepad.

3. Start WinHex, and click **File, Open** from the menu. Navigate to your work folder, and then double-click **Bit_shift.txt**. Figure 9-12 shows the file open in WinHex.

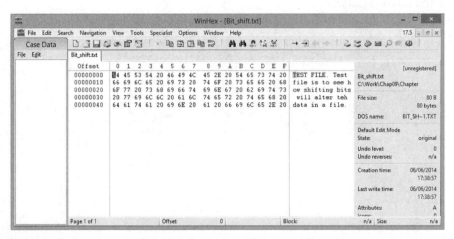

Figure 9-12 Bit_shift.txt open in WinHex
Courtesy of X-Ways AG, *www.x-ways.net*

4. To set up WinHex for bit-shifting, click **Options, Edit Mode** from the menu. Click **Default Edit Mode** (=editable), if necessary, and then click **OK**.

5. Highlight all the data in the file by clicking **Edit, Select All** from the menu.

6. Click **Edit, Modify Data** from the menu. In the Modify Block Data dialog box, click the **Left shift by 1 bit** option button (see Figure 9-13), and then click **OK**.

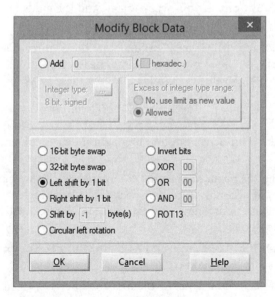

Figure 9-13 The Modify Block Data dialog box
Courtesy of X-Ways AG, *www.x-ways.net*

7. Click **File, Save As** from the menu, and save the file as `Bit_shift_left.txt` in your work folder. As you can see in Figure 9-14, the text has changed to random values. Exit and then restart WinHex.

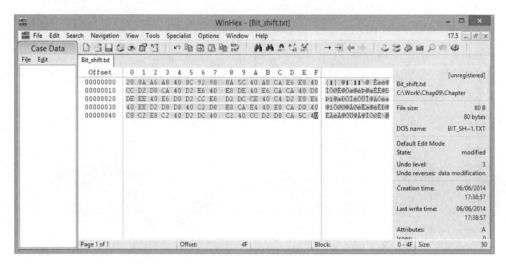

Figure 9-14   Viewing the shifted bits
Courtesy of X-Ways AG, *www.x-ways.net*

8. To return the file to its original configuration, you need to bit-shift it back to the right. Make sure the data is highlighted, and then click **Edit, Modify Data** from the menu. In the Modify Block Data dialog box, click **Right shift by 1 bit**, and then click **OK**.

9. Save the file as `Bit_shift_right.txt` in your work folder, and leave this file open in WinHex for the next activity.

Now you can use WinHex to find the MD5 hash values for these three files and determine whether `Bit_shift.txt` is different from `Bit_shift_right.txt` and `Bit_shift_left.txt`. To check the MD5 values in WinHex, follow these steps:

1. With `Bit_shift_right.txt` open in WinHex, click **File, Open** to open `Bit_shift.txt`, and then repeat to open `Bit_shift_left.txt`.

2. Click the **Bit_shift.txt** tab to make it the active file, and highlight the file's content by clicking **Edit, Select All**.

3. Click **Tools, Compute Hash** from the menu to open the Compute hash dialog box. In the list box, click **MD5 (128 bit)**, if necessary, and then click **OK**. Copy the MD5 hash value of `Bit_shift.txt`, and paste it in a new text document in Notepad. Click **Close** in the MD5 (128 bit) dialog box.

4. Repeat Steps 2 and 3 for `Bit_shift_left.txt` and `Bit_shift_right.txt`, pasting their hash values in the same Notepad text file.

5. Compare the MD5 hash values to determine whether the files are different. When you're finished, exit WinHex. In Notepad, save the text file as `Bit_shift_recovery.txt` in your work folder, and exit Notepad. If your output is correct, the `Bit_shift.txt` and `Bit_shift_right.txt` files should have the same MD5 hash values.

Typically, antivirus tools run hashes on potential malware files, but some advanced malware uses bit-shifting as a way to hide its malicious code from antivirus tools. With the bit-shifting functions in WinHex, however, you can inspect potential malicious code manually. In addition, some malware that attacks Microsoft Office files consists of executable code that's embedded at the end of document files and hidden with bit-shifting. When an Office document is opened, the malware reverses the bit-shifting on the executable code and then runs it.

Understanding Steganalysis Methods

As discussed in Chapter 8, the term **steganography** comes from the Greek word for "hidden writing." It's defined as hiding messages in such a way that only the intended recipient knows the message is there. The term for detecting and analyzing steganography files is "steganalysis."

In addition to steganography, digital watermarking was developed as a way to protect file ownership. Some digital watermarks are designed to be visible—for example, to notify users that an image is copyrighted. The digital watermarks used for steganography aren't usually visible. For example, when viewing two files that look the same, but one has an invisible digital watermarking, they appear to be the same file. Their file sizes might even be identical. However, if you run an MD5 or SHA-1 hash comparison on both files, you'll find that the hash values aren't equal. Chapter 8 described a few steganography tools available for lossy graphics files. These tools insert data into the graphics file but often alter the original file in size and clarity.

One way to hide data is to use steganography tools, many of which are freeware or shareware, to insert information into a variety of files. If you encrypt a plaintext file with PGP and insert the encrypted text into a steganography file, for example, cracking the encrypted message is extremely difficult.

Neil F. Johnson and Sushil Jajodia, authors of the white paper "Steganalysis of Images Created Using Current Steganography Software" (1998, *www.jjtc.com/ihws98/jjgmu.html*, *www.jjtc.com/Steganography*, or *http://143.132.8.23/cms/tues/docs/Steganography/Basics-Steganography-Security.pdf*), described these steganalysis methods ("attacks"):

- *Stego-only attack*—Used when only the file containing the possible steganography content is available for analysis; it's similar to a cyphertext attack. This attack is one of the most difficult to perform because all you have to analyze is the suspected steganography file.

- *Known cover attack*—Used when the **cover-media**, the original file with no hidden message, and the **stego-media**, the converted cover-media file that stores the hidden message, are available for analysis. By analyzing the original and steganography files, further comparisons can be made to identify common patterns that might help decipher the message.

- *Known message attack*—Used when the hidden message is revealed later, allowing further analysis of new messages. Similar to the known cover attack, this method uses comparative analysis to decipher the message. Because the message is known, deciphering it takes less effort.

- *Chosen stego attack*—Used when a steganography tool and stego-media were used to hide the message content. Because this method uses a known steganography tool, the analyst applies password or passphrase recovery techniques to decipher the message.

- *Chosen message attack*—Used to identify corresponding patterns used in stego-media. This technique creates stego-media and then analyzes them to determine how data is configured in the file. The analyst then uses these known configuration patterns to compare with suspected stego-media to determine what the message might be.

Examining Encrypted Files

People who want to make data unreadable can use advanced encryption programs, such as PGP or BestCrypt. Encrypted files are encoded to prevent unauthorized access. To decode an encrypted file, users supply a password or passphrase. Without the passphrase, recovering the contents of encrypted files is difficult. Many commercial encryption programs use a technology called "key escrow," which is designed to recover encrypted data if users forget their passphrases or if the user key is corrupted after a system failure. Forensics examiners can also use **key escrow** to attempt to recover encrypted data. Although some vendors have developed key recovery tools, the resources needed to crack encryption schemes are usually beyond what's available to small or medium organizations. If you do encounter encrypted data in an investigation, make an effort to persuade the suspect to reveal the encryption passphrase.

Some encryption schemes are so complex that the time to crack them can be measured in days, weeks, years, and even decades. Key sizes of 128 bits to 4096 bits make the job of breaking them with a brute-force attack nearly impossible with current technology. The development of quantum computing will probably make current encryption schemes obsolete. Until then, some will remain unbroken with commercially available tools.

Recovering Passwords

Password recovery is becoming more common in digital forensics analysis. Several password-cracking tools are available for handling password-protected data or systems. Some of these products are integrated into a digital forensics tool, such as OSForensics. Others, including the following, are stand-alone tools that typically require extracting password files or accessing a suspect's disk or image file directly:

- Last Bit (*http://lastbit.com/password-recovery-methods.asp*)
- AccessData PRTK (*www.accessdata.com/products/digital-forensics/decryption*)
- ophcrack (*http://ophcrack.sourceforge.net*)
- John the Ripper (*www.openwall.com/john*)
- Passware (*www.lostpassword.com/kit-forensic.htm*)

These tools use a dictionary attack or brute-force attack to crack passwords. Brute-force attacks use every possible letter, number, and character found on a keyboard. Eventually, a brute-force attack can crack any password; however, this method can require a lot of time and processing power, especially if the password is very long. In a dictionary attack, the program uses common words found in the dictionary and tries them as passwords. Most password crackers have dictionaries in a variety of languages, including English, French, Russian, and even Swahili. With some password-cracking tools, you can import additional unique words extracted from evidence. In FTK, for example, you can export a word list to PRTK that can be added to the dictionary.

With many of these programs, you can build profiles of a suspect to help determine his or her password. These programs consider information such as names of relatives or pets, favorite colors, and schools attended. The principle behind these programs is that people have a habit of using things they're comfortable with, especially if it requires memorizing something secret, such as a password. This method of password cracking is known as a "hybrid attack."

Many password-protected OSs and applications store passwords in the form of MD5 or SHA hash values. Because of this storage method, a brute-force attack requires converting a dictionary password from plaintext to a hash value. This process requires additional CPU cycle time to process each attempt to match the dictionary password to the OS or application password.

Another method has been developed that hashes passwords in a dictionary. A **rainbow table** is a file containing the hash values for every possible password that can be generated from a computer's keyboard. Because rainbow tables already contain these hash values and no conversion is necessary, this method is much faster than a dictionary or brute-force attack. For more information on rainbow tables and where to download them, see *http://project-rainbowcrack.com* and *http://project-rainbowcrack.com/table.htm*. As good as rainbow tables are for cracking passwords, however, a new scheme of protecting passwords has been developed that adds extra bits to a password and then hashes it. This technique, called **salting passwords**, alters hash values, which makes cracking passwords more difficult.

For more information on salting passwords, see *http://web.cs.du.edu/~mitchell/forensics/information/pass_crack.html* and *https://crackstation.net/hashing-security.htm*.

It should be noted that algorithms for password encryption vary from simple to complex. When attempting to crack a password, research the encryption method used by the application or OS. You might be able to identify known weaknesses that could help you determine the password.

Chapter Summary

- Examining and analyzing digital evidence depend on the nature of the investigation and the amount of data to process. You begin a forensics case by creating an investigation plan that defines the investigation's goal and scope, the materials needed, and the tasks to perform. Depending on the evidence you find, you might have to modify your investigation plan at some point.

- For most forensics investigations, you follow the same general procedures: Wipe and prepare target drives, document all hardware components on the suspect's computer, check date and time values in the suspect computer's CMOS, acquire data and document your steps, list all folders and files on the suspect system and examine their contents, attempt to open any password-protected files, determine the function of executable files, and document all your steps, making sure to follow evidence preservation procedures.

- Advanced digital forensics tools have features such as indexing text data that make keyword searches much faster. They also allow integrating the NIST National Software Resource Library (NSRL) to get MD5 and SHA1 hash values for known OSs and applications.

- One of the most critical aspects of digital forensics is validating digital evidence because ensuring the integrity of data you collect is essential for presenting evidence in court. Forensics tools have built-in validation features, but hexadecimal editors offer more advanced features. All data needs to be validated before and during analysis because digital evidence can be corrupted easily. Use hash values such as MD5 and SHA-1 to verify that data hasn't changed.

- Data hiding involves changing or manipulating a file to conceal information. Data-hiding techniques include changing file extensions, setting file attributes to hidden, hiding partitions, bit-shifting, using steganography, and using encryption and password protection.

- There are three ways to recover passwords: dictionary attacks, brute-force attacks, and rainbow tables. Rainbow tables are the quickest method because they contain predefined hash values of all known passwords. If passwords have been salted, however, recovering them can take much longer, and some might not be recoverable at all.

Key Terms

bit-shifting The process of shifting one or more digits in a binary number to the left or right to produce a different value.

block-wise hashing The process of hashing all sectors of a file and then comparing them with sectors on a suspect's disk drive to determine whether there are any remnants of the original file that couldn't be recovered.

cover-media In steganalysis, the original file with no hidden message. *See also* stego-media.

key escrow A technology designed to recover encrypted data if users forget their passphrases or if the user key is corrupted after a system failure.

Known File Filter (KFF) An AccessData database containing the hash values of known legitimate and suspicious files. It's used to identify files for evidence or eliminate them from the investigation if they are legitimate files.

rainbow table A file containing the hash values for every possible password that can be generated from a computer's keyboard.

salting passwords Adding bits to a password before it's hashed so that a rainbow table can't find a matching hash value to decipher the password. *See also* rainbow table.

scope creep The result of an investigation expanding beyond its original description because the discovery of unexpected evidence increases the amount of work required.

steganography A cryptographic technique for embedding information in another file for the purpose of hiding that information from casual observers.

stego-media In steganalysis, the file containing the hidden message. *See also* cover-media.

Review Questions

1. Which of the following represents known files you can eliminate from an investigation? (Choose all that apply.)

    a. Any graphics files

    b. Files associated with an application

    c. System files the OS uses

    d. Any files pertaining to the company

2. For which of the following reasons should you wipe a target drive?

    a. To ensure the quality of digital evidence you acquire

    b. To make sure unwanted data isn't retained on the drive

    c. Neither of the above

    d. Both a and b

3. The Known File Filter (KFF) can be used for which of the following purposes? (Choose all that apply.)

    a. Filter known program files from view.

    b. Calculate hash values of image files.

    c. Compare hash values of known files with evidence files.

    d. Filter out evidence that doesn't relate to your investigation.

4. Password recovery is included in all forensics tools. True or False?

5. After you shift a file's bits, the hash value remains the same. True or False?

6. Which forensic image file format creates or incorporates a validation hash value in the image file? (Choose all that apply.)

    a. Expert Witness

    b. SMART

    c. AFF

    d. dd

7. _____ happens when an investigation goes beyond the bounds of its original description.

9

8. Suppose you're investigating an e-mail harassment case. Generally, is collecting evidence for this type of case easier for an internal corporate investigation or a criminal investigation?

   a. Criminal investigation because subpoenas can be issued to acquire any needed evidence quickly

   b. Criminal investigation because law enforcement agencies have more resources at their disposal

   c. Internal corporate investigation because corporate investigators typically have ready access to company records

   d. Internal corporate investigation because ISPs almost always turn over e-mail and access logs when requested by a large corporation

9. You're using Disk Management to view primary and extended partitions on a suspect's drive. The program reports the extended partition's total size as larger than the sum of the sizes of logical partitions in this extended partition. What might you infer from this information?

   a. The disk is corrupted.

   b. There's a hidden partition.

   c. Nothing; this is what you'd expect to see.

   d. The drive is formatted incorrectly.

10. Commercial encryption programs often rely on _____ technology to recover files if a password or passphrase is lost.

11. Steganography is used for which of the following purposes?

   a. Validating data

   b. Hiding data

   c. Accessing remote computers

   d. Creating strong passwords

12. The National Software Reference Library provides what type of resource for digital forensics examiners?

   a. A list of digital forensics tools that make examinations easier

   b. A list of MD5 and SHA1 hash values for all known OSs and applications

   c. Reference books and materials for digital forensics

   d. A repository for software vendors to register their developed applications

13. In steganalysis, cover-media is which of the following?

   a. The content of a file used for a steganography message

   b. The type of steganographic method used to conceal a message

   c. The file a steganography tool uses to host a hidden message, such as a JPEG or an MP3 file

   d. A specific type of graphics file used only for hashing steganographic files

14. Rainbow tables serve what purpose for digital forensics examinations?

   a. Rainbow tables contain computed hashes of possible passwords that some password-recovery programs can use to crack passwords.

   b. Rainbow tables are a supplement to the NIST NSRL library of hash tables.

   c. Rainbow tables are designed to enhance the search capability of many digital forensics examination tools.

   d. Rainbow tables provide a scoring system for probable search terms.

15. The likelihood that a brute-force attack can succeed in cracking a password depends heavily on the password length. True or False?

16. If an application uses salting when creating passwords, what concerns should a forensics examiner have when attempting to recover passwords?

   a. There are no concerns because salting doesn't affect password-recovery tools.

   b. Salting can make password recovery extremely difficult and time consuming.

   c. Salting applies only to OS startup passwords, so there are no serious concerns for examiners.

   d. The effect on the computer's CMOS clock could alter files' date and time values.

17. Block-wise hashing has which of the following benefits for forensics examiners?

   a. Allows validating sector comparisons between known files

   b. Provides a faster way to shift bits in a block or sector of data

   c. Verifies the quality of OS files

   d. Provides a method for hashing sectors of a known good file that can be used to search for data remnants on a suspect's drive

9

Hands-On Projects

If necessary, create a *Work*\Chap09\Projects folder on your system before starting the projects; it's referred to as your "work folder" in steps. Then extract all files from the Chap09\Projects folder on the DVD to your work folder.

Hands-On Project 9-1

In this project, you perform bit-shifting on a file and verify that the file can be restored.

1. Start Notepad and type the following in a new text document: **This document contains very sensitive information. We do not want the competition to be able to read it if they intercept the message.**

2. Save the file as **correspondence.txt** in your work folder, and then exit Notepad.

3. Start WinHex, and open the **correspondence.txt** file.

4. In the in-chapter activity, you used the left and right shift options. For this project, you use the Circular left rotation option in the Modify Block Data dialog box. (*Note*: Because this text file is ASCII, returning it to a readable state takes eight circular left rotations.) Click **Edit, Select All** from the menu.

5. Click **Edit, Modify Data** from the menu. In the Modify Block Data dialog box, click the **Circular left rotation** option button, and then click **OK**.

6. Save the file as **correspondence1.txt**, and exit WinHex.

7. Restart WinHex, and open **correspondence1.txt**. Click **Edit, Select All** from the menu.

8. With the file's contents highlighted, click **Edit, Modify Data** from the menu. In the Modify Block Data dialog box, click the **Circular left rotation** option button, if necessary, to rotate the bits, and then click **OK**. Repeat this step seven times to verify that you can recover the data.

9. When you have recovered the text to its readable state, save it as **correspondence2.txt**.

10. Write a short paper stating whether you think this method is a reliable one for encrypting. Leave WinHex running for the next project.

Hands-On Project 9-2

Before conducting a forensics analysis, you should validate image files you've acquired. In this project, you validate the files analyzed in Hands-On Projects 9-3 and 9-4 to verify that they aren't corrupt. Chris Murphy, a Superior Bicycles employee suspected of industrial espionage, had a Windows drive formatted in NTFS that was seized as part of the investigation. For this project, you use the gcfi-ntfs.dd image file that was used earlier in this chapter.

1. Start Microsoft Word, and open the **GCFI-NTFS hash values.doc** file from your work folder. Print the file so that you can compare it with your results later in this project, and then exit Word.

2. Start WinHex, if necessary, and open **gcfi-ntfs.dd** from your work folder.

3. Click **Tools, Compute Hash** from the menu. In the Compute hash dialog box, click the list arrow, click **MD5 (128 bit)**, if necessary, and then click **OK**.

4. When the checksum process is finished, check the MD5 hash value in WinHex, and compare it with the value in the document you printed in Step 1.

5. After you have verified all the files, make a note in your log listing the file you examined and its hash value, and then exit WinHex.

Hands-On Project 9-3

In this project, you search the GCFI-NTFS drive image that belonged to Chris Murphy. You should have completed Hands-On Project 9-2 before beginning this one. Chris is suspected by his manager of leaking company secrets and possibly engaging in industrial espionage. Conduct a search to ascertain whether any evidence exists to support this claim.

1. Start OSForensics with the **Run as administrator** option, and start a new case. Enter **Superior Bicycles** for the case name. Enter your name as the investigator, your class name as organization, and your telephone number in the Contact Details text boxes in the New Case dialog box, and click **OK**.

2. To mount the disk image, scroll down the navigation bar on the left, and click **Mount Drive Image**. In the Mounted virtual disks window, click the **Mount new** button. In the OSFMount - Mount drive dialog box that opens, click the **...** button next to the Image file text box, navigate to your work folder, click **gcfi-ntfs.dd**, click **Open**, and then click **OK**.

3. Click the **Create Index** button in the left pane to start the Create Index Wizard. In the Step 1 of 5 window, click the **Use Pre-defined File Types** option button, if necessary. Click the **Emails, Attachments, Office + PDF Documents, Web Files + XML**, and **Zip Files** check boxes, and then click **Next**. In the Step 2 of 5 window, click the **Add** button. In the Add Start Location dialog box, click the **Whole Drive** option button if necessary, click the list arrow, click the mounted image drive letter, and then click **OK**. Click **Next**. In the Step 3 of 5 window, click **Start Indexing**.

4. When the indexing has finished, click **OK** in the message box informing you that errors reading some files might have occurred in the indexing process, if necessary. Click **Search Index** in the left pane. Type **chris** in the Enter Search Words text box, and then click **Search**.

5. Click the **Emails** tab, if necessary, and then double-click each e-mail message from baspen99@aol.com to view its contents. Click the **Add E-mail to Case** icon on the toolbar. In the Please Enter Case Export Details window, type **Bob Aspen message** in the Title text box, and then click **Add**. Repeat until all relevant e-mails have been added. If you get an error message at any time, click **Yes**. When you're finished, close the E-mail Viewer window.

6. Click **Start** in the left pane, and then click **Generate Report** in the right pane. In the Export Report dialog box, click the **Copy files to report location** button, click **Browse**, navigate to and click your work folder, and then click **OK**. OSForensics opens the report in your default Web browser.

7. After reviewing the report, exit your Web browser, and write a short memo to Ileen Johnson, the lead investigator in this case, summarizing your findings and what they indicate.

8. In File Explorer, navigate to your work folder where you saved the report, and rename the case folder **HOP09-3Case Report**. Keep OSForensics running for the next project.

Hands-On Project 9-4

In this project, you determine whether Chris transmitted any e-mails with information about the new kayak. Make sure you have finished Hands-On Project 9-3 before starting this one.

1. If necessary, start OSForensics with the **Run as administrator** option, and open the Superior Bicycles case. If necessary, mount the **gcfi-ntfs.dd** image file.

2. As mentioned, Chris is suspected of leaking information about the new kayak prototypes. You need to determine what he or someone else might have sent by e-mail. Click **Search Index** in the left pane. In the Enter Search Words text box, type **kayak**, and then click **Search**.

3. Click the **Emails** tab, if necessary, and then double-click the first e-mail message in the results. Click the **Add E-mail to Case** icon on the toolbar. In the Please Enter Case Export Details window, type **Kayak Search** in the Title text box, and then click **Add**. Repeat until all relevant e-mails have been added. If you get an error message at any time, click **Yes**. When you're finished, close the E-mail Viewer window.

4. Next, click the **Files** tab. Right-click the file in the search results and click **Add to Case**, and then click **List of Selected Items**. In the Please Enter New Case Item Details window, type **Kayak Document** in the Title text box, and then click **OK**.

5. Click **Start** in the left pane, and then click **Generate Report**. In the Export Report dialog box, click the **Copy files to report location** button, and then click **Browse**, navigate to and click your work folder, and click **OK**.

6. Exit OSForensics. Print the report that opens in your Web browser, and turn it in to your instructor.

7. In File Explorer, navigate to your work folder where you saved the report, and rename the case folder **HOP09-4Case Report**. Close any open windows.

Case Projects

Case Project 9-1

As part of the duties of a digital forensics examiner, creating an investigation plan is a standard pactice. Write a paper that describes how you would organize an investigation for a potential fraud case. In addition, list methods you plan to use to validate the data collected from drives and files, such as Word and Excel, with hashes. Specify the hash algorithm you plan to use, such as MD5 or SHA1.

Case Project 9-2

Several graphics files were transmitted via e-mail from an unknown source to a suspect in an ongoing investigation. The lead investigator gives you these graphics files and tells you that at least four messages should be embedded in them. Use your problem-solving and brainstorming skills to determine a procedure to follow. Write a short report outlining what to do.

Case Project 9-3

A drive you're investigating contains several password-protected files and other files with headers that don't match the extension. Write a report describing the procedures for retrieving the evidence with some of the forensics tools and hexadecimal editors discussed in this chapter and Chapter 8. Explain how to identify the file headers and determine how their extensions are mismatched. Then discuss what techniques and tools you can use for recovering passwords from the protected files.

9

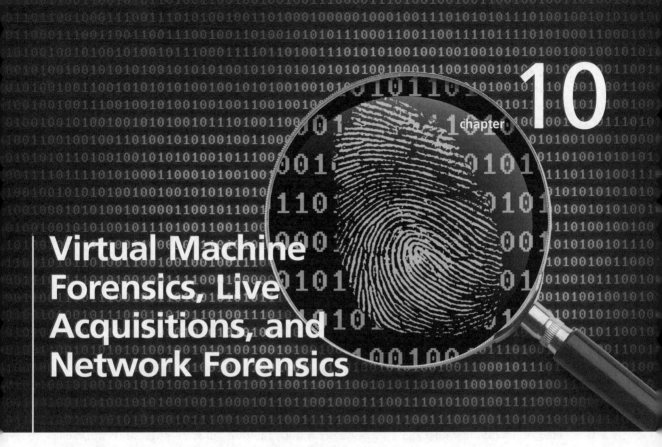

chapter 10

Virtual Machine Forensics, Live Acquisitions, and Network Forensics

After reading this chapter and completing the exercises, you will be able to:

- Explain standard procedures for conducting forensic analysis of virtual machines

- Describe the process of a live acquisition

- Explain network intrusions and unauthorized access

- Describe standard procedures in network forensics and network-monitoring tools

This chapter explores procedures for virtual machine forensics, live acquisitions, and network forensics. You learn about virtualization and virtual machine components and see how to detect that a virtual machine has been set up on a host computer and how to acquire an image of a virtual machine. Network forensics enable you to determine how an intruder gained access to a network's resources and information, and you use live acquisitions to capture an image while a machine is running, which is necessary in many situations, such as concerns about losing data if a system is shut down. For these procedures, you need to understand how to analyze RAM and network traffic.

An Overview of Virtual Machine Forensics

Virtual machine use has become common. Forensics investigators need to know how to analyze virtual machines and use them to analyze other suspect drives as well as systems containing malware. Later in this chapter, you open virtual machines from a USB drive that are used to perform live acquisitions on suspect drives.

As you've learned, virtual machines (VMs) help offset hardware costs for companies and are handy when you want to run legacy or uncommon OSs and software along with the other software on your computer. The software that runs virtual machines is called a "hypervisor." There are two types of hypervisors: a type 1 and a type 2 hypervisor. A **type 1 hypervisor** runs on "bare metal," meaning it loads on physical hardware and doesn't require a separate OS, although many type 1 hypervisors incorporate Linux-based operating systems (explained later in "Working with Type 1 Hypervisors"). Literally thousands of VMs can be hosted on a single type 1 hypervisor and many more on a cluster of these hosts. A **type 2 hypervisor** rests on top of an existing OS, such as Windows, Linux, or Mac OS. Figure 10-1 illustrates the difference between the two.

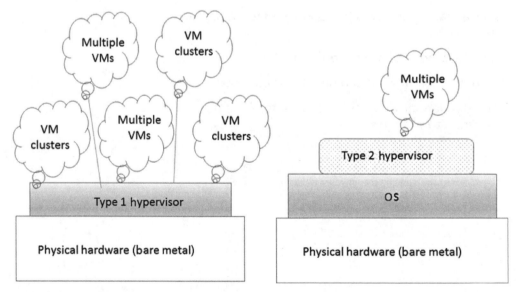

Figure 10-1 Type 1 and type 2 hypervisors
© 2016 Cengage Learning®

Much of the following information on virtual forensics comes from "Virtual Forensics: A Discussion of Virtual Machines Related to Forensic Analysis" (B. Shavers, Seattle, WA, 2008). For more details, download this white paper at *www.forensicfocus.com/downloads/virtual-machines-forensics-analysis.pdf*.

With rising hardware and software costs, companies have to pay careful attention to making the best investments for IT infrastructures. New versions of software require more RAM, hard drive space, and resources, and redeploying new versions of OSs and applications two or three times a year isn't cost effective. Enter virtual machines, which make it possible for one server to support an entire department or company. With virtual machines in use, a well-equipped workstation or reasonably priced server can take care of all a small company's needs. For all these reasons, virtual networks are now a standard part of doing business.

Type 2 hypervisors are usually the ones you find loaded on a suspect machine. Type 1 hypervisors are typically, but not exclusively, loaded on servers or workstations with a lot of RAM and storage. The next sections describe these hypervisors in more detail. Because users tend to be more familiar with type 2 hypervisors, you examine them first before moving on to type 1 hypervisors.

Type 2 Hypervisors

Type 2 hypervisors can be used on a laptop, a desktop, or even a tablet to simulate an OS environment, such as running a Windows Server 2008 VM on a Linux host. Companies often use these hypervisors to run legacy hardware that works only with a specific OS, such as Windows XP. Although VMs should be kept on a separate network, this setup can be a useful solution if hardware replacement costs are beyond a company's budget.

Before attempting to install a type 2 hypervisor, you need to enable virtualization in the BIOS before attempting to create a VM. Intel **Virtualization Technology (VT)** has responded to the need for security and performance by producing different CPU designs. With one design, you must go into the BIOS to enable virtualization (which is a hardware function, not an OS function). The other CPU design doesn't support virtualization. To determine whether your CPU supports virtualization, go to *http://ark.intel.com/Products/VirtualizationTechnology*. Instruction sets called **Virtual Machine Extensions (VMX)** are necessary to use virtualization; without these instruction sets, virtualization software doesn't work. (For a more detailed explanation, refer to *www.hardwaresecrets.com/article/Everything-You-Need-to-Know-About-the-Intel-Virtualization-Technology/263*.) The following sections give you an overview of the most widely used type 2 hypervisors.

As a result of more people using mobile devices to connect to company networks, type 2 hypervisors for smartphones are being developed (Marissa Tejada, "Smartphone Virtualization for MidSize Firms," *http://midsizeinsider.com/en-us/article/smartphone-virtualization-for-midsize-fi#.VAQ_bWM0-eM*, September 2013). With this software, employees can connect to company resources and keep personal information stored on their smartphones private. VMware introduced a type 2 hypervisor called Horizon Mobile Manager, and BlackBerry has been working on a similar product (Lucas Mearian, "VMware launches dual persona feature for Verizon smartphones," *www.computerworld.com/article/2497432/mobile-wireless/vmware-launches-dual-persona-feature-for-verizon-smart-phones.html*, May 2013). By 2018, type 2 hypervisors should be available for all smartphones.

10

Parallels Desktop Parallels Desktop (*www.parallels.com/products/desktop/*) was created for Macintosh users who also use Windows applications. It runs both legacy and current Windows OSs as well as Linux. Unlike most type 2 hypervisors, it isn't free but is generally under US$100.

KVM The KVM (Kernel-based Virtual Machine; *www.linux-kvm.org/page/Main_Page*) hypervisor is for the Linux OS. This open-source hypervisor enables you to choose between an Intel and an AMD CPU and to run Linux or Windows VMs. Like many type 2 hypervisors, it supplies virtualized hardware, such as graphics cards and network adapters.

Microsoft Virtual PC If you download older versions, such as Virtual PC 2007 or 2004, you can create VMs that run non-Windows OSs. However, the most recent version supports only VMs that run Windows. You can still download older versions from the Microsoft Web site, but you might get error messages during installation stating that your OS is incompatible with the virtualization software. These messages indicate a conflict between the 32-bit Virtual PC and a 64-bit OS (Microsoft Corporation, "Windows Virtual PC Tips," May 2009, *www.microsoft.com/en-us/download/details.aspx?id=14645*). On most Windows systems, you can simply click OK to bypass these messages and install the software. Be sure to download the right version—32-bit or 64-bit—for your OS (*www.microsoft.com/en-us/download/details.aspx?id=3702*).

VMware Workstation and Player VMware Workstation (*www.vmware.com/products/workstation*) is a solid workhorse, and although the standard version isn't free, a trial version is available. Take a look at some of its features:

- Can be installed on almost any device, including tablets
- Can install Microsoft Hyper-V Server on it
- Can create encrypted VMs
- Capable of supporting up to 16 CPUs, 8 TB of storage, and 20 virtual networks

Most current hypervisors can encrypt VMs to send sensitive information to clients. They can also be used to send new or proprietary software for testing to clients.

Older versions of VMware Player could run only VMs that had already been created. The current version, however, allows you to create and run VMs but not connect to other devices. You can download VMware Player and Workstation from the VMware Web site (*www.vmware.com*). When installing VMware Player, be sure to select the option for installing VMware Tools, which adds sharing folders with the host, dragging and dropping, and other features to make working with VMs easier.

Figure 10-2 shows the default location of files for a Windows installation of VMware Player. On a Linux installation, the files are in the /var/lib/vmware/virtual machines directory.

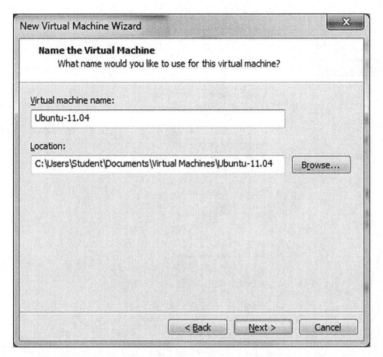

Figure 10-2 The default location of VMware Player files
Source: VMware, *www.vmware.com*

10

Table 10-1 lists some files associated with VMware. For more information on VMware Workstation, go to *www.vmware.com/support*.

Table 10-1 Files associated with VMware

File extension	Description
.vmx	Stores configuration files
.log	Contains logs of information such as when a VM was powered off, virtual appliances added, and so on
.nvram	Keeps track of the state of a VM's BIOS
.vmdk	Stores the virtual hard drive's contents
.vmem	Stores VM paging files, which serve as RAM
.vmsd	Contains information about snapshots

Source: VMware, *www.vmware.com*

After VMware Player is installed, you see the opening window shown in Figure 10-3. You can create a VM, open an existing VM, or upgrade to VMware Workstation.

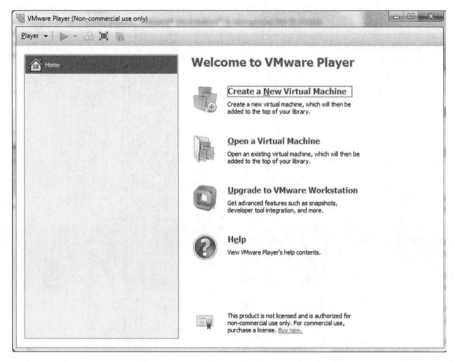

Figure 10-3 The VMware Player opening window
Source: VMware, *www.vmware.com*

VirtualBox Oracle VirtualBox (*www.virtualbox.org*) supports all Windows and Linux OSs as well as Macintosh and Solaris. This shareware can be downloaded and installed on both Windows and Linux host systems. Table 10-2 shows the file types associated with VirtualBox.

Table 10-2 Files associated with VirtualBox

File extension	Description
.ova or .ovf	File used to create a virtual machine; OVF stands for "Open Virtualization Format"
.vdi	Disk image file
.r0	Default libraries
.vbox	Saved settings of virtual hard drives
.vbox-extpack	Plug-ins
.vbox-prev	Backups of VMs
.xml-prev	Backups of XML settings
.log	Log files containing information such as a VM being powered on and off, whether it's in hibernation mode, virtual appliances added, and so on

© 2016 Cengage Learning®

As with most other type 2 hypervisors, you can select different virtual hard drive types when you're creating a VM (see Figure 10-4). VirtualBox even allows selecting types associated with other applications, such as the VMware VMDK type or the Parallels HDD type. Keep in mind, however, that virtual machines created with one type 2 hypervisor might not be able to be read by another. For example, VMware doesn't read the Parallels format. Later in the chapter, you learn that some virtual hard drive types can't be mounted as a virtual drive by forensics software, such as OSForensics or FTK Imager.

Figure 10-4   Types of virtual hard drives
Source: Oracle VirtualBox

Type 2 hypervisors also come with templates for different operating systems. For example, if the VM's filename includes the word "Ubuntu," the hypervisor assumes it's running a 64-bit Linux OS. After a VM has been created, several files are associated with it, as you've seen in Tables 10-1 and 10-2. Figure 10-5 shows some files associated with a VM running Fedora Linux. The .vbox file stores settings for the virtual hard drive, the .vbox-prev file contains backups of the VM, and the .vhd file contains the VM's virtual hard drive. There's also a folder for log files.

Name	Date modified	Type	Size
Logs	2/7/2014 4:35 PM	File folder	
Fedora 20.vbox	2/6/2014 8:10 AM	VirtualBox Machine Definition	8 KB
Fedora 20.vbox-prev	2/6/2014 7:48 AM	VBOX-PREV File	8 KB
Fedora 20.vhd	2/6/2014 8:10 AM	Virtual Hard Disk	4,252,752 KB

Figure 10-5   VM files in VirtualBox
Source: Oracle VirtualBox

Conducting an Investigation with Type 2 Hypervisors

On the surface, an investigation involving virtual machines doesn't differ much from a standard investigation. You begin by acquiring a forensic image of the host computer (the physical machine the VM runs on) as well as network logs. By linking the VM's IP address to log files, you might be able to determine what Web sites the VM accessed. After acquiring a forensic image of the host, export associated VM files, such as the ones listed in Tables 10-1 and 10-2. A VM shares the host's physical devices, such as DVD/CD players and USB drives, and can access files from peripheral devices and shared folders.

Detecting whether virtual machines are on a host computer can be challenging for digital investigators. On a Windows host, you usually look in the Users or Documents folder. On a Linux host, the files might be in /usr/bin/software-center or another folder in the /usr directory. Files associated with VMs, such as log files, should be extracted and examined to determine the crime or incident's timeline and to find relevant information, such as Web sites and network files that were accessed as well as downloads that occurred from the VM's IP address, which might include penetration-testing software or malware. Figure 10-6 shows part of a log file, including a VM powering off and other activities.

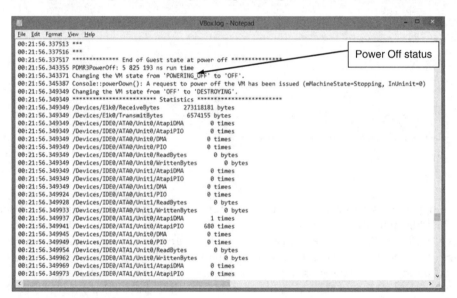

Figure 10-6 A VM log file
Source: Oracle VirtualBox

 Older OSs, such as Windows XP, often have a My Virtual Machines folder.

The next step is to check the host's Registry for clues that VMs have been installed or uninstalled. For example, the HKEY_CLASSES_ROOT Registry key contains associations for file extensions. If you see one of the file extensions listed in Tables 10-1 and 10-2, you know to search for a VM. Another clue to a VM being installed is the existence of a virtual network adapter. Figure 10-7 shows an unidentified network on a Windows 8 machine. If you open

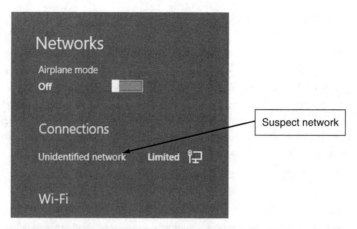

Figure 10-7   A suspect network on a Windows 8 machine
Courtesy of Microsoft Corporation

the Network and Sharing Center, you see VirtualBox Host-Only Network (see Figure 10-8). To see all network adapters on a system, you can also use the Windows `ipconfig` or Linux `ifconfig` command. In Windows PowerShell, you can also use the `Get-VM` cmdlet and pipe the output to the `Get-VMNetworkAdapter` cmdlet:

```
Get-VM -comp hyperv3 | Get-VMNetworkAdapter
```

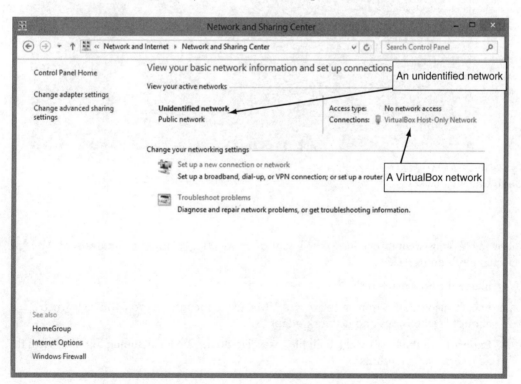

Figure 10-8   A suspect network viewed in the Network and Sharing Center
Courtesy of Microsoft Corporation

In VirtualBox, six types of virtual network adapters are possible, such as AMD and Intel Pro adapters. Refer to the user documentation for hypervisor software to find the names of virtual adapters to look for.

In addition to searching for network adapters, you need to determine whether USB drives have been attached to the host because they could have live VMs running on them. These VMs might have been used to access files and then disconnect without installing anything on the host. A VM can also be nested inside other VMs on the host machine or a USB drive (see Figure 10-9). Some newer Windows systems log when USB drives are attached, but there are other ways to determine whether this happened. After imaging the host's drive, search the Windows Registry or the system log files.

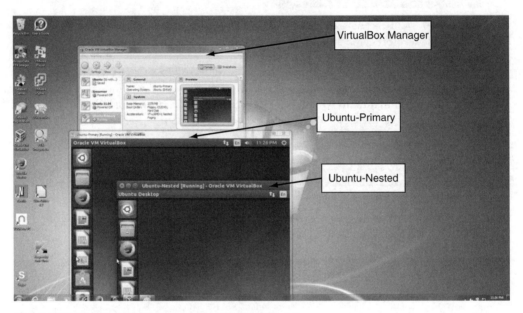

Figure 10-9   A VM nested inside another VM
Source: Oracle VirtualBox

Following a consistent procedure when you're conducting a forensic analysis of VMs is crucial. Here's an overview:

1. Image the host machine.

2. Locate the virtualization software and VMs, using the information you've learned about file extensions and network adapters.

3. Export from the host machine all files associated with VMs, including log files, virtual adapters, and snapshots.

4. Record the hash values of these associated files. Typically, forensics software can perform this task as part of the export function.

5. Next, you can open a VM as an image file in forensics software and create a forensic image of it or mount the VM as a drive and then image it or do a live search.

Live acquisitions of VMs are often necessary because they include all snapshots. A snapshot simply records the state of a VM at a particular moment. However, it's recording only changes in state; it's *not* a complete backup. Many network administrators depend on snapshots when working with VMs in case updates or software installations fail. When you're acquiring an image of a VM file, snapshots might not be included, depending on the software you're using. In this case, you have only the original VM, which might not have any of the changes made to it after it was created. Therefore, doing live acquisitions of VMs is important to make sure snapshots are incorporated.

Create a *Work*\Chap10\Chapter work folder on your system. The work folder path shown in screenshots might differ slightly from yours.

If necessary, download VMware Player from *https://my.vmware.com/web/vmware/downloads* and install it. You also need FTK Imager Lite, which you installed in Chapter 3. In this activity, you examine your own system for evidence of a VM:

1. Start FTK Imager Lite, and click **File, Add Evidence Item** from the menu.

2. In the Select Source dialog box, click the **Logical Drive** option button, and then click **Next**.

3. In the Select Drive dialog box, click the **Source Drive Selection** list arrow, click the drive where you installed VMware Player, and then click **Finish**.

4. In the upper-left pane, expand the drive where VMware Player is installed until you see a folder with "[root]" next to it. Expand this folder, and navigate to the **Windows\System32** folder.

5. Right-click the **config** folder and click **Export Files**.

6. In the Browse For Folder dialog box, navigate to and click your work folder (*Work*\Chap10\Chapter), and then click **OK**. Click **OK** in the Export Results dialog box, and then exit FTK Imager.

7. Start OSForensics, and start a new case. When you're prompted for a case folder, create one under your work folder called **InChap10-1**.

8. In the left pane, click **Registry Viewer**, which opens to a listing of Registry keys.

9. Click the **Software** folder in the right pane and click **Open**. In the left pane of the window that opens, expand the **SOFTWARE** node, scroll down, and then expand **C:\VMware, Inc.** and **VMware Drivers**. The drivers shown in Figure 10-10 are examples of what you might see in the Registry as evidence of a VM's presence on the system. Exit OSForensics.

10

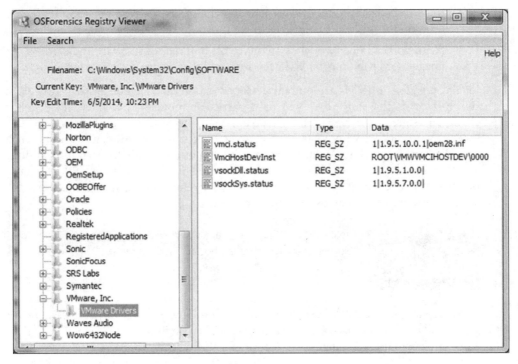

Figure 10-10   Viewing VMware in the Registry
Source: PassMark Software, *www.osforensics.com*

After determining that a VM was installed on the host, the next step is finding it. In VMware, you look for files with `.vmdk`, `.vmsd`, or `.vmx` extensions as well as `nvram` (virtual RAM) files. Next, you need to acquire an image of the VM. Follow these steps:

In this activity, an Ubuntu Linux 14.04 virtual machine is used. You should already have VirtualBox installed.

1. Start your Web browser, and go to **www.ubuntu.com/download/desktop**. Download an ISO image of Ubuntu Linux 14.04.

2. Start VirtualBox. Create a virtual machine named **Ubuntu 14.04,** and install Ubuntu 14.04 as the guest OS.

3. Start FTK Imager Lite, and click **File, Add Evidence Item** from the menu.

4. In the Select Source dialog box, click the **Image File** option button, and then click **Next.**

5. Click the **Browse** button, navigate to **\users*username*\VirtualBox VMs\Ubuntu 14.04,** click the **Ubuntu 14.04** folder, and double-click the **.vmdk** file. Then click **Finish.**

6. Click to expand the Evidence Tree in the left pane. Typically, in an Ubuntu installation, three partitions are listed: partition 1, containing the root partition; partition 5, containing the swap partition (see Figure 10-11); and unallocated space.

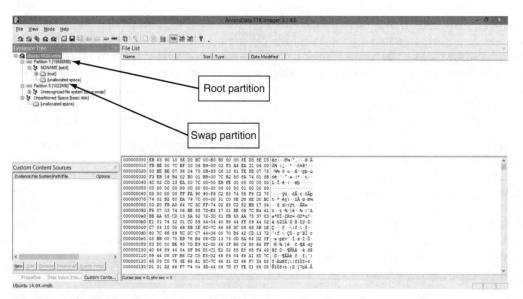

Figure 10-11 Examining a virtual machine's root and swap partitions in FTK Imager Lite
© 2014 AccessData Group, Inc. All Rights Reserved.

In Linux, the swap partition can be set up as virtual memory. It serves as RAM and might contain important information, such as passwords.

TIP

7. Now that you have the virtual machine file open, acquire an image of it by clicking **File, Create Disk Image** from the menu.

8. In the Select Source dialog box, click the **Image File** option button, and then click **Next**.

9. In the Select File dialog box, click the **Browse** button, and then navigate to and double-click the **.vmdk** file. Click **Finish**.

10. In the Create Image dialog box, click the **Add** button in the Image Destination section.

11. In the Select Image Type dialog box, verify that **Raw (dd)** is selected for the image format, and then click **Next**.

12. In the Evidence Item Information dialog box, enter today's date for the evidence number, your name, and any other pertinent information, and then click **Next**.

13. In the Select Image Destination dialog box, click the **Browse** button, navigate to and click your work folder, and then click **OK**. In the Image Filename (Excluding Extension) text box, type **C10InChap-2**. In the Image Fragment Size (MB) text box, type **0** so that FTK Imager Lite doesn't attempt to break the image file into chunks that fit on a CD.

14. Click **Finish**, and then click **Start** to begin the image acquisition. This process might take a few minutes. When it's finished, exit FTK Imager Lite. You can then examine the image with the tool of your choice.

Other VM Examination Methods In much the same way that Linux systems mount OSs or peripheral devices, forensics tools can mount VMs as an external drive. Both FTK Imager and OSForensics have this feature built in. By mounting a VM as a drive, you can make it behave more like a physical computer, which means you can use the standard examination procedures for a static hard drive. Imaging the host machine enables you to retrieve and examine log files as well as associated VM files (for example, .vbox-prev files or .vmdk files) to determine what the VM was used for. You mount a VM as a drive in Hands-On Project 10-1.

Another method of examining a VM is making a copy of its forensic image and opening this copy while it's running—in other words, starting it as a live virtual machine. From a forensics standpoint, this method alters the evidence, so it might be considered a nonstandard approach. However, this method makes it possible to run forensics software on the image to search for clues, such as finding malware and penetration-testing tools. For example, typical users shouldn't have tools such as Metasploit, W3AF, PortSwigger, Cain and Abel, or Wireshark installed on their work machines. These tools can be used to monitor network traffic, conduct brute-force attacks on passwords, perform SQL injections, and so forth.

Here are the basic steps:

1. Acquire a forensic image of the VM, and make a copy of this image.

2. Verify the copy's hash value (as you learned in Chapter 3), and then start the VM from the copy and explore its contents.

3. Your objective is to find evidence you can extract with a forensics software tool. Look for malware or network-monitoring tools, as discussed previously. Document what you find.

4. Create a snapshot of the running VM, and then power off the VM and exit the virtualization software.

5. Now that you have documented what's on the VM by doing a live examination, you need to follow standard forensics procedures for the evidence to be admissible in court. Open the original forensic image of the VM, and find the malware or tools you discovered in the live analysis. Prepare a written report of your findings.

Using VMs as Forensics Tools In addition to the many ways VMs can be used, investigators can use them to run forensics tools stored on USB drives. Being able to use a USB drive to acquire an image of a system is convenient. In this section, you set up two VMs on a USB drive, with one running Ubuntu 14.04 and the other running SANS Investigative Forensics Toolkit (SIFT), an open-source VMware appliance with guidelines and procedures for digital investigations; it can be installed only with Ubuntu 12.04. For these activities, you need a 16 GB or larger USB drive. You use VirtualBox because as of this writing, VMware has no portable version.

The SANS SIFT currently works only with Ubuntu 12.04, so in the next activity, you download and install this version.

1. Most USB drives still use FAT32, so first reformat the drive as NTFS. Insert the USB drive, open File Explorer, click the USB drive, and do a quick format to NTFS, making sure to set the cluster size to **8192**.

2. Start a Web browser, and go to **www.vbox.me**. Click the **Portable-VirtualBox_v4.3.6-Starter_v6.4.9-Win_all.exe** link. Download the `*.exe` file, and install it on your USB drive.

3. In File Explorer, create a folder on your USB drive called **VirtualMachine VMs**. Next, navigate to your USB drive, and double-click the `Portable-VirtualBox.exe` file (see Figure 10-12). If necessary, click **Yes** in the UAC message box.

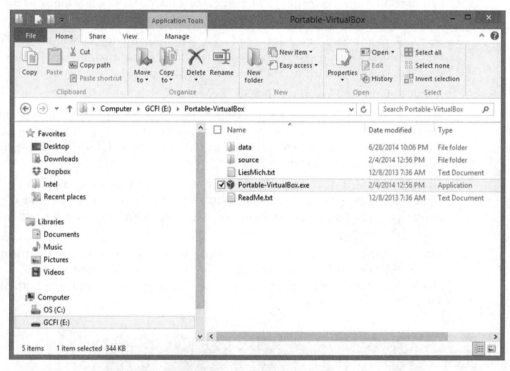

Figure 10-12   Starting Portable-VirtualBox from the USB drive
Courtesy of Microsoft Corporation

4. In the main Portable-VirtualBox window, click **File, Preferences** from the menu to open the VirtualBox - Settings dialog box. In the right pane, click the **Default Machine Folder** list arrow, click the **VirtualMachine VMs** folder you created, and click **OK**.

5. Click the **New** icon to create a VM. Enter the name **Ubuntu-portable**, and then click **Next**.

6. Increase the amount of memory to **1024**, and click **Next**. In the Create Virtual Machine window, click **Create**.

7. In the Create Virtual Hard Drive dialog box, click the **VMDK (Virtual Machine Disk)** option button, and then click **Next**. Accept the default settings in the remaining windows.

8. In the main window, click the **Ubuntu-portable** VM, and click the **Settings** icon.

9. Click **Storage** in the left pane. In the Storage Tree section, click **Empty** under Controller: IDE, and then click the down arrow next to the CD icon. Click **Choose a virtual CD/DVD disk file**. Navigate to the folder where the Ubuntu 14.04 ISO file is stored, double-click the ISO file, and then click **OK**.

10. Click the **Ubuntu-portable** VM, and then click the green **Start** icon. Install Ubuntu 14.04, accepting the default settings.

11. When the installation has finished, restart the **Ubuntu-portable** VM. After making sure it starts successfully, power it off. Leave Portable-VirtualBox running.

Installing the SANS SIFT takes about an hour. Follow these steps:

1. Click the **New** icon to create a VM, and name it **SANS SIFT**. Click **Linux** as the OS type, and then click **Next**. Use the default settings in the remaining windows.

2. Start a Web browser, if necessary, and go to **www.ubuntu.org**. Download the ISO file for Ubuntu 12.04, and save it in on your USB drive. (After Ubuntu 12.04 has been installed, you can delete the ISO file from your USB drive.)

3. Install Ubuntu 12.04 on the SANS SIFT VM.

4. Start the SANS SIFT VM. Open a Web browser in the VM and go to **http://digital-forensics.sans.org/community/downloads** to register. When your registration has been accepted, you're e-mailed a link to download the installation file SIFT Workstation 3.0.7z. Download it to the SANS SIFT VM.

5. On the SANS SIFT VM, open a terminal window. Type `wget --quiet -O -https://raw.github.com/sans-dfir/sift-bootstrap/master/ bootstrap.sh | sudo sh -s -- -i -s -y` and press **Enter** to run a script that installs SANS SIFT for you.

6. After the SANS SIFT has been installed, your window should look similar to what's shown in Figure 10-13. Open the `windows-to-unix-cheatsheet.pdf` file and look over it to get an idea of its contents. When you're finished, exit Portable-VirtualBox.

Figure 10-13 The SANS SIFT tools
Source: Oracle VirtualBox

Working with Type 1 Hypervisors

This section isn't intended as complete coverage of type 1 hypervisors and virtual networks; it's meant to help you understand the impact they have on forensic investigations. Having a good working relationship with network administrators and lead technicians can be extremely helpful in these investigations, particularly when you're a law enforcement officer or work for an outside company.

Type 1 hypervisors are installed directly on hardware, although for testing purposes, you can install them on a VM. Some are freeware, and some are proprietary and quite expensive. The capability of type 1 hypervisors is limited only by the amount of available RAM, storage, and throughput. Most type 1 hypervisors come in different levels, such as free, standard, and enterprise. Each type 1 hypervisor can host from a few to several hundred VMs per host, and the IBM hypervisor can even host thousands of VMs per host. The following are some common type 1 hypervisors:

- VMware vSphere (*https://my.vmware.com/web/vmware/downloads*)—Available in free, Enterprise, ESXi, and Enterprise Plus editions
- Microsoft Hyper-V 2012 (*www.microsoft.com/en-us/download/details.aspx?id=29189*)
- Citrix XenServer—Free edition (*www.citrix.com/products/xenserver/overview.html*) and Platinum, the advanced edition (*www.citrix.com/products.html?posit=glnav*)
- IBM PowerVM (*www-03.ibm.com/systems/power/software/virtualization/*)—Express and Standard editions
- Parallels Bare Metal (*http://sp.parallels.com/products/pcs/download/*)

Training to use these products can be expensive; for example, one week of training on VMware vSphere 5.5 can cost thousands of dollars. To manage these products, you also need a thorough understanding of virtual networks, IP addressing, hardware, and security.

The two most readily available products are Citrix XenServer and VMware ESXi. In this activity, you install XenServer as a VM in VirtualBox:

1. Start your Web browser, and go to **www.citrix.com/products/xenserver/overview.html**. Download the free ISO image for XenServer, and make note of where you stored this file.
2. Start VirtualBox, and click the **New** icon. In the dialog box that opens, type **XenServer** for the virtual machine name.
3. Click the **Type** list arrow, and click **Other**. Click the **Version** list arrow, and click **Other/Unknown (64 bit)**. If you aren't using a 64-bit machine, click **Other**. Click **Next**.
4. For the memory size, specify **1024** (or 25% of your available RAM), and then click **Next**.
5. Click **Create**. The Create Virtual Hard Drive dialog box opens. For the hard drive type, click the **VMDK (Virtual Machine Disk)** option button, and then click **Next**.
6. In the next dialog box, accept the default setting **Dynamically allocated** for the hard drive, and click **Next**. In the File location and size window, change the file size to **20 GB**, and then click **Create**.
7. In the Oracle VM VirtualBox Manager window, click the **XenServer** VM you just created. Click the **Settings** icon at the top. On the left side, click **Storage**.

8. In the Storage Tree section, click the **CD** icon. On the right side, you should see a CD icon under Attributes to the right of the CD/DVD Drive label. Click the **CD** icon, and click **Choose a virtual CD/DVD disk file**.

9. Navigate to the folder where the XenServer ISO image is stored, click the `XenServer-6.2.0-install-cd.iso` file, click **Open**, and then click **OK**.

10. In the Oracle VM VirtualBox Manager window, click the **Start** icon, and follow the wizard to install XenServer.

11. If you're prompted to restart, press **Enter**, and wait for your system to finish restarting. Figure 10-14 shows the XenServer VM in the Preview window on the right.

Figure 10-14 The XenServer VM running in VirtualBox
Source: Oracle VirtualBox

12. Power off the XenServer VM, and exit VirtualBox.

Performing Live Acquisitions

As you learned in Chapter 3, live acquisitions are especially useful when you're dealing with active network intrusions and attacks or if you suspect employees are accessing network areas they shouldn't. Live acquisitions done before taking a system offline are also becoming a necessity because attacks might leave footprints only in running processes or RAM; for example, some malware disappears after a system is restarted. In addition, information in RAM is lost after you turn off a suspect system. However, after you do a live acquisition, information on the system has changed because your actions affect RAM and running processes, which also means the information can't be reproduced. Therefore, live acquisitions don't follow typical forensics procedures.

The problem investigators face is the **order of volatility (OOV)**, which determines how long a piece of information lasts on a system. Data such as RAM and running processes might exist for only milliseconds; other data, such as files stored on the hard drive, might last for years. The following steps show the general procedure for a live acquisition, although investigators differ on exact steps:

1. Create or download a bootable forensic CD or USB drive, and test it before using it on a suspect drive. If the suspect system is on your network and you can access it remotely, add the necessary network forensics tools to your workstation. If not, insert the bootable forensics CD/USB drive in the suspect system.

2. Make sure you keep a log of all your actions; documenting your actions and reasons for these actions is critical.

3. A network drive is ideal as a place to send the information you collect. If you don't have one available, connect an external drive to the suspect system for collecting data. Be sure to note this step in your log.

4. Next, copy the physical memory (RAM). WindowsScope (*www.windowsscope.com*), OSForensics, FTK Imager, and similar tools can copy the RAM for you.

5. The next step varies, depending on the incident you're investigating. With an intrusion, for example, you might want to see whether a rootkit exists by using a tool such as RootKit Revealer (*http://technet.microsoft.com/en-us/sysinternals/bb897445*). You can also access the system's firmware to see whether it has changed, create an image of the drive over the network, or shut down the system and make a static acquisition later.

6. Be sure to get a forensically sound digital hash value of all files you recover during the live acquisition to make sure they aren't altered later.

Performing a Live Acquisition in Windows

Several tools are available for capturing RAM. For example, Mandiant Memoryze (*www.mandiant.com/resources/download/memoryze*) lists all open network sockets, including those hidden by rootkits. It also works on both 32-bit and 64-bit systems. Belkasoft RamCapturer (*http://forensic.belkasoft.com/en/ram-capturer*) is available in 32-bit and 64-bit versions and can run from a USB drive. Another tool is Kali Linux, the updated version of BackTrack (covered in more detail in Chapter 7). It still has more than 300 tools, but outdated or obsolete ones have been eliminated. Kali Linux contains password crackers, network sniffers, and freeware forensics tools. For more details, go to *www.kali.org/official-documentation/*.

GUI tools are easy to use, but keep in mind that they often require a lot of system resources. In addition, some GUI tools might get false readings in Windows OSs, and command-line tools often give you more control. For these reasons, you should become familiar with some command-line forensics tools, such as Sleuth Kit, introduced in Chapter 7. Covering the more than 300 available command-line tools is beyond the scope of this book, but investigating them on your own is highly recommended.

Network Forensics Overview

Network forensics is the process of collecting and analyzing raw network data and tracking network traffic systematically to ascertain how an attack was carried out or how an event occurred on a network. Because network attacks are on the rise, there's more focus on this field and an increasing demand for skilled technicians. Labor forecasts predict a shortfall of 50,000 network forensics specialists in law enforcement, legal firms, companies, and universities.

When intruders break into a network, they leave a trail. Being able to spot variations in network traffic can help you track intrusions, so knowing your network's typical traffic patterns is important. For example, if a company's peak use is typically between 6 a.m. and 6 p.m., that's when you should expect spikes. If a usage spike occurs during the night, the network administrator should recognize it as unusual activity and take steps to investigate it.

Network forensics can also help you determine whether a network is truly under attack or a user has inadvertently installed an untested patch or custom program, for example. A lot of time and resources can be wasted determining that a bug in a custom program or an untested open-source program caused an "attack."

The Need for Established Procedures

Network forensics examiners must establish standard procedures for how to acquire data after an attack or intrusion incident. Typically, network administrators want to find compromised machines, get them offline, and restore them as quickly as possible to minimize downtime. However, taking the time to follow standard procedures is essential to ensure that all compromised systems have been found and to ascertain attack methods in an effort to prevent them from happening again.

Procedures must be based on an organization's needs and should complement the network infrastructure. The increase in cybercrimes has prompted many groups to begin compiling procedures and protocols to follow when a network intrusion occurs. Network administrators need to learn how to stop intruders and determine how they got in; what they copied, altered, or deleted; and whether they're still on the network. To address these needs, NIST created "Guide to Integrating Forensic Techniques into Incident Response" (*http://csrc.nist. gov/publications/nistpubs/800-86/SP800-86.pdf*, 2006). In addition, the paper "Identifying Critical Features for Network Forensics Investigation Perspectives (Adeyemi, Razak, and Azhan, *http://arxiv.org/ftp/arxiv/papers/1210/1210.1645.pdf*, 2012) explores network investigations from the perspectives of the military, law enforcement, and industry. A group from India has also come up with a general framework for network forensics (*www.ijcaonline.org/ journal/number11/pxc387408.pdf*, 2010). These approaches are discussed in more detail in "Developing Procedures for Network Forensics."

Securing a Network

Network forensics is used to determine how a security breach occurred; however, steps must be taken to harden networks before a security breach happens, particularly with recent increases in network attacks, viruses, and other security incidents. Hardening includes a range of tasks, from applying the latest patches to using a **layered network defense strategy**, which sets up layers of protection to hide the most valuable data at the innermost part of the network. It also ensures that the deeper into the network an attacker gets, the more difficult access becomes and the more safeguards are in place. The National Security Agency (NSA) developed a similar approach, called the **defense in depth (DiD)** strategy. DiD has three modes of protection:

- People
- Technology
- Operations

If one mode of protection fails, the others can be used to thwart the attack. Listing people as a mode of protection means organizations must hire well-qualified people and treat them well so that they have no reason to seek revenge. In addition, organizations should make sure employees are trained adequately in security procedures and are familiar with the organization's security policy. Physical and personnel security measures are included in this mode of protection.

The technology mode includes choosing a strong network architecture and using tested tools, such as intrusion detection systems (IDSs) and firewalls. Regular penetration testing coupled with risk assessment can help improve network security, too. Having systems in place that allow quick and thorough analysis when a security breach occurs is also part of the technology mode of protection.

Finally, the operations mode addresses day-to-day operations. Updating security patches, antivirus software, and OSs falls into this category, as does assessment and monitoring procedures and disaster recovery plans.

If you're interested in more information on DiD, visit *www.nsa.gov/ia/_files/support/defenseindepth.pdf*.

10

Testing networks is as important as testing servers. You need to be up to date on the latest methods intruders use to infiltrate networks as well as methods internal employees use to sabotage networks. In the early and mid-1990s, approximately 70% of network attacks were caused by employees. Since then, this problem has been compounded by contract employees, who often have the same level of network privileges as full-time employees.

In addition, small companies of fewer than 10 employees often don't consider security precautions against internal threats necessary, so they can be more susceptible to problems caused by employees revealing proprietary information to competitors. However, increasing use of the Internet has caused a sharp rise in external threats, so internal and external threats are currently about 50-50.

Developing Procedures for Network Forensics

As you have seen, log files are often examined along with forensic image files collected from devices. To get these files, you need to establish a good working relationship with network administrators and technicians. Network forensics can be a long, tedious process, and unfortunately, the trail can go cold quickly. A standard procedure often used in network forensics is as follows:

1. Always use a standard installation image for systems on a network. This image isn't a bit-stream image but an image containing all the standard applications used. You should also have MD5 and SHA-1 hash values of all application and OS files.

2. When an intrusion incident happens, make sure the vulnerability has been fixed to prevent other attacks from taking advantage of the opening.

3. Attempt to retrieve all volatile data, such as RAM and running processes, by doing a live acquisition before turning the system off.

4. Acquire the compromised drive and make a forensic image of it.

5. Compare files on the forensic image with the original installation image. Compare hash values of common files, such as `Win.exe` and standard dynamic link libraries (DLLs), and ascertain whether they have changed.

In digital forensics, you can work from the image to find most of the deleted or hidden files and partitions. Sometimes you restore the image to a physical drive so that you can run programs on the drive. In network forensics, you have to restore the drive to see how malware that attackers have installed on the system works. For example, intruders might have transmitted a Trojan program that gives them access to the system and then installed a rootkit, which is a collection of tools that can perform network reconnaissance tasks (using the `ls` or `netstat` command to collect information, for instance), keylogging, and other actions.

Reviewing Network Logs Network logs record traffic in and out of a network. Network servers, routers, firewalls, and other devices record the activities and events that move through them. A common way of examining network traffic is running the `tcpdump` command-line program (*www.tcpdump.org*), which can produce hundreds or thousands of lines of records. A sample output is shown here:

```
TCP log from 2015-12-16:15:06:33 to 2015-12-16:15:06:34.
Tue Dec 16 15:06:33 2015; TCP; eth0; 1296 bytes; from
   204.146.114.10:1916 to 156.26.62.201:126
Tue Dec 16 15:06:33 2015; TCP; eth0; 625 bytes; from
   192.168.114.30:289 to 188.226.173.122:13
Tue Dec 16 15:06:33 2015; TCP; eth0; 2401 bytes; from
   192.168.5.41:529 to 188.226.173.122:31
Tue Dec 16 15:06:33 2015; TCP; eth0; 1296 bytes; from
   206.199.79.28:1280 to 10.253.170.210:168;first packet
```

The first line of the output is simply the header. The rest of the lines follow the format *time*; *protocol*; *interface*; *size*; *source and destination addresses*. Take another look at the second line from the previous output:

```
Tue Dec 16 15:06:33 2015; TCP; eth0; 1296 bytes; from
   204.146.114.10:1916 to 156.26.62.201:126
```

This line shows that data was transmitted on Tuesday, December 16, 2015, at 15:06:33. It was a TCP packet sent via the Ethernet 0 interface of 1296 bytes. The packet was sent from 204.146.114.10:1916 to 156.26.62.201:126. In these IP addresses, the numbers after the colon represent the port number.

When viewing network logs, port information can give you clues to investigate. For example, you might notice that a particular IP address is coming in frequently on an unusual port. A receiving port above 1024, for example, should also raise a flag. You can check the Internet Assigned Numbers Authority Web site (*www.iana.org/assignments/port-numbers*) for a list of assigned port numbers.

Using a network analysis tool such as Wireshark (which you use later in this chapter), you could generate a list of the top 10 Web sites users in your network are visiting. As shown in the following output, the number of bytes being transferred is listed first, followed by the IP address of the site:

```
Top 10 External Sites Visited:
    4897   188.226.173.122
    2592   156.26.62.201
    4897   110.150.70.190
    4897   132.130.65.172
    4897   192.22.192.204
    4897   83.141.167.38
    1296   167.253.170.210
    1296   183.74.83.174
    625    6.234.186.83
    789    89.40.199.255
```

You could also generate a list of the top 10 internal users, as shown:

```
Top 10 Internal Users:
    4897   192.168.5.119
    4897   192.168.5.41
    4897   192.168.5.44
    4897   192.168.5.5
    2401   204.146.114.50
    1296   192.168.5.95
    1296   204.146.114.10
    1296   204.146.114.14
    1296   206.199.79.28
    625    192.168.5.72
```

These network logs can show you patterns, such as an employee transmitting data to or from a particular IP address frequently. Further investigation of the IP address could show that this employee is accessing an online shopping site during company time, for example.

 Automated software packages, such as Tripwire (*www.tripwire.com*), can tell you when suspicious network activity has occurred. Tripwire is an audit control program that detects anomalies in traffic and sends **NOTE** alerts automatically.

As with all investigations, keep preservation of evidence in mind. Your investigation might turn up other companies that have been compromised. In much the same way you wouldn't turn over proprietary company information to become public record, you shouldn't reveal information discovered about other companies. In these situations, the best course of action is to contact the companies and enlist their aid in tracking down network intruders. Depending on the situation, at some point you might have to report the incident to federal authorities.

Using Network Tools A variety of tools are available for network administrators to perform remote shutdowns, monitor device use, and more. The tools covered in this chapter are freeware and work in Windows and Linux. Sysinternals (*http://technet.microsoft.com/ en-us/sysinternals/bb842062.aspx*), for example, is a collection of free tools for examining Windows products. Created by Mark Russinovich and Bryce Cogswell and acquired by

Microsoft, it gives you a choice of file, system, networking, process, and security tools, among others. The following list describes a few of the powerful Windows tools it includes:

- RegMon shows all Registry data in real time.
- Process Explorer shows what files, Registry keys, and DLLs are loaded at a specific time.
- Handle shows what files are open and which processes are using these files.
- FileMon shows file system activity.

Far too many tools are available to list here, but you should take some time to explore the site and see what's available. One in particular that's worth investigating is PsTools, a suite that includes the following tools:

- *PsExec*—Runs processes remotely
- *PsGetSid*—Displays the security identifier (SID) of a computer or user
- *PsKill*—Kills processes by name or process ID
- *PsList*—Lists detailed information about processes
- *PsLoggedOn*—Displays who's logged on locally
- *PsPasswd*—Allows you to change account passwords
- *PsService*—Enables you to view and control services
- *PsShutdown*—Shuts down and optionally restarts a computer
- *PsSuspend*—Allows you to suspend processes

These tools help you monitor your network efficiently and thoroughly. For example, you can consult records that PsTools generates to prove an employee ran a program without permission. You can also monitor your network and shut down machines or processes that could be harmful.

Although these tools are helpful for network administrators, imagine what would happen if an attacker (or even an internal user) could get administrative rights to the network and start using these tools. For example, in a networking class, students had to install their own servers and then harden their systems. One student was able to use PsShutdown to log on to another student's server and shut it down remotely because no password for the default user account had been created.

Using Packet Analyzers

Packet analyzers are devices or software placed on a network to monitor traffic. Most network administrators use them for increasing security and tracking bottlenecks. However, attackers can use them to get information covertly. Most packet analyzers work at Layer 2 or 3 of the OSI model. To understand what's happening on a network, often you have to look at the higher layers by using custom software that comes with switches and routers, however.

Some analyzers perform packet captures, some are used for analysis, and some handle both tasks. Your organization needs to have policies about using these tools to comply with new federal laws on digital evidence. Windows has many tools capable of capturing and analyzing packets, but you can't feed the data they collect directly into other tools. Most tools can read anything captured in Pcap (packet capture) format. (Libpcap is the version for Linux, and Winpcap is the version for Windows.) Programs such as tcpdump and Wireshark (*www.wireshark.org*) use the Pcap format, for example.

As a forensics expert, you must choose the tool that best suits your purposes. For example, if your network is being hit with SYN (the synchronize portion of the TCP handshake) flood attacks, you want to find packets with the SYN flag set. In a SYN flood attack, the attacker keeps asking your server to establish a connection. Although your server can handle thousands of connections, it can handle only a limited number of establishing connections. To find these packets, tcpdump and tethereal (a network protocol analyzer) can be programmed to examine TCP headers to find the SYN flag. Figure 10-15 shows a TCP header; the Flags area contains several flags, including the SYN flag (denoted as S in the figure).

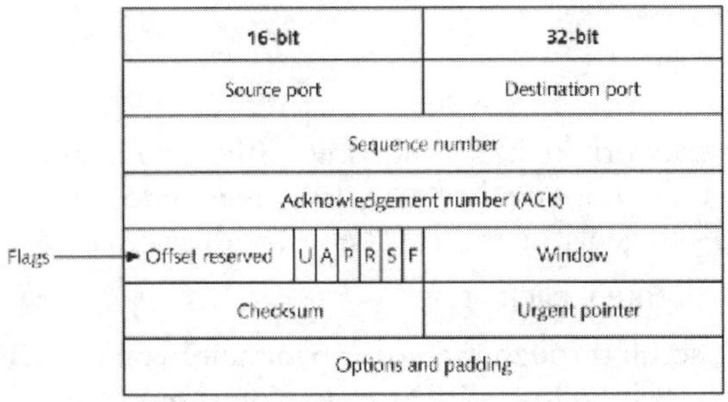

16-bit	32-bit
Source port	Destination port
Sequence number	
Acknowledgement number (ACK)	
Offset reserved U A P R S F	Window
Checksum	Urgent pointer
Options and padding	

Flags ——▶ Offset reserved

Figure 10-15   A TCP header
© Cengage Learning®

Tcpslice (*http://sourceforge.net/projects/tcpslice/*) is a good tool for extracting information from large Libpcap files; you simply specify the time frame you want to examine. It's also capable of combining files. A suite of tools called Tcpreplay (*http://tcpreplay.synfin.net/trac/*) can be used to replay network traffic recorded in Libpcap format; you use this information to test network devices, such as IDSs, switches, and routers. Another tool, Tcpdstat (*www.freebsdsoftware.org/net/tcpdstat.html*), works close to real time to generate Libpcap statistics and break packets down by protocol so that you can get a quick overall view of network traffic, including average and maximum transfer rates.

Ngrep (*http://ngrep.sourceforge.net*) can be used to examine e-mail headers or chat logs. It collects and hashes data for verification. It's similar to tcpdump but can be used to identify network communication between worms and viruses. Etherape (*http://etherape.sourceforge.net*) is a tool for viewing network traffic graphically. Another GUI tool, Netdude (*http://netdude. sourceforge.net/*), was designed as an easy-to-use interface for inspecting and analyzing large tcpdump files (sometimes several gigabytes). Argus (*www.qosient.com/argus*) is a session data probe, collector, and analysis tool. This real-time flow monitor can be used for security, accounting, and network management.

Wireshark can be used in a real-time environment to open saved trace files from packet captures. An important feature is its capability to rebuild sessions. To use this feature, right-click a frame in the upper pane and click Follow TCP Stream. Wireshark then traces the packets associated with an exploit. To see how this tool works, download the most recent version of Wireshark for Windows (*www.wireshark.org/download.html*) and install it on your workstation. Then follow these steps:

1. Start Wireshark, and click **Capture, Interfaces** from the menu to open the Capture Interfaces dialog box (see Figure 10-16).

10

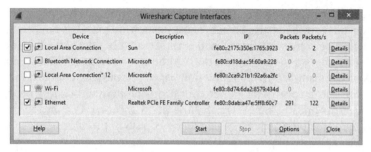

Figure 10-16 The Capture Interfaces dialog box
Source: Wireshark Foundation

2. Click the check box next to the network interface showing traffic, and then click the **Start** button at the bottom. (If you're not on a live network, ping another student or yourself and visit some Web sites to generate traffic. Then start this activity again.)

3. After several frames have been captured, click **Stop**.

4. After the trace has been loaded, scroll through the upper pane until you see a TCP frame. Right-click the frame and click **Follow TCP Stream**. You should see a window similar to Figure 10-17.

Figure 10-17 Following a TCP stream
Source: Wireshark Foundation

5. Review the information displayed in this window, and then exit Wireshark.

You can find information on network forensics tools at many of the Web sites mentioned in this chapter. If you're interested in learning even more about network forensics, the next section covers the Honeynet Project.

Examining the Honeynet Project

The Honeynet Project (*https://www.honeynet.org*) was developed to make information widely available in an attempt to thwart Internet and network attackers. Many people participate in this worldwide project. The objectives are awareness, information, and tools. The first step is to make people and organizations aware that threats exist and they might be targets. The second is to provide information on how to protect against these threats, including how attackers operate, how they communicate, and what tactics they use. Finally, for people who want to do their own research, the Honeynet Project offers tools and methods.

A major threat is **distributed denial-of-service (DDoS) attacks**. A trace of a DDoS attack might go through other organizations' networks, not just yours or your ISP's. In DDoS attacks, hundreds or even thousands of machines can be used. These machines are known as **zombies** because they have unwittingly become part of the attack. When the first DDoS attacks began, the main concerns were the high monetary impact and the amount of time it took to track down these attacks.

Another major threat is **zero day attacks**. Attackers look for holes in networks and OSs and exploit these weaknesses before patches are available. Vendors usually aren't aware that these vulnerabilities exist, so they haven't developed and released patches for them. Penetration testers attempt to break into networks to find undiscovered vulnerabilities and then predict where the next onslaught of network attacks will come from.

In any organization, you have to determine the value of the data you're protecting and weigh it against the price of the defense system you plan to install. When an attack strikes, your first response is to stop it and prevent it from going further. Then you need to see what defense procedures worked and what additional procedures might be needed. Training and informing IT staff are critical.

The Honeynet Project was set up as a resource to help network administrators deal with DDoS and other attacks. It involves installing honeypots and honeywalls at different locations in the world. A **honeypot** is a computer set up to look like any other machine on your network; its purpose is to lure attackers to your network, but it contains no information of real value. You can take the honeypot offline to analyze it and not affect the running of your network. **Honeywalls** are computers set up to monitor what's happening to honeypots on your network and record what attackers are doing (see *www.honeynet.org/papers/cdrom/*). Honeypots and honeywalls are commonly used to attract intruders and see what they're attempting to do on a network.

10

Chapter Summary

- Virtual machines are used extensively in organizations and are a common part of forensic investigations. Investigators must be familiar with file extensions that indicate the existence of VMs.

- There are two types of hypervisors for running virtual machines. Type 1 hypervisors contain their own OSs and are loaded directly on physical hardware. Type 2 hypervisors are applications installed on top of an OS.

- Virtualization Technology is Intel's CPU design for security and performance enhancements that enable the BIOS to support virtualization. Virtual Machine Extensions (VMX) are instruction sets created for Intel processors to handle virtualization.

- Forensic procedures for VMs start by creating an image of the host machine, and then exporting files associated with a VM. Next, you create an image of the VM. Virtual machines can be imaged by using forensics software tools, mounting the VM as a drive, or doing a live acquisition.

- Live acquisitions are necessary to retrieve volatile items, such as RAM and running processes. They're also useful when taking systems offline would affect business functioning adversely. Investigators must be concerned with the order of volatility (OOV), which determines how long a piece of information lasts on a system.

- Network forensics is the process of collecting and analyzing raw network data and systematically tracking network traffic to ascertain how an attack took place. Organizations should develop standard procedures for network forensics.

- Steps must be taken to harden networks before a security breach happens, which includes applying layered defense strategies to the network architecture, installing the latest software patches, and making employees aware of security procedures.

- Being able to spot variations in network traffic can help you track intrusions, so knowing a network's typical traffic patterns is important.

- Several tools are available for monitoring network traffic, such as packet analyzers and honeypots. Tools such as `tcpdump` and Wireshark offer support groups and online training. Keep in mind that network tools can also be used by intruders who obtain administrative rights to attack networks from the inside.

- The Honeynet Project is designed to help people learn the latest intrusion techniques that attackers are using. The project disseminates information and provides tools for research.

Key Terms

defense in depth (DiD) The NSA's approach to implementing a layered network defense strategy. It focuses on three modes of protection: people, technology, and operations.

distributed denial-of-service (DDoS) attacks A type of DoS attack in which other online machines are used, without the owners' knowledge, to launch an attack.

honeypot A computer or network set up to lure an attacker.

honeywalls Intrusion prevention and monitoring systems that track what attackers do on honeypots.

layered network defense strategy An approach to network hardening that sets up several network layers to place the most valuable data at the innermost part of the network.

network forensics The process of collecting and analyzing raw network data and systematically tracking network traffic to determine how security incidents occur.

order of volatility (OOV) A term indicating how long an item on a network lasts. RAM and running processes might last only milliseconds; items stored on hard drives can last for years.

packet analyzers Devices and software used to examine network traffic. On TCP/IP networks, they examine packets (hence the name).

type 1 hypervisor A virtual machine interface that loads on physical hardware and contains its own OS.

type 2 hypervisor A virtual machine interface that's loaded on top of an existing OS.

Virtualization Technology (VT) Intel's CPU design for security and performance enhancements that enable the BIOS to support virtualization.

Virtual Machine Extensions (VMX) Instruction sets created for Intel processors to handle virtualization.

zero day attacks Attacks launched before vendors or network administrators have discovered vulnerabilities and patches for them have been released.

zombies Computers used without the owners' knowledge in a DDoS attack.

Review Questions

1. Virtual Machine Extensions (VMX) are part of which of the following?
   a. Type 1 hypervisors
   b. Type 2 hypervisors
   c. Intel Virtualized Technology
   d. AMD Virtualized Technology

2. You can expect to find a type 2 hypervisor on what type of device? (Choose all that apply.)
   a. Desktop
   b. Smartphone
   c. Tablet
   d. Network server

3. Which of the following file extensions are associated with VMware virtual machines?
   a. `.vmx`, `.log`, and `.nvram`
   b. `.vdi`, `.ova`, and `.r0`
   c. `.vmx`, `.r0`, and `.xml-prev`
   d. `.vbox`, `.vdi`, and `.log`

4. In VirtualBox, a(n) _____ file contains settings for virtual hard drives.
   a. `.vbox-prev`
   b. `.ovf`
   c. `.vbox`
   d. `.log`

5. The number of VMs that can be supported per host by a type 1 hypervisor is generally determined by the amount of _____ and _____.

10

6. A forensic image of a VM includes all snapshots. True or False?

7. Which Registry key contains associations for file extensions?
   a. HFILE_CLASSES_ROOT
   b. HKEY_CLASSES_ROOT
   c. HFILE_EXTENSIONS
   d. HKEY_CLASSES_FILE

8. Which of the following is a clue that a virtual machine has been installed on a host system?
   a. Network logs
   b. Virtual network adapter
   c. Virtualization software
   d. USB drive

9. To find network adapters, you use the _____ command in Windows and the _____ command in Linux.

10. What are the three modes of protection in the DiD strategy?

11. A layered network defense strategy puts the most valuable data where?
    a. In the DMZ
    b. In the outermost layer
    c. In the innermost layer
    d. None of the above

12. Tcpslice can be used to retrieve specific timeframes of packet captures. True or False?

13. Packet analyzers examine what layers of the OSI model?
    a. Layers 2 and 4
    b. Layers 4 through 7
    c. Layers 2 and 3
    d. All layers

14. When do zero day attacks occur? (Choose all that apply.)
    a. On the day the application or OS is released
    b. Before a patch is available
    c. Before the vendor is aware of the vulnerability
    d. On the day a patch is created

Hands-On Projects

The objective of these projects is to give you practice in mounting and imaging virtual machines. Before beginning, create a *Work*\Chap10\Projects folder on your system.

Hands-On Project 10-1

In this project, you mount a VM as a drive in OSForensics, using the Ubuntu-portable VM you created for the in-chapter activity. The VM is assigned the next available drive letter on your system in read-only mode, and then you do an image acquisition.

1. Start OSForensics. In the left pane, scroll down and click **Mount Drive Image** to open the PassMark OSFMount utility.

2. In the lower-left corner, click **Mount new** to open the OSFMount - Mount drive window.

3. Make sure **Image file** is selected, and click the **...** button. Scroll to the location of VMware VMs, and double-click the **Ubuntu-portable.vmdk** file. In the "Select a partition in image" window, accept the default option, **Use entire image file**, and click **OK**.

4. Accept the defaults, and click **OK**. This process should take only a few minutes. The .vmdk file should be displayed as a mounted drive, as shown in Figure 10-18.

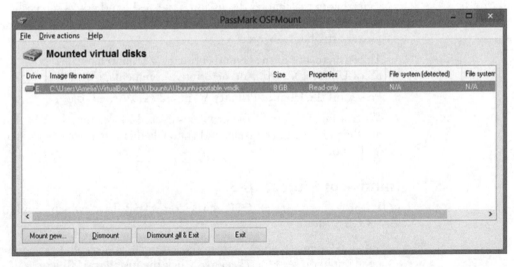

Figure 10-18 A VM mounted as a read-only drive
Source: PassMark Software, *www.osforensics.com*

5. Double-click the drive to display its contents, and take a screenshot. Make a note of the new drive letter, and click **Exit**.

6. In the left pane, scroll up and click the **Manage Case** button. In the right pane, click any current case, and then click the **Add Device** button.

7. In the "Select device to add" dialog box, click the **Drive Letter** list arrow. The drive letter you noted in Step 5 is listed, and you can add it to a case when you're doing a standard static analysis. Click **Cancel**.

8. Write a short report of your results, and include the screenshots you took.

Hands-On Project 10-2

In this project, you examine a virtual machine nested inside another virtual machine. Keep in mind that the number of VMs you can nest depends on the host machine's hardware.

1. Start VirtualBox. Create a VM called **Ubuntu-Primary**, and install Ubuntu 14.04 as a guest OS.

2. Start the **Ubuntu-Primary** VM. Start a Web browser in the VM, and go to **https://www.virtualbox.org/wiki/Downloads**. Download VirtualBox, and install it on the **Ubuntu-Primary** VM. Start a Web browser from the virtual machine, go to **www.ubuntu.org**, and download the ISO image for Ubuntu 14.04.

3. Start VirtualBox on the **Ubuntu-Primary** VM, and create a VM called **Ubuntu-Nested**. Click the **VMDK (Virtual Machine Disk)** option button for the hard drive type, and leave the default settings in the remaining windows. Install Ubuntu 14.04 on this VM, too.

4. Take a screenshot of Ubuntu-Nested running inside Ubuntu-Primary. Navigate to where virtual machine files are stored on Ubuntu-Primary (referring to the chapter discussion, if needed), and take a screenshot showing where files for Ubuntu-Nested are located. When you're finished, power off **Ubuntu-Nested**.

5. Take a snapshot of the Ubuntu-Primary VM, and name it **SS_of_Ubuntu_Nested**. Add descriptive comments, if you like.

6. Power off the **Ubuntu-Primary** VM, and exit VirtualBox.

7. Write a short report on the problems caused by deleting the VM that another VM is nested inside, and state whether any trace of the primary VM would be left.

Hands-On Project 10-3

In this project, you install OSForensics on a USB drive, which should have at least 8 GB of storage.

1. Start OSForensics. Click **Start** in the left pane, and scroll down in the right pane until you see Housekeeping. Click the **Install to USB** icon.

2. In the "Install OSForensics to USB drive or an optical disk" window, click **Browse** next to the USB directory text box, click your USB drive, and then click **OK**.

3. In the Installation type section, click the **Evaluation** option button, and then click **Install**. In the message box stating that the installation is finished, click **OK**, and then click **Exit** in the left pane.

4. Remove the USB drive from your computer. Take it to another machine and start OSForensics from this device. Take a screenshot of OSForensics running.

5. Perform two tasks, such as mounting a VM or starting a new case.

6. Write a short paper explaining how having a forensics tool on a USB drive can be useful in the field. Exit OSForensics, and retrieve your USB drive.

Hands-On Project 10-4

For this project, you must have installed OSForensics on a USB drive in Hands-On Project 10-3. Follow these steps to examine your physical machine's RAM:

1. Start OSForensics from your USB drive. On the left, click the **Memory Viewer** button. In the warning message box that opens, click **OK**.

2. Take a screenshot of the opening window, which displays running processes. In the upper pane on the right, click the **Dump Physical Memory** button. In the "Save file as" dialog box, navigate to your *Work***Chap10****Projects** folder. Save the file as **testdump**. When the dump is finished, click **OK**.

3. Using WinHex, the hex editor you used in earlier chapters, open the testdump file and examine its contents. Do a search for keywords you'd expect to find in a physical machine's RAM, such as Microsoft, From, To, Subject, and http. If you find other keywords, make note of them. Take screenshots of the search results.

4. Exit OSForensics and WinHex. Write a short paper on your findings, and describe the challenges and possibilities of using OSForensics for a memory dump in an actual investigation.

Hands-On Project 10-5

This project gives you a chance to explore the SANS SIFT tools. If you didn't install it in the in-chapter activity, do so before starting this project.

1. Start Portable-VirtualBox, and start the **SANS SIFT** VM.

2. Open **sift-cheatsheet.pdf**. It gives instructions on how to mount drives and examine files and has resources for sample images. Take a screen capture of the VM with this file open.

3. Open **memory-forensics-cheatsheet.pdf**. One of the resources it lists is the volatility tool. Start a Web browser, go to **https://code.google.com/p/volatility/wiki/SampleMemoryImages**, and write down the resources this tool offers.

4. On the left, scroll down and click **DFF (Digital Forensics Framework)**. Click the second icon from the left to add a local device. Click the **VBOX Hard drive** device, and click **OK**. If anything had been loaded on the USB drive, this tool would enable you to search for terms and examine the contents. Click **File, Exit** from the menu.

10

5. Wireshark is another tool available in the SIFT toolkit. Click the **Wireshark** icon on the left. In the Capture Help section, click the **How to Capture** link.

6. Step-by-step instructions open in Firefox. Make note of the warnings, such as making sure you have permission before doing packet captures. Exit Firefox. Write a one- to two-page paper summarizing the information in the two cheatsheets you examined and listing warnings for using Wireshark.

Case Projects

CASE PROJECTS

Case Project 10-1

As you have seen, some virtual machines can be loaded on a USB drive. Research which type 2 hypervisors fit on a USB drive of less than 16 GB. Which OS and forensics tools could you load on this drive?

Case Project 10-2

Your company wants to send a working VM to customers with a sample of its new software, but you're concerned about the security of the software and data. What precautions can you take?

Case Project 10-3

You have acquired a forensic image of a suspect's laptop. After doing an examination, you discover at least one VM installed, and you think more data can be found, but you aren't sure. You decide to make a copy of the VM's files and mount the VM as an external drive. Write the best procedure for this situation.

Case Project 10-4

Go to *http://docs.kali.org/installation/kali-linux-live-usb-install* and follow the instructions for installing Kali Linux on a USB drive. Try at least three of the tools it includes, and take screenshots of the tools you selected. Write a one- to two-page paper summarizing each tool's functions.

chapter 11

E-mail and Social Media Investigations

After reading this chapter and completing the exercises, you will be able to:

- Explain the role of e-mail in investigations
- Describe client and server roles in e-mail
- Describe tasks in investigating e-mail crimes and violations
- Explain the use of e-mail server logs
- Explain how to approach investigating social media communications
- Describe some available e-mail forensics tools

This chapter explains how to trace, recover, and analyze e-mail messages by using forensics tools designed for investigating e-mail and general-purpose tools, such as disk editors. E-mail is a major means of communication, and e-mail programs differ in how and where they store and track e-mail. Some are installed separately from the OS and require their own directories and information files on the local computer. Others take advantage of existing software, such as Web browsers, and install no additional software on the client computer. In addition, many people communicate through social media sites, such as LinkedIn, Facebook, and Twitter. Throughout this chapter, you see how e-mail programs on the server interact with e-mail programs on the client, and vice versa. You also learn how to recover deleted e-mail from a client computer, regardless of the e-mail program used, and how to trace an e-mail back to the sender. You also get an overview of the legal issues affecting social media communications.

Exploring the Role of E-mail in Investigations

E-mail evidence is an important part of any computing investigation, so digital forensics investigators must know how e-mail is processed to collect this essential evidence. In addition, with the increase in e-mail scams and fraud attempts with phishing or spoofing, investigators need to know how to examine and interpret the unique content of e-mail messages.

As a computing investigator, you might be called on to examine a phishing e-mail to see whether it's authentic. Later, in "Tracing an E-mail Message," you learn about resources for looking up e-mail and Web addresses to verify whether they're associated with a spoofed message. The Internet links in a phishing e-mail often appear to be correct, such as the U.S. Internal Revenue Service's Web page, *www.irs.gov*. Typically, **phishing** e-mails contain links to text on a Web page. By using this technique, a phishing message attempts to get personal information by luring readers with false promises. When **pharming** is used, readers might go to the correct Web site address, but DNS poisoning takes them to a fake site. To determine whether redirection has been used, you need to view the message's HTML source code and check whether an Internet link is a label with a redirect to a different Web address.

For more information on phishing, see *www.wordspy.com/words/phishing.asp*.

One of the most noteworthy e-mail scams was 419, or the Nigerian Scam, which originated as chain letters from Nigeria, Africa, in the 1970s and 1980s before switching to fax machines and then e-mail. Fraudsters need only access to Internet e-mail to solicit victims, thus saving the costs of international mail and phone calls. Unlike newer, more sophisticated phishing e-mail frauds, 419 messages have certain characteristic ploys and a typical writing style. For example, the sender asks for access to your bank account so that he can transfer his money to it as a way to prevent corrupt government officials in his homeland from confiscating it. The sender often promises to reward you financially if you make a minor payment or allow access to your bank account. The messages are usually in uppercase letters and use poor grammar. Another common scam is a sender stating you have won a sweepstake and asking you to send money to claim the prize. You can find samples of 419 scam messages at *www.hoax-slayer.com/nigerian-scam-list.shtml*.

One noteworthy example of a lawsuit involving **spoofing** e-mail occurred in February 2001 in the Superior Court of Massachusetts: *Suni Munshani v. Signal Lake Venture Fund II, LP et al.* Suni Munshani claimed he received an e-mail from the CEO of Signal Lake Venture Fund instructing him to purchase options (financial warrants) for a total of $25 million. Signal Lake Venture Fund investigated its e-mail servers and didn't find the e-mail Munshani claimed he received.

In preparation for the trial, Signal Lake Venture Fund conducted a discovery demand for all of Munshani's e-mail. Because of the sensitive information Munshani had on his e-mail server, the court appointed an impartial discovery firm to examine the e-mail. The discovery firm found that Munshani had used a text editor to alter an e-mail the CEO of Signal Lake Venture Fund had sent. The clue to the e-mail being a fake was the **Enhanced/Extended Simple Mail Transfer Protocol (ESMTP)** number in the message's header, which is unique to each message an e-mail server transmits. The e-mail Munshani claimed was a legitimate message instructing him to purchase options had the same ESMTP value as the other message the CEO sent. This level of examination revealed that Munshani committed fraud. For more information on this case, see *www.signallake.com/email_forensics_library/SMunshaniVsSL.pdf*.

Exploring the Roles of the Client and Server in E-mail

You can send and receive e-mail in two environments: via the Internet or an intranet (an internal network). In both e-mail environments, messages are distributed from a central server to many connected client computers, a configuration called a **client/server architecture**. The server runs an e-mail server program, such as Microsoft Exchange Server, to provide e-mail services. Client computers use e-mail programs (also called e-mail clients), such as Microsoft Outlook, to contact the e-mail server and send and retrieve e-mail messages (see Figure 11-1).

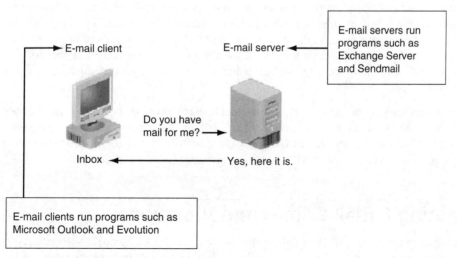

Figure 11-1   E-mail in a client/server architecture
© Cengage Learning®

Regardless of the OS or e-mail program, users access their e-mail based on permissions the e-mail server administrator grants. These permissions prevent users from accessing each other's e-mail. To retrieve messages from the e-mail server, users identify themselves to the server, as when logging on to the network. Then e-mails are delivered to their computers.

E-mail services on both the Internet and an intranet use a client/server architecture, but they differ in how client accounts are assigned, used, and managed and in how users access their e-mail. Overall, an intranet e-mail system is for the private use of network users, and Internet e-mail systems are for public use. On an intranet, the e-mail server is generally part of the local network, and an administrator manages the server and its services. In most cases, an intranet e-mail system is specific to a company, used only by its employees, and regulated by its business practices, which usually include strict security and acceptable use policies. For example, network users can't create their own e-mail accounts, and usernames tend to follow a naming convention that the e-mail administrator determines. For example, for John Smith at Some Company, jsmith is the username, and it's followed by the company's domain name, somecompany.com, to create the e-mail address jsmith@somecompany.com.

 In an e-mail address, everything after the @ symbol represents the domain name. You need to know the domain information when you investigate e-mail to identify the point of contact at a domain, and you need the domain administrator's assistance to collect evidence.

In contrast, a company that provides public e-mail services, such as Google, Hotmail, or Yahoo!, owns the e-mail server and accepts everyone who signs up for the service by providing a username and password. E-mail companies also provide their own servers and administrators. After users sign up, they can access their e-mail from any computer connected to the Internet. In most cases, Internet e-mail users aren't required to follow a standardized naming convention for usernames. They can choose their own usernames (but not the domain name), as long as they aren't already in use.

For digital investigators, tracking intranet e-mail is easier because accounts use standard names the administrator establishes. For example, jane.smith@mycompany.com is easily recognized as the e-mail address for an employee named Jane Smith. Tracking Internet e-mail users is more difficult because these accounts don't always use standard naming schemes, and e-mail administrators aren't familiar with all the user accounts on their servers. Identifying the owner of an e-mail account with an address such as itty_bitty@gmail.com, for example, isn't easy.

With the expansion of cloud service providers, many companies are migrating their e-mail services to the cloud. This setup is convenient because employees can easily access their e-mail from anywhere in the world, but it adds a layer of complexity for investigations, depending on the service level agreement with the cloud provider (covered in Chapter 13).

Investigating E-mail Crimes and Violations

Investigating crimes or policy violations involving e-mail is similar to investigating other types of computer abuse and crimes. Your goal is to find out who's behind the crime or policy violation, collect the evidence, and present your findings to build a case for reprimands, prosecution, or arbitration. Make sure you know the applicable privacy laws for your jurisdiction; for example, in the United States, the **Electronic Communications Privacy Act (ECPA)** and the **Stored Communications Act (SCA)** apply to e-mail.

E-mail crimes and violations depend on the city, state, and country in which the e-mail originated. For example, in Washington State, sending unsolicited e-mail is illegal. However, in other states, it isn't considered a crime. Consult with an attorney for your organization to determine what constitutes an e-mail crime.

Committing crimes with e-mail is common, and more investigators are finding communications that link suspects to a crime or policy violation through e-mail. For example, some people use e-mail when committing crimes such as narcotics trafficking, extortion, sexual harassment, stalking, fraud, child abductions, terrorism, child pornography, and so on. Because e-mail has become a major communication medium, any crime or policy violation can involve e-mail.

Examining E-mail Messages

After you have determined that a crime has been committed involving e-mail, access the victim's computer or mobile device to recover the evidence on it. Using the victim's e-mail client, find and copy any potential evidence. It might be necessary to log on to the e-mail service and access any protected or encrypted files or folders. With a corporate investigation, be sure policies are in place for this action. For a criminal investigation, you need warrants to access or get copies of files on a server. When dealing with a stalker, if you can't actually sit down at the victim's computer, you might have to guide the victim on the phone to open and print a copy of an offending message, including the header. The header contains unique identifying numbers, such as the IP address of the server that sent the message. This information helps you trace the e-mail to the suspect.

TIP Before you work with a victim on the phone, create written procedures for opening and printing an e-mail header and message text with a variety of e-mail programs, according to your state, county, or company's laws or policies. These steps help you give consistent instructions and can be useful when training new investigators.

In some cases, you might have to recover e-mail after a suspect has deleted it and tried to hide it. You see how to recover these messages later in "Using OSForensics to Recover E-mail." For now, you continue working with a victim's computer as a digital investigator.

Copying an E-mail Message Before you start an e-mail investigation, you need to copy and print the e-mail involved in the crime or policy violation. You might also want to forward the message as an attachment to another e-mail address, depending on your organization's guidelines. This section gives procedures for different e-mail programs. You might not have access to all of them, but these procedures can serve as a guideline for when you encounter them in investigations.

The following activity shows you how to use Outlook 2013, included with Microsoft Office, to copy an e-mail message to a USB drive. (*Note*: Depending on the Outlook version you use, the steps might vary slightly.) You use a similar procedure to copy messages in other e-mail programs. If Outlook or Outlook Express is installed on your computer, follow these steps:

1. Insert a USB drive into a USB port.

2. Open File Explorer, navigate to the USB drive, and leave this window open.

3. Start Outlook by going to the Start screen, typing **Outlook**, and pressing **Enter**.

4. In the Mail Folders pane, click the folder containing the message you want to copy. For example, click the **Inbox** folder. A list of messages in that folder is displayed in the pane in the middle. Click the message you want to copy.

5. Resize the Outlook window so that you can see the message you want to copy and the USB drive icon in File Explorer.

6. Drag the message from the Outlook window to the USB drive icon in File Explorer.

7. Click the **File** tab, and then click **Print** to open the Print pane. After printing the e-mail so that you have a copy to include in your final report, exit Outlook.

Instead of dragging, you can click a message in the Inbox, click the File tab, and click Save As. In the Save As dialog box, navigate to where you want to copy the message, making sure you select Outlook Message Format if you want to make a copy. If you select the Text Only format, you get only the message contents. Finally, click the Save button.

With many GUI e-mail programs, you can copy an e-mail by dragging it to a storage medium, such as a folder or drive, or by saving it in a different location. For e-mail programs you run from the command line, however, open the message, and then use the option to copy it, usually located at the bottom of the screen. After you copy an e-mail, work only with the copy, not the original version, to avoid altering the original evidence by mistake.

Viewing E-mail Headers

After you copy and print a message, use the e-mail program that created it to find the e-mail header. This section includes instructions for viewing e-mail headers in a variety of e-mail programs, including Windows GUI clients and some common Web-based e-mail providers. After you open e-mail headers, copy and paste them into a text document so that you can read them with a text editor, such as Windows Notepad, Linux vim, Nano (used with UNIX), or Apple TextEdit. You examine headers in the next section.

Whether you're working in a forensics lab or elsewhere, installing and becoming familiar with as many e-mail programs as possible is beneficial. Often more than one e-mail program is installed on a computer, and you need to find out which one the suspect is using.

Before beginning the next activity, create a *Work*\Chap11\Chapter work folder on your system. Then extract all files from the Chap11 folder on the book's DVD to your work folder. The work folder path shown in screenshots might differ slightly from yours.

To retrieve an Outlook e-mail header, follow these steps:

1. Start Outlook, and then select the message you copied in the previous section.

2. Double-click the message, and then click **File, Properties**. The "Internet headers" text box at the bottom contains the message header, shown in Figure 11-2.

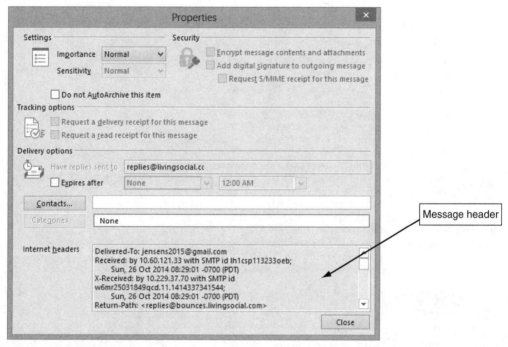

Figure 11-2 An Outlook e-mail header
Courtesy of Microsoft Corporation

3. Select the message header text, and then press **Ctrl+C** to copy it to the Clipboard.

4. Start Notepad, and then press **Ctrl+V** in a new document window to paste the message header text.

5. Save the document as **Outlook Header.txt** in your work folder. Then close the document and exit Outlook.

Some popular Web-based e-mail service providers are Gmail, AOL, Hotmail, and Yahoo!, and you work with a few in the following activities. You can use any computer connected to the Internet to send and receive e-mail, which makes Web-based e-mail messages more difficult to trace. To view AOL Web e-mail headers, follow these steps:

1. Start your Web browser and log on to AOL. On AOL's main page, click the **Options** link, and then click **E-mail Settings**.

2. Click the **Always show full headers** check box, and then click **Save Settings**. Click the **Back to E-mail** button to return to the mail folders.

3. Select an e-mail. In the reading pane, click the **Print Message** button. Exit AOL.

Follow these steps to view e-mail headers in Yahoo!:

1. Log on to your Yahoo! mail account, and click **Inbox** to view a list of messages.

2. Above the message window, click the **More** list arrow, and click **View Full Header** (see Figure 11-3).

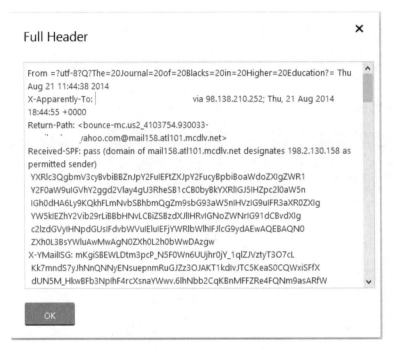

Figure 11-3   Viewing headers in Yahoo!
Source: Yahoo! Inc.

3. In the Full Header window, select all the text, press **Ctrl+C** to copy it, and then click **OK**.

4. Start Notepad, and then press **Ctrl+V** in a new document window to paste the message header text. Save the document as **Yahoo Header.txt** in your work folder. Log off Yahoo!, and exit your Web browser.

The e-mail programs reviewed in this section supply similar information in the message header. The methods for retrieving headers vary, but you can usually find information about displaying message headers in the program's Help files.

Examining E-mail Headers

The next step is examining the e-mail header you saved to gather information about the e-mail and track the suspect to the e-mail's originating location. The main piece of information you're looking for is the originating e-mail's domain address or an IP address. Other helpful information includes the date and time the message was sent, filenames of any attachments, and unique message number, if it's supplied.

For more detailed information on e-mail headers, see *www.stopspam. org/index.php.*

To open and examine an e-mail header, follow these steps:

1. Open File Explorer and navigate to your work folder.

2. Double-click a `.txt` file containing message header text, such as **Outlook Header.txt**. The message header opens in Notepad.

Figure 11-4 shows a message header copied from an Outlook e-mail. (The e-mail addresses are not real addresses.) Line numbers have been added for reference.

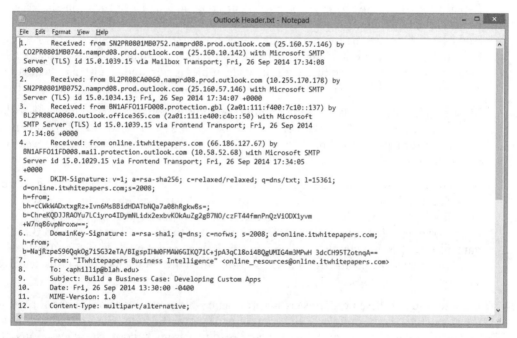

Figure 11-4   An e-mail header with line numbers added
Courtesy of Microsoft Corporation

The e-mail header in Figure 11-4 supplies useful information. Lines 1 through 4 show the servers the message passed through. Lines 3 and 4 include "via Frontend Transport," which is a stateless proxy for inbound traffic on Microsoft Exchange Server. Line 5 shows "DKIM-Signature," which stands for DomainKeys Identified Mail (*www.dkim.org*). It's a way to verify the names of domains a message is flowing through and was developed to help cut down on spam. Line 6 is the verification from DKIM. Lines 7 through 10 are simply the From, To, Subject, and Date fields in the e-mail. Lines 11 and 12 show the MIME-Version and Content-Type information.

If there were an attachment, it would be listed in a later line. An attachment can be any type of file, from a program to a picture. If a message includes an attachment, investigate it as a supporting piece of evidence. If you're working with the victim, the attachment is usually still attached to the e-mail. If you're investigating a suspect's computer, remember to work with the copied version. On a suspect's computer or a forensic image, search for the attached file with a forensics tool or the OS's Search or Find feature to determine whether the file was saved and still exists on the drive. If you're investigating an e-mail attachment with an unfamiliar file extension, such as .mdf, you can search the Internet to find out what program creates a file of this type.

To search for specific files in e-mail headers, use a forensics tool. You can also use a forensics tool to search for unique header information, such as an ID number.

Examining Additional E-mail Files

E-mail programs save messages on the client computer or leave them on the server. How e-mails are stored depends on settings on the client and server. On the client computer, you could save all your e-mail in a separate folder for record-keeping purposes. For example, in Outlook, you can save sent, draft, deleted, and received e-mails in a .pst file, or you can save offline files in an .ost file. With these client files (.pst and .ost), users can access and read their e-mail offline (when their computers aren't connected to the central e-mail server).

Most e-mail programs also include an address book of contacts, and many offer calendars, task lists, and memos. A suspect's address book, calendar, task list, and memos can contain valuable information that links e-mail crimes or abuse to other parties and reveal the suspect's physical address and even involvement in other crimes.

In Web-based e-mail, messages are displayed and saved as Web pages in the browser's cache folders. Many Web-based e-mail providers offer instant messaging (IM) services, such as Yahoo! Messenger and Google Talk, that can save message contents in proprietary and nonproprietary file formats. These files are usually stored in different folders than Internet data files are. For example, in Windows 8.1, you can find IM files and folders under Users*username*\AppData or under Program Files. IM and chat programs usually have their own folder names.

Because some of these programs create proprietary files, you might need special tools to read their contents. For example, Yahoo Message Archive Decoder 4.5 (*http://yahoo-message-archive-decoder.soft112.com*) can open and read files from Yahoo! Messenger. Some IM programs are configured to not save chat content unless users change the default setting, so you might need to search the suspect's Pagefile.sys file to find message fragments. Unlike Yahoo!'s proprietary file format, Windows Messenger stores messages in RTF format that most word processors can read. When you're working on the victim's computer, these files can help you document corroborating evidence for the investigation.

Tracing an E-mail Message

As part of the investigation, you need to determine an e-mail's origin by further examining the header with one of many free Internet tools. Determining message origin is referred to as "tracing." In this section, you learn about some Internet lookup tools that can be used to trace where an e-mail originated.

For example, if a company is listed in an e-mail address, you can visit the company's site to find out who administers the domain. If the point of contact isn't listed on the Web site or the domain doesn't have a Web site, you need to use a registry site, such as those in the following list, to determine the point of contact:

- *www.arin.net*—Use the American Registry for Internet Numbers (ARIN) to map an IP address to a domain name and find the domain's point of contact.

- *www.internic.com*—Like *www.arin.net*, you use this site to find a domain's IP address and point of contact.

- *www.google.com*—Use this search engine and others to look for more information and additional postings on discussion boards.

Using one of these Web sites, you can find the suspect's full e-mail address, such as jim.shu@superiorbicycles.biz, and contact information. Keep in mind that the suspect might have posted false information, so verify your findings by checking network e-mail logs against e-mail addresses, as described in the next section.

Using Network E-mail Logs

Network administrators maintain logs of the inbound and outbound traffic routers handle. Routers have rules to allow or deny traffic based on source or destination IP address. In most cases, a router is set up to track all traffic flowing through its ports. Using these logs, you can determine the path a transmitted e-mail has taken. The network administrator who manages routers can supply the log files you need. Review the router logs to find the victim's (recipient's) e-mail, and look for the unique ID number. Network administrators also maintain logs for firewalls that filter Internet traffic; these logs can help verify whether an e-mail message passed through the firewall. Firewalls maintain log files that track Internet traffic destined for other networks or the network the firewall is protecting. When a network administrator provides firewall log files, you can open them in a text editor, such as Notepad in Windows or vim in Linux. (Some firewalls, however, require special programs to read their log files.) Figure 11-5 shows a typical Windows firewall log.

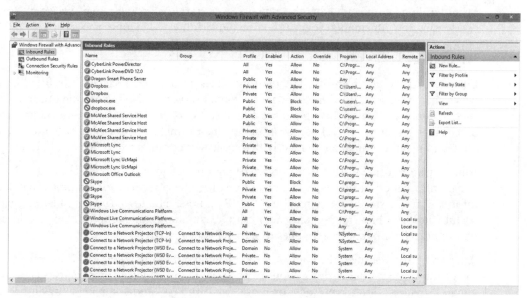

Figure 11-5 A Windows firewall log
Courtesy of Microsoft Corporation

Understanding E-mail Servers

An e-mail server is loaded with software that uses e-mail protocols for its services and maintains logs you can examine and use in your investigation. As a digital forensics investigator, you can't know everything about e-mail servers. Your focus is not to learn how a particular e-mail server works but how to retrieve information about e-mails for an investigation. Usually, you must work closely with the network administrator or e-mail administrator, who is often willing to help you find the data or files you need and might even suggest new ways to find this information. If you can't work with an administrator, conduct research on the Internet or use the forensics tools discussed later in this chapter to investigate the e-mail server software.

To investigate e-mail abuse, you should know how an e-mail server records and handles the e-mail it receives. Some e-mail servers use databases that store users' e-mails, and others use a flat file system. All e-mail servers can maintain a log of e-mails that are processed. Some e-mail servers are set up to log e-mail transactions by default; others must be configured to do so. Most e-mail administrators log system operations and message traffic for the following reasons:

- Recover e-mails in case of a disaster.
- Make sure the firewall and e-mail filters are working correctly.
- Enforce company policy.

However, the e-mail administrator can disable logging or use circular logging (also called "log rotation"), which overwrites the log file when it reaches a specified size or at the end of a specified time frame. It's similar to the standard backup rotations used for file servers. Circular logging saves valuable server space, but you can't recover a log after it's overwritten. For example, on Monday the e-mail server records traffic in the Mon.log file. For the next six days, the e-mail server uses a log for each day, such as Tues.log, Wed.log, and so forth. On Sunday at midnight, the e-mail server starts recording e-mail traffic in Mon.log, overwriting the information logged the previous Monday. The only way to access the log file information is from a backup file, which many e-mail administrators create before a log file is overwritten.

E-mail logs generally identify the e-mail messages an account received, the IP address from which they were sent, the time and date the e-mail server received them, the time and date the client computer accessed the e-mail, the e-mail contents, system-specific information, and any other information the e-mail administrator wants to track. These e-mail logs are usually formatted in plain text and can be read with a basic text editor, such as Notepad or vim.

Administrators usually set e-mail servers to continuous logging mode. They can also log all e-mail information in the same file, or use one log file to record, for example, date and time information, the size of the e-mail, and the IP address. These separate log files are extremely useful when you have an e-mail header with a date and time stamp and an IP address, and you want to filter or sort the log files to narrow your search.

After you have identified the source of the e-mail, contact the network or e-mail administrator of the suspect's network as soon as possible. Some e-mail providers, especially Internet e-mail providers, don't keep logs for more than 30 days (and some keep logs for less time), and their logs might contain key information for your investigation.

In addition to logging e-mail traffic, e-mail servers maintain copies of clients' e-mail, even if the users have deleted messages from their inboxes. Some e-mail servers don't completely delete messages until the system is backed up. Sometimes the e-mail administrator can recover deleted e-mail without restoring the entire e-mail server, but some e-mail servers require recovering the entire server to retrieve one deleted message.

This process is similar to deleting files on a hard drive; the file is marked for deletion, but it's not truly unrecoverable until another piece of data is written in the same place. E-mail servers wait to overwrite disk space until the server has been backed up. If you have a date and time stamp for an e-mail, the e-mail administrator should be able to recover it from backup media if the message is no longer on the e-mail server.

Examining UNIX E-mail Server Logs

More than a dozen UNIX e-mail server programs are available. Most produce log files similar to the ones discussed previously. Postfix and Sendmail are two common UNIX e-mail servers. Sendmail is the default for FreeBSD systems, such as CentOS.

Log files and configuration files can provide helpful information. The configuration file for Sendmail is /etc/mail/sendmail.cf, which can help you determine where log files are stored. Sendmail refers to the sendmail.cf file to find out what to do with an e-mail after it's received. For example, if the server receives an e-mail from an unsolicited site, a line in the sendmail.cf file can tell the Sendmail server to discard it.

Similar to the sendmail.cf file, the /etc/syslog.conf file includes e-mail logging instructions so that you can determine how Sendmail is set up to log e-mail events and which events are logged. The syslog.conf file's configuration in the /etc directory contains three pieces of information that tell you what happened to an e-mail when it was logged: the event, the priority level of concern, and the action taken when it was logged. By default, Sendmail can display an event message, log the event message to a log file, or send an event message to a remote log host. E-mail files are typically found at /var/mail.

Postfix is another common UNIX e-mail server. Similar to Sendmail, it has configuration files, master.cf and main.cf, in the /etc/postfix directory, and e-mails are stored in /var/spool/postfix.

Because a UNIX system has a variety of e-mail servers available, the syslog.conf file simply specifies where to save different types of e-mail log files. The first log file it configures is /var/log/maillog, which usually contains a record of **Simple Mail Transfer Protocol (SMTP)** communication between servers.

The IP address (10.0.1.1) and the timestamp in the maillog file are important information in an e-mail investigation. You can compare this information with the header of the e-mail the victim received to confirm the sender. The maillog file also contains information about **Post Office Protocol version 3 (POP3)** and **Internet Message Access Protocol 4 (IMAP4)** events. This information includes an IP address and a timestamp that you can compare with the e-mail the victim received.

Typically, UNIX systems are set to store log files in the /var/log directory. However, an administrator can change the log location, especially when an e-mail service specifies a different location. If you're examining a UNIX computer and don't find the e-mail logs in /var/log, you can use the `find` or `locate` command to find them. For example, type `locate .log` at a UNIX command prompt.

Recall that the forward slash (/) is used in UNIX/Linux file paths, and the backslash (\) is used in Windows file paths.

If you need more assistance to find where a file is created by default, you can use the UNIX man pages for the e-mail service running on the computer. A new directory—/home/ *username*/mail—is created on the client computer when a user logs on for the first time and runs the e-mail program. If the server has been configured to deliver e-mail to client machines but not store copies of e-mails on the server, the only copy of the e-mail is on the client computer in the user's mail folder.

If the UNIX e-mail server is set to store all messages on the server, you can access them by requesting that the UNIX administrator create e-mail groups and add you to the same group as the suspect. UNIX e-mail servers don't usually use groups to prevent users from accidentally viewing e-mail that doesn't belong to them. However, e-mail groups can be useful for investigative purposes, as long as you have secured a warrant.

Examining Microsoft E-mail Server Logs

Exchange Server, generally called Exchange, is the Microsoft e-mail server software. Exchange uses an Exchange database and is based on the Microsoft Extensible Storage Engine (ESE), which uses several files in different combinations to provide e-mail service. The files most useful to an investigation are `.edb` database files, checkpoint files, and temporary files.

In older versions of Exchange, `.edb` files were the database files you needed. An `.edb` file is responsible for messages formatted with **Messaging Application Programming Interface (MAPI)**, a Microsoft system that enables different e-mail applications to work together. As a database server, Exchange logs information about changes to its data, also called transactions, in a transaction log. To prevent loss of data from the most recent backup, a checkpoint file, or marker, is inserted in the transaction log to mark the last point at which the database was written to disk. With these files, e-mail administrators can recover lost or deleted messages in the event of a disaster, such as a power failure. Exchange also creates `.tmp` (temporary) files to prevent loss when it's busy converting binary data to readable text.

Like UNIX e-mail servers, Exchange maintains logs to track e-mails. To retrieve them, you can use the Windows PowerShell cmdlet `GetTransactionLogStats.ps1 -Gather` (*http://blogs.technet.com/b/exchange/archive/2013/10/07/analyzing-exchange-transaction-log-generation-statistics.aspx*).

Exchange servers can also maintain a log called `Tracking.log` that tracks messages. If the Message Tracking feature has been enabled and the e-mail administrator selects verbose (detailed) logging, you can see the timestamp, IP address of the sending computer, and the e-mail's contents or body. Except for special forensics tools, the message-tracking log in verbose mode provides the most information about messages sent and received in Exchange.

Another log used for troubleshooting and investigating the Exchange environment is the troubleshooting log. You can read this log, also known as a "diagnostic log," by using Windows

Event Viewer, shown in Figure 11-6, which is available in Administrative Tools. Each event logged has an ID number and a severity level.

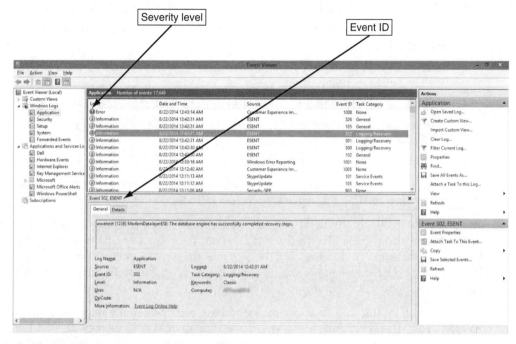

Figure 11-6   Viewing a log in Event Viewer
Courtesy of Microsoft Corporation

To examine the details of an e-mail event, double-click the event to open its Event Properties dialog box. This dialog box shows date and time information that might be useful if, for example, you suspect the e-mail server has been tampered with to alter its contents.

Using Specialized E-mail Forensics Tools

For many e-mail investigations, you can rely on e-mail message files, e-mail headers, and e-mail server log files. However, if you can't find an e-mail administrator willing to help with the investigation, or you encounter a highly customized e-mail environment, you can use data recovery tools and forensics tools designed to recover e-mail files.

As technology has progressed in e-mail and other services, so have the tools for recovering information lost or deleted from a hard drive. In previous chapters, you have reviewed many tools for data recovery, such as ProDiscover Basic and OSForensics. You can also use these tools to investigate and recover e-mail files. Other tools, such as the ones in the following list, are specifically created for e-mail recovery, including recovering deleted attachments from a hard drive:

- DataNumen for Outlook and Outlook Express (*www.datanumen.com/products.htm*)
- FINALeMAIL for Outlook Express and Eudora (*http://finalemail-1-2.en.softonic.com*)

- Sawmill-Novell GroupWise for log analysis (*www.sawmill.net/formats/groupwise_post_office_agent.html*)

- DBXtract for Outlook Express (*www.oehelp.com/DBXtract/Default.aspx*)

- Fookes Aid4Mail and MailBag Assistant for Outlook, Thunderbird, and Eudora (*www.fookes.com*)

- Paraben E-Mail Examiner, configured to recover several e-mail formats (*www.paraben.com/email-examiner.html*)

- AccessData FTK for Outlook and Outlook Express (*www.accessdata.com*)

- Ontrack EasyRecovery EmailRepair for Outlook and Outlook Express (*www.ontrackdatarecovery.ie/email-repair-recovery/*)

- R-Tools R-Mail for Outlook and Outlook Express (*www.outlook-mail-recovery.com*)

- OfficeRecovery's MailRecovery for Outlook, Outlook Express, Exchange, Exchange Server, and IBM Notes (*www.officerecovery.com*)

When you use a third-party tool to search for a `.db` file, for example, you can find where the administrator stores these files for the e-mail server; they could be on the server or in a remote location for backup. To find log files, use `.log` as the search criteria. You're likely to find at least two logs related to e-mail—one listing logged events for messages and the other listing logged events for accounts accessing e-mail.

Forensics tools enable you to find e-mail database files, personal e-mail files, offline storage files, and log files. With some tools, you use a special viewer to see messages and other files; others require using a text editor to compare information, such as the timestamp, username, domain, and message contents, to determine whether it matches what was found on the victim's computer.

One advantage of using data recovery tools is that you don't need to know how the e-mail server or e-mail client operates to extract data from these computers. Data recovery tools do the work for you and allow you to view evidence on the computer. However, if you're serving as an expert witness, you do need to understand the e-mail system's functions and be able to explain them to laypeople.

After you compare e-mail logs with the messages, you should verify the e-mail account, message ID, IP address, and date and time stamp to determine whether there's enough evidence for a warrant. If so, you can obtain and serve your warrant for the suspect's computer equipment. Remember to follow the evidence-handling rules and control measures your organization uses, as described in previous chapters.

When requesting a search warrant, consider whether you're looking for evidence of more than one crime. If you intend to investigate different crimes, make sure to include probable cause for each crime so that you need only a single warrant covering all areas of interest. Your investigation might require a second warrant, however. For example, if you're investigating a drive for evidence of harassment and you come across e-mail suggesting that the suspect is also selling controlled substances over the Internet, you need a second warrant to investigate this crime.

After collecting evidence, you begin copying it to another source for the examination while documenting everything you're doing. If you create an image, document the procedure and tool you use. If you're just collecting a specific folder, such as the `.evolution` directory, document the command you use to copy data. With some tools, you can scan e-mail database files on a suspect's Windows computer, locate any e-mails the suspect has deleted—these messages don't have data location information—and restore them to their original state. You can also search a computer for other files associated with e-mail, such as databases, and see whether any attachments were sent with an e-mail and view them.

Using OSForensics to Recover E-mail

OSForensics isn't task or file specific, as other tools are. However, it indexes data on a disk image or an entire drive for faster data retrieval. It can also filter or find files specific to e-mail clients and servers. You can configure these filters when you enter search parameters. In this activity, you learn how to use OSForensics to recover e-mails:

1. Start OSForensics and start a new case. In the New Case dialog box, enter your name. For the case name, type **InChap11**. Fill in the contact details and the organization, and then click **OK**. Create a subfolder of your work folder called **Chap11**, and then create a subfolder called **Terry**.

2. Click the **Add Device** button. Navigate to the folder where you stored the M57 case files, click the hard drive file **terry-2009-12-11-002.e01**, and click **OK**.

3. Click the **Create Index** button in the left pane to start the Create Index Wizard. In the Step 1 of 5 window, click the **Use Pre-defined File Types** option button, if necessary. Click the **Emails** and **Attachments** check boxes, and then click **Next**. In the Step 2 of 5 window, click the **Add** button. In the Add Start Location dialog box, click the **Whole Drive** option button, if necessary. Click the list arrow, click **terry-2009-12-11-002.e01**, and then click **OK**. Click **Next**. In the Step 3 of 5 window, click **Start Indexing**. When the indexing has finished, click **OK** in the message box informing you that errors reading some files might have occurred in the indexing process, if necessary.

4. Click **Search Index** in the left pane. In the Enter Search Words text box, type **money**, and then click **Search**.

5. Click the **Emails** tab, if necessary. The search should have returned 10 e-mails. Right-click the first e-mail with the subject line "Computer Equipment" and click **Open**.

6. To see more details, click **View, Headers** from the menu. Figure 11-7 shows the results.

7. When you're finished examining the e-mail, close the Email Viewer window, and exit OSForensics.

11

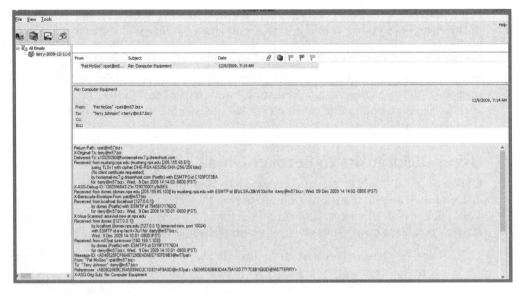

Figure 11-7 Viewing e-mail headers in OSForensics
Source: PassMark Software, *www.osforensics.com*

Using a Hex Editor to Carve E-mail Messages

Few vendors have products for analyzing e-mail in systems other than Microsoft, such as Apple Mail or Evolution. In this section, you learn about a method for acquiring Evolution e-mail directories and extracting messages with Hex Workshop. These techniques can be used with all e-mail systems that create flat plaintext files, known as an **mbox** format, to store messages. Vendor-unique e-mail file systems, such as Microsoft .pst or .ost, typically use **Multipurpose Internet Mail Extensions (MIME)** formatting, which can be difficult to read with a text or hexadecimal editor.

To carve e-mail messages from Evolution, you need to copy the .evolution directory, its subdirectories, and content to another storage medium that can be transported to your forensic workstation. One way is to export this directory and subdirectories from an image file to a target drive path you designate by using a forensics tool. For an e-mail recovery that requires extracting only e-mail data from a computer, the Linux tar command is easy to use. You can create a tarball of the entire .evolution directory and uncompress it so that a hexadecimal editor on any OS can read it.

For this case, you're acquiring the .evolution directory from Martha Dax's Linux computer to see whether you can find the same e-mail you found in the Jim_shu's.pst file. Then you compare the message headers of the two e-mails to detect any differences and perhaps discover e-mail addresses other than Terry Sadler's and Martha Dax's. To make a tarball of the .evolution directory, you would follow these steps:

Because you don't have an .evolution directory on your system, just read through these steps as an example of extracting this file to a USB drive. In the next activity, you use a data file from the book's DVD.

1. Start Linux and open a terminal window. Type **su** and press **Enter,** and then type your password and press **Enter.**

2. Connect a USB drive to your computer and mount it, if it's not mounted automatically.

3. Navigate to the user's home directory. For example, type **cd /home/martha** and press **Enter.**

4. To determine whether the .evolution directory is in this location, type **ls -a** and press **Enter.** Examine the output. If you don't see an .evolution directory in the home directory, type **ls -aR** to list all subdirectories. When you have located the .evolution directory, use the **cd** command to navigate to the parent directory so that you can copy the .evolution directory and its subdirectories.

5. Type **tar cf martha-evolution.tar .evolution** and press **Enter.**

6. Using File Manager or another GUI utility, copy **martha-evolution.tar** to a USB drive.

7. Type **exit** and press **Enter,** and then log out of your Linux computer.

All mbox-formatted messages start with the word "From" followed by a space (the character 0x20). To carve e-mail messages from martha-evolution.tar (which you copied from the DVD to your work folder), follow these steps:

1. Start WinHex. Click **File, Open** from the menu, navigate to your work folder, click **martha-evolution.tar,** and then click **Open.** Click **View, Text Display Only** from the menu, and then click **View,** point to **Character Set,** and click **ANSI ASCII.**

2. To locate the e-mail from Terry Sadler, click **Search, Find Text** from the menu.

3. In the Find Text dialog box, type **terrysadler** in the "The following text string will be searched" text box, make sure **ASCII/Code page** is selected in the drop-down list, and then click **OK.** If necessary, click **OK** in the "Search complete" message box.

4. Place the cursor in front of the letter "F" in the word "From" (see the third line in Figure 11-8). Notice the offset byte count 000710EF at the bottom.

Figure 11-8 WinHex displaying the beginning of the e-mail from Terry Sadler
Courtesy of X-Ways AG, *www.x-ways.net*

5. Click at offset **000710EF** in the middle pane and drag down until you reach the end of the e-mail, as shown in Figure 11-9. (*Note*: Your screen might look a little different.)

Figure 11-9   WinHex displaying the ending position of the e-mail from Terry Sadler
Courtesy of X-Ways AG, *www.x-ways.net*

6. Right-click the highlighted text and click **Edit**, point to **Copy Block**, and click **Into New File**.

7. In the Save File As dialog box that opens, save the file as **Martha-evolution.txt** in your work folder, and exit Hex Workshop.

8. Start Notepad and open the **Martha-evolution.txt** file (see Figure 11-10) so that you can refer to it in the next few paragraphs, and then exit Notepad when you've finished reading this section.

The ending position of this message is at offset 000720F1. With mbox-formatted files, typically you find the end of the message at the next "From_" occurrence. Because this message is the last in the inbox, it terminates with "0A, 0A, 0A."

After carving an e-mail message from a tarball .evolution file, you have a plaintext file with no line breaks. The text pasted into Notepad wraps, making it difficult to find reference points. To make this file's header and content readable, you need to enter line breaks at logical places, which can be tedious. The effort pays off, however, because you can find information of interest to your investigation more easily.

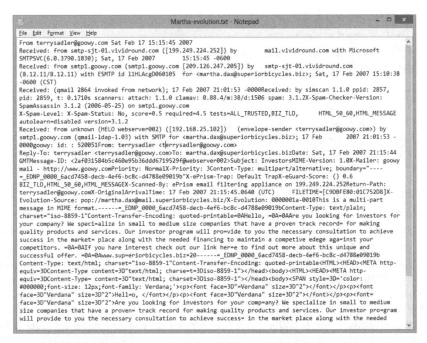

Figure 11-10   The Terry Sadler e-mail in Notepad
Courtesy of Microsoft Corporation

For example, you might notice that the only addresses visible are terrysadler@goowy.com and martha.dax@superiorbicycles.biz. The next step is to see whether you can find Jim Shu's e-mail. His e-mail address hasn't been listed in the results so far. By comparing these two messages from the Jim_shu's.pst file and Martha Dax's .evolution inbox, you determine that Terry Sadler blind-copied (bcc) Jim Shu. This information might be of interest to Martha Dax because it shows that Jim Shu and Terry Sadler have a relationship involving a business proposal. By further examining Jim Shu's e-mail and other Superior Bicycles employees' e-mail, you might be able to learn what the relationship is and whether it should be of concern to Martha Dax and Superior Bicycles.

Recovering Outlook Files

As a forensics examiner recovering e-mail messages from Outlook, you might need to reconstruct .pst files and messages. With many advanced forensics tools, such as OSForensics, X-Ways Forensics, AccessData FTK, and Guidance Software EnCase, deleted .pst files can be partially or completely recovered. Typically, additional effort is required to reconstruct these recovered files so that their content can be extracted as part of a data recovery or forensics examination.

The scanpst.exe recovery tool comes with Microsoft Office and can repair .ost files as well as .pst files. You run this tool from File Explorer or a command prompt and use it with any data that looks like a .pst or an .ost file. It processes the data and rebuilds it into a .pst file that can be accessed with Outlook or other tools discussed in this chapter.

For more information on scanpst.exe, see *http://office.microsoft.com/ en-001/outlook-help/repair-outlook-data-files-pst-and-ost-HA010075831. aspx, www.outlook-tips.net/beginner/scanpst.htm*, and *www.slipstick. com/outlook/config/recover-deleted-messages-pst-files/*.

Guidance Software uses the SysTools plug-in (*http://encase-forensic-blog.guidancesoftware. com/2014/04/systools-outlook-exporter-for-encase-no.html*) for Outlook e-mail through version 2013. SysTools extracts .pst files from EnCase Forensic for analysis. An advantage of this plug-in is that you don't have to install Outlook to examine Outlook e-mails.

Other recovery tools are designed to reconstruct e-mail data in Outlook and other e-mail formats. One tool that has been well tested is DataNumen Outlook Repair (*www.datanumen. com/outlook-repair*); it's one of the better e-mail recovery tools on the market. It can recover files from VMware and Virtual PC as well as ISO images and other types of file backups. You install and use it later in the hands-on projects.

E-mail Case Studies

Throughout this book, you have been using the M57 case, and in the hands-on projects, you work with some .pst files in this case. Another major case involving corporate e-mail is the Enron case, which required retrieving thousands of e-mails at a time when few policies for collecting this information existed. When the Electronic Discovery Reference Model (EDRM; *www.edrm.net*) group acquired the right to store and distribute these e-mails, it discovered how much personally identifiable information they contained. Another company worked with the EDRM to correct the problem by removing the personal information. In the end, more than 10,000 e-mails were collected (*http://info.nuix.com/Enron.html*). The following list gives you an idea of how much personal information these e-mails contained:

- 60 containing credit card numbers
- 572 containing thousands of Social Security or other identity numbers
- 292 containing birth dates
- 532 containing information of a highly personal nature, such as medical or legal matters

As a regular part of doing business, employees sent internal e-mails with spreadsheet attachments containing personal information about employees and customers. Now spreadsheets are typically password-protected or encrypted, but these documents weren't. In the hands-on projects, you download some .pst files of Enron employees and examine them with tools discussed in this chapter to get an idea of what kind of information can be found in corporate e-mails.

Applying Digital Forensics to Social Media

Social media sites, such as Twitter, Facebook, LinkedIn, and YouTube, aren't just a way of communicating with friends and family. These **online social networks** (OSNs) are also used to conduct business, brag about criminal activities, raise money, and have class discussions. You can also use OSNs to build a profile of a prospective client, a business partner, a suspect in a murder trial, and more.

Social media can contain a lot of information, including the following:

- Evidence of cyberbullying and witness tampering
- A company's position on an issue

- Whether intellectual property rights have been violated
- Who posted information and when

The number of cases involving social media is growing, and social media evidence often substantiates a party's claims. For example, in an intellectual property case, evidence gathered from the public side of an employee's LinkedIn profile showed that she had copied thousands of records from her company laptop to a USB drive and started working at a competing company before quitting her job ("Elephant in the Room: Case Studies of Social Media in Civil and Criminal Cases," Mark Lanterman, *http://blog.x1discovery.com/2014/06/10/elephant-in-the-room-case-studies-of-social-media-in-civil-and-criminal-cases/*, June 2014). In his article on social media forensics (*http://mashable.com/2012/02/13/social-media-forensics/*), Todd Piett noted that 88% of the law enforcement groups surveyed use social media as a tool for doing background checks, corroborating data, verifying alibis, and finding suspects and witnesses. For example, in one case, a 19-year-old was accused of a crime, but police were able to use his Facebook posts as proof he was somewhere else when the crime occurred (*http://edition.cnn.com/2009/CRIME/11/12/facebook.alibi/index.html*, 2009).

In another case, police were able to arrest a gang member because one of his friends boasted about a murder on his MySpace page ("Police embrace social media as crime-fighting tool," *www.cnn.com/2012/08/30/tech/social-media/fighting-crime-social-media/*, 2012).

Digital investigators can mine social media sites to find information, too. The challenge is that even though much of YouTube and Facebook content is public, the data is spread over many servers, providers, and users. Facebook alone surpassed 1.23 billion users in 2014. The amount of data on social media sites is staggering: 250 million pictures and 200 million tweets a day, for example. There's so much information that analyzing it requires techniques referred to as "big data analytics," which is the study of dissimilar types of data in huge quantities. Investigators might have to sift through videos, pictures, GPS locations, text messages, e-mails, tweets, and posts in just one case, and trying to analyze so many types of data has an effect on what approach is used.

In addition, OSNs involve multiple jurisdictions that might even cross national boundaries, and social media vendors prohibit access to their servers. As an investigator, you're not allowed to physically touch or retrieve information from these machines. A warrant or subpoena is needed to get the information, and then vendors have to supply the information for you. In cases involving imminent danger, law enforcement can file for emergency requests, however. Facebook, MySpace, and other OSNs usually have legal staff who evaluate these requests. Twitter vehemently opposes government requests and cites the U.S. Fourth Amendment to refuse all requests. Facebook, however, has begun accommodating international requests.

Facebook has two types of profiles: basic subscriber info and extended subscriber info (called Neoprint). Basic subscriber info simply tells you the last time a person logged on, his or her e-mail address and associated mobile number, and whether the account can be viewed publicly. The Neoprint profile includes friends, groups, video feeds, and undeleted photos ("U.S. Law Enforcement obtaining warrants to search Facebook Profiles," *www.foxnews.com/tech/2011/07/12/us-law-enforcement-obtain-warrants-to-search-facebook-profiles/*, 2011). Typically, this profile is given to law enforcement only with a warrant.

11

Stroz-Freidburg, an established company specializing in e-discovery, digital forensics, and fraud accounting, has created procedures on how to approach social media forensics (*www.strozfriedberg.com/ category/services/forensics-investigations-services/digital-forensics/ social-networking-forensics*), such as collecting and validating social media content, determining what data should be collected, and maintaining the chain of custody with evidence that's variable in nature.

Many types of cases involve social media. For example, a company selling illegal knock-offs might use social media to sell its merchandise. As an investigator, you need a big-picture perspective to determine what evidence might apply to a case and where to look for information. With the advent of social media and the cloud, locations to examine for evidence are no longer limited to physical devices, such as cell phones and laptops.

Forensics Tools for Social Media Investigations

Software for social media forensics is being developed, but not many tools are available now. In addition, there are many questions about how the information these tools gather can be used in court or in arbitration. Investigators often run into the problem of finding information unrelated to a case, and sometimes it requires stopping to get another warrant or subpoena, such as investigating a claim of fraud and finding evidence of corporate espionage. Using social media forensics software might also require getting the permission of the people whose information is being examined.

Many OSN tools use customized Web crawlers to find data, but they take too long to find information to make them efficient. A few helpful software packages are available now, however. The Afentis Forensics group (*http://afentis.com/expert-witness/forensic-software/*) has several tools, including Facebook Forensics, YouTube Forensics, Twitter Forensics, and LinkedIn Forensics. With Facebook Forensics, for example, you can download a person's complete profile. Another tool, X1 Social Discovery (*www.x1.com/products/x1_social_discovery/*), can be used in two modes in Facebook: a credentialed user account (which requires the username and password of the person under investigation) and a public account (created to examine the publicly accessible posts of people or groups). X1 also has tools for Twitter and YouTube. In addition, researchers created an open-source tool to target Facebook accounts (Huber, Mulazzani, et al, "Social Snapshots: Digital Forensics for Online Social Networks," ACSAC '11, Proceedings of the 27th Annual Computer Security Applications Conference, December 2011). This tool was used with Facebook users' permission to take snapshots of posted information; it's not currently available for distribution.

Chapter Summary

- E-mail fraudsters use phishing, pharming, and spoofing scam techniques. Phishing e-mails typically lure users to sites or ask for sensitive information. Pharming e-mails redirect users to Web sites that look like legitimate businesses or official government Web sites and solicit personal identity information from victims.

- In both Internet and intranet e-mail environments, e-mail messages are distributed from one central server to connected client computers, a configuration called a client/server architecture. The server uses server e-mail software to provide e-mail services. Client computers use e-mail programs (also called e-mail clients) to contact the e-mail server and send and retrieve e-mails.

- Investigating crimes or policy violations involving e-mail is similar to investigating other types of computer abuse and crimes. Your goal is to find out who's behind the crime, collect the evidence, and build a case.

- After determining that a crime has been committed involving e-mail, access the victim's computer, if possible, and then use the installed e-mail program to find the e-mail the victim received. Next, copy and print the e-mail. You might also want to forward the message to another e-mail address, depending on your organization's guidelines.

- The next step is using the e-mail program that created the message to find the e-mail header, which provides supporting evidence and can help you track the suspect to the e-mail's originating location by finding the domain or IP address. Also helpful are the date and time the message was sent, the filenames of any attachments, and the unique ID number, if it's supplied. When you find the originating e-mail address, you can track the message to a suspect by doing reverse lookups.

- To investigate e-mail abuse, you should know how an e-mail server records and handles e-mail. Some e-mail servers use databases that store users' e-mails; others use a flat file system. E-mail servers also maintain a log (by default or through configuration settings) of all e-mails that are processed.

- For many e-mail investigations, you can rely on e-mail message files, e-mail headers, and e-mail server log files. However, if the e-mail administrator isn't willing to turn over records and files, or you encounter a highly customized e-mail environment, you can use data recovery tools and forensics tools designed to recover e-mail files.

- For other e-mail applications that use the mbox format, a hexadecimal editor can be used to carve messages manually. This technique requires perseverance because it's tedious and time consuming.

- Social media, or online social networks (OSNs), can provide evidence in criminal and civil cases, so software for collecting OSN information is being developed. Because of the variety and amount of data involved in OSN investigations, techniques of big data analytics are usually needed.

- Social media forensics tools are still very new. They're designed to access Facebook, Twitter, and other OSN user accounts and examine pictures, postings, videos, friend lists, and so forth. These tools can be used to find out which people users have been in touch with, when, and how often.

Key Terms

client/server architecture A network architecture in which each computer or process on the network is a client or server. Clients request services from a server, and a server processes requests from clients.

Electronic Communications Privacy Act (ECPA) A law enacted in 1986 to extend the Wiretap Act to cover e-mail and other data transmitted via the Internet.

Enhanced/Extended Simple Mail Transfer Protocol (ESMTP) An enhancement of SMTP for sending and receiving e-mail messages. ESMTP generates a unique, nonrepeatable number that's added to a transmitted e-mail. No two messages transmitted from an e-mail server have the same ESMTP value. *See also* Simple Mail Transfer Protocol (SMTP).

Internet Message Access Protocol 4 (IMAP4) A protocol for retrieving e-mail messages; it's slowly replacing POP3. *See also* Post Office Protocol 3 (POP3).

mbox A method of storing e-mail messages in a flat plaintext file.

Messaging Application Programming Interface (MAPI) The Microsoft system that enables other e-mail applications to work with each other.

Multipurpose Internet Mail Extensions (MIME) A specification for formatting non-ASCII messages, such as graphics, audio, and video, for transmission over the Internet.

online social networks (OSNs) A term researchers use for social media.

pharming A type of e-mail scam that uses DNS poisoning to redirect readers to a fake Web site.

phishing A type of e-mail scam that's typically sent as spam soliciting personal identity information that fraudsters can use for identity theft.

Post Office Protocol version 3 (POP3) A protocol for retrieving e-mail messages from an e-mail server.

Simple Mail Transfer Protocol (SMTP) A protocol for sending e-mail messages between servers.

spoofing Transmitting an e-mail message with its header information altered so that its point of origin appears to be from a different sender; typically used in phishing and spamming to hide the sender's identity. *See also* phishing.

Stored Communications Act (SCA) Part of the Electronic Communications Privacy Act that extends to the privacy of stored communications, such as e-mail.

Review Questions

1. E-mail headers contain which of the following information? (Choose all that apply.)
   a. The sender and receiver e-mail addresses
   b. An ESMTP number or reference number
   c. The e-mail servers the message traveled through to reach its destination
   d. The IP address of the receiving server
   e. All of the above

2. What's the main piece of information you look for in an e-mail message you're investigating?
   a. Sender or receiver's e-mail address
   b. Originating e-mail domain or IP address
   c. Subject line content
   d. Message number

3. In Microsoft Outlook, what are the e-mail storage files typically found on a client computer?

   a. `.pst` and `.ost`

   b. `res1.log` and `res2.log`

   c. `PU020102.db`

   d. `.evolution`

4. When searching a victim's computer for a crime committed with a specific e-mail, which of the following provides information for determining the e-mail's originator? (Choose all that apply.)

   a. E-mail header

   b. Username and password

   c. Firewall log

   d. All of the above

5. Phishing does which of the following?

   a. Uses DNS poisoning

   b. Lures users with false promises

   c. Takes people to fake Web sites

   d. Uses DHCP

6. Which of the following is a current formatting standard for e-mail?

   a. SMTP

   b. MIME

   c. Outlook

   d. HTML

7. All e-mail headers contain the same types of information. True or False?

8. When you access your e-mail, what type of computer architecture are you using?

   a. Mainframe and minicomputers

   b. Domain

   c. Client/server

   d. None of the above

9. To trace an IP address in an e-mail header, what type of lookup service can you use? (Choose all that apply.)

   a. Intelius Inc.'s AnyWho online directory

   b. Verizon's *http://superpages.com*

   c. A domain lookup service, such as *www.arin.net*, *www.internic.com*, or *www.whois.net*

   d. Any Web search engine

10. Router logs can be used to verify what types of e-mail data?

    a. Message content

    b. Content of attached files

    c. Tracking flows through e-mail server ports

    d. Finding blind copies

11. Logging options on many e-mail servers can be:

    a. Disabled by the administrator

    b. Set up in a circular logging configuration

    c. Configured to a specified size before being overwritten

    d. All of the above

12. On a UNIX-like system, which file specifies where to save different types of e-mail log files?

    a. `maillog`

    b. `/var/spool/log`

    c. `syslog.conf`

    d. `log`

13. What information is *not* in an e-mail header? (Choose all that apply.)

    a. Blind copy (bcc) addresses

    b. Internet addresses

    c. Domain name

    d. Contents of the message

    e. Type of e-mail server used to send the e-mail

14. Which of the following types of files can provide useful information when you're examining an e-mail server?

    a. `.dbf` files

    b. `.emx` files

    c. `.log` files

    d. `.slf` files

15. Internet e-mail accessed with a Web browser leaves files in temporary folders. True or False?

16. When confronted with an e-mail server that no longer contains a log with the date information you need for your investigation, and the client has deleted the e-mail, what should you do?

    a. Search available log files for any forwarded messages.

    b. Restore the e-mail server from a backup.

    c. Check the current database files for an existing copy of the e-mail.

    d. Do nothing because after the file has been deleted, it can no longer be recovered.

17. You can view e-mail headers in Notepad with all popular e-mail clients. True or False?

18. To analyze e-mail evidence, an investigator must be knowledgeable about an e-mail server's internal operations. True or False?

19. Sendmail uses which file for instructions on processing an e-mail message?
    a. `sendmail.cf`
    b. `syslogd.conf`
    c. `mese.ese`
    d. `mapi.log`

20. The term "via Frontend Transport" in a header indicates that the e-mail is on which of the following?
    a. UNIX server
    b. Older NetWare server
    c. Microsoft Exchange Server
    d. Mac server

Hands-On Projects

Create a *Work*\Chap11\Projects folder on your system for this chapter's projects. The only data files you need for these projects are from the Enron and M57 cases.

If your instructor hasn't already done so, go to *http://info.nuix.com/Enron.html* to register for the Enron data set and get information on downloading the cleansed Enron e-mail.

Hands-On Project 11-1

For this project, you use Aid4Mail to examine an Enron employee's e-mail.

1. First, create a subfolder of your work folder called **HandsOn11-1**. Then start your Web browser, and go to **www.aid4mail.com/downloads**. Download and install Aid4Mail.

2. Next, go to **http://enrondata.org/assets/edo_enron-custodians-data.html** to see a list of Enron employees and what position they held in the company. Find Eric Saibi and read his description. He was a trader for Enron, which gives you some clues for search keywords.

3. Go to the link you received for cleansed Enron e-mail. There are two options: downloading the complete Enron EDRM data set of 16.8 GB or selecting one of the 130 files listed. To save time, right-click and download **File 31** (or copy **eric_saibi.zip** to your work folder). Uncompress the file.

4. Start Aid4Mail. Click **Next** in the Welcome window. Click **Office Outlook PST file**, and then click **Next**.

5. Navigate to and click the Eric Saibi PST file, and then click **Next**. In the Source MAPI Folders window, click **Next**.

6. In the Filter Options window, you can select a range of dates and words to search for. For now, leave the default settings, and click **Next**.

7. In the Target Format window, scroll to the bottom and examine the export options shown in Figure 11-11. You can export metadata in CSV or XML format, for example. Click **Convert emails to CSV**, and then click **Next**.

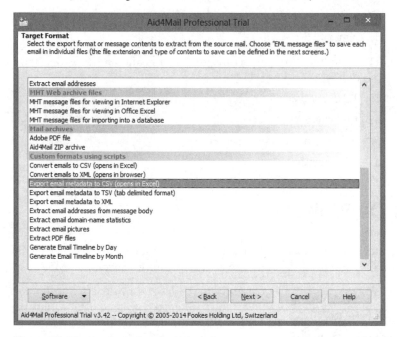

Figure 11-11   Export options in Aid4Mail
Source: Fookes Software, *www.aid4mail.com*

8. In the Target Settings window, click *Work***Chap11****Projects****HandsOn11-1**, and enter the filename **Eric_Saibi.CSV**. Click **Next**, and then click **Start**.

9. After Aid4Mail has finished converting the e-mail to CSV format, open the file in Microsoft Excel (or any spreadsheet program), and exit Aid4Mail. Scroll through Eric Saibi's e-mail data and look for messages that might contain personal information or be related to the Enron scandal. Go to the Aid4Mail Web site and read the user manual. What can be done to make viewing data easier? Write a short paper describing the options.

Hands-On Project 11-2

In this project, you use ProDiscover Basic to retrieve mail in the M57 case. Jo Smith, one of the M57 patent researchers, likes to trade illicit photos, illustrated in the M57 case as cats and kittens.

1. Start ProDiscover Basic with the **Run as administrator** option, and start a new project. Enter today's date for the project number and **Jos hard drive** for the project name. Click **OK**.

2. In the tree view, click to expand **Add**, and click **Image File**. Navigate to where you stored the M57 files, click **jo-2009-12-11.001.E01**, and click **Open**. If the Auto Verify Image Checksum message box opens, click **Yes**.

3. Click the **Search** toolbar button, and then click the **Content Search** tab, if necessary. In the Search for the pattern(s) text box, type *.**pst**. Under Select the Disk(s)/Image(s) you want to search in, click the .**E01** image file, and then click **OK**.

4. Few search results are returned. Try entering at least three other keywords that might return results in a search for e-mail. When you're finished, exit ProDiscover Basic.

5. Write a report describing your results. Do your results show that Jo was dealing in illicit photos or corporate espionage? What's your assessment of using this tool to retrieve e-mail?

Hands-On Project 11-3

In this project, you use Facebook Forensic Toolkit by Afentis Software to discover the friends and other information of a public Facebook profile. Although you can use your own Facebook logon for this project, creating a logon connected to your professional e-mail account is highly recommended for working on actual cases.

1. Start a Web browser, go to **www.facebookforensics.com**, and download the trial version of Facebook Forensic Toolkit. Install the software, and then start it.

2. In the opening window (see Figure 11-12), click the **Examine Profile and Clone Data** option.

3. In the New Case - Information window, click the **browse** button next to "Location of examination results." Create a subfolder of your work folder called **HandsOn11-3**, and click **OK**.

4. Enter today's date for the case number and your name for the examiner. Enter **Test** for the other information. Click the **blue right arrow** in the upper-left corner.

5. Enter the URL for the Facebook page of a topic you're interested in. Click the **blue right arrow** to continue. Adjust the Profile/Content information as needed. Click the **blue right arrow** to continue, and then click **Authenticate**. When prompted to authenticate with a valid logon, enter valid Facebook logon credentials, and click **Log In**. If you're asked to allow fbcrawler to post to Facebook for you, click **Not Now**.

6. Click **Start** on the right, and examine the information in each category (see Figure 11-13).

7. Next, click **HOME** at the top, enter the Facebook page of a famous person, repeat the authentication process in Step 5, and then repeat Step 6. When you're finished, exit the program.

8. Write a one- to two-page paper describing the information you expected to find and what you actually found.

11

Examine Profile
and Clone Data

Keyword / Username
Search on Facebook

Case Management

ntis Facebook #Forensic Toolkit (FFT) v2 - social media #eDiscovery and electronic Best Evidence http://www.facebookf(

Figure 11-12   The opening window of Facebook Forensics
Source: Afentis Forensics, *www.facebookforensics.com*

Figure 11-13   The Results window
Source: Afentis Forensics, *www.facebookforensics.com*

Case Projects

Case Project 11-1

You get a call from a high school student named Marco who claims he has just received an e-mail from another student threatening to commit suicide. Marco isn't sure where the student sent the e-mail from. Write a brief report explaining how you should proceed, including what you should do first in this situation.

Case Project 11-2

A mother calls you to report that her 15-year-old daughter has run away from home. She has access to her daughter's e-mail account and says her daughter has a number of e-mails in her inbox suggesting she has run away to be with a 35-year-old woman. Write a brief report explaining how you should proceed.

Case Project 11-3

X1 Social Discovery is a forensics package for OSNs. The orientation videos advise that investigators create a Facebook or similar OSN profile without friends, groups, or associates attached to it. Go to *www.x1.com/products/x1_social_discovery/* and download the user information. Write a one- to two-page paper in which you support or argue against these safeguards that are recommended before you use Social Discovery to gather information on a social media account.

11

chapter **12**

Mobile Device Forensics

After reading this chapter and completing the exercises, you will be able to:

- Explain the basic concepts of mobile device forensics
- Describe procedures for acquiring data from mobile devices

This chapter explains how to retrieve information from a cell phone, smartphone, tablet, or other mobile device and explores social media content on mobile devices in more depth. Although some free and demo software is used in projects, the software and hardware discussed in this chapter are usually expensive and not supplied on the book's DVD. Check with your instructor to see whether any is available at your organization.

The field of mobile device forensics changes rapidly and poses challenges in trying to retrieve information. Unlike what you might see in television shows, you don't just start scrolling through contact lists or most recent calls. As with all digital investigations, you need to follow the forensics procedures described in this chapter.

Understanding Mobile Device Forensics

People store a wealth of information on cell phones and smartphones, and the thought of losing your phone and, therefore, the information stored on it can be a frightening prospect. Despite this concern, not many people think about securing their phones, although they routinely lock and secure laptops or desktops. Depending on your phone's model, the following items might be stored on it:

- Incoming, outgoing, and missed calls
- Multimedia Message Service (MMS; text messages) and Short Message Service (SMS) messages
- E-mail accounts
- Instant messaging (IM) logs
- Web pages
- Pictures, videos, and music files
- Calendars and address books
- Social media account information
- GPS data
- Voice recordings and voicemail

Many people store more information on phones than on computers; indeed, Lessard and Kessler state that mobile devices contain "more probative information per byte examined than traditional computers" ("Android Forensics: Simplifying Cell Phone Examinations," *Small Scale Digital Device Forensics Journal*, September 2010). Often piecing together a case's facts with just the information stored on mobile devices is possible. In many countries, phones are used to log in to bank accounts, make deposits, and transfer funds from one device to another, which provides even more potential evidence.

The use of smartphones for illicit activities—such as identity theft, child pornography, and bank fraud—has become more prevalent.

Because mobile devices are seized at the time of arrest, police used to look through them as a routine matter. The Supreme Courts of Oregon and Ohio, however, ruled that a search warrant is needed to examine these devices because of all the information they can contain. More recently the U.S. Supreme Court ruled unanimously in *Riley v. California* that a search warrant is required before an arresting officer can begin examining a phone's contents (*www.newrepublic.com/article/118396/supreme-court-cellphone-case-went-further-privacy-advocates-hoped*, June 2014). Furthermore, because phones often contain private or sensitive information, any information that doesn't pertain to the case must be redacted from the public record.

Despite the usefulness of these devices in providing clues for investigations, investigating smartphones and other mobile devices is one of the more challenging tasks in digital forensics. No single standard exists for how and where phones store messages, although many phones use similar storage schemes. In addition, new phones come out about every six months, and they're rarely compatible with previous models. Therefore, the cables, software, and accessories used for forensics acquisitions can become obsolete in a short time.

Mobile Phone Basics

Mobile phone technology has advanced rapidly in the past few decades and developed far beyond what its inventors could have imagined. Gone are the days of two-pound cell phones that only the wealthy could afford. By the end of 2008, mobile phones had gone through three generations: analog, digital personal communications service (PCS), and **third-generation** (3G). 3G introduced unheard-of capabilities, such as being able to download while you were walking or in a moving vehicle. Sprint Nextel introduced the **fourth-generation** (4G) network in 2009. Several technologies can be used for 4G networks and are discussed later in this section.

Many digital networks are used in the mobile phone industry, and Table 12-1 lists the main ones. Much of this table is taken from the National Institute of Standards and Technology (NIST) document "Guidelines on Mobile Device Forensics" (Special Publication [SP] 800-101, Revision 1, May 2014; *http://nvlpubs.nist.gov/nistpubs/SpecialPublications/NIST.SP.800-101r1.pdf*). You can download this document to learn more.

Table 12-1 Digital networks

Digital network	Description
Code Division Multiple Access (CDMA)	Developed during World War II, this technology was patented by Qualcomm after the war. One of the most common digital networks, it uses the full radio frequency spectrum to define channels. In the United States, Sprint, U.S. Cellular, and Verizon, for example, use CDMA networks.
Global System for Mobile Communications (GSM)	Another common digital network, it's used by AT&T and T-Mobile in the United States and is the standard in Europe and Asia.
Time Division Multiple Access (TDMA)	This digital network uses the technique of dividing a radio frequency into time slots; GSM networks use this technique. It also refers to a specific cellular network standard covered by Interim Standard (IS) 136.
Integrated Digital Enhanced Network (iDEN)	This Motorola protocol combines several services, including data transmission, into one network.
Digital Advanced Mobile Phone Service (D-AMPS)	This network is a digital version of the original analog standard for cell phones.

(continues)

Table 12-1 Digital networks (*Continued*)

Digital network	Description
Enhanced Data GSM Environment (EDGE)	This digital network, a faster version of GSM, is designed to deliver data.
Orthogonal Frequency Division Multiplexing (OFDM)	This technology for 4G networks uses energy more efficiently than 3G networks and is more immune to interference.

© 2016 Cengage Learning®

Most **Code Division Multiple Access (CDMA)** networks conform to IS-95, created by the **Telecommunications Industry Association (TIA)**. These systems are referred to as CDMAOne, and when they went to 3G services, they became CDMA2000.

Global System for Mobile Communications (GSM) uses the **Time Division Multiple Access (TDMA)** technique, so multiple phones take turns sharing a channel on a round-robin basis. As noted in Table 12-1, TDMA also refers to the IS-136 standard, which introduced sleep mode to enhance battery life. TDMA can operate in the cell phone (800 to 1000 MHz) or PCS (1900 MHz) frequency, so it's compatible with several cell phone networks.

The 3G standard was developed by the **International Telecommunication Union (ITU)** under the United Nations. It's compatible with CDMA, GSM, and TDMA. The **Enhanced Data GSM Environment (EDGE)** standard was developed specifically for 3G.

GSM carriers, by definition, must accept any GSM phone. CDMA carriers have locked phones and don't have to accept any users who aren't subscribers. Until recently, users who traveled frequently between the United States, Africa, Europe, and parts of Asia needed separate phones for each place. With GSM phones, you simply pop in a SIM card for the country you're currently in.

In 2008, the International Telecommunication Union Radio (ITU-R) created the requirements for carriers to be considered 4G (*www.whatsag.com/G/Understanding_4G.php*). 4G networks can use the following technologies:

- *Orthogonal Frequency Division Multiplexing*—The **Orthogonal Frequency Division Multiplexing (OFDM)** technology uses numerous parallel carriers instead of a single broad carrier and is less susceptible to interference (*http://bwrcs.eecs.berkeley.edu/ Classes/EE225C/Lectures/Lec16_ofdm.pdf*).

- *Mobile WiMAX*—This technology uses the IEEE 802.16e standard and Orthogonal Frequency Division Multiple Access (OFDMA) and supports transmission speeds of 12 Mbps. Sprint chose this technology for its 4G network, although some argue it's not true 4G.

- *Ultra Mobile Broadband (UMB)*—Also known as CDMA2000 EV-DO, this technology was used by CDMA network providers to switch to 4G and supports transmission speeds of 275 Mbps for downlinks and 75 Mbps for uplinks. It has been replaced by LTE (described later in this list).

- *Multiple Input Multiple Output (MIMO)*—This technology, developed by Airgo and acquired by Qualcomm, supports transmission speeds of 312 Mbps and is used by 4G, WiMAX, and other technologies.

- *Long Term Evolution (LTE)*—This technology, designed for GSM and Universal Mobile Telecommunications Systems (UMTS) technology, supports 45 Mbps to 144 Mbps transmission speeds. Commonly called "4G LTE."

As an investigator, you should research these technologies to make sure you stay up to date.

Although digital networks use different technologies, they operate on the same basic principles. Geographic areas are divided into cells resembling honeycombs. As described in NIST SP 800-101 (mentioned earlier in this section), three main components are used for communication with these cells:

- *Base transceiver station (BTS)*—This component is made up of radio transceiver equipment that defines cells and communicates with mobile phones; it's sometimes referred to as a "cell phone tower," although the tower is only one part of the BTS equipment.

- *Base station controller (BSC)*—This combination of hardware and software manages BTSs and assigns channels by connecting to the mobile switching center.

- *Mobile switching center (MSC)*—This component connects calls by routing digital packets for the network and relies on a database to support subscribers. This central database contains account data, location data, and other key information needed during an investigation. If you have to retrieve information from a carrier's central database, you usually need a warrant or subpoena.

Inside Mobile Devices

Mobile devices can range from simple phones to small computers, also called **smartphones**. The hardware consists of a microprocessor, ROM, RAM, a digital signal processor, a radio module, a microphone and speaker, hardware interfaces (such as keypads, cameras, and GPS devices), and an LCD display. Many have removable memory cards and up to 64 GB of internal memory, and Bluetooth and Wi-Fi are included in most mobile devices ("Guidelines on Mobile Device Forensics," SP 800-101, Revision 1, May 2014; *http://nvlpubs.nist.gov/nistpubs/SpecialPublications/NIST.SP.800-101r1.pdf*).

Most basic phones have a proprietary OS, although smartphones use the same OSs as PCs (or stripped-down versions of them). These OSs include Windows Mobile, RIM OS, Android (based on Linux), Google OS, and iOS (for Apple devices). Typically, phones store system data in **electronically erasable programmable read-only memory (EEPROM)**, which enables service providers to reprogram phones without having to access memory chips physically. Many users take advantage of this capability by reprogramming their phones to add features or switch to different service providers. Although this reprogramming isn't supported officially by service providers, instructions on how to do so are readily available on the Internet.

The OS is stored in ROM, which is nonvolatile memory, so along with other data, it's available even if the phone loses power. Acquiring data from ROM is covered in more detail later in "Understanding Acquisition Procedures for Mobile Devices."

For personal use, **personal digital assistants (PDAs)** have been mostly replaced by iPods, iPads, and other mobile devices. Their use has shifted to more specific markets, such as medical or industrial PDAs (*www.medindia.net/pda/pda_manufacturers.asp*). Palm Pilot and

Microsoft Pocket PC were popular models when PDAs came on the market in the 1990s, and stand-alone PDAs are still made by companies such as Sharp and HP. Similar to smartphones, PDAs house a microprocessor, flash ROM, RAM, and other hardware components. As with smartphones, the amount of information on a PDA varies depending on the model. Usually, you can retrieve a user's calendar, address book, Web access, and other items.

A number of peripheral memory cards are used with PDAs:

- *Compact Flash (CF)*—CF cards were used for extra storage and work much the same way as PCMCIA cards.
- *MultiMediaCard (MMC)*—MMC cards were designed for mobile phones, but they can be used with PDAs to provide another storage area.
- *Secure Digital (SD)*—SD cards are similar to MMCs but have added security features to protect data; they're now used on smartphones.

Most PDAs were designed to synchronize with a computer, so they had built-in slots for that purpose (whether hard-wired or wireless synchronization).

SIM Cards Subscriber identity module (SIM) cards are usually found in GSM devices and consist of a microprocessor and internal memory. SIM cards are similar to standard memory cards, except the connectors are aligned differently. iPhones and many Android phones have micro SIM and nano SIM slots. However, some can be accessed only if the phone has been unlocked.

GSM refers to mobile phones as "mobile stations" and divides a station into two parts: the SIM card and the mobile equipment (ME), which is the remainder of the phone. The SIM card is necessary for the ME to work and serves these additional purposes:

- Identifies the subscriber to the network
- Stores service-related information
- Can be used to back up the device

SIM cards come in two sizes, but the most common is the size of a standard U.S. postage stamp and about 0.75 mm thick. Portability of information is what makes SIM cards so versatile. By switching a SIM card between compatible phones, users can move their provider usage and other information to another phone automatically without having to notify the service provider. For example, if you travel between neighboring countries often, you could have a GSM phone and two SIM cards. When you travel to another country, you simply switch to the other SIM card. With phones on which this switching is allowed, information such as your contact list is stored on the phone, so when you switch to another carrier, all you have to do is change the SIM card. Another common practice is switching to another SIM card when you have used most of your monthly minutes on your main SIM card.

Older CDMA phones don't use SIM cards; they incorporate the card's functions into the phone. Newer TDMA phones in North America do use SIM cards, however, and they are sealed so that users must contact the service provider when changing phones or providers.

As mentioned, many phones now include SD cards for external storage. They range from 16 GB to 64 GB and can be part of a mobile device or game console.

Understanding Acquisition Procedures for Mobile Devices

Search and seizure procedures for mobile devices are as important as procedures for computers. The main concerns are loss of power, synchronization with cloud services, and remote wiping. All mobile devices have volatile memory, so making sure they don't lose power before you can retrieve RAM data is critical. At the investigation scene, determine whether the device is on or off. If it's off, leave it off, but find the charger and attach it as soon as possible. Note this step in your log if you can't determine whether the device was charged at the time of seizure. If the device is on, check the display for the battery's current charge level.

Because mobile devices are often designed to synchronize with applications on a user's laptop or tablet, any mobile device attached to a PC or tablet via a USB cable or micro USB cable should be disconnected immediately. Many people use their smartphones to get Internet access for tablets or laptops, so you might find these devices already connected to the Internet. Disconnecting them immediately helps prevent synchronization that might occur automatically on a preset schedule and overwrite data on the device. In addition, collect the laptop and any peripheral devices to determine whether the hard drive contains any information that's been transferred and then deleted from the mobile device, including pictures, videos, and other files that have been transferred and then deleted.

Depending on the warrant or subpoena, the time of seizure might be relevant. In addition, messages might be received on the mobile device after seizure that may or may not be admissible in court. If you determine that the device should be turned off to preserve battery power or a possible attack, note the time and date at which you take this step. The alternative is to isolate the device from incoming signals with one of the following options:

- Place the device in airplane mode, if this feature is available.
- Place the device in a paint can, preferably one that previously contained radio wave–blocking paint, or use the Paraben Wireless StrongHold Bag (*www.paraben.com/stronghold-bags.html*), which conforms to Faraday wire cage standards.
- Turn the device off.

The drawback of using these isolating options is that the mobile device is put into roaming mode, which accelerates battery drainage. Most mobile devices shut themselves off or enter a "sleep state" after reaching a certain low battery level.

Make sure you handle all components with care and protect them from environmental factors and sources of electromagnetic interference (EMI).

SANS DFIR Forensics (*http://digital-forensics.sans.org/blog/2014/06/24/getting-the-most-out-of-smartphone-forensic-exams-sans-advanced-smartphone-forensics-poster-release*) has a slightly different process that handles other possible problems. It lists three conditions: The device is on and unlocked, the device is on and locked, and the device is off. If it's on and unlocked, you must isolate it from the network, disable the screen lock, and remove the passcode, among other tasks. If the device is on and locked, what you can and can't do varies depending on the type of device, such as whether it's a BlackBerry, an iPhone, or an Android. If the device is off, you should attempt a physical static acquisition and then turn the device on, determine whether it's locked, and then follow the procedure for either a locked or unlocked condition. As devices become more sophisticated, turning them off means removing the battery.

When you're back in the forensics lab, you need to assess what can be retrieved. To determine whether you should do a logical acquisition or physical acquisition, you need to know where information is stored. As with laptops and desktops, a logical acquisition involves accessing files and folders as you would see them when looking at them in File Explorer. A physical acquisition is a bit-by-bit acquisition done to find deleted files or folders. You should check the following locations for information, keeping in mind that with mobile devices, often you need manufacturers' tools:

- Internal memory
- SIM card
- Removable or external memory cards
- Network provider

Because of wiretap laws, checking providers' servers requires a search warrant or subpoena, so you need one if you want to check voicemail stored by the provider or another third party, for example. In addition, because most newer phones and phone plans store voicemail on the phone, you need a search warrant for the device, too. You might also need information from the service provider to determine where the suspect or victim was at the time of a call, to access backups of contacts, and more. In the past, you had to serve the provider with a warrant to have a triangulation of a cell tower done to determine location. This is still true if you're doing an ongoing investigation and don't have the device. If, however, you have the device, you can usually retrieve GPS data from it.

Checking with the service provider has been further complicated because backups might be stored in a cloud provided by the carrier or a third party. For iPods and iPads, syncing and backups tend to occur in the iCloud; other providers offer a similar cloud backup. In addition, because of the growing problem of mobile devices being stolen, service providers have started using remote wiping to remove a user's personal information stored on a stolen device, and this procedure often results in the loss of valuable information for investigations. Remote wiping is usually done to remove an account so that a thief can't use the phone and rack up charges. It can also erase all contacts, the calendar, and other personal information, such as photos, stored on the device. In some instances, it restores the device to the original factory settings. Depending on the device and service provider, the device owner or the service provider can do the remote wipe.

Memory storage on a mobile device is usually a combination of volatile and nonvolatile memory. Volatile memory requires power to maintain its contents, but nonvolatile memory doesn't. Although the locations of data vary from one phone model to the next, volatile memory usually contains data that changes frequently, such as missed calls, text messages, and sometimes even user files. Nonvolatile memory, on the other hand, contains OS files and stored user data, such as a personal information manager (PIM) and backed-up files.

As mentioned, memory resides in the phone and in the SIM card, if the device is equipped with one. The file system for a SIM card is a hierarchical structure (see Figure 12-1). This file structure begins with the root of the system (MF). The next level consists of directory files (DF), and under them are files containing elementary data (EF). In this figure, the EFs under the GSM and DCS1800 DFs contain network data on different frequency bands of operation. The EFs under the Telecom DF contain service-related data.

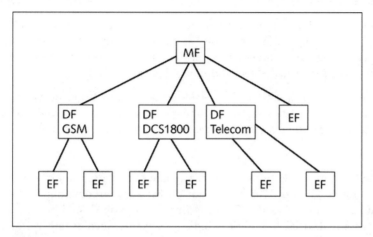

Figure 12-1   SIM file structure
© Cengage Learning®

You can retrieve quite a bit of data from a SIM card, depending on whether the phone is GSM or CDMA. The information that can be retrieved falls into four categories:

- Service-related data, such as identifiers for the SIM card and subscriber
- Call data, such as numbers dialed
- Message information
- Location information

If power has been lost, you might need PINs or other access codes to view files. Typically, users keep the original PIN assigned to the SIM card, so when you're collecting evidence at the scene, look for users' manuals and other documentation that can help you access the SIM card. With most SIM cards, you have three attempts at entering an access code before the device is locked, which then requires calling the service provider to get the PIN unlock key (PUK) and waiting a certain amount of time before trying again. Common codes to try are 1-1-1-1 or 1-2-3-4.

Mobile Forensics Equipment

Mobile forensics is an evolving science, with the biggest challenge being constantly changing phone models. What works today might not work on a model that comes out tomorrow. This section gives you an overview of procedures for working with mobile forensics software, and specific tools are discussed in the following sections.

The first step is identifying the mobile device. Most users don't alter their devices, but some file off serial numbers, change the display to show misleading data, and so on. When attempting to identify a phone, you can make use of several online sources, such as *www.phonescoop.com* and *www.mobileforensicscentral.com*.

Next, make sure you have installed the mobile device forensics software. As mentioned, not all facilities are equipped with the necessary software because many tools are cost prohibitive. Some vendors offer tools that simply take pictures of screens as you scroll through them. Forensically, this approach isn't the best, but you can use it if no other alternatives are available.

The next step is to attach the phone to its power supply and connect the correct cables. Most phones now have a combination USB/power cable, and many are interchangeable. For older phones, often you have to rig cables together. Some vendors have toolkits with an array of cables you can use (discussed later in "Mobile Forensics Tools in Action").

After you've connected the device, start the forensics software and begin downloading the available information. If your forensics software doesn't support the model you're investigating, you might need to acquire other tools. Your main concern should be that the software is forensically sound.

SIM Card Readers With GSM phones and many newer models of mobile devices, the next step is accessing the SIM card, which you can do by using a combination hardware/software device called a "SIM card reader." To use this device, you should be in a forensics lab equipped with antistatic devices. In addition, biological agents, such as fingerprints, might be present on the inside of the case, so you should consult the lead investigator when you're ready to proceed to this step. The general procedure is as follows:

1. Remove the back panel of the device.
2. Remove the battery.
3. Remove the SIM card from its holder.
4. Insert the SIM card into the card reader, which you insert into your forensic workstation's USB port.

A variety of SIM card readers are available. Some are forensically sound and some are not; make sure you note this feature in your investigation log. Another problem with SIM card readers is dealing with text and SMS messages that haven't been read yet. After you view a message, the device shows the message as opened or read. For this reason, documenting messages that haven't been read is critical. Using a tool that takes pictures of each screen can be valuable because these screen captures can provide additional documentation.

Mobile Phone Forensics Tools and Methods The best method of retrieving information, of course, is acquiring a forensic image, which enables you to recover deleted text messages and similar data. With Android devices, the process can be as simple as using AccessData FTK Imager to perform a logical acquisition and a low-level analysis ("Android Forensics, Part I: How we recovered (supposedly) erased data," July 2014, *http://blog.avast. com/2014/07/09/android-foreniscs-pt-2-how-we-recovered-erased-data/*).

iPhone acquisition procedures are similar, and several good tools are available, such as MacLockPick 3.0 (*www.macforensicslab.com/ProductsAndServices/index.php?main_page= product_info&cPath=12&products_id=2*), which is designed to deal with iPhones, iPads, iOS, and Mac OS X Lion. It can also extract iPhoto information, handle plug-in apps, and pull the user's online history.

The NIST guidelines (*http://nvlpubs.nist.gov/nistpubs/SpecialPublications/NIST.SP.800-101r1. pdf*) list six types of mobile forensics methods:

- *Manual extraction*—If investigators can't do a logical or physical extraction, this method involves looking at the device's content page by page and taking pictures.

- *Logical extraction*—The mobile device is connected to a forensic workstation via a wired (USB cable, for example) or wireless (such as Bluetooth) connection, and then a forensic copy of the device is made.

- *Hex dumping and Joint Test Action Group (JTAG) extraction*—Hex dumping involves using a modified boot loader to access the RAM for analysis (*http://digital-forensics.sans.org/blog/2008/09/03/hex-dumping-flash-from-a-mobile*). The JTAG extraction method gets information from the processor, flash memory, or other physical components. It's a highly invasive method.

- *Chip-off*—This method requires physically removing flash memory chip and gathering information at the binary level.

- *Micro read*—This method looks at logic gates with an electron microscope and can be used even when data has been overwritten on magnetic media. It's very expensive, however, so it's typically used only in cases involving national security.

Paraben Software (*www.paraben.com*), a vendor of mobile forensics software, offers several tools, including Device Seizure, used to acquire data from a variety of phone models. Paraben also has the Device Seizure Toolbox containing assorted cables, a SIM card reader, and other equipment for mobile device investigations. DataPilot (*www.datapilot.com*) has a similar collection of cables that can interface with Nokia, Motorola, Ericsson, Samsung, Audiovox, Sanyo, and others.

Another tool is BitPim (*www.bitpim.org*), used to view data on many CDMA phones, including LG, Samsung, Sanyo, and others. It offers versions for Windows, Linux, and Mac OS X. It's not a forensics tool, but it can be used in read-only mode. In Windows, BitPim stores files in Documents\BitPim by default, so when you start a new case, make sure you move these files to another location first so that they're not overwritten. BitPim Cleaner 2.1.0 by Mobile Forensics, Inc. (MFI, *www.mobileforensicsinc.com/store_files/Products.htm*), moves these files for you. MFI, a vendor of mobile forensics software, offers several affordable products as well as training. Susteen Inc. (*http://susteen.com*) also has a tool for mobile forensics analysis, Secure View 3 (*http://secureview.us*).

Keep in mind that you should validate any new tool and verify its claims with rigorous testing.

Cellebrite UFED Forensic System (*www.cellebrite.com*) works with smartphones, PDAs, tablets, and GPS devices. This kit comes with several hundred cables, includes handset support for phones from outside the United States, and handles multiple languages. A lesser known tool used widely by government agencies is Micro Systemation XRY (*https://www.msab.com*), which retrieves data from smartphones, GPS devices, tablets, and music players.

12

MOBILedit Forensic (*www.mobiledit.com*) is a forensics software tool containing a built-in write-blocker. It can connect to phones directly via Bluetooth, irDA, or a cable and can read SIM cards by using a SIM reader. It's also notable for being very user friendly.

Another tool is SIMcon (*www.simcon.no*), used to recover files on a GSM/3G SIM or USIM card, including stored numbers and text messages. SIMcon's features include the following:

- Reads files on SIM cards
- Analyzes file content, including text messages and stored numbers
- Recovers deleted text messages
- Manages PIN codes
- Generates reports that can be used as evidence
- Archives files with MD5 and SHA-1 hash values
- Exports data to files that can be used in spreadsheet programs
- Supports international character sets

Software tools differ in the information they display and the level of detail, and some tools are designed for updating files, not retrieving data. In general, tools designed to edit information, although they are user friendly, usually aren't forensically sound. You might be able to view some data with one of these tools that you can't view with a forensics tool, but note this step in your log and state that the tool isn't typically used for forensics purposes. Every program has its idiosyncrasies, so be aware of the shortcomings of the tools you use, and document every step you take during an investigation.

Social Media Forensics on Mobile Devices Roughly half of Facebook users access their accounts via mobile devices (smartphones and tablets), and they tend to be the most active users of social media (Noora Al Mutawa et al, "Forensic analysis of social networking applications on mobile devices," *Digital Investigation 9*, 2012, *www.dfrws.org/ 2012/proceedings/DFRWS2012-3.pdf*). Al Mutawa et al examined Facebook, Twitter, and MySpace use on BlackBerries, iPhones, and Android devices and discovered, for example, that physical acquisitions of iPhones required "jailbreaking," meaning they got root access to the device's OS to bypass the provider's codes for preventing users from switching to other providers and preventing unauthorized people from taking actions an investigator would take.

In addition, they found that evidence artifacts vary depending on the social media channel and the device. For example, on iPhones, a SQLite database for Facebook was found that lists friends, their ID numbers, and phone numbers as well as files that tracked all uploads, including pictures. Similar databases were found on Twitter. On Android devices, Facebook friends were found in the contacts list because these devices synchronized with Facebook. Forensic analysis also showed that iPhone and Android devices yielded the most information, and much of the data was stored in SQLite databases. Following standard procedures—doing a logical acquisition followed by a physical acquisition—can yield solid evidence, especially with devices that aren't locked.

Mobile Forensics Tools in Action

Now that you have a good idea of the types of tools and procedures needed for a mobile device investigation, you can see some of these tools in action and the results—both successful and unsuccessful. Cellebrite, for example, is a widely used mobile forensics tool, often used by law enforcement. With this straightforward tool, you determine the device's make and model, hook up the correct cable, turn the device on, and retrieve the data. In many cases, it works flawlessly. However, keep in mind that there are more than half a million apps for mobile devices, and Cellebrite can analyze data from only a few hundred.

In this case you're examining, Randall Simpson, the CIO of Flashbills, and Sarah Jensen, the lead developer at Desert Oasis Funding, are suspected of intellectual property theft. Randall is unhappy that his share of the profits has gone down since his partner's son was hired, and Sarah has been after the code for a new app from Flashbills. The corporate investigator is aware that the two have been calling and e-mailing each other, so he attempted to do a logical acquisition of Sarah's TracFone (a low-cost, prepaid phone often referred to as a "burner phone"). To keep customers from switching to other plans, these phones are code-locked to prevent a USB connection and even jailbreaking. Cellebrite was able to read the SIM card data but found no text messages, SMS messages, phone numbers, or other data. Figure 12-2 shows a Cellebrite report, and Figure 12-3 shows some plists (discussed in Chapter 7) found on the device.

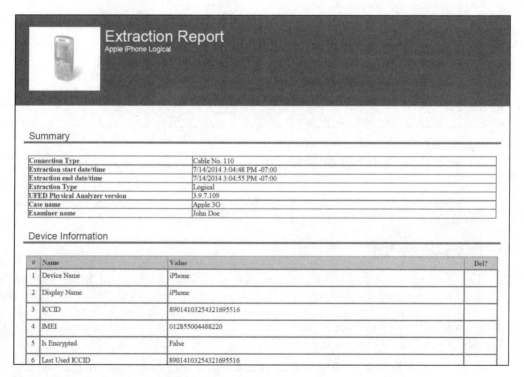

Figure 12-2 A Cellebrite report
Source: Cellebrite Mobile Synchronization LTD

	Name:		Size (Bytes):		
9	Name: Path: MD5: SHA256:	clients.plist /Library/Caches/locationd/clients.plist f8dd4daca97c53c07880b25cd06fffd9 4f341dfec01f3bdf44ee8910c33ca510 65eb52fc2deb02b405ffb43b0ab4a2ad	Size (Bytes): Created: Modified: Accessed:	1803 4/10/2014 3:44:42 PM(UTC+0) 7/14/2014 9:58:22 PM(UTC+0) 7/14/2014 9:58:22 PM(UTC+0)	
10	Name: Path: MD5: SHA256:	ClientTruth.plist /Library/ConfigurationProfiles/ClientTruth.plist 2de6a04cdba79ed13580c47dfd70cc5f 97704a8960b4facceef54397a08fb5d0 a456247c3627359215aa2a27df22656c	Size (Bytes): Created: Modified: Accessed:	181 4/10/2014 3:44:29 PM(UTC+0) 4/10/2014 3:44:29 PM(UTC+0) 4/10/2014 3:44:29 PM(UTC+0)	
11	Name: Path: MD5: SHA256:	com.apple.Accessibility.plist /Library/Preferences/com.apple.Accessibility.plist 9218fbd80b4ff9d26e6e3e8ab10ad871 c3a0d76325b270fe26167b38439b1e9a a255d5f7d4fe0215cf5767c6195b12b6	Size (Bytes): Created: Modified: Accessed:	288 7/14/2014 10:03:24 PM(UTC+0) 7/14/2014 10:03:24 PM(UTC+0) 7/14/2014 10:03:24 PM(UTC+0)	
12	Name: Path: MD5: SHA256:	com.apple.accounts.exists.plist /SystemConfiguration/com.apple.accounts.exists.plist 16422e4b7e14e9dde66ef63e727ede0f a6c9ced9eedcacdbd6546765a15eb855 0be51bcee24e8f8f8ed3e6c27c96c3ed	Size (Bytes): Created: Modified: Accessed:	111 7/14/2014 9:23:04 PM(UTC+0) 7/14/2014 9:23:04 PM(UTC+0) 7/14/2014 9:23:04 PM(UTC+0)	
13	Name: Path: MD5: SHA256:	com.apple.accountsettings.plist /Library/Preferences/com.apple.accountsettings.plist b433aabe90564192ad12c4ee589fb524 ee1a3d4c3e381c0ee92319dd48e33c4c 0ebce4c48edfc7334fcc0848b1fe94a1	Size (Bytes): Created: Modified: Accessed:	4079 7/14/2014 10:03:46 PM(UTC+0) 7/14/2014 10:03:46 PM(UTC+0) 7/14/2014 10:03:46 PM(UTC+0)	
14	Name: Path: MD5: SHA256:	com.apple.aggregated.plist /Library/Preferences/com.apple.aggregated.plist 91a20145343d0872b4d4ce4a70053c6a 19ccf13caed4d725a1271bd4cae6f1c9 5bfc6f47d0dd4f0a83fe708ef9dc4aff	Size (Bytes): Created: Modified: Accessed:	78 7/14/2014 7:13:13 PM(UTC+0) 7/14/2014 7:13:13 PM(UTC+0) 7/14/2014 7:13:13 PM(UTC+0)	
15	Name: Path: MD5: SHA256:	com.apple.AppSupport.plist /Library/Preferences/com.apple.AppSupport.plist 2444b5d902ed0e78d0c34edad8cc1237 d15afc98d9dd1d6b3a3552b005a90c8a 57fb4ae32f8b7c51fa50c8c9356c4290	Size (Bytes): Created: Modified: Accessed:	98 7/14/2014 7:17:42 PM(UTC+0) 7/14/2014 7:17:42 PM(UTC+0) 7/14/2014 7:17:42 PM(UTC+0)	
16	Name: Path: MD5: SHA256:	com.apple.apsd.plist /Library/Preferences/com.apple.apsd.plist 218d6fe6891aa9b5224964520c30e1aa 23cdb2be51f32441ba37b470c3c62c0b 4793645a71ed37d141f97d394f4d6d73	Size (Bytes): Created: Modified: Accessed:	152 7/14/2014 10:03:49 PM(UTC+0) 7/14/2014 10:03:49 PM(UTC+0) 7/14/2014 10:03:49 PM(UTC+0)	
17	Name: Path: MD5: SHA256:	com.apple.awdd.persistent.plist /Library/Preferences/com.apple.awdd.persistent.plist d130d96fbc5a49e22a74a01acb7d425b 61114c7b4f401acdbca40a52ed846dbd 5c80fb9e1c8e19f8dbc464de4dd59e38	Size (Bytes): Created: Modified: Accessed:	177 7/14/2014 10:03:48 PM(UTC+0) 7/14/2014 10:03:48 PM(UTC+0) 7/14/2014 10:03:48 PM(UTC+0)	
18	Name: Path: MD5:	com.apple.awdd.persistent.plist.GclkAKj /Library/Preferences/com.apple.awdd.persistent.plist.G clkAKj d99173f4a3dfc852ce1b05289c30674f	Size (Bytes): Created: Modified: Accessed:	177 7/14/2014 7:17:44 PM(UTC+0) 7/14/2014 7:17:44 PM(UTC+0) 7/14/2014 7:17:44 PM(UTC+0)	

Figure 12-3   Plists found on an iPhone 3G
Source: Cellebrite Mobile Synchronization LTD

Create a *Work*\Chap12\Chapter work folder on your system. The work folder path shown in screenshots might differ slightly from yours.

The investigator was able to get a warrant for cloud backups of Randall's and Sarah's mobile devices. In the following activity, you gather these files. Before starting, copy the InCh12Randall.exe and InCh12Sarah.exe files from the DVD to your work folder, and run both to extract the evidence files. (When you do, the file extension becomes .001 for these files.) Then follow these steps:

1. Start OSForensics with the **Run as administrator** option, if necessary, and click **Yes** in the UAC message box. If you're prompted with a warning dialog box and/or notification, click **Continue Using Free Version**.

2. In the left pane, click **Manage Case**, if necessary, and click the **New Case** button on the right. In the New Case dialog box, type **Randall's e-mail** in the Case Name text box and

your name in the Investigator text box. For the Case Folder setting, click **Custom Location**, and then click **Browse**. Create a **Randall** subfolder of your work folder, and then click **OK**.

3. Click **Add Device**. In the "Select device to add" dialog box, click the **Image File** option button. Click the **...** button, navigate to and click your work folder, and click the **InCh12Randall.001** file. Click **Open**, and then click **OK**.

4. Click **Create Index** in the left pane to start the Create Index Wizard. In the Step 1 of 5 window, click the **Use Pre-defined File Types** option button, if necessary. Click to select the **Emails** and **Attachments** check boxes, and then click **Next**.

5. In the Step 2 of 5 window, click **Add**. In the Add Start Location dialog box, browse to and click the **InCh12Randall.001** file, click **OK**, and then click **Next**. In the Step 3 of 5 window, click **Start Indexing**. When the indexing has finished, click **OK** in the message box informing you that errors reading some files might have occurred in the indexing process, if necessary.

6. Repeat the preceding steps with the **InCh12Sarah.001** file, creating a **Sarah** subfolder this time.

7. Search both files for the keyword **Flashbills**. Make a note of the number of e-mails they sent each other and the kind of information they exchanged. Exit OSForensics.

You can also simply connect a mobile device to a computer to browse the file system and examine and retrieve files. Figure 12-4, for example, shows the file system on an Android device connected by USB cable to a computer. To do an acquisition, you just need a USB write-blocker. This method isn't ideal, but you can use it to gather basic information.

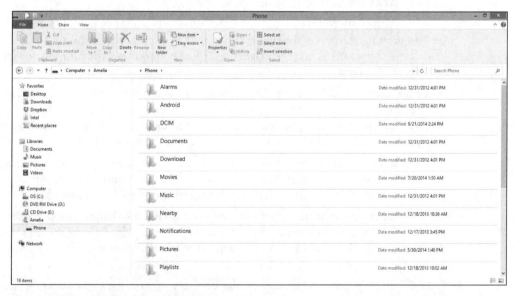

Figure 12-4 Viewing the Android file system
Courtesy of Microsoft Corporation

In this activity, you have the opportunity to examine some demo software for mobile forensics:

1. Start a Web browser, go to **www.paraben.com**, and download the demo version of Device Seizure. Install the software, accepting the default settings.

2. After installing Device Seizure, start it. If you get a message about the time remaining for the demo, click **OK**.

3. In the welcome window of the Device Seizure Wizard, click the **Create Case** button. In the New Document window, type **Test Case** as the filename, and then click **Save**.

4. In the Case Information window, type today's date in the Case Number text box, **174** in the Property/Evidence Number text box, and **ABC Corporation** in the Company/Agency Name text box. Click **Next**.

5. Enter your first name in the Examiner text box, and click **Next**. Examine the information in the Summary window, and click **Next** and then **Finish**.

6. Explore the available functions in this tool, such as importing iPhone backup files, creating emulations, and acquiring data. When you're finished, exit the program.

Next, you examine a Galaxy mini device with Oxygen Forensics. First, go to *www.oxygen-forensic.com* and register for the freeware. After getting the registration code, which could take a few days, download and install the software. Then follow these steps:

1. Start a Web browser, if necessary, and go to **www.oxygen-forensic.com/en/download/ devicebackups**. Download the **Samsung Galaxy Mini** file to your work folder. Unzip the file, which is `Patrick Payge's Galaxy Mini.ofb`.

2. Start Oxygen Forensic Suite 2014, and click the **Import backup file** list arrow.

3. Click **Import OFB backup**. Navigate to your work folder, click the `Patrick Payge's Galaxy Mini.ofb` file, and click **Open**.

4. In the Oxygen Forensic Extractor v. 5.1.303 dialog box that opens, click **Extract**. (The version number shown on the dialog box might differ, depending on when you down-loaded the software.) When the extraction is finished, you see the "Import finished" message. Click **Finish**.

5. In the left pane, click **Brooklyn maniac**, expand the tree structure, and click `Patrick Payge's Galaxy Mini.ofb`. Notice all the information available in the right pane. Some items have an "unregistered" status or a red exclamation mark, which indicates that you're using the free version, and these features aren't available.

6. At the lower right, click **Device Information**. In the message box about collecting infor-mation on account data, click **Start**. After the collection is finished, you should see owner account information, including names, password hashes, and so forth.

7. Click the **back arrow** at the upper left, and then click the **Event Log** icon. At the upper right, you should see a date filter. Change the start date to **06/08/2011** and the end date to **07/01/2011**. Notice the number of calls involving Dan Espozito. If time permits, do a search on his name to find more information.

8. Click the **back arrow**, and then click **File Browser** to view the Galaxy mini's file system. Take a screenshot with the tree structure expanded. Click **File**, **Exit** from the menu.

Many mobile forensics tools are available, but most aren't free. As the market continues to expand and mature, the methods and techniques for acquiring evidence will change.

Subscribe to user groups and professional organizations to stay abreast of what's happening in the industry.

New Technologies and Challenges As mentioned in Chapter 10, both VMware and BlackBerry are developing type 2 hypervisors for mobile devices. They're useful for security and protecting personal information but add another layer of complexity to forensics investigations. In corporate investigations, for example, you need to take care to separate personal information from business-related data. Knowledge of privacy laws is especially crucial in this task.

The Internet of Things (IoT) also brings new challenges to the field of mobile forensics. The number of devices that connect to the Internet is higher than the number of people, and this number is expected to reach 50 billion in the next few decades (*http://share.cisco.com/internet-of-things.html*). Although jokes about "The fridge did it" are rampant, the concerns are real. From a mobile device, you can turn on lights in your home, lock or unlock doors, adjust the thermostat, and more, and all these appliances and devices can be interconnected. LG already offers a refrigerator that can order groceries for you, and it's connected to an established payment method, such as a digital wallet. So in an investigation, determining who actually ordered food and unlocked the door when the delivery was made could be difficult. In the very near future, investigators might face these challenges and more.

Research on wearable computers has been conducted at MIT labs for more than a decade, and these computers are now moving into working reality. For example, workers in warehouses can wear rings to scan inventory, Google Glass to access the Internet or take pictures while walking is available, and the Apple Watch will be on the market in 2015 (*www.apple.com/watch/*). In addition, IBM has created a unique mobile phone as jewelry. Earrings are the speakers, a necklace is the microphone, a ring notifies you of incoming calls, and a bracelet identifies the caller (*http://electronics.howstuffworks.com/gadgets/home/digital-jewelry1.htm*). Collecting information from wearable computers will pose many new challenges for investigators.

12

Chapter Summary

- People store a wealth of information on smartphones, including calls, text messages, picture and music files, address books, and more. These files can give you a lot of information when investigating cases.

- Mobile phones have gone through four generations: analog, digital personal communications service (PCS), third-generation (3G), and fourth-generation (4G). Two major digital networks currently used in the United States are Code Division Multiple Access (CDMA) and Global System for Mobile Communications (GSM).

- 4G technology is the current generation of mobile phones. It has faster data transfer rates than previous generations.

- Mobile devices range from basic, inexpensive phones used primarily for phone calls to smartphones that integrate a phone, PDA, camera, music player, and more into one device.

- Data can be retrieved from several different places in phones, including volatile memory, nonvolatile memory, and Secure Digital, MultiMediaCard, and Compact Flash cards.

- The use of personal digital assistants (PDAs) has declined because smartphones incorporated all their features and added more. They're still used for specialized applications, such as medical and industrial PDAs.

- As you do with computers, you must follow correct search and seizure procedures for mobile devices. In particular, investigators must take care to ensure that mobile devices remain connected to a power source so that they don't lose data in volatile memory. Also, suspect devices should be disconnected from PCs as soon as possible to prevent any synchronization that might overwrite data on the device.

- To isolate a mobile device from incoming messages, you can put it in airplane mode, turn the device off, or place it in a specially treated paint can or evidence bag.

- SIM cards store data in a hierarchical file structure containing a system root, which holds directory files that store elementary data.

- Mobile device forensics is becoming more important as these devices grow in popularity. Accessing backup files from the cloud or SIM cards is the easiest way to retrieve information from these devices, but acquiring an image is more accurate and produces more detailed data.

- Many software tools are available for reading data stored in mobile devices. Typically, these devices connect to the phone wirelessly (through Bluetooth or irDA) or with a cable. Some also read SIM cards by using a SIM card reader, which is a combination hardware/software device.

- The Internet of Things (IoT) has resulted in yet another challenge to forensics. The number of devices that connect to the Internet is expected to reach 50 billion in the next few decades. Because mobile devices and appliances are so interconnected, determining a timeline or who actually performed an action can be difficult. In addition, collecting information from wearable computers will pose many new challenges for investigators.

Key Terms

Code Division Multiple Access (CDMA) A widely used digital cell phone technology that makes use of spread-spectrum modulation to spread the signal across a wide range of frequencies.

electronically erasable programmable read-only memory (EEPROM) A type of nonvolatile memory that can be reprogrammed electrically, without having to physically access or remove the chip.

Enhanced Data GSM Environment (EDGE) An improvement to GSM technology that enables it to deliver higher data rates. *See also* Global System for Mobile Communications (GSM).

fourth-generation (4G) The current generation of mobile phone standards, with technologies that improved speed and accuracy.

Global System for Mobile Communications (GSM) A second-generation cellular network standard; currently the most used cellular network in the world.

International Telecommunication Union (ITU) An international organization dedicated to creating telecommunications standards.

Orthogonal Frequency Division Multiplexing (OFDM) A 4G technology that uses numerous parallel carriers instead of a single broad carrier and is less susceptible to interference.

personal digital assistants (PDAs) Handheld electronic devices that typically contain personal productivity applications used for calendaring, contact management, and note taking. Unlike smartphones, PDAs don't have telephony capabilities.

smartphones Mobile telephones with more features than a traditional phone has, including a camera, an e-mail client, a Web browser, a calendar, contact management software, an instant-messaging program, and more.

subscriber identity module (SIM) cards Removable cards in GSM phones that contain information for identifying subscribers. They can also store other information, such as messages and call history.

Telecommunications Industry Association (TIA) A U.S. trade association representing hundreds of telecommunications companies that works to establish and maintain telecommunications standards.

third-generation (3G) The preceding generation of mobile phone standards and technology; had more advanced features and faster data rates than the older analog and personal communications service (PCS) technologies.

Time Division Multiple Access (TDMA) The technique of dividing a radio frequency into time slots, used by GSM networks; also refers to a cellular network standard covered by Interim Standard (IS) 136. *See also* Global System for Mobile Communications (GSM).

Review Questions

1. List four places where mobile device information might be stored.

2. Typically, you need a search warrant to retrieve information from a service provider. True or False?

3. The term TDMA refers to which of the following? (Choose all that apply.)

    a. A technique of dividing a radio frequency so that multiple users share the same channel

    b. A proprietary protocol developed by Motorola

    c. A specific cellular network standard

    d. A technique of spreading the signal across many channels

4. What's the most commonly used cellular network worldwide?

5. Which of the following relies on a central database that tracks account data, location data, and subscriber information?

    a. BTS

    b. MSC

    c. BSC

    d. None of the above

6. GSM divides a mobile station into _____ and _____.

7. SD cards have a capacity up to which of the following?

    a. 100 MB

    b. 4 MB

    c. 64 GB

    d. 500 MB

8. Describe two ways you can isolate a mobile device from incoming signals.

9. Which of the following categories of information is stored on a SIM card? (Choose all that apply.)

    a. Volatile memory

    b. Call data

    c. Service-related data

    d. None of the above

10. Most SIM cards allow _____ access attempts before locking you out.

11. SIM card readers can alter evidence by showing that a message has been read when you view it. True or False?

12. List two peripheral memory cards used with PDAs.

13. When acquiring a mobile device at an investigation scene, you should leave it connected to a laptop or tablet so that you can observe synchronization as it takes place. True or False?

14. Remote wiping of a mobile device can result in which of the following? (Choose all that apply.)

    a. Removing account information

    b. Enabling a GPS beacon to track the thief

    c. Returning the phone to the original factory settings

    d. Deleting contacts

15. In which of the following cases did the U.S. Supreme Court require using a search warrant to examine the contents of mobile devices?

    a. *Miles v. North Dakota*

    b. *Smith v. Oregon*

    c. *Riley v. California*

    d. *Dearborn v. Ohio*

16. When investigating social media content, evidence artifacts can vary, depending on the social media channel and the device. True or False?

Hands-On Projects

If necessary, extract all data files in the Chap12\Projects folder on the book's DVD to the *Work*\Chap12\Projects folder on your system. (Create this folder on your system before starting the projects; it's referred to as your "work folder" in steps.)

Hands-On Project 12-1

In this case, Sebastian and Nau are suspected of drug dealing, and their phones were seized with the other digital evidence. One of your colleagues has a licensed version of SIMcon. You were able to go to her forensics lab and examine the SIM cards of both phones. In this project, you examine the exported Excel files.

1. Start Excel, and open the **Messages_Sebastian's_phone.xls** and **Messages_Nau's_phone.xls** files.

2. If the messages aren't currently in chronological order, change the display to sort them in this order.

3. Establish the timeline for what transpired between these two employees. Note items such as when they respond to each other's messages, dates and times, and what numbers they call.

4. Write a short report summarizing the data you examined and stating any conclusions you can draw from the SMS messages.

Hands-On Project 12-2

SIMcon is a forensics software tool that can generate information for mobile device investigations. In Hands-On Project 12-1, you examined SMS messages on two phones that had been generated by SIMcon. In this project, you view the report with additional details that was generated. Be prepared to do research for this assignment.

1. Start Notepad, and open **Report_Nau's_phone.txt**. Start a second instance of Notepad, and open **Report_Sebastian's_phone.txt**.

2. As you examine the reports, find definitions for the following items: International Mobile Subscriber Identity (IMSI), PLMN selector, HPLMN search period, and Cell Broadcast Message Identifier (CBMI). Note any other items of interest.

3. Explain what "SIM Phase: phase 2 - profile download required" means.

4. You notice "Originating Address (TP-OA): 264813358947" in the report for Nau's phone. The number breaks down into 264-81-3358947. Explain what the first two numbers—264 and 81—designate.

5. Explain what the following originating addresses mean:

    *   Originating Address (TP-OA): 123
    *   Originating Address (TP-OA): 131

6. Next, compare the two files. If you didn't complete Hands-On Project 12-1, create a timeline of the SMS messages.

7. Write a report with answers to the preceding questions, and include any conclusions you drew about the messages' contents.

Hands-On Project 12-3

As mentioned in the chapter, many SIM card reader tools aren't forensically sound. In this project, you use one of these tools to examine SIM cards.

1. Start a Web browser, go to **www.dekart.com/products/card_management/ sim_manager**, and download **SIMManager.exe**, which has a 30-day free trial.

2. Install SIMManager and start the program. If you get a message stating that this copy of the program isn't registered, click **OK**.

3. Click the **Open** toolbar icon, navigate to your work folder, click the **Phonebook_Sebastian's.phn** file, and click **Open**.

4. Click to select **Phonebook_Sebastian's** on the left; his name and the cell phone number are then displayed on the right.

5. Click the **SMS messages** icon on the left. Examine the messages displayed on the right.

6. Click the **Print** toolbar icon to print the messages. Accept the default selections, click **Print**, and then click **Print** in the Print dialog box.

7. Examine the menu items, and notice that this tool is used for altering or updating a SIM card, not for investigative purposes. Click **File, Close** from the menu.

8. Click the **Open** toolbar icon, navigate to your work folder, click the **Phonebook_Nau's.phn** file, and then click **Open**.

9. Determine Nau's full first name. Next, click the **SMS messages** icon on the left.

10. Notice that two different SMS Centers are listed on the left. Draw a conclusion as to what the difference might be.

11. Print the messages, following the procedure in Step 6.

12. Compare the two sets of messages, and correlate the timestamps. Create a timeline based on this information. Write a short report on your findings and any relevant conclusions.

Hands-On Project 12-4

In this project, you use Oxygen Forensics to examine a BlackBerry device. If you haven't already done so, go to *www.oxygen-forensic.com* and request a registration code for downloading the demo version of Oxygen Forensics. (Keep in mind that getting the registration code might take a few days, and plan accordingly.) When you get it, download and install the software.

1. Start a Web browser, if necessary, and go to **www.oxygen-forensic.com/ en/download/devicebackups**. Download the **Blackberry 9520** file to your work folder. Unzip the file, which is **Greg Bramson's BlackBerry 9520.ofb**.

2. Start Oxygen Forensic Suite 2014, and click the **Import backup file** list arrow.

3. Click **Import OFB backup**. Navigate to your work folder, click the `Greg Bramson's BlackBerry 9520.ofb` file, and click **Open**.

4. In the Oxygen Forensic Extractor v. 5.1.303 dialog box that opens, click **Extract**. When the extraction is complete, click **Finish**.

5. When the file opens, click **Brooklyn maniac**, expand the tree structure, and then click `Greg Bramson's BlackBerry 9520.ofb`.

6. Notice at the lower right that the listing varies from what you saw for Patrick Payge's Galaxy Mini in the in-chapter activity. The Device Information and File Browser entries are the same, but this BlackBerry device has an entry called Phone Call Logs instead of an Event Log. Click the **Device Information** icon to see the owner, number, and service provider.

7. Return to the main window by clicking the **back arrow** at the upper left, and then click the **File Browser** icon. Click the **Geo files** tab (scrolling to the right to find it, if necessary), and examine the files listed. What can they tell you about the owner?

8. Click the **Images** tab, and scroll down until you get to the `.jpg` files. What types of pictures are stored? What can they tell you?

9. Return to the main window, and click **Messages** at the lower right. Examine the messages listed. Combined with the other files and pictures, what sort of timeline can you construct for the owner?

10. Exit the program. Write a two- to three-page paper with your findings.

Case Projects

12

CASE PROJECTS

Case Project 12-1

Download the most current version of the NIST Mobile Device Forensics Guidelines at *http://nvlpubs.nist.gov/nistpubs/SpecialPublications/NIST.SP.800-101r1.pdf*. Page 17 lists classifications of mobile device tools. For the tools covered in this chapter, determine what type each one is based on these NIST guidelines. Write a one- to two-page paper explaining the uses and limitations of each tool.

Case Project 12-2

For this project, you need access to a mobile forensics toolkit. Select a cell phone model for which you have no cable. After doing Internet research for possible options, write a plan for approaching the problem. Remember that you don't want to destroy data, so make sure you include a step to test the equipment before using it.

chapter 13

Cloud Forensics

After reading this chapter and completing the exercises, you will be able to:

- Describe the main concepts of cloud computing
- Summarize the legal challenges in conducting cloud forensics
- Give an overview of the technical challenges with cloud forensics
- Describe how to acquire cloud data
- Explain how to conduct a cloud investigation
- Explain what remote access tools can be used for cloud investigations

This chapter explains how to apply forensics skills and techniques to a cloud environment. First, you get an overview of cloud computing so that you understand how clouds are configured and how they operate. Next, you review some of the legal and technical challenges in conducting cloud forensics and get an overview of some related issues with acquisitions and encryption.

This chapter also gives you guidance on creating a plan for conducting a cloud investigation and describes how to gather evidence from cloud service providers and customers. Because of rapid changes in cloud storage models and methods, you need to continue researching changes in cloud computing and how to apply digital forensics techniques to the cloud.

An Overview of Cloud Computing

The cloud has introduced ways of managing data that didn't exist five years ago. For this reason, cloud investigations have some unique challenges. This section gives you background on cloud computing, including a brief history, cloud service levels and deployment methods, cloud vendors, and basic concepts of cloud forensics. You also learn about new standards being developed to improve security practices and incident responses in cloud environments.

History of the Cloud

The idea of cloud computing came from several people. Professor John McCarthy of MIT and Dr. J. C. R. Licklider, director at the U.S. Department of Defense Advanced Research Projects Agency (ARPA), are generally given credit for developing the concept (*www.computerweekly. com/feature/A-history-of-cloud-computing*). In 1961, McCarthy proposed selling computing resources, such as processing data, and software as a service through a public utility, similar to how water, sewer, and electrical power are made available to the public. This idea was based on hosting services and software on a mainframe computer. In an April 25, 1963, memo, "Members and Affiliates of the Intergalactic Computer Network," Dr. Licklider proposed interconnecting programs and data to share resources. In 1968, the ARPA Program Plan No. 723, Resource Sharing Computer Networks, was initiated to engineer a solution of sharing networked resources. It then developed into the Advanced Research Projects Agency Network (ARPANET), which later became the Internet (*www.dod.mil/pubs/foi/ Science_and_Technology/DARPA/977.pdf*).

In 1999, Salesforce.com developed a customer relationship management (CRM) Web service that applied digital marketing research to business subscribers so that they could do their own market analysis; this service eventually led the way to the cloud. Amazon created Amazon Mechanical Turk in 2002, which provided storage, computations, and human intelligence, and then started its Elastic Compute Cloud (EC2) in 2006, a Web service aimed at supporting small businesses. It enabled people and small businesses to rent processing time to run their own applications from a centralized source. After Web 2.0 in 2009, other providers started their own cloud services, such as Google Apps, Apple iCloud, Microsoft OneDrive, and more.

Cloud Service Levels and Deployment Methods

The National Institute of Standards and Technology defines cloud computing in its NIST Special Publication 800-145 document "The NIST Definition of Cloud Computing" (*http://csrc.nist.gov/publications/nistpubs/800-145/SP800-145.pdf*, 2011) as a computing storage system that provides on-demand network access for multiple users and can allocate storage to users to keep up with changes in their needs. The cloud has three service levels:

- *SaaS*—With **software as a service (SaaS)**, applications are delivered via the Internet. A familiar one is Google Docs, which is similar to office suites such as Microsoft Office or LibreOffice. Data is stored in the cloud, and files can be accessed and shared with others.

- *PaaS*—**Platform as a service (PaaS)** means an OS, such as Linux or Windows, has been installed on a cloud server. Users can then install their own applications, settings, and tools in the cloud environment. The cloud provider maintains just the hardware for customers, who are responsible for their own system administration and application support.

- *IaaS*—**Infrastructure as a service (IaaS)** means customers can rent hardware, such as servers and workstations, and install whatever OSs and applications they need. IaaS can come in handy when customers can't afford to purchase hardware or pay someone to maintain it but can afford to rent. In addition, this service level makes it easy to add hardware during peak business periods, such as tax season or end-of-year accounting, and then cut back on hardware when it's not needed during slow periods.

 NIST currently has only the three types of cloud services described in the preceding list. However, some vendors are developing new types of specialized cloud services, so keep in mind that NIST might consider adding other definitions of cloud services.

Table 13-1 describes where investigators find evidence of cloud access, depending on the type of cloud service level.

Table 13-1 Locations of evidence in different service levels

Service level	Locations of evidence
SaaS	Most likely stored on a desktop, laptop, tablet, or smartphone.
PaaS	Most likely found on a desktop or server, although it could also be stored on a company network or the remote service provider's infrastructure.
IaaS	Usually found on a desktop or server; infrastructure equipment can be owned by the company or the remote service provider.

© 2016 Cengage Learning®

As an investigator, the location of evidence affects what you can get access to and what laws regulate your actions. If, for example, you're conducting a corporate investigation and policies and procedures are in place, you can do a static acquisition of the device that accessed cloud data and a remote acquisition of files on the cloud server. If the company has its own cloud server, the acquisition might be even more straightforward, particularly if the cloud server has built-in forensics and e-discovery tools. These tools speed up an investigation and reduce its costs.

The deployment methods for a cloud are public, private, community, and hybrid. A **public cloud** is accessible to anyone, and typically, the only identification required is an e-mail address. This deployment method offers no security, but it's popular because of its ease of use. Next is a **private cloud**, which can be accessed only by people who have the necessary credentials, such as logon names and passwords; sometimes location is used as a way to restrict access, too. Most companies have private clouds. A **community cloud** is a way to bring people together for a specific purpose. For example, say a city wants all small businesses to have access to the same documents and templates. By creating a community cloud, the city can make these files accessible to those who have a current business license. A **hybrid cloud** enables a company to keep some information private and designate other files as public or community information.

Cloud Vendors

Many **cloud service providers** (**CSPs**) and products are available. CSPs use a variety of approaches and systems to build their cloud systems, such as servers using distributive processing methods with data farms for storage or mainframes running OSs as virtual machines. The following are some CSPs and cloud applications:

- *Salesforce (www.salesforce.com)*—Offers a variety of cloud services, including automation and CRM, cloud application development, and Web site marketing

- *IBM Cloud (www.ibm.com/cloud-computing/us/en/)*—Provides cloud development and mobile applications for several platforms

- *Cisco Cloud Computing (www.cisco.com/web/solutions/trends/cloud/index.html)*— Has cloud applications for a wide assortment of businesses, ranging from enterprise and midsize businesses to resellers of cloud services

- *Amazon EC2 (http://aws.amazon.com/ec2/)*—Offers a Web service run from the cloud that allows scalability

- *AT&T Synaptic (http://cloudarchitect.att.com/Home/* and *www.synaptic.att.com/clouduser/)*—Provides onsite data storage and the capability of a hybrid cloud system

- *Google Cloud Storage (https://cloud.google.com/products/cloud-storage/)*—Offers virtual machines with tools for analyzing large data sets

- *HP Helion (www8.hp.com/us/en/cloud/helion-overview.html)*—Provides a hybrid cloud environment with a wide range of products that can integrate into a business's storage needs

- *Microsoft Azure Blob Storage (http://azure.microsoft.com/en-us/documentation/services/storage/)*—Offers tiered support for large organizations

- *XenServer and XenCenter Windows Management Console (http://xenserver.org/overview-xenserver-open-source-virtualization/download.html)*—Has a freeware type 1 hypervisor used for public and private clouds

Basic Concepts of Cloud Forensics

Cloud forensics procedures are needed in many situations, such as cyber criminals attacking a cloud, policy violations in accessing a cloud, data recovery, reports of suspicious activity, fraud, and data breaches (Stephen Coty, AlertLogic, Inc., RSAConference, *www.rsaconference.com/writable/presentations/file_upload/anf-t07a-computer-forensics-and-incident-response-in-the-cloud.pdf*, 2014). Cloud forensics can be defined as simply as applying digital forensics to cloud computing and is considered a subset of network forensics (Keyun Ruan et al, "Cloud forensics: An overview," *www.academia.edu/2821856/Cloud_forensics_An_overview*, 2012). This article describes cloud forensics as having three dimensions: organizational, legal, and technical. The organizational dimension addresses the structure of the cloud, such as location of data storage and administration of services. The legal dimension covers service agreements and other jurisdictional matters because a cloud's data storage can be located anywhere in the world and even cross nations' boundaries. The technical dimension deals with procedures and specialized applications designed to perform forensics recovery and analysis in the cloud. The following are capabilities forensics tools should have to handle acquiring data from a cloud:

- *Forensic data collection*—Tools must be able to identify, label, record, and acquire data from the cloud.

- *Elastic, static, and live forensics*—To meet the elastic nature of clouds, tools must be able to expand and contract their data storage capabilities as the demand for services changes.

- *Evidence segregation*—Clouds are set up for **multitenancy**, meaning many different unrelated businesses and users share the same applications and storage space, so forensics tools must be able to separate each customer's data.

- *Investigations in virtualized environments*—Because cloud operations typically run in a virtual environment, forensics tools should have the capability to examine virtual systems.

Legal Challenges in Cloud Forensics

Because cloud computing is a rapidly changing technology, laws haven't kept up with the implications of storing files and data in locations that aren't physically within reach. For this reason, when you're investigating a cloud system, you need to consider many factors involving a CSP's relationship with cloud users. This section explains a CSP's contract obligations with cloud users and how warrants and subpoenas are applied to CSPs and users. Understanding these legal issues can help you prepare for an investigation more effectively.

Service Level Agreements

Organizations that sell cloud services have **service level agreements (SLAs)** with their customers, which are also called "master service agreements." An SLA is a contract between a CSP and the customer that describes what services are being provided and at what level. It should also specify support options, penalties for services not provided, system performance (periods of downtime and uptime, for example), fees, provided software or hardware, and so forth (*www.webopedia.com/TERM/S/Service_Level_Agreement.html*). It's important that SLAs define in detail the scope of services the CSP provides and what responsibilities are expected of the customer, including the following:

- Service hours
- Restrictions applied to the customer by the CSP
- Availability of the cloud to the customer
- Levels of support for the customer
- Response time for data transfers
- Throughput, limitations
- Contingency plan for incident response

- Business continuity and disaster recovery plan
- Fees for the subscription to the cloud and fees for additional services as they occur
- Security measures
- Terminology of the cloud's systems and applications

Digital forensics examiners should be most concerned with restrictions applied to customers and security measures. These CSP components must state who is authorized to access data and what the limitations are in conducting acquisitions for an investigation. Because many cloud vendors spread data storage systems across multiple countries, the CSP should also address any multijurisdiction concerns and define how conflicts between laws of different countries will be resolved.

Even if a contract delineates access to data and processes for acquiring it, a country's laws might expand, limit, or even reject the rights specified in the contract's terms.

CAUTION

Policies, Standards, and Guidelines for CSPs CSPs have policies, standards, and guidelines for their daily operations, and digital forensics investigators should review them carefully when preparing a cloud investigation plan. This section summarizes recommendations for these policies, standards, and guidelines from the SANS organization (*www.sans.org/security-resources/policies/#name* and *www.sans.org/security-resources/policies/computer.php*).

Policies are detailed rules for a CSP's internal operation and typically include personnel responsibilities, management structure, delegation authority, contracting authority, expectations of protecting data, and the authorization to distribute information. Standards give guidance to staff for unique operations, hardware, and software and describe their obligations in daily operations and security of the CSP's environment. Although guidelines aren't required, they describe best practices for cloud processes and give staff an example of what they should strive to achieve in their work.

For more information on policy, standards, and guidelines, see *www.itmanagerdaily.com/cloud-computing-policy-template/* and *https://cloudsecurityalliance.org*.

TIP

CSP Processes and Procedures Processes and procedures are detailed documents that define workflow and step-by-step instructions for CSP staff. They often include hardware configuration diagrams, network maps, and application processing flowcharts. Digital forensics examiners can use these documents to understand how data is stored, manipulated, secured, backed up, restored, and accessed by CSP staff and customers.

Additional documents of interest are the CSP's business continuity and disaster recovery plans, which can be helpful in recovering and analyzing data you need for your investigation. These documents are particularly useful if you have large quantities of data to collect and examine without adequate storage. If the CSP has a backup site designated in its business continuity plan, you might be able to use it for storing digital evidence you've collected and analyzing extremely large data sets.

Jurisdiction Issues

Although there are plans to revise current laws, many cross-jurisdiction legal issues haven't been resolved. No law ensures uniform access or required handling procedures for the cloud, so cases that encompass multiple jurisdictions as well as the cloud's multitenancy nature are concerns for any investigation. In addition, investigators should be concerned about cases involving data commingled with other customers' data that's unrelated to the investigation (*www.researchgate.net/publication/221352825_A_Survey_of_the_Legal_Issues_Facing_Digital_Forensic_Experts*). If government regulations and agreements haven't been developed in other countries, investigators might be limited in what they can do to process a case.

Often simply figuring out what law controls data stored in the cloud is a challenge. Although the SLA or associated contracts and addenda can prescribe what laws are enforceable, they don't usually control privacy issues and criminal or civil procedures. (An addendum is used to add or change a contract without having to re-create it.) Many countries with legal systems derived from a common source, such as English common law, might have similar laws but vary in procedures. In addition, how privacy rights are defined in different jurisdictions is a major factor in problems with the right to access data. For example, EU Directive 95/46/EC (*http://searchsecurity.techtarget.co.uk/definition/EU-Data-Protection-Directive*) is more restrictive than rules in other countries, including the United States. This directive protects private information for all EU citizens, stating that EU citizens must be notified before their personal information is accessed, and this information can be accessed only with their consent.

Some problems are as fundamental as establishing definitions of terms and roles and determining which law is applicable. As mentioned, when data is stored in muliple countries, conflicts in laws can happen. For this reason, digital forensics examiners could be held liable when conducting an investigation involving cloud data. Consult with legal experts when conducting cloud examinations to make sure you're aware of possible restrictions in collecting evidence.

Accessing Evidence in the Cloud

Cloud forensics typically involves litigation of criminal or civil matters. When information or evidence is needed, warrants and subpoenas are used to get it from parties involved in the investigation or litigation. When evidence needs to be seized, warrants are used in criminal cases and issued by law enforcement. When only information is needed, subpoenas are typically issued for civil and criminal cases.

In the United States, the Electronic Communications Privacy Act (ECPA) describes five mechanisms the government can use to get electronic information from a provider: search warrants, subpoenas, subpoenas with prior notice to the subscriber or customer, court orders, and court orders with prior notice to the subscriber or customer. The following sections describe these mechanisms in more detail as they apply to cloud investigations.

Search Warrants A search warrant can be used only in criminal cases, and it must be requested by a law enforcement officer who has evidence of probable cause that a crime was committed and evidence of it can be found at the location specified in the warrant. There has been a lot of litigation over the concept of "probable cause," but not much case law applies to searches conducted in the cloud.

13

 To obtain a search warrant, a government entity must show that there's probable cause to believe the contents of a wire or electronic communication or other records are relevant to an ongoing criminal investigation.

The law requires search warrants to contain specific descriptions of what's to be seized. For cloud environments, the property to be seized usually describes data rather than physical hardware, unless the CSP is a suspect. Generally, however, seizing hardware yields no benefit that seizing just data can't provide.

Seizing hardware can also be disruptive to other customers sharing it with the suspect. For example, FBI agents seized computers from a data center in Dallas, Texas, to gather evidence in an investigation of two men accused of defrauding telecommunication providers. Seizing these computers had the unintended consequence of disrupting the business operations of around 50 companies with data hosted on these systems. The FBI's main motivation in seizing these computers was that the CSP was also a suspect. As a result, however, Liquid Motors, a company providing inventory management services to car dealers, had to shut down its operations and filed a temporary restraining order (TRO) against the FBI the same day to get its data back. Although the TRO was denied, the FBI made mirror images of the data over the weekend to give to Liquid Motors (*Liquid Motors, Inc. v. Lynd*, No. 3:09-cv-0611-N, N.D. Tex, April 3, 2009).

Search warrants must also describe the location of items to be seized. This step is straightforward when describing physical locations, but it's less clear when dealing with online data because servers are often dispersed across state or national borders. The near-instant **provisioning** and **deprovisioning** of resources pose a serious legal challenge in cloud forensics. Unless physical machines are seized or virtual machines are turned off, executing a warrant is unlikely to affect the data owner, but the trade-off is that the risk of **spoliation** (failing to preserve evidence) increases if the search is announced. The FBI faced this risk in the Liquid Motors case, which is why hardware was seized along with the data.

Finally, a search warrant must establish how it will be carried out. Safeguards in federal search warrants include specifying the date and time of day to minimize disruptions to people and business operations.

Subpoenas and Court Orders Under the U.S. federal judicial system, there are government agency subpoenas, non-government and civil litigation subpoenas, and court orders:

- *Government agency subpoenas*—U.S. Code 18 states that customer communications and records can't be knowingly divulged to any person or entity, although it allows specific exceptions to government agencies. This type of subpoena is used to get information when it's believed there's a danger of death or serious physical injury or for the National Center for Missing and Exploited Children. U.S. federal courts interpret this as meaning that no Stored Communications Act provision permits disclosure for a civil discovery order unless the order comes from a government entity: "Subpoena may not be enforced consistent with the plain language of the Privacy Act because the exceptions enumerated in § 2702(b) do not include civil discovery subpoenas." Most courts have concluded that third parties can't be compelled to disclose electronic communications pursuant to a civil discovery subpoena (*Crispin v. Christian Audigier, Inc.*, 717 F. Supp. 2d 965 [C.D. Cal. 2010], and *Mintz v. Mark Bartelstein & Associates, Inc.*, 885

F. Supp. 2d 987, 991 [C.D. Cal. 2012]). The SCA doesn't contain an exception for civil discovery subpoenas. See *www.law.cornell.edu/uscode/text/18/2702* for more information about this statute.

- *Non-government and civil litigation subpoenas*—These subpoenas are used to produce information from private parties for litigation. An example of how they apply to a CSP can be seen in *Flagg v. City of Detroit* (252 F.R.D. 346, E.D. Mich., 2008). A CSP received a civil subpoena for the production of electronically stored information (ESI) in the cloud, including text messages sent or received by city employees who used mobile devices supplied by SkyTel. Although the court determined that this data could be subject to discovery under the Federal Rules of Civil Procedure, it denied the subpoena because the evidence could have been acquired more easily by making an ESI discovery request to the cloud users. For more information on this case, see *www.ca6.uscourts.gov/opinions.pdf/13a0119p-06.pdf* and *www.ediscoverylaw.com/2008/03/articles/case-summaries/court-sets-protocol-for-production-and-review-of-text-messages/*.

- *Court orders*—Court orders are written by judges to compel someone to do or not do something, such as a CSP producing user logon activities. Under U.S. Code 18, court orders are available only to government agencies. In U.S. federal courts, it's interpreted as meaning that a court order can be issued by "any court that is a court of competent jurisdiction" only if the government agency "offers specific and articulable facts showing that there are reasonable grounds to believe that the contents of a wire or electronic communication, or the records or other information sought, are relevant and material to an ongoing criminal investigation." When a state government agency is involved, a court order can't be issued if the laws of the state prohibit it. For more information, see *www.law.cornell.edu/uscode/text/18/2703*.

The burden of proof (reasonable grounds) to get a court order is lower than the probable cause required for a search warrant.

Technical Challenges in Cloud Forensics

13

Cloud forensics procedures combine many computing and networking tasks, such as data recovery, network analysis to detect intrusions, database administration and security, software security, and international relations. In the following sections, you learn about some common technical concerns you'll encounter when performing cloud forensics.

The NIST Cloud Computing Forensic Science Working Group (*www.sensei-iot.org/Presentations/MHerman_CC_FSWG.pdf*, 2014) developed the following list of challenges in conducting cloud forensics. Some of these challenges are discussed in more detail in the following sections:

- Architecture
- Data collection
- Analysis of cloud forensic data
- Anti-forensics
- Incident first responders

- Role management
- Legal issues
- Standards and training

NIST is building standards for cloud forensics procedures. For the most current information, see *www.nist.gov/itl/itl-cloud-computing-forensic-science.cfm*.

Architecture

Clouds vary in their architecture, so no two CSPs are configured in exactly the same way. Depending on the type of cloud architecture, customers' data might be commingled, making it difficult to sort through data to determine what's relevant to an investigation. Identifying data storage locations can be a problem, too, because most CSPs keep these locations secret for security reasons. In addition, differences in recording procedures or log keeping can make it difficult to determine data's origin and complicate an investigation's chain of evidence.

Analysis of Cloud Forensic Data

Analyzing digital evidence collected from a cloud requires verifying the data with other data and log records. You might need to reconstruct the data to determine what actually occurred during an incident and compare network records to make sure servers' internal clocks are synchronized correctly. Examining logs can be useful to compare the modified, last access, and create (MAC) dates and times for files. Metadata from affected files should be examined, too, to validate file accesses. All this information is used to build a timeline to show what happened when an incident occurred.

Anti-Forensics

Destroying ESI that's potential evidence is called "anti-forensics." Anti-forensics tactics are used in cloud environments as well as in other network environments. Hackers might obfuscate incriminating files or hide them by the simple technique of changing file extensions. Specialized malware for defeating evidence collection can add time to an investigation and result in the loss of valuable evidence. Additonal methods for anti-forensics include inserting malware programs in other files, using encryption to obfuscate malware programs activated through other malware programs, and using data-hiding utilities that append malware to existing files. Other techniques affect file metadata by changing the modify and last access times. Changing file timestamps can make it difficult to develop a timeline of a hacker's activities. Calculating hash values of files and comparing the results with known good files' hash values can help identify files that might have been altered. (For a reminder on hashing and using known good files, refer to Chapter 9.)

Incident First Responders

Typically, CSPs have personnel trained to respond to network incidents, such as system and network administrators who handle normal support services for the cloud. When a network intrusion occurs, they become first responders to the incident. If a CSP doesn't have an internal first responder team, the forensics examiner should organize CSP staff to handle these tasks. Some factors to address include the following:

- Will the CSP's operations staff be cooperative and follow directions, and will management issue orders stating that you're the leader of the investigation?

- Do you need to brief staff about operations security? For example, you might need to explain that they should talk only to others who have a need to know about the incident and the investigation's activities.

- Do you need to train staff in evidence collection procedures, including the chain of custody?

Role Management

Role management in the cloud covers data owners, identity protection, users, access controls (a list of access privileges and restrictions for each user), and so forth. As an investigator, you need to collect this information so that you can identify additional victims or suspects. Identity protection, for example, means you need to determine whether sensitive personally identifiable information (PII) was compromised, which broadens the investigation's scope. You might also need to determine whether a PII compromise was intentional or accidental, and knowing cloud users' access permissions can help with this task.

Standards and Training

As the cloud becomes more widely used, there's an effort to standardize cloud architectures for operating procedures, interoperability, testing, validation, and so on, and there should be common standards that all CSPs follow. The Cloud Security Alliance (CSA; *https:// cloudsecurityalliance.org*) is one organization that has developed resource documentation for CSPs and their staff. It provides guidance for privacy agreements, security measures, questionnaires, and more.

Training in cloud security and cloud forensics is also continuing to develop. Cloud investigators should have an understanding of cloud architecture in addition to basic digital and network forensics skills. Some sources for cloud forensics training are (ISC)^2's Certified Cyber Forensics Professional (*www.isc2.org/ccfp/Default.aspx*), INFOSEC Institute (*http://resources. infosecinstitute.com/overview-cloud-forensics/*), SANS Cloud Forensics with F-Response (*http:// digital-forensics.sans.org/blog/2013/04/09/cloud-forensics-with-f-response*), National Institute of Justice Digital Forensics Training (for law enforcement only; *www.nij.gov/topics/forensics/ evidence/digital/training/Pages/welcome.aspx*), and University College Dublin Centre for Cybersecurity and Cybercrime Investigation (*www.ucd.ie/cci/training.html*).

13

Acquisitions in the Cloud

The methods used to collect evidence in cloud investigations depend on the nature of the case. For example, an incident involving a network penetration through a CSP's firewall requires collecting and examining firewall and server logs for attacker activities and ensuring that the company's database hasn't been accessed or corrupted. Investigating an unauthorized database access, on the other hand, means focusing on transaction logs, too.

For e-discovery and investigations that require collecting specific files and recovering deleted artifacts, the standard acquisition methods discussed in previous chapters must be used, whether they're static or remote acquisitions. Recovering deleted data from cloud storage might be limited to the type of file system the CSP uses. For example, if a CSP uses a Microsoft NTFS RAID system, you can probably recover deleted data. This task might be more difficult if providers use Linux, UNIX, or another file system.

As you learned in Chapter 3, remote acquisitions are often more difficult because you're usually dealing with large volumes of data and can be limited by the network speed. You might need to negotiate with attorneys and the CSP about limiting the collection to specific files to prevent scope creep. You can also set up another cloud system dedicated to the investigation, which should grant access only to authorized users, such as digital forensics examiners and first responders. If external network connections are needed, make sure they're protected and monitored through a firewall to guard against unauthorized accesses.

With cloud systems running in a virtual environment, snapshots can give you valuable information before, during, and after an incident. Forensics examiners should re-create separate cloud servers from each snapshot, acquire an image of each server, and calculate an MD5 or SHA1 hash for all files. They can then compare hash values, modified, MAC (modified, last accessed, and created) dates and times, and file access permission to see what changed between snapshots. With this information, they can determine what files were altered and a time range for when they were altered as well as what files need further inspection of their contents to see what was altered.

To learn more about this technique, see "Forensic Acquisition and Analysis of VMware Hard Disk" (Manish Hirwani, Yin Pan, Bill Stackpole, and Daryl Johnson, Rochester Institue of Technology, July 5, 2012, *https://ritdml.rit.edu/bitstream/handle/1850/15922/SAM3427.pdf?sequence=1*).

Encryption in the Cloud

Many CSPs and third parties offer encryption services for cloud users as a security measure, so you should expect to encounter encrypted files in cloud investigations. Knowing how encryption is used in cloud computing helps you plan your investigation and data acquisition. Capturing encrypted data in the cloud is handled the same way as acquiring any encrypted digital evidence, as discussed in Chapter 5. You need assistance from the data owner (the cloud user) or the CSP to decrypt data with the right encryption key. If the data owner is uncooperative, you might need to turn to the attorneys handling the case or the data owner's management and have them direct the data owner to provide the information needed to access files.

Encrypted data in the cloud is in two states: data at rest (data that has been written to disk) and data in motion (data being transmitted over a network). Some systems also have encryption for data in use (data that's in RAM).

Some public CSPs, such as Google Cloud Storage and Microsoft OneDrive, provide encryption for data stored in the cloud and automatically decrypt it when data is accessed. Accessing data encrypted on these servers might require a live acquisition.

More CSPs and third-party vendors are offering cloud encryption tools for cloud customers. If you encounter encrypted data, you need to find out from the CSP what type of encryption was used and who knows how to recover this encrypted data. Some vendors that offer encryption services for cloud data are as follows:

- AFORE CloudLink Secure VSA from RSA (*www.emc.com/collateral/white-papers/ h11748-rsa-data-protection-manager-afore-cloudlink-seucre-vsa.pdf*) encrypts data in motion and data at rest and ensures data segregation. Encryption keys are stored on a CSP's *non-cloud* servers.

- Atalla Cloud Encryption from Hewlett-Packard (*www8.hp.com/us/en/software-solutions/ software.html?compURI=1669398#.U8MjxLGTE08*) provides trusted key management and data layer encryption that can encrypt virtual disks, databases, files, and more.

- SecureCloud from Trend Micro (*www.trendmicro.com/us/enterprise/cloud-solutions/ secure-cloud/*) combines encryption with key management based on an organization's security policies. SecureCloud can also wipe data after it's deleted from cloud storage areas. Knowing about this feature is important when attempting to recover deleted data.

- SafeGuard Encryption for Cloud Storage from Sophos (*www.sophos.com/en-us/ products/safeguard-encryption.aspx*) provides automatic encryption and decryption for users' uploads and downloads of data. Some public cloud services that can use this application are Dropbox and OneDrive.

Craig Gentry of IBM, a cryptography researcher, invented an encryption method called "fully homomorphic encryption." Homomorphic encryption uses an "ideal lattice" mathematical formula to encrypt data. This formula uses abstract algebra's ring theory to make encryption more difficult to break. For an explanation of ideal lattices and their use, see "On Ideal Lattices and Learning with Errors over Rings" (Vadim Lyubashevsky et al, *http://link.springer.com/ chapter/10.1007%2F978-3-642-13190-5_1*, 2010) and "Ideal Lattices" (Eva Bayer-Fluckiger, *http://alg-geo.epfl.ch/~bayer/files/Baker.pdf*, 2002). IBM is continuing research on homomorphic encryption, as it's believed to be a major breakthrough in cloud security.

For more information on homomorphic encryption, see the following white papers: "A Fully Homomorphic Encryption Scheme" (Craig Gentry, *https://crypto.stanford.edu/craig/craig-thesis.pdf*), "Can Homomorphic **NOTE** Encryption be Practical?" (Kristin Lauter, Michael Naehrig, and Vinod Vaikuntanathan of Microsoft Research, *http://research.microsoft.com/ pubs/148825/ccs2011_submission_412.pdf*), "Fully Homomorphic Encryption over the Integers" (Marten van Dijk, MIT, and Craig Gentry, Shai Halevi, and Vinod Vaikuntanathan, IBM Research, *https://eprint.iacr.org/ 2009/616.pdf*, June 8, 2010), and "Fully Homomorphic Encryption Using Ideal Lattices" (Craig Gentry, *http://paul.rutgers.edu/~jasperry/ light-sp13/gentry09.pdf*).

Conducting a Cloud Investigation

In Chapter 1, you learned about taking a systematic approach to digital forensics examinations, and you should use this same approach in investigating cloud incidents. The type of incident determines how to proceed with planning the investigation. For example, if a CSP is a victim of a cyberattack, the investigation should follow network forensics techniques (covered in Chapter 10). If the investigation involves searching for and recovering data from cloud storage or cloud customers, follow the methods described in Chapters 3, 5, and 9.

Investigating CSPs

As mentioned, CSPs usually have incident response teams trained to handle events such as cyberattacks and responding to e-discovery demands. How much support they offer to forensics investigators is affected by the SLA with cloud customers. If a CSP has no team or limited staff to handle these tasks, investigators should ask the following questions to understand how the CSP is set up:

- Does the investigator have the authority to use cloud staff and resources to conduct an investigation?

- Is detailed knowledge of the cloud's topology, policies, data storage methods, and devices available?

- Are there any restrictions on collecting digital evidence from remote cloud storage?

- For e-discovery demands on multitenant cloud systems, is the data to collect commingled with other cloud customers' unrelated data? Is there a way to separate the data to prevent violating privacy rights or confidentiality agreements?

- Is the data of interest to the investigation local or remote? If it's in a remote location, can the CSP provide a forensically sound connection to it?

For additional guidance on cloud investigations, see "NIST Cloud Computing Forensic Science Challenges," Draft NISTIR 8006 (*http://csrc.nist.gov/publications/drafts/nistir-8006/draft_nistir_8006.pdf*, 2014).

Investigating Cloud Customers

Cloud customers access CSPs through both computers and mobile devices, such as tablets and smartphones, and can do this through a Web site, an app, or other methods. If a cloud customer doesn't have the CSP's application installed, you might find cloud-related evidence in a Web browser's cache file. If the CSP's application is installed, you can find evidence of file transfers in the application's folder, usually found under the user's account folder, such as C:\Users*username*. You can find more information about cloud application activities on a user's computer in the Windows Prefetch folder (C:\Windows\Prefetch). For more information on investigating cloud activity on a computer, refer to Chapter 9; for cloud activity on mobile devices, see Chapter 12.

Understanding Prefetch Files

To reduce the time it takes to start applications, Microsoft has created prefetch files, which contain the DLL pathnames and metadata used by an application. The OS reads the associated prefetch file and loads its information into the computer's memory to speed an application's start time. This way, the OS can handle other tasks instead of waiting for an application to load the libraries it needs. Metadata in a prefetch file contains, for example, an application's MAC times in UTC format and a counter of how many times the application has run since the prefetch file was created. If a prefetch file is deleted, Windows re-creates one that resets the MAC times and the counter.

In a prefetch file, the application's create date and time are at offset 0x80, the modified date and time are at offset 0x88, the last access date and time are at offset 0x90, and the record date and time are at offset 0x98. The counter listing the number of times the application has run since creating the prefetch file is at offset 0xD4, as shown in Figure 13-1. (Review Chapter 5 for interpreting these dates and times.)

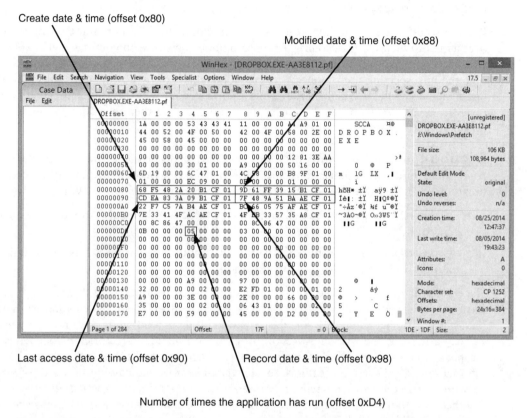

Figure 13-1   Showing offset positions for the counter and the dates and times for `Dropbox.exe`
Courtesy of X-Ways AG, *www.x-ways.net*

Examining Stored Cloud Data on a PC

Several vendors offer cloud storage to the public. Three widely used services are Dropbox, Google Drive, and OneDrive. These services are free for storage up to 2 GB for Dropbox and up to 15 GB for Google Drive and OneDrive. Users can get more storage for a monthly subscription fee.

When Dropbox or Google Drive is installed on a computer, File Explorer shows it as a separate folder, and data can be copied from and to it. OneDrive is already installed with Windows, and is also shown as a folder in File Explorer when a user activates his or her OneDrive account. If a user's computer is offline, these services have storage on a user's computer, and when Internet connectivity is restored, they update cloud-stored files based on the user's stored files. If the user accesses the cloud service via the Web on the same computer or a different computer, updates to the original computer are made automatically when the Internet connection is reestablished.

Cloud applications from Dropbox, Google Drive, and OneNote have Registry entries, so even if a suspect uninstalls a cloud application, you can usually find information to show it was installed previously. The following sections describe what data to look for in Windows 7 and 8 systems that reveals an association with one of these cloud services. The locations of this data might vary in older Windows versions. For other OSs, such as Linux and Mac, you need to do more research to test how cloud services interact with them.

Because security is such an important issue with cloud storage, users must maintain control over access to their cloud accounts. An unscrupulous person who cracks a user's cloud password could upload illegal or compromising data to that user's cloud via the Web. The next time the unsuspecting user connects to the cloud, this data is downloaded automatically to his or her computer's synchronized folder. To determine whether this happened, you can review a CSP's Web-connected login records and compare them with date and time values for the suspected files.

Dropbox In addition to providing secure online data storage, Dropbox (*www.dropbox. com*) offers third-party applications, such as e-mail, chat, Cisco WebEx, and other collaboration tools. Files that show use of Dropbox are usually in these folders in Windows 7 and 8:

- C:\Users*username*\Dropbox (contains the folders and files also stored in the Dropbox cloud)

- C:\Users*username*\AppData\Roaming\Dropbox (synchronizes files between the Dropbox cloud and the client workstation)

Since 2012, Dropbox has used base-64 format to store the contents of these files, so reading them requires specialized software. Magnet Forensics has a tool called Internet Evidence Finder (IEF) Triage designed for this purpose. It can read and interpret the Dropbox `filecache.dbx` file, which stores information on shared directories associated with a Dropbox user account and file transfers between Dropbox and the client's system. For more information on IEF Triage's features, see *www.magnetforensics.com/mfsoftware/ief-portable-solutions/ief-triage/* and *www.magnetforensics.com/mfsoftware/internet-evidence-finder/*. Another free tool that can read Dropbox files is Dropbox Reader (*www.net-security.org/secworld.php?id=11194*). This utility consists of six Python scripts:

- `read_config.py`—Converts `config.db` into a readable text file.

- `read_filecache_config`—Reads and reports the contents of `filecache.db`.

- `read_filejournal`—Supplies information on synchronized files stored in `filecache.db` as well as metadata and hashes for synchronized files.

- `read_sigstore`—Lists additional hashes of files that have been uploaded.

- `hash_blocks`—Lists additional hashes that can be matched to hashes found in `read_filejournal` and `read_sigstore` output files.

- `dropbox_contains_file`—Provides hashes by block to verify partial or exact matches of files recorded in `filecache.db` and `filejournal.db`.

Dropbox prefetch files also create several files: C:\Windows\Prefetch\DROPBOXDECRYPTOR-*nnnnnnnn*.pf, C:\Windows\Prefetch\DROPBOX.EXE-*nnnnnnnn*.pf, C:\Windows\Prefetch\ DROPBOXDECRYPTORV*nnn*NSETUP.TMP-*nnnnnnnn*.pf, and C:\Windows\Prefetch\ DROPBOXINSTALLER.EXE-*nnnnnnnn*.pf.

Google Drive Gmail users have access to Google Drive (*https://drive.google.com/*) for cloud data storage and applications such as Google Docs (a word processor), Google Drawings (a graphics program for charts), Google Forms (an online form and survey tool), Google Sheets (a spreadsheet tool), Google Slides (a slide presentation tool), and PDFzen (a PDF viewer and editor). Users can access Gmail and Google Drive from any Internet-connected computer running Windows Vista or later, Mac OS X, or Linux and smartphones running Android or iOS.

Google Drive is installed in C:\Program Files (x86)\Google\Drive. Each user has a configuration file, called a "user profile," stored in C:\Users*username*\AppData\Local\Google\ Drive. If Google Drive has been installed, it creates a folder in the path C:\Users\ *username*\Google Drive\. This folder contains the contents of what has been uploaded to Google Drive cloud storage.

When Google Drive is installed, it adds the following Registry entries:

- SOFTWARE\Microsoft\Windows\CurrentVersion\Installer\Folder
- SOFTWARE\Google Drive
- NTUSER\Software\Microsoft\Windows\CurrentVersion\Run\GoogleDriveSync
- NTUSER\Software\Classes

It also creates these additional files:

- C:\User*username*\Desktop\Google Drive.lnk
- C:\Windows\Prefetch\GOOGLEDRIVESYNC.EXE-*nnnnnnnn*.pf
- C:\Windows\Prefetch\GOOGLEUPDATE.EXE-*nnnnnnnn*.pf

The C:\Users*username*\AppData\Local\Google\Drive folder contains the synchronization file sync_config.db, which is an SQL database file with the Google Drive upgrade number, the highest application version number, the local synchronization root path, and other parameters. To view this file, extract it to a work folder from the disk or image and use a SQL viewer program, such as the freeware SQLite Database Browser at SourceForge (*http:// sourceforge.net/projects/sqlitebrowser/*).

Google Drive also creates a snapshot database in the C:\Users*username*\AppData\Local\ Google\Drive folder that lists information about local cloud entries. The snapshot.db file contains information about each file accessed, the URL pathname, the modified and created dates and times in UNIX timestamp format, and the file's MD5 value and size. This file can be read by an SQL viewer, such as SQLite Database Browser. To decipher the UNIX times, see *www.onlineconversion.com/unix_time.htm* or *http://unixtime-converter.com/*. When files are deleted, Google Drive removes all this information from the snapshot.db file.

The Google Drive file sync_log.log in C:\Users*username*\AppData\Local\Google\ Drive has a detailed list of a user's cloud transactions. You can open this file with any text editor. The create, modify, and delete dates and times in this file are of special interest. Dates and times are formatted as UNIX timestamps. To find this information, search for these string values: RawEvent (CREATE, RawEvent (MODIFY, and RawEvent (DELETE.

If Google Drive has been uninstalled, search for the Web browser's cache and history, shadow volume restore points, Pagefile.sys, Hiberfile.sys, prefetch files, Registry keys of recent file activities, and shortcut files (link files with an .lnk extension).

13

OneDrive Microsoft created SkyDrive as a cloud service that later became OneDrive (*https://onedrive.live.com/about/en-us/*); it's available with Windows 8. OneDrive is similar to Dropbox and Google Drive in function and features, such as handling many cloud storage tasks automatically for users. It also offers subscription services for Microsoft software, such as Microsoft Office.

OneDrive stores user profile data in the user's account path, and logs and synchronized files are stored in the following paths:

- Windows 7 log files are in C:\Users*username*\AppData\Local\Microsoft\ OneDrive\logs.

- Windows 8 log files are in C:\Users*username*\AppData\Local\Microsoft\Windows\ SkyDrive\logs (or OneDrive\logs).

- Windows 7 synchronized files are in C:\Users*username*\AppData\OneDrive.

- Windows 8 synchronized files are in C:\Users*username*\AppData\SkyDrive\OneDrive.

- Windows 8 OneDrive prefetch files are named ONEDRIVEREBRAND.EXE-*nnnnnnnn* and stored in C:\Windows\Prefetch.

- In older versions of Windows, the Windows\Prefetch folder typically contains the prefetch filenames SKYDRIVE.EXE-*nnnnnnnn*.pf, SKYDRIVECONFIG.EXE-*nnnnnnnn*.pf, and SKYDRIVESETUP.EXE-*nnnnnnnn*.pf.

 You might find OneDrive folders and files listed as SkyDrive when looking for the preceding files and paths. SkyDrive folders are typically found in older releases of Windows 8. In addition, some pathnames might vary with the Windows release. When you're looking for OneDrive log files, searching all folders is best.

Some Registry files of interest that Windows 8 uses for OneDrive are as follows:

- SOFTWARE\Microsoft\Windows\CurrentVersion\Explorer\FolderDescriptions\ *nnnnnnnn-nnnn-nnnn-nnnn-nnnnnnnnnnnn*

- SOFTWARE\Microsoft\Windows\CurrentVersion\Explorer\SyncRootManager\ SkyDrive

- SOFTWARE\Microsoft\Windows\CurrentVersion\Explorer\SyncRootManager\ SkyDrive\UserSyncRoots

- SOFTWARE\Microsoft\Windows\CurrentVersion\Live\Roaming

- SOFTWARE\Microsoft\Windows\CurrentVersion\PushNotifications\Applications\ MoSkyFileSync

- SOFTWARE\Microsoft\Windows\CurrentVersion\SettingSync\WindowsSettingHandlers\ SkyDriveSettings

- SOFTWARE\Microsoft\Windows NT\CurrentVersion\Schedule\TaskCache\Tasks\ *nnnnnnnn-nnnn-nnnn-nnnn-nnnnnnnnnnnn*

- SOFTWARE\Microsoft\Windows Search\FileChangeClientConfigs*nnnnnnnn-nnnn-nnnn-nnnn-nnnnnnnnnnnn*

- NTUSER\Software\Microsoft\Windows\CurrentVersion\SkyDrive
- NTUSER\Software\Microsoft\Windows NT\CurrentVersion\Winlogon

Most Registry entries are listed as SkyDrive, but in future Windows updates, this name might change to OneDrive.

You can find more information in the following Windows 8 log files, which are in the C:\Users*username*\AppData\Local\Microsoft\Windows\SkyDrive\logs folder:

- SyncEngine-*yyyy-mm-ddnn.nnn-n*.etl manages synchronization between OneDrive and a user's computer. It contains timestamps for activities that have been performed.
- SyncDiagnostics.log contains cid (client ID), clientType, clientVersion, device, deviceID, and timeUtc values. The cid, deviceID, and timeUtc values can be useful for confirming the relationship between OneDrive and a user's computer.

Windows Prefetch Artifacts

You can collect prefetch file artifacts with a disk editor or forensics tool. In the following activity, you use WinHex's Data Interpreter to find an application's MAC dates and times and the number of times Dropbox has run. You need WinHex, OSForensics, and the image file InCh05.img from Chapter 5. Follow these steps:

Before beginning this activity, create the *Work*\Chap13\Chapter folder (referred to as your "work folder" in the following steps).

1. Copy **InCh05.img** from Chapter 5 to your work folder. Start OSForensics with the **Run as administrator** option. In the left pane, click **Manage Case**, if necessary. In the right pane, click the **New Case** button. In the New Case dialog box, type **InChap13** in the Case Name text box and your name in the Investigator text box. For the Acquisition Type setting, click the **Investigate Disk(s) from Another Machine** option button, and click **Custom Location** for the Case Folder setting. Click the **Browse** button, navigate to and click your work folder, and then click **OK** twice.

2. To mount the disk image, scroll down the left pane and click **Mount Drive Image**. In the Mounted virtual disks window, click the **Mount new** button. In the OSFMount - Mount drive dialog box that opens, click the **...** button next to the Image file text box, navigate to the folder where you saved InCh05.img, click **InCh05.img**, click **Open**, and then click **OK**.

3. Click **File Name Search** in the left pane, click the **...** button next to the Config button, navigate to and click the drive letter where you mounted InCh05.img, and then click **OK**. In the Search String text box, type **DROPBOX**, and then click **Search**.

4. When the search is finished, scroll through the list of results and find the DROPBOX.EXE-AA3E8112.pf file in the path C:\Windows\Prefetch (although your drive letter might differ). Right-click this file and click **Open With**.

13

5. In the How do you want to open this file? dialog box, click **Look for another app on this PC.** In the "Open with" window, navigate to **C:\Program Files (x86)\WinHex** (or the location where you installed WinHex), and click `WinHex.exe`.

6. In WinHex, click **View** from the menu, point to **Show**, and click **Data Interpreter**. Click **Options, Data Interpreter** from the menu to open the Data Interpreter Options dialog box. Click the **Win32 FILETIME (64 bit)** check box, if necessary, and then click **OK**.

7. Click offset **0x80**, and notice the date and time displayed in the Data Interpreter window. Repeat by clicking at offsets **0x88, 0x90,** and **0x98** to view the other dates and times.

8. Click **Options, Data Interpreter** from the menu again, click to clear the **Win32 FILETIME (64 bit)** check box, click the **8 bit, unsigned** check box, and then click **OK**.

9. Move the cursor and click at offset **0xD4** to see how many times this application has been run. When you're finished, exit WinHex.

For more information on recovering evidence from computers using Dropbox, Google Drive, and OneDrive, review "Cloud Forensics" (Maegan Katz and Ryan Montelbano, *www.champlain.edu/Documents/ LCDI/CloudForensics.pdf*, 2013) and "Cloud Storage Forensics" (Mattia Epifani, *https://digital-forensics.sans.org/summit-archives/Prague_Summit/ Cloud_Storage_Forensics_Mattia_Eppifani.pdf*, 2013).

Tools for Cloud Forensics

Very few tools designed for cloud forensics are available, but many digital, network, and e-discovery tools can be combined to handle collecting and analyzing data from the cloud. Some vendors with integrated tools that can be applied to cloud forensics include the following:

- Guidance Software EnCase eDiscovery and its incident response and EnCase Cybersecurity tools

- AccessData Digital Forensics Incident Response services, and AD eDiscovery

- F-Response and its cloud server forensics utility

- ProDiscover Incident Response and Forensics editions

Forensic Open-Stack Tools

Forensic Open-Stack Tools (FROST) integrates with OpenStack running in IaaS cloud environments and adds forensics response capabilities for a CSP. OpenStack is an open-source computing platform intended for public and private cloud services, and FROST is the first known effort to provide a forensics response process for a cloud service. A feature of FROST is that it bypasses a virtual machine's hypervisor. Collected data is placed in the cloud's **management plane,** which is a tool with application programming interfaces (APIs) that allow reconfiguring a cloud on the fly; it's accessed through the application's Web interface. Because the hypervisor is bypassed, special malware can take control of the virtual session and deny or alter access. It can also prevent or interfere with forensic anlaysis and data collection.

For more information on FROST, see "Design and implementation of FROST: Digital forensic tools for the OpenStack cloud computing platform" (*www.cisa.umbc.edu/papers/DFRWS2013_Dykstra_FROST.pdf*).

F-Response for the Cloud

F-Response is a remote access tool introduced in Chapter 3 that can be applied to cloud forensics. It uses USB forwarding techniques to allow non-remote-capable forensics tools, such as X-Ways Forensics, to access remote servers and their data storage. For remote access with F-Response, two tools are needed: F-Response Enterprise or Consultant (*www.f-response.com*) and KernelPro USB-Over-Ethernet (*www.usb-over-ethernet.com*). For information on using F-Response, see *www.f-response.com/assets/pdfs/CloudForensicsWithF-Response.pdf*.

Chapter Summary

- Three service levels are available for the cloud: software as a service, platform as a service, and infrastructure as a service. These services can be deployed as public clouds, private clouds, community clouds, or hybrid clouds.

- CSPs use servers on distributive networks or mainframes that allow elasticity of resources for customers. Some of these CSPs are IBM Cloud, Cisco Cloud Computing, AT&T Synaptic, Google Cloud Storage, HP Helion, and Microsoft Azure Blob Storage.

- With multinational clouds, you should seek legal counsel before proceeding with an investigation to make sure you aren't violating another country's privacy laws and to identify all jurisdictions where data is stored.

- Cloud investigations are necessary in cases involving cyberattacks, policy violations, data recovery, and fraud complaints. Cloud forensics is considered a subset of network forensics.

- Before initiating a cloud investigation, you should review the SLA to identify any restrictions that might limit collecting and analyzing data. You should also review the CSP's policies and be aware of contract obligations between the CSP and cloud customers. Some CSPs have customers sharing resources that might cross international boundaries, which is a concern for digital forensics examiners.

- Law enforcement uses search warrants to acquire evidence in a criminal case. For criminal and civil cases, subpoenas and court orders are used to collect evidence. There are three types of subpoenas: government agency, non-government and civil litigation, and court orders.

- Five mechanisms are used to collect digital evidence under the U.S. Electronic Communications Privacy Act (ECPA): search warrants, subpoenas, subpoenas with prior notice to the subscriber or customer, court orders, and court orders with prior notice to the subscriber or customer. A search warrant can be used by law enforcement only when there's evidence of probable cause that a crime was committed and evidence can be found at a specific location.

- Technical challenges in cloud forensics involve cloud architecture, data collection, analysis of cloud forensic data, anti-forensics, incident first responders, role management, legal issues, and standards and training.

13

- Customer data at CSPs might be commingled, which can make separating it difficult for investigations of a specific customer. Data might also be stored in geographic locations other than where the investigation is taking place, making it difficult to collect evidence and even resulting in conflicts in privacy laws.

- Anti-forensics is an effort to alter log records as well as date and time values of important system files and install malware to hide hackers' activities.

- CSPs should have an incident response team ready to respond to network intrusions. In the absence of this team, it's up to the digital forensics examiner to develop a plan for responding to the incident.

- Role management defines the duties of CSP staff and customers, such as who's the data owner, who's in charge of identity protection, who are the users, and who allows user account access to the CSP. A digital forensics examiner needs this information to determine where data is stored and the impact of its loss to the CSP and customers.

- The Cloud Security Alliance is developing resources that guide CSPs in privacy agreements and security measures. Security and digital forensics training for clouds are sponsored by organizations such as SANS, ISC[2], the INFOSEC Institute, and the National Institute of Justice.

- Procedures for acquiring cloud evidence include examining network and firewall logs, performing disk acquisitions of a cloud system's OS, and examining data storage devices. Data in clouds can be encrypted in two states: at rest and in motion.

- When investigating a cloud incident, apply a systematic approach to planning and processing the case. CSPs typically have incident response teams consisting of system administrators, network administrators, and legal advisors.

- The three cloud services Dropbox, Google Drive, and Microsoft OneDrive contain data on a user's computer or mobile device that can reveal what files were copied or accessed along with dates and times they were accessed.

- Prefetch files, which help speed applications' startups, contain metadata on the last date and time an application was run and how many times it has run since being installed. Interpreting this metadata requires a hex editor or forensics tool.

- Vendors offer tools that can be combined for cloud forensics. Specific forensics tools for the cloud are FROST for OpenStack cloud IaaS platforms and F-Response's cloud server utility.

Key Terms

cloud service providers (CSPs) Vendors that provide on-demand network access to a shared pool of resources (typically remote data storage or Web applications).

community cloud A shared cloud service that provides access to common or shared data.

deprovisioning Deallocating cloud resources that were assigned to a user or an organization. *See also* provisioning.

hybrid cloud A cloud deployment model that combines public, private, or community cloud services under one cloud. Segregation of data is used to protect private cloud storage and applications.

infrastructure as a service (IaaS) With this cloud service level, an organization supplies its own OS, applications, databases, and operations staff, and the cloud provider is responsible only for selling or leasing the hardware.

management plane A tool with application programming interfaces (APIs) that allow reconfiguring a cloud on the fly.

multitenancy A principle of software architecture in which a single installation of a program runs on a server accessed by multiple entities (tenants). When software is accessed by tenants in multiple jurisdictions, conflicts in copyright and licensing laws might result.

platform as a service (PaaS) A cloud is a service that provides a platform in the cloud that has only an OS. The customer can use the platform to load their own applications and data. The CSP is responsible only for the OS and hardware it runs on; the customer is responsible for everything else that they have loaded on to it.

private cloud A cloud service dedicated to a single organization.

provisioning Allocating cloud resources, such as additional disk space.

public cloud A cloud service that's available to the general public.

service level agreements (SLAs) Contracts between a cloud service provider and a cloud customer. Any additions or changes to an SLA can be made through an addendum.

software as a service (SaaS) With this cloud service level, typically a Web hosting service provides applications for subscribers to use.

spoliation Destroying, altering, hiding, or failing to preserve evidence, whether it's intentional or a result of negligence.

Review Questions

1. Amazon was an early provider of Web-based services that eventually developed into the cloud concept. True or False?

2. What are the three levels of cloud services defined by NIST?
   a. CRC, DRAM, and IMAP
   b. OpenStack, FROST, and management plane
   c. SaaS, PaaS, and IaaS
   d. Hybrid, private, and community clouds

3. What capabilities should a forensics tool have to acquire data from a cloud? (Choose all that apply.)
   a. Identify and acquire data from the cloud.
   b. Expand and contract data storage capabilities as needed for service changes.
   c. Circumvent firewalls to access cloud data.
   d. Examine virtual systems.

4. Commingled data isn't a concern when acquiring cloud data. True or False?

5. A(n) _____ is a contract between a CSP and the customer that describes what services are being provided and at what level.

13

6. Which of the following is a mechanism the ECPA describes for the government to get electronic information from a provider? (Choose all that apply.)

   a. Subpoenas with prior notice

   b. Temporary restraining orders

   c. Search warrants

   d. Court orders

7. In which cloud service level can customers rent hardware and install whatever OSs and applications they need?

8. What are the two states of encrypted data in a secure cloud?

   a. RC4 and RC5

   b. CRC-32 and UTF-16

   c. Homomorphic and AES

   d. Data in motion and data at rest

9. Evidence of cloud access found on a smartphone usually means which cloud service level was in use?

   a. IaaS

   b. HaaS

   c. PaaS

   d. SaaS

10. Which of the following cloud deployment methods typically offers no security?

    a. Hybrid cloud

    b. Public cloud

    c. Community cloud

    d. Private cloud

11. The multitenancy nature of cloud environments means conflicts in privacy laws can occur. True or False?

12. To see Google Drive synchronization files, you need a SQL viewer. True or False?

13. A CSP's incident response team typically consists of which staff?

14. Any text editor can be used to read Dropbox files. True or False?

15. When should a temporary restraining order be requested for cloud environments?

    a. When cloud customers need immediate access to their data

    b. To enforce a court order

    c. When anti-forensics techniques are suspected

    d. When a search warrant requires seizing a CSP's hardware and software used by other parties not involved in the case

Hands-On Projects

Create a *Work*\Chap13\Projects folder on your system before starting these projects; it's referred to as your "work folder" in steps. Then extract all files from the Chap13\Projects folder on the DVD to your work folder.

Hands-On Project 13-1

You have been asked to identify any files that might have been uploaded from Denise Robinson's computer to the Dropbox cloud service. To determine whether files were uploaded, you must find the Dropbox folder where files are synchronized to see what it contains. For this project, you examine the InCh05.img image file from Chapter 5. Follow these steps:

1. Start OSForensics with the **Run as administrator** option. If you dismounted the InCh05.img image file after the in-chapter activity, mount it again.

2. Click the **Manage Case** button, and verify that the InChap13 case has a green checkmark next to it in the Select Case window. If not, right-click the case name and click **Open**. If the case isn't displayed, click **Import Case**, navigate to and click the case location folder, and then click **OK**.

3. You need to find Denise Robinson's account name listed in *drive*:\Users*username*\Dropbox. To find this information, click **File System Browser** in the left pane. In the "Select device to add" dialog box, click the **Drive Letter** option button, if necessary. Click the **Drive Letter** list arrow (see Figure 13-2), click the drive letter assigned to the InCh05.img file, and then click **OK**.

Figure 13-2 The "Select device to add" dialog box
Source: PassMark Software, *www.osforensics.com*

4. In the File System Browser window, navigate to *drive*Users (substituting the correct drive letter for *drive*) and expand the file listings. Click to expand the **Denise** user account folder, and then click the **Dropbox** subfolder, as shown in Figure 13-3.

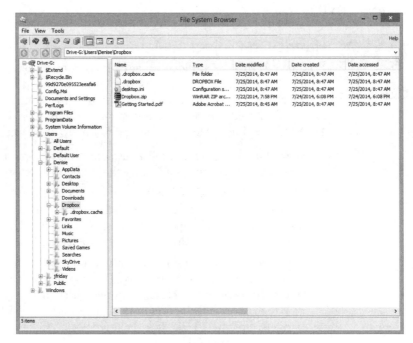

Figure 13-3 The File System Browser window
Source: PassMark Software, *www.osforensics.com*

5. Right-click the `Getting Started.pdf` file in the right pane and click **View with Internal Viewer** to display its contents. In the viewer window, click the **File Viewer** tab (see Figure 13-4), if necessary, and scroll through the document, which is a welcome notice from Dropbox. Close this viewer window, and repeat this step for other files in this folder to determine their contents.

Figure 13-4 Viewing the file's contents
Source: PassMark Software, *www.osforensics.com*

6. In the File System Browser window, right-click the **Dropbox.zip** file and click **Save to disk**. In the "Save file as" dialog box, navigate to your work folder, click **Save**, and then click **OK**. Close the File System Browser window.

7. Open File Explorer, navigate to your work folder, and extract (unzip) **Dropbox.zip**. Examine the extracted data, and write a memo to the attorney stating that you recovered the Dropbox.zip file and describing its contents.

8. Leave the InChap13 case open and OSForensics running for the next project.

Hands-On Project 13-2

The attorney managing the case discovered that Denise Robinson's computer contains the IMG_3646.png file that might have been uploaded to Google Drive. To determine whether it has, you need to examine the Google Drive file sync_log.log. For this project, you need a text editor (Notepad, WordPad, or any word processor), OSForensics, a Web browser, and the image file InCh05.img you saved in Hands-On Project 13-1. Follow these steps:

1. If you exited OSForensics, restart it, and open the InChap13 case and the InCh05.img file.

2. Click **File System Browser** and navigate to **C:\Users\Denise\AppData\Local\Google\Drive**. Right-click **sync_log.log** and click **View with Internal Viewer**.

3. In the viewer window, click the **Text Viewer** tab, if necessary. In the text box, type **IMG_3646**, and then click the **>>** button. Finding the file confirms that it was uploaded to Google Drive.

4. Scroll to the right to view the modified=1406307808 and created= 1406307808 values. Because both timestamp values are identical, you need to convert only one of them. Highlight the modified timestamp **1406307808**, as shown in Figure 13-5, and then right-click it and click **Copy**.

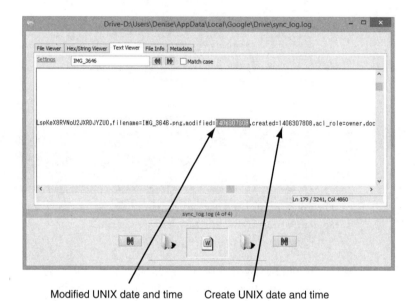

Modified UNIX date and time   Create UNIX date and time

Figure 13-5 Searching for a file uploaded to Google Drive
Source: PassMark Software, *www.osforensics.com*

5. Start a Web browser, go to **http://unixtime-converter.com**, paste the numbers into the UNIX TimeStamp text box, as shown in Figure 13-6, and click **Convert**. (*Note*: If you can't access this Web site, try *www.onlineconversion.com/unix_time.htm*.)

Figure 13-6 A UNIX timestamp converter
Source: *http://unixtime-converter.com*

In this book's examples, all date and time values are in the U.S. Pacific time zone, which is -0800 from UTC time for Pacific standard time or -0700 from UTC time for Pacific daylight time. Depending on the conversion utility you're using, these values might be converted to your local time zone. It's important to note the time zone where evidence was collected to make sure you have the correct local time for file activities.

6. In the Result text box, highlight the converted date and time value, and then right-click it and click **Copy**.

7. Start a text editor and type **IMG_3646.png** in the first line. Press **Enter** to add a blank line, and then press **Enter** again. Create two columns by typing **Last modified date**, pressing Tab eight times, and typing **Created date**. Place the cursor under the "Last modified date" column, and then right-click and click **Paste**. Repeat to paste the same date and time value under the "Created date" column.

8. Save the file as **Google Drive IMG_3646 date stamps.txt**. Exit the text editor, and turn this file in to your instructor. Leave OSForensics running for the next project.

Hands-On Project 13-3

The case attorney asked you to examine the OneDrive synchronization folder for Denise Robinson to look for any e-mail correspondence. Follow these steps:

1. If you exited OSForensics, restart it, and open the InChap13 case and InCh05.img file. In the left pane, click **File System Browser**.

2. In the File System Browser window, navigate to *drive*:\Users\Denise\SkyDrive\OneDrive\E-mails. Extract all files with the extension .oxps by right-clicking each file and clicking **Save to disk**, and then clicking **OK** in the message box about saving the file successfully. Exit OSForensics.

3. Open File Explorer, navigate to your work folder, and open each file to view its contents. Write a one-page memo describing the contents of each file you recovered, and then close File Explorer. Turn the memo in to your instructor.

Hands-On Project 13-4

The case attorney wants to know the last time Denise Robinson accessed Google Drive. To find this information, use the following steps. If you need help, refer to the in-chapter activity.

1. Start WinHex, and open the *drive*:\Windows\Prefetch\GOOGLEDRIVESYNC(1).EXE-67B59A2.pf file.

2. Find the Windows date and time at offset 0x80 and the number of times this file has been run since it was installed at offset 0xD4.

3. Write a memo stating the date, time, and number of times this program has been run. Turn the memo in to your instructor.

Case Projects

CASE PROJECTS

Case Project 13-1

Privacy laws in other countries are an important concern when performing cloud forensics and investigations. You've been assigned a case involving PII data stored on a cloud in Australia. Before you start any data acquisiton from this cloud, you need to research what you can access under Australian law. For this project, look for information on Australia's Privacy Principles (APP), particularly Chapter 8: APP 8—Cross-border disclosure of personal information. Write a one- to two-page paper summarizing disclosure requirements, steps for storing PII data in Australia, requirements for getting consent from data owners, and any exceptions allowed by this law.

Case Project 13-2

As a digital forensics examiner, it's a good idea to build a list of references for information on privacy laws in other countries, which can be useful in cases involving cloud storage. Using the search term "world privacy laws," look for at least three Web sites with references to laws in other countries. Write a one-page paper listing the URL for each site, summarizing what kind of information it offers, and evaluating its ease of use.

Case Project 13-3

A cloud customer has asked you to do a forensics analysis of data stored on a CSP's server. The customer's attorney explains that the CSP offers little support for data acquisition and analysis but will help with data collection for a fee. The attorney asks you to prepare a memo with detailed questions of what you need to know to perform this task. She plans to use this memo to negotiate for services you'll provide in collecting and analyzing evidence. Write a one- to two-page memo with questions to ask the CSP.

Case Project 13-4

To examine a cloud environment, you must have the latest knowledge on cloud encryption. Conduct online research, and write a two-page report about current vendors and services for encrypting data stored in the cloud. List the vendors, their products, and what type of cloud service level each tool is intended for, such as PaaS, IaaS, or SaaS.

chapter 14

Report Writing for High-Tech Investigations

After reading this chapter and completing the exercises, you will be able to:

- Explain the importance of reports
- Describe guidelines for writing reports
- Explain how to use forensics tools to generate reports

This chapter gives you guidelines on writing reports of your findings in digital forensics investigations. You learn about different types of reports and what to include in a typical report and examine how to generate report findings with forensics software tools.

Understanding the Importance of Reports

You write a report to communicate the results of your forensic examination of a computer, network system, or digital device. A forensic report presents evidence that might support further investigation and, in some situations, be admissible in court, at an administrative hearing, or as an affidavit to support issuing an arrest or a search warrant. A report can also provide justification for collecting more evidence and be used at a probable cause hearing, as evidence in a grand jury hearing, or at a motion hearing. In addition, if an employer is investigating employee misconduct, a report might be the basis for disciplinary action. Besides presenting facts, reports can communicate expert opinion. You should look at your report as your first testimony in a case. You must expect to be examined and cross-examined about it. Opposing counsel will look for an opportunity to attack the facts you present, whether you determined them yourself or extracted them from other reports or the expected testimony of other witnesses. You need to know what facts affect your opinion and what facts don't.

For civil cases, including those involving digital forensics investigations, U.S. district courts require that expert witnesses submit written reports; state courts are also starting to require reports from expert witnesses, although the details of these requirements vary. Therefore, if you're a digital forensics examiner involved in a civil case, you must write a report explaining your investigation and findings. Specifically, Rule 26, Federal Rules of Civil Procedure (FRCP; see *www.law.cornell.edu/rules/frcp/Rule26.htm*), requires that parties who anticipate calling an expert witness to testify must provide a copy of the expert's written report that includes all opinions, the basis for the opinions, and the information considered in coming to those opinions. The report must also include related exhibits, such as photographs or diagrams, and the witness's curriculum vitae listing all publications he or she contributed to during the preceding 10 years. (These publications don't have to be relevant to the case.)

In addition, federal courts, as a matter of rule, require all fact or expert witnesses to provide a report before trial in civil cases. See FRCP 26 (a) (2); Federal Rules of Evidence (FRE) 702, 703, and 705; and the rule stated in *Daubert v. Merrell Dow Pharmaceuticals, Inc.*, 509 U.S. 579, which is that testimony is based on sufficient facts or data, testimony is the product of reliable principles and methods, and the witness has applied the principles and methods reliably to the facts of the case. This rule is followed in more than half the states. The remaining states generally follow the rule established in *Frye v. United States*, 293 F. 1013 (D.C. Cir. 1923), which states that testimony is inadmissible unless it is "testimony deduced from a well-recognized scientific principle or discovery; the thing from which the deduction is made must be sufficiently established to have gained general acceptance in the particular field in which it belongs."

In addition to opinions and exhibits, the written report must specify fees paid for the expert's services and list all other civil or criminal cases in which the expert has testified (in trials and depositions) for the preceding 4 years. This list doesn't need to include cases in which the expert acted as a consulting expert and didn't provide expert testimony or cases in which the expert testified as a **lay witness** (a witness testifying to personally observed facts).

Although the requirements for information in reports aren't specific, you should keep a copy of any deposition notice or subpoena so that you can include the following information:

- Jurisdiction (for example, U.S. District Court for Eastern District of Washington)
- Style of the case (the format used for official court documents—for example, using a header such as *John Smith, Plaintiff v. Paul Jones, Defendant*)
- Cause number
- Date and location of the deposition
- Name of the deponent (the person testifying at deposition)

There are no requirements to include details of your previous testimony in a report, although you should summarize key points of your testimony for future reference and keep transcripts of your previous testimony, if available.

As an expert witness, you should be aware that lawyers use services called **deposition banks** (libraries), which store examples of expert witnesses' previous testimony. Some of these services have hundreds of thousands of depositions on file and might have several depositions for expert witnesses who testify regularly. After a case is resolved, a lawyer sends copies of the opposing expert witnesses' depositions to the bank to be stored. In preparation for a trial, when the opposing party has identified an expert witness, the attorney might request copies of this witness's previous testimony. Lawyers might also request transcripts of previous testimony by their own potential experts to ensure that the experts haven't previously testified to a contrary position. Lawyers who are members of associations also use electronic mailing lists to ask other members for copies of previous depositions by a specific expert witness.

Attorneys can submit documents electronically in many courts; the standard format in federal courts is Portable Document Format (PDF).

Limiting a Report to Specifics

The client (who might be an attorney, a detective, or an investigator) should define the investigation's goal or mission. All reports to the client should start by stating this mission or goal, which is usually to find information on a specific subject, recover certain important documents, or recover certain types of files or files with specific dates and times. Clearly defining the goals reduces the time and cost of the examination and is especially important with the increasing size of hard drives and complexity of networks.

Before you begin writing, identify your audience and the purpose of the report to help you focus on specifics. Remember that if the audience has little technical knowledge, you might have to dedicate part of the report to educating readers on technical issues. You can do this with a set of several stock paragraphs that you keep on hand, although you should update these stock definitions periodically.

Types of Reports

Digital forensics examiners are required to create different types of reports, such as a formal report consisting of facts from your findings, a preliminary written or verbal report to your attorney, and an examination plan for the attorney who has retained you.

An **examination plan** is a document that serves as a guideline for knowing what questions to expect when you're testifying (see Figure 14-1). Your attorney uses the examination plan to guide you in your testimony. You can propose changes to clarify or define information or to include substantive information the attorney might have omitted. You can also use the examination plan to help your attorney learn the terms and functions used in digital forensics.

WITNESS EXAMINATION PLAN

WITNES: ___Joseph Friday___ /Factors:___ Expert Digital Forensic Examiner.

Direct Examination: Expert Testimony   Objective/Rule/

Testimony CV

Identity and Address Iowa Bureau of Criminal Investigations

Position (Current) Digital Forensic Examiner

Undergraduate   Iowa State University summa cum laude 1990 BS Computer Science

Master's Degree Purdue University, 1992 MS Electrical Engineering

Summer Internship 1989 Des Moines Police Department

Academic Appointments

Lecturer, Dept. of Computer Science, University of Iowa 1998-Current

Instructor, Iowa Police Academy

Professional Society Certifications

P.E. 1990

CISSP 2001

Memberships

American Society of Industrial Security

Publications

Journal of the Iowa State Bar Association, May 1999, "Computer Forensics on RAID Servers-Testifying to Reasonable Certainty"

Experience

How many systems have you conducted forensic examinations on?

The Client

What is your relationship to the Plaintiff? Retained by his attorney to examine the hard drive of his computer for all financial records. I have never actually met or talked to Mr. Smith.

The Specific Examination

How long does it take you to conduct this examination?

What type of files were you looking for? Why those types of files? Where did you find those files?

What condition were the files in?

What is your opinion as to the cause of that condition?

Can you say for a reasonable certainty that the financial data files were deleted intentionally? Yes.

Are you able to state to a reasonable certainty who deleted the financial data files? Yes.

What is your fee for examining the hard drive, preparing a report and testifying?

Anticipated Cross Examination – Expert Testimony

How many times have you worked for Mr. Sawyer as an expert witness? I've done 16 contracts as a consultant expert or expert witness.

Have you ever previously testified that overwriting utilities are not 100% reliable? Yes, but that was in 1994 and utilities are so far as I can tell are 100% reliable today.

Figure 14-1 A sample examination plan
© Cengage Learning®

A verbal report is less structured than a written report. Typically, it takes place in an attorney's office, where the attorney requests your consultant's report. As an expert hired as a trial consultant, you'll use verbal reports often. Keep in mind that others can't force your attorney to repeat what you've told him or her in a verbal report. A verbal report is usually a preliminary report and addresses areas of investigation yet to be completed, such as the following:

- Tests that haven't been concluded
- Interrogatories that the lawyer might want to address to opposing parties
- Document production, either requests for production (to parties) or subpoenas (to non-parties, people who have information but aren't a named party in the case)
- Determining who should be deposed and the plan for deposing them

With preliminary reports, mention to your client that your factual statement and opinion are still tentative and subject to change as more information comes in.

A written report is frequently an affidavit or a declaration. Because this type of report is sworn to under oath (and penalty of perjury or comparable false swearing statute), it demands attention to detail, carefully limiting what you write, and thorough documentation and support of what you write. See the following section for more guidelines on written reports.

Guidelines for Writing Reports

The method for expressing an opinion is to have an attorney frame a hypothetical question based on available factual evidence. The law requires that an expert who doesn't have personal knowledge about the system or occurrence must state opinions by response to hypothetical questions, which ask the expert witness to express an opinion based on hypothetical facts without referring to a particular system or situation. In this regard, you as a forensics investigator (an expert witness) differ from an ordinary witness. You didn't see or hear the incident in dispute; you're giving evidence as an opinion based on professional knowledge and experience, even if you might never have seen the system, data, or scene.

Although the rules of evidence have relaxed requirements on the way an expert renders an opinion, structuring hypothetical questions for your own use helps ensure that you're basing your opinion on facts expected to be supported by evidence. State the facts needed to answer the question, and don't include any unnecessary facts. You might want to address alternative facts, however, if they allow your opinion to remain the same. The expression "alternative facts" might seem contradictory, but it simply means competing facts. In a civil case, if there weren't alternative possible facts, the case wouldn't be at trial; it would have been decided at summary judgment.

An expert's opinion is governed by FRE, Rule 705, and the corresponding rule in many states. For more information on Rule 705, visit *www.law.cornell.edu/rules/fre/rule_705*.

The following text from a court transcript illustrates an exchange using a hypothetical question between an attorney and a digital forensics expert. Note that the word "presented" is used in this transcript; it means that the attorney handed the expert something while asking a question.

Mr. Stiubhard: Mr. Noriki, presented with a hard drive of 1 TB, an attached Maxtor manufacturer's data sheet that indicated it was manufactured in May 2014, previous testimony by a detective that the notebook computer in which this drive

> was found was manufactured by Dell Computer Corporation in June 2014 and purchased by the owner in June 2014. Based on these facts testified to, do you have an opinion whether this is original equipment on this system?

Mr. Noriki: Yes.

Mr. Stiubhard: Mr. Noriki, what is your opinion on whether this hypothetical hard drive would be the original equipment with the system?

Mr. Noriki: Based on facts you have provided, it's my professional opinion that the hard drive would …

Hypothetical questions can be abused and made so complex that the finder of fact (the expert) might not be able to remember enough of the question to evaluate the answer. Another abuse of the hypothetical question is that it effectively allows attorneys to recite their favored facts to the jury repeatedly and in the order and with the emphasis they want to use.

As an expert witness, you can testify to an opinion or a conclusion, if these basic conditions are met:

- The opinion, inferences, or conclusions depend on special knowledge, skill, or training not within the ordinary experience of lay witnesses or jurors.
- The witness must be shown to be qualified as a true expert in the field (which is why the curriculum vitae is important).
- The witness must testify to a reasonable degree of certainty (probability) regarding his or her opinion, inference, or conclusion.
- At minimum, expert witnesses must know the relevant data (facts) on which their opinion, inference, or conclusion is based, and they must be prepared to testify in response to a hypothetical question that sets forth the underlying evidence.

What to Include in Written Preliminary Reports

Remember that anything you write down as part of your examination for a report is subject to **discovery** from the opposing attorney, meaning what you write can or will be given to the opposing attorney. Discovery is the process of opposing attorneys seeking information from each other. Therefore, a written preliminary report is considered a **high-risk document** because opposing counsel can demand discovery on it. If the written preliminary report states a contrary or more equivocal position than you take in your final report or testimony, you should expect opposing counsel to try to discredit your testimony by using the written report. It's simply better if there's no written report to provide. If you must write a preliminary report, don't use words such as "preliminary copy," "draft copy," or "working draft." These words give opposing counsel an opening for discrediting you and make it seem as though the attorney who retained you contributed to what should be your independent professional judgment. In addition, if you do write a preliminary report, don't destroy it before a final resolution of the case or any discovery issue related to the report. Destroying the report could be considered destroying or concealing evidence; among lawyers, this action is called spoliation, and it could subject your client to monetary or evidentiary sanctions. If you've been identified on a witness list provided to the court and opposing counsel, all your work related to the case is potentially subject to discovery.

For written preliminary reports, therefore, include the same information you would supply in an informal verbal report. First, restate the assignment to confirm with your client that the work you have done is focused correctly. Next, summarize what has been accomplished. Identify the systems you have examined, what tools you have used, and what you have seen. State evidence preservation or protection processes you have used. (See Chapters 3 and 9 for more information on these processes.) The following list shows additional items to include in your report:

- Summarize your billing to date and estimate costs to complete the effort.
- Identify the tentative conclusion (rather than the preliminary conclusion).
- Identify areas for further investigation and get confirmation from the attorney on the scope of your examination.

Report Structure

A report usually includes the sections shown in the following list, although the order varies depending on organizational guidelines or case requirements:

- Abstract (or summary)
- Table of contents
- Body of report
- Conclusion
- References
- Glossary
- Acknowledgments
- Appendixes

Each section should have a title indicating what you're discussing, so make sure it conveys the essential point of the section. For example, the body of your report might be titled "Investigation Findings for ABC Bicycle, Inc.: Intellectual Property Theft."

If the report is long and complex, you should include an abstract. More people read the abstract than the entire report, so writing one for your report is important. The abstract and table of contents give readers an overview of the report and its points so that they can decide what they need to review. An abstract simply condenses the report to concentrate on the essential information. It should be one or two paragraphs totaling about 150 to 200 words. Remember that the abstract should describe the examination or investigation and present the report's main ideas in a summarized form. Informative abstracts don't duplicate references or tables of results. As with any research paper, write the abstract last.

The body consists of the introduction and discussion sections. The introduction should state the report's purpose and show that you're aware of its terms of reference. You should also state any methods used and any limitations and indicate how the report is structured. It's important to justify why you're writing the report, so make sure you answer the question "What is the problem?" You should also give readers a map of what you're delivering. Introduce the problem, moving from broader issues to the specific problem, finishing the introduction with the precise aims of the report (key questions). Craft this introduction carefully, setting up the processes you used to develop the information in logical order. Refer to

14

relevant facts, ideas, and theories as well as related research by other authors. Organize discussion sections logically under headings to reflect how you classify information and to ensure that your information remains relevant to the investigation.

Two other main sections are the conclusion and supporting materials (references and appendixes). The conclusion starts by referring to the report's purpose, states the main points, draws conclusions, and possibly renders an opinion. References and appendixes list the supporting material to which your work refers. Follow a style manual's guidelines on format for presenting references, such as *Gregg Reference Manual: A Manual of Style, Grammar, Usage, and Formatting; The Chicago Manual of Style: The Essential Guide for Writers, Editors, and Publishers;* or the *MLA Style Manual and Guide to Scholarly Publishing* from the Modern Language Association. Appendixes provide additional resource material not included in the body of the report.

Writing Reports Clearly

To produce clear, concise reports, you should assess the quality of your writing, using the following criteria:

- *Communicative quality*—Is it easy to read? Think of your readers and how to make the report appealing to them.

- *Ideas and organization*—Is the information relevant and clearly organized?

- *Grammar and vocabulary*—Is the language simple and direct so that the meaning is clear and the text isn't repetitive? However, technical terms should be used consistently; you shouldn't try to use variety for these terms. Using different words for the same thing might raise questions.

- *Punctuation and spelling*—Are they accurate and consistent?

Good expert reports share many of the qualities of other kinds of writing. To write is to think, so a report should lay out ideas in a logical order that facilitates logical thinking. Make each sentence follow from the previous one, building an argument piece by piece. Group related ideas and sentences into paragraphs, and group paragraphs into sections. Create a flow from the beginning of the report to the end.

The report should be grammatically sound, use correct spelling, and be free of writing errors. Avoid jargon, slang, or colloquial terms. Most lawyers, judges, and jurors aren't technically trained, so if technical terms must be used, define them in ordinary language (or refer readers to your glossary). Defining acronyms and any abbreviations not used as standard measurement units is particularly important; spell out all acronyms the first time they're used. If there's any possibility of misinterpreting an abbreviation, define it or use the full expression. For example, "m" is used routinely in scientific and technical writing as an abbreviation for "meter," but nontechnical readers (especially in the United States) might assume it's an abbreviation for "mile."

Considering Writing Style
Style means the tone of language you use to address the reader. When writing a report, use a natural language style. For instance, talk about yourself in the first person, not the third person; don't call yourself "your affiant" when "I" is appropriate and clearly more natural. (However, keep in mind that too many sentences containing "I" can become repetitive.) A natural language style helps keep readers interested in what

you have to say. However, you should also follow formal writing guidelines, so pay attention to word usage, grammar, and spelling.

Be sure to avoid vague language and generalizations, as in "There was a problem." Instead, state the problem specifically and describe what you or others did to solve it. Be careful about repetition, too; repeat only what's necessary, such as key words or technical terms.

Most of the report describes what you did, so it should be in past tense, but use present or future tense as appropriate. Use active rather than passive voice to avoid boring writing and contorted phrases. For example, "The software recovered the following data" is more direct and, therefore, more interesting to read than "The following data was recovered by the software."

Avoid including too many details and personal observations. Your only agenda should be finding the truth, so don't think in terms of catching somebody or proving something. It's not your job to win the case. Don't become an advocate for anything other than the truth and your honest objective opinion.

A final caution in writing style: Project objectivity. You must communicate calm, detached observations in your report, so don't become emotionally involved in the investigation. Always try to identify the flaws in your thinking or examination; it's better to identify flaws than allow opposing counsel to do it for you at an embarrassing moment.

Including Signposts Another aspect of writing clearly is choosing language that gives your readers signposts to what you're trying to communicate, draws their attention to a point, and shows them the sequence of a process. Signposts assist readers in scanning the text quickly by highlighting the main points and logical development of information.

For example, the first substantive section of your report could start with "This is the report of findings from the forensic examination of computer SN 123456." The discussion of your examination procedures could be introduced with "The first step in this examination was," "The second step in this examination was," and so on. "First" and "second" are signposts that show the sequence of information or tasks. When you want to evaluate something, you might include a signpost such as "The problem with this is …" To show that you're drawing a conclusion, introduce the point with "This means that …" or "The result shows that …"

Designing the Layout and Presentation of Reports

Layout and presentation involve many factors, including using clear titles and section headings. A numbering system is also part of the layout. Typically, report writers use one of two numbering systems: decimal numbering or legal-sequential numbering. After you choose a system, be sure to follow it consistently throughout the report.

A report using the decimal numbering system divides material into sections and restarts numbering with each main section, as shown in the following example. With this system, readers can scan the headings and understand how one part of the report relates to the other.

I. Abstract

1.1. This report includes a review of data found on hard drives on Computer A and Computer B. Both systems were Dell desktop computers. Computer A had no image files other than those that would have been found in routine office applications. Computer B had more than 60 GB of image data (approximately 120,000 JPG files with dates from January 30, 2013, to March 15, 2014).

II. Detailed Analysis

Computer A

2.1. The hard drives of Computer A are designated drive C and drive D.

2.2. Both hard drives are 100 GB Maxtor drives.

2.3. Both hard drives are less than 20% full.

Computer B

2.4. The hard drives of Computer B are designated drive C and drive D.

2.5. Both hard drives are 80 GB Seagate drives.

2.6. Both drives are more than 90% full.

The legal-sequential numbering system is often used in legal pleadings. Each Roman numeral represents a major aspect of the report, and each Arabic numeral is an important piece of supporting information, as shown in the following example. This system is meaningful to lawyers but might not be as effective with nonlawyers because the sequential numbering doesn't indicate a hierarchy that shows the relative importance of information in the report.

I. Abstract

1. This report includes a review of data found on hard drives on Computer A and Computer B. Both systems were Dell desktop computers. Computer A had no image files other than those that would have been found in routine office applications. Computer B had more than 60 GB of image data (approximately 120,000 JPG files with dates from January 30, 2013, to March 15, 2014).

II. Detailed Analysis

Computer A

2. The hard drives of Computer A are designated drive C and drive D.

3. Both hard drives are 100 GB Maxtor drives.

4. Both hard drives are less than 20% full.

Computer B

5. The hard drives of Computer B are designated drive C and drive D.

6. Both hard drives are 80 GB Seagate drives.

7. Both drives are more than 90% full.

Providing Supporting Material Use material such as figures, tables, data, and equations to help tell the story as it unfolds. Refer to this material in the text and integrate the points they make into your writing. Number figures and tables sequentially as they're introduced (for example, Figure 1, Figure 2, and so forth with another sequence for Table 1, Table 2, and so on).

Figure captions should supply descriptive information. In charts, label all axes and include units of measure. Insert a figure or table after the paragraph in which it's first mentioned, or gather all supporting material in one place after the references section (before any appendixes).

Formatting Consistently How you format text is less important than being consistent in applying formatting. For example, if you indent paragraphs, be sure all are indented. Use fonts consistently, and use consistent heading styles throughout (for example, major headings in bold with initial capitals, minor headings in italics, and so forth). Follow the same guideline throughout for units of measure; for example, use "%" or "percent," but don't use both. In other words, establish a template and stick to it.

Explaining Examination and Data Collection Methods Explain how you studied the problem, which should follow logically from the report's purpose. Depending on the kind of data, this section might contain subsections on examination procedures, materials or equipment, data collection and sources, and analytical or statistical techniques. Supply enough detail for readers to understand what you did.

Data collection is a critical portion of the report. Without good data recording in a lab notebook or record, completing a report beyond this point is futile. If your data collection process becomes the subject of discovery or examination, presenting data in a well-organized manner is important. Use tables in your report to illustrate how data was handled and examined. As mentioned, tables should be labeled clearly as to their content and numbered for easy referral.

Including Calculations In most cases, hashing algorithms are calculated in digital forensics investigations. If you use any hashing algorithms, be sure to give the common name, such as "Message Digest 5 (MD5) hash." Generally, you don't need to give examples of each type of hash if you're using standard tools; you explain generally what they do and cite the authority or policy you rely on for using the tool. For example, to explain why you're using the MD5 hash, you might cite the National Software Reference Library (NSRL; *www.nsrl.nist.gov*) as an authority. You could also cite a court case in which a tool's validity had been accepted previously.

Providing for Uncertainty and Error Analysis In digital forensics, many results can be absolutely true if stated conservatively but might be a guess if you overreach. Therefore, a statement of limitations of knowledge and uncertainty is necessary to protect your credibility. For example, if you're using the timestamp for a file in a Windows OS to indicate that the file was created at a certain time, you need to acknowledge that a PC clock could be reset easily. In addition, you should state that there's no absolute assurance that a file's timestamp is a reflection of its creation time, but there might be other reliable indicators, such as timestamps of other files, creation timestamps for directories, creation order of certain files, and information in automatic backups.

14

Explaining Results and Conclusions Explain your findings, using subheadings to divide the discussion into logical parts. Make comments on results as they're presented, discussing the importance of what you found in light of the overall report objectives. Take a step back from the details and synthesize what has (and has not) been learned about the problem and what the information means. Describe what you actually found, not what you hoped to find. Including this discussion as you present results can often improve clarity and readers' understanding.

Link your discussion to figures and tables as you present results, and describe and interpret what these supporting materials show. If you have many similar figures, select representative examples for the main report and put the rest in an appendix.

Save broader generalizations and summaries for the report's conclusion. The conclusion should restate the objectives, aims, and key questions and summarize your findings with clear, concise statements. Keep the conclusion brief and to the point.

Providing References When you write a report, you must cite references to all material you have used as sources for the content of your work. These citations are made wherever you quote, paraphrase, or summarize someone else's opinions, theories, or data. References can include books, periodicals, newspapers, Web sites, conference proceedings, personal communications, and interviews.

In the main section of your report, typically you cite references with the author's last name and year of publication enclosed in parentheses. (Sometimes page numbers are required, too; check the style manual you're following for guidance.) In the references section, you list sources alphabetically by author and provide publication information. Give enough detail so that someone else could track down the information. Follow a standard format, such as the one shown in the following examples, for use of italics, capitalization, volume and page numbers, publisher address, and other style concerns. Many good style manuals are available, and having one handy is worthwhile.

The following examples show how different sources are presented in the references section; keep in mind that formatting might differ slightly depending on the style manual you follow:

Personal (unpublished) communications:

Cited in the text only, as in "x is recoverable by using tool A (Koenick, F., pers. comm.)."

Lecture notes:

Stiubhard, C. K. "The Curriculum Vitae." Lecture for CIS 411/511, CTIN and City University, Seattle, WA, May 1, 2014.

Web site:

Law Office of Christopher K. Stiubhard. *www.stiubhardlaw.com*, 2011.

Single-author journal article:

O'Herlighy, T. A. "Development of Relationships on the Internet." *Journal of the Advocate* 7, 2012, pp. 130–142.

Multiple-author journal article:

Noriki, H. W., C. K. Stiubhard, and M. D. Clay. "Investigation of Counterfeiting of Spare Parts—A Statistical Analysis." *The Frontline Journal of Aviation* 8, 2009, pp. 150–152.

Book:

Clark, F. and K. Diliberto. *Investigating Computer Crime*. CRC Press, New York, 2006.

Government/technical report:

U.S. Department of Justice. "The Examination of Computers." Report XYZ-001, Washington, DC, 2008.

Chapter in an edited volume:

Pellegrino, A. "Investigation of the Automated Backup Copies of Microsoft Application Files." In Noriki, H. W. et al, *Computer Forensics*. Learning Technology, Springfield, MA, 2010.

Including Appendixes If necessary, you can include appendixes containing material such as raw data, figures not used in the body of the report, and anticipated exhibits. Arrange them in the order referred to in the report. They are considered additional material and might not be examined by readers. Some portions of appendixes might be considered optional, but others are required. For example, exhibits are required under FRCP, Rule 26, as is your curriculum vitae (unless bona fides are integrated into the report).

Whether you're working for a law firm, digital forensics company, research lab, or law enforcement agency, these organizations have established formats for reports. Be sure to get samples from them before beginning your report.

Generating Report Findings with Forensics Software Tools

With many forensics software tools, such as ProDiscover, X-Ways Forensics, OSForensics, FTK, ILookIX, and EnCase, log files of analysis activities and reports can be created that provide information about the findings for a case. Although forensics software reports what was found and where, remember that it's your responsibility to explain the significance of the evidence you recover and, if necessary, define any limitations or uncertainty that applies to your findings. These reports and logs are typically in text, word processing, or HTML format. In this section, you learn how to integrate a software-generated report into the official investigation report that you present to your attorney or client.

As an example of a report from a digital investigation, you reexamine a case from Chapter 9. Before starting the activity, create a *Work\ Chap14\Chapter* folder on your system (referred to as your "work folder" in steps). Your folder name will likely differ from what's shown in screenshots.

For this activity, the general counsel for Superior Bicycles, Ileen Johnson, has asked you to look for correspondence to employee Denise Robinson in a forensic image of an old Windows 98 system taken more than seven years ago. Ileen wants to know what messages Denise received from Terry Sadler and whether she has any accounting data, such as spreadsheets, on her old computer. Ileen says she doesn't know Mr. Sadler's full e-mail address, only that it starts with "terrysadler." She gives you a USB drive containing an image file, GCFI-Win98.eve, from Denise's computer and tells you she believes Denise uses an old version of OpenOffice as her office application.

Using ProDiscover Basic to Generate Reports

You need to look for spreadsheet accounting information that might have been created with OpenOffice Calc and e-mail correspondence created in Outlook Express. For OpenOffice Calc, search for files with .ods and .sxc extensions. For Outlook Express, look for files with a .dbx extension. When you have found files matching these extensions, bookmark them and generate a report in ProDiscover. Then export the files for further examination in OSForensics.

14

For this activity, you need to install OpenOffice or LibreOffice. Both are free and can be downloaded at *www.openoffice.us.com/download-openoffice-free.php* or *www.libreoffice.org/download/libreoffice-fresh/*.

First, you need to convert the ProDiscover image file GCFI-Win98.eve to a raw (dd) file named GCFI-Win98.dd. You can read this file in OSForensics, which you do in the next activity. Follow these steps:

1. Copy **GCFI-Win98.eve** from where you moved it in Chapter 9 to this chapter's work folder.

2. Start ProDiscover Basic with the **Run as administrator** option. If the Launch Dialog dialog box opens, click **Cancel**.

3. To create the raw version of GCFI-Win98.eve, click **Tools**, point to **Image Conversion Tools**, and click **Convert ProDiscover Image to "DD"**.

4. In the Convert ProDiscover Image to "DD" Image dialog box, click **Browse** next to the Source ProDiscover Image text box, navigate to where you stored GCFI-Win98.eve, click **GCFI-Win98.eve**, and then click **Open**.

5. Click **Browse** next to the Destination DD Image text box. In the Save As dialog box, navigate to where you stored GCFI-Win98.eve, type **GCFI-Win98.dd** in the File name text box, click **Save**, and then click **OK**.

6. To start the analysis of GCFI-Win98.dd, click **File, New Project** from the menu. In the New Project dialog box, type **InChap14** for the project number and filename, and then click **OK**. Save the project in your work folder.

7. In the tree view, click to expand **Add** and then click **Image File**.

8. In the Open dialog box, navigate to your work folder, click the **GCFI-Win98.dd** file, and click **Open**.

9. Click to expand **Images** under Content View, and then expand the **GCFI-Win98.dd** file path so that you can see the folders and files in the work area.

10. Click the **Search** toolbar button. In the Search dialog box, click the **Search for files named** option button, and in the text box underneath, type the following extensions (see Figure 14-2), pressing **Enter** after each one: **.ods, .sxc,** and **.dbx**.

11. Under "Select the Disk(s)/Image(s) you want to search in," click the **GCFI-Win98.dd** image file, and then click **OK**.

12. In the search results, click the check box next to **Inbox.dbx**. In the Add Comment dialog box, type **Files for case report InChap14** in the Investigator comments text box, click the **Apply to all items** check box, and then click **OK**.

13. In the search results, click the check boxes next to **Sent Items.dbx, Speedy Financials2.sxc, Speedy Financials 1.sxc, Speedy Financials.sxc,** and **Speedy Financials3.sxc**, as shown in Figure 14-3.

14. Click the **Add to Report** button, and then double-click **Inbox.dbx** to return to the work area.

15. In the work area, right-click **Inbox.dbx** and click **Copy All Selected Files**.

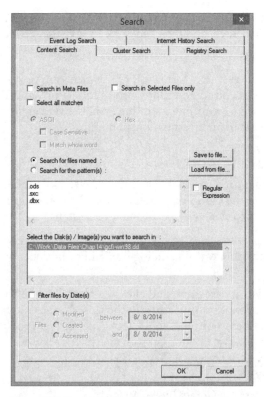

Figure 14-2 Searching for file extensions
Courtesy of Technology Pathways, LLC

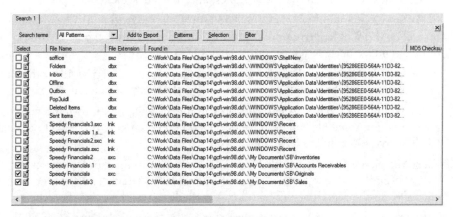

Figure 14-3 Selecting files in the search results
Courtesy of Technology Pathways, LLC

16. In the Choose Destination dialog box, click the **Browse** button, browse to your work folder, and click **OK** twice. Click **OK** in the message box about files being copied successfully.

17. In the tree view, click **Report**, and then click **Action, Export** from the menu to open the Export dialog box.

18. In the File Name text box, type **InChp14-prodiscover**. Click **Browse**, navigate to and double-click your work folder, click **Save**, and then click **OK** to save the report.

19. Exit ProDiscover. If you're prompted to save the project, click **Yes**.

ProDiscover's report generator defaults to rich text format (RTF), which can be opened by most word processors. This format enables you to add more information, such as a detailed narrative. In the following section, you see how to integrate this ProDiscover report into an OSForensics report that can be used as part of an investigation's findings.

Using OSForensics to Generate Reports

OSForensics has some unique features that aren't available in ProDiscover Basic. The following steps show you how to further analyze the Outlook Express .dbx files you exported with ProDiscover. First, load the case data for processing by performing these steps:

1. Start OSForensics with the **Run as administrator** option, and click **Yes** in the UAC message box. If you're prompted with a warning dialog box and/or notification, click **Continue Using Free Version**.

2. In the left pane, click **Manage Case**, if necessary, and click the **New Case** button on the right. In the New Case dialog box, type **InChap14** in the Case Name text box and your name in the Investigator text box. For the Acquisition Type setting, click the **Investigate Disk(s) from Another Machine** option button, and then click **OK**.

3. Mount the image file **GCFI-Win98.dd**, using the **Mount Drive Image** option in the left pane (referring to Chapter 5 for a reminder on using OSFMount, if needed). Click **Create Index** in the left pane to start the Create Index Wizard.

4. In the Step 1 of 5 window, click the **Use Pre-defined File Types** option button, if necessary. Click to select all the check boxes, and then click **Next**.

5. In the Step 2 of 5 window, click the **Add** button. In the Add Start Location dialog box, click the **Whole Drive** option button, if necessary. Click the list arrow, click the mounted image drive letter, and then click **OK**. Click **Next**.

6. In the Step 3 of 5 window, click **Start Indexing**. The Step 4 of 5 window displays a progress bar, and then the Step 5 of 5 window shows the files being indexed.

7. When the indexing has finished, click **OK** in the message box informing you that errors reading some files might have occurred in the indexing process, if necessary. Click **Search Index** in the left pane.

8. Click **File Name Search**, and click the **...** button next to the Config button. Navigate to and click the drive letter where you mounted **GCFI-Win98.dd** in Step 3, and then click **OK**. In the Search String text box, type ***.dbx**, and then click **Search**.

9. When the search is finished, right-click **Deleted Items.dbx** and click View with Internal Viewer to open the E-mail Viewer window.

10. Click the message in the upper pane to display its contents (see Figure 14-4). Read the message's content in the lower pane; it seems to be a message about a board meeting. Because it's a normal business communication, right-click the message in the upper pane, point to **Bookmark**, and click **Green**. Close this window.

11. Repeat Steps 9 and 10 for the **Inbox.dbx** and **Sent Items.dbx** files. After you read each message, decide whether to bookmark it as Green, Yellow, or Red,

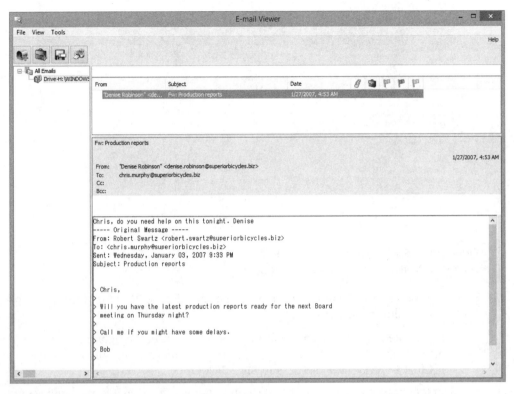

Figure 14-4 Viewing an e-mail's contents
Source: PassMark Software, *www.osforensics.com*

according to its contents. Normal correspondence should be flagged Green, messages that look suspicious should be flagged Yellow, and correspondence that looks very suspicious should be flagged Red. When you're finished, close this window.

12. In the File Name Search window, right-click **Inbox.dbx** and click **View with Internal Viewer** again. In the upper pane, click the **Yellow** flag column and then the **Red** flag column to sort the messages.

13. Ctrl+click each **Red** flagged message to highlight it (see Figure 14-5).

14. Right-click the highlighted messages and click **Add Email to Case**. In the Please Enter Case Export Details window, type **Message describing potential fraud** in the Export Title text box, click the **Use same details for all** check box, and then click **Add**.

15. Ctrl+click each **Yellow** flagged message. Right-click the highlighted messages and click **Add Email to Case**. In the Please Enter Case Export Details window, type **Messages of interest** in the Export Title text box, click the **Use same details for all** check box, and then click **Add**. Close the E-mail Viewer window.

16. Repeat Step 15 for all **Green** flagged messages, but type **Routine messages** in the Export Title text box.

17. Repeat Steps 12 through 16 for the **Sent Items.dbx** file. Leave OSForensics running for the next activity.

14

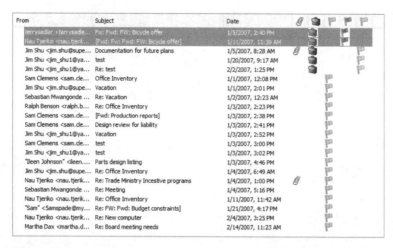

From	Subject	Date					
terrysadler <terrysadle...	Fw: Fwd: FW: Bicycle offer	1/5/2007, 2:40 PM					
Nau Tjeriko <nau.tjerik...	[Fwd: Fw: Fwd: FW: Bicycle offer]	1/11/2007, 11:39 AM					
Jim Shu <jim.shu@supe...	Documentation for future plans	1/5/2007, 8:28 AM					
Jim Shu <jim_shu1@ya...	test	1/20/2007, 9:17 AM					
Jim Shu <jim_shu1@ya...	Re: test	2/2/2007, 1:25 PM					
Sam Clemens <sam.cle...	Office Inventory	1/1/2007, 12:08 PM					
Jim Shu <jim.shu@supe...	Vacation	1/1/2007, 2:01 PM					
Sebastian Mwangonde ...	Re: Vacation	1/2/2007, 12:23 AM					
Ralph Benson <ralph.b...	Re: Office Inventory	1/3/2007, 2:23 PM					
Sam Clemens <sam.cle...	[Fwd: Production reports]	1/3/2007, 2:38 PM					
Sam Clemens <sam.cle...	Design review for liability	1/3/2007, 2:41 PM					
Jim Shu <jim_shu1@ya...	Vacation	1/3/2007, 2:52 PM					
Sam Clemens <sam.cle...	test	1/3/2007, 3:00 PM					
Jim Shu <jim_shu1@ya...	test	1/3/2007, 3:02 PM					
"Ileen Johnson" <ileen...	Parts design listing	1/3/2007, 4:46 PM					
Jim Shu <jim.shu@supe...	Re: Office Inventory	1/4/2007, 6:49 AM					
Nau Tjeriko <nau.tjerik...	Re: Trade Ministry Incestive programs	1/4/2007, 1:00 PM					
Sebastian Mwangonde ...	Re: Meeting	1/4/2007, 5:16 PM					
Nau Tjeriko <nau.tjerik...	Re: Office Inventory	1/11/2007, 11:42 AM					
"Sam" <Samspade@my...	Re: FW: Fwd: Budget constraints]	1/21/2007, 4:17 PM					
Nau Tjeriko <nau.tjerik...	Re: New computer	2/4/2007, 3:25 PM					
Martha Dax <martha.d...	Re: Board meeting needs	2/14/2007, 11:23 AM					

Figure 14-5   Selecting an e-mail message
Source: PassMark Software, *www.osforensics.com*

Next, you generate an OSForensics report that includes the ProDiscover report you created previously. Follow these steps:

1. In OSForensics, click **Manage Case** in the left pane. In the right pane, click **Add Attachment**. In the "Select a file to open" dialog box, navigate to your work folder, click the **InChp14-prodiscover** report, and then click **Open**.

2. In the Please Enter Case Export Details window, type **ProDiscover Findings** in the Export Title text box, and then click **Add**.

3. In the Manage Case window, click **Generate Report**. In the Export Report dialog box, click **Copy files to report location**, click **Browse** and navigate to your work folder, and then click **OK**.

4. When the report generator is finished, it opens the report in your Web browser automatically. Inspect the report and test the links, and then exit the Web browser and OSForensics.

If you need to close your Web browser, you can open the OSForenics report later by navigating to the C:*Work*\Chap14\Case Report folder in File Explorer and double-clicking the `report.html` file.

Chapter Summary

- All U.S. district courts and many state courts require expert witnesses to submit written reports.

- Rule 26 of the FRCP in the United States requires expert witnesses who anticipate that they will have to testify to submit written reports. The report must include the expert's opinion along with the basis for the opinion.

- Attorneys use deposition banks to research expert witnesses' previous testimony and to learn more about expert witnesses hired by opposing counsel.

- Reports should answer the questions you were retained to answer and keep information that doesn't support specific questions to a minimum.

- A well-defined report structure contributes to readers' ability to understand the information you're communicating. Make sure your report includes clearly labeled sections and follows a numbering scheme consistently. Ensure that supporting materials, such as figures and tables, are numbered and labeled clearly.

- Clarity of writing is critical to a report's success. Make sure to include signposts to give readers clues about the sequence of information, and avoid vague wording, jargon, and slang.

- Convey a tone of objectivity, and be detached in your observations. Synthesize what has (and has not) been learned about the problem and what the information means.

Key Terms

deposition banks Libraries of previously given testimony that law firms can access.

discovery Efforts to gather information before a trial by demanding documents, depositions, interrogatories (written questions answered in writing under oath), and written requests for admissions of fact.

examination plan A document that lets you know what questions to expect when you're testifying.

high-risk document A written report containing sensitive information that could create an opening for the opposing attorney to discredit you.

lay witness A person whose testimony is based on personal observation; not considered to be an expert in a particular field.

Review Questions

1. Which of the following rules or laws requires an expert to prepare and submit a report?
   a. FRCP 26
   b. FRE 801
   c. Neither
   d. Both

2. For what purpose have hypothetical questions traditionally been used in litigation?
   a. To frame the factual context of rendering an expert witness's opinion
   b. To define the case issues for the finder of fact to determine
   c. To stimulate discussion between a consulting expert and an expert witness
   d. To deter a witness from expanding the scope of his or her investigation beyond the case requirements
   e. All of the above

14

3. If you were a lay witness at a previous trial, you shouldn't list that case in your written report. True or False?

4. Which of the following is an example of a written report?

    a. A search warrant

    b. An affidavit

    c. Voir dire

    d. Any of the above

5. What is destroying a report before the final resolution of a case called?

6. An expert witness can give an opinion in which of the following situations?

    a. The opinion, inferences, or conclusions depend on special knowledge, skills, or training not within the ordinary experience of laypeople.

    b. The witness is shown to be qualified as a true expert in the field.

    c. The witness testifies to a reasonable degree of certainty (probability) about his or her opinion, inference, or conclusion.

    d. All of the above

7. Which of the following is the standard format for reports filed electronically in federal courts?

    a. Word

    b. Excel

    c. PDF

    d. HTML

    e. Any of the above

8. When writing a report, what's the most important aspect of formatting?

    a. A neat appearance

    b. Size of the font

    c. Clear use of symbols and abbreviations

    d. Consistency

9. Automated tools help you collect and report evidence, but you're responsible for doing which of the following?

    a. Explaining your formatting choices

    b. Explaining the significance of the evidence

    c. Explaining in detail how the software works

    d. All of the above

10. What can be included in report appendixes?

11. Which of the following statements about the legal-sequential numbering system in report writing is true?

    a. It's favored because it's easy to organize and understand.

    b. It's most effective for shorter reports.

    c. It doesn't indicate the relative importance of information.

    d. It's required for reports submitted in federal court.

12. What is a major advantage of automated forensics tools in report writing?

Hands-On Projects

In this chapter's projects, several of the data files have been used in previous chapters. Because some of these extracted files are very large and might take up too much room on your computer's drive, move them from these previous folders to this chapter's *Work*\Chap14\Projects folder. Create this folder on your system before beginning the projects.

Hands-On Project 14-1

This project is a continuation of the in-chapter activities. The general counsel for Superior Bicycles, Ileen Johnson, has asked you to locate a file that might contain information about the construction of a new bicycle frame. She tells you that the file she's interested in recovering is named "Materials," but she doesn't know the file extension. Follow these steps:

1. If necessary, start OSForensics and load the **InChap14** case. In the Manage Case window, double-click **InChap14**. If you have dismounted GCFI-Win98.dd, remount it as described in the in-chapter activity.

2. Click **Search Index** in the left pane of OSForensics. In the Enter Search Words text box, type **Materials**. Click the **Index to Search** list arrow, navigate to and click the drive where you mounted the image, and then click **Search**.

3. In the Search Index Results window, click the **Files** tab, and examine the search hits to find any files with the name Materials.

4. Next, click the **Emails** tab. Right-click each message and click **Open** to examine its contents. For messages with a file named Materials attached, right-click the filename in the lower pane and click **Add Attachment(s) to Case**. In the Please Enter Case Export Details window, type **File named Materials.rtf** in the Export Title input box, and then click **Add**.

5. Double-click the e-mail with the subject line "Documentation for future plans" containing the Materials.rtf file. In the Documentation for future plans window, click **View, Headers**. In the lower pane, select the header contents. Right-click this highlighted material and click **Copy**. Close the Documentation for future plans and the E-mail Viewer windows.

14

6. In the Manage Case window, click **Add Note**. Type **Header information - Documentation for future plans** in the Name text box. In the lower pane, right-click and click **Paste** to paste the e-mail header information. Click **Save**.

7. Click **Start** in the left pane, and then click **Generate Report** in the right pane. In the Export Report window, click the **Copy files to report location** option button. Click **Browse**, navigate to and click your work folder, and then click **OK** twice.

8. Review the report in your Web browser, and then print it. Turn it in to your instructor, and then exit your Web browser and OSForensics.

Hands-On Project 14-2

Ileen Johnson has sent you another image file collected from employee Chris Murphy's computer, which uses a different file system than Denise Robinson's computer uses. She's conducting a follow-up investigation of a case that's several years old and deals with some very old file formats. You need to locate and extract files using these file formats and generate a report for Ileen.

For this project, you use the GCFI-NTFS.dd image file used in Chapter 9's hands-on projects. You need to look for spreadsheet accounting information created with OpenOffice Calc (files with .ods and .sxc extensions) and e-mail correspondence created with Outlook Express (.dbx and .pst extensions). When you find any files with these extensions, add them to the case in OSForensics. This project continues in Hands-On Project 14-3.

 For this project and the next, you need to install OpenOffice or LibreOffice. Both are free and can be downloaded at *www.openoffice.us.com/download-openoffice-free.php* or *www.libreoffice.org/download/libreoffice-fresh/*.

Follow these steps to find e-mail messages containing attached spreadsheets:

1. Start OSForensics, and create a new case named **HOP14-2**. Use OSFMount to select the drive for the image file GCFI-NTFS.dd.

2. Click **Create Index** in the left pane. In the Step 1 of 5 window, click the **Use Pre-defined File Types** option button, click the **Emails, Attachments, Office + PDF Documents, Zip Files, Images,** and **Plain Text Files** check boxes, and then click **Next**. In the Step 2 of 5 window, click **Add**. If the drive used in Hands-On Project 14-1 is listed in the Start Folder window, click it and then click **Remove**. In the Add Start Location dialog box, click the **Whole Drive** option button, click the list arrow, click the drive letter where GCFI-NTFS.dd is mounted, and click **OK**. Click **Next**, and in the Step 3 of 5 window, click **Start Indexing**.

3. When the indexing has finished, click **OK**, if necessary, in the message box informing you that errors reading some files might have occurred in the indexing process.

4. Next, click **File Name Search** in the left pane. In the Search String text box, type ***.ods;*.sxc;*.dbx;*.pst**, click the **...** button next to the Start Folder text box, click the drive where you mounted GCFI-NTFS.dd, click **OK**, and then click **Search**.

5. When the search is finished, click the **Sorting** list arrow, and then click **Type**.

6. Right-click **Inbox.dbx** and click **View with Internal Viewer**. In the E-mail Viewer window, click the **Paperclip** toolbar icon to sort all messages containing attachments.

7. In the E-mail Viewer window, examine each message. Right-click any message with an .ods or .sxc file attached and click **Add Email to Case**. In the Please Enter Case Export Details window, type **Spreadsheet file found in message** in the Export Title text box, and then click **Add**.

8. Right-click the spreadsheet file in the message header and click **Add Attachment(s) to Case**. In the Please Enter Case Export Details window, type **Found spreadsheet** in the Export Title text box, and then click **Add**. Close the E-mail Viewer window.

9. Click **File Name Search** in the left pane. If the File List window is blank, move the scrollbar up or down to display the contents. Examine the other .dbx files to determine whether there are more messages with attached spreadsheets. If you find other spreadsheets, repeat Steps 6 through 8. Leave this case loaded and OSForensics running for the next project.

Hands-On Project 14-3

In this continuation of Hands-On Project 14-2, you search for spreadsheets with an .ods or .sxc extension that aren't attached to e-mails. Follow these steps:

1. Click **File Name Search** in the left pane, if necessary. Double-click the first file with an .ods or .sxc extension in the search results to open it. If a file contains spreadsheet data, right-click the file, point to **Add to Case**, and click **File(s)**. In the Please Enter Case Export Details window, type **Spreadsheet not attached to e-mail** in the Export Title text box, and click **Add**.

2. Repeat Step 1 for all other spreadsheet files in the search results window. When you're finished, exit OSForensics.

14

Hands-On Project 14-4

For this project, print all e-mails and spreadsheets from the case you processed in Hands-On Projects 14-2 and 14-3. Then write a one- to two-page report addressed to Ileen Johnson that explains the steps you have taken and the evidence you found in your examination. In the conclusion, state your opinion about the nature of the correspondence, based on the e-mails you collected and compared for these cases. Include any supporting materials as appendixes, and be sure to follow the writing guidelines described in this chapter for your report.

Case Projects

Case Project 14-1

The county prosecutor has hired you to investigate a case in which the county treasurer has been accused of embezzlement. What additional resources, such as other experts, might you need to collect data for this investigation? Write a one-page paper outlining what resources you should consider to help you with the evidence collection process.

Case Project 14-2

Your digital forensics company has been hired to verify the local police department's findings on a current case. Tension over the case is running high in the city. What do you need to ask the police investigator for, and what procedures should you follow? Consider what test you might use to validate the police department's findings. Write a one- to two-page report outlining what you need to do.

Case Project 14-3

Your manager has asked you to research and recommend a writing guide that examiners in your digital forensics company can use for all official written reports. Conduct research on the Internet to find information about style manuals and technical and legal writing guides. You should also research writing guides from professional associations, such as the IEEE and the American Psychological Association. Write a two- to three-page report recommending a style manual or technical/legal writing guide for your company to use and explain the reasons for your recommendations. You might want to combine guidelines from different sources in coming up with recommendations for digital forensics reports.

chapter

15

Expert Testimony in Digital Investigations

After reading this chapter and completing the exercises, you will be able to:

- Explain guidelines for giving testimony as a fact witness or an expert witness
- Describe guidelines for testifying in court
- Explain guidelines for testifying in depositions and hearings
- Describe procedures for preparing forensics evidence for testimony

This chapter explains the rules of evidence and procedure as they apply to testimony. You learn about the types of testimony—for trials, depositions, and hearings—and the difference between a fact witness and an expert witness. In addition, you learn how to avoid some common problems of testimony and learn some techniques you can use to increase the value of your testimony. This chapter also offers an example of how to prepare forensics evidence for testimony.

Preparing for Testimony

When cases go to trial, you as a forensics examiner can play one of two roles: a **fact witness** providing technical or scientific evidence or an **expert witness**. As a fact witness, you provide only the facts you have found in your investigation—any evidence that meets the relevance standard and is more probative than prejudicial. When you give technical or scientific testimony, you present this evidence and explain what it is and how it was obtained. You don't offer conclusions, only the facts. However, as an expert witness, you have opinions about what you have found or observed. You form these opinions from experience and deductive reasoning based on facts found during an investigation. In fact, it's your opinion that makes you an expert witness.

For either type of testimony, you need to prepare thoroughly. Establish communication early with your attorney. Before you start processing evidence, learn about the victim, the complainant, opposing experts or fact witnesses, and the opposing attorney as soon as possible. Learn the basic points of the dispute. As you learn about the case, take notes, but keep them in rough draft form and record only the facts, keeping your opinions to a minimum. (As explained in Chapter 14, any written material is subject to discovery, so use caution in what you put in written form.)

 Your attorney can give you specific guidelines in preparing for the case. Remember that as an expert witness, you work for the attorney, not the client (plaintiff or defendant), so if you discover negative findings, communicate them as soon as possible to your attorney.

As part of your preparation, confirm your findings with your own documentation and by corroborating with other digital forensics professionals. Return to the notes you took during your investigation. If you're working with electronic notes, use care in storing them. In your analysis and reporting, develop and maintain a standard method of processing to minimize confusion and help you prepare for testimony later. Digital forensics is only now developing a peer review process. To get a peer review, often you have to search outside your region. Learn to take advantage of your professional network and request peer reviews to help support your findings.

You might also want to use the Internet to learn about opposing experts and try to find their strengths and weaknesses in previous testimony. Review their curriculum vitae, if possible, and see how they present themselves. To do otherwise is to go into battle without trying to know your opponent. Your attorney might be able to get copies of depositions they have given in other cases, usually from the deposition banks mentioned in Chapter 14. Some organizations of forensics investigators also maintain e-mail lists that you can use to query members about other expert witnesses.

Review the following questions when preparing your testimony:

- What's my story of the case (the central facts relevant to my testimony)?
- What can I say with confidence?
- What is the client's overall theory of the case?
- How does my opinion fit into the theory of the case?
- What's the scope of the case? Have I gone too far?
- Have I identified the client's needs for how my testimony fits into the overall theory of the case?

Documenting and Preparing Evidence

As emphasized in previous chapters, document your steps in gathering and preserving evidence to make sure they're repeatable, in case you're challenged. If your findings can't be repeated, they lose credibility as evidence. In addition, validate your tools and verify your evidence with hash algorithms to ensure its integrity. (Refer to Chapter 5 for guidelines on using hash algorithms.) The following guidelines are also useful in ensuring the integrity of your evidence:

- If you need a checklist to analyze evidence, create it only for a specific case. Don't create a formal checklist of your procedures that's applied to all your cases or include such a checklist in your report. If opposing counsel gets this checklist through discovery, you might be challenged during cross-examination about inconsistencies in your performance if you deviated from the checklist.
- As a standard practice, collect evidence and record the tools you used in designated file folders or evidence containers. This method helps organize your evidence and tools. Follow a system to record where items are kept for each case and how documentation is stored.
- Remember that the chain of custody of evidence supports the integrity of your evidence; do whatever you can to prevent contamination of the evidence. You should also document any lapse or gap in evidence preservation or custody. Lapses and gaps don't necessarily result in evidence being inadmissible, but they might affect the weight given to the evidence.
- When collecting evidence, be careful not to get too little or too much information. For litigation, you're responsible for collecting only what's asked for, no more. In some circumstances, collecting and identifying evidence on facts unrelated to the case could cause problems for your attorney.
- Make sure you note the date and time of your forensic workstation when starting your analysis. If precise time is an issue, consider using an Internet clock, such as the one at *www.time.gov* or *www.nist.gov/pml/div688/grp40/its.cfm* (downloading `nistime-32bit.exe`), or an atomic clock to verify the accuracy of your workstation's clock. Many retailers, such as Walmart and Radio Shack, now sell atomic clocks.
- Keep only successful output when running analysis tools; don't keep previous runs, such as those missing necessary switch or output settings. Note that you used the tool, but it didn't generate results because of these missing settings.

15

- When searching for keyword results, rerun searches with well-defined keywords and search parameters. You might even want to state how they relate to the case, such as being business or personal names. Narrow the search to reduce false hits, and eliminate search results containing false-positive hits.

- When taking notes of your findings, keep them simple and specific to the investigation. You should avoid any personal comments so that you don't have to explain them to opposing counsel.

- When writing your report, list only the evidence that's relevant to the case; do not include unrelated findings.

- Define any procedures you use to conduct your analysis as scientific and conforming to your profession's standards. Listing textbooks, technical books, articles by recognized experts, and procedures from authoritative organizations that you relied on or referenced during your examination is a common way to prove your conformity with scientific and professional standards.

Reviewing Your Role as a Consulting Expert or an Expert Witness

Depending on your attorney's needs, you might give him or her just your opinion and technical expertise instead of testifying in court; this role is called a "consulting expert." If your role changes from consulting expert to expert witness later, however, your previous work as a consulting expert is subject to discovery by opposing counsel. For this reason, don't record conversations or phone calls.

When you appear in a federal court as an expert witness, Federal Rules of Civil Procedure (FRCP) 26 (2) (B) requires that you provide the following information:

- Other cases in which you have testified as an expert at a trial or in a deposition in the preceding four years

- Ten years of any published writings

- Previous compensation you received when giving testimony

In addition, the court can appoint its own expert witnesses. Court-appointed expert witnesses must be neutral in their opinions, and they must be knowledgeable in their field. As an expert hired by the defense or plaintiff, you need to evaluate the court's expert. Make sure you brief your attorney on your findings and opinion of the court's expert to help your attorney deal with any testimony the court-appointed expert provides.

When approached to give expert testimony, find out whether you're the first one asked. If you aren't, find out why other experts might have been contacted but not retained.

Creating and Maintaining Your CV

Your **curriculum vitae** (CV) lists your professional experience and is used to qualify your testimony. For forensics examiners, keeping this document updated and complete is crucial to supporting your role as an expert and showing that you're constantly enhancing your skills through training, teaching, and experience.

Your CV should describe tasks you've performed that define specific accomplishments and your basic and advanced skills. You should also list your general and professional education and professional training. If the list of training is extremely lengthy, use a heading such as "Selected Training Attended." Be sure to include coursework sponsored by government agencies or organizations that train government agency personnel and courses sponsored or approved by professional associations, such as bar associations. Also, note any professional training you provided or contributed to. You must also include a testimony log that reflects every testimony you have given as an expert.

Make sure your CV reflects your professional background. Unlike a job resume, it should not be geared toward a specific trial. Most important, keep your CV current and date it for version control. If your CV is more than three months old, you probably need to update it to reflect new cases and additional training.

Keep a separate list of books you've read on your area of expertise, but don't include this list in your CV because it might suggest that you approve of everything written in these books.

Preparing Technical Definitions

Before you testify in court, prepare definitions of technical concepts that you can use when questioned by your attorney and the opposing attorney. Make sure you use your own words, and remember that you're explaining these concepts for a nontechnical audience. You don't need to make the jury subject matter experts; you're simply explaining the general meaning of these terms. The following are examples of definitions to prepare ahead of time for your testimony:

- Digital forensics or computer forensics
- CRC-32, MD5, and SHA-1 hashing algorithms
- Image files and bit-stream copies
- File slack and unallocated (free) space
- File timestamps
- Computer log files
- Folder or directory
- Hardware
- Software
- Operating system

Preparing to Deal with the News Media

Some legal actions generate interest from the news media, but you should avoid contact with news media, especially during a case, for the following reasons:

- Your comments could harm the case and create a record that can be used against you.
- You have no control over the context of the information a journalist publishes.

15

- You can't rely on a journalist's promises of confidentiality. Journalists have been known to be aggressive in getting information, and their interests do not coincide with yours or your client's. Be on guard at all times because your comments could be interpreted in a manner that taints your impartiality in this case and future cases. Even after the case is resolved, avoid discussing details with the press.

If you're solicited for information or opinions by journalists (or anyone else), refrain from saying anything, and refer them to your client (the attorney who retained you). If you can't avoid a journalist, consult with your attorney and determine how to handle the situation. Plan to record any attempted interviews so that you have your own record of what occurred. (Note, however, that state laws on consent for recording vary.) This recording can be important if you're misquoted or quoted out of context. Reporters often look for a sensational sound bite or controversial quote.

Testifying in Court

Before you're called to testify in court, you should become familiar with the usual procedures followed during a trial. First, your attorney examines you about your qualifications to demonstrate to the court that you're competent as an expert witness or a fact witness. The opposing counsel might then cross-examine you on your qualifications (perhaps in an attempt to discredit you). Next, your attorney guides you through your testimony, and then opposing counsel can cross-examine you on your testimony. Your attorney might then have an opportunity for redirect examination of material addressed in cross-examination. After your testimony, you might be called back to update your testimony, or you might be called as a rebuttal witness.

Understanding the Trial Process

The typical order of trial proceedings, whether civil or criminal, is as follows:

- *Motion in limine*—A pretrial motion to exclude certain evidence because it would prejudice the jury. Effectively, this motion is a written list of objections to certain testimony or exhibits. It allows the judge to decide whether certain evidence should be admitted when the jury isn't present. Some evidence is so prejudicial that just the jury knowing it exists is enough to damage the case. In this situation, getting a ruling on the evidence before trial is crucial.

- *Impaneling the jury*—This process includes voir dire of venireman (questioning potential jurors to see whether they're qualified), strikes (rejecting potential jurors), and seating of jurors.

- *Opening statements*—Both attorneys provide an overview of the case, with the plaintiff's attorney going first.

- *Plaintiff*—The plaintiff's attorney presents the case.

- *Defense*—The defense's attorney presents the case.

- *Rebuttal*—Rebuttal from both the plaintiff's and defense's attorneys is an optional phase of the trial. Generally, it's allowed to cover an issue raised during cross-examination of a witness.

- *Closing arguments*—Statements that organize the evidence and state the applicable law. The plaintiff's attorney goes first and gets a rebuttal opportunity at the end, which should be limited to issues raised by the defense's attorney.

- *Jury instructions*—The attorneys propose instructions to the jury on how to consider the evidence, and then the judge approves or disapproves; if the instructions are approved, the judge reads them to the jury.

Providing Qualifications for Your Testimony

During the qualification phase of your testimony, your attorney asks questions to elicit the qualifications that make you an expert witness. This qualification phase is called **voir dire** (from the French, literally "to see, to say"). Typically, your attorney guides you through your CV. The amount of detail in this examination depends on several factors, but they all relate to how much advantage the attorney sees in your qualifications. After your attorney has completed this examination, he or she asks the court to accept you as an expert on digital forensics. However, opposing counsel might object and is allowed to examine you, too; usually, cross-examination happens only if the opposing attorney thinks there's something to gain from it.

If you know that the opposing expert witness taught or took a course that used a publication you wrote or co-authored, tell your attorney about it. He could emphasize that you're the author and examine the opposing witness on this fact to give you more credibility as a recognized expert in the field.

The following example is a short direct-examination voir dire:

Q: Please state your name and spell your last name for the record.
A: William Nokiki, N-O-K-I-K-I.
Q: What is your profession?
A: I am a digital forensics examiner.
Q: How long have you been a digital forensics examiner?
A: Twelve years.
Q: Where are you currently employed?
A: I am currently employed by IT Forensics, Incorporated, of Seattle, Washington.
Q: How long have you been with IT Forensics?
A: Eight years.
Q: What is your title with IT Forensics?
A: I am a senior case manager.
Q: What training have you received in digital forensics?
A: I have been trained at the Federal Law Enforcement Training Center in 2000, I trained with NTI in 1996, and I have received training from the International Association of Computer Investigative Specialists since 1999, most recently on large disk acquisitions and network monitoring. I have taken dozens of short courses with many different investigative training organizations over the past fifteen years.
Q: Where have you been an instructor?
A: I have taught classes on digital forensics at City College, Highline Community College, Bellevue Community College, and Lake Washington Technical College. I taught the digital forensics instructors for the state of Washington in 2002. I have made many shorter presentations, including continuing legal education programs approved by the Washington State Bar Association.

15

Q: Have you been published?

A: Yes, I am co-author of the college textbook Digital Investigations and Forensics.

Q: Have you testified previously?

A: Yes, I have most recently in United States v. Smith. A detailed list of occasions in which I have testified is in my CV.

Plaintiff's Attorney:	Your witness.
Defense Attorney:	No questions for the witness.
Plaintiff's Attorney:	Your Honor, Plaintiff would move that Mr. Nokiki be accepted as an expert witness on digital forensics.
Judge:	Any objection, Mr. Defense Attorney?
Defense Attorney:	No objection, Your Honor.
Judge:	Mr. Nokiki is accepted as an expert witness on digital forensics. You may proceed, Mr. Plaintiff's Attorney.

If you have especially strong qualifications and have been qualified as an expert on several occasions, opposing counsel might offer to accept you as an expert without your qualifications being stated formally. Generally, your attorney bypasses that offer in favor of impressing the jury with your qualifications.

General Guidelines on Testifying

Whether you're serving as an expert witness or a fact witness, be professional and polite when presenting yourself to any attorney or the court. Before the trial, try to learn the jury, judge, and attorneys' level of knowledge on and attitudes toward computers and technology. Talk to local attorneys to learn more about the type of people typically serving on local juries. With this knowledge, you can gauge your presentation to your audience's educational level, and incorporate appropriate analogies into your explanations. Remember that the judge is well educated but not necessarily in the field of digital evidence. Jurors typically average around 12 years of education and an eighth-grade reading level. The attorneys might have a thorough background in the field, but you're the expert with experience. You could also be dealing with an arbiter or mediator who may or may not have a background in digital forensics.

There are two responses you use often as a witness. First, if asked a question you can't answer, respond by saying, "That is beyond the scope of my expertise" or "I was not asked to investigate that." These statements make it clear that you understand your limitations. You won't seem less of an expert for knowing and expressing your limitations. If anything, acknowledging your limitations enhances your standing with a jury. Second, if you don't understand a question or find it confusing, simply say, "Can you please rephrase the question?" Typically, this response gets the attorney to reorganize the question and is one method you can use to control the pace and direction of the examination. If the question is stated awkwardly or you aren't sure of the intent, ask the attorney for clarification.

If opposing counsel tries to reframe your answer in a way that you don't believe is accurate, reject his restatement by saying "No, that isn't what I said," and then restate your position accurately, starting with "What I said was." Be respectful and even pleasant, but be firm.

Another aspect of acknowledging your limitations is making sure you avoid overstating opinions. Part of what you have to deliver to the jury is a person they can trust to help them figure out something that's beyond their expertise. Overstating an opinion creates the potential for the jury to mistrust or doubt you; like a teacher, you should admit your limitations and the limitations of your results.

Your delivery is an important part of how you answer questions and affects the impact you have on the jury. The following list offers some general guidelines on delivery and presentation:

- Always acknowledge the jury and direct your testimony to them, using an enthusiastic, sincere tone to keep the jury interested in what you have to say. When an attorney or the judge asks you a question, turn toward the questioner, and then turn back to the jury to give the answer.

- If a microphone is present, place it 6 to 8 inches from you, and remember to speak loudly and clearly so that the jury can hear and understand you.

- Use simple, direct language to help the jury understand you. For example, use "test" instead of "analyze," as in "I ran a test on the files I found." Also, make sure you use specific, articulate speech when speaking; for clarity, avoid contractions and slang, unless you're quoting a fact related to the case.

- Avoid humor. What one person thinks is funny, another won't. In addition, limit your responses to what you perceive as attempts at humor from anybody else.

- Build repetition into your explanations and descriptions for the jury.

- Use chronological order to describe events when testifying, and use hand gestures to help the audience understand what you're emphasizing. For example, point to graphics while talking. (Graphics are discussed more later in "Using Graphics During Testimony.")

- If you're using technical terms, identify and define these terms for the jury, using analogies and graphics as appropriate. List any important technical elements, showing how you verified and validated each element.

- When giving an opinion, cite the source of the evidence the opinion is based on. Then express your opinion and explain your methodology—how you arrived at your opinion.

- If the witness chair is adjustable, make sure the height is comfortable, and turn the chair so that it faces the jury.

- To enhance your image with the jury, dress in a manner conforming to the community's dress code for business professionals, or dress like the attorneys in the case. If your testimony is being videotaped, avoid fine stripes in suits or ties because they can generate a strobing effect in video recordings under artificial light. Men should wear conservative ties with a base color of red; women should wear suits in conservative colors or a dress that allows freedom of movement.

- Don't memorize your testimony; you should strive for a natural, extemporaneous tone. Also, make sure you have alternative ways to describe or explain key facts.

- For direct examinations, state your opinion, identify evidence to support your opinion, explain the method you used to arrive at your opinion from your analysis, and then restate your opinion.

As mentioned, have definitions and explanations aimed at a nontechnical audience ready for technical terms you must use in your testimony. Learn how to describe the tools you use as a standardized process for your work. Make sure you're knowledgeable about the fallibility of digital forensics so that you can resist counterattacks from opposing counsel. Lengthy explanations might be good for some jury cases but not for others, so seek your attorney's opinion.

15

Prepare your testimony with the attorney who hired you. The following are specific questions you should prepare for:

- How is data (or evidence) stored on a hard drive?
- What is an image or a bit-stream copy of a drive?
- How is deleted data recovered from a drive?
- What are Windows temporary files, and how do they relate to data or evidence?
- What are system or network log files?

Using Graphics During Testimony Graphical exhibits, such as charts and tables, illustrate and clarify your findings. As a general rule, memory retention is much weaker for audio material and slightly stronger for visual material. Therefore, oral testimony supported by graphical presentations is an effective way to impart information and help your listeners retain it. Your exhibits must be clear and easy to understand. Graphics should be big, bold, and simple so that the jury can see them easily, and consider factors such as glare and adequate contrast to ensure easy visibility. If necessary, make smaller copies of graphics for jurors so that they can see details better.

The goal of using graphics is to provide information the jury needs to know (such as how hardware and software work), an explanation of your findings, and the role the evidence plays in the case. Make sure each graphic conveys only one concept or point; don't try to include too much information in a single graphic. If you're using graphics to explain a complex technical concept or procedure, use two or more graphics, with the first graphic providing an overview.

Don't include vendor logos on your charts, and don't use charts created by someone else, unless you commissioned someone to create them, to avoid possible copyright issues. Another advantage of creating your own charts is that you can make sure you're comfortable with what's in them and can explain the material in them.

Review all graphics with your attorney before trial, and make sure you've practiced using them so that you appear comfortable and confident. In most courts, you need at least three extra copies of your graphics: one for your attorney, one for the opposing attorney, and one for the judge. However, it's the attorney's responsibility to have graphical exhibits admitted into evidence.

Courtrooms are becoming more audiovisual capable, and you might be able to use a projector system. If one is available, discuss using it with your attorney. You might also talk about the possibility of giving jurors copies of your presentation on CD or DVD.

Make sure the jury can see your graphics, and face the jury during your presentation. If your graphics haven't been placed near the jury box, ask the judge if you can move them so that the jury can see them better. When you're talking about specific areas of an illustration, use a pointer to direct jurors' attention to details. You can also use your hands to help emphasize certain information or direct attention to specific points. Make sure any gestures are above the waist so that the jury can see them. If an attorney asks you questions as you explain the graphics, face the jury and answer the questions in full sentences.

When you're standing in front of the jury, leave your jacket unbuttoned and keep your elbows bent to show that you're comfortable, confident, and at ease.

Avoiding Testimony Problems Although you should recognize when conflict-of-interest issues apply to your case and discuss any concerns with the attorney who hires you, be aware of a practice called **conflicting out**. It's an attempt by opposing attorneys to prevent you from serving on an important case and is most common in the private sector when you work as an independent consultant. Opposing attorneys might call to discuss the case with you and then claim you can't testify because of a conflict of interest caused by you discussing the case with another attorney besides the one who hired you. As a result, you might be excluded from working for an attorney needing your services. (The issue of conflict is raised by motion after witness lists are exchanged.)

In addition, avoid agreeing to review a case unless you're under contract with that person. Also, avoid conversations with opposing attorneys—there's no such thing as an "off the record" conversation with opposing attorneys after you have been retained; refer them to the attorney who retained you. Have a fee agreement ready to e-mail or fax to opposing attorneys to protect yourself from this practice; this agreement serves as proof that they didn't want to retain you. If you aren't retained, you're in a better position to collect a fee for the service you did provide, and it deters them from attempting to manufacture a conflict issue to disqualify you later as an expert witness.

Early in direct examination, your attorney should ask whether you were hired to perform an analysis and testify. He or she might ask how much you charged for your services and whether you have already been paid; you should receive payment before testifying. If you haven't been paid, it might seem that you have a contingent interest in the litigation—that your payment depends on the resolution of the case. Fees and payment schedules are appropriate subjects for examination, although the judge might limit these questions. If your attorney doesn't ask you questions about payment, the opposing counsel could examine you on it in an effort to discredit you or lessen your credibility as a witness. However, the opposing counsel knows that this tactic might be used on his expert witnesses, too, so he might touch on the subject but not dwell on it, unless you say you haven't been paid completely.

When you're testifying, don't talk to anyone during court recess. If the opposing attorney sees you having a conversation with anyone, including the attorney who retained you, he or she could cross-examine you again and demand that you explain and repeat your conversation. However, be aware that your attorney might want to notify you of updates during breaks, so make sure you conduct any conferences in a private setting. If a juror approaches and says anything to you, decline to talk with him or her and promptly report the contact to the attorney who retained you. This event must be reported to the court.

15

Understanding Prosecutorial Misconduct If you're working for a prosecutor in a criminal case and believe you have found exculpatory evidence (evidence that exonerates or diminishes the defendant's liability), you have an obligation to ensure that the evidence isn't concealed. Initially, you should report the evidence (emphasizing its exculpatory nature) to the prosecutor handling the case. Be sure you document communicating your concern to the prosecutor. If this information isn't disclosed to the defense attorney in a reasonable time, you can report it to the prosecutor's supervisor. Be sure to document this communication, too. Documentation of each attempt to induce disclosure and your reasoning is important to protect your reputation.

If these efforts still don't result in disclosure, you can report the lack of disclosure to the judge. Be sure you have documented your attempts to bring the matter to the prosecutor's attention before bringing it to the judge. Don't communicate directly with the defense attorney; reporting evidence to the judge fulfills your obligation. The rules that apply to defense expert witnesses are different.

Testifying During Direct Examination

You provide direct testimony when you answer questions from the attorney who hired you. This direct examination is the most important part of testimony at a trial. Cross-examination is not as important, even if the opposing attorney is attempting to discredit you.

When preparing your testimony for direct examination, keep some guidelines and techniques in mind. You should work with your attorney to get the right language that communicates your message to the jury effectively. Also, your attorney might advise you to be wary of your inclination to be helpful. This trait is natural, but it can hurt your testimony. You shouldn't volunteer any information or be overly friendly (or hostile) to the opposing attorney.

Review the examination plan your attorney has prepared to see whether you can make any suggestions for improvement; this plan is structured to ensure that questions elicit relevant evidence during direct examination. Make sure you've prepared a clear overview of your findings and have a systematic and easy-to-follow plan for describing your evidence-collection methods. Practice testifying with your graphics so that you're comfortable using them.

Your attorney might also help you develop a theme to follow when presenting your testimony, but make sure you use your own words when answering questions. Generally, the best approach your attorney can take in direct examination is to ask you open-ended questions and let you give your testimony.

In addition, make sure you know the following terms before giving testimony because your attorney will likely use them during the direct examination:

- *Independent recollection*—Information you know about this case and others without being prompted
- *Customary practice*—Procedures that are traditionally followed in similar cases
- *Documentation of the case*—The written records you have maintained

When your attorney questions you about your background and qualifications, your answers should show why you are an expert able to give testimony. Give answers that emphasize your factual findings and opinions. Remember to tailor your language to the jury's educational level, and try to strike a balance between technical language and layperson language when describing complex matters.

Avoid vagueness in your wording choices, too. For example, don't use expressions such as "very large" or "a long time." The meaning of these expressions varies, depending on what they're compared with, and this comparison might be different for every juror. Use precise numbers and units of measurement, and if relevant, cite numbers' statistical position, relationship to the mean, or an expected value or range.

When you're using graphics in a presentation, keep in mind that you're instructing the jury in what you did to collect evidence, so follow some of the same guidelines teachers use in a classroom to make sure the jury understands your explanations.

Testifying During Cross-Examination

When answering questions from the opposing attorney, use your own words. Keep in mind that certain words have additional meanings that an opposing attorney can exploit. For example, the word "suspicious" is more value laden than the more neutral "concerned."

During cross-examination, opposing attorneys sometimes use the trick of interrupting you as you're answering a question. In a trial, a judge usually doesn't allow this trick, but in a deposition, there's no independent arbiter of procedure. Be aware of leading questions from the opposing attorney, too. An ambiguous question, such as "Isn't it true that forensics experts always destroy their handwritten notes?" is an attempt to lead you to say something that could be construed as wrong. (The answer to that question should be "I don't know.") Leading questions call for yes or no answers and are sometimes referred to as "setup questions"— setting you up for a response that could be damaging to your client's case. They're often phrased in a complex structure, designed to limit your freedom in answering. Getting to the real question opposing counsel is asking might take many questions.

If opposing attorneys ask you a question such as "Did you use more than one tool to verify the evidence?" they're checking to make sure you validated the findings from one tool by using another tool. Opposing attorneys often ask the following questions, too:

* What are the tools you used, and what are their known problems or weaknesses?
* Are the tools you used reliable? Are they consistent, and do they produce the same results?
* Have other professionals called on you as a consultant on how to use tools?
* Do you keep up with the latest technologies used in digital forensics, such as by reading journal articles?

During examinations, lawyers aren't supposed to ask another question until you have finished answering the current question. However, the opposing counsel sometimes uses rapid-fire questions during cross-examination that are meant to throw you off. Taking a moment to turn toward the jury before you answer gives you more control over the timing and speed of the opposing attorney's examination. Even though your attorney should object by saying, "Counsel has not allowed the witness to answer the question," don't be afraid to regroup and restate your answers if you get confused during your testimony. Jurors will sympathize because often they're confused by the opposing attorney's questions, too.

If the opposing attorney declares that you aren't answering the questions, she could be making an attempt to get you to change your testimony. You aren't giving the answer she wants, or she's attempting to get you to say something that contradicts part of your previous testimony. Don't take this attempt personally, but think carefully about what the opposing attorney is trying to do.

During a jury trial, keep a comfortable level of eye contact with the jury. You might find yourself competing with the opposing attorney, but do your best to keep the jury's attention on you during your testimony. As the opposing attorney asks you questions, avoid strict yes

15

or no answers, if possible; add facts to clarify your answer, when appropriate, before the opposing attorney can hit you with a "killer question." This type of question, contrived based on a change in a basic underlying fact, is one that you seemingly can't answer or deny. It can derail your testimony and your client's case; however, the judge will usually support you in stating conditions or limits.

Sometimes opposing attorneys ask several questions inside one question; this practice is called a compound question, and your attorney should object to it. If your attorney doesn't, you can respond by saying, "Could you please break your last question into separate questions?" Another tactic opposing attorneys use in cross-examinations is to make a speech and phrase it as a question. You have no obligation to respond to statements by opposing counsel. The judge usually catches this error, and your attorney should also object. Other methods opposing attorneys use to challenge your credibility are putting words in your mouth and summarizing your testimony to fit their needs, creating assumptions or speculation, and controlling the pace of your testimony. Other tactics are stating minor inconsistencies that cause you to make conflicting statements and encouraging you to volunteer information.

Your response to cross-examination tactics should challenge the opposing attorney to be more sensible, a response that often plays well with juries. Take your time answering questions. Be thoughtful, professional, and courteous in your responses. The more patient you are during cross-examination, the better you'll weather any possible attacks. If the opposing attorney becomes assertive or upset with your testimony, be as professional and courteous as possible. If he continues to lose control, staying calm and professional strengthens your image by comparison. Responding to a question with a sentence that communicates limitations or qualifications might be important, if a simple yes or no doesn't answer the question completely and accurately. If you need to have your attorney expand a line of questions on redirect, have an agreed-on expression you can use to signal him, such as "This question requires a more complex answer, but the short answer is yes (or no)."

In addition to direct examination and cross-examination, most jurisdictions now allow the judge and jurors to ask questions. These questions are subject to the same rules of evidence that any other question is. Attorneys can object to these questions but generally won't unless they are an especially serious breach of the rules, such as a question that was specifically excluded in a motion in limine. Answering a question from the judge or a juror should be viewed as an opportunity. As a witness, you usually have to guess at what's important to the judge and jury, but you don't when responding to a question directly from them.

Many factors contribute to your stress when testifying, including the judge, the attorneys, the jury, and the feeling of losing control. Don't think you're responsible for the outcome. If you make a mistake, correct it, and get back on track with your testimony. You should avoid showing that you have lost control, such as by the following behaviors:

- Being argumentative when being badgered by the opposing attorney or being nervous about testifying

- Having poor listening skills or using defensive body language, such as crossing your arms

- Being too talkative or talking too fast when answering questions

- Being too technical for the jury to understand your testimony

- Acting surprised and unprepared to respond when presented with unknown or new information

Never have unrealistically high self-expectations when testifying; everyone makes mistakes. Who controls the testimony is the most important part for the attorney, in both direct examination and cross-examination. The key to successful cross-examination is to continue selling yourself to the jury, no matter how much the opposing attorney tries to discredit you or your testimony. In addition, remember that for every expert witness, there's a first time testifying. Good technical credentials and related experience are the most effective defense against cross-examination voir dire when testifying. You should also remember that the number of times you've testified isn't a condition of qualifying as an expert witness.

Preparing for a Deposition or Hearing

A **deposition** differs from trial testimony because there's no jury or judge. Both attorneys are present and ask you questions. The purpose of the deposition is for the opposing attorney to preview your testimony before trial. The attorney who requests a deposition usually establishes its location, which might be in his or her office or your forensics laboratory.

There are two types of depositions: discovery and testimony preservation. A **discovery deposition** is part of the discovery process for trial. The opposing attorney who requested the deposition often conducts the equivalent of a direct examination and a cross-examination. Your attorney usually asks only questions needed to clarify a point that could be subject to misinterpretation in your direct testimony. Although a discovery deposition can be video recorded, a written transcript is more common and is required in addition to the video recording. If the deposition *is* video recorded, court rules generally require a longer notice period to schedule it than a stenographically recorded one.

A **testimony preservation deposition** is usually requested by your client to preserve your testimony in case of schedule conflicts or health problems. These depositions are often video recorded in addition to the written transcript, and your testimony is entered by playing the video recording for the jury. In some cases, you can set the deposition at your laboratory or have lab facilities available, which can make it easier to conduct demonstrations and produce better testimony. This deposition follows the pattern of trial testimony, with your attorney calling you as a witness and conducting a direct examination, opposing counsel conducting cross-examination, and the attorneys conducting redirect and recross examination, if necessary. The judge rules on objections and, based on objections that are sustained, decides which portions of the testimony are omitted from the copy presented to the jury.

Guidelines for Testifying at Depositions

Often attorneys are more combative during discovery depositions than they are during trial (or video-recorded depositions). For this reason, a deposition can be more stressful than trial testimony. Therefore, strive to stay calm and convey a relaxed, confident appearance during a deposition. For example, try to keep your hands on top of the table, and make sure your chair is at the right height to avoid sitting below the opposing attorney's eye level. Maintain a professional demeanor and try not to be influenced by the opposing attorney's tone, expression, or tactics. Learn the opposing attorney's name before the deposition and include it in your responses to project a sense of equality in position between you and the opposing attorney. Look the opposing attorney directly in the eyes, even if she attempts to avoid eye contact.

15

Remember that during a deposition, opposing attorneys use all the techniques available to them at trial, so keep the guidelines for testimony in mind when answering questions, and be assertive in your responses. If you're particularly concerned about the deposition, ask your attorney to record a practice session, and then evaluate your performance. Here are some general rules to follow during depositions:

- Be professional and polite.
- Use facts when describing your opinion.
- Understand that being deposed in a discovery deposition is an unnatural process; it's intended to get you to make mistakes.

If you prepared a written report, the opposing attorney might attempt to use it against you by leading you to testify contrary to what you had previously written. If the attorney is concealing the report or any other document from your view, ask to see the document. When the opposing attorney asks you about something specific in your written report, ask what page number he's referring to. If you don't have the report in your hands, you can ask to review it.

If your attorney objects to a question from the opposing attorney, pause and think of what direction your attorney might want you to go in your answer. Keep your answers short and simple. Strive for a relaxed, friendly demeanor, especially if you're being recorded. To gain time and control, ask the opposing attorney questions to clarify what he's asking for, such as asking him to repeat the question.

Be prepared at the end of a deposition to spell any specialized or technical words you used. To aid court reporters, give them a list of technical or scientific words you use often, including definitions and correct spellings.

Recognizing Deposition Problems Discuss any potential problems with your attorney before the deposition. Identify anything that might affect your client negatively and could be used by opposing counsel. If you don't disclose this information, the opposing attorney might use it against you in court. Be prepared to defend yourself if there are problems. The following guidelines can also help you avoid problems during depositions:

- Avoid omitting information in your testimony; omissions can cause major problems. Although you don't have to volunteer more information than an attorney asks for, make sure you're telling the truth at all times.
- To respond to difficult questions that could jeopardize your client's case, pause before answering, allowing your attorney to object before you answer.
- To avoid having the opposing attorney box you into a corner or lead you to contradict previous statements, answer only the questions you're asked, using short answers that are narrow in scope when possible.
- Realize that excessively detailed questions from opposing counsel are an attempt to get you to contradict yourself. Avoid trying to educate the opposing attorney, especially if the questions seem to be beyond the scope of your expertise or the questions you were retained to answer. Feel free to give answers such as "I don't know" or "I don't understand."
- When asked whether you know about an opposing fact or expert witness, your response should be as professional as possible. A good standard answer is "I have

heard Mr. Smith is a competent examiner, but I have not reviewed his work." If you have specific and verifiable information that's damaging to the opposing expert's reputation, you can note it, but do it in an understated manner. This technique emphasizes your professional demeanor, especially if you have negative information about the opposing expert's skills or competency.

- Keep in mind that you can correct any minor errors you make during your examination by referring back to the error and correcting it. You also have an opportunity after the deposition, but you have to ask for it. You'll be asked at the end of the deposition if you waive signature; if you want to review the deposition, you shouldn't waive signature because you then get a chance to review, make corrections on the corrections page, and sign the deposition.

- Discovery deposition testimony generally doesn't make it to the jury, except for the purpose of showing previous inconsistent testimony by the witness. This process is called "publishing the deposition." The witness can then be examined about inconsistent testimony in the deposition.

Guidelines for Testifying at Hearings

Testifying at a hearing is generally comparable to testifying at a trial, so follow the same general guidelines you would for courtroom testimony. A hearing can be before an administrative agency or a legislative body or in a court (when it typically addresses specific issues). An administrative or legislative hearing generally addresses the agency's or committee's subject matter and seeks evidence in your testimony on a subject for which it's contemplating making a rule or legislation. A presiding officer or committee chairperson is present, and the format of questioning depends on the agency's or committee's rules and the purpose of the hearing. Often administrative or legislative hearings are related to events that previously resulted in litigation. Testifying at administrative hearings isn't as common as testifying in depositions or at trials.

The federal government has thousands of administrative agencies, and states often have hundreds of administrative agencies.

A judicial hearing is held in court to determine the admissibility of certain evidence before trial. No jury is present, but evidentiary suppression hearings are usually held early in the case to determine whether a criminal case moves forward or is dismissed. Generally, they focus more on your procedure in obtaining and preserving evidence than on the substance of the evidence or your opinion. They can also include the basis or authority (warrant or probable cause) for you conducting the examination. In most criminal cases, the defense attorney seeks to suppress any evidence for which there's an arguable basis for rejection.

15

Preparing Forensics Evidence for Testimony

In this section, you learn the steps for extracting information to be presented to a court. You also learn how to prepare to testify on digital evidence you have collected. You should be ready to answer specific questions from your attorney as well as opposing counsel.

In the following example, the general counsel at Flashbills has asked you to find a specific e-mail from Randall Simpson's personal e-mail account that's stored on his work computer. You're directed to search for and recover any message containing the word "offshore." The company's computing use policy states that the employer reserves the right to inspect and access all data on employees' computers, including personal data, such as stored e-mail. The general counsel also tells you that you need to testify on the data you extract to show the chain of custody for your findings. Another examiner has already created a forensic image of Mr. Simpson's computer, and a paralegal gives you this file, InCh12Randall.001.

 Before beginning the following activity, create a folder called *Work* *Chap15\Chapter* for your work folder, and move or copy the InCh12Randall.001 file from Chapter 12 to it.

To perform this task, you use OSForensics to extract and examine e-mails in the forensic image InCh12Randall.001. Follow these steps:

1. Start OSForensics with the **Run as administrator** option, and click **Yes** in the UAC message box. If you're prompted with a warning dialog box and/or notification, click **Continue Using Free Version**.

2. In the left pane, click **Manage Case**, if necessary, and click the **New Case** button on the right. In the New Case dialog box, type **InChap15** in the Case Name text box and your name in the Investigator text box. For the Acquisition Type setting, click the **Investigate Disk(s) from Another Machine** option button, and then click **OK**.

3. Mount the image file **InCh12Randall.001**, using the **Mount Drive Image** option in the left pane (referring to Chapter 5, if necessary, on using OSFMount). Click **Create Index** in the left pane to start the Create Index Wizard.

4. In the Step 1 of 5 window, click the **Use Pre-defined File Types** option button, if necessary. Click to select the **Emails** and **Attachments** check boxes, and then click **Next**.

5. In the Step 2 of 5 window, click the **Add** button. In the Add Start Location dialog box, click the **Whole Drive** option button, if necessary. Click the list arrow, click the mounted image drive letter, and then click **OK**. Click **Next**.

6. In the Step 3 of 5 window, click **Start Indexing**. When the indexing has finished, click **OK** in the message box informing you that errors reading some files might have occurred in the indexing process, if necessary.

7. Click **Search Index** in the left pane. In the Enter Search Words text box, type **offshore**. Click the **Index to Search** list arrow, click **My Index - *drive_letter*** (substituting the correct drive for *drive_letter*) for **InCh12Randall.001**, and then click **Search**.

8. When the search is finished, click the **Emails** tab, if necessary. Right-click the first e-mail message and click **Open**. If necessary, click **Yes** in the Security Alert message box.

9. In the E-mail Viewer window, read the message and find the word **offshore**. Right-click the message in the upper pane and click **Add Email to Case** (see Figure 15-1).

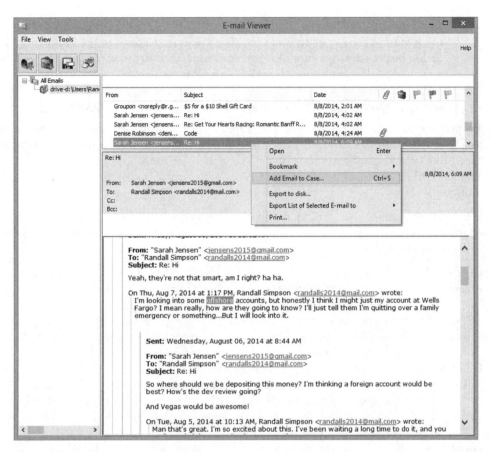

Figure 15-1 Adding an e-mail as evidence
Source: PassMark Software, *www.osforensics.com*

10. In the Please Enter Case Export Details window, type **Message with reference to Offshore** in the Export Title text box, type **Search request by General Counsel, Flashbills, LLC** in the Notes text box (see Figure 15-2), and click **Add**. Click **File, Close** from the menu.

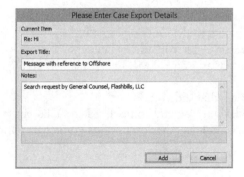

15

Figure 15-2 Entering case details to export to a report
Source: PassMark Software, *www.osforensics.com*

11. Repeat Steps 8 through 10 for all other messages containing the keyword **offshore**.

12. Click **Start** in the left pane, and then click **Generate Report**. In the Export Report dialog box, click **Copy files to report location**. Click **Browse**, navigate to and click your work folder, and then click **OK**. Exit OSForensics.

Preparing a Defense of Your Evidence-Collection Methods

To prepare for testimony, you should prepare answers for questions on what steps you took to extract e-mails from the image of Randall Simpson's computer. You might also be asked to explain specific features of the computer, OS, and applications (such as Mozilla Thunderbird or Microsoft Outlook) and explain how these applications and digital forensics tools work.

Ms. Johnson plans to ask you the following questions when you're called to testify. Prepare your answers, referring to these examples as guidelines, so that you can answer the questions with confidence and professionalism.

Question 1: How did you locate e-mails in the image of Mr. Simpson's computer?

Answer 1: I used PassMark Software OSForensics to access and search the InCh12Randall.001 image of Mr. Simpson's computer.

Question 2: How did you search for e-mails on Mr. Simpson's computer?

Answer 2: Using OSForenics, I indexed all data on Mr. Simpson's computer, and then searched for e-mails containing the word "offshore," as instructed.

Question 3: Can you please explain what an index is?

Answer 3: In digital forensics, an index lists all the words or terms in documents or unallocated space along with their locations in the forensic image. By indexing, which can take a few minutes or several hours, you can find keywords of interest to an investigation quickly.

Question 4: What's an image file?

Answer 4: An image file is a copy of a computer's disk drive. It copies all areas of a disk drive, including deleted files.

Question 5: When did you perform this examination?

Answer 5: I performed this examination on September 5, 2014, at about 4:00 p.m.

Question 6: How many e-mails on Mr. Simpson's computer containing the word "offshore" did you find?

Answer 6: I found seven e-mails.

Question 7: After you found these e-mails, what did you do?

Answer 7: I added them to the OSForensics case.

Question 8: What do you mean by "adding them to the OSForensics case"?

Answer 8: OSForensics has a report generator. After you add evidence, such as an e-mail, to the case, the report generator creates an HTML report file containing all the evidence you've added.

Question 9: After finishing your examination, what did you do?

Answer 9: I sent the HTML report to the Flashbills general counsel, exited OSForensics, and secured the external disk drive containing the forensic image of Mr. Simpson's computer in the evidence locker.

Chapter Summary

- When cases go to trial, you as the forensics expert play one of two roles: a fact witness or an expert witness. As a fact witness, you're providing only the facts you discovered in your investigation. However, as an expert witness, you have opinions about what you have observed. In fact, it's your opinion that makes you an expert witness.

- If you're called as a fact witness or an expert witness in a digital forensics case, you need to prepare for your testimony thoroughly. Establish communication early with your attorney. Substantiate your findings with your own documentation and by collaborating with other digital forensics professionals.

- When you're called to testify in court, your attorney examines you on your qualifications to establish your competency as an expert witness or a fact witness. Opposing counsel might attempt to discredit you based on your past record. Your attorney then leads you through the evidence, followed by the opposing counsel cross-examining you. Redirect examinations and recross examinations of limited scope might follow.

- Make sure you're prepared for questions opposing counsel might use to discredit you, confuse you, or throw you off the track. Stay calm and project professionalism in your behavior and appearance.

- Know whether you're being called as a fact witness or an expert witness (or both) and whether you're being retained as a consulting expert or expert witness. Also, be familiar with the contents of your curriculum vitae.

- A deposition differs from a trial because there's no jury or judge. Both attorneys and a court reporter are present, and the attorney asks you questions. There are two types of depositions: discovery and testimony preservation. Testimony preservation depositions are often recorded.

- Hearings are typically administrative hearings or judicial hearings. Guidelines for testifying at depositions and hearings are much the same as the guidelines for courtroom testimony. Keep in mind that attorneys at discovery depositions might be more combative, so striving to maintain a calm, professional appearance can be critical.

- Make sure you prepare answers for questions on what steps you took to collect and analyze evidence and questions on what tools you used and how they work.

Key Terms

15

conflicting out The practice of opposing attorneys trying to prevent you from testifying by claiming you have discussed the case with them and, therefore, have a conflict of interest.

curriculum vitae (CV) An extensive outline of your professional history that includes education, training, work, and what cases you have worked on as well as training you have conducted, publications you have contributed to, and professional associations and awards.

deposition A formal examination in which you're questioned under oath with only the opposing parties, your attorney, and a court reporter present. There's no judge or jury. The purpose of a deposition is to give the opposing counsel a chance to preview your testimony before trial.

discovery deposition The opposing attorney sets the deposition and often conducts the equivalent of both direct and cross-examination. A discovery deposition is considered part of the discovery process. *See also* deposition.

expert witness This type of testimony reports opinions based on experience and facts gathered during an investigation.

fact witness This type of testimony reports only the facts (findings of an investigation); no opinion is given in court.

testimony preservation deposition A deposition held to preserve your testimony in case of schedule conflicts or health problems; it's usually videotaped as well as recorded by a stenographer. *See also* deposition.

voir dire In this qualification phase of testimony, your attorney asks you questions to establish your credentials as an expert witness. The process of qualifying jurors is also called voir dire.

Review Questions

1. Which of the following describes fact testimony?
   a. Scientific or technical testimony describing information recovered during an examination
   b. Testimony by law enforcement officers
   c. Testimony based on observations by lay witnesses
   d. None of the above

2. Which of the following describes expert witness testimony? (Choose all that apply.)
   a. Testimony designed to assist the jury in determining matters beyond the ordinary person's scope of knowledge
   b. Testimony that defines issues of the case for determination by the jury
   c. Testimony resulting in the expression of an opinion by a witness with scientific, technical, or other professional knowledge or experience
   d. Testimony designed to raise doubt about facts or witnesses' credibility

3. When using graphics while testifying, which of the following guidelines applies? (Choose all that apply.)
   a. Make sure the jury can see your graphics.
   b. Practice using charts for courtroom testimony.
   c. Your exhibits must be clear and easy to understand.
   d. Make sure you have plenty of extra graphics, in case you have to explain more complex or supporting issues.

4. What kind of information do fact witnesses provide during testimony? (Choose all that apply.)
   a. Their professional opinion on the significance of evidence
   b. Definitions of issues to be determined by the finder of fact
   c. Facts only
   d. Observations of the results of tests they performed

5. What expressions are acceptable to use in testimony to respond to a question for which you have no answer? (Choose all that apply.)
   a. No comment.
   b. That's beyond the scope of my expertise.
   c. I don't want to answer that question.
   d. I wasn't asked to investigate that.
   e. That's beyond the scope of my investigation.

6. What should you do if you realize you have made a mistake or misstatement during a deposition? (Choose all that apply.)
   a. If the deposition is still in session, refer back to the error and correct it.
   b. Decide whether the error is minor, and if so, ignore it.
   c. If the deposition is over, make the correction on the corrections page of the copy provided for your signature.
   d. Call the opposing attorney and inform him of your mistake or misstatement.
   e. Request an opportunity to make the correction at trial.

7. List two types of depositions.

8. At trial as a fact or expert witness, what must you always remember about your testimony?
   a. You're responsible for the outcome of the case.
   b. Your duty is to report your technical or scientific findings or render an honest opinion.
   c. Avoid mentioning how much you were paid for your services.
   d. All of the above

9. Before testifying, you should do which of the following? (Choose all that apply.)
   a. Create an examination plan with your retaining attorney.
   b. Make sure you've been paid for your services and the estimated fee for the deposition or trial.
   c. Get a haircut.
   d. Type all the draft notes you took during your investigation.

10. Voir dire is the process of qualifying a witness as an expert. True or False?

15

11. What is a motion in limine?

    a. A motion to dismiss the case

    b. The movement of molecules in a random fashion

    c. A pretrial motion for the purpose of excluding certain evidence

    d. A pretrial motion to revise the case schedule

12. During your cross-examination, you should do which of the following? (Choose all that apply.)

    a. Maintain eye contact with the jury.

    b. Pay close attention to what your attorney is objecting to.

    c. Help the attorneys, judge, and jury in understanding the case, even if you have to go a bit beyond the scope of your expertise.

    d. Pay close attention to opposing counsel's questions.

    e. Answer opposing counsel's questions as briefly as is practical.

13. Your curriculum vitae is which of the following? (Choose all that apply.)

    a. A necessary tool to be an expert witness

    b. A generally required document to be made available before your testimony

    c. A detailed record of your experience, education, and training

    d. Focused on your skills as they apply to the current case

14. The most reliable way to ensure that jurors recall testimony is to do which of the following?

    a. Present evidence using oral testimony supported by hand gestures and facial expressions.

    b. Present evidence combining oral testimony and graphics that support the testimony.

    c. Wear bright clothing to attract jurors' attention.

    d. Emphasize your points with humorous anecdotes.

    e. Memorize your testimony carefully.

15. If you're giving an answer that you think your attorney should follow up on, what should you do?

    a. Change the tone of your voice.

    b. Argue with the attorney who asked the question.

    c. Use an agreed-on expression to alert the attorney to follow up on the question.

    d. Try to include as much information in your answer as you can.

16. In answering a question about the size of a hard drive, which of the following responses is appropriate? (Choose all that apply.)

    a. It's a very large hard drive.

    b. The technical data sheet indicates it's a 3 terabyte hard drive.

    c. It's a 3 terabyte hard drive configured with 2.78 terabytes of accessible storage.

    d. I was unable to determine the drive size because it was so badly damaged.

17. List three items you should include in your CV.

18. When working for a prosecutor, what should you do if the evidence you found appears to be exculpatory and isn't being released to the defense?

    a. Keep the information on file for later review.

    b. Bring the information to the attention of the prosecutor, then his or her supervisor, and finally to the judge (the court).

    c. Destroy the evidence.

    d. Give the evidence to the defense attorney.

Hands-On Projects

The projects in this chapter have you acting as an expert witness and rendering an opinion on a case. It's assumed you know how to retrieve data from an image file and document your evidence. For these projects, you need `InCh05.img`, `InCh12Randall.001`, and `InCh12Sarah.001` from Chapters 5 and 12. Before beginning, create a *Work*\Chap15\ Projects folder, and move all image files to this subfolder.

Hands-On Project 15-1

After reviewing the e-mails you recovered during the in-chapter activity, the general counsel has found new information that Randall Simpson is involved in some sort of negotiations for a new program's source code. The general counsel asks you to reexamine Mr. Simpson's computer to see whether you can locate any files containing source code. For this project, you search the `InCh12Randall.001` image in allocated and unallocated space for files starting with the name "flashbills":

1. Start OSForensics with the **Run as administrator** option, and click **Yes** in the UAC message box. If you're prompted with a warning dialog box and/or notification, click **Continue Using Free Version**.

2. In the left pane, click **Manage Case**, if necessary, and double-click **InChap15** so that a green check mark is displayed next to the case title name.

3. If necessary, mount the image file **InCh12Randall.001**, using the **Mount Drive Image** option in the left pane, and then click **Create Index** in the left pane to start the Create Index Wizard.

4. In the Create Index window, click **New Index**. In the Step 1 of 5 window, click the **Use Pre-defined File Types** option button, if necessary. Click to select the **Emails, Attachments, Office + PDF Documents, Zip Files, Images, Plain Text Files, Web Files + XML, All Other Supported File Types**, and **Unknown Files** check boxes, and then click **Next**.

5. In the Step 2 of 5 window, click the **Add** button. In the Add Start Location dialog box, click the **Whole Drive** option button, if necessary. Click the list arrow, click the mounted image drive letter, and then click **OK**. Click **Next**.

15

6. In the Step 3 of 5 window, click **Start Indexing**. When the indexing has finished, click **OK** in the message box informing you that errors reading some files might have occurred in the indexing process, if necessary.

7. Click **File Name Search** in the left pane. In the Search String text box, type **flashbills*.***. Click the **...** button, click the drive mounted in Step 3, click **OK**, and then click **Search**.

8. When the search is finished, click the **File List** tab, if necessary. Right-click the first file and click **View with Internal Viewer**.

9. In the Internal Viewer window, click the **Hex/String Viewer** tab, if necessary. Highlight the pathname and filename, and then right-click the selection and click **Carve Selection to Case** (see Figure 15-3).

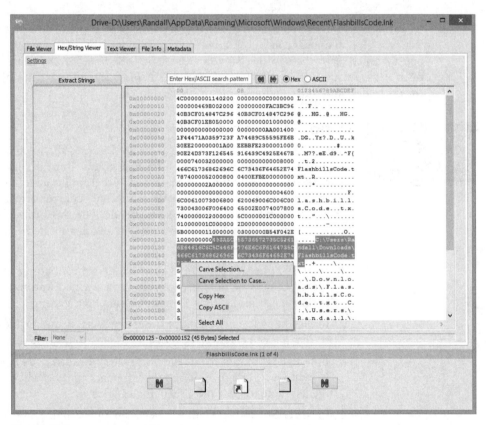

Figure 15-3 Carving text data
Source: PassMark Software, *www.osforensics.com*

10. In the Please Enter New Case Item Details window, type **Found reference to file named FlashbillsCode** in the Title text box, and then click **OK** twice. Close the Internal Viewer window.

If the filename is blank after you exit the internal viewer, click the File List tab to see the list of search results again.

11. In the File Name Search results window, right-click the next search result and click **Open**. OSForensics opens the default text editor (such as Notepad). In the text editor, click **File, Save As** from the menu. Navigate to your work folder, type **FlashbillsCode-1.txt** in the File name text box, and click **Save**. Exit the text editor.

12. Repeat Step 11 for the remaining search results and increment each filename by 1, such as **FlashbillsCode-2.txt** and **FlashbillsCode-3.txt**.

13. Click **Manage Case** in the left pane, and then click **Add Attachment**. In the "Select a file to open" dialog box, navigate to your work folder, click the **FlashbillsCode-1.txt** file saved in Step 11, and then click **Open**.

14. In the Please Enter Case Export Details window, type **Randall's Discovered Source Code** in the Export Title text box, and then click **Add**.

15. Repeat Steps 13 and 14 to attach the **FlashbillsCode-2.txt** and **FlashbillsCode-3.txt** files to this case.

16. Leave OSForensics running for the next project.

Hands-On Project 15-2

This project is a follow-up from Chapter 12 of possible intellectual property theft from Flashbills, LLC, that involved Randall Simpson's and Sarah Jensen's cell phones. The e-mail evidence you collected from Randall Simpson's computer in this chapter has given the general counsel additional information about the theft of intellectual property. These e-mails also show additional correspondence between Randall Simpson and Sarah Jensen discussing a source code file. The general counsel's attorney assigned to the case was able to get a subpoena that required Sarah Jensen to allow Flashbills, LLC, to copy her computer's hard drive. Another digital forensics firm acquired a forensic image of Sarah Jensen's hard drive and transferred the image file InCh12Sarah.001 and a chain of evidence form to you. For this project, you're asked to confirm that e-mails and source code files found on Randall Simpson's computer are also on Sarah Jensen's computer. Follow these steps:

15

1. Start OSForensics, if necessary. Mount the image file **InCh12Sarah.001**, using the **Mount Drive Image** option in the left pane, and click **Create Index** in the left pane to start the Create Index Wizard.

2. If necessary, click **New Index**. In the Step 1 of 5 window, click the **Use Pre-defined File Types** option button, if necessary. Click to select the **Emails, Attachments, Office + PDF Documents, Zip Files, Images, Plain Text Files, Web Files + XML, All Other Supported File Types**, and **Unknown Files** check boxes, and then click **Next**.

3. Because the image file `InCh12Randall.001` is still mounted from Hands-On Project 15-1, you need to remove it in the Step 2 of 5 window. To remove it, click the drive letter selected previously for the mounted image, and then click **Remove**. Click the **Add** button. In the Add Start Location dialog box, click the **Whole Drive** option button, if necessary. Click the list arrow, click the drive letter for the `InCh12Sarah.001` image mounted in Step 1, and then click **OK**. Click **Next**.

4. In the Step 3 of 5 window, click **Start Indexing**. When the indexing has finished, click **OK** in the message box informing you that errors reading some files might have occurred in the indexing process, if necessary.

5. Click **File Name Search** in the left pane. In the Search String text box, type **flashbillsCode.txt**. Click the **...** button, click the drive mounted in Step 3, click **OK**, and then click **Search**.

6. When the search is finished, click the **File List** tab, if necessary. Right-click the first file and click **Open**. OSForensics starts your default text editor (such as Notepad). In the text editor, click **File, Save As** from the menu. Navigate to your work folder, type **FlashbillsCode-A.txt** in the File name text box, and click **Save**. Exit the text editor.

7. Repeat Step 6 for the second search result in the File Name Search window, typing the filename **FlashbillsCode-B.txt**.

8. Click **Manage Case** in the left pane, and then click **Add Attachment**. In the "Select a file to open" dialog box, navigate to your work folder, click the `FlashbillsCode-A.txt` file saved in Step 6, and click **Open**.

9. In the Please Enter Case Export Details window, type **Sarah's Discovered Source Code** in the Export Title text box, and then click **Add**.

10. Repeat Steps 8 and 9 to attach the `FlashbillsCode-B.txt` file to this case. Leave OSForensics running for the next project.

Hands-On Project 15-3

The general counsel's attorney has asked you to search for any e-mails containing the word "code" on Randall's computer. The attorney is interested only in e-mails that are to or from someone besides Randall and Sarah. For this project, you do a search of the `InCh12Randall.001` image file, adding any relevant e-mails and attachments:

1. Start OSForensics, if necessary. Click **Search Index** in the left pane. In the Enter Search Words text box, type **code**. Click the **Index to Search** list arrow, click the **My Index - *drive_letter* (1)** index for `InCh12Randall.001`, and then click **Search**.

When you create an index in OSForensics, a version number is added to its name. For example, in Hands-On Project 15-1, the second index you created is named My Index - *drive_letter* (1). The *drive_letter* is the one OSFMount assigns to the mounted image.

2. When the search is finished, click the **Emails** tab, if necessary, and examine each e-mail. When you find an e-mail from someone other than Randall and Sarah, right-click the e-mail and click **Open**.

3. In the E-mail Viewer window, read the contents of all e-mails. If an e-mail has an attachment, right-click the attached file and click **Add Attachment(s) to Case** (see Figure 15-4). In the Please Enter Case Export Details window, type **Denise's e-mail message containing an attached file** in the Export Title text box, and then click **Add**.

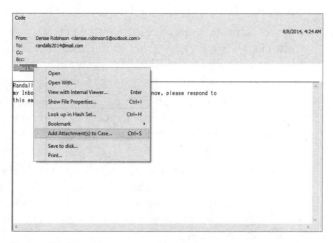

Figure 15-4 Adding an attachment from an e-mail
Source: PassMark Software, *www.osforensics.com*

4. In the upper pane, right-click the e-mail and click **Add E-mail to Case**. In the Please Enter Case Export Details window, type **Denise's e-mail message** in the Export Title text box, and click **Add**. Click **File, Close** from the menu. Leave OSForensics running for the next project.

Hands-On Project 15-4

In Hands-On Project 15-3, you found an e-mail from Denise Robinson with an attachment named `Bio1.txt`. According to your attorney, this file contains proprietary source code from Flashbills, LLC. With this information, the attorney was able to get a subpoena to acquire a forensic image of Denise Robinson's computer to determine whether she's the source of the leaked source code. The attorney had the same digital forensics firm used in Hands-On Project 15-2 give you a copy of the `InCh05.img` file of Denise Robinson's computer. Follow these steps to search this image for any evidence of the `Bio1.txt` file:

1. Start OSForensics, if necessary. Mount the image file **InCh05.img**, using the **Mount Drive Image** option in the left pane. Click **Create Index** in the left pane and then click **New Index** to start the Create Index Wizard.

15

2. Follow the steps in Hands-On Project 15-2 to create an index for the `InCh05.img` file. When the indexing is finished, click **Search Index** in the left pane.

3. In the Enter Search Words text box, type **Bio**. Click the **Index to Search** list arrow, click the **My Index -** *drive_letter* index for `InCh05.img`, and then click **Search**.

4. Click the **Email Attachments** tab. Right-click the first search result for `Bio1.txt`, point to **Export List of All Items to,** and click **html.** In the Export List to window, navigate to your work folder, type **Denise Robinson's Bio1.txt file** in the File name text box, and click **Save.**

5. Right-click the first search result for `Bio1.txt` and click **Add to Case.** Click **File(s).** In the Please Enter Case Export Details window, type **Bio1.txt file from Denise Robinson's computer** in the Export Title text box, and then click **Add.**

6. Click the **Emails** tab. Right-click the first e-mail, point to **Export List of All Items to,** and click **html.** In the Export List to window, navigate to your work folder, type **Denise Robinson's e-mail messages** in the File name text box, and click **Save.**

7. Right-click the first e-mail again and click **Open.** In the E-mail Viewer window, right-click the highlighted e-mail and click **Add E-mail to Case.** In the Please Enter Case Export Details window, type **Denise Robinson's e-mail messages** in the Export Title text box, and click **Add.** Click **File, Close** from the menu.

8. Repeat Step 7 for all other e-mails in the Emails tab.

9. Click **Manage Case** in the left pane, and then click **Add Attachment.** In the "Select a file to open" dialog box, navigate to your work folder, click **Denise Robinson's Bio1.txt file.html,** and then click **Open.** In the Please Enter Case Export Details window, type **Denise Robinson's source code** in the Export Title text box, and click **Add.**

10. Click **Add Attachment.** In the "Select a file to open" dialog box, navigate to your work folder, click **Denise Robinson's e-mail messages.html,** and then click **Open.** In the Please Enter Case Export Details window, type **Denise Robinson's e-mail source code** in the Export Title text box, and click **Add.**

11. Click **Start** in the left pane, and then click **Generate Report** in the right pane. In the Export Report dialog box, click the **Copy files to report location** button, click **Browse,** navigate to and click your work folder, and then click **OK** twice.

12. After the report opens in your Web browser, print the main Web page and all linked Web pages for this report, and then turn them in to your instructor.

Case Projects

Case Project 15-1

For this project, you create a brief outline of the steps you used for the in-chapter activity and hands-on projects. This project helps you review your work so that you can testify competently on your findings and the procedures you used. The outline doesn't need detailed steps; it serves as a way to trigger your memory about what you did.

Case Project 15-2

You have been approached by an attorney who needs you as a fact witness and possibly an expert witness in a criminal case. The attorney has requested your curriculum vitae so that she can review it and prepare questions for you to answer during the pretrial qualifications. Prepare a draft of your CV and turn it in to your instructor for review. Your CV will be an ongoing project in your career.

Case Project 15-3

The attorney who retained you has given you a list of digital forensics terms and asked you to write definitions for these terms. These definitions will be given to the jury to help them better understand the case's subject matter. Do research online to define the following terms, making sure you target your definitions to nontechnical readers:

- Hashes for Cyclic Redundancy Check, Message Digest, and Secure Hash Algorithm
- A drive image
- Static versus live data acquisition of drives
- Data carving
- Digital forensics tool validation

When you're finished, submit the definitions to your instructor.

Case Project 15-4

15

The general counsel for Flashbills has asked you to create a Microsoft PowerPoint, LibreOffice Impress, or HTML presentation on the work you've done for him (in the in-chapter activity and hands-on projects). He plans to have you make this presentation to the jury during the trial. Integrate portions of your OSForensics reports and findings from e-mail and source code files that might be of use for testimony. When you're finished, submit the presentation's files to your instructor.

chapter 16

Ethics for the Expert Witness

After reading this chapter and completing the exercises, you will be able to:

- Explain how ethics and codes apply to expert witnesses
- Explain how other organizations' codes of ethics apply to expert testimony
- Describe ethical difficulties in expert testimony
- Explain the process of carving data manually

For digital forensics examiners, maintaining the highest level of ethical behavior in their work is essential. In this chapter, you learn how digital forensics experts and other professionals apply ethics and codes of conduct to their work and to giving expert testimony. Forensics examiners are responsible for meeting the highest standards when conducting examinations, preparing reports, and giving testimony to ensure that evidence is accurate, reliable, and impartial. In addition, you must know when to disqualify yourself from an investigation. Knowing what to look for when taking a new case helps you avoid potential ethical problems.

Applying Ethics and Codes to Expert Witnesses

Ethics are the rules you internalize and use to measure your performance. The standards that others apply to you or that you're compelled to adhere to by external forces, such as licensing bodies, can be called ethics, but they're more accurately described as rules of conduct. Many professions now call these rules **codes of professional conduct or responsibility**. Both concepts of ethics are addressed in this chapter.

People need ethics to help maintain their balance, especially in difficult and contentious situations, and for guidance on their values. Ethics also help you maintain self-respect and the respect of your profession. Because forensics examiners don't have the same formal, detailed codes of conduct that professions such as medicine and the law have, relying on an internal code of ethics might be more critical. In addition, your internal standards, related to a philosophical, religious, or moral position, can be higher than standards established by codes of professional conduct. Laws governing codes of professional conduct or responsibility define the lowest level of action or performance required to avoid liability. Even with these low standards, there are still violations.

One of the most effective mechanisms for protecting yourself at a personal level and a legal level is to have nothing to hide. This ethical position allows people to be self-critical and critical of others. People who fear having their improper acts revealed feel as though they must protest the improper acts of others being revealed. Being able to engage in criticism of yourself or others, however, makes it possible to refine and strengthen personal codes of ethics or codes of professional responsibility.

Expert witnesses are expected to present unbiased, specialized, and technical evidence to a jury. However, experts, like the attorneys who hire them, have biases and other ethical failings. As a professional, you must control your biases, not allow them to control you. Ethics are a tool you can use to identify and control your biases or prejudices.

Currently, expert witnesses testify in more than 80% of trials, and in many trials, multiple expert witnesses testify. The courts are clearly aware of the importance of expert witnesses to the legal system and are concerned about expert witnesses' ethics and the challenges experts face in reconciling their ethical standards and court practice. Awareness of this challenge is evident in the following statement from *Kenneth C. v. Delonda R.* (814 N.Y.S.2d 562, 2006):

> ... the topic of expert witness ethics and professionalism is largely undeveloped and there are few definitive statements about what exactly the expert witness's ethical obligations are and how they are to handle the subtle as well as the more blatant attempts to influence them. While some expert witnesses belong to professions that have an established code ..., many experts come from

professions that are not self-governing with a uniform code of ethics.... Even where professional associations have established ethical guidelines for conducting investigations, forming opinions ... very few explain how the ethical boundaries imposed on judges and lawyers may bear on the performance of their role in the legal system.

Included in most professions' codes of professional conduct is an admonition to adhere to or comply with the law. The most important laws applying to attorneys and witnesses are the rules of evidence. As mentioned in Chapter 15, the Federal Rules of Evidence (FRE) prescribe the methods by which experts appear before the court. Codes of professional conduct or responsibility affect attorneys who hire experts, but experts are bound by their personal ethics and the ethics of their professional organizations. Professional organizations' guidelines are often vague and broad and might do little to enforce experts' ethical conduct, however. Finding examples of experts' ethically questionable behavior in court isn't difficult. For example, in an investigation of the West Virginia State Police Crime Lab (438 S.E.2d 501, W. Va. 1993), a former officer in the Serology Division was found to have falsified evidence in criminal prosecutions. In addition, the article "Geoffrey Campbell, Erdmann Faces New Legal Woes: Pathologist Indicted for Perjury in Texas Murder Trial" (*American Bar Association Journal*, November 1995) describes how a former Texas pathologist faked autopsies to aid in criminal trials. For a general discussion of expert witness ethics, see *http://ir.lawnet. fordham.edu/cgi/viewcontent.cgi?article=4332&context=flr*.

In the United States, there's no state or national licensing body for digital forensics examiners. Some states have licensing requirements for private investigators and classify forensics examiners with private investigators, but the work private investigators usually do bears little resemblance to the work of forensics examiners. Therefore, your sources for ethical standards are your internal values (ethics) and the codes of professional associations you belong to and certifying bodies that have granted you a certification as well as your employer's rules of professional conduct. Most examiners rely on a combination of these standards to construct their professional ethical codes.

A movement is underway to create a general code of ethics for expert witnesses. At least one proposal includes the topics of confidentiality, fees, ex parte communication, conflicts of interest, and professionalism. Generally, the positions advocated for in these proposals reflect the experience of other professional organizations, court rulings, and court rules but seek to consolidate these scattered resources into a codified system. For more information, see *http:// blogs.findlaw.com/strategist/2011/03/should-there-be-an-expert-witness-code-of-ethics.html*.

Forensics Examiners' Roles in Testifying

As you learned in Chapter 15, in testifying, forensics examiners have two roles: testifying to the facts found during evidence recovery (fact witness) and rendering an opinion based on education, training, and experience (expert witness).

As an expert witness, you can testify even if you weren't present when the event occurred or didn't handle the data storage device personally. Because of an expert's important role in litigation, attorneys often shop for experts who can support their cases, and experts' fees might be only a secondary consideration. Criticism of expert witnesses is widespread in the legal community because it's possible to find and hire an expert to testify to almost any opinion on any topic. As a result, the impartiality of expert testimony and the potential for misconduct have become concerns.

16

If you're going to have a long and productive career as an expert witness, beware of attorneys' opinion shopping. An attorney might be willing to risk your career to improve the prospect of success in a case—and can always find another expert for the next case. The most effective way to prevent opinion shopping is to require that the attorney retaining your services send you enough material on the case for you to make an evaluation. Distinguishing opinion shopping from the process of attempting to disqualify experts by creating conflicts can be difficult, however.

Conversely, attorneys should be cautious of expert witnesses who will tailor an opinion. If witnesses will tailor opinions for you, they might have tailored opinions for somebody else. When an expert witness is discredited, it can affect the attorney's credibility, too.

Considerations in Disqualification

One of the effects of violating court rules or laws is **disqualification**. This outcome isn't usually punitive, but it can be embarrassing for you as a professional and potentially for the attorney who retained you. A disqualification based on an ethical lapse could effectively be a death sentence for a career as an expert witness, as you can expect it to come up in any case you're involved in.

Opposing counsel might attempt to disqualify you based on any deviations from opinions you've given in previous cases. Any testimony you give at trials or depositions is on record and available to attorneys. (As mentioned in Chapter 14, attorneys search deposition banks for information on expert witnesses.) If there's a change in your position on a point, be sure to explain why you have changed it, such as recent developments in technology, new tools with new capabilities, or the facts of the current case differing from a previous case. An apparent change of position could be a subject for cross-examination, and you must be able to explain what appears to be contradictory opinions, or you'll be seen as tailoring testimony to your client's needs.

Some attorneys contact many experts as a ploy to disqualify them or prevent opposing counsel from hiring them; as explained in Chapter 15, this practice is called "conflicting out." Although attorneys might merely be scouting the field for information, you should always note calls from attorneys and the nature of the communication. Have a standard response, such as "Before we go beyond the general nature of the case and my expertise, you need to complete a client questionnaire and send me an investigation retainer." The retainer can be small, perhaps 2 to 8 hours of your usual billable rate for a simple case; the purpose of requesting the retainer is to deter attorneys from communicating with you solely for the purpose of disqualifying you. No explicit rule in the code of professional conduct prohibits attorneys from engaging in this process, but there are general prohibitions on engaging in actions designed to delay or be obstructive without legitimate purpose. These types of actions are unlikely to result in a bar association taking disciplinary action against attorneys, however.

Before allowing an attorney to describe any case details, determine who the parties are to reduce the possibility of a conflict. Although you aren't bound by the rigid rules on conflict of interest that bind attorneys, you might be working for an attorney on a case opposing the attorney who called you, and this conflict could reflect on the attorney.

When you're aware of a possible disqualification issue, bring it to the attention of the attorney who has retained you. The attorney then can get an early determination on the disqualification issue. There are rules to determine whether you can be disqualified from working on a case merely because you discussed general aspects of it. The rules for disqualification are derived from court decisions. Factors courts have used in determining whether to disqualify an expert include the following:

- Whether the attorney informed the expert that their discussions were confidential
- Whether the expert reviewed materials marked as confidential or attorney work product
- Whether the expert was asked to sign a confidentiality agreement
- Number of discussions held over a period of time
- The type of documents that were reviewed (publicly filed or confidential)
- The type of information conveyed to the expert—whether it included general or specific data or included confidential information, trial strategies, plans for method of proof, and so forth
- The amount of time involved in discussions or meetings between the expert and attorney
- Whether the expert provided the attorney with confidential information
- Whether the attorney formally retained the expert
- Whether the expert voiced concerns about being retained
- Whether the expert was requested to perform services for the attorney
- Whether the attorney compensated the expert

Numerous cases describe disqualification under the communication standards. For example, in *Wang Laboratories, Inc. v. Toshiba Corp.* (762 F. Supp. 1246 [E.D. Va. 1991]), the court summarized the process of determining whether an expert should be disqualified because of previous contact with an opposing party. The test is in two parts. First, was it objectively reasonable for the first party who claims to have previously retained the consultant to conclude that a confidential relationship existed? Second, was any confidential or privileged information disclosed by the first party to the consultant?

Similarly, there's extensive case law in which experts were not disqualified and allowed to testify over the objection of opposing counsel. For example, in *Hewlett-Packard Co. v. EMC Corp.* (330 F. Supp. 2d 1087 [N.D. Cal. 2004]) and *Tidemann v. Nadler Golf Car Sales, Inc.* (224 F.3d 719 [7th Cir. 2000]), the other side's lawyer merely served a subpoena on the expert to get factual testimony. If you don't know which standards for disqualification are being applied or how they are being applied in your jurisdiction, you should research the applicable state's court rulings on these issues. States often refer to already established rulings in other states or federal courts, and you can use an online search to find cases in the applicable jurisdiction. You might also want to have a standing relationship with an attorney who can advise you on these issues.

16

Traps for Unwary Experts

Expert witnesses should be cautious about the following potential traps, even though some aren't laid deliberately:

- What are some differences between the attorney's motives and the investigator's duty that might affect how the investigator acts, or is expected to act, as an expert witness?

- Is the function of the expert witness in conflict with the investigator's code of professional responsibility?

- Attorneys look at witnesses' codes of professional responsibility based on organizations they are members of. As an expert witness, you should anticipate that the opposing counsel will look at your organization memberships and those organizations' codes of professional responsibility.

Contingency fees aren't allowed except in certain limited circumstances; for example, consultants who don't testify can earn a contingency fee for locating testifying experts or investigative leads. However, an expert's activities leading to testimony can't be compensated on a contingent basis. Even the appearance of testimony on a contingent basis is dangerous. Therefore, experts should be paid in full for all previous work and for the anticipated time required for testimony.

It's unlikely you will encounter these situations, but if you do, it's wise to ask the hiring attorney to file a motion with the court requesting a ruling on disqualification. This process protects you from future liability or ethical complaints. If the attorney doesn't want to follow this procedure, consider withdrawing from the employment.

In addition, avoid obvious ethical errors, such as the following:

- Don't present false data or alter data.

- Don't report work that was not done.

- Don't ignore available contradictory data.

- Don't do work beyond your expertise or competence.

- Don't allow the attorney who retained you to influence your opinion in an unauthorized way. (Keep in mind that there are authorized points of influence, such as the attorney framing a hypothetical question for you or asking you to answer specific questions.)

- Don't accept an assignment if it can't be done reasonably in the allowed time.

- Don't reach a conclusion before doing complete research.

- Don't fail to report possible conflicts of interest.

Determining Admissibility of Evidence

Although stating hypothetical questions during examination is no longer required in court, these questions can give you the factual structure to support and defend your opinion. You owe your client a full understanding of the facts relevant to your opinion, and you can ask him or her to establish that there's evidence supporting the facts your opinion is based on.

Although expert opinions can be presented without stating the underlying factual basis, the testimony isn't admissible if the facts on which the opinion is based are inadequate or there's insufficient evidence to allow stating a legitimate opinion. FRE 702 (whether the expert is qualified and whether the expert opinion can be helpful) and FRE 703 (whether basis for the testimony is adequate) are considered in determining admissibility. If a question on admissibility arises under FRE 702 or 703, the court might require underlying facts or data to determine whether or to what extent the expert should be permitted to testify. Obviously, opposing counsel has an opportunity to explore and challenge the underlying facts and data on cross-examination. However, experts who provide explanations for how they reached their conclusions are far more persuasive to a judge or jury.

Organizations with Codes of Ethics

No single source offers a definitive code of ethics for expert witnesses, so you must draw on standards from other organizations to form your own ethical standards. This section discusses the impact that other organizations' ethical guidelines can have on expert testimony. Many professional organizations have rules to guide their members in areas such as interaction with patients/clients, objectivity, role in society, fees, solicitation, independence, and contractual relationships. The more restrictive and specific ethical rules are, the more impact they have in curbing unethical expert testimony.

For a detailed discussion and comparison of codes of professional responsibility of these groups, see "Expert witnesses at trial: Where are the ethics?" (Murphy, Justin P., *Georgetown Journal of Legal Ethics* 14: 217–240, 2000). You can read a copy of this article free (and get a free 7-day trial of the High Beam article service) at *www.highbeam. com/doc/1P3-70439645.html*.

International Society of Forensic Computer Examiners

The International Society of Forensic Computer Examiners (ISFCE) Code of Ethics and Professional Responsibility provides guidelines for its members on how they are expected to perform their duties as forensics examiners. These guidelines include specific instructions on how members must maintain their professional standing and define what members must do and not do when performing their duties as forensics examiners. For example, the ISFCE code of ethics includes guidelines such as the following:

- Maintain the utmost objectivity in all forensic examinations and present findings accurately.
- Conduct examinations based on established, validated principles.
- Testify truthfully in all matters before any board, court, or proceeding.
- Avoid any action that would appear to be a conflict of interest.
- Never misrepresent training, credentials, or association membership.
- Never reveal any confidential matters or knowledge learned in an examination without an order from a court of competent jurisdiction or the client's express permission.

In addition, members are expected to maintain their integrity by reporting other members who violate the code of conduct to the ISFCE.

The ISFCE also offers a Certified Computer Examiner (CCE) certification and includes ethical standards for examiners holding this certification. For more information on the ISFCE Code of Ethics and Professional Responsibility, see *www.isfce.com/ethics2.htm*.

16

International High Technology Crime Investigation Association

In its bylaws, the International High Technology Crime Investigation Association (HTCIA) provides a detailed Code of Ethics of Professional Standards Conduct for its members. HTCIA core values include the following requirements related to testifying:

- The HTCIA values the Truth uncovered within digital information and the effective techniques used to uncover that Truth, so that no one is wrongfully convicted.

- The HTCIA values the Integrity of its members and the evidence they expose through common investigative and digital forensics best practices, including specialized techniques used to gather digital evidence.

For more information on the HTCIA code of ethics, see *www.htcia.org/code-of-ethics-bylaws/*.

International Association of Computer Investigative Specialists

The International Association of Computer Investigative Specialists (IACIS) provides a well-defined, simple guide for expected behavior of forensics examiners. These standards follow the principles defined by other professional organizations for investigations and testimony. The standards for IACIS members that apply to testifying include the following:

- Maintain the highest level of objectivity in all forensic examinations and accurately present the facts involved.

- Examine and analyze evidence in a case thoroughly.

- Conduct examinations based on established, validated principles.

- Render opinions having a basis that is demonstratively reasonable.

- Not withhold any findings, whether inculpatory or exculpatory, that would cause the facts of a case to be misrepresented or distorted.

For more information on the IACIS code of ethics, see *www.iacis.com/membership/overview*.

American Bar Association

As a forensics examiner, you deal with attorneys, so you should be aware of the basic rules of professional conduct they must follow. The American Bar Association (ABA) is not a licensing body, but the ABA's Model Code of Professional Responsibility (Model Code) and its successor, the Model Rules of Professional Conduct (Model Rules), are the basis of state licensing bodies' codes. In the United States, attorneys are licensed by states.

These codes are quite extensive, so only a few relevant sections are given here. To read the codes in their entirety, go to *www.americanbar.org/content/dam/aba/migrated/cpr/mrpc/mcpr.authcheckdam.pdf* for the Model Code and *www.americanbar.org/groups/professional_responsibility/publications/model_rules_of_professional_conduct.html* for the Model Rules.

The ABA has stated that, unlike attorneys, expert witnesses do not owe a duty of loyalty to their clients. However, this doesn't absolve them of a duty to truth in facts they've observed or opinions they've rendered.

American Psychological Association

For psychologists, the broadly accepted guidelines governing their conduct as experts are the American Psychological Association's (APA's) Ethical Principles of Psychologists and Code of Conduct (commonly referred to as the "Ethics Code"). These guidelines offer comprehensive regulations, with an entire section devoted to forensics activities. The Ethics Code (*www.apa.org/ethics/code/index.aspx*) consists of standards that are enforceable rules for the conduct of psychologists and applies only to psychologists' activities in scientific and professional functions that are psychological in nature.

Ethical Difficulties in Expert Testimony

Despite the professional guidelines described in the previous section, problems still exist with expert witness testimony. There are inherent conflicts between the goals of attorneys and the goals of scientists or technicians (experts). Attorneys work in an adversarial system and look to sway the judge or jury with the most articulate, understandable expert, who is generally the most persuasive expert rather than the best scientist. In contrast, science requires experts to focus on the evidence without the influence of others' objectives.

As a result, *Daubert* and the APA's forensics guidelines can challenge experts to choose between complete impartiality and responsible advocacy. On one hand, an expert can appear in the role of impartial educator, whose purpose is to help the judge or jury understand a fact or an issue. According to *Daubert*, to provide reliable and valid testimony, the expert has the "ethical responsibility to present a complete and unbiased picture of the … research relevant to the case at hand." With an adversarial system, pressures from hiring attorneys, and a tendency to identify with the side you're working for, educating impartially is difficult. Therefore, experts should accept the position they have been placed in and act as responsible advocates. Ethical problems surface when experts decide to advocate for one side, as they must consider the line between using research to argue one side of an issue fairly and distorting and misrepresenting available research. *Daubert* cautions that if an expert falsifies, distorts, or misrepresents the facts while advocating his or her position, opinion testimony will not be deemed reliable or valid.

Enforcing any professional organization's ethical guidelines is difficult. The principles can be enforced only against members of the organization, and if the expert chooses to withdraw from the organization, there's no effective mechanism to enforce the guidelines, unless the organization is a licensing agency. For forensics examiners testifying as experts, this means an organization has limited influence over examiners as witnesses in the form of peer pressure and reputation among peers. In addition, without a specific organization to oversee and comment on current expert testimony standards or transgressions, it's difficult to identify and investigate violations or to apprise an organization's members of acceptable methodologies and standards.

As a result, even the most specific guidelines, such as Section 7.0 of the APA Ethics Code, are as challenging to enforce as the broader restrictions the AMA has established. All guidelines rely primarily on internalization of the codes and witnesses' analysis of when and how they

16

will participate in a case. The available guidelines also fail to ensure superior quality expert testimony because along with applicable laws, they set only a minimum level of acceptable performance or competence as the standard.

Ethical Responsibilities Owed to You

The attorney who has retained you, opposing counsel, and the court also owe you ethical responsibilities as an expert witness. Your attorney owes you a fair statement of the case or situation, adequate time to review evidence and prepare your report, and a reasonable opportunity to examine data, conduct testing, and investigate the matter before rendering an opinion. If the attorney wants you to render an opinion quickly and without adequate opportunity to review, be cautious. He might be trying to get you to commit based on inadequate information, or he's trying to rush you because he hasn't kept track of critical dates and is under pressure to meet a deadline. The attorney might also hold you under subpoena for an excessive amount of time waiting to testify. This might reflect difficulties in anticipating the amount of time required for other witnesses' testimony; however, you should be paid for the waiting time per the fee agreement. Making any portion of your fee dependent on a favorable report is inappropriate and should be a breach of the fee agreement. You are owed fair compensation for your time and work under the terms of the fee agreement.

Most attorneys, including opposing counsel, are competent, courteous professionals, but if they aren't, you can expect abuses that might include inquiry into your personal finances; unless this inquiry is about compensation terms for the current case, it's inappropriate. In addition, some opposing counsel attempt to make discovery depositions physically uncomfortable, such as using an excessively warm or cool room, having you face into the sun, or refusing to take comfort breaks. You don't need to endure the situation in silence, but you should be practical. Note the conditions to the attorney who set the deposition and ask him or her to correct the situation. If the situation is not corrected, you should note these conditions in the record, and continue noting them as long as the conditions persist.

After you have noted a problem in the record, you can refuse to continue with the deposition; however, these situations are rare and even more rare in court. Generally, you should consult with an attorney before taking that last step. If you think the behavior was serious enough that you can justify refusing to continue, you should also consider reporting the attorney to the state bar association. Other tactics include the attorney who set the deposition neglecting to have payment ready for you; you can refuse to attend the deposition if payment isn't tendered. An opposing attorney might also ask repetitive questions; the attorney who retained you should object to these techniques. For a testimony preservation deposition, however, you can expect that the attorney calling for your testimony will try to make you as comfortable as possible because he or she wants your best performance.

As a measure of protection, you might want to have your personal attorney attend the deposition; this attorney can't object to questions but is available to advise the attorney who retained you or to advise you during breaks. Whether this precaution is necessary depends on the issues involved, how confrontational opposing counsel is expected to be, and whether the retaining attorney might need immediate advice on questions. A less costly alternative is arranging to have your attorney available by phone during the deposition. In this case, you could bring your own recorder to the deposition and play back portions to your attorney, unless there's an order to the contrary. In most jurisdictions, attendees are allowed to record depositions, so unless somebody objects, record your testimony. A recording is also useful when you review your deposition testimony before signing the transcript.

Standard and Personally Created Forensics Tools

The tools you use to recover, control, and track evidence are subject to review by opposing parties. If the court deems them unreliable, the evidence you recovered with those tools might not be admitted or be admitted with a limiting instruction. If you use standard tools—commonly used tools or commercially available tools—you simplify the process of validating them.

Personally created tools, if they're designed to serve a specific purpose and have been adequately tested to validate their accuracy for that purpose, might have advantages that you can demonstrate to a judge, who ultimately determines whether evidence is admissible. For example, a tool you've created could be more compact or run more efficiently than other comparable tools. You're still required to validate these tools, however, and might have to share their source code for analysis. Remember that "borrowing" code from other products or incorporating other tools into your own without acknowledgment or paying royalties could be a violation of copyright and is considered theft. In addition, it can result in a major embarrassment for you, could have serious criminal and civil liability implications, and could adversely affect the attorney who retained you. (For opinions related to the advisability of using your own tools, you can read about the *Daubert v. Merrell Dow Pharmaceuticals, Inc.,* case at *www.law.cornell.edu/supct/html/92-102.ZS.html*.)

An Ethics Exercise

In any investigation, examination, or expert opinion, ethical issues can arise. For this final chapter, you're asked to analyze a forensics image from a computer that was unintentionally reformatted and had a new Windows OS installed. Ileen Johnson, retained as special counsel to Superior Bicycles, is following up on an ethics case from her former employer. This computer was under the control of an employee suspected of accessing and possibly transmitting a proprietary photo of the bow construction of a new kayak design developed by Superior Bicycles. Your task is to analyze the forensic image, InCh16.dd, to see whether you can find and recover a file named Kayak4 with an unknown extension.

Before beginning these activities, refer to the information in the "Examining NTFS Disks" section of Chapter 5 on FILE0 records in the MFT file. Then extract files from the Chap16 folder on the book's DVD to your *Work*\Chap16\Chapter folder. If necessary, create this folder first. The work folder pathname you see in screenshots might differ.

The tools on this book's DVD have limitations in searching for Unicode data strings. The following information guides you on how to search for Unicode text with the hex search function in ProDiscover Basic. To build search strings for this purpose, you must also use a hexadecimal editor, such as WinHex, to convert text characters to their hexadecimal values.

16

Determining Hexadecimal Values for Text Strings

A forensics examiner's technical capability requires being able to work around problems and challenges when dealing with digital evidence. ProDiscover Basic is an introductory tool with limitations that the licensed versions of ProDiscover Forensics Edition and Incident Response Edition don't have. Specifically, you can't search for Unicode text data in ProDiscover Basic. As a workaround, however, you can search for the hexadecimal equivalents of string text values. When converting plain text to hexadecimal, you need to place null (00) values between each character's hexadecimal values because Unicode values stored on NTFS drives are 16 bits each. The first 8 bits are character values, such as 0 through 9, uppercase and lowercase A to Z, and other special characters, such as !, ?, and #; the remaining 8 bits identify the language, such as the Latin alphabet, which is 0x00.

To begin examining the forensic image, you start by determining the hexadecimal values for the text string "Kayak4." Follow these steps to convert the text values into hexadecimal values, and save the results to a text file so that you can refer to them easily when performing searches for Unicode data.

1. Start WinHex. Click **File, New** from the menu, type **32** in the Desired file size text box, and then click **OK**.

2. Move the cursor to the input area on the right, and type **K A Y A K 4,** as shown in Figure 16-1. (Make sure you insert a null (0x00) space between each character by pressing the right arrow key.)

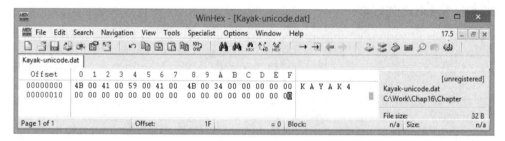

Figure 16-1 Determining hexadecimal values
Courtesy of X-Ways AG, *www.xways.net*

3. Write down this hexadecimal value for KAYAK4: **4B 00 41 00 59 00 41 00 4B 00 34 00.**

4. Save this file as **InChp16-unicode.dat** in your work folder, and then exit WinHex.

Searching for Unicode Data in ProDiscover Basic

With the collected information from the previous steps, now it's time to examine the anonymous user's disk image:

1. Start ProDiscover Basic with the **Run as administrator** option, and start a new project, using **InCh16** for the project number and filename.

2. Click **Action** from the menu, point to **Add**, and click **Image File**.

3. In the Open dialog box, navigate to and click the image file **InCh16.dd**, and then click **Open**.

4. Click **Action, Search** from the menu. In the Search dialog box, click the **Content Search** tab, and then click the **Hex** option button. Click the **Search for the pattern(s)** option button, if necessary, and in the Search text box, type the hexadecimal value for KAYAK4 that you wrote down in the preceding activity. Under Select the Disk(s)/Image(s) you want to search in, click the image file (see Figure 16-2), and then click **OK**.

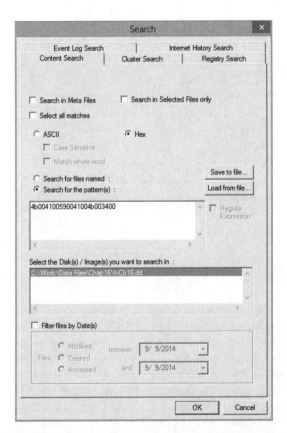

Figure 16-2 Searching for hexadecimal files in ProDiscover
Courtesy of Technology Pathways, LLC

5. In the search results window, click **pagefile.sys**, and scroll down through the contents until you have located string data matching the search criteria (shown in Figure 16-3).

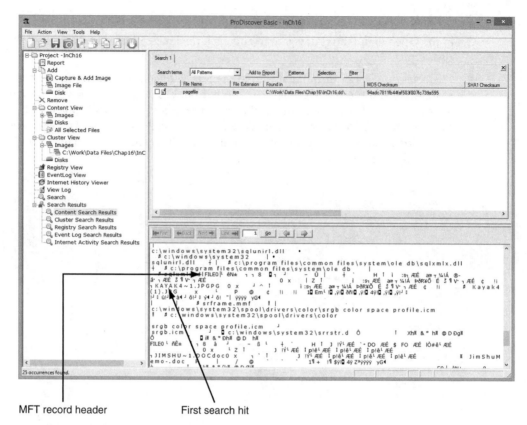

MFT record header   **First search hit**

Figure 16-3   Viewing search results
Courtesy of Technology Pathways, LLC

The lower pane of the search results contains a portion of what seems to be a previously created MFT file. The FILE0 header appears to be associated with files starting with "KAYAK4." This finding could mean that an MFT file occupied this space where `pagefile.sys` is located now. How this result might occur varies; the cause might be a reformatted disk or a new OS installation. Reformatting or reinstalling an OS doesn't completely overwrite previous data on a disk, thus revealing residual data, such as previous MFT records and their associated files.

6. Next, double-click **pagefile.sys** to view the file in the main ProDiscover window. Scroll down, and then right-click the **pagefile.sys** file and click **Copy File**. Click **Save** to copy it to your work folder.

7. Exit ProDiscover Basic, saving when prompted.

Interpreting Attribute 0x80 Data Runs

The next task is a detailed examination of the `pagefile.sys` file in WinHex. You learn how to interpret data runs from the MFT file's fragments found in `pagefile.sys`.

Navigating Through an MFT Record For this task, you need WinHex and a spreadsheet program, such as Microsoft Excel or LibreOffice Calc. To examine `pagefile.sys` with WinHex, follow these steps:

1. Start WinHex. Click **File, Open** from the menu, navigate to and click **`pagefile.sys`**, and then click **Open**.

2. Click **Search, Find Text** from the menu. In the Find Text dialog box, type **KAYAK4** in the text box at the top, if necessary. Click the **Match case** check box, if necessary. Click **Unicode** in the list box underneath (see Figure 16-4), and then click **OK**.

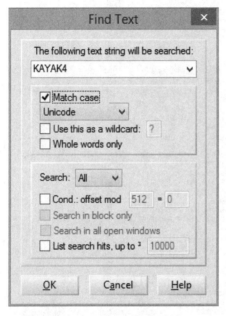

Figure 16-4 The Find Text dialog box
Courtesy of X-Ways AG, *www.xways.net*

NOTE

When searching for specific record information, sometimes there are duplicate files with the same name that have different data runs, meaning the file was written more than one time to disk on separate occasions. When performing a search, you need to examine all search results, compute their data run values, and attempt to recover the files. If your first effort doesn't produce successful results, continue searching for other occurrences.

3. In the main window, the cursor is placed in the right pane at the start of the first occurrence of the Unicode string KAYAK4. From this position, scroll upward until you see FILE0.

4. To position the cursor at the start of the next attribute, place the cursor in the middle pane where FILE0 starts, and drag down 0x38 hexadecimal bytes (see Figure 16-5), using the offset counter in the lower-right corner as a guide.

Highlighted bytes for record header
from starting position 0x00 to 0x37

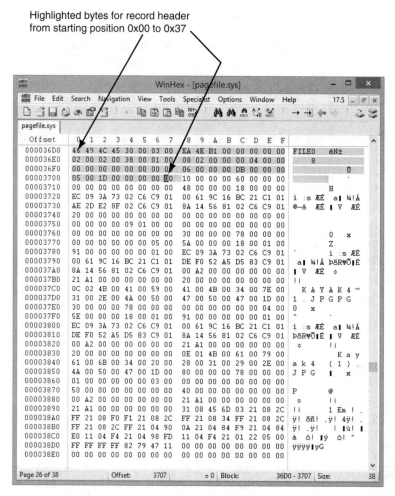

Figure 16-5 An MFT record header
Courtesy of X-Ways AG, *www.xways.net*

All numeric values in these steps are hexadecimal. If the offset counter is in decimal mode, click the row of numbers to the right of the hexadecimal section once. Each time you click here, WinHex toggles between decimal and hexadecimal modes.

5. Place the cursor at the beginning of attribute 0x10, and drag down 0x60 hexadecimal bytes until you reach the next attribute, 0x30 (see Figure 16-6).

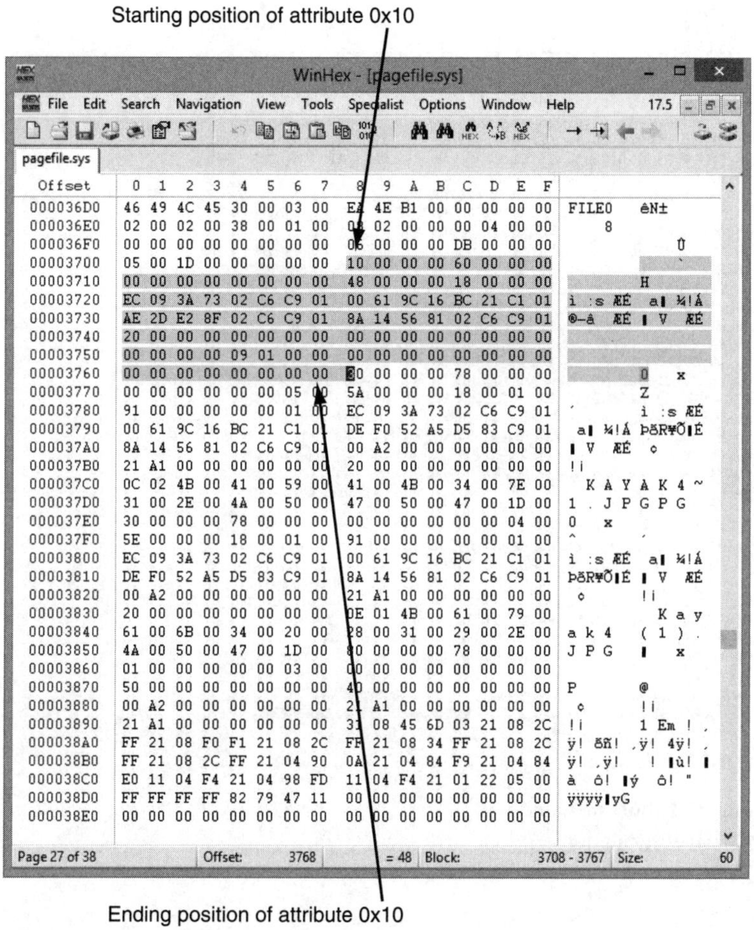

Starting position of attribute 0x10

Figure 16-6 Viewing attribute 0x10
Courtesy of X-Ways AG, *www.xways.net*

Ending position of attribute 0x10

6. The next two sections of the file are the short and long filename attribute 0x30. (Figure 16-7 shows the short filename attribute.) Both have lengths of 0x78 hexadecimal bytes. Repeat the previous step until you reach attribute 0x80.

16

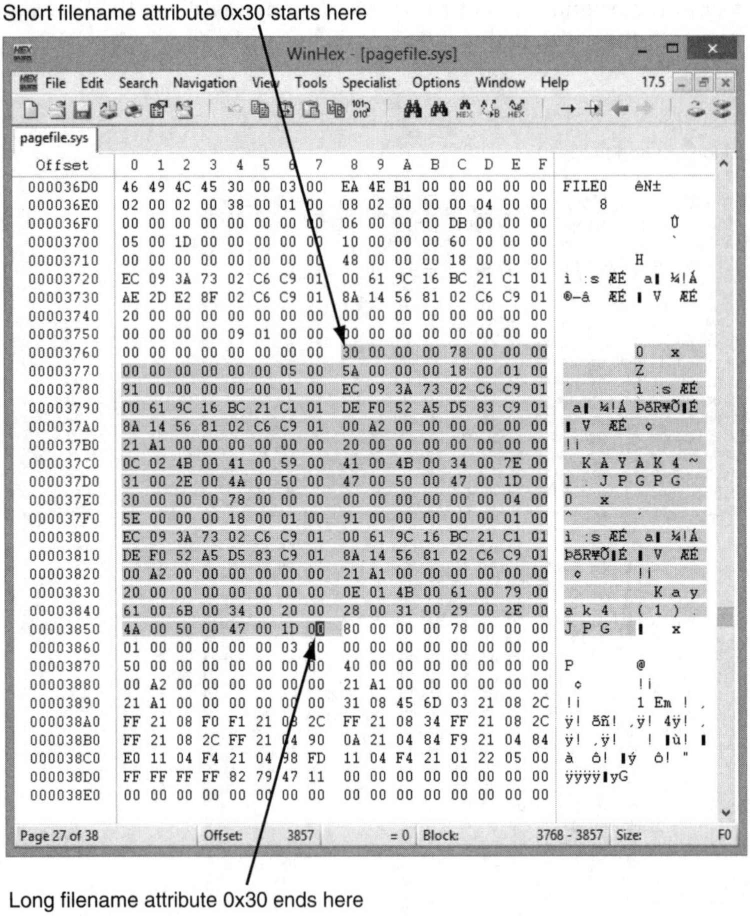

Short filename attribute 0x30 starts here

Figure 16-7 Attribute 0x30: short filename
Courtesy of X-Ways AG, *www.xways.net*

Long filename attribute 0x30 ends here

7. From the starting position of attribute 0x80, count 0x40 hexadecimal bytes to the beginning of the first data run, as shown in Figure 16-8. Leave WinHex open for the next activity.

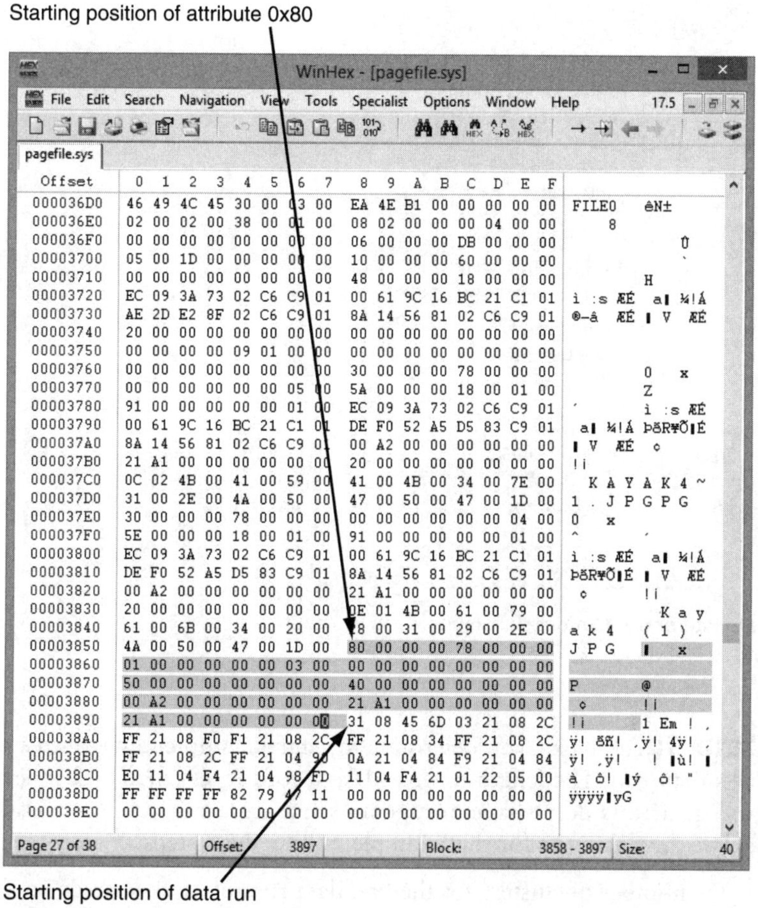

Starting position of attribute 0x80

Starting position of data run

Figure 16-8 Attribute 0x80: the beginning of the first data run
Courtesy of X-Ways AG, *www.xways.net*

Now that you have located the data run's starting position, the next task is to calculate the starting and ending cluster positions of each data run fragment. (For more detailed information on calculating data runs, refer back to Figures 5-19, 5-20, and 5-21 in Chapter 5.)

Configuring the Data Interpreter Window in WinHex Typically, when WinHex starts, the Data Interpreter window opens, where you can convert data formats into easy-to-read values, such as converting hexadecimal values into decimal values. For the following activities, you need to know how to configure the Data Interpreter window to perform data run calculations. Follow these steps:

1. Start WinHex, if necessary. If the Data Interpreter window doesn't open, click **View** from the menu, point to **Show**, and click the check box next to **Data Interpreter**.

2. Click **Options, Data Interpreter** from the menu to open the Data Interpreter Options dialog box. Click the **8 bit, signed, 16 bit, signed**, and **24 bit, signed** check boxes (clearing any other check boxes that are selected), as shown in Figure 16-9, and then click **OK**. Leave WinHex open for the next activity.

16

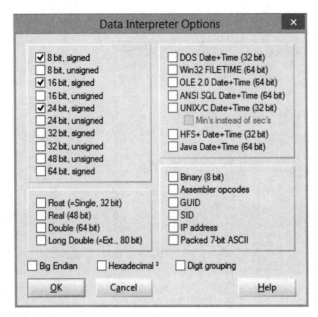

Figure 16-9 The Data Interpreter Options dialog box
Courtesy of X-Ways AG, *www.xways.net*

Calculating Data Runs Next, you determine the starting and ending cluster numbers for the MFT record's data run. The length of this MFT record is less than 512 bytes (0x200 hexadecimal), so the data runs don't have an update sequence array value, as described in Chapter 5. To calculate the data runs for this example, follow these steps:

1. To determine the number of clusters for the first data run, place the cursor on the data run position immediately to the right of the first data run position 31, as shown in Figure 16-10. Because it's only 1 byte long, the 0x08 converts to 8 in decimal (as shown in the Data Interpreter window), which indicates 8 clusters in the first data run.

```
00003800   EC 09 3A 73 02 C6 C9 01   00 61 9C 16 BC 21 C1 01   ì :s ÆÉ    a  ¼!Á
00003810   DE F            1         8A 14 56 81 02 C6 C9 01   ÞðR¥Õ¦É ¦ V  ÆÉ
00003820   00 A                      21 A1 00 00 00 00 00 00   ¢         !¡
00003830   20 0    8 Bit (±): 8      0E 01 4B 00 61 00 79 00             K a y
00003840   61 0    16 Bit (±): 17672  28 00 31 00 29 00 2E 00   a k 4    ( 1 ) .
00003850   4A 0    24 Bit (±): 7161096  80 00 00 00 78 00 00 00   J P G    ¦   x
00003860   01 0                      00 00 00 00 00 00 00 00
00003870   50 00 00 00 00 00 00 00   40 00 00 00 00 00 00 00   P        @
00003880   00 A2 00 00 00 00 00 00   21 A1 00 00 00 00 00 00   ¢         !¡
00003890   21 A1 00 00 00 00 00 00   31 08 45 6D 03 21 08 2C   !¡       1 Em ! ,
000038A0   FF 21 08 F0 F1 21 08 2C   FF 21 08 34 FF 21 08 2C   ÿ! ðñ! ,ÿ! 4ÿ! ,
000038B0   FF 21 08 2C FF 21 04 90   0A 21 04 84 F9 21 04 84   ÿ! ,ÿ!   ! ù! ¦
000038C0   E0 11 04 F4 21 04 98 FD   11 04 F4 21 01 22 05 00   à ô! ¦ý ô! "
000038D0   FF FF FF FF 82 79 47 11   00 00 00 00 00 00 00 00   ÿÿÿÿ¦yG
```

Figure 16-10 Number of clusters in the first data run
Courtesy of X-Ways AG, *www.xways.net*

2. To determine the starting logical cluster number (LCN) position for this data run, place the cursor to the left of the 4 in the string **45 6D 03**. This address location is 3 bytes, or 24 bits, as shown in Figure 16-11. Therefore, the starting LCN position for the first data run is 224581, as shown in the Data Interpreter window.

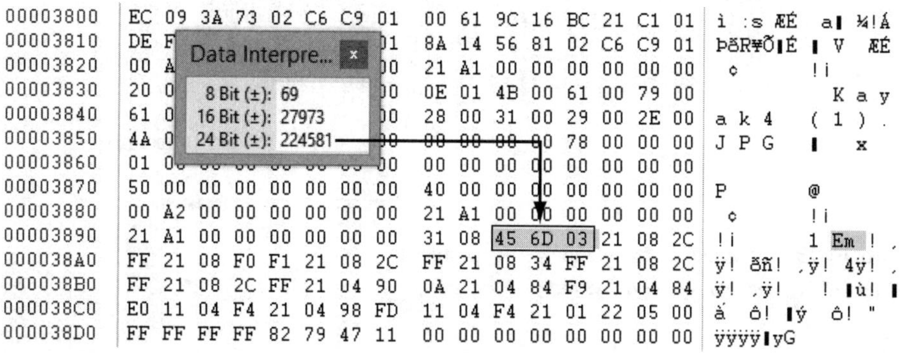

```
00003800   EC 09 3A 73 02 C6 C9 01   00 61 9C 16 BC 21 C1 01   ì :s ÆÉ  a▌ ¼!Á
00003810   DE F┌──────────────────┐1  8A 14 56 81 02 C6 C9 01   ÞŏR¥Ŏ▐É ▌V ÆÉ
00003820   00 A│ Data Interpre...  ✕│0  21 A1 00 00 00 00 00 00   ¢        !¡
00003830   20 0│                   │0  0E 01 4B 00 61 00 79 00          K a y
00003840   61 0│ 8 Bit (±): 69     │0  28 00 31 00 29 00 2E 00   a k 4   ( 1 ) .
00003850   4A 0│ 16 Bit (±): 27973 │0  00 00 00 00 78 00 00 00   J P G  ▌  x
           4A 0│ 24 Bit (±): 224581─│──── 00 00 00 00
00003860   01 0└──────────────────┘0  00 00 00 00 00 00 00 00
00003870   50 00 00 00 00 00 00 00   40 00 00 00 00 00 00 00   P        @
00003880   00 A2 00 00 00 00 00 00   21 A1 00 00 00 00 00 00   ¢        !¡
00003890   21 A1 00 00 00 00 00 00   31 08 45 6D 03 21 08 2C   !¡       1 Em !
000038A0   FF 21 08 F0 F1 21 08 2C   FF 21 08 34 FF 21 08 2C   ÿ! ðñ! .ÿ! 4ÿ! ,
000038B0   FF 21 08 2C FF 21 04 90   0A 21 04 84 F9 21 04 84   ÿ! .ÿ!   ! ▌ù! ▌
000038C0   E0 11 04 F4 21 04 98 FD   11 04 F4 21 01 22 05 00   à ó! ▌ý  ó! "
000038D0   FF FF FF FF 82 79 47 11   00 00 00 00 00 00 00 00   ÿÿÿÿ▌yG
```

Figure 16-11 Starting LCN position for the first data run
Courtesy of X-Ways AG, *www.xways.net*

3. Next, move the cursor to the next data run's cluster count position; it also has the hexadecimal value 0x08, which converts to decimal 8. The next 2 bytes (16 bits) display the virtual cluster number (VCN) 2C FF, which converts to -212 in decimal (see Figure 16-12).

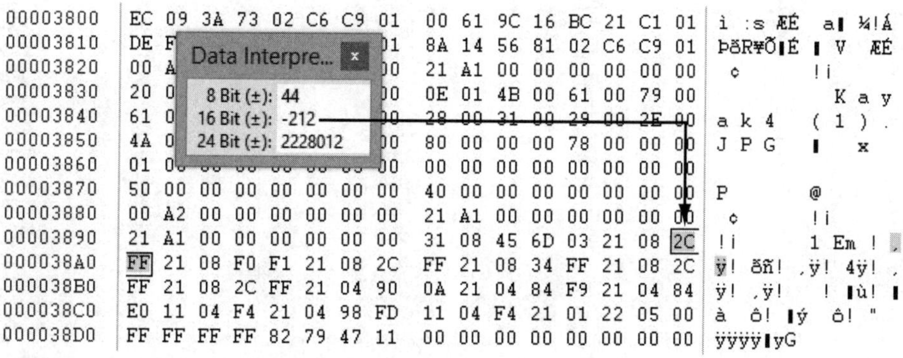

```
00003800   EC 09 3A 73 02 C6 C9 01   00 61 9C 16 BC 21 C1 01   ì :s ÆÉ  a▌ ¼!Á
00003810   DE F┌──────────────────┐1  8A 14 56 81 02 C6 C9 01   ÞŏR¥Ŏ▐É ▌V ÆÉ
00003820   00 A│ Data Interpre...  ✕│0  21 A1 00 00 00 00 00 00   ¢        !¡
00003830   20 0│                   │0  0E 01 4B 00 61 00 79 00          K a y
00003840   61 0│ 8 Bit (±): 44     │0  28 00 31 00 29 00 2E 00   a k 4   ( 1 ) .
00003850   4A 0│ 16 Bit (±): -212──│──── 80 00 00 00 78 00 00 00   J P G  ▌  x
           4A 0│ 24 Bit (±): 2228012│0
00003860   01 0└──────────────────┘0  00 00 00 00 00 00 00 00
00003870   50 00 00 00 00 00 00 00   40 00 00 00 00 00 00 00   P        @
00003880   00 A2 00 00 00 00 00 00   21 A1 00 00 00 00 00 00   ¢        !¡
00003890   21 A1 00 00 00 00 00 00   31 08 45 6D 03 21 08 2C   !¡       1 Em ! ▌
000038A0   FF 21 08 F0 F1 21 08 2C   FF 21 08 34 FF 21 08 2C   ÿ! ðñ! .ÿ! 4ÿ! ,
000038B0   FF 21 08 2C FF 21 04 90   0A 21 04 84 F9 21 04 84   ÿ! .ÿ!   ! ▌ù! ▌
000038C0   E0 11 04 F4 21 04 98 FD   11 04 F4 21 01 22 05 00   à ó! ▌ý  ó! "
000038D0   FF FF FF FF 82 79 47 11   00 00 00 00 00 00 00 00   ÿÿÿÿ▌yG
```

Figure 16-12 Starting VCN position for the second data run
Courtesy of X-Ways AG, *www.xways.net*

16

4. Repeat Steps 1 to 3 to find the remaining clusters per fragment and the VCN values, as shown in Figure 16-13. (Refer to Chapter 5 for information on how NTFS manages MFT records.)

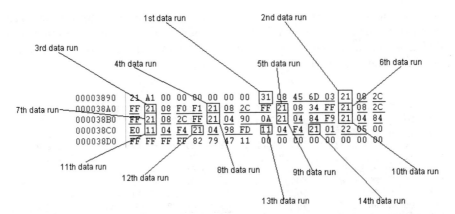

Figure 16-13   All data runs for the `Kayak4.jpg` file

Courtesy of X-Ways AG, *www.xways.net*

5. To simplify the calculations, enter the LCN and VCN values in a spreadsheet, as shown in Figure 16-14. When you're finished, exit WinHex. Note that columns C and E of the spreadsheet have formulas that compute the LCN value from the VCN value in column B and the ending LCN in column D.

	A	B	C	D	E
1	**File name:**	**Kayak4.jpg**			
2	**Data Run**	**VCN**	**Starting Cluster**	**Clusters per fragment**	**Ending Cluster**
3	1	LCN starting no.	224581	8	224588
4	2	-212	224369	8	224376
5	3	-3600	220769	8	220776
6	4	-212	220557	8	220564
7	5	-204	220353	8	220360
8	6	-212	220141	8	220148
9	7	-212	219929	8	219936
10	8	2704	222633	4	222636
11	9	-1660	220973	4	220976
12	10	-8060	212913	4	212916
13	11	-12	212901	4	212904
14	12	-616	212285	4	212288
15	13	-12	212273	4	212276
16	14	1314	213587	1	213587
17					

```
Formulas for Column C              Formulas for Column E

=C3         starting LCN           =(C3+D3)-1    for cell E3
=C3+B4      for cell C4            =(C4+D4)-1    for cell E4
=C4+B5      for cell C5            =(C5+D5)-1    for cell E5
=C5+B6      for cell C6            =(C6+D6)-1    for cell E6
=C6+B7      for cell C7            =(C7+D7)-1    for cell E7
=C7+B8      for cell C8            =(C8+D8)-1    for cell E8
=C8+B9      for cell C9            =(C9+D9)-1    for cell E9
=C9+B10     for cell C10           =(C10+D10)-1  for cell E10
=C10+B11    for cell C11           =(C11+D11)-1  for cell E11
=C11+B12    for cell C12           =(C12+D12)-1  for cell E12
=C12+B13    for cell C13           =(C13+D13)-1  for cell E13
=C13+B14    for cell C14           =(C14+D14)-1  for cell E14
```

Figure 16-14   Converted data run values in a spreadsheet

Source: The Document Foundation

Carving Data Run Clusters Manually

Now that you have calculated the starting and ending cluster positions for the `Kayak4.jpg` file, it's time to recover the fragments in ProDiscover. To begin data carving, follow these steps:

1. Start ProDiscover Basic, and click the **Open Project** toolbar icon. In the Open dialog box, navigate to and click the **Ch16.dft** project, and then click **Open**.

2. In the tree view, click to expand **Cluster View** and **Images**, if necessary, and then click **InCh16.dd**.

3. In the spreadsheet you created in the previous activity, locate the starting cluster position (224581) in cell C3, and then locate the clusters per fragment (8) in cell D3.

4. In ProDiscover's work area, click the **Decimal** check box under the Cluster text box, type the decimal value **224581** in the text box, and then click **Go**.

5. Click cluster position **224581**, hold the **Shift** key down, and press the **right arrow** key to highlight the seven additional clusters shown in Figure 16-15.

 When extracting fragments, it's important to recover only the clusters from the starting and ending cluster positions. Adding extra clusters produces a corrupted file that the intended application, such as Microsoft Word, Excel, or a graphics application, can't read.

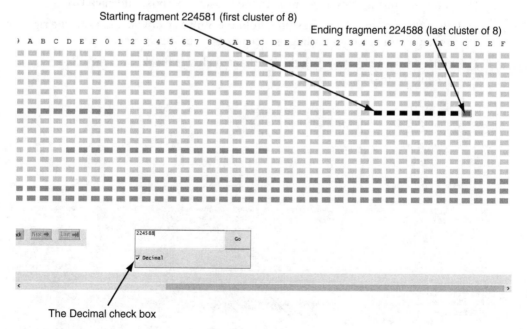

Figure 16-15 Highlighted cluster for the first fragment
Courtesy of Technology Pathways, LLC

6. In the work area, right-click the highlighted cluster blocks and click **Recover**.

7. In the Recover Clusters dialog box, click the **Recover all clusters to a single file** option button, if necessary, and then click the **Recover Binary** check box (see Figure 16-16). Click **Browse**, navigate to and click your work folder, and then click **OK** twice. Leave ProDiscover Basic running.

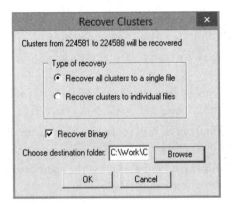

Figure 16-16   The Recover Clusters dialog box
Courtesy of Technology Pathways, LLC

Return to the spreadsheet and find the starting cluster for the second through fourteenth data run fragments. Follow these steps for each remaining data run fragment:

1. Enter the starting cluster position in the Cluster text box, and click **Go**.

2. Click this starting cluster position, hold the **Shift** key down, and press the **right arrow** key until you reach the ending cluster position for the data run.

3. In the work area, right-click the highlighted cluster blocks and click **Recover** (see Figure 16-17).

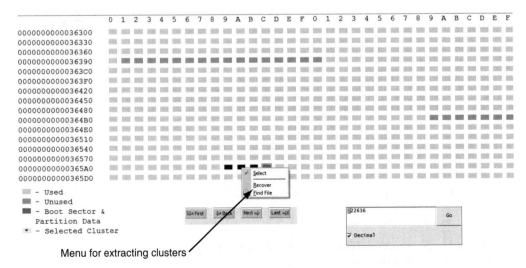

Menu for extracting clusters

Figure 16-17   Menu for extracting clusters from an image file
Courtesy of Technology Pathways, LLC

4. In the Recover Clusters dialog box, click the **Recover all clusters to a single file** option button, if necessary, and click the **Recover Binary** check box. Click **Browse**, navigate to and click your work folder, and then click **OK** twice.

5. Refer to your spreadsheet for the remaining data run fragments, and repeat Steps 1 through 4 to recover them. Exit ProDiscover.

When you have finished carving the fragmented data runs, the next step is appending the fragments into one file. To combine all fragments, they must be in the correct order, according to what's listed in the data runs. If you switch the order of any fragment, the recovered file is unreadable. Follow these steps:

1. Start WinHex, if necessary. Click **Tools** on the menu, point to **File Tools**, and click **Concatenate**. In the Select Destination File window, type **Kayak4.jpg** in the File name text box (see Figure 16-18), navigate to and click your work folder, and click **Save**.

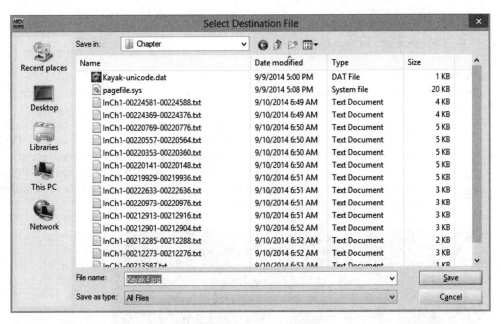

Figure 16-18   The Select Destination File window
Courtesy of X-Ways AG, *www.x-ways.net*

The demo version of WinHex can save only files of less than 200 KB at a time. The licensed version of WinHex and X-Ways Forensics has no limit on file sizes that can be saved.

2. In the Choose Source File #1 window, click the `InCh1-00224581-00224588.txt` file (see Figure 16-19), and then click **Append**.

3. Repeat Step 2 to append the remaining file fragments. Refer to Figure 16-14, if needed, to make sure you're appending them in the correct order.

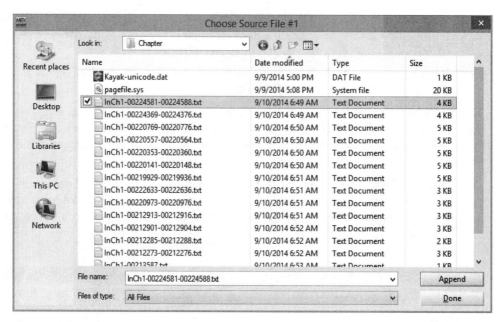

Figure 16-19   The Choose Source File window
Courtesy of X-Ways AG, *www.x-ways.net*

4. When you have finished appending the file fragments, click **Done**. In the message
asking you to confirm that 14 files were concatenated to Kayak4.jpg, click **OK**. In
File Explorer, navigate to your work folder, and double-click **Kayak4.jpg** to
view the recovered file (see Figure 16-20). If it fails to open or only a partial image is
displayed, review your steps to make sure you collected the correct clusters and have
appended them in the correct order. Exit WinHex.

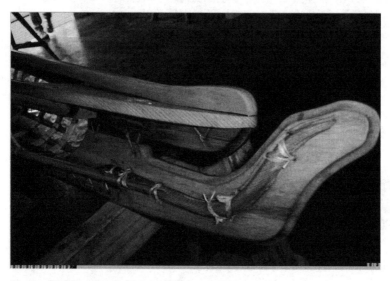

Figure 16-20   Viewing the recovered Kayak4.jpg file

Chapter Summary

■ Ethics can be defined as rules you internalize and use to measure your performance (internal standards) or standards that you're compelled to adhere to by external forces, such as licensing bodies (codes of professional conduct or responsibility). Laws governing codes of professional conduct or responsibility typically define the lowest level of action or performance required to avoid liability.

■ Digital forensics examiners don't have the same formal, detailed codes of conduct that professions such as medicine and the law have, so relying on an internal code of ethics might be more critical. Additional sources include codes of professional associations you belong to, certifying bodies that have granted you a certification, and your employer's rules of professional conduct. Most examiners rely on a combination of these standards to construct their professional ethical codes.

■ You owe your client a full understanding of the facts relevant to your opinion, and you can ask him or her to establish that there's evidence supporting the facts your opinion is based on.

■ Be aware of attempts to disqualify you as an expert. Opposing counsel might attempt to disqualify you based on any deviations from opinions you've given in previous cases, so be prepared to explain the reason for any changes in your position. Some attorneys might contact you solely for the purpose of discrediting or disqualifying you (conflicting out). Always note calls from attorneys and the nature of the communication, and require that the attorney complete a client questionnaire and send you an investigation retainer.

■ Courts use many factors in determining whether to disqualify an expert, such as whether an expert was formally retained and compensated, whether an expert was informed that discussions were confidential, and so on.

■ Be aware of obvious ethical errors, such as ignoring contradictory data, performing work beyond your expertise or competence, allowing the attorney who hired you to influence your opinion improperly, and reaching a conclusion before completing your research.

■ No single source offers a definitive code of ethics for expert witnesses, so you must draw on standards from other organizations to form your own ethical standards. Many professional organizations, such as the ABA and APA, have rules to guide their members in areas such as interaction with patients/clients, objectivity, role in society, fees, solicitation, independence, and contractual relationships.

■ The International Society of Forensic Computer Examiners (ISFCE) Code of Ethics and Professional Responsibility provides guidelines for its members, and the International Association of Computer Investigative Specialists (IACIS) has a well-defined, simple guide for the expected behavior of forensics examiners.

16

■ The inherent conflict between the needs of the justice system and your obligations for professional conduct can create ethical difficulties. With an adversarial legal system, pressures from hiring attorneys, and a tendency to identify with the side you're working for, maintaining impartiality can be difficult. Digital forensics examiners should consider their personal values, review the codes of conduct that apply to other professions, and develop a personal code of conduct that will protect them from ethical errors.

- The attorney who has retained you, opposing counsel, and the court owe you ethical responsibilities as an expert witness. For example, your attorney owes you a fair statement of the case or situation, adequate time to review evidence and prepare your report, and a reasonable opportunity to examine data, conduct testing, and investigate the matter before rendering an opinion.

- As a forensics examiner, you deal with attorneys, so be aware of the basic rules of professional conduct they must follow. The American Bar Association is not a licensing body, but its Model Code of Professional Responsibility (Model Code) and its successor, the Model Rules of Professional Conduct (Model Rules), are the basis of state licensing bodies' codes.

- To give reliable and valid testimony, an expert has the ethical responsibility to present a complete, unbiased picture of the research related to the case. With an adversarial system, pressures from hiring attorneys, and a tendency to identify with the side you're working for, educating impartially is difficult.

- The attorney who has retained you, opposing counsel, and the court also owe you ethical responsibilities as an expert witness.

- The tools you use to recover, control, and track evidence are subject to review by opposing parties. If the court deems them unreliable, the evidence you recovered with those tools might not be admitted or be admitted with a limiting instruction. If you create tools for your own use, you must still validate them and submit them for review.

- After carving data artifacts, analyzing as much of the information as possible is critical. This information includes the create, modified, last access, and record timestamps in a recovered MFT record in addition to any recovered data runs. Collecting as many facts as possible provides more complete findings for your final report.

Key Terms

codes of professional conduct or responsibility External rules that often have the effect of law in limiting professionals' actions; breach of these rules can result in discipline, including suspension or loss of a license to practice and civil and criminal liability.

contingency fees Payments that depend on the content of the expert's testimony or the outcome of the case.

disqualification The process by which an expert witness is excluded from testifying.

ethics Rules that you internalize and use to measure your performance; sometimes refers to external rules (codes of professional conduct or responsibility).

Review Questions

1. Describe two types of ethical standards.

2. Ethical obligations are duties that you owe only to others. True or False?

3. List three sound reasons for offering a different opinion from one you testified to in a previous case.

4. List three or more factors courts have used in determining whether to disqualify an expert.

5. All expert witnesses must be members of associations that license them. True or False?

6. Contingency fees can be used to compensate an expert under which circumstances?
   a. When the expert is too expensive to compensate at the hourly rate
   b. When the expert is willing to accept a contingency fee arrangement
   c. When the expert is acting only as a consultant, not a witness
   d. All of the above

7. List three organizations that have a code of ethics or conduct.

8. In the United States, no state or national licensing body specifically licenses forensics examiners. True or False?

9. When you begin a conversation with an attorney about a specific case, what should you do? (Choose all that apply.)
   a. Ask to meet with the attorney.
   b. Answer his or her questions in as much detail as possible.
   c. Ask who the parties in the case are.
   d. Refuse to discuss details until a retainer agreement is returned.

10. What purpose does making your own recording during a deposition serve?
    a. It shows the court reporter that you don't trust him or her.
    b. It assists you with reviewing the transcript of the deposition.
    c. It allows you to review your testimony with your attorney during breaks.
    d. It prevents opposing counsel from intimidating you.

11. Externally enforced ethical rules, with sanctions that can restrict a professional's practice, are more accurately described as which of the following?
    a. Laws
    b. Objectives
    c. A higher calling
    d. All of the above

12. Describe an unethical technique opposing counsel might use to make a deposition difficult for you.

16

13. What are some risks of using tools you have created yourself?
    a. The tool might not perform reliably.
    b. The judge might be suspicious of the validity of results from the tool.
    c. You might have to share the tool's source code with opposing counsel for review.
    d. The tool doesn't generate reports in a standard format.

14. List four steps you should take, in the correct order, to handle a deposition in which physical circumstances are uncomfortable.

15. List three obvious ethical errors.

16. Codes of professional conduct or responsibility set the highest standards for professionals' expected performance. True or False?

Hands-On Projects

The following projects produce correspondence that might contain attorney-client privileged information. Your task is to locate and recover the data and report to Ileen Johnson on your findings. Before beginning these projects, create a *Work*\Chap16\Projects folder on your system and move the file used with in-chapter activities to this folder.

Hands-On Project 16-1

For this project, Ileen Johnson wants you to recover a spreadsheet file starting with the name "Baidar" in InCh16.dd. She also needs to know the following:

- When the file was created and last modified
- How many versions of this file are on the drive
- How many versions of this file can be recovered

To find this information, you need WinHex and ProDiscover to examine the pagefile.sys file in InCh16.dd. As described in the in-chapter activity, use WinHex to find the date and time values, find the cluster addresses from each data run, concatenate data run fragments, and use ProDiscover to extract clusters. To determine the date and time values with WinHex, refer to Chapter 5, if needed. When you have finished this examination, write a one-page report describing your findings and any irregularities in date and time values. Then turn the report in to your instructor for review.

Hands-On Project 16-2

Ileen Johnson has new information that the InCh16.dd image might contain additional evidence for you to recover. All she knows is that the file might be named "tourguide." She has no idea what type of file it is and wants you to determine its file extension and whether the file can be recovered. Using ProDiscover, conduct a search for the "tourguide.*" keyword (see Figure 16-21). Examine the file's contents and perform any steps needed to extract it from the image file and make it readable. Save the file in your work folder, and give a copy to your instructor.

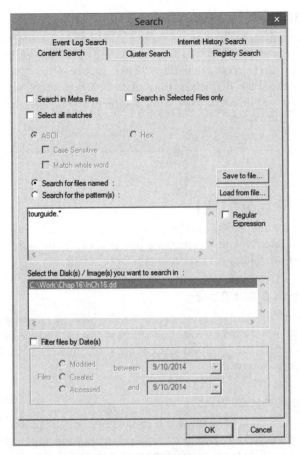

Figure 16-21 Searching for PDF files in ProDiscover
Courtesy of Technology Pathways, LLC

Hands-On Project 16-3

After reviewing the files you recovered, Ileen Johnson needs to know the create date for the Kayak4.jpg file. Using the information in Chapter 5 (refer to Figure 5-14 for a reference on how to interpret date and time values), locate the create date value for this file, and use WinHex to extract this information from the pagefile.sys file you used in the in-chapter activity. After determining this information, write a short report listing the file's create date, and turn it in to your instructor.

16

When using the Data Interpreter window for date and time values, place the cursor at the beginning of the date field. For example, if the date and time string is EC 09 3A 73 02 C6 C9 01, place the cursor on the EC value.

Hands-On Project 16-4

Ileen Johnson wants you to retrieve a PDF file with a message addressed to Jim Shu from the `InCh16.dd` image. Using ProDiscover, reopen the in-chapter case file `Ch16.dft`, and do a search on the term "*.pdf." When you have found this PDF file, make note of the path to it. Navigate to this path, and examine the file's contents. Save the file in your work folder, and give a copy to your instructor.

Case Projects

Case Project 16-1

Write a code of ethics for an organization you belong to or a school you attend, and explain the purpose of the code. Your code of ethics should have at least three items of expected ethical behavior.

Case Project 16-2

Write a one- to two-page paper on the basic tenets of your personal ethical code and the sources your code is based on. It should be based on your personal experiences with ethical conflicts and how your understanding of ethics has played a part in your life.

Case Project 16-3

Examine a code of ethics for a professional organization, business, or government agency, and write a critique of it. In your paper, determine the entity's priorities and whose interests the code serves.

Case Project 16-4

Write a critique of your personal code of ethics from Case Project 16-2. How can you tell when you have followed (or not followed) the precepts of your personal code of ethics? Include your experiences with personal ethical conflicts and whether you were able to resolve them.

Case Project 16-5

Write an opinion paper of two or more pages describing your findings in the in-chapter activities and hands-on projects. Review the contents of the files you extracted, and make your own conclusion about what Jim Shu might be up to, based on this collected data. You should also take date and time values into consideration as part of your opinion on the files' validity. In addition, give an opinion on any legal correspondence you found in this examination.

Certification Test References

This appendix gives you an overview of National Institute of Standards and Technology (NIST) testing processes for certification of digital forensics tools and digital forensics training programs offering certificates.

NIST Digital Forensics Tool Testing

NIST provides several resources on digital forensics tool testing. Check these resources regularly for the latest updates and test results. The following links on the NIST Web site are of specific interest to forensics examiners:

- The Computer Forensics Tool Testing (CFTT) Project (*www.cftt.nist.gov*)
- The National Software Reference Library (NSRL) Project (*www.nsrl.nist.gov/index.html*)

The CFTT Project was developed to give the legal community, law enforcement, and forensics tool vendors a program to validate the reliability of these tools. As part of the validation, this project is intended to help vendors improve their products to ensure that their results stand up in court.

The NSRL is a repository of known software and files from computer vendors. OS and application files are identified by their unique hash values, usually MD5 and SHA-1 hashes. Forensics examiners can filter out known files by their hash values, which reduces the number of files they need to inspect for possible digital evidence. The NSRL also contains hash values for known bad files, typically computer viruses and contraband material.

Types of Digital Forensics Certifications

Several organizations, both public and private, have developed certification programs for digital forensics examiners. Some organizations specialize in certain areas, and others take a general overview approach, but all provide a baseline for what examiners are supposed to be proficient in when conducting computer investigations. These organizations typically have fees for membership and certification exams.

Some of these organizations have come and gone for a variety of reasons. If you decide to get a certification, examine the sponsoring organization's history and management and check the board of directors' or advisers' credentials. With this information, you can determine an organization's focus. For example, if an organization's members are well known for disk and media forensics, you know the certification is oriented toward stand-alone computing exams. If an organization's members are well known for network and intrusion forensics, you know the certification focuses on network firewalls and other related network intrusion topics. In addition, the older the organization is, the better the chances are that it will be around for future support.

Digital forensics certification organizations can be divided into three categories:

- Professional certifying organizations
- Application vendor certifying companies
- Digital forensics public and private training groups

The following sections describe some well-known certifying organizations, but many other organizations provide certification. When selecting a certification program, research it thoroughly to make sure it fits your needs. All these programs require a sizable investment of your time and money.

Professional Certifying Organizations

These organizations are typically nonprofit or not-for-profit groups that have specific missions to provide guidelines and training for digital forensics.

IACIS Certification The International Association of Computer Investigative Specialists (IACIS) is a nonprofit organization formed to promote professional standards and certify forensics examiners. Through IACIS, you can become a Certified Forensic Computer Examiner (CFCE). To qualify to take the CFCE exam, you must be an active law enforcement officer or other person qualified to be an IACIS member. For more information on qualification requirements, visit *www.iacis.com*.

IACIS offers an extensive testing program to verify competence in performing a computing investigation. The examination process is not a training program; it's strictly a testing program. Applicants are screened before acceptance into the certification program, and IACIS is the sole decision maker for all applicants. Applying for the certification requires completing an application form and paying the associated fee. For the latest information on fees, go to *www.iacis.com/certification/overview*. If you're rejected for any reason, your fee is returned. If you're accepted into the program, a monitor (an IACIS CFCE member) directs you through the testing.

ISFCE Certification Similar to IACIS, the International Society of Forensic Computer Examiners (ISFCE) provides guidelines for training for its Certified Computer Examiner (CCE) certification. You can find current information on ISFCE at *www.isfce.com* and more information on the CCE certification at *www.certified-computer-examiner.com*. Presently, several universities and colleges sponsor credited and noncredited digital forensics classes for this certification. In addition, many commercial forensics training companies offer CCE training.

GIAC Certification The SysAdmin, Audit, Network, Security (SANS) Institute offers extensive training in all aspects of computing security, including forensics. The SANS certification program is called Global Information Assurance Certification (GIAC; *www.giac.org/ overview*) and has several training tracks. One track, Global Certified Forensic Analyst (GCFA), provides unique training in network intrusion response forensics for computer media. Tools used for GCFA training are open source and require extensive knowledge of UNIX and Linux. For more information on this program, visit *www.giac.org/certifications/ security/gcfa.php*.

Application Vendor Certifying Companies

Several digital forensics application vendors have developed their own certification programs. These programs follow standard guidelines for practices used in all digital forensics investigations and examinations. In addition, these vendor-specific exams certify that people earning these certifications are competent in using their forensics tools. Two well-established vendor certification programs are Guidance Software EnCase Certified Engineer (EnCE) and AccessData Certified Examiner (ACE).

EnCE Certification For acceptance into the EnCE certification program, you must meet one of several prerequisite options defined at *www.guidancesoftware.com/training/Pages/ ence-certification-program.aspx*.

ACE Certification For acceptance into the ACE certification program, you must meet one of several prerequisite options defined at *http://accessdata.com/training/computer-forensics/ certification*.

Digital Forensics Public and Private Training Groups

Several small businesses, universities, and colleges have developed program certificates for successful completion of their coursework; these organizations can be divided into academic institutions and private training companies. The programs range from one day to several months of classroom work. Most academic institutions offer college credit for their courses, and private training companies typically offer continuing education credits. For more information on these programs, refer to the Web sites listed in the following sections. To find other programs, do a search on "digital forensics certificates."

Academic Institutions Here are some leading schools offering digital forensics certificates:

- British Columbia Institute of Technology, *www.bcit.ca/study/programs/526cascert*
- California State at Fullerton, *http://extension.fullerton.edu/ProfessionalDevelopment/ Certificates/Computer-Forensics1*
- Century College (cloud virtualization forensics), *www.century.edu/futurestudents/ programs/pnd.aspx?id=9*
- Champlain College, *http://digitalforensics.champlain.edu*
- College of San Mateo, *http://collegeofsanmateo.edu/cis/degrees_forensics_cs.asp*
- DeVry University, *www.devry.edu/degree-programs/college-engineering-information- sciences/computer-forensics-about.html*

- University of Central Florida, *http://programs.online.ucf.edu/wp-content/themes/ programs/catalog-archive/20122013/programs.online.ucf.edu/current/grad/college-of- engineering-and-computer-science-graduate-degree-programs/digital-forensics-ms/*

- University of Maryland University College, *www.umuc.edu/academic-programs/ masters-degrees/digital-forensics-and-cyber-investigations.cfm*

- University of Rhode Island, *www.dfcsc.uri.edu/academics/*

- West Virginia University, *www.lcsee.statler.wvu.edu/forensics/*

- Wilber Wright College, *www.ccc.edu/colleges/wright/programs/Pages/Computer- Security-and-Forensic-Investigation-Basic-Certificate.aspx*

Private Training Companies The following list shows a few private training companies offering digital forensics certificates:

- ed2go, *www.ed2go.com/career/training-programs/forensic-computer-training*

- Computer Forensic Training Center Online, *www.cftco.com*

- NW3C, *www.nw3c.org/home*

Web Site References The following Web sites collect and list resources for digital forensics training:

- Guide to Online Programs for Digital Forensics, *http://programs.online.ucf.edu/current/ grad/college-of-engineering-and-computer-science-graduate-degree-programs/digital- forensics-ms/*

- Computer Forensics Education - Course Directory, *www.forensicfocus.com/computer- forensics-education-directory*

Digital Forensics References

This book is only the beginning of digital forensics and investigations. To master all levels of digital forensics, you should familiarize yourself with the works of other authors who have made significant contributions to this profession. This appendix lists international standards, digital forensics books, operating system books, and legal references that can expand your skills and understanding of conducting digital investigations. In addition, you'll find helpful Web links, e-mail lists, professional journals, and a sample cloud service level agreement.

International Organization of Standards 27000

The International Organization of Standards (ISO) is an organization that publishes guidelines for many manufactured items as well as digital forensics functions. It's in the process of developing additional standards for digital forensics so that collected evidence can be shared more easily. The 27000 series of ISO documents deals with digital security, and the following relate to digital forensics:

- ISO/IEC 27037:2012 – Information technology – Security techniques – Guidelines for identification, collection, acquisition, and preservation of digital evidence

- ISO/IEC 27038:2014 – Information technology – Security techniques – Specification for digital redaction

- ISO/IEC 27039 – Information technology – Security techniques – Selection, deployment and operation of intrusion detection and prevention systems

- ISO/IEC 27040 – Information technology – Security techniques – Storage security

- ISO/IEC 27041 – Information technology – Security techniques – Guidelines for assuring suitability and adequacy of incident investigative methods

- ISO/IEC 27042 – Information technology – Security techniques – Guidelines for the analysis and interpretation of digital evidence

- ISO/IEC 27043 – Information technology – Security techniques – Incident investigation principles and processes

- ISO/IEC 27050 – Information technology – Security techniques – Electronic discovery

For more information, see *www.iso27001security.com/html/27000.html*.

Digital Forensics Reference Books

In recent years, several books on digital forensics have been published. The following sections list a variety of books that can expand your technical skills and understanding of digital investigations. Some of these books might be out of print and not available through retail bookstores, such as Amazon and Barnes & Noble. For out-of-print books, check with Abe Books (*www.abebooks.com*) to see whether books you're looking for are in stock. Abe Books and other used book dealers can search other resources for unique out-of-print books.

Brown, Christopher L. T. *Computer Evidence: Collection & Preservation*. Course Technology, 2009 (ISBN 10:1584506997).

Bunting, Steve and William Wei. *EnCase Computer Forensics: The Official EnCE: EnCase Certified Examiner Study Guide*. Sybex, 2012 (ISBN 0470901063).

Caloyhannides, Michael A. *Computer Forensics and Privacy*. Artrech House Publishers, 2001 (ISBN 1580532837).

Carrier, Brian. *File System Forensic Analysis*. Addison-Wesley Professional, 2005 (ISBN 0321268172).

Carvey, Harlan. *Windows Forensic Analysis DVD Toolkit*, 2nd ed. Syngress, 2009 (ISBN 1597494224).

Casey, Eoghan, ed. *Digital Evidence and Computer Crime*. Academic Press, 2011 (ISBN 0123742684).

Casey, Eoghan, ed. *Handbook of Computer Crime Investigation, Forensic Tools and Technology*. Academic Press, 1997 (ISBN 0121631036).

Clark, Franklin and Ken Diliberto. *Investigating Computer Crime*. CRC Press, 1996 (ISBN 0849381584).

Fowler, Kevvie. *SQL Server Forensic Analysis*. Addison-Wesley Professional, 2008 (ISBN 0321544366).

Garrison, Clint P. *Digital Forensics for Network, Internet, and Cloud Computing: A Forensic Evidence Guide for Moving Targets and Data*. Syngress, 2010 (ISBN 1597495379).

Icove, David, Karl Seger, and William VonStorch. *Computer Crime, A Crimefighter's Handbook*. O'Reilly & Associates, Inc., 1995 (ISBN 1565920864).

Jones, Keith J., Richard Bejtlich, and Curtis W. Rose. *Real Digital Forensics: Computer Security and Incident Response*. Addison-Wesley Professional, 2005 (ISBN 0321240693).

Kruse II, Warren G. and Jay G. Heiser. *Computer Forensics: Incident Response Essentials*. Pearson Education, 2001 (ISBN 0201707195).

Kubansiak, Ryan R., Sean Morrissey, and Jesse Varsalone (tech. ed.). *Mac OS X, iPod, and iPhone Forensic Analysis DVD Toolkit*. Syngress, 2008 (ISBN 1597492973).

Malin, Cameron H., James M. Aquilma, and Eoghan Casey. *Malware Forensics: Investigating and Analyzing Malicious Code*. Syngress, 2008 (ISBN 159749268X).

Martin, James P. and Harry Cendrowski. *Cloud Computing and Electronic Discovery*. Wiley, 2014 (ISBN 1118764307).

Mel, H. X. and Dons Baker. *Cryptography Decrypted*. Addison-Wesley, 2001 (ISBN 0201616475).

Pogue, Chris, Cory Altheide, and Todd Haverkos. *UNIX and Linux Forensic Analysis DVD Toolkit*. Syngress, 2008 (ISBN 1597492698).

Prosise, Chris, Kevin Mandia, and Matt Pepe. *Incident Response: Computer Forensics*. McGraw-Hill, 2014 (ISBN 0071798684).

Quick, Darren, Ben Martini, and Raymond Choo. *Cloud Storage Forensics*. Syngress, 2013 (ISBN 9780124199705).

Rosenblatt, Kenneth S. *High-Technology Crime*. KSK Publications, 1995 (ISBN 0964817101).

Ruan, Keyun. *Cybercrime and Cloud Forensics: Applications for Investigation Processes*. IGI Global, 2012 (ISBN 1466626623).

Sammes, A. J. and Brian Jenkinson. *Forensic Computing*, 2nd ed. Springer, 2007 (ISBN 1846283973).

Shavers, Brett, and Eric Zimmerman. *X-Ways Forensics Practitioner's Guide*. Syngress, 2009 (ISBN 0124116051).

Stephenson, Peter. *Investigating Computer-Related Crime*. CRC Press, 2000 (ISBN 0849322189).

MS-DOS Reference Books

The following books are good references on how to use MS-DOS and how to create your own DOS batch files. Some of these books might be out of print. If you can't find them at a local bookstore, try searching for them on eBay or at *www.half.com*.

Cooper, Jim. *Special Edition Using MS-DOS 6.22*, 3rd Edition. Que, 2002 (ISBN 0789725738).

Gookin, Dan. *DOS for Dummies*, 3rd Edition. Wiley Publishing, Inc., 1999 (ISBN 0764503618).

Menefee, Craig and Nick Anis. *Harnessing DOS 6.0, Batch File and Command Macro Power*. Bantam Computer Books, 1993 (ISBN 0553351885).

Windows Reference Books

The better you understand the many versions of Windows operating systems, the better you understand what data you're looking for and recovering. For a current list of Windows OS and application books, see Microsoft Press (*www.microsoftpressstore.com*). In addition, you should search for the latest Windows books at your favorite retail provider's Web site.

Linux Reference Books

Linux is becoming more popular with end users and digital forensics examiners. The more you know and understand about Linux, the easier it is to use. It makes dynamic control of processes possible, which is beneficial to digital forensics examiners.

Helmke, Matthew. *Ubuntu Unleashed*. Sams Publishing, 2014 (ISBN 0672336936).

Rankin, Kyle. *Knoppix Hacks: 100 Industrial-Strength Tips and Tools*. O'Reilly Media, Inc., 2004 (ISBN 0596007876).

Siever, Ellen, et al. *Linux in a Nutshell: A Desktop Quick Reference.* O'Reilly Media, Inc., 2000 (ISBN 0596000251).

Sobell, Mark G. *A Practical Guide to Linux Commands, Editors, and Shell Programming.* Prentice Hall PTR, 2012 (ISBN 013308504X).

Tyler, Chris. *Fedora Linux: A Complete Guide to Red Hat's Community Distribution.* O'Reilly Media, Inc., 2006 (ISBN 0596526822).

Legal Reference Books

The following books are guides on expert testimony:

Babitsky, Steven and James J. Mangraviti, Jr. *How to Become a Dangerous Expert Witness: Advanced Techniques and Strategies.* SEAK, Inc., 2005 (ISBN 1892904276).

Babitsky, Steven, James J. Mangraviti, Jr., and Christopher J. Todd. *The Comprehensive Forensic Services Manual: The Essential Resources for All Experts.* SEAK, Inc., 2000 (ISBN 1892904071).

Babitsky, Steven, James J. Mangraviti, Jr., and Christopher J. Todd. *The Comprehensive Forensic Services Manual: The Essential Resources for All Experts.* SEAK, Inc., 2002 Supplement (ISBN 1892904225).

Smith, Fred Chris and Rebecca Gurley Bace. *A Guide to Forensic Testimony: The Art and Practice of Presenting Testimony as an Expert Technical Witness.* Addison-Wesley Professional, 2002 (ISBN 0201752794).

Web Sites

Association of Certified Fraud Examiners, *www.acfe.com*

CERIAS, *www.cerias.purdue.edu/site/research/forensics/*

CERT, *www.cert.org*

Champlain College, Computer & Digital Forensics, *http://digitalforensics.champlain.edu*

Computer Crime Research Center, *www.crime-research.org*

Computer Forensic Analysis, *www.porcupine.org/forensics/*

Computer Forensics, Cybercrime and Steganography Resources, *www.forensics.nl*

Computer Technology Investigators Network, *www.ctin.org*

Digital Forensic Investigator, *www.dfinews.com*

Digital Forensic Research Workshop, *www.dfrws.org*

FBI Laboratory, *www.fbi.gov/news/stories/2013/january/piecing-together-digital-evidence*

FBI's Forensic Science Communications, *www.fbi.gov/about-us/lab/forensic-science-communications*

Forensic Focus, *www.forensicfocus.com*

High Tech Crime Consortium, *www.hightechcrimecops.org*

International Federation for Information Processing, *www.ifip.org*

International High Technology Crime Investigation Association, *www.htcia.org*

Journal of Digital Forensics, Security and Law, *www.jdfsl.org*

Open Source Digital Forensics, *www.opensourceforensics.org*

Penguin Sleuth, *http://penguinsleuth.org*

SANS, *www.sans.org*

Sleuth Kit, *www.sleuthkit.org*

Source Forge, Digital Forensics Tool Testing Images, *http://dftt.sourceforge.net*

US-CERT, *www.us-cert.gov*

Steganalysis References The following are useful references for learning more about steganalysis methods:

"Multi-class Blind Steganalysis for JPEG Images" (Tomas Pevny and Jessica Fridrich, *http:// dde.binghamton.edu/tomas/pdfs/pev06-spie.pdf*, 2010)

"JPEG steganography detection with Benford's Law" (Panagiotis Andriotis, George Oikonomou, and Theo Tryfonas, *www.fortoo.eu/m/page-media/4/jpeg-steganography.pdf*, 2013)

"Steganalysis of Images Created Using Current Steganography Software" (Neil F. Johnson and Sushil Jajodia, *www.jjtc.com/ihws98/jjgmu.html*, 1998)

E-mail Lists

Computer Forensics World, *www.computerforensicsworld.com/index.php*

Mobile Phone Forensics, *www.mobilephoneforensics.com*

X-Ways Support Forum, *www.winhex.net*

Yahoo! Groups

Computer Forensics Tool Testing (CFTT), *https://groups.yahoo.com/neo/groups/cftt/info*

Mobile Phone Forensics, *https://groups.yahoo.com/neo/groups/mobile-cell-phone-forensics/info*

Professional Journals

Digital Forensics Magazine (www.digitalforensicsmagazine.com)

Digital Investigations (www.journals.elsevier.com/digital-investigation)

Forensic Science Communications (www.fbi.gov/about-us/lab/forensic-science-communications)

International Journal of Cyber Criminology (www.cybercrimejournal.com)

International Journal of Cyber-Security and Digital Forensics (http://sdiwc.net/security-journal/ index.php)

International Journal of Electronic Security and Digital Forensics (www.inderscience.com/ jhome.php?jcode=ijesdf)

International Journal of Forensic Computer Science (www.ijofcs.org)

Journal of Digital Forensics, Security and Law (www.jdfsl.org)

Digital Forensics Lab Considerations

In Chapter 2, you learned what's needed for a digital forensics lab. This appendix addresses some additional considerations for planning and operating a lab.

International Lab Certification

In addition to the American Society of Crime Laboratory Directors (ASCLD; *www.ascld. org*), the International Organization of Standards (ISO) has requirements for standard processes that transcend national boundaries. An organization can become ISO certified when it has integrated processes to ensure that established requirements in products and services are met consistently. Of special interest to digital forensics examiners are the following ISO standards that can be applied to lab operation:

- ISO 9000: Quality management system in production environments
- ISO 9001: Quality management
- ISO 9069: Software quality model
- ISO 9241: Ergonomic requirements for office work with visual display
- ISO 17025: General requirements for competence of test and calibration laboratories
- ISO 27001: Information technology–Security techniques–Information security management systems

NOTE

For more information on ISO standards, visit *www.iso.org*, *www.ansi. org/standards_activities/iso_programs/overview.aspx?menuid=3*, and *www.fasor.com/iso25*.

Considering Office Ergonomics

Because digital investigations often require hours of processing drives for evidence, your workspace should be as comfortable as possible to prevent repetitive-motion injuries and other computer work-related injuries. Ergonomics is the study of designing equipment to meet the human need for comfort and allow improved productivity and involves psychology, anatomy, and physiology. Understanding psychology helps designers create equipment that people can easily understand how to use. Ergonomic design also considers anatomy to make sure the equipment correctly fits the person using it. Physiology helps determine how much effort or energy the person using the equipment must expend.

To ensure an ergonomic workspace, review the following questions when arranging your workspace and selecting lab furniture:

- *Desk or workstation table*—Is the desk placed at the correct height for you? Do you need a chair that's lower or higher than normal to make the desktop easy to reach and comfortable to use? Are your wrists straight when sitting? Is this position comfortable? Are the heels of your hands in a comfortable position? Do they exert too much pressure on the desktop? Do you need a keyboard or mouse pad?

- *Chair*—Can your chair's height be adjusted? Is the back of the chair too long or too short? Is the seat portion too long or too short for your thighs? Are the seat and back padded enough to be comfortable? Can you sit up straight when viewing the monitor? Are your elbows in a comfortable position while working? How do your shoulders and back feel while sitting and working at the workstation? Is your head facing the monitor, or do you have to turn your head because you can't position the chair in front of the monitor?

- *Workbench*—Is the workbench for your lab facility at the correct height when you're standing in front of it? Can you reach the back of the bench easily without having to stand on a stool?

Besides furniture, consider the ergonomics of your keyboard and mouse. These two items probably contribute to more repetitive-motion injuries than any other devices because they were designed for moderate but not extensive use. Using the keyboard for several hours at a time can be painful and cause physical problems. Make sure your wrists are straight when you're working with a keyboard or mouse, even if these items are ergonomically designed.

If you work with computers for hours in one position, you'll injure yourself. No matter how well the furniture, keyboard, or mouse is designed, always take breaks to stretch and rest your body.

Considering Environmental Conditions

Your lab's ventilation and temperature also contribute to your comfort and productivity. Although a typical desktop computer uses standard household electricity, computers get warm as they run. Unless you invest in a liquid-cooled computer case for your forensic workstation, a standard desktop computer generates heat. The more workstations you're running, the hotter your lab, so the room needs adequate air conditioning and ventilation. Consult with your building's facility coordinator to determine whether the room can be upgraded to handle your current and expected computing needs.

Use the following checklist of heating, ventilation, and air-conditioning (HVAC) system questions when planning your digital forensics laboratory:

- How large is the room, and how much air moves through it per minute?

- Can the room handle the increased heat that workstations generate?

- How many workstations will be placed in this room? What's the maximum number of workstations the room can handle?

- Can the room handle the heat output from a small RAID server?

Lighting

Lighting is often an overlooked environmental issue in digital forensics labs. Most offices have too many lights at the wrong illumination, which can cause headaches and eyestrain. Several vendors offer natural or full-spectrum lighting, which is less fatiguing than standard incandescent or fluorescent lights, although it doesn't have any health benefits.

In 1986, the Food and Drug Administration (FDA) issued a Health Fraud Notice about "false and misleading" claims and "gross deceptions" by light bulb and lamp manufacturers on the benefits of full-spectrum lighting (*FDA Enforcement Report: Health Fraud Notice*, 1986, WL 59812).

If the lighting in your lab is a problem, consult with facility management and find out what products can best meet your needs. For additional information on dealing with eyestrain, see *www.apple.com/about/ergonomics/vision.html*.

Considering Structural Design Factors

The physical construction of your digital forensics lab is another factor to consider. Your lab should be a safe, secure, lockable room. Processing a drive or creating an image can take anywhere from a few hours to several days or weeks. When you must leave evidence unattended overnight, you need a secure location—a room that no unauthorized people can access without your control.

The National Industrial Security Program Operating Manual (NISPOM), Chapter 5, Section 8, page 1, "Construction Requirements," gives an overview of how to build a secure lab. See *www.dss.mil/documents/ odaa/nispom2006-5220.pdf* for details.

To ensure physical security, examine the facility's hardware, walls, ceiling, floors, and windows. Make sure only heavy-duty building material has been used in the construction. All hardware, such as door hinges on the outside of the lab, should be peened, pinned, brazed, or spot-welded to prevent removal.

Walls can be constructed of plaster, gypsum wallboard, metal panels, hardboard, wood, plywood, glass, wire mesh, expanded metal, or other materials offering resistance to and evidence of unauthorized entry. If you use insert panels, you need to install material that can reveal evidence of an attempt to gain entry.

Ceilings, like walls, can be constructed of plaster, gypsum wallboard, acoustic ceiling panels, hardboard, wood, plywood, ceiling tile, or other material that offers some sort of resistance and makes detection possible if access is attempted. False or drop ceilings in which the walls don't extend to the true ceiling because of hanging ceiling tile must be reinforced with wire mesh or 18-gauge expanded metal that extends from the top of the false wall to the true ceiling.

This material must overlap adjoining walls and should provide resistance so that attempted access can be detected.

If you have raised floors, which are common in data centers, look for large openings in the perimeter walls. If you find any, use the same types of material described for ceilings to make sure the floor provides resistance and shows evidence of someone attempting to access the lab.

Avoid windows on the lab exterior. If you're assigned a room with exterior windows, install additional material, such as wire mesh, on the inside to improve security. If your lab must be placed on an exterior wall, request an upper floor, not a ground floor. Also, make sure monitors face away from windows to prevent unauthorized people from being able to see what you're working on.

Doors can be wood (solid core) or metal and shouldn't have windows. If the door does have a window, it should have wire mesh in the glass for resistance so that attempted entries can be detected. The door's locking device should have a heavy-duty, built-in combination device or a high-quality key-locking doorknob. If you're using a key-locking doorknob, only authorized personnel should have a copy of the key.

Depending on your lab's location, you might need to install intrusion detection systems and fire alarms. Consult and contract with a bonded alarm company.

Determining Electrical Needs

You need enough electrical power to run workstations and other equipment; 15- and 20-amp service is preferred for electrical outlets. In addition, you should have enough electrical outlets spaced throughout the lab for easy access, eliminating the need for extension cords or electrical plug strips, which are potential fire hazards.

If you have adequate electrical power for your operation, power fluctuations aren't usually a problem unless you're in an area with poor electrical service. Most computers are fairly tolerant of power fluctuations, although they do cause electrical wear and tear on computer components. However, all electrical devices eventually fail, usually because of accumulated electrical voltage spikes. If your lab equipment exhibits unexplained failures, consult with your facilities manager to check for problems with electrical power.

In addition, uninterruptible power supply (UPS) units must be connected to all forensic workstations to reduce electrical problems. If a power failure occurs, a UPS unit enables you to continue working until you can shut down your computer safely. Most UPS units also block or filter electrical fluctuations, which helps minimize computer component problems that might corrupt and destroy evidence stored on sensitive magnetic media.

Planning for Communications

When you're planning voice and data communications, keep in mind that each examiner needs a telephone. Unless you're working in a TEMPEST environment, which has special voice and data access requirements, you can install a multiline Integrated Services Digital Network (ISDN) phone system in the lab. ISDN is the easiest way for lab personnel to handle incoming calls.

You also need dial-up or broadband Internet access. Digital forensics software vendors often provide updates and patches on their Web sites, and you need to be able to download them. Internet access is also needed to conduct research on evidence you find and to consult with other forensics professionals. However, don't keep your workstation connected to the Internet while conducting your analysis unless absolutely necessary. Internet connections can compromise your system's security, even with a firewall installed.

Setting up a local area network (LAN) for workstations in a lab enables you to transfer data to other examiners easily and makes operations run more smoothly. For example, you can share a RAID file server and printers on a LAN. This setup is especially useful when you have specialty printers connected to a print server. Using a central RAID server also saves time when you're copying large files, such as image files.

If your organization is part of a wide area network (WAN), consider having a separate computer used only to connect to the WAN to protect the security of your forensic workstations. By keeping your forensic workstations physically separate from the WAN, you eliminate any intentional or unintentional access to your evidence or work product. For example, although workstations on a WAN can receive notices to upgrade software, doing so while your forensic workstation is connected to the WAN can corrupt evidence. Isolating systems prevents this corruption.

Installing Fire-Suppression Systems

Any electrical device can cause a fire, although fires aren't common with computers. However, an electrical short in a computer might destroy a cable. If the power on a low-voltage cable is high enough, it could ignite other combustible items nearby. Computers can also cause fires if a hard disk's servo-voice coil actuators freeze because of damage to the drive. When this happens, the head assembly can't move. The disk's circuit card then applies more electrical power to actuators to try to move the head assembly, which passes too much power through the disk. Disk components can handle only so much power before they fail and overload the cables connecting the drive to the computer. When too much power is applied to these low-voltage cables, especially ribbon cables, sparks can fly, causing a fire.

Most offices are equipped with fire sprinkler systems and dry chemical fire extinguishers (B rated). For most forensics lab operations, these fire-suppression systems work well, and no additional protection is required. However, if your lab facility has raised floors, you might need to install a dry chemical fire-suppression system. If you have any concerns, contact your facility coordinator or the local fire marshal. For additional information on best practices for fire extinguishers, see *www.fia.uk.com/filemanager/root/site_assets/news/fia_best_practice_guide_2014_final_version_46193.pdf*. For information on computer room fire-suppression systems, see *www.cfm.va.gov/til/dManual/dmfpfire.pdf*.

DOS File System and Forensics Tools

This appendix gives you information about older file systems, such as Microsoft File Allocation Table (FAT) and Mac HFS and HFS+, and MS-DOS tools. It also introduces the MS-DOS forensics tools X-Ways Replica and Digital Intelligence DriveSpy, and there's a short discussion of how hexadecimal numbers relate to binary setting in bytes.

Overview of FAT Directory Structures

When Microsoft created the MS-DOS operating system, data was stored on floppy disks. Floppy disks have a limited maximum size, so the addressable storage space is small compared with modern hard disks. All floppy disks for Microsoft OSs use the FAT12 file system. (FAT file systems are explained in more detail in Chapter 5.) Because of the limited disk and memory space on older computers, Microsoft engineered FAT12 so that directory names could be only one to eight characters. Filenames could be up to eight characters, and file extensions could be zero to three characters. This naming scheme is often called the "8.3 naming convention." The characters in file extensions identify the file type, such as .doc for a Word document or .xls for an Excel spreadsheet.

When larger drives were developed, Microsoft reengineered FAT and created FAT16, which allows up to 2 GB of addressable storage space for drive partitions. With further advances in disk technologies, Microsoft created FAT32, which can access up to 2 terabytes (TB) or more of storage space. In MS-DOS 6.22, the same directory and filename conventions from FAT12 were carried over to FAT16. In Windows 95 and later, FAT32 maintains the eight-character maximum for filenames and three-character limit for file extensions.

When larger filenames than FAT12 and FAT16 allowed were needed, Microsoft developed Virtual FAT (VFAT). VFAT provides two filenames for every file: a long filename in what looks like Unicode format, displayed in a hexadecimal editor with null (00) values between each character, and a short filename that uses eight-character filenames and three-character extensions. The purpose of having both filenames is backward-compatibility with older Microsoft OSs and file systems. For example, Figure D-1 shows four files, one with a long filename (Market_Plan-31.txt) and three with short filenames. When you view Market_Plan-31.txt in MS-DOS with the dir command, you see its name converted to the short filename: Market~1.txt (see Figure D-2).

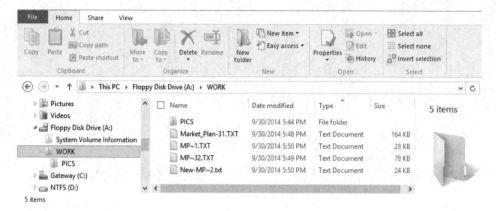

Figure D-1 Viewing filenaming in File Explorer
Courtesy of Microsoft Corporation

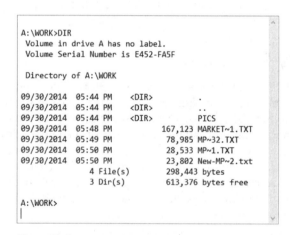

Figure D-2 Viewing filenaming in MS-DOS with the `dir` command
Courtesy of Microsoft Corporation

For older Windows OSs that run only FAT file systems, the forensics tool DriveSpy from Digital Intelligence (*www.digitalintelligence.com/software/disoftware/drivespy*) has excellent analysis and recovery capabilities. DriveSpy runs only from an MS-DOS prompt in Windows Vista or older OSs.

With DriveSpy, you can examine a directory structure to find its cluster position in a FAT file system. Continuing with the previous example, you can locate the cluster number for the Work directory with the DriveSpy `dir` command (see Figure D-3).

To display information listed in the directory, use the DriveSpy `cluster` command. Note that the cluster number for the Work directory is 2 in Figure D-3. To view this cluster's content, type Cluster 2 and press Enter (see Figure D-4).

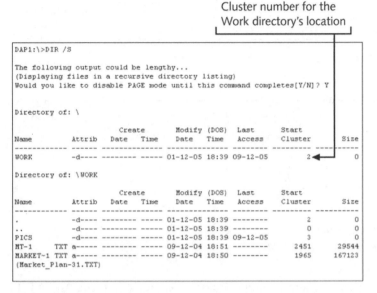

Figure D-3 illustration labels:

Cluster number for the Work directory's location

```
DAP1:\>DIR /S

The following output could be lengthy...
(Displaying files in a recursive directory listing)
Would you like to disable PAGE mode until this command completes[Y/N]? Y


Directory of: \

                     Create          Modify (DOS)  Last       Start
Name        Attrib   Date    Time    Date    Time  Access     Cluster    Size
----------  ------   ------- -----   ------- ----- -------    -------    ----
WORK        -d----   -------- -----  01-12-05 18:39 09-12-05       2          0

Directory of: \WORK

                     Create          Modify (DOS)  Last       Start
Name        Attrib   Date    Time    Date    Time  Access     Cluster    Size
----------  ------   ------- -----   ------- ----- -------    -------    ----
.           -d----   -------- -----  01-12-05 18:39 --------        2          0
..          -d----   -------- -----  01-12-05 18:39 --------        0          0
PICS        -d----   -------- -----  01-12-05 18:39 09-12-05        3          0
MT-1   TXT  a-----   -------- -----  09-12-04 18:51 --------     2451      29544
MARKET~1 TXT a-----  -------- -----  09-12-04 18:50 --------     1965     167123
(Market_Plan-31.TXT)
```

Figure D-3 Finding the Work directory's cluster number
Courtesy of Microsoft Corporation

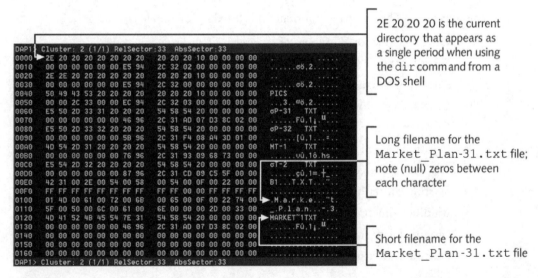

Figure D-4 callout labels:

2E 20 20 20 is the current directory that appears as a single period when using the dir command and from a DOS shell

Long filename for the Market_Plan-31.txt file; note (null) zeros between each character

Short filename for the Market_Plan-31.txt file

Figure D-4 Viewing the directory cluster content
Source: Digital Intelligence, *www.digitalintelligence.com*

Another useful tool that can run in Windows is the shareware Directory Snoop from Briggs Softworks (*www.briggsoft.com*). Directory Snoop is a convenient GUI tool for inspecting and recovering deleted data from disks. Figure D-5 shows an example of using Directory Snoop for FAT partitions. Note that no long filenames are listed in the bottom pane, which indicates that MS-DOS 6.22 or earlier was used to format the floppy disk and write data to it.

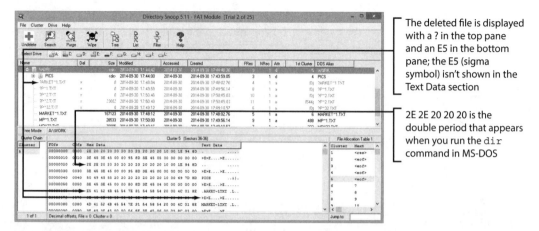

The deleted file is displayed with a ? in the top pane and an E5 in the bottom pane; the E5 (sigma symbol) isn't shown in the Text Data section

2E 2E 20 20 20 is the double period that appears when you run the `dir` command in MS-DOS

Figure D-5   Using Directory Snoop
Source: Briggs Softworks, *www.briggsoft.com*

FAT directories contain specific information about the files stored in them. All FAT directories start with a hexadecimal 2E followed by several hexadecimal 20 values. A hexadecimal 2E converts to the ASCII value for a period, and a hexadecimal 20 represents a space. (For an explanation of hexadecimal numbers, see "An Overview of Hexadecimal Numbering" later in this appendix.) The following information is listed for all files in a directory:

- Long filename for Windows 95 or later FAT disks
- Short filename (8.3 naming convention)
- Attributes assigned to the file
- Case and creation time in milliseconds
- Creation time of the file
- Creation date of the file
- Last access date of the file
- Starting cluster high-word for FAT32 file systems
- Modified timestamp
- Modified date stamp
- Starting cluster of the file (assigned by FAT when all links to the file are listed)
- File size

When a file is deleted in a FAT directory, a hexadecimal E5 is inserted as the filename's first character (see the callout in Figure D-5). If the file is renamed, an entry with the new filename is created, and the old filename is marked as deleted with the E5 value, just as though the file had been deleted. These entries aren't usually deleted from the directory. Figure D-6 shows a renamed file in a directory on a FAT12 drive. Notice the size of this renamed file and the byte size of the deleted file and the renamed file.

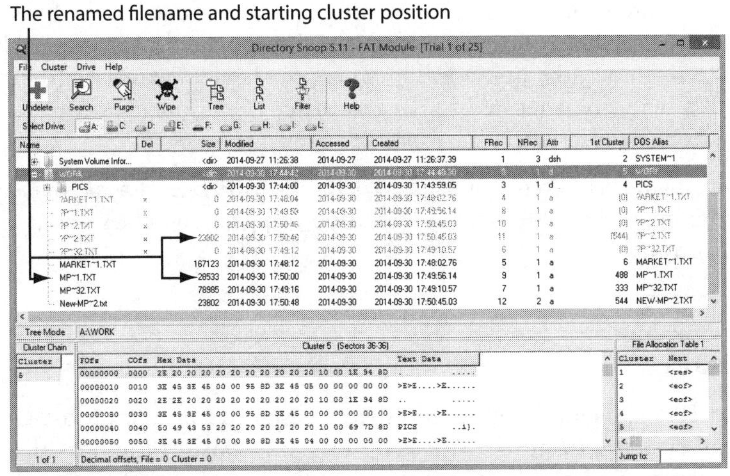

The renamed filename and starting cluster position

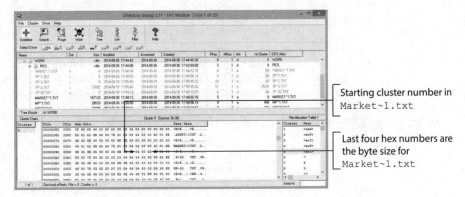

Figure D-6 Using Directory Snoop with a FAT12 drive
Source: Briggs Softworks, *www.briggsoft.com*

You can also reverse-engineer the starting cluster position and file size. These values are listed in hexadecimal format in the directory. To convert hexadecimal values to decimal, use the Windows scientific calculator:

1. In Windows, click **Start**, type **Calculator**, and click the third **Calculator** icon in the list of calculators.

2. Click **View**, **Programmer** from the Calculator menu.

3. In the Programmer Calculator window, click the **Hex** option button.

4. Using the keyboard or number buttons, enter the hexadecimal value you want to convert, and then click the **Dec** option button.

As shown in Figure D-7, the last four hexadecimal numbers are the byte size for the `Market~1.txt` file. When converting these numbers from hex to decimal, you read them from right to left: 00 02 8C D3, in this example. What's displayed with the `dir` command or in File Explorer might be slightly smaller than what's converted. Figure D-7 also shows `Market-1.txt`'s starting cluster number in hex. To convert these numbers to decimal, you enter them from right to left: 00 06.

Figure D-7 Converting from hexadecimal to decimal
Source: Briggs Softworks, *www.briggsoft.com*, and Microsoft Corporation

Note the decimal value 6 entered in the calculator. In FAT directory entries, the file's starting cluster position is at offset 1A hexadecimal or 26 decimal from the first position where the filename is displayed. Remember, the first position where the filename appears has the starting value of 0. The file's byte size is located starting at offset 1C hexadecimal or 28 decimal. These values are read from right to left.

In digital forensics investigations, often you need to determine the size of a file that has been deleted and overwritten by a newer file. This information can give you clues about copies of the deleted file on other disks.

DOS Forensics Tools

During the 1980s and 1990s, digital forensics tools were designed to run on MS-DOS. These tools can collect digital evidence from FAT drives on PCs and consist of utilities that handle tasks such as data acquisitions of file slack space and unallocated space, text string searches, and other functions. Most of these tools can fit on a forensic boot floppy disk, which is used to access a PC's drive to acquire and examine its contents. Currently, only a few vendors still sell DOS forensics tools, such as these two:

- *X-Ways Replica*—This disk forensic acquisition program can run from a floppy disk or CD running Microsoft DOS 6.22. For more information, see *www.x-ways.net/replica.html*.
- *DriveSpy*—This DOS command-line program can acquire forensic images, search for text and hexadecimal data strings, view FAT links showing the cluster where data is located (useful for finding fragments of residual data), and other analysis functions. For more information, see *www.digitalintelligence.com/software/disoftware/drivespy*.

Legacy Mac File Systems

Chapter 7 mentioned legacy Mac file systems. Table D-1 shows the Hierarchical File System (HFS) block positions, and Table D-2 shows the Extended Format File System (HFS+) byte offset positons.

Table D-1 HFS system files

HFS block position	HFS structure	Purpose of structure
0 and 1	Boot block	Startup volume containing boot instructions; also stores system files and Finder information.
2	Master Directory Block (MDB)	Contains volume creation date and time and location of other system files, such as Volume Bitmap. A duplicate of this file called the Alternate MDB is located at the second-to-last block on the volume. Its purpose is to provide information to OS disk utilities.
3	Volume Bitmap	Tracks used and unused blocks on the volume.
	Catalog	Lists all files and directories on the volume. It's a B*-tree file that uses the extents overflow file to coordinate all file allocations to the volume.
	Extents overflow file	This B*-tree file lists the extra extents, which are the allocated blocks used to store data files.

Table D-2 HFS+ system files

HFS+ byte offset (fixed starting position)	HFS+ structure	Purpose of structure
	Boot blocks	No change from HFS.
1024	Volume Information Block (VIB)	Replaces the MDB used in HFS.
Not fixed	Allocation file	Tracks available free blocks on the volume; replaces the HFS Volume Bitmap.
Not fixed	Extents overflow file	For files with more than eight extents, additional extents are recorded and managed through this B*-tree system file.
Not fixed	Catalog	Similar to an HFS catalog, this improved version allows up to eight extents for each file's forks. It's a B*-tree file.
Not fixed	Attributes file	Stores new file attribute information that isn't available in HFS. The new attributes are inline data attribute records, fork data attribute records, and extension attribute records.
Not fixed	Startup file	New to HFS+, this file can boot non-HFS and non-HFS+ volumes.
Not fixed	Alternate VIB	Same file as the HFS Alternate MDB.
	Reserved (512 bytes)	Last sector of the volume; used by Apple during manufacturing.

© 2016 Cengage Learning®

For more information on B*-tree and HFS, see *http://tldp.org/HOWTO/Filesystems-HOWTO-7.html*.

An Overview of Hexadecimal Numbering

To understand hexadecimal numbering, you need to understand binary data. Information in a computer is stored in binary digits called "bits." Like a light switch, a bit is either off or on. Bits set to off are given the value 0, and bits set to on are given the value 1. Bits can be turned on or off, depending on what values they're assigned by programs. ASCII has established a list of bit patterns associated with letters, numbers, and other symbols. These bits are grouped into bytes, which consist of 8 consecutive bits.

Computers communicate and store data only in binary fashion: 0s and 1s. When you're looking at raw binary data, it's difficult to interpret all these 0s and 1s and determine where bytes start and end. To make binary data easier to view, computer scientists apply the base-16 numbering system to bits. You're familiar with base-10 numbering, in which numbers are represented as 0, 1, 2, 3, 4, 5, 6, 7, 8, and 9, and the next number after 9 is 10. In base-16 numbering (also called "hexadecimal" or just "hex"), the symbols are 0, 1, 2, 3, 4, 5, 6, 7, 8, 9, A, B, C, D, E, and F, and the next number after F is defined as 10. Counting bits in base-16 numbering is much easier than in base-10 numbering. Typically, a 0x is added at the front of a number to indicate that it's a hexadecimal value. So, for example, the hexadecimal number 9 is written as 0x09, and the number B is written as 0x0B. The 0 between the x and the hexadecimal number is used to provide a place for numbers greater than 0x09, such as 0x12 (with the equivalent decimal value of 18).

To determine the numeric value for decimal or hexadecimal binary digits, you read the pattern from right to left and add the value of the bit's position. For example, the letter A pattern of 01000001 is 0x41 in hexadecimal, as shown in Table D-3, and for the lowercase letter a, the pattern is 01100001, as shown in Table D-4.

Table D-3 Calculating decimal and hexadecimal bit patterns for the letter A

Hexadecimal numbers	80	40	20	10	8	4	2	1
Binary numbers	0	1	0	0	0	0	0	1
Decimal numbers	128	64	32	16	8	4	2	1

© 2016 Cengage Learning®

Adding the decimal values in Table D-3 from right to left results in $1 + 64 = 65$. For the hexadecimal values, it's $0x01 + 0x40 = 0x41$.

Table D-4 Calculating decimal and hexadecimal bit patterns for the letter a

Hexadecimal numbers	80	40	20	10	8	4	2	1
Binary numbers	0	1	1	0	0	0	0	1
Decimal numbers	128	64	32	16	8	4	2	1

© 2016 Cengage Learning®

For the lowercase letter a, add the decimal values in Table D-4 from right to left: $1 + 32 + 64 = 97$. For the hexadecimal values, it's $0x01 + 0x20 + 0x40 = 0x61$.

For more information on bits, bytes, and hexadecimal numbering, refer to the following Web sites:

- *www.theproblemsite.com/codes/hex.asp*
- *http://homepage.smc.edu/morgan_david/cs40/hex-system.htm*
- *www.mathsisfun.com/hexadecimals.html*
- *http://whatis.techtarget.com/definition/hexadecimal*
- *www.tcpipguide.com/free/t_BinaryInformationandRepresentationBitsBytesNibbles-2.htm*

acquisition The process of creating a duplicate image of data; one of the required functions of digital forensics tools.

Advanced Forensic Format (AFF) An open-source data acquisition format that stores image data and metadata. File extensions include .afd for segmented image files and .afm for AFF metadata.

affidavit A notarized document, given under penalty of perjury, that investigators create to detail their findings. This document is often used to justify issuing a warrant or to deal with abuse in a corporation. Also called a "declaration" when the document is unnotarized.

allegation A charge made against someone or something before proof has been found.

allocation block In the Mac file system, a group of consecutive logical blocks assembled in a volume when a file is saved. *See also* logical block.

alternate data streams Ways in which data can be appended to a file (intentionally or not) and potentially obscure evidentiary data. In NTFS, alternate data streams become an additional file attribute.

American Society of Crime Laboratory Directors (ASCLD) A national society that sets the standards, management, and audit procedures for labs used in crime analysis, including digital forensics labs used by the police, FBI, and similar organizations.

American Standard Code for Information Interchange (ASCII) An 8-bit coding scheme that assigns numeric values to up to 256 characters, including letters, numerals, punctuation marks, control characters, and other symbols.

approved secure container A fireproof container locked by a key or combination.

areal density The number of bits per square inch of a disk platter.

attorney-client privilege (ACP) Communication between an attorney and client about legal matters is protected as confidential communications. The purpose of having confidential communications is to promote honest and open dialogue between an attorney and client. This confidential information must not be shared with unauthorized people.

attribute ID In NTFS, an MFT record field containing metadata about the file or folder and the file's data or links to the file's data.

authorized requester In a private-sector environment, the person who has the right to request an investigation, such as the chief security officer or chief intelligence officer.

Automated Fingerprint Identification System (AFIS) A computerized system for identifying fingerprints that's connected to a central database; used to identify criminal suspects and review thousands of fingerprint samples at high speed.

B*-tree A Mac file that organizes the directory hierarchy and file block mapping for File Manager. Files are represented as nodes (objects); leaf nodes contain the actual file data.

bad block inode In the Linux file system, the inode that tracks bad sectors on a drive.

bitmap images Collections of dots, or pixels, in a grid format that form a graphic.

bit-shifting The process of shifting one or more digits in a binary number to the left or right to produce a different value.

bit-stream copy A bit-by-bit duplicate of data on the original storage medium. This process is usually called "acquiring an image," "making an image," or "forensic copy."

bit-stream image The file where the bit-stream copy is stored; usually referred to as an "image," "image save," or "image file."

block-wise hashing The process of hashing all sectors of a file and then comparing them with sectors on a suspect's disk drive to determine whether there are any remnants of the original file that couldn't be recovered.

boot block A block in the Linux file system containing the bootstrap code used to start the system.

Boot.ini A file that specifies the Windows path installation and a variety of other startup options.

BootSect.dos If a machine has multiple booting OSs, NTLDR reads BootSect.dos, which is a hidden file, to determine the address (boot sector location) of each OS. *See also* NT Loader (Ntldr).

bootstrap process Information contained in ROM that a computer accesses during startup; this information tells the computer how to access the OS and hard drive.

brute-force attack The process of trying every combination of characters—letters, numbers, and special characters typically found on a keyboard—to find a matching password or passphrase value for an encrypted file.

business case A document that provides justification to upper management or a lender for purchasing new equipment, software, or other tools when upgrading your facility. In many instances, a business case shows how upgrades will benefit the company.

carving The process of recovering file fragments that are scattered across a disk.

catalog An area of the Mac file system used to maintain the relationships between files and directories on a volume.

Certified Computer Examiner (CCE) A certification from the International Society of Forensic Computer Examiners.

Certified Cyber Forensics Professional (CCFP) A certification from ISC^2 for completing the education and work experience and passing the exam.

Certified Forensic Computer Examiner (CFCE) A certificate awarded by IACIS at completion of all portions of the exam.

chain of custody The route evidence takes from the time the investigator obtains it until the case is closed or goes to court.

client/server architecture A network architecture in which each computer or process on the network is a client or server. Clients request services from a server, and a server processes requests from clients.

cloud service providers (CSPs) Vendors that provide on-demand network access to a shared pool of resources (typically remote data storage or Web applications).

clumps In the Mac file system, groups of contiguous allocation blocks used to keep file fragmentation to a minimum.

clusters Storage allocation units composed of groups of sectors. Clusters are 512, 1024, 2048, or 4096 bytes each.

Code Division Multiple Access (CDMA) A widely used digital cell phone technology that makes use of spread-spectrum modulation to spread the signal across a wide range of frequencies.

codes of professional conduct or responsibility External rules that often have the effect of law in limiting professionals' actions; breach of these rules can result in discipline, including suspension or loss of a license to practice and civil and criminal liability.

community cloud A shared cloud service that provides access to common or shared data.

Computer Forensics Tool Testing (CFTT) A project sponsored by the National Institute of Standards and Technology to manage research on digital forensics tools.

computer-generated records Data generated by a computer, such as system log files or proxy server logs.

computer-stored records Digital files generated by a person, such as electronic spreadsheets.

Computer Technology Investigators Network (CTIN) A nonprofit group based in Seattle-Tacoma, WA, composed of law enforcement members, private corporation security professionals, and other security professionals whose aim is to improve the quality of high-technology investigations in the Pacific Northwest.

configuration management The process of keeping track of all upgrades and patches you apply to your computer's OS and applications.

conflicting out The practice of opposing attorneys trying to prevent you from testifying by claiming you have discussed the case with them and, therefore, have a conflict of interest.

contingency fees Payments that depend on the content of the expert's testimony or the outcome of the case.

cover-media In steganalysis, the original file with no hidden message. *See also* stego-media.

covert surveillance Observing people or places without being detected, often using electronic equipment, such as video cameras or key stroke/screen capture programs.

curriculum vitae (CV) An extensive outline of your professional history that includes education, training, work, and what cases you have worked on as well as training you have conducted, publications you have contributed to, and professional associations and awards.

Cyclic Redundancy Check (CRC) A mathematical algorithm that translates a file into a unique hexadecimal value.

cylinder A column of tracks on two or more disk platters.

data block A block in the Linux file system where directories and files are stored on a drive.

data compression The process of coding data from a larger form to a smaller form.

data fork The part of a Mac file containing the file's actual data, both user-created data and data written by applications, as well as resource map and header information, window locations, and icons. *See also* resource fork.

data recovery Retrieving files that were deleted accidentally or purposefully.

data runs Cluster addresses where files are stored on a drive's partition outside the MFT record. Data runs are used for non-resident MFT file records. A data run record field consists of three components; the first component defines the size in bytes needed to store the second and third components' content.

defense in depth (DiD) The NSA's approach to implementing a layered network defense strategy. It focuses on three modes of protection: people, technology, and operations.

demosaicing The process of converting raw picture data to another format, such as JPEG or TIF.

deposition A formal examination in which you're questioned under oath with only the opposing parties, your attorney, and a court reporter present. There's no judge or jury. The purpose of a deposition is to give the opposing counsel a chance to preview your testimony before trial.

deposition banks Libraries of previously given testimony that law firms can access.

deprovisioning Deallocating cloud resources that were assigned to a user or an organization. *See also* provisioning.

device drivers Files containing instructions for the OS for hardware devices, such as the keyboard, mouse, and video card.

digital evidence Evidence consisting of information stored or transmitted in electronic form.

Digital Evidence First Responder (DEFR) A professional who secures digital evidence at the scene and ensures its viability while transporting it to the lab.

Digital Evidence Specialist (DES) An expert who analyzes digital evidence and determines whether additional specialists are needed.

digital forensics Applying investigative procedures for a legal purpose; involves the analysis of digital evidence as well as obtaining search warrants, maintaining a chain of custody, validating with mathematical hash functions, using validated tools, ensuring repeatability, reporting, and presenting evidence as an expert witness.

digital forensics lab A lab dedicated to digital investigations; typically, it has a variety of computers, OSs, and forensics software.

digital investigations The process of conducting forensic analysis of systems suspected of containing evidence related to an incident or a crime.

discovery Efforts to gather information before a trial by demanding documents, depositions, interrogatories (written questions answered in writing under oath), and written requests for admissions of fact.

discovery deposition The opposing attorney sets the deposition and often conducts the equivalent of both direct and cross-examination. A discovery deposition is considered part of the discovery process. *See also* deposition.

disqualification The process by which an expert witness is excluded from testifying.

distributed denial-of-service (DDoS) attacks A type of DoS attack in which other online machines are used, without the owners' knowledge, to launch an attack.

double-indirect pointers The inode pointers in the second layer or group of an OS. *See also* inodes.

drive slack Unused space in a cluster between the end of an active file and the end of the cluster. It can contain deleted files, deleted e-mail, or file fragments. Drive slack is made up of both file slack and RAM slack. *See also* file slack *and* RAM slack.

Electronic Communications Privacy Act (ECPA) A law enacted in 1986 to extend the Wiretap Act to cover e-mail and other data transmitted via the Internet.

electronically erasable programmable read-only memory (EEPROM) A type of nonvolatile memory that can be reprogrammed electrically, without having to physically access or remove the chip.

Encrypting File System (EFS) A public/private key encryption first used in Windows 2000 on NTFS-formatted disks. The file is encrypted with a symmetric key, and then a public/private key is used to encrypt the symmetric key.

Enhanced Data GSM Environment (EDGE) An improvement to GSM technology that enables it to deliver higher data rates. *See also* Global System for Mobile Communications (GSM).

Enhanced/Extended Simple Mail Transfer Protocol (ESMTP) An enhancement of SMTP for sending and receiving e-mail messages. ESMTP generates a unique, nonrepeatable number that's added to a transmitted e-mail. No two messages transmitted from an e-mail server have the same ESMTP value. *See also* Simple Mail Transfer Protocol (SMTP).

ethics Rules that you internalize and use to measure your performance; sometimes refers to external rules (codes of professional conduct or responsibility).

evidence bags Nonstatic bags used to transport computer components and other digital devices.

evidence custody form A printed form indicating who has signed out and been in physical possession of evidence.

examination plan A document that lets you know what questions to expect when you're testifying.

Exchangeable Image File (Exif) A file format the Japan Electronics and Information Technology Industries Association (JEITA) developed as a standard for storing metadata in JPEG and TIF files.

exculpatory evidence Evidence that indicates the suspect is innocent of the crime.

exhibits Evidence used in court to prove a case.

expert witness This type of testimony reports opinions based on experience and facts gathered during an investigation.

Extended Format File System (HFS+) File system used by Mac OS 8.1 and later. HFS+ supports smaller file sizes on larger volumes, resulting in more efficient disk use.

extensive-response field kit A portable kit designed to process several computers and a variety of operating systems at a crime or incident scene involving computers. This kit should contain two or more types of software or hardware computer forensics tools, such as extra storage drives.

extents overflow file A file in HFS and HFS+ that's used by the catalog to coordinate file allocations to a volume when the list of a file's contiguous blocks becomes too long. Any file extents not in the MDB or a VCB are also contained in this file. *See also* catalog, Master Directory Block (MDB), *and* Volume Control Block (VCB).

extraction The process of pulling relevant data from an image and recovering or reconstructing data fragments; one of the required functions of digital forensics tools.

fact witness This type of testimony reports only the facts (findings of an investigation); no opinion is given in court.

false positives The results of keyword searches that contain the correct match but aren't relevant to the investigation.

File Allocation Table (FAT) The original Microsoft file structure database. It's written to the outermost track of a disk and contains information about each file stored on the drive. PCs use the FAT to organize files on a disk so that the OS can find the files it needs. The variations are FAT12, FAT16, FAT32, VFAT, and FATX.

file slack The unused space created when a file is saved. If the allocated space is larger than the file, the remaining space is slack space and can contain passwords, logon IDs, file fragments, and deleted e-mails.

file system The way files are stored on a disk; gives an OS a road map to data on a disk.

forensic workstation A workstation set up to allow copying forensic evidence, whether it's on a hard drive, flash drive, or the cloud. It usually has software preloaded and ready to use.

Fourth Amendment The Fourth Amendment to the U.S. Constitution in the Bill of Rights dictates that the government and its agents must have probable cause for search and seizure.

Fourth Extended File System (Ext4) A Linux file system that added support for partitions larger than 16 TB, improved management of large files, and offered a more flexible approach to adding file system features.

fourth-generation (4G) The current generation of mobile phone standards, with technologies that improved speed and accuracy.

geometry A disk drive's internal organization of platters, tracks, and sectors.

Global System for Mobile Communications (GSM) A second-generation cellular network standard; currently the most used cellular network in the world.

Hal.dll The Hardware Abstraction Layer dynamic link library allows the OS kernel to communicate with hardware.

hard link In the Linux file system, a pointer that allows accessing the same file by different filenames, which refer to the same inode and physical location on the drive.

hash value A unique hexadecimal value that identifies a file or drive.

hazardous materials (HAZMAT) Chemical, biological, or radiological substances that can cause harm to people.

head The device that reads and writes data to a disk drive.

head and cylinder skew A method manufacturers use to minimize lag time. The starting sectors of tracks are slightly offset from each other to move the read-write head.

header node A node that stores information about the B*-tree file. *See also* B*-tree.

Hierarchical File System (HFS) An older Mac OS file system, consisting of directories and subdirectories that can be nested.

High Performance File System (HPFS) The file system IBM uses for its OS/2 operating system.

high-risk document A written report containing sensitive information that could create an opening for the opposing attorney to discredit you.

High Tech Crime Network (HTCN) A national organization that provides certification for computer crime investigators and digital forensics technicians.

honeypot A computer or network set up to lure an attacker.

honeywalls Intrusion prevention and monitoring systems that track what attackers do on honeypots.

host protected area (HPA) An area of a disk drive reserved for booting utilities and diagnostic programs. It's not visible to the computer's OS.

hostile work environment An environment in which employees cannot perform their assigned duties because of the actions of others. In the workplace, these actions include sending threatening or demeaning e-mail or a co-worker viewing pornographic or hate sites.

hybrid cloud A cloud deployment model that combines public, private, or community cloud services under one cloud. Segregation of data is used to protect private cloud storage and applications.

inculpatory evidence Evidence that indicates a suspect is guilty of the crime with which he or she is charged.

index node A B*-tree node that stores link information to the previous and next nodes. *See also* B*-tree.

indirect pointers The inode pointers in the first layer or group of an OS. *See also* inodes.

industrial espionage Theft of company sensitive or proprietary company information often to sell to a competitor.

Info2 file In Windows NT through Vista, the control file for the Recycle Bin. It contains ASCII data, Unicode data, and date and time of deletion.

infrastructure as a service (IaaS) With this cloud service level, an organization supplies its own OS, applications, databases, and operations staff, and the cloud provider is responsible only for selling or leasing the hardware.

initial-response field kit A portable kit containing only the minimum tools needed to perform disk acquisitions and preliminary forensics analysis in the field.

innocent information Data that doesn't contribute to evidence of a crime or violation.

inode blocks Blocks in the Linux file system that contain the first data after the superblock and consist of a grouping of inodes. *See also* inodes.

inodes A key part of the Linux file system, these information nodes contain descriptive file or directory data, such as UIDs, GIDs, modification times, access times, creation times, and file locations.

International Association of Computer Investigative Specialists (IACIS) An organization created to provide training and software for law enforcement in the digital forensics field.

International Telecommunication Union (ITU) An international organization dedicated to creating telecommunications standards.

Internet Message Access Protocol 4 (IMAP4) A protocol for retrieving e-mail messages; it's slowly replacing POP3. *See also* Post Office Protocol 3 (POP3).

interrogation The process of trying to get a suspect to confess to a specific incident or crime.

interview A conversation conducted to collect information from a witness or suspect about specific facts related to an investigation.

ISO image A bootable file that can be copied to CD or DVD; typically used for installing operating systems. It can also be read by virtualization software when creating a virtual boot disk.

key escrow A technology designed to recover encrypted data if users forget their passphrases or if the user key is corrupted after a system failure.

keychains A Mac feature used to track a user's passwords for applications, Web sites, and other system files.

keyed hash set A value created by an encryption utility's secret key.

keyword search A method of finding files or other information by entering relevant characters, words, or phrases in a search tool.

Known File Filter (KFF) An AccessData database containing the hash values of known legitimate and suspicious files. It's used to identify files for evidence or eliminate them from the investigation if they are legitimate files.

lay witness A person whose testimony is based on personal observation; not considered to be an expert in a particular field.

layered network defense strategy An approach to network hardening that sets up several network layers to place the most valuable data at the innermost part of the network.

least significant bit (LSB) The lowest bit value in a byte. In Microsoft OSs, bits are displayed from right to left, so the rightmost bit is the LSB. OSs that read bits from right to left are called "little endian." OSs that display the LSB from left to right are called "big endian."

limiting phrase Wording in a search warrant that limits the scope of a search for evidence.

line of authority The order in which people or positions are notified of a problem; these people or positions have the legal right to initiate an investigation, take possession of evidence, and have access to evidence.

link count A field in each inode that specifies the number of hard links. *See also* hard link.

live acquisitions A data acquisition method used when a suspect computer can't be shut down to perform a static acquisition. Captured data might be altered during the acquisition because it's not write-protected. Live acquisitions aren't repeatable because data is continually being altered by the suspect computer's OS.

logical acquisition This data acquisition method captures only specific files of interest to the case or specific types of files, such as Outlook .pst files. *See also* sparse acquisition.

logical addresses When files are saved, they are assigned to clusters, which the OS numbers sequentially starting at 2. Logical addresses point to relative cluster positions, using these assigned cluster numbers.

logical block In the Mac file system, a collection of data that can't exceed 512 bytes. Logical blocks are assembled in allocation blocks to store files in a volume. *See also* allocation block.

logical cluster numbers (LCNs) The numbers sequentially assigned to each cluster when an NTFS disk partition is created and formatted. The first cluster on an NTFS partition starts at count 0. LCNs become the addresses that allow the MFT to read and write data to the disk's nonresident attribute area. *See also* data runs *and* virtual cluster number (VCN).

logical EOF In the Mac file system, the actual ending of a file's data.

lossless compression A compression method in which no data is lost. With this type of compression, a large file can be compressed to take up less space and then uncompressed without any loss of information.

lossy compression A compression method that permanently discards bits of information in a file. The removed bits of information reduce image quality.

low-level investigations Corporate cases that require less investigative effort than a major criminal case.

management plane A tool with application programming interfaces (APIs) that allow reconfiguring a cloud on the fly.

map node A B*-tree node that stores a node descriptor and map record. *See also* B*-tree.

Master Boot Record (MBR) On Windows and DOS computers, this boot disk file contains information about partitions on a disk and their locations, size, and other important items.

Master Directory Block (MDB) On older Mac systems, the location where all volume information is stored. A copy of the MDB is kept in the next-to-last block on the volume. Called the Volume Information Block (VIB) in HFS+.

Master File Table (MFT) NTFS uses this database to store and link to files. It contains information about access rights, date and time stamps, system attributes, and other information about files.

mbox A method of storing e-mail messages in a flat plaintext file.

Message Digest 5 (MD5) An algorithm that produces a hexadecimal value of a file or storage media. Used to determine whether data has been changed.

Messaging Application Programming Interface (MAPI) The Microsoft system that enables other e-mail applications to work with each other.

metadata In NTFS, this term refers to information stored in the MFT. *See also* Master File Table (MFT).

metafile graphics Graphics files that are combinations of bitmap and vector images.

most significant bit (MSB) The highest bit value in a byte.

multi-evidence form An evidence custody form used to list all items associated with a case. See also evidence custody form.

Multipurpose Internet Mail Extensions (MIME) A specification for formatting non-ASCII messages, such as graphics, audio, and video, for transmission over the Internet.

multitenancy A principle of software architecture in which a single installation of a program runs on a server accessed by multiple entities (tenants). When software is accessed by tenants in multiple jurisdictions, conflicts in copyright and licensing laws might result.

National Institute of Standards and Technology (NIST) One of the governing bodies responsible for setting standards for some U.S. industries.

National Software Reference Library (NSRL) A NIST project with the goal of collecting all known hash values for commercial software and OS files.

network forensics The process of collecting and analyzing raw network data and systematically tracking network traffic to determine how security incidents occur.

network intrusion detection and incident response Detecting attacks from intruders by using automated tools; also includes the manual process of monitoring network firewall logs.

nonkeyed hash set A unique hash number generated by a software tool and used to identify files.

nonstandard graphics file formats Less common graphics file formats, including proprietary formats, newer formats, formats that most image viewers don't recognize, and old or obsolete formats.

NT File System (NTFS) The file system Microsoft created to replace FAT. NTFS uses security features, allows smaller cluster sizes, and uses Unicode, which makes it a more versatile system. NTFS is used mainly on newer OSs, starting with Windows NT.

NT Loader (Ntldr) A program located in the root folder of the system partition that loads the OS. *See also* BootSect.dos.

NTBootdd.sys A device driver that allows the OS to communicate with SCSI or ATA drives that aren't related to the BIOS.

NTDetect.com A 16-bit program that identifies hardware components during startup and sends the information to Ntldr.

Ntoskrnl.exe The kernel for the Windows NT family of OSs.

one-time passphrase A password used to access special accounts or programs requiring a high level of security, such as a decryption utility for an encrypted drive. This passphrase can be used only once, and then it expires.

online social networks (OSNs) A term researchers use for social media.

order of volatility (OOV) A term indicating how long an item on a network lasts. RAM and running processes might last only milliseconds; items stored on hard drives can last for years.

Orthogonal Frequency Division Multiplexing (OFDM) A 4G technology that uses numerous parallel carriers instead of a single broad carrier and is less susceptible to interference.

packet analyzers Devices and software used to examine network traffic. On TCP/IP networks, they examine packets (hence the name).

Pagefile.sys At startup, data and instruction code are moved in and out of this file to optimize the amount of physical RAM available during startup.

partition A logical drive on a disk. It can be the entire disk or part of the disk.

Partition Boot Sector The first data set of an NTFS disk. It starts at sector [0] of the disk drive and can expand up to 16 sectors.

partition gap Unused space or void between the primary partition and the first logical partition.

password dictionary attack An attack that uses a collection of words or phrases that might be passwords for an encrypted file. Password recovery programs can use a password dictionary to compare potential passwords to an encrypted file's password or passphrase hash values.

person of interest Someone who might be a suspect or someone with additional knowledge that can provide enough evidence of probable cause for a search warrant or arrest.

personal digital assistants (PDAs) Handheld electronic devices that typically contain personal productivity applications used for calendaring, contact management, and note taking. Unlike smartphones, PDAs don't have telephony capabilities.

personal identity information (PII) Any information that can be used to create bank or credit card accounts, such as name, home address, Social Security number, and driver's license number.

pharming A type of e-mail scam that uses DNS poisoning to redirect readers to a fake Web site.

phishing A type of e-mail scam that's typically sent as spam soliciting personal identity information that fraudsters can use for identity theft.

physical addresses The actual sectors in which files are located. Sectors reside at the hardware and firmware level.

physical EOF In the Mac file system, the number of bytes allotted on a volume for a file.

pixels Small dots used to create images; the term comes from "picture element."

plain view doctrine When conducting a search and seizure, objects in plain view of a law enforcement officer, who has the right to be in position to have that view, are subject to seizure without a warrant and can be introduced as evidence. As applied to executing searches of computers, the plain view doctrine's limitations are less clear.

platform as a service (PaaS) A cloud is a service that provides a platform in the cloud that has only an OS. The customer can use the platform to load their own applications and data. The CSP is responsible only for the OS and hardware it runs on; the customer is responsible for everything else that they have loaded on to it.

plist files In Mac, preference files for installed applications on a system.

Post Office Protocol version 3 (POP3) A protocol for retrieving e-mail messages from an e-mail server.

private cloud A cloud service dedicated to a single organization.

private key In encryption, the key used to decrypt the file. The file owner keeps the private key.

probable cause The standard specifying whether a police officer has the right to make an arrest, conduct a personal or property search, or obtain a warrant for arrest.

professional conduct Behavior expected of an employee in the workplace or other professional setting.

professional curiosity The motivation for law enforcement and other professional personnel to examine an incident or crime scene to see what happened.

provisioning Allocating cloud resources, such as additional disk space.

public cloud A cloud service that's available to the general public.

public key In encryption, the key used to encrypt a file; it's held by a certificate authority, such as a global registry, network server, or company such as VeriSign.

rainbow table A file containing the hash values for every possible password that can be generated from a computer's keyboard.

RAM slack The unused space between the end of the file (EOF) and the end of the last sector used by the active file in the cluster. Any data residing in RAM at the time the file is saved, such as logon IDs and passwords, can appear in this area, whether the information was saved or not. RAM slack is found mainly in older Microsoft OSs.

raster images Collections of pixels stored in rows rather than a grid, as with bitmap images, to make graphics easier to print; usually created when a vector graphic is converted to a bitmap image.

raw file format A file format typically found on higher-end digital cameras; the camera performs no enhancement processing—hence the term "raw." This format maintains the best picture quality, but because it's a proprietary format, not all image viewers can display it.

raw format A data acquisition format that creates simple sequential flat files of a suspect drive or data set.

reconstruction The process of rebuilding data files; one of the required functions of digital forensics tools.

recovery certificate A method NTFS uses so that a network administrator can recover encrypted files if the file's user/creator loses the private key encryption code.

redundant array of independent disks (RAID) Two or more disks combined into one large drive in several configurations for special needs. Some RAID systems are designed for redundancy to ensure continuous operation if one disk fails. Another configuration spreads data across several disks to improve access speeds for reads and writes.

Registry A Windows database containing information about hardware and software configurations, network connections, user preferences, setup information, and other critical information.

repeatable findings Being able to obtain the same results every time from a digital forensics examination.

Resilient File System (ReFS) A new file system developed for Windows Server 2012. It allows increased scalability for disk storage and improved features for data recovery and error checking.

resolution The density of pixels displayed onscreen, which governs image quality.

resource fork The part of a Mac file containing file metadata and application information, such as menus, dialog boxes, icons, executable code, and controls. Also contains resource map and header information, window locations, and icons. *See also* data fork.

risk management The process of determining how much risk is acceptable for any process or operation, such as replacing equipment.

salting passwords Adding bits to a password before it's hashed so that a rainbow table can't find a matching hash value to decipher the password. *See also* rainbow table.

salvaging Another term for carving, used outside North America. *See* carving.

Scientific Working Group on Digital Evidence (SWGDE) A group that sets standards for recovering, preserving, and examining digital evidence.

scope creep The result of an investigation expanding beyond its original description because the discovery of unexpected evidence increases the amount of work required.

search and seizure The legal act of acquiring evidence for an investigation. *See also* Fourth Amendment.

search warrants Legal documents that allow law enforcement to search an office, a home, or other locale for evidence related to an alleged crime.

Second Extended File System (Ext2) An early Linux file system.

sector A section on a track, typically made up of 512 bytes.

secure facility A facility that can be locked and allows limited access to the room's contents.

Secure Hash Algorithm version 1 (SHA-1) A forensic hashing algorithm created by NIST to determine whether data in a file or on storage media has been altered.

service level agreements (SLAs) Contracts between a cloud service provider and a cloud customer. Any additions or changes to an SLA can be made through an addendum.

Simple Mail Transfer Protocol (SMTP) A protocol for sending e-mail messages between servers.

single-evidence form A form that dedicates a page for each item retrieved for a case. It allows investigators to add more detail about exactly what was done to the evidence each time it was taken from the storage locker. *See also* evidence custody form.

smartphones Mobile telephones with more features than a traditional phone has, including a camera, an e-mail client, a Web browser, a calendar, contact management software, an instant-messaging program, and more.

sniffing Detecting data transmissions to and from a suspect's computer and a network server to determine the type of data being transmitted over a network.

software as a service (SaaS) With this cloud service level, typically a Web hosting service provides applications for subscribers to use.

sparse acquisition Like logical acquisitions, this data acquisition method captures only specific files of interest to the case, but it also collects fragments of unallocated (deleted) data. *See also* logical acquisition.

spoliation Destroying, altering, hiding, or failing to preserve evidence, whether it's intentional or a result of negligence.

spoofing Transmitting an e-mail message with its header information altered so that its point of origin appears to be from a different sender; typically used in phishing and spamming to hide the sender's identity. *See also* phishing.

standard graphics file formats Common graphics file formats that most graphics programs and image viewers can open.

static acquisitions A data acquisition method used when a suspect drive is write-protected and can't be altered. If disk evidence is preserved correctly, static acquisitions are repeatable.

steganography A cryptographic technique for embedding information in another file for the purpose of hiding that information from casual observers.

stego-media In steganalysis, the file containing the hidden message. *See also* cover-media.

Stored Communications Act (SCA) Part of the Electronic Communications Privacy Act that extends to the privacy of stored communications, such as e-mail.

subscriber identity module (SIM) cards Removable cards in GSM phones that contain information for identifying subscribers. They can also store other information, such as messages and call history.

superblock A block in the Linux file system that specifies and keeps track of the disk geometry and available space and manages the file system.

symbolic links Pointers to other files; they can point to items on other drives or other parts of the network and don't affect the link count. *See also* hard link.

tarball A highly compressed data file containing one or more files or directories and their contents.

Telecommunications Industry Association (TIA) A U.S. trade association representing hundreds of telecommunications companies that works to establish and maintain telecommunications standards.

TEMPEST A term referring to facilities that have been hardened so that electrical signals from digital devices, computer networks, and telephone systems can't be monitored or accessed easily by someone outside the facility.

testimony preservation deposition A deposition held to preserve your testimony in case of schedule conflicts or health problems; it's usually videotaped as well as recorded by a stenographer. *See also* deposition.

Third Extended File System (Ext3) A Linux file system that made improvements to Ext2, such as adding journaling as a built-in file recovery mechanism.

third-generation (3G) The preceding generation of mobile phone standards and technology; had more advanced features and faster data rates than the older analog and personal communications service (PCS) technologies.

Time Division Multiple Access (TDMA) The technique of dividing a radio frequency into time slots, used by GSM networks; also refers to a cellular network standard covered by Interim Standard (IS) 136. *See also* Global System for Mobile Communications (GSM).

track density The space between tracks on a disk. The smaller the space between tracks, the more tracks on a disk. Older drives with wider track densities allowed the heads to wander.

tracks Concentric circles on a disk platter where data is stored.

triple-indirect pointers The inode pointers in the third layer or group of an OS. *See also* inodes.

type 1 hypervisor A virtual machine interface that loads on physical hardware and contains its own OS.

type 2 hypervisor A virtual machine interface that's loaded on top of an existing OS.

unallocated disk space Partition disk space that isn't allocated to a file. This space might contain data from files that have been deleted previously.

Unicode A character code representation that's replacing ASCII. It's capable of representing more than 64,000 characters and non-European-based languages.

Uniform Crime Report Information collected at the federal, state, and local levels to determine the types and frequencies of crimes committed.

UTF-8 (Unicode Transformation Format) One of three formats Unicode uses to translate languages for digital representation.

validation A way to confirm that a tool is functioning as intended; one of the functions of digital forensics tools.

vector graphics Graphics based on mathematical instructions to form lines, curves, text, and other geometric shapes.

vector quantization (VQ) A form of compression that uses an algorithm similar to rounding off decimal values to eliminate unnecessary bits of data.

verdict The decision returned by a jury.

verification The process of proving that two sets of data are identical by calculating hash values or using another similar method.

virtual cluster number (VCN) When a large file is saved in NTFS, it's assigned a logical cluster number specifying a location on the partition. Large files are referred to as nonresident files. If the disk is highly fragmented, VCNs are assigned and list the additional space needed to store the file. The LCN is a physical location on the NTFS partition; VCNs are the offset from the previous LCN data run. *See also* data runs *and* logical cluster numbers (LCNs).

virtual hard disk (VHD) A file representing a system's hard drive that can be booted in a virtualization application and allows running a suspect's computer in a virtual environment.

Virtual Machine Extensions (VMX) Instruction sets created for Intel processors to handle virtualization.

virtual machines Emulated computer environments that simulate hardware and can be used for running OSs separate from the physical (host) computer. For example, a computer running Windows Vista could have a virtual Windows 98 OS, allowing the user to switch between OSs.

Virtualization Technology (VT) Intel's CPU design for security and performance enhancements that enable the BIOS to support virtualization.

voir dire In this qualification phase of testimony, your attorney asks you questions to establish your credentials as an expert witness. The process of qualifying jurors is also called voir dire.

Volume Control Block (VCB) An area of the Mac file system containing information from the MDB. *See also* Master Directory Block (MDB).

vulnerability/threat assessment and risk management The group that determines the weakest points in a system. It covers physical security and the security of OSs and applications.

warning banner Text displayed on computer screens when people log on to a company computer; this text states ownership of the computer and specifies appropriate use of the machine or Internet access.

wear-leveling An internal firmware feature used in solid-state drives that ensures even wear of read/writes for all memory cells.

whole disk encryption An encryption technique that performs a sector-by-sector encryption of an entire drive. Each sector is encrypted in its entirety, making it unreadable when copied with a static acquisition method.

write-blocker A hardware device or software program that prevents a computer from writing data to an evidence drive.

Software write-blockers typically alter interrupt-13 write functions to a drive in a PC's BIOS. Hardware write-blockers are usually bridging devices between a drive and the forensic workstation.

zero day attacks Attacks launched before vendors or network administrators have discovered vulnerabilities and patches for them have been released.

zombies Computers used without the owners' knowledge in a DDoS attack.

zone bit recording (ZBR) The method most manufacturers use to deal with a platter's inner tracks being shorter than the outer tracks. Grouping tracks by zones ensures that all tracks hold the same amount of data.

Index

Numerics

3DES (Triple Data Encryption Standard) encryption, 124

3G (Third-generation), 459–460

4G (Fourth-generation), 459–460

419 scams, 424–425

7Zip, 261

A

ABA (American Bar Association), 574–575

Abstracts, 517, 519–520

Acceptance testing, 84, 155

AccessData BootCamp and Windows forensics courses, 70

AccessData Certified Examiners (ACEs), 70, 601

AccessData Digital Forensics AD eDiscovery, 500

AccessData Digital Forensics Incident Response services, 500

AccessData Forensic Toolkit (FTK), 8, 37, 92, 253–254

  carving, 326

  compared to other tools, 264

  e-mail investigations, 438, 443

  as "flagship" suite, 273

  Linux forensics, 304

  Macintosh forensics, 303

  report generation, 263

  validation and verification, 256

AccessData Forensic Toolkit (FTK) Imager, 95–96

  acquisition, 111–115

  Creating Image dialog box, 114–115

  Drive/Image Verify Results dialog box, 164

Evidence Item Information dialog box, 113

main window, 111

mobile device forensics, 466

obtaining digital signature of files, 163–165

Select Drive dialog box, 112

Select Image Destination dialog box, 114

Select Image Type dialog box, 113

validation, 118, 370

virtual machines, 399–401

AccessData GUI forensics tools, 267

AccessData Known File Filter (KFF) database, 369

AccessData Password Recovery Toolkit (PRTK), 378

AccessData Registry Viewer, 31, 223

AccessData Ultimate Toolkit, 70

Accreditation, 64–70

  budget planning, 65–68

  certification and training, 68–70

  duties of manager and staff, 64–65

ACDSee, 78

ACEs (AccessData Certified Examiners), 70, 601

ACP (attorney-client privilege), 31–32

Acquisition, 89–125, 254–256, 264

  cloud computing, 483, 491–493

  contingency planning for, 94–95

  data-copying methods, 255

  defined, 90, 254

  determining best method for, 92–94

  live, 21, 90, 92–93, 267, 399, 406–407

  logical, 93–94, 255

  Macintosh file structures, 303

  from mobile devices, 463, 465–473

  RAID data, 118–122

  remote network, 122–125

  sparse, 93–94, 159

  static, 90, 92–93

  storage formats, 90–92

  subfunctions of, 254

  tools for, 95–115, 125, 254–256

  validating acquisitions, 115–118

Addenda, 487

Adobe Freehand MX, 319–320

Adobe Illustrator, 319

Adobe Photoshop, 319

Advanced Forensic Format (AFF), 92

Advanced Research Projects Agency Network (ARPANET), 482

Afentis Forensics group, 446

Affidavits (declarations), 13–14, 515

AFIS (Automated Fingerprint Identification System), 155

AFORE CloudLink Secure VSA, 493

.ai (Illustrator) format, 320

Aid4Mail, 438

Allegations, defined, 12

Allocation blocks, 299–300

Alternate data streams, 213–215

Amazon Elastic Compute Cloud (EC2), 482, 484

Amazon Mechanical Turk, 482

American Bar Association (ABA), 574–575

American Express v. Vinhnee (2005), 140

American Psychological Association (APA), 575

American Registry for Internet Numbers (ARIN), 433